S0-BES-064

CRITICAL SURVEY
OF GRAPHIC NOVELS

HEROES & SUPERHEROES

CRITICAL SURVEY OF GRAPHIC NOVELS

HEROES & SUPERHEROES

Volume 1
100 Bullets – Lucifer

Editors

Bart H. Beaty
University of Calgary

Stephen Weiner
Maynard Public Library

SALEM PRESS
Ipswich, Massachusetts   Hackensack, New Jersey

PROPERTY OF MURRELL LIBRARY
VALLEY COLLEGE
MO 65340

Cover images (clockwise from top left): *Ultimates*, Marvel Comics; *Daredevil: Born Again*, Marvel Comics; *Hellboy*, Dark Horse; *Cerebus* (center), Aardvark-Vanheim; *The Uncanny X- Men*, Marvel Comics

Copyright © 2012, by Salem Press, A Division of EBSCO Publishing, Inc.

All rights reserved. No part of this work may be used or reproduced in any manner whatsoever or transmitted in any form or by any means, electronic or mechanical, including photocopy, recording, or any information storage and retrieval system, without written permission from the copyright owner. For permissions requests, contact proprietarypublishing@ebscohost.com.

The paper used in these volumes conforms to the American National Standard for Permanence of Paper for Printed Library materials, X39.48-1992 (R1997).

LIBRARY OF CONGRESS CATALOGING-IN-PUBLICATION DATA

Critical survey of graphic novels : heroes and superheroes / editors, Bart H. Beaty, Stephen Weiner.

    p. cm.

Includes bibliographical references and index.

ISBN 978-1-58765-865-5 (set) -- ISBN 978-1-58765-866-2 (vol. 1) -- ISBN 978-1-58765-867-9 (vol. 2)

1. Graphic novels. 2. Comic books, strips, etc. 3. Superheroes in literature. 4. Heroes in literature. I. Beaty, Bart. II. Weiner, Stephen, 1955-

PN6725.C75 2012

741.5'0973--dc23

2011046278

First Printing

Printed in the United States of America

CONTENTS

MASTER LIST OF CONTENTS

Heroes Volume 1

Heroes Volume 2

PUBLISHER'S NOTE

Graphic novels have spawned a body of literary criticism since their emergence as a specific category in the publishing field, attaining a level of respect and permanence in academia previously held by their counterparts in prose. Salem Press's *Critical Survey of Graphic Novels* series aims to collect the preeminent graphic novels and core comics series that form today's canon for academic coursework and library collection development, offering clear, concise, and accessible analysis of not only the historic and current landscape of the interdisciplinary medium and its consumption, but the wide range of genres, themes, devices, and techniques that the graphic novel medium encompasses.

The combination of visual images and text, the emphasis of art over written description, the coupling of mature themes with the comic form—these elements appeal to the graphic novel enthusiast but remain a source of reluctance to other readers. Designed for both popular and scholarly arenas and collections, the series provides unique insight and analysis into the most influential and widely-read graphic novels with an emphasis on establishing the medium as an important academic discipline. We hope researchers and the common reader alike will gain a deeper understanding of these works, as the literary nature is presented in critical format by leading writers in the field of study.

Heroes and Superheroes is the first title of the *Critical Survey of Graphic Novels* series, to be followed by *Independents and Underground Classics*; *Manga*; and *History, Theme, and Technique*. This title collects the heroic tales of the superpowered crusader or the exploits of the morally ambiguous or derisive anti-hero that have become the seminal classics in the graphic novel landscape. Whether it is the vigilantism of Batman, the doubts of Spider-Man, or the tales of Norse myth in *Thor*, the techniques and traditions of literature are perpetuated in this medium of heroes and superheroes. Stories from the Silver Age of comics through the current day have been compiled and dissected to provide viewpoints that are easily missed during initial readings.

SCOPE AND COVERAGE

This two-volume set covers over 130 well-regarded works of the hero or superhero genre, summarizing plots and analyzing the works in terms of their literary integrity and overall contribution to the graphic novel landscape. It contains works from prominent publishers as well as leading hero or superhero titles published by alternative and independent houses. The entries in this encyclopedic set also cover a wide range of periods and trends in the heroes and superheroes genre, from the social relevance of *Green Lantern/Green Arrow* during the Bronze Age of Comic Books to the grim satire of *Watchmen* in the Modern Age; from watershed events such as the death of Captain America to the trudging narrative and complexity of *Cerebus* and from the caped and costumed crusaders who justly contest evil with supernatural abilities to the flawed and tragic antihero or the unheroic, brooding vigilante and their moral struggles and complexity.

In writing these essays, contributors worked from original sources, providing new criticism and content aimed at deconstructing the centuries-old heroic story and portraying the graphic novel as literature. To that end, essays look beyond the popular-culture aspects of the medium to show the wide range of literary devices and overarching themes and styles used to convey beliefs and conflicts. Furthermore, critical attention was paid to originators of the graphic novel and the birth of well-known characters, as well as panel selection and relevancy, and a particular work's influence on the creators' careers, other graphic novels, or literature as a whole.

The graphic novels field is defined by tremendous complexity; to that end, many important works and creators have been omitted. Lastly, while the series has an international scope, attention has been focused on translated works that have been influential in the development of a specific graphic novel tradition.

ORGANIZATION AND FORMAT

The essays in *Heroes and Superheroes* appear alphabetically and are approximately 4 to 5 pages in length. Each essay is heavily formatted and begins with full ready-reference top matter that includes the primary author or authors; illustrators and other artists who contributed to the work; and the first serial and book publication. This is followed by the main text, which is divided into "Publication History," "Plot," "Volumes," "Characters," "Artistic Style," "Themes," and "Impact." A list of films or television series based on the work and a user-friendly bibliography complete the essay. Cross-references direct readers to related topics, and further reading suggestions accompany all articles.

Publication History presents an overview of the work's origin and publication chronology. Many graphic novels were first serialized in comic book form, often as a limited series, and were later collected or republished in book format, while other graphic novels were conceptualized as novelistic works.

Plot provides an in-depth synopsis of the main story progression and other story arcs. As an aid to students, this section focuses on the most critically important plot turns in the series or work and why these were important.

Where applicable, *Volumes* orients the reader or researcher to the accepted reading order of the work. For series, it lists individual volumes or collections, often comprising different story arcs. The year when each collection was published is provided. Also identified are the issues that were collected within a volume, a synopsis of the volume's main focus, and its significance within the entire collection.

Characters presents detailed descriptions of major characters in the story, beginning with the main protagonists and antagonists. The section discusses physical description, character traits and significant characteristics, the character's relationship with others, and the primary role a character plays in advancing the plot of the work or series. To aid readers, descriptions include "also known as" names and monikers.

Artistic Style provides analysis of the work's visual content, especially as it relates to characterization, plot, and mood; analysis of the illustrative use of color versus black and white; discussion of any changes in style as the story progresses; and the use of elements and devices such as dialogue, captions, panels, penciling, inking, and backgrounds.

Themes identifies the central themes in the work, how they are expressed—for example, through plot or layout—and how they relate to characterization and style. It also discusses, when applicable, whether a major thematic point is a chronicle of the author's personal development, or a projection of it, and how this may resonate with readers.

Impact covers the work's influence on the creators' careers, publishing houses, the medium of graphic novels itself, and literature in general. The section also analyzes the impact of the creation of new characters or series. Of focus is the critical reception of the work or series and whether it was atypical for its historical period.

Bibliography lists secondary print sources for further study and examination, annotated to assist readers in evaluating focus and usefulness.

APPENDIXES AND OTHER SPECIAL FEATURES

Special features help to further distinguish this reference series from other works on graphic novels. This includes appendixes listing major graphic novel awards and a general bibliography. These resources are complemented by a timeline discussing significant events and influential graphic novel predecessors which spans the ancient world through the Middle Ages and the Renaissance to the present. Another key feature of the essays in this publication is a biographical sidebar on an author or illustrator related to the work profiled. Additionally, the two-volume set features nearly 100 pictures, including full-page images and panels from the actual work. Four indexes round out the set, illustrating the breadth of the reference work's coverage: Works by Publisher, Works by Author, Works by Artist, and a subject index.

ACKNOWLEDGMENTS

Many hands went into the creation of this work, and Salem Press is grateful for the effort of all involved. This includes the original contributors of these essays, whose names can be found at the end of each essay and also found in the "Contributors List" that follows the Introduction. Special mention must be paid to Lisa Schimmer, who played an invaluable role in shaping some of the reference content. Finally, we are indebted to our editors, Bart Beaty, Professor of English at the University of Calgary, and Stephen Weiner, Director of Maynard Public Library in Maynard, Massachusetts, for their advice in selecting works and their writing contributions. Both are published in the field of comics and graphic novels studies. Beaty is the author of *Fredric Wertham and the Critique of Mass Culture, Unpopular Culture: Transforming the European Comic Book in the 1990s*, and *David Cronenberg's "A History of Violence."* Weiner is the author or co-author of *The 101 Best Graphic Novels, Faster Than a Speeding Bullet: The Rise of the Graphic*

Novel, *The Hellboy Companion*, *The Will Eisner Companion*, and *Using Graphic Novels in the Classroom*. Their efforts in making this resource a comprehensive and indispensible tool for students, researchers, and general readers alike are gratefully acknowledged.

INTRODUCTION

Heroism has been a part of the human story since the beginning of recorded time. Archaeological excavations often unearth fragments of tablets that depict heroic stories, and the stories that have survived from early civilizations are almost exclusively those of heroes. Heroes serve as a collective moral compass and present humanity with an ideal to which to aspire. Over time, the hero tale has been adapted handily to different storytelling methods, from the narrative poems of the ancient Greeks to the novels of Alexandre Dumas to action films starring Errol Flynn, Sean Connery, and Tom Cruise.

The comic book came into existence in 1933 and was a longer, more involved format than its predecessor the cartoon panel, or newspaper cartoon strip. Comic books embraced the hero story naturally, and many hero tales appeared during the 1930's. Often cited as the creator of the graphic novel form, comics pioneer Will Eisner began his career drawing the action-packed comics *The Flame* and *Hawks of the Seas* during the years prior to 1938.

The world of both hero stories and comic books in general changed dramatically when Superman, the first superhero, appeared in the pages of *Action Comics*. Superman was so successful that the term "superhero" was coined in an effort to describe the parade of costumed adventurers that followed in his wake. Superheroes differed from "regular" heroes because the latter were normal people who performed admirably during extraordinary circumstances; superheroes, on the other hand, had something extra that the rest of humanity could never have. That extra asset made them "super."

After the success of Superman, numerous costumed heroes were created. Many were forgettable, but others, such as Batman, Wonder Woman, and Captain America, have made lasting impressions on popular culture. Superpowered heroes meant the villains had to be endowed with superpowers also, so the fights would be even. As a result, early comic books were concerned with the battle of good against evil, in the same manner as the pulp magazines that had preceded them. Superheroes also provided a vibrant metaphor during World War II. While the United States was at war, superhero comics were extremely popular.

After the war, interest in superheroes waned to the point that few superhero comic books were published in the late 1940's and early 1950's. However, by 1956, superhero comics were back, as DC Comics began publishing stories featuring updated versions of the heroes that had been popular in the 1940's. The first superhero to be revived was the Flash. Other costumed heroes followed. Comic books published by DC in the late 1950's and early 1960's were well produced, smart, and often based on science-fiction concepts.

The superhero comic received a major facelift in the 1960's, when Marvel Comics created new heroes and new kinds of superhero stories as a result of the success DC enjoyed by reviving the superhero concept. Whereas DC Comics focused on tight stories that wrapped up in a few pages, Marvel stories were sprawling, continuing from one issue to the next. Because Marvel had only a few heroes worth reviving from the World War II era, new heroes were created against the backdrop of real-world tensions over a potential nuclear holocaust. Marvel heroes were flawed and, in some cases, tragic, another departure from the DC Comics model. Just as the war had pervaded the superhero comic books of the 1940's, real-world problems seeped into Marvel comic book stories; these problems were not always world-shaking, however. Problems tackled by Marvel characters could be as mundane as paying a utility bill before the power was cut off, or struggling with a tumultuous love life.

Although DC Comics had created most of its signature heroes in the late 1930's and early 1940's, Marvel's best known superheroes, Spider-Man, the X-Men, and the Fantastic Four, were created in the early 1960's. Marvel also discovered creative ways to integrate its 1940's superheroes into its new superhero universe. The *Fantastic Four* featured a remodeled Human Torch; the Avengers were led by Captain America; and the Sub-Mariner, a hero in the 1940's, was reincarnated as a villain. Because the Marvel stories focused more on character than on plot, and because they were longer, they signified another step in the evolution of the cartoon format: the graphic novel.

One of the earliest superhero graphic novels was published in 1978 and featured the tragic Marvel character the Silver Surfer, a powerful alien stranded on Earth. Although the content was similar to that generally found in comic books of the time, the story was longer, fuller, and better developed. DC Comics had also experimented with a similar format for a few years, collecting and republishing selected superhero story lines in single volumes, printing them in a larger-than-usual format, and selling them at a higher price.

By the 1980's, the hero stories of the 1960's, so innovative at the time, were growing stale, and another revision of the superhero was in order. This was partly a response to an aging segment of the comic book readership that demanded more sophisticated stories. Many of these more mature tales were published by upstart comic book publishers attempting to give Marvel and DC a run for their money. The growth of the graphic novel format also allowed creators the freedom to tell stories that could not fit into the monthly comic book format. Thus, the rise of the graphic novel contributed to the evolution of the superhero story.

At the same time, a new periodical format emerged. Promoted by DC Comics and Dark Horse Comics primarily, the "limited series" was a complete story of a hero featured in monthly or bimonthly comic books; these stories tended toward dark versions of heroes. The limited series was then sometimes collected and republished as a single volume. Many signature superhero graphic novels emerged in the 1980's, among them Frank Miller's *Batman: The Dark Knight Returns* (1986); *Watchmen* (1986-1987), by Alan Moore and Dave Gibbons; *Batman: Year One* (1987), by Miller and David Mazzucchelli; *Daredevil: Born Again* (1986), also by Miller and Mazzucchelli; Howard Chaykin's *American Flagg!* (1983-1988); and Richard and Wendi Pini's *ElfQuest* (1978-1985).

In the 1990's, as the format became more popular, graphic novels became more diverse in their subject matter and didn't always feature superheroes. One of the most recognized is *The Sandman* series, written by Neil Gaiman. Numerous others, such as Jeff Smith's *Bone* (1991-2004) and Mike Mignola's *Hellboy* (first published in 1994), also appeared in graphic novel format. As the 1990's progressed, almost every comic book publishing company made a greater effort to republish popular superhero stories as graphic novels; they often featured "extras," enticing the reader to purchase both the limited series and the collected versions of the same story.

As the 1990's came to a close, the graphic novel had taken off, riding on the back of the superhero. Likewise, the graphic novel became a new avenue for the dissemination of the centuries-old hero story throughout popular culture. Graphic novels continued their rise into the first part of the twenty-first century, with many books landing on best-seller lists and winning major prizes.

The entries in this encyclopedia cover the gamut of heroes and superheroes, from some of the earliest hero graphic novels such as Jack Kirby's *Fourth World* books to more recent works, such as *The Death of Captain America* (2007-2008), by Ed Brubaker and Steve Epting, and *Omega the Unknown* (2007-2008), by Jonathan Lethem and Karl Rusnak. The volume contains works from major publishers as well as a strong sampling of hero graphic novels published by smaller comic book houses.

The graphic novel has become a useful vehicle for the hero and the superhero story, and this volume gives the scholar the critical tools to place these graphic novels in the broader context of popular literature.

Stephen Weiner

CONTRIBUTORS

Linda Alkana
*California State University,
Long Beach*

Katherine Allocco
*Western Connecticut State
University*

Stephen Aubrey
Brooklyn College

Bart Beaty
University of Calgary

Richard A. Becker
Pasadena, CA

Arnold T. Blumberg
University of Baltimore

Mark Brokenshire
Hove, South Australia, Australia

Stefan Buchenberger
Kanagawa University

Christopher B. Bundrick
*University of South Carolina,
Lancaster*

Thomas Gregory Carpenter
Lipscomb University

Julian C. Chambliss
Rollins College

Jean-Christophe Cloutier
Columbia University

Brian A. Cogan
Molloy College

Rikke Platz Cortsen
University of Copenhagen

Joseph J. Darowski
Michigan State University

Jim Davis
Kennesaw State University

Ryan P. Donovan
Mid-Manhattan Library

Damian Duffy
*University of Illinois at Urbana-
Champaign*

Randy Duncan
Henderson State University

Lance V. Eaton
Emerson College

Andrew Edwards
Glyndwr University

Thomas R. Feller
Nashville, TN

Rachel E. Frier
Rockville, MD

Jeff Geers
Bowling Green State University

Rebecca Gorman
*Metropolitan State College
of Denver*

Charles Gramlich
Xavier University of Louisiana

Diana Green
*Minneapolis College of Art
and Design*

Robert Greenberger
Fairfield, CT

Florian Gross
Leibniz Universitat Hannover

Taylor Hagood
Florida Atlantic University

Ben Hall
Manchester, MO

Stefan Hall
Defiance College

Matthew Halm
Washington State University

Darren Harris-Fain
Auburn University, Montgomery

Bob Hodges
University of Mississippi

David Huxley
*Manchester Metropolitan
University*

Patrick D. Johnson
Washington State University

Sheila Johnson
Tinley Park, IL

Benjamin Kahan
University of Pennsylvania

Jason Knol
Arlington Heights, IL

Thomas Knowlton
Mid-Manhattan Library

Walter Lai
University of Toronto

Jason M. LaTouche
Tarleton State University

Peter Lee
Simi Valley, CA

A. David Lewis
Boston University

Adam Lipkin
Brandeis University

Wim Lockefeer
Bilzen, Belgium

Anna Lohmeyer
University of Nebraska, Kearney

Brian A. Lynch
Villanova University

Tyler J. Manolovitz
Sam Houston State University

Jessica McCall
Las Vegas, NV

Ora C. McWilliams
University of Kansas

Hannah E. Means-Shannon
Georgian Court University

Julia M. Meyers
Duquesne University

P. Andrew Miller
Northern Kentucky University

Ross Murray
Coburg, Victoria, Australia

Daniel J. O'Rourke
Ashland University

Sam Otterbourg
University of North Carolina, Greensboro

Peter Y. Paik
University of Wisconsin, Milwaukee

Martyn Pedler
University of Melbourne

Marco Pellitteri
London Metropolitan University

Katharine Polak
University of Cincinnati

Doré Ripley
Diablo Valley College

Michael Robinson
Lynchburg College

Eddie Robson
Lancaster, UK

Anderson Rodriguez
The Woodlands, TX

Joseph Romito
University of Pennsylvania

Robert Sabella
Budd Lake, NJ

Allen Sallee
Burbank, IL

Elizabeth D. Schafer
Loachapoka, AL

David S. Serchay
Broward County Library System

Shannon Blake Skelton
University of Wisconsin, Madison

Matthew J. Smith
Wittenberg University

Michael Smith
James Madison University

Gregory Steirer
University of Pennsylvania

Benjamin Stevens
Bard College

P. L. Thomas
Furman University

Shaun T. Vigil
Harvard University

Robert G. Weiner
Texas Tech University

Stephen Weiner
Maynard Public Library

Marise Williams
University of Melbourne

Joseph Willis
Southern Utah University

Nathan Wilson
Tulsa, OK

Wayne Wise
Chatham University

Kent Worcester
Marymount Manhattan College

Scott D. Yarbrough
Charleston Southern University

A

100%

Author: Pope, Paul
Artist: Paul Pope (illustrator); Lee Loughridge (colorist); John Workman (letterer)
Publisher: DC Comics
First serial publication: 2002-2003
First book publication: 2005

Publication History

100% is a black-and-white comic first published by Vertigo Comics, an imprint of DC Comics, in five single issues. It was Paul Pope's second full-length publication for Vertigo (after *Heavy Liquid* in 2001). Throughout the 1990's Pope had numerous short stories published in anthologies, most notably *Dark Horse Presents* and *Negative Burn*.

Pope negotiated successfully with DC for *100%* to be published in black and white rather than color. The majority of *100%* was completed between August, 2000, and January, 2003.

Pope has stated that inspiration for *100%* was writer Philip K. Dick's novel *Man in the High Castle* (1962), and that it was initially conceived of as a series of loosely connected, old-fashioned short romance stories in a science-fiction setting. Instead, Vertigo solicited Pope to create just one story. Pope took what he considered the best elements and created one complete story. Parts of *100%* are based on real experiences involving Pope's family and friends. The title *100%* is intended to be perceived as a catchy slogan, similar to the title of a rock album. Pope has also stated that though *Heavy Liquid* is set in 2075 and *100%* and *Batman: Year 100* (2006) are set in 2038, all three stories occupy the same universe.

Pope based the six main characters on superhero and other comic-character archetypes, giving each a "costume" and look. Daisy is intentionally based on the Vertigo character Death, Haitous is inspired

by Frankenstein and the Hulk, and John wears Hercules-like armbands and a T-shirt with a logo on the chest.

Paul Pope

Paul Pope is one of the most acclaimed comics creators to have crossed over from independent comics to the mainstream. Beginning his career with self-published graphic novels *Sin Titulo* and *The Ballad of Dr. Richardson*, Pope rose to fame with his work on *THB*, a manic and sporadically published science-fiction story about a young woman on Mars. This work was followed by a number of popular limited series, including *Heavy Liquid, Batman: Year 100*, and *100%*. Pope is celebrated for his striking visuals, and his illustrations have been collected into art books. His work features heavy, inky blacks with strong erotic undercurrents that have made him a favorite among the style-conscious and with advertisers. His stories tend to focus on independent heroes and heroines who implicitly promote Pope's libertarian political philosophy.

Plot

Set in New York over a two-week period in 2038, *100%* tells the story of three relationships of six connected people: Strel and Haitous, Kimberley (also known as Kim) and Eloy, and John and Daisy. The story is told in twenty-five chapters of varying length.

Kim, a young bar worker at the Cat Shack Nite Club, decides to buy a gun after a girl is murdered in the club's back alley. Strel, Kim's friend and coworker, helps her negotiate a deal in a crowded and noisy nightclub. Later, they discuss Strel's dream of owning her own coffee business.

John, a busboy at the Cat Shack, meets Daisy, a new "gastro" dancer starting at the club. (Gastro dancing is a type of strip tease that uses magnetic resonance imaging, or MRI, technology, allowing a dancer's internal organs to be seen.) Daisy accidentally leaves her diary at the club, and John takes it for safekeeping. When they next meet, Daisy accuses John of stealing and reading the diary. When she realizes he has done neither, Daisy storms off, forbidding him to watch her dance. As Daisy readies herself to become her onstage persona, "Dollar Bill," she takes mood-altering pills that help her perform her athletic and erotic act. After her performance, Daisy checks to see whether or not John kept his word not to watch her perform; he has. Their attraction is evident; they kiss, though both seem surprised they have done so.

Cleaning the backstage employee room, John notices Daisy's stage clothes. In a spur-of-the-moment action, he pockets a pair of her underpants. When he realizes she is showering, he quickly leaves with the underwear. On her way home, Daisy agrees to go on a date with a very nervous John.

Haitous, Strel's estranged partner, who has returned from a year-long Eurasian G-Fight tour, watches footage of his next opponent, a vicious young fighter named Wallman. G-Fight uses the same technology as gastro dancing, allowing spectators to see the internal organs of a boxer during a match. Haitous calls Strel via a videophone, but she hangs up.

Strel introduces Kim to her cousin Eloy, who is immediately enamored with her. Eloy is creating an art project in which one hundred kettles boil at the same time, with all their whistles tuned to a "C" note. Kim is overwhelmed when Eloy tests his artwork for her and Strel. On a date, Kim tells Eloy how she feels buried under "bad stuff" happening all the time, but Eloy helps her find a different perspective. On their way home, they kiss, cementing their new relationship.

While on a date, Daisy tells John of a violent story that may or may not be about her, in which a woman witnesses her father kill her mother and mother's friend. On their way home, John gets soaked from water splashed by a passing vehicle. They go to her place so John can dry off, and she finds her underwear

in his coat pocket. At first angry, she soon relents, and they spend the night together.

Haitous is preoccupied with thoughts of Strel. His trainers advise him to work out something before the fight, or he will get beaten. Haitous corners Strel at work, pleading to see her later. Strel initially refuses but eventually relents, though reluctantly. Strel had wanted Haitous to retire from boxing, but he went on the Eurasian tour; thus, Strel kicked him out.

Eloy returns home to find Haitous waiting to ask him if, as a favor, he would bet a large sum of money on the long odds of Haitous winning his fight in the last round. Eloy then attends a funding meeting for his art project, but the backers make it clear Eloy must change the project to secure the money. Kim is adamant that Eloy should not change the project, accusing him of hypocrisy if he does. Eloy turns down the funding offer. Sullen, he decides to scrap the kettle project and his artistic ambitions; he soon changes his mind, however.

Haitous and Strel agree to start seeing each other again. He makes Strel promise to check the contents of a safety-deposit box after his fight. Haitous wins the brutal bout in the last round. After the fight, Strel finds the deposit box filled with money: the winnings of Eloy's proxy bet and enough to start a coffee business. Strel visits a severely battered Haitous and returns the money, stressing she cannot accept it unless they are together. That is fine by Haitous, as he is giving up boxing for good.

After freaking out when she hears John say "I love you" in his sleep, Daisy stresses out about their quickly developing relationship. John finds her vomiting in the toilet after the drugs she has taken for her gastro performance make her sick, and he nurses her to health. John asks Daisy to open up to him, but she deflects his attempts at intimacy, claiming she is "disappearing." Scared of John's growing attachment to her, she decides to leave New York and is gone the next day. Deeply upset, John decides he needs to do "something crazy" like traveling to an exotic location. He throws a dart at a world map; where it hits is where he will go. Unfortunately, it seems fate is against him: The dart lands in the middle of New York City.

Characters

- *Kimberly*, a.k.a. *Kim*, is a young, good-natured bar worker at the Cat Shack. A feeling of helplessness spurs her to buy a gun. Her idealistic attitude helps Eloy remain true to his artistic vision. At first a timid character, she becomes more trusting and matures throughout the story.
- *Strel* is the shift manager at the Cat Shack and Haitous's estranged wife. She has a matter-of-fact attitude but a stubborn streak when it comes to Haitous, as she is wary of renewing their relationship. She has dreams of running her own business. She is friend and mentor to Kim.
- *Daisy* is an itinerant gastro dancer going by the stage name "Dollar Bill." She works for a short time at the Cat Shack. She has a drug habit and a troubled past. Her real name is Jennifer, and she is reluctant to open up to anyone, deflecting any attempts at intimacy. She has a brief and intense relationship with John but leaves New York when she realizes John is falling in love with her.
- *John* is a good-looking and hardworking busboy at the Cat Shack. After ditching his education, focused on medieval literature, he decides to do something different with his life. He has a short but intense relationship with Daisy. Generally levelheaded but prone to angry outbursts, he yearns to be more spontaneous and impulsive. His emotional attachment to Daisy scares her away.
- *Haitous* is Strel's estranged husband. He is a huge man, formerly of the Navy, and a somewhat battered G-Fight champion. A melancholy and brooding character, he has been away on tour for a year and is now genuinely trying to fix his relationship with Strel. He decides his fight against the vicious Wallman will be his last.
- *Eloy* is a tall and bald African American. He is an experimental modern artist who develops a relationship with Kim. He is Strel's cousin. He is highly intelligent but slightly nerdy. His artwork garners interest from wealthy art patrons, who agree to grant him money to finish the project if he will change it. He refuses.

Artistic Style

Pope's style is influenced by a combination of Japanese manga and European comics artists, such as Hergé (*The Adventures of Tintin*, 1929-1976), Daniel Torres (*Rocco Vargas*, 1997), and Bruno Premiani (*Tomahawk*, 1950's; *Doom Patrol*, 1960's). Pope is the only Western artist to have worked for Kodansha, Japan's premier publisher of manga comics, for more than five years.

Pope uses a brush for all his artwork, which has been likened to calligraphy instead of the traditional comic pen-and-ink style. His art has also been compared to David Mazzucchelli's (*City of Glass,* 1994; *Asterios Polyp*, 2009) and Eddie Campbell's (*From Hell*, 1989-1996).

Pope's visually complex layouts are considered technically perfect and constantly inventive. His panels express a congested world without being cluttered, whether they depict the streets of a future New York, a night club, a sushi bar, or a run-down apartment. His work is both subjective enough to immerse the reader in the *100%* world of a future New York and objective in the portrayal of characters and their relationships, deftly using black, white, and gray-scale production to provide a measure of emotional distance from the characters.

The liberal use of sound effects, from the lighting of a cigarette to the oppressively loud music beats in a night club, evokes the constant noise of the constantly busy New York urban landscape. Using primarily rectangular panels that are always offset provides a subtle pace of events happening in the narrative in uneven and varying time frames.

Themes

The themes of trust and intimacy in relationships are strong in *100%*. Pope employs symbolism and metaphor in the objects and actions around each relationship. John and Daisy's relationship burns quickly, like the firecoat she uses in her gastro act. For John, Daisy is like the mood-altering drugs she uses. The initial "high" of the relationship is tempered by the emotional "low" of her leaving. Kim and Eloy's relationship is mirrored in Eloy's kettle art project. Like a kettle boiling slowly, their relationship builds to "100 percent" intensity.

The metaphor of boxing looms over Strel and Haitous's relationship, which is characterized by "rounds." Haitous, who loses the first encounters with Strel when she refuses to talk to him, wins over Strel eventually. Just as Haitous goes the distance to beat Wallman, Strel and Haitous's relationship has "gone the distance" to the final round.

The theme of the body as an emotional barrier is also prevalent. *100%* draws parallels between stripping and boxing as "sports" heavily invested in the exploitation of the body; both professions offer financial rewards at the physical and emotional expense of the participant. Daisy and Haitous trade on their body—how it looks and what it can do.

Haitous is unable to be completely honest and emotional with Strel until he relinquishes the body-focused G-Fight. He finally decides that he would prefer to be with Strel than be seen by G-Fight patrons. Daisy prefers to be exposed on stage rather than "open up" to John. While she allows John access to her body, like her diary, her inner thoughts are off-limits. Telling John her real name, Jennifer, is the most she can afford of her real self.

Impact

100% was Pope's second work for Vertigo and one of his few full-length works for a major publisher. Pope's work for Vertigo propelled him to his highest-profile work, *Batman: Year 100*, for which he won two Eisner Awards. Pope's status as an artist was raised in the wider art community, and in 2008, he branched into fashion, designing a collection for DKNY Jeans.

100% crosses romance with science fiction and is clearly influenced by the cyberpunk science-fiction genre, specifically the stories of novelist William Gibson, which often intertwine technological and artistic aesthetics. The idea of gastro on both strip club dancers and boxers is a unique concept not only in comics but also in the genre of literature in general. Gastro is the culmination of voyeurism and pornography, allowing the innards of the body to be seen. However, Pope is particularly adept in handling the idea, never actually showing either Daisy's or Haitous's internals.

Ross Murray

Further Reading

Mazzucchelli, David. *Asterios Polyp* (2009).

Pope, Paul. *Batman: Year 100* (2006).

_____. *Heavy Liquid* (2001).

Bibliography

Pope, Paul. "Paul Pope Interview, Part One." Interview by Ray Mescallado. *The Comics Journal* 191 (November, 1996): 98.

_____. "Paul Pope Interview, Part Two." Interview by Ray Mescallado. *The Comics Journal* 192 (December, 1996): 91.

_____. *Pulphope: The Art of Paul Pope*. Richmond, Va.: AdHouse Books, 2007.

See also: *Batman: Year 100; Doom Patrol*

100 Bullets

Author: Azzarello, Brian
Artist: Eduardo Risso (illustrator); Grant Goleash (colorist); Patricia Mulvihill (colorist); Clem Robins (letterer); Dave Johnson (cover artist)
Publisher: DC Comics
First serial publication: 1999-2009
First book publication: 2000-2009

Publication History

The DC Comics imprint Vertigo ran one hundred issues of *100 Bullets* between 1999 and 2009, and the title was collected in thirteen trade paperbacks; the title of each collection was a pun on its volume number. *100 Bullets* represented a landmark in long-running Vertigo series, which tend to stop in the range of sixty to seventy-five issues. The same creative team, excepting changes in colorist and editor in the first two years and ten pages of pinups drawn by an all-star roster of guests integrated into the story for issue 26, produced all 100 issues and more than 2,200 pages of story over ten years. Before *100 Bullets*, the American Brian Azzarello was an unknown and the Argentine Eduardo Risso was not well known in the United States, despite European collaborations such as *Boy Vampiro* and *Chicanos* with fellow Argentine Carlos Trillo. Azzarello and Risso's only collaboration prior to *100 Bullets* was in 1998, on the four-issue private-detective series *Jonny Double*. The character Dex from that limited series makes a cameo in issues 1 and 43 of *100 Bullets*. Because of *100 Bullets*' critical success, Azzarello and Risso went on to work together on mainstream characters, including a six-issue run on *Batman* entitled *Broken City*, in which Agent Graves makes a cameo. After finishing *100 Bullets*, Risso collaborated with Brian K. Vaughan on *Logan* for Marvel. Azzarello started a spaghetti Western series, *Loveless*, that ran for twenty-four issues and collaborated on a *Sgt. Rock* graphic novel with Joe Kubert.

Plot

100 Bullets has its genesis in the moral dilemmas Agent Graves offers many of the characters throughout

Brian Azzarello

Award-winning writer Brian Azzarello is best known for *100 Bullets*, a title that revived the moribund crime comics genre when it debuted from DC's Vertigo imprint in 1999. Working with Argentine illustrator Eduardo Risso, Azzarello plunged into the noir conventions of old-time crime novels while updating the genre with a fantastic contemporary setting. Beginning as a series of unrelated episodic stories, *100 Bullets* gradually transformed into a complexly plotted criminal masterpiece. Azzarello's comics are noteworthy for the pitch-perfect use of regional dialects and slang. The image that emerges from his work is bleakly dystopic, and he has been drawn to developing highly flawed characters. His widely praised *Joker* one-shot, with Lee Bermejo, is an attempt to flesh out the psychological drives of the most significant villain in the Batman mythos.

the series. Graves appears in a variety of American cities, seeming to represent some sort of law enforcement or intelligence agency, and presents a person with an attaché case containing irrefutable evidence that that person has been wronged by someone, a gun, and one hundred untraceable bullets. The recipients are always skeptical; however, through experimentation with the gun, the person verifies that if he or she uses the bullets, no law enforcement will interfere. It emerges that some, though not all, of the cases Graves hands out advance his campaign against the Trust.

Thirteen powerful European family heads began the Trust in the wake of the European discovery of the American continent. These thirteen brokered a deal with the monarchs of Europe to leave the Old World and have total control in the New World. Members of the Trust typically passed down their positions to their children, though houses can be dissolved and new houses created to maintain the balance of voting power at thirteen. To enforce their will, the Trust formed a band of seven elite killers, the Minutemen.

The Minutemen had strict instructions to eliminate the Trust's opponents and to curb infighting within the Trust by exacting eye-for-eye retribution whenever one house of the Trust moved against another house. The Minutemen worked under the command of an agent, and the warlord, a former Minuteman, served as a liaison between the Trust and the Minutemen.

This arrangement lasted for 400 years, until the Trust voted to dissolve the Minutemen. Agent Graves and his Minutemen react by burning alive a member of the Trust in Atlantic City. Graves then has the warlord, Mr. Shepherd, report all of the Minutemen dead to the Trust. Graves and Shepherd hide six of the seven Minutemen and alter their memories according to their personalities. The seventh Minuteman, Lono, was not in Atlantic City and is allowed to freelance.

Graves continues to use his connections to the Trust in order to distribute attaché cases even while he is supposed to be dead. After an unspecified time, concurrent with the series beginning, Graves gives a man a case that sends him after Megan Dietrich, a member of the Trust, alerting the Trust that Graves is alive. Graves begins awakening the Atlantic City Minutemen and uses the cases to begin the training of at least two potential new Minutemen: Dizzy Cordova and Loop Hughes. Shepherd assists Graves in these endeavors but continues to work for the Trust and its most powerful member, Augustus Medici. As Graves's war against Augustus and the Trust escalates, various characters begin to wonder why every move Graves makes helps Augustus consolidate more power. Gradually, a forty-year-old conspiracy to change the nature of the Trust is revealed.

Volumes
- *100 Bullets: First Shot, Last Call* (2000). Collects issues 1-5 and a short from *Vertigo: Winter's Edge 3*, introducing Dizzy, Graves, Graves's cases and accompanying moral dilemmas, Shepherd, Lono, Megan, and Augustus.
- *100 Bullets: Split Second Chance* (2000). Collects issues 6-14, featuring two stand-alone stories, awakening the first-seen Atlantic City Minuteman, and introducing Mr. Branch, who explains the Trust to Dizzy.
- *100 Bullets: Hang Up on the Hang Low* (2001). Collects issues 15-19, featuring the story of Loop Hughes reconnecting with his absent father.
- *100 Bullets: A Foregone Tomorrow* (2002). Collects issues 20-30, introducing Benito Medici, three more Minutemen, and the full membership of the Trust and featuring a stand-alone story about the Kennedy assassination.
- *100 Bullets: The Counterfifth Detective* (2003). Collects issues 31-36, featuring Milo Garret as a Los Angeles private eye with a bandaged face and a case from Graves.
- *100 Bullets: Six Feet Under the Gun* (2003). Collects issues 37-42, featuring six stand-alone stories moving different characters along in the plot.
- *100 Bullets: Samurai* (2004). Collects issues 43-49, featuring the stories of Loop and Lono in prison and of Jack in a zoo in the New Jersey woods.
- *100 Bullets: The Hard Way* (2005). Collects issues 50-58, introducing Victor Ray, explaining the origin of the Trust, and featuring Wylie Times facing off with Shepherd.
- *100 Bullets: Strychnine Lives* (2006). Collects issues 59-67, featuring Lono and Loop free from prison, working with Victor for Augustus, and Benito and Branch meeting with Megan and then Dizzy.
- *100 Bullets: Decayed* (2006). Collects issues 68-75, featuring Graves activating the last Minuteman and a flashback to 1962 showing the elevation of Graves as the agent of the Minutemen.
- *100 Bullets: Once Upon a Crime* (2007). Collects issues 76-83, featuring Lono and Graves's Minutemen in a confrontation over Dizzy and a flashback to Shepherd's recruitment by Graves and Mr. Hughes.
- *100 Bullets: Dirty* (2008). Collects issues 84-88, featuring five stand-alone stories, including the introduction of Will Slaughter.
- *100 Bullets: Wilt* (2009). Collects issues 89-100, featuring the fiery and violent end of the series.

Characters

- *Agent Graves* is the central character, appearing in the most issues. He appears to be playing a moralistic game by offering the chance of revenge to unwitting recipients, but his larger plan emerges. Graves never lies, and he sincerely offers people opportunities to change their lives.
- *Isabella "Dizzy" Cordova*, a.k.a. *The Girl*, is the point-of-view character as she becomes a Minuteman. A former Chicago gang member, Dizzy lost her husband and son in a drive-by shooting. Graves selects Dizzy for her strong sense of morality, and Shepherd and Graves compete over their plans for her.
- *Mr. Shepherd* works as the Trust's warlord and is in charge of training potential Minutemen. It is never clear how much of his agenda is his own, how much is the Trust's, and how much is Graves's.
- *Lee Dolan* was an awarded-winning restaurateur in Los Angeles before allegations of child pornography cost him his position and family. He is working as a bartender when Graves approaches him.
- *Megan Dietrich* is the head of the House of Dietrich in Los Angeles. She resents her father's death, has prickly relationships with Benito Medici and others, and is racist and sexist.
- *Lono*, a.k.a. *The Dog*, is a Hawaiian mercenary who kills and rapes with no conscience and was difficult to control as a Minuteman. Shepherd grooms Lono to be his successor as warlord.
- *Augustus Medici* has been the head of the House of Medici in Miami since the 1960's and is the most powerful member of the Trust. He uses Graves to consolidate his power.
- *Sophie* was a waitress in Miami and Loop's cousin's girlfriend before Lono raped her repeatedly and killed her boyfriend.
- *Cole Burns*, a.k.a. *The Wolf*, works as an ice cream man in New York before Graves reawakens his memories of being a Minuteman. Subsequent events test his loyalty to Graves.
- *Mr. Branch* was a journalist before receiving a case from Graves and investigating it, then learning about the Trust from Lono and Shepherd. He exiles himself to Paris to escape the corruption of the Trust, and Shepherd sends Dizzy to learn from him. Branch has a vexed friendship with and fear of Cole.
- *Mr. Curtis Hughes* is a former associate of Graves whom the Trust would not allow to be a Minuteman because of his race. He works in Philadelphia as collector for Italian gangsters and has never met his son.
- *Louis "Loop" Hughes*, a.k.a. *The Boy*, is a young man to whom Graves offers a chance to kill his absentee father. Loop instead begins working with Curtis. Graves arranges for Loop to be sent to prison to continue his training as a Minuteman.
- *Benito Medici* is the privileged son of Augustus who avoids the responsibilities of his birth, but an assassination attempt makes him reconsider.
- *Jack Daw*, a.k.a. *The Monster*, is a heroin addict and a massive man who is an occasional bouncer in Boston. He persists as a junkie, criminal, and street fighter before rejoining the Minutemen.
- *Echo Memoria* is an Italian thief who seduces many of the series' men as she seeks a painting important to the Trust.
- *Milo Garret*, a.k.a. *The Bastard*, is a disfigured Minuteman who works as a private eye in Los Angeles and prefers it to his old job.
- *Wylie Times*, a.k.a. *The Point Man*, was the head Minuteman. As a drunken gas station attendant in El Paso, Texas, he resists his tragic past and deep grudge against Shepherd and the Trust.
- *Victor Ray*, a.k.a. *The Rain*, was the Minuteman Graves activated first while in Chicago, but he is one of the last he contacted despite being the most loyal to Graves.
- *Remi Rome*, a.k.a. *The Saint*, is a scarred, sadistic, volatile, and arrogant Minuteman hidden as a meatpacker and trapped in a love-hate relationship with his Cleveland mob enforcer brother, Ronnie.
- *Will Slaughter* is a retired Minuteman who works as a hit man to support his family.

Artistic Style

The use of perspective is one of the most striking aspects of *100 Bullets'* artistic style. The viewer looks through panels at angles foreign to the normal camera placement of most comics, such as through the bullet hole in a character's head and out from pinball machines and paintings. Risso's panels sometimes jump between radically different perspectives within scenes. Writer and artist Darwyn Cooke has commented that the effect of Risso's stylizations is a rare artistic reality that totally encapsulates the work's themes, much as Chester Gould does in *Dick Tracy* or Steve Ditko in *Spider-Man*.

Patricia Mulvihill's coloring and Dave Johnson's covers work in a similar suggestive and expressionistic vein. Mulvihill often uses repeated color associations to depict the emotions and moralities of the various characters. Johnson's covers evoke character, setting, and cultural references without a narrative reliance on the details of plot.

Risso's storytelling often shows the actions of two different story lines within a single panel. The most prominent example of this feature is issue 20, "The Mimic," which juxtaposes Shepherd and Benito's conversation about the Trust in a New York City park with a drug dealer's realization that a more powerful rival will force him out of the park. This construction allows the stories of street crime and elite crime to complement each other and brings their similarities into focus.

Themes

Class structure is a major thematic concern in *100 Bullets*, as it is in a good deal of contemporary crime fiction. Reviews had described *100 Bullets* as a combination of the noir novels of Jim Thompson, the television urban procedural *The Wire*, and Howard Zinn's *A People's History of the United States*. *100 Bullets* reimagines in pulp terms the historical critique that Zinn and other radical historians mount of a United States founded through, and often perpetuating, genocide, slavery, war, and class exploitation. Azzarello and Risso's reimagining may lack the nuance of an academic critique, but it dramatizes a United States led by the lies of an organization of elite thieves, the Trust, for their own enrichment.

As previously noted, Risso's layouts and artwork frequently reinforce the relationship between the powerful and the disenfranchised; this relationship is also mirrored in the interactions between the Trust and the Minutemen. The Minutemen are composed primarily of working-class killers, many of whom are ex-convicts, yet these are the people whom the Trust selects to police its membership. There are limits to the disenfranchised composition of the Minutemen, however, as Dizzy and Loop are likely the first exceptions to the Minutemen's white, male membership, given the bigotry of many members of the Trust, including younger members such as Megan.

With his mission of pitting the disenfranchised against the powerful through his use of the attaché cases, Agent Graves can be read as a class warrior. He hides the Minutemen in a variety of blue-collar jobs: ice cream man, bouncer, private investigator, gas-station attendant, and meatpacker. Precisely what Graves seeks as an endgame remains unclear, but he admits it will not be perfect and seems to want to ensure a peaceful balance of power by destroying, altering, or greatly weakening the Trust.

Impact

100 Bullets was the first long-running Vertigo series devoid of fantasy and supernatural elements and was one of the first major Vertigo series written by an American instead of a British writer. Azzarello paved the way for subsequent writers Jason Aaron, Howard Chaykin, Joshua Dysart, David Lapham, Brian K. Vaughan, and Brian Wood to create non-fantasy series for the imprint. The success and notoriety of Risso's European style helped lead to more non-American artists on Vertigo titles, including Riccardo Burchielli, Werther Dell'Edera, Marcelo Frusin, Davide Gianfelice, R. M. Guéra, M. K. Perker, Alberto Ponticelli, Victor Santos, and Danijel Žeželj.

In terms of crime comics, *100 Bullets* is the second-longest-running series of all time after the true-crime anthology *Crime Does Not Pay*, which ran for 125 issues in the 1940's and early 1950's. With its wide variety of protagonists set in a single universe, *100 Bullets* is similar to *Sin City* and *Stray Bullets* but tells a more cohesive and unified story. The series has been a major influence on the resurgence of crime comics and publishing ventures such as the launch of DC Comics' Vertigo Crime subimprint and the translation of European crime comic albums for American markets by publishers such as Dark Horse, Fantagraphics, and IDW.

Bob Hodges

Further Reading

Brubaker, Ed, and Sean Phillips. *Criminal* (2006-   ).

Cooke, Darwyn. *Richard Stark's Parker* (2009-   ).

Lapham, David. *Stray Bullets* (1995-   ).

Rucka, Greg, and Matthew Southworth. *Stumptown* (2009-   ).

Bibliography

Benton, Mike. *Crime Comics: An Illustrated History*. Dallas: Taylor, 1993.

Cooke, Darwyn. Introduction to *100 Bullets: Decayed*. Edited by Scott Nybakken. New York: Vertigo, 2006.

Haut, Woody. *Neon Noir: Contemporary American Crime Fiction*. London: Serpent's Tail, 1999.

Horsley, Lee. *The Noir Thriller*. New York: Palgrave Macmillan, 2009.

Lindenmuth, Brian. "The Fall (and Rise) of the Crime Comic." http://www.mulhollandbooks.com/2010/12/14/a-history-of-and-appreciation-for-crime-comics.

Moore, Stuart. "Graphic Violence: A Talented New Generation of Writers Brings Crime to the Comics." *Mystery Scene* 77 (2002): 32-35.

Savage, Bill. Introduction to *100 Bullets: A Foregone Tomorrow*. New York: DC Comics, 2002.

See also: *Blacksad; Criminal*

ALIAS

Author: Bendis, Brian Michael

Artist: Michael Gaydos (illustrator); Matt Hollingsworth (colorist); Cory Petit (letterer); David Mack
(cover artist)

Publisher: Marvel Comics

First serial publication: 2001-2004

First book publication: 2003-2004

Publication History

According to its creator, Brian Michael Bendis, *Alias*
originated in a discussion between Bendis and then
Marvel editor in chief Joe Quesada about writing a
crime comic. Bendis wrote part of it as a screenplay,
without editing himself. He took it to Marvel publisher Bill Jemas, who decided to rethink the company's lack of titles for mature readers. Michael
Gaydos, with whom Bendis had gone to art school
years earlier, was hired as the artist. The series also
occasionally featured work by additional artists, including Mark Bagley, David Mack, Bill Sienkiewicz,
and Matt Hollingsworth. *Alias* launched in 2001 as
the first title of Marvel's mature-rated MAX Comics
line.

The first issue of *Alias* was published in November, 2001, and the series ran for twenty-eight issues, until January, 2004. Various collected editions
followed, starting in 2003. *Alias* introduces former
superhero Jessica Jones, who works as a private investigator. The character had not existed prior to
this series; however, she is treated as though she has
had numerous previous interactions with established
Marvel characters. Many of the characters included
in *Alias*, such as Luke Cage, J. Jonah Jameson, and
Jessica herself, moved to *The Pulse*, Bendis's mainstream Marvel Universe series that followed the completion of *Alias*.

No connection exists between *Alias* and Chuck
Dixon's comic book of the same name from the 1980's
or the American Broadcasting Company (ABC) television crime series. Bendis derived the title by rear-
ranging the letters of his wife Alisa's name.

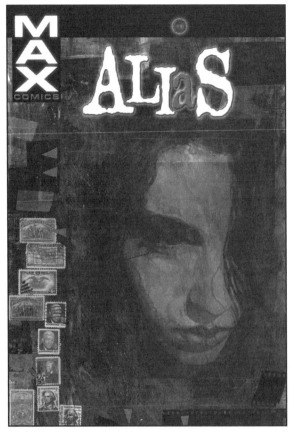

Alias. (Courtesy of Marvel Comics)

Plot

Jessica Jones, a former superhero, is a cynical private
investigator whose relationships with other superheroes, many of whom are incorporated into the series,
are filled with tension. In the first issue, she and Luke
Cage, a former friend of Jessica and a superhero sometimes known as Power Man, have a one-night stand.

While on a case for a client, Jessica inadvertently
captures the secret identity of Captain America on tape.
Made paranoid by this discovery, Jessica wonders if
she has been set up, especially when her client is murdered. Fearing the worst, she goes to Luke's apartment
but is turned away. Jessica is arrested for the murder,
but the police seem to care more about her former life
as a superhero than the crime. Lawyer Matt Murdock,

also known as the superhero Daredevil, keeps her out of jail at Luke's request. Carol Danvers, also known as Ms. Marvel, reluctantly helps Jessica find out who has set her up. The culprit is revealed to be a tycoon seeking political gain by discrediting Captain America. SHIELD agent Clay Quartermain exposes the tycoon, and Steve Rogers, the civilian identity of Captain America, thanks Jessica and secures the tape. Carol warns Jessica that Luke is a "cape chaser" and sets her up with Scott Lang, also known as Ant-Man, instead.

A new client hires Jessica to find her husband, Rick Jones, a missing superhero sidekick who is related to Jessica. Although the Rick Jones that Jessica finds is an imposter, the reader gets a chance to read part of the real Jones's autobiography, *Sidekick*, which briefly revisits past story lines of the Marvel Universe.

Another client, J. Jonah Jameson, the antisuperhero editor of *The Daily Bugle*, hires Jessica to learn Spider-Man's secret identity but offends her in the process. She scams him in return, using the fee she is paid to help orphans and AIDS patients. A case dealing with bigotry against mutants in a small town in New York leads Jessica to get involved with the sheriff, a reporter, a family, and a murder. After resolving the case, she connects with Scott Lang by phone on her drive back to the city, confiding in him and beginning a romantic relationship marked by misunderstandings.

For the following six months, Jessica deals with two Spider-Women, one of whom is the first Spider-Woman, Jessica Drew, and the other the victim of a drug dealer who exploits superheroes. She again encounters *Bugle* editor Jameson, and a mystic, Madame Web, who sees how Jessica's past haunts her.

The series then explores Jessica's origin story, flashing back fifteen years to when she was a teenager. At that time, Jessica attended the same high school as Peter Parker, who developed superpowers and became Spider-Man. Like Peter, Jessica gained her superpowers in an accident, hers involving large quantities of radioactive chemicals. Her parents and younger brother were killed in the accident, and Jessica was adopted by the Jones family.

In the story's present time frame, Jessica accepts a case that entails obtaining confessions from the incarcerated supervillain Zebediah Killgrave, the Purple Man. This leads Jessica to confide in Luke and explain her history with Killgrave, who had controlled her mind and subjected her to psychological torture years before. This event led her to give up her superhero identity of Jewel.

Knowing she must confront Killgrave, Jessica visits him in prison. He greets her as Jessica Jones, his favorite comic book character, and continues to insist that they are all characters in a comic book as she attempts to get the confessions. Killgrave escapes and continues to play with Jessica's mind, but Jessica regains control and punches Killgrave into unconsciousness just as the Avengers arrive to help her. Feeling that they have experienced something important, Scott realizes he wants to be with Jessica. However, she tells him she is pregnant and that the child is not his, ending their intermittent attempts at a relationship. At the end of the series, Luke tells Jessica that she has become more important to him than he would have thought and that he wants to be there for her. She tells him that she is pregnant with his child, and the two begin a long-term relationship that continues in two of Bendis's next works, *The Pulse* and *New Avengers*.

Volumes

- *Alias* (2003). Collects issues 1-9, featuring Jessica's reconnection with Luke, her ambivalent relationship with other superheroes, and several cases.
- *Alias: Come Home* (2003). Collects issues 11-15, featuring Jessica's developing relationships with both Scott and Luke and a case involving bigotry and prejudice against mutants in a small town.
- *Alias: The Underneath* (2003). Collects issues 10 and 16-21, featuring J. Jonah Jameson, *The Daily Bugle*, and two Spider-Women.
- *Alias: The Secret Origins of Jessica Jones* (2004). Collects issues 22-28, linking Jessica's past with her present.
- *Alias Omnibus* (2006). Collects issues 1-28 and *What If Jessica Jones Had Joined the Avengers?*
- *Alias, Ultimate Collection* Book 1 (2009). Collects *Alias*, issues 1-15.
- *Alias, Ultimate Collection* Book 2 (2009). Collects *Alias*, issues 16-28.

Characters

- *Jessica Jones*, the protagonist, is the owner and sole employee of Alias Investigations. She had a brief career as the superheroes Jewel and Knightress, but after a traumatic encounter with the supervillain the Purple Man, she decided to give up superheroics altogether. However, she retains her powers, including superstrength, relative invulnerability, and flight, which she has yet to fully master. Her past has given her some friends and contacts within the superhero community.

- *Luke Cage*, a.k.a. *Power Man*, is a friend to and on-and-off lover of Jessica. He is part of an organization called Heroes for Hire. His powers are superstrength and near invulnerability due to his unbreakable skin. Luke and Jessica's awkward early relationship grows more meaningful as the series progresses.

- *Carol Danvers*, a.k.a. *Ms. Marvel*, has been a friend to Jessica since Jessica's days as Jewel. She sends Jessica on a date with Scott Lang but also gossips behind her back. It is implied that Carol and Jessica had a past love triangle with SHIELD agent Clay Quartermain.

- *Scott Lang*, a.k.a. *Ant-Man*, dates Jessica at different times throughout the series. They were originally set up by their mutual friend Carol Danvers. The two connect, but their attempts at a relationship end when Jessica finds out she is pregnant with Luke Cage's child.

- *Matt Murdock*, a.k.a. *Daredevil*, is a lawyer in his civilian life and represents Jessica when she is wrongfully arrested. Later, he hires her and Luke Cage as bodyguards to further assert that he is not Daredevil after his identity is revealed by a tabloid newspaper.

- *J. Jonah Jameson* is the publisher of the New York newspaper *The Daily Bugle*. He has an irrational antisuperhero agenda and hires Jessica to uncover and expose Spider-Man's secret identity. He is also the foster father of Mattie Franklin, the third Spider-Woman, whom Jessica rescues from the clutches of a drug dealer. Jameson later hires Jessica as a superhero liaison in the series *The Pulse*.

Artistic Style

Gaydos's art is gritty, with bold lines and abundant use of shadows. This gives the series a film-noir effect that is fitting, as the main character is a private eye. Additionally, Hollingsworth's muted color palette enhances the somber mood displayed throughout the series.

The ability to convey characters' expressions is one of Gaydos's significant talents. He is able to suggest different emotions in panels that do not have word balloons or captions, giving the series the quality of "good acting." Information and emotion are also conveyed through the strategic use of page layouts. An interesting technique is repeatedly used when a client is telling Jessica his or her story. The panel is split into two parts: The top half shows Jessica listening, while the lower half features the clients' changes in expressions and mannerisms as they explain their stories. This technique reinforces Jessica's character and provides a certain cohesion to the storyline.

Consistency is one of the art's strongest qualities. When the art does change, it does so to further the verisimilitude of the story. For example, in "The Secret Origin of Jessica Jones," Gaydos illustrates a flashback to Jessica's teenage years, during which she went to school with Peter Parker, by drawing in a style similar to the early Spider-Man comics of the 1960's.

Although Gaydos supplies the vast majority of the art, *Alias* features guest artists a few times throughout the series. This is done purposely to reflect different eras of the Marvel Universe. For example, for flashbacks of Jessica as Jewel, the art is penciled by Mark Bagley, an experienced Marvel artist whose work reflects the visual style of early 1980's and 1990's comics. Furthermore, the lettering, coloring, and page format also reflect this era, giving the reader the feeling that the episodes did happen and could have been published years ago. When Jessica reads Rick Jones's autobiography, *Sidekick*, the accompanying one-page illustrations are drawn by Bill Sienkiewicz, another veteran artist with a distinct style. These "photos" from the book therefore separate themselves visually from the narrative reality contained within *Alias*.

Cover artist Mack uses a complex, layered approach. He employs a collage technique featuring the juxtaposition of realistic illustrations, childlike line drawing, and photos. This unique style separates *Alias*'s covers from those of other superhero books and gives depth to the characters. Overall, its unique style of art makes *Alias* stand out among other superhero titles and gives the series a visual maturity that accompanies Bendis's adult themes.

Themes

Alias explores themes of identity, manipulation, self-control, escape from one's past, and the possibility of happiness. From exposed secret identities to characters finding themselves, identity is the main theme in this series. Jessica is embarrassed by her past superhero personas. Her first adventure finds her accidentally filming Captain America as he changes into his costume, and she struggles with what to do with this information about his identity. When hired to find the missing former Hulk sidekick Rick Jones, she discovers that the man she is looking for is merely a Rick Jones impersonator. Neither the civilians nor the superheroes in *Alias* have a fixed identity.

Brian Michael Bendis

One of the most acclaimed comic book writers of the 2000's, Brian Michael Bendis is the chief architect of Marvel's Ultimate universe and the author of a wide range of company-wide crossovers, including *House of M*, *Secret War*, *Secret Invasion*, and *Siege*. Bendis began his career working in independent comics, where his crime titles *A.K.A. Goldfish* and *Jinx* brought him to the attention of Todd McFarlane. Working with McFarlane, Bendis wrote *Sam and Twitch* and *Hellspawn*. With Michael Oeming, he created *Powers*, a superhero/crime hybrid that won numerous industry awards. At Marvel Comics, he began writing *Ultimate Spider-Man* in 2001 and has written many other titles set in that universe. His work on *Daredevil* (with Alex Maleev) and *Alias* (with Alex Gaydos) are considered his finest work at Marvel, where he has become one of the most important writers on staff. Bendis is known for combining superhero comics storytelling with crime elements and for his ability to breathe new life into outdated comics concepts.

Manipulation is demonstrated most blatantly in the story line "Purple," in which the sociopathic Zebediah Killgrave, the Purple Man, is the villain. He possesses the ability to control people's minds, and as the flashback sequence reveals, Killgrave had previously manipulated and tortured Jessica, causing her to relinquish her superhero identity.

The theme of self-control manifests itself through Jessica's inability to fly. She can get off the ground, but not always reliably, and landing is a problem. In addition, she finds it difficult to remember and process what her own thoughts and desires were before Killgrave began controlling her mind. She remembers loving Killgrave, even though she knows he planted those thoughts in her head. Thus, the themes of identity, manipulation, and self-control are manifest in Jessica's situation.

After alluding to it for most of the series, the story arc "The Secret Origin of Jessica Jones" shows the effects of a traumatic event from Jessica's early years on her adult life. Jessica gained her powers as a teen when the car carrying her family crashed into a vehicle transporting radioactive material. In this single event, her family died and she developed powers as a result of her exposure to the chemicals. Jessica is unable to use her powers without being reminded of how she got them, manipulated by her past just as she was manipulated by Killgrave, and this contributes to her ambivalent feelings about being a superhero. Nevertheless, her triumph over Killgrave and her happy union with Luke at the end of the series demonstrate a final theme in the *Alias* series: the possibility of happiness in a world of dubious identity and past regrets.

Impact

Alias was the first title published by Marvel's mature-rated line, MAX Comics, and was more of a critical success than a financial one, in part because of its mature-readers label. The label not only restricted sales to minors but also prevented Bendis from using popular Marvel characters such as Spider-Man and Wolverine in the series because of their appeal to younger readers. When Spider-Man, for example, does appear in *Alias*, he is only shown peripherally as teenage Peter Parker. However, the mature label enabled the characters to

Alias. (Courtesy of Marvel Comics)

enter into more realistic relationships and adult situations, allowing them to develop as individuals both in *Alias* and in the works that followed.

In addition to introducing protagonist Jessica Jones, *Alias* served as a springboard for the reintroduction and further development of an earlier superhero, Luke Cage. The relationship, including their child and their marriage, continues beyond *Alias*, and they are featured in *The Pulse* and the *New Avengers* comics, in which Luke leads the team of superheroes.

Alex Alkana

Further Reading

Bendis, Brian Michael, and Mark Bagley. *The Pulse* (2004-2006).

Bendis, Brian Michael, and Alexander Maleev. *Scarlett* (2010-).

Bendis, Brian Michael, and Michael Avon Oeming. *Powers* (2000-).

Vaughan, Brian K., and Tony Harris. *Ex Machina* (2004-2010).

Bibliography

Giles, Keith. "Bendis Reflects on Comic-Con International 2001." *Comic Book Resources*, July 27, 2001. http://comicbookresources.com/print.php?type=ar&id=176.

Yarbrough, Beau. "Marvel Grows up with Mature Readers Line as Bendis Gets Down and Dirty with *Alias*." *Comic Book Resources*, May 7, 2001. http://www.comicbookresources.com/print.php?type=ar&id=224.

_____. "Would an *Alias* by Any Other Name Smell as Sweet?" *Comic Book Resources*, May 10, 2001. http://comicbookresources.com/?page=article&id=226.

See also: *Daredevil: Born Again; Daredevil: The Man Without Fear; Death of Captain America; Fallen Son: The Death of Captain America; Powers; Ex Machina*

ALL-STAR BATMAN AND ROBIN, THE BOY WONDER

Author: Miller, Frank
Artist: Jim Lee (penciller and cover artist); Scott Williams (inker and cover artist); Alex Sinclair (colorist and cover artist); Jared K. Fletcher (letterer)
Publisher: DC Comics
First serial publication: 2005-2008
First book publication: 2008

Publication History

All-Star Batman and Robin, the Boy Wonder was first published by DC Comics in nine single issues and is Frank Miller's fifth work in his Dark Knight Universe, which also includes *Batman: The Dark Knight Returns* (1986), *Batman: Year One* (1987), *Spawn/Batman* (1994), and *Batman: The Dark Knight Strikes Again* (2002). In 2008, the nine issues were collected in *All-Star Batman and Robin, the Boy Wonder,* Volume 1. The proposed six-issue *Dark Knight: Boy Wonder*, which was scheduled to be released in 2011, is supposed to finish the All-Star Batman and Robin story line. The stories of Miller's Dark Knight Universe occur on DC Comics' Earth-31, one of fifty-one realities created after the events of *Infinite Crisis* (2005-2006). *All-Star Batman and Robin* is placed chronologically after *Batman: Year One*.

In retelling Robin's origin story Miller borrows copiously from *Detective Comics*, issue 38 (1940), in which Dick Grayson/Robin is introduced as Batman's sidekick. In that issue, Dick's parents refuse to pay extortion money to gangsters, who place acid on the Grayson's trapeze ropes, which break during a performance; thus, they plunge to their deaths. Miller's version has Dick's parents shot by a sniper in front of him and a circus crowd.

The comic was initially a monthly publication but became bimonthly after issue 5. Issues 4-6 were up to five months late because penciller Jim Lee was involved in the production of the DC Universe Online video game.

Controversy surrounded issue 10, which went on sale more than four months late. The issue had already been distributed to retailers when DC noticed a printing

(WireImage)

Jim Lee

The artist who produced the best-selling single comics issue of all time with *X-Men* issue 1 (1991), Jim Lee is one of the most acclaimed artists to have emerged in the comics industry in the past quarter-century. Lee broke into comics as the artist on *Alpha Flight* and *Punisher War Journal* in the late-1980's. He rose to fame as the artist on *Uncanny X-Men*, prompting Marvel to create a new X-Men title to showcase his talents, which broke all sales records. A year later, Lee and six other artists left Marvel to create Image Comics, for which Lee created *WildCATs* under the Wild-Storm Productions banner. He illustrated *Batman: Hush* with writer Jeph Loeb and *Superman: For Tomorrow* with Brian Azzarello before becoming co-publisher of DC in 2010 and guiding the re-launch of all of that company's titles. Lee is known for his dynamic figure drawing and use of crowquill hatching to define depth, and his art largely defined the early-1990's superhero style.

error: Profane dialogue between Batgirl and several thugs had been blacked out but was still visible through the ink. DC asked retailers to destroy any copies that they had received in lieu of replacement copies. However, many copies had already been sold to the public.

Plot

All-Star Batman and Robin tells of how twelve-year-old Dick Grayson becomes Batman's crime-fighting partner, Robin. It also shows the emergence of the costumed superheroes Black Canary and Batgirl and the early foundation of the Justice League, consisting of Wonder Woman, Superman, Green Lantern Hal Jordan, and Plastic Man.

Dick Grayson, a circus acrobat and member of his family's trapeze group, the Flying Graysons, watches as his parents are shot in front of him and a circus audience that includes Bruce Wayne and reporter Vicki Vale. Inconceivably, Batman appears quickly and stops the fleeing killer, Jocko-Boy Vanzetti. The corrupt police take Dick to a known body-dumping ground, as Vale and Bruce's butler, Alfred, follow in Bruce's limousine. Batman follows in the Batmobile, and using a sonic device, he summons a flock of bats to scare the police away. Batman then crashes the Batmobile into both police car and limousine, seriously injuring Vale, and absconds with Dick.

Before passing out, Vale tells Alfred she saw Batman kidnap Dick. Batman's attempts to impress and intimidate Dick fail. More police pursue Batman until he engages the Batmobile's flight mode and heads to the Batcave. Internally, Batman questions whether or not he has done the right thing in recruiting Dick to his "mission" against crime as Dick struggles to make sense of his parents' murders.

Superman is angered after learning that Batman has reportedly kidnapped Dick Grayson. At the hospital, Vale is close to death as the result of her injuries. Batman advises Alfred to contact Superman via Clark Kent to retrieve a special doctor from Paris, which Superman does. Vale later makes a full recovery.

When finally arriving at the Batcave, Dick is impressed with its technological wonders and Batman's impressive array of vehicles, but he feigns disinterest. Unexpectedly, Batman leaves Dick alone in the Batcave to fend for himself. Later, Alfred provides Dick with food and clothes, which displeases Batman.

Wonder Woman, Superman, Green Lantern, and Plastic Man—the newly formed Justice League—debate Batman's alleged kidnapping of Dick Grayson and his violent crime-fighting methods. Superman proposes they turn him over to the authorities, Green Lantern believes they should reason with him, while Plastic Man thinks they should offer him membership. A seething Wonder Woman stridently opposes these actions, preferring to kill Batman as a sign that superheroes police their own kind. Green Lantern's proposal is adopted.

While investigating the freedom of Jocko-Boy Vanzetti, Batman intervenes in a melee involving Black Canary and numerous thugs. She is so impressed that she kisses him passionately. The text infers that they have intercourse. Later, Batman delivers Jocko-Boy to Dick and asks him to decide the killer's fate. Dick lets Jocko-Boy live but interrogates him viciously, finding out that the Joker hired him to kill Dick's parents. Dick wants to pursue the Joker immediately, but Batman refuses, telling Dick he is not ready. Batman tasks him with creating a secret identity and costume. Unimpressed with Dick's choice of "Hood," based on Robin Hood, Batman instead names him "Robin."

Batman reluctantly meets with Green Lantern, whom he thinks is a "moron." The meeting is brief, and Batman relocates the time and place to one of his Gotham safe houses. Knowing that Green Lantern's power ring cannot operate against anything yellow, Batman paints himself, Robin, and his safe house completely yellow. Batman mockingly denies the kidnapping accusations and dismisses the request to tone down his harsh methods. Robin pilfers Green Lantern's power ring. When Green Lantern tries to retrieve it, Dick punches him in the throat. Batman performs an emergency tracheotomy to save Green Lantern's life. After the incident, Batman realizes Dick must grieve and takes him to his parents' grave.

Captain James Gordon secretly delivers a note from Catwoman to Batman requesting Batman meet her. He finds her terribly injured at the hands of the Joker.

Gordon is confronted by his wife's life-threatening alcoholism after she is involved in a serious car accident. He also finds out his daughter, Barbara, has been moonlighting as Batgirl.

Characters

- *Batman*, a.k.a. *Bruce Wayne*, the protagonist, is brutal and arrogant in his mission to eradicate crime in Gotham. He is supremely confident and physically strong. He is also periodically moody and harsh when dealing with Dick/Robin. His crime-fighting methods draw the ire of the Justice League.
- *Robin*, a.k.a. *Dick Grayson*, is a twelve-year-old trapeze artist who sees his parents murdered in front of him. He is a brilliant acrobat, highly intelligent, and a fast learner. He struggles throughout to come to terms with his parents' murders and Batman's contradictory treatment of him. He soon embraces the Robin identity to help Batman fight crime.
- *Alfred Pennyworth* is Batman/Bruce Wayne's butler and confidante. He is a former member of the Air Force and trained in combat medicine. He is frequently sarcastic toward Batman/Bruce but kind and caring toward Dick.
- *Black Canary* is a blond Irish bar attendant working in a dingy Gotham bar who, inspired by Batman, decides to rob lowlifes rather than serve them drinks. She is a trained martial artist and is strongly attracted to Batman.
- *Green Lantern*, a.k.a. *Hal Jordan*, is an easily confused and flustered hero. He tries to convince Batman to tone down his crime-fighting methods but is enraged at his refusal. An overzealous Robin punches him in the throat, and Batman performs an emergency tracheotomy to save his life.
- *Catwoman*, a.k.a. *Selina Kyle*, a burglar, is a sultry former lover of Batman. She appears briefly, accepting the Joker's offer of creating "mischief," but she is later viciously assaulted by him.
- *Captain James Gordon* is perhaps the only honest cop in the Gotham City Police Department. A stoic figure, he has accepted Batman's vigilantism and enjoys an unstable alliance with the crime fighter.
- *Vicki Vale* is an attractive blond reporter who is injured while zealously pursuing the story of Dick Grayson's kidnapping.
- *Superman*, a.k.a. *Clark Kent*, is the "all-American" superhero. He is the first to call for calm but is easily incensed. He is particularly concerned about Batman's brutal crime-fighting activities. He is yet to realize he can fly.
- *Wonder Woman*, a.k.a. *Diana*, is a raven-haired Amazonian princess with a healthy disrespect for men and the world they have built. She is harsh, vocal, and dismissive of the other exploits of heroes and wants Batman "taken out."
- *Batgirl*, a.k.a. *Barbara Gordon*, is the redheaded teenage daughter of Gordon. Inspired by Batman, she takes on the role of Batgirl; however, her efforts come to nothing, and she is arrested by the police.
- *The Joker* is a white-skinned, melancholic, and psychopathic criminal sporting a large Chinese dragon tattoo across his back. He appears briefly, murdering a young female attorney and propositioning Catwoman about partnering in crime.

Artistic Style

Lee's comic style has become a benchmark for comic superhero art since he came to prominence in the 1990's. *All-Star Batman and Robin* provides more of his instantly and much-copied style of hyperkinetic action, extreme close-ups, and stilted poses. Lee's heroes are statuesque, sporting exaggerated musculature and dynamic lines. His facial expressions have a tendency to repeat, most notably Batman's continually "gritted-teeth" face, which is presented from every angle. Lee's art, which overwhelms panels, is highly subjective, placing the reader in the middle of the action.

Lee has stated that he could have easily created a Miller-style comic from the script but wanted to impose his own style, which required a conscious effort on his part to create something different. Issues contain between two and seven full-page splash panels, and apart from issues 1, 2, and 8, also contain up to three double-page spreads.

Issue 4 includes a six-page foldout of the Batcave. While splash and double-page spreads are indicative of Lee's style, their prevalence may well have been an attempt to complete issues quickly because of missed deadlines. Overall the comic becomes more of a vehicle for Lee's artwork than a solid attempt at comic storytelling.

As used previously in *Batman: Year One*, each character has personalized lettering for voice-over captioning, using a variety of fonts, styles, and coloring. Most notable is Batman's precisely italicized font, the Joker's scratchily chaotic handwritten script, Wonder Woman's elaborate cursive, and Gordon's typewriter font.

Each issue of the series was released with variant covers by Neal Adams, Miller, and Frank Quitely. Lee's cover illustration of issue 9 is an homage to Jack Burnley's cover of *Batman*, issue 9 (February-March, 1942). Miller's alternate cover of issue 2 references David Mazzucchelli's cover of the *Batman: Year One* trade paperback. An alternate cover for the unreleased issue 12 by Bill Sienkiewicz can be found online.

Themes

The theme of corruption is strong in *All-Star Batman and Robin*. While the endemic corruption of the Gotham City Police Department and Gotham as a city corrupted by crime are obvious examples of this theme, the idea of corruption extends into all facets of the story. Dick Grayson's childhood is corrupted by his parent's murder, Wonder Woman believes that men have corrupted the world, and Gordon's marriage has been corrupted by his wife's alcoholism. In his brief appearance, the Joker corrupts the trust of both the young attorney he murders and Catwoman, whom he initially treats as an equal but later assaults. To Batman, grief is also a corrupting influence: "Grief turns into acceptance. Forgiveness. Grief forgives what never can be forgiven." Grief corrupts a crime fighter's ability to do his job properly. Batman's methods corrupt the idea of a "hero," threatening to sully the image of other heroes.

Miller's solution to corruption, crime, and, indeed, grief, is that it can only be dealt with through uncompromising brute force. Batman reasons that causing "terror" is the best part of the job and that costumed crime fighters are themselves criminals. Thus, to allow Batman to be a "hero," crime and corruption in Gotham must be portrayed as much worse, more criminal, than Batman.

Impact

The teaming of Lee and Miller, two long-standing heavyweights of the comics industry, promised a Batman story to rival that of any era and a lucrative venture for DC Comics. Interest in the series was healthy; the first issue sold more than 300,000 copies. However, while both *Batman: The Dark Knight Returns* and *Batman: Year One* were praised as landmark comics, *All-Star Batman and Robin* was received with almost universal disdain. Criticism was aimed at the story's slow pace and Miller's use of repeating the same or similar phrases ad nauseam. Characters also tend to draw from the same vocabulary, conveying a lack of character definition. After Batman refers to Robin as a "little snot" for much of the book, Hal Jordan does the same. Similarly, Vicki Vale and Black Canary use the same expressions as Batman. None of the subtlety of *Batman: Year One* and *Batman: The Dark Knight Returns* is on display in *All-Star Batman and Robin*.

All-Star Batman and Robin is in no way a "traditional" portrayal of the brooding and usually stoic crime fighter. Batman's arrogance and his reveling in excessive violence are particularly jarring. His disdain for other heroes presents him as condescending and disrespectful. Because of his lack of compassion for Robin/Dick's situation and his consistent treatment of him as a burden and an annoyance, this Batman was one that readers found hard to embrace. To Miller's credit, he has created a unique portrayal of a supremely confident Batman enjoying his crime-fighter role.

Marise Williams

Further Reading

Miller, Frank. *Batman: The Dark Knight Returns* (1986).

Miller, Frank, and David Mazzucchelli. *Batman: Year One* (1987).

Miller, Frank, Lynn Varley, and Todd Klein. *Batman: The Dark Knight Strikes Again* (2002).

Bibliography

Adams, Sam, et al. "Reinventing the Pencil: Twenty-one Artists Who Changed Mainstream Comics (For Better or Worse)." *A.V. Club*, July, 2009. http://www.avclub.com/articles/reinventing-the-pencil-21-artists-who-changed-main,30528.

Murray, Ross. "Dissecting Why All-Star Batman and Robin Leaves Fans Cold." *Mapping the Multiverse: Comics Superheroes and Research in the Age of Now*, June 18, 2010. http://mapping-the-multiverse.blogspot.com/2010/06/dissecting-why-all-star-batman-and.html.

Tantimedh, Adi. "New York Comic Con, Day One: Jim Lee Spotlight." *Comic Book Resources*, February 25, 2006. http://www.comicbookresources.com/?page=article&id=6523.

See also: *Batman: Black and White,* Volume 1*; Batman: Dark Victory; Batman: The Dark Knight Returns; Batman: The Dark Knight Strikes Again; Batman: The Killing Joke; Batman: The Long Halloween; Batman: Year One; Batman: Year 100*

ALL-STAR SUPERMAN

Author: Morrison, Grant
Artist: Frank Quitely (pseudonym of Vincent Deighan; illustrator); Jamie Grant (colorist and inker); Phil Balsman (letterer); Travis Lanham (letterer)
Publisher: DC Comics
First serial publication: 2005-2008
First book publication: 2007, 2009

Publication History

All-Star Superman was conceived by Grant Morrison as a way to revitalize and to simplify DC Comics' oldest and most renowned superhero. Morrison was already a popular author for both Marvel Comics and DC Comics, part of the "British wave" of writers, which included Neil Gaiman and Alan Moore, who made a collective splash in American comics starting in the 1980's. For DC, Morrison had already revitalized such minor characters as Animal Man and Doom Patrol before reviving the moribund Justice League of America. He also created and wrote the acclaimed series *The Invisibles*, a mature comic book for DC's Vertigo imprint.

All-Star Superman was originally published as a twelve-issue, ongoing comic by DC Comics as part of its All-Star project. For that imprint, DC hired the finest writers and artists to reconstruct its most iconic heroes, by eliminating considerable baggage that had accumulated in those heroes' various comics over many decades of publication, and give those creators free rein to tell out-of-continuity stories. The intent was for readers who were unfamiliar with the heroes' entire history, or perhaps those who had never read them at all, to appreciate them as much as long-established readers of Superman had.

The series was later collected in two volumes by DC Comics in 2007 and 2009. A one-volume compilation, entitled *Absolute All-Star Superman,* was published in 2010.

Plot

The series begins with Superman rescuing Earth from an attempt by Lex Luthor to implant a high-powered nuclear bomb in the sun, which would have dire effects

(Getty Images)

Frank Quitely

Frank Quitely is the pen name of Scottish comics artist Vincent Deighan, one of the most acclaimed illustrators of the 2000's. After breaking into the American comic book industry as the artist on Grant Morrison's 1996 *Flex Mentallo* miniseries, Quitely undertook a number of works for DC and its Vertigo imprint. In 2000 he collaborated with Morrison on *JLA: Earth 2* and replaced Bryan Hitch as the artist on *The Authority*. By the time he helped to reboot the X-Men franchise with *New X-Men*, he had become one of the most sought-after names in comics. His collaborations with Morrison since that time have included *We3*, *All-Star Superman*, and *Batman and Robin*. Quitely's art is defined by its open, uncluttered sensibility where posture is given predominance in the construction of meaning and characterization. His images are reminiscent of Geoff Darrow and rely on similarly thin lines, but are considerably more minimalist.

on the planet. In doing so, Superman enters the outskirts of the sun itself. Since Superman was born on a planet under a red sun, many of his powers come from exposure to the yellow sun. He experiences two side effects as the result of such close contact: his superpowers have increased at least threefold, but also that his exposure to such high levels of solar radiation is slowly killing him.

Superman decides to temporarily keep the latter information private, and he immediately pursues his relationship with Lois Lane before he dies, a relationship that he had shunned previously out of fear for Lois's life at the hands of his enemies. He brings Lois to his Fortress of Solitude for a private dinner and a birthday gift of artificial Superman-like powers, which she will possess for only twenty-four hours. During this episode, hindrances to their relationship become apparent—Lois is intimidated by Superman, and she is insecure being in his fortress alone with him.

Immediately upon their return to Metropolis, Superman and Lois encounter a series of emergencies that require Superman's help. First is an invasion of subterranean reptiles. Their attempts to overcome the reptiles are hindered by Samson and Atlas, two strongmen who are also attracted to Lois Lane and who encourage a competition with Superman for her affection. Samson is a time traveler who tells Superman that he (Superman) will be remembered by future generations for successfully handling twelve legendary challenges before he dies. These challenges provide the structure for the remaining chapters in the series.

Although *All-Star Superman* was designed in part to streamline the Superman legend, Morrison still introduces many of the familiar characters who had become part of the Superman mythology over the previous seven decades. Within the series, Superman shares an adventure with his pal Jimmy Olsen; spends time at his childhood home with his adoptive parents Jonathan and Martha Kent, and attends his father's funeral after his sudden heart attack; visits with his superdog Krypto, who returns from his frequent travels in space; becomes trapped on the Bizarro world, a square planet filled with beings who are the opposite of their counterparts on Earth; and finally frees the miniaturized inhabitants of Kandor, the last surviving city from his home

planet of Krypton. Throughout the story, Superman performs the twelve heroic feats that had been predicted by Samson: saving the manned mission to the sun, brewing an elixir that gives Lois Lane temporary superpowers, answering the Ultrasphinx's "unanswerable" question, chaining the Chronovore, saving Earth from the inhabitants of the Bizarro world, returning alive from the Ultraverse, creating life, freeing the inhabitants of Kandor, defeating Solaris, conquering death, building an artificial heart for the sun, and inventing a formula to create a second Superman.

Volumes

- *All-Star Superman,* Volume 1 (2007). Collects issues 1-6, in which Superman first learns of his impending death and strives to cope with it by solidifying his relationship with Lois Lane.
- *All-Star Superman,* Volume 2 (2009). Collects issues 7-12, featuring Superman's last legendary challenges, his final encounter with his nemesis Lex Luthor, and his inevitable death.
- *Absolute All-Star Superman* (2010). Collects issues 1-12.

Characters

- *Superman* (original name, *Kal-El*; secret identity, *Clark Kent*) was born on the planet Krypton but was sent to Earth by his parents shortly before Krypton exploded. Because of Earth's lower gravity and yellow sun, Superman has superpowers such as invulnerability, the ability to fly, super strength, and X-ray vision. He devotes his life to fighting crime and saving people from disasters on his adopted planet.
- *Lois Lane* is the ace reporter for *The Daily Planet*, where Superman works in the guise of Clark Kent. Lois is in love with Superman, who has mixed feelings toward her, being fearful that his enemies might attack her to get at him.
- *Lex Luthor* is an unstable genius who seeks to be the most powerful person on Earth. He hates Superman intensely for having usurped that position. He regularly devises schemes to kill Superman. As many of the schemes fail, Luthor spends considerable time in prison.

- *Jimmy Olsen* is a junior reporter and photographer for *The Daily Planet*. A naïve young man, he is one of Superman's only friends. Because Olsen's public image as a friend of Superman might cause Superman's numerous enemies to strike at him, Superman gave him a "signal watch" that summons Superman in an emergency.

- *Dr. Leo Quintum* is Superman's confidant and serves as his sounding board. He examines Superman after his return from the sun and determines that he is dying. Ultimately, he holds the secret for the formula that can create another Superman.

- *The Superman Squad* is a group of superpowered supermen from future eras who time travel to Superman's era to help him in his battle with the Chronovore as part of their mission to protect space-time.

- *Bizarro* is a strange opposite of Superman. Bizarro's thought processes are backward from those of normal humans, as everything he says and does is the reverse of the truth. While his actions often seem evil, he actually believes he is doing good. When Superman is trapped on the Bizzaro world, he must speak in reverse logic in order to elicit Bizarro's help.

- *Bar-El* and *Lilo*, were Krypton's first astronauts. The couple survived the planet's destruction as they were in space when the planet exploded. They consider all humans inferior and think Superman is a failure for mourning the destruction of Krypton. They are determined to make Krypton's culture live again. Like Superman, they possess superpowers. While Superman was trapped on the Bizarro world, Bar-El and Lilo take over the Fortress of Solitude. When he returns to Earth, weakened by his exposure to solar radiation, they use his weakness to their advantage and hurl him at the moon, which breaks in two from the impact. Later, Superman shows compassion toward the two when he saves them and places them in the Phantom Zone.

Artistic Style

Many artists have contributed to the *Superman* continuity since the character was first introduced in 1938, each bringing his or her own personal style to it. During the 1970's, DC Comics made a deliberate effort to raise its literary standards by emphasizing characterization and thematic plots, which had been a successful approach for Marvel Comics the previous decade. This affected the art as well, which was heavily influenced by Neal Adams's style, in which the main characters were more realistic. The background of the frames became nearly as important as the foreground. Since *All-Star Superman* was partly an attempt to simplify the Superman legend, artist Frank Quitely opted to simplify the art as well. His work recalls the *Superman* artists of the 1950's, such as Curt Swan and Wayne Boring, who emphasized the action in the panel foregrounds (the backgrounds were considerably less important). In *All-Star Superman*, the panel backgrounds are often blank or are filled with complementary colors so that the figures in the foreground stand out. At times, the foreground is brightly colored while the background is darker by contrast. Overall, the panels are considerably less crowded than had become the norm, with an open, vibrant feel to them.

The characters are drawn in the traditional, simple, comic style reminiscent of the 1950's and 1960's versions. While Superman is square-jawed and an imposing figure, he is never particularly detailed or well-muscled. His hair has the recognizable curl over his forehead and is combed in a more traditional style when he is disguised as Clark Kent.

The series chronicles the heroic feats and eventual death of Superman, and as the series progresses, Quitely shows Superman's physical deterioration. His features become less clearly defined, which gives him a slightly unkempt appearance, and facial markings mar the clean features that defined Superman earlier in the series.

Captions and splash panels have become common techniques in graphic storytelling. However, Morrison and Quitely avoid virtually all captions, opting instead to tell their story exclusively through pictures and cartoon balloons. This simplification, along with the less cluttered panels, speeds up the pacing of the story while adding to an open, free-flowing feel.

Quitely first drew the panels in blue line, then used graphic pencils on top of that to achieve his desired line thickness. Inker Jamie Grant scanned the panels into Photoshop, which he used for the inking. This method enabled Grant to maintain the correct thickness throughout, which is sometimes lost in the manual inking process.

Themes

According to author Morrison, there are several themes flowing through *All-Star Superman*. Perhaps the most dominant is Superman's optimistic outlook for the goodness and future of humanity, in spite of his own impending death. Morrison intended for Superman to be a Christlike figure in a way that was subtle and without religious undertones. Similar to Christ, Superman was sent to Earth by his father and uses his talents to try to save humanity from its own weaknesses. Morrison deliberately removes all traces of doubt and dark thoughts from Superman, which had become a popular trend, so that Superman's only concern is for the good of others.

This leads to another important theme (and another similarity between Superman and Christ)—the tendency to "turn the other cheek." No matter how cruel another person might be in the series, Superman never descends to a spiteful level, always showing respect and kindness to everybody he meets. This is most apparent in a scene involving Steve Lombard, an egotistical *Daily Planet* employee who constantly degrades Superman in front of other employees, including Clark Kent. When Superman encounters Lombard, he treats him with humility. In another demonstration of Superman's benevolence, he shows respect to Lex Luthor, when, as Clark Kent, he interviews Luthor in prison, even though he knows Luthor is responsible for his impending death.

Another theme, which initially seems almost contradictory, is Morrison's attempt to show that Superman is not "above" or "better than" humans but is, rather, a traditional everyman—a representative man rather than the ideal man. This is evident in Superman's upbringing, as he was raised as Clark Kent, an average

man with no spectacular talents. Kent's clumsiness—a common aspect of his personality for many decades—is a frequent reminder of his humanity. Bar-El and Lilo recognize Superman's humanity, which perhaps prompts their frustration with humans and Superman, who has embraced his adopted planet and its culture. Superman is not intended to be just a Christlike figure saving humanity; he also represents the potential of all humans to save themselves.

Impact

The vast majority of DC Comics have a regular continuity, with events in each comic having an impact on others. Although its All-Star line of comics was a deliberate departure from this tradition, intended to be outside DC's regular continuity, the change is part of a continuing trend in that direction. Two of its influences were Frank Miller's *The Dark Knight Returns* and Moore's *Watchmen*, both of which sought to create more realistic views of superheroes. Writers like Morrison, Moore, and Miller are all often concerned with treating their characters as people rather than as icons encumbered by all the trappings that have accumulated in the works of numerous writers and artists over the years.

An immediate influence on *All-Star Superman* is DC's *One Million*, a crossover event that featured many of the company's superheroes and villains. It was designed by Morrison in 1998 and showed the descendants of DC's twentieth- and twenty-first-century heroes. Some critics have surmised that *All-Star Superman* was written as a prequel to *One Million*, which Morrison neither affirms nor denies.

All-Star Superman was an immediate critical and popular success; its most notable impact on comics was demonstrating that allowing writers and artists to alter the basic framework of even iconic characters did not alienate either longtime or new readers. In a similar vein, Morrison and Quitely later worked together on a new continuing series, *Batman and Robin*, which was not intended to mimic *All-Star Superman,* but took a similar approach in its willingness to discard much of the traditional baggage that had accumulated in previous *Batman* story lines.

Robert Sabella

Films

All-Star Superman. Directed by Sam Liu. DC Entertainment/Warner Bros. Animation, 2011. This direct-to-DVD animated film is based directly on Morrison and Quitely's comic series.

Television Series

Smallville. Developed by Alfred Gough and Miles Millar. Warner Bros., 2001-2011. At the beginning, this series focused on Clark Kent as a high school student before he became Superman. In later seasons, the show shifted to Kent's adult life.

Further Reading

Bendis, Brian Michael, and Mark Bagley. *Ultimate Spider-Man* (2002-2010).

Millar, Mike, and Brian Michael Bendis. *Ultimate X-Men* (2006-2010).

Miller, Frank, and Jim Lee. *All-Star Batman and Robin, the Boy Wonder* (2009).

Morrison, Grant, Andy Clarke, and Cameron Stewart. *Batman and Robin,* Volume 2*: Batman and Robin* (2010).

Morrison, Grant, Frank Quitely, and Phillip Tan. *Batman and Robin,* Volume 1*: Batman Reborn* (2010).

Bibliography

Klaehn, Jeffrey. "Grant Morrison, Batman, and the Superhero Genre." *Publishers Weekly*, January 13, 2009.

See also: *All Star Batman and Robin, the Boy Wonder; Watchmen; Batman: The Dark Knight Returns*

A*MAZING* A*DVENTURES OF THE* E*SCAPIST*, T*HE*

Author: Chabon, Michael; Chaykin, Howard; Mc-Carthy, Kevin; Pekar, Harvey; Vaughan, Brian K.

Artist: Eduardo Barreto (illustrator); Eddie Campbell (illustrator); Will Eisner (illustrator); Dean Haspiel (illustrator); Eric Wight (illustrator); Paul Hornschemeier (colorist); Dan Jackson (colorist); Michelle Madsen (colorist); Sean Konot (letterer); Tom Orzechowski (letterer); Brian Bolland (cover artist); Mike Mignola (cover artist); Chris Ware (cover artist)

Publisher: Dark Horse Comics

First serial publication: 2004-2005

First book publication: 2004-2006

Publication History

The Amazing Adventures of the Escapist originated in Michael Chabon's Pulitzer Prize-winning novel *The Amazing Adventures of Kavalier and Clay* (2000), in which two Jewish cousins invent the superhero the Escapist during the Golden Age of comic books. After the success of the novel, Dark Horse Comics secured the rights to publish a real-life comic featuring Chabon's metafictional character. Along with editor Diana Schutz, Chabon oversaw the production of *The Amazing Adventures of the Escapist* and also made occasional contributions. The bulk of the comic was created by an array of contemporary artists and writers.

Although *The Amazing Adventures of the Escapist* consists entirely of original material, it continues the novel's pretense that the character was part of a hugely successful but now forgotten Golden Age franchise and that its creators actually existed. Various explanatory passages, written mostly by Chabon (sometimes under a pseudonym), contend that the series collects recently discovered documents from the Escapist's history.

Dark Horse published eight quarterly collections of nonserialized Escapist stories during 2004 and 2005 before the series was canceled due to poor sales. The first six issues were collected in three trade paperbacks and published by Dark Horse Books. The last issue of *The Amazing Adventures of the Escapist* contained the first issue of *The Escapists*, an attempt to offset the

(Getty Images)

Michael Chabon

Michael Chabon combines elements of literary fiction and genres such as fantasy and adventure into novels centered on story, character, and a love of language. In his writing for both adults and teens, Chabon tells complex stories about multifaceted characters whose motivations and lives reflect the realities of the worlds in which they live. Even when examining philosophical or social issues, Chabon adds witty dialogue and a comedic touch that ranges from academic humor to light-hearted whimsy.

commercially unsuccessful anthology character of the series through the inclusion of a continued narrative. *The Escapists* evolved into a six-issue spin-off series, also published by Dark Horse and later collected in graphic novel form.

Plot

The Amazing Adventures of the Escapist, a collection of stories with unrelated plots and without a particular reading order, tells the story of the eponymous hero and other characters created by Joe Kavalier and Sam Clay. In addition to superhero stories, the series also includes several short, often childlike comics. Acting as a sort of continuation of Chabon's novel, the comic series repeatedly supplements its stories with essays that explain the fate of the franchise after the novel's end in 1954, thus constructing an alternate history of comics centered on the Escapist.

The origin story, "The Passing of the Key," is set in Empire City, a Gotham-esque version of New York City. The young Tom Mayflower is one of the assistants of his uncle Max, the escape artist Misterioso. During one of his performances, Max is shot and lies dying in the backstage area. In his final minutes, he tells Tom how he was recruited by The League of the Golden Key, an ancient secret society that has the mission of freeing captives and liberating the oppressed. The league's prime enemy is the nefarious Iron Chain, an equally ancient society that is now covertly ruling Nazi Germany. Max gives Tom a magic key that he got from the league and thus passes the torch to his nephew, who begins to call himself the Escapist and fight the Iron Chain and other villains.

The first volume presents two different 1950's incarnations of the Escapist. In "Are You Now or Have You Ever Been. . . ." he takes on a Joseph McCarthy-like witch-hunting senator who tries to hide his masochistic practices by killing the owners of incriminating material. In "Sequestered," Tom Mayflower has to appear for jury duty and ends up freeing the defendant, who was framed by the Iron Chain. In "Prison Break," he infiltrates a prison and uncovers the corrupt machinations of the prison management with the help of his archenemy, the Saboteur. An aged Escapist rescues a crashed submarine in "Three Hundred Fathoms Down," while "Divine Wind" is an Escapist manga. In "The Lady or the Tiger," the Escapist falls in love with a female Escapist but learns that she was created by the Iron Chain. The latter part of the first volume focuses on another major character of the Escapist universe, Luna Moth. A librarian by day and a flying superhero by night, she takes on a crazy villain ("The Mechanist"), a devilish creature ("Old Flame"), and Death himself ("Reckonings").

Volume two begins with "Heil and Fear Well," a story reminiscent of 1950's horror tales published by EC Comics, in which surviving Nazis, headed by Josef Mengele, try to put Adolf Hitler's mind into the brain of a U.S. senator. The story "The Escapist 2966" depicts a future Escapist on whom centuries of escaping and liberating have left an indelible mark of doubt. "Chain Reaction" is a further Escapist-versus-Saboteur story, while "The Boy Who Would Be the Escapist" depicts how a boy escapes his miserable state through fantasizing about the Escapist. "The Trial of Judy Dark" is a Luna Moth tale in which a good deal of her origin story is told, and "To Reign in Hell" shows how the Escapist's assistant Big Al is tempted by an Iron Chain agent to defect.

Volume three opens with a meeting between the Escapist and one of his most important role models, the Spirit. Then, in "The Death of the Escapist," a present-day Escapist plants the germ of liberation in an Asian dictatorship by feigning his own death. "Liberators" shows a postwar Escapist team up with former Resistance members in the attempt to salvage art, only to learn that parts of the group work for the Soviet Union. In "A Fair to Remember," the Iron Chain plots against the 1939-1940 New York World's Fair but is stopped by the Escapist, while the Escapist's assistant Omar uses his hypnotic powers to bring down the villain in "Doc Hypnosis vs. The Escapist." "Another Man's Escape," which shows an undisguised Tom Mayflower as a soldier in Vietnam, precedes the troubling "Electricity," in which the only connection to the Escapist is Sam Clay, who supposedly penned the story. The 1960's "The Siren Song of Circe O'Shaughnessy" puts the Escapist in New York bohemia, while the 1980's indie-style "The Escapist Escapes Again!" depicts another failed plan of the Iron Chain to capture the Escapist. A Bronze Age story about euthanasia, "The Final Curtain" concludes the volume on a somber note.

Issue 7 consists of only one story, written by Chabon and not featuring the Escapist. "Arms and the Man I Sing" features Mr. Machine Gun, a marginal character in the Escapist universe. Equipped by mad Nazis with a mechanical arm that can transform into a machine gun, he becomes an instrumental weapon in World War II and the Korean War. Now, during the 1970's, he is a U.S. senator, but the weapon takes increasing control of his actions and turns him into a brutal avenger of the night.

Along with the Harvey Pekar-penned "Escape from the Hospital," a war story titled "Powder Burns," and the carnival story "The Escapist at the Royal Festival of Magic," issue 8 contains the first episode of *The Escapists*. In this spin-off, a young comic fan, son of the most ardent collector of Escapist memorabilia, teams up with two other teenagers to revive the comic book.

Volumes

- *The Amazing Adventures of the Escapist,* Volume 1 (2004). Collects issues 1-2, featuring the Escapist's origin story and several stories about Luna Moth. With multiple stories taking place in the 1950's, this volume focuses on a corrupt, witch-hunting senator and the nefarious activities of the Iron Chain.
- *The Amazing Adventures of the Escapist,* Volume 2 (2004). Collects issues 3-4, highlighting the origin story of Luna Moth and features an Escapist-versus-Saboteur story, "Chain Reaction."
- *The Amazing Adventures of the Escapist,* Volume 3 (2006). Collects issues 5-6, featuring "The Escapist and the Spirit," Will Eisner's last work. The volume also includes stories of the Escapist set in the 1960's and the 1980's.

Characters

- *Tom Mayflower*, a.k.a. *the Escapist*, the protagonist, is a young man with a lame left leg. He was rescued from an orphanage in central Poland by Max Mayflower and raised as his nephew. After receiving the golden key, he loses his physical impediment and becomes the agile Escapist. With his domino mask and occasional hat, team of assistants, magic key that helps him out of traps and desperate situations, and suit with a key symbol, he is essentially a pastiche of several pulp and comics figures.

- *Max Mayflower*, a.k.a. *Misterioso*, is a Harry Houdini-like escape artist and Tom's uncle. He was abducted as a rich, irresponsible young man, but he was then freed by the League of the Golden Key and given the golden key, which he gives to Tom shortly before his death.
- *Dr. Alois Berg*, a.k.a. *Big Al*, is one of the Escapist's assistants. Endowed with incredible strength and intellect, he was kept in a cage as a circus freak until liberated by Max Mayflower. The mustached Big Al is eight feet tall and constantly wears a bowler hat. Reciting from works by William Shakespeare and Sir Isaac Newton while engaging in fisticuffs, he resembles the X-Men's Beast in character.
- *Omar* is the turban-clad Asian assistant of the Escapist. Also freed by Max, he is a former slave of the sultan of Khurvistan. Omar is a taciturn character who occasionally uses his hypnotic powers to help the Escapist.
- *Miss Plum Blossom* is the third major assistant in the series. Like Big Al and Omar, she was freed by Max Mayflower, in her case from a sweatshop in Macau. A submissive and silent figure, she is responsible for creating the Escapist's masks and wardrobe.
- *Judy Dark*, a.k.a. *Luna Moth*, is the latest avatar of the Cimmerian moth goddess Lo. A shy librarian at the Empire City Public Library, she becomes the voluptuous Luna Moth after she is shot to death during the exhibition of the mysterious Book of Lo. She closely resembles a gender-inverted version of Clark Kent/Superman.
- *Officer Francis O'Hara* is a hapless police officer. He dates Judy Dark but is secretly enamored of her alter ego, Luna Moth, who repeatedly has to rescue him.
- *The Saboteur* is the only villain to appear in more than one story. In his maniacal attempt to rule over Empire City, he engages in several plots against the Escapist but also fights the Iron Chain, since he claims Empire City for himself.
- *Ben Vanderslice*, a.k.a. *Mr. Machine Gun*, is the heir of an arms empire and was captured by Nazis while working as an Office of Strategic Services

(OSS) agent in World War II. Through the Nazis' implantation of a machine-gun hand, he becomes the invincible Mr. Machine Gun, a strategic asset for the United States; however, he resigns after a massacre during the Korean War. During the 1970's, he works as a pacifist senator and is an advocate of gun control. When his machine-gun hand takes control of his mind and turns him into a brutal avenger at night, he nearly kills himself to become free of the gun.

Artistic Style

Given the large group of contributors, the breadth of artistic styles on display in *The Amazing Adventures of the Escapist* is extensive. Realistic drawings of the Escapist alternate with highly hypertrophied renditions of him, and perfectly conventional superhero styles are supplemented by stories drawn as children's comics, manga, or in anthropomorphic styles. Crude artwork is contrasted with highly ornate stories in lush watercolors or even computer-rendered panels. Contemporary styles are sometimes contrasted and sometimes integrated with older styles from earlier ages. Nonetheless, the various artistic approaches share one common denominator. Every story is evocative of a certain artist, style, genre, or historical period; however, hardly ever does the art recreate the historical styles verbatim. Rather, the series depicts a precarious combination of contemporary, state-of-the-art illustrations, panel structures, and colorings with classic styles. Thus, the series both plays with nostalgia and belies its own historical context. Still, this playful reconstruction of comics history often creates impressive pastiche work. More explicit cases of quotation can also be seen, as, for example, on the cover of issue 3. Drawn by Mike Mignola, it shows the Escapist punching Hitler in the jaw, a clear allusion to Captain America, issue 1.

Themes

The linchpin of both *The Amazing Adventures of Kavalier and Clay* and *The Amazing Adventures of the Escapist* is the metaphorical usage of the terms "escape" and "liberation." On one hand, the series continues the novel's broad interrogations of literal and symbolic escapes, featuring a shell-shocked G.I. who has become the prisoner of his mind, a terminally ill man for whom death means escape, a depressive Pekar, and the Escapist, who sometimes wishes nothing more than to be able to escape from his own destiny.

On the other hand, the series continues the novel's engagement with the superhero. In the novel, this is closely linked to the Jewish background of the comic book's creators. Mirroring the Jewish subtext of many other superheroes, the Escapist is rendered as a therapeutic attempt by Kavalier to assuage his inability to rescue his family from the Nazis and their ultimate fate in the Holocaust. With *The Amazing Adventures of the Escapist*, the reader witnesses a slight change of emphasis. Rather than primarily examining the relation between superheroes and Jewish identity, it examines the relationship between superheroes and comics history. The series' work with history and genre highlights the superhero's central features and muses on the nature of the respective genres. The sincere take on the genre as a whole, which already characterized the novel, allows for an affectionate portrayal of the Escapist's fate throughout the decades as well as an analysis of the history of comics. Also, through its depiction of the obscure ownership history of the Escapist and the role several publishers play in its demise, it also pleads for the escape of comics artists from the debilitating control of copyright-owning publishers.

Impact

The Amazing Adventures of the Escapist is unique in origin, as a fictional hero from a literary novel became real on the pages of a comic book. However, given mixed reviews and overall weak sales, the project was rather short-lived. Although it did result in the publication of the six-issue spin-off *The Escapists*, neither series caused any significant trend.

However, the impact of *The Amazing Adventures of the Escapist* cannot be gauged without considering the novel that spawned the comic book. *The Amazing Adventures of Kavalier and Clay* is an influential literary engagement with the comic medium and has proven to be a factor in the increasing cultural respectability of and academic interest in comics. *The Amazing Adventures of the Escapist* continues Chabon's original project insofar as it calls for an understanding of comics that highlights the artistic and intellectual potential of the medium while embracing formerly denigrating terms such as "escapist entertainment". For Chabon, these are the factors that make comics what they are, and it would be detrimental to the form if the reader forgot about them in favor of "serious" work alone.

Florian Groß

Further Reading

Chaykin, Howard. *American Flagg!* (1983-1989).
Eisner, Will, et al. *The Spirit* (1941-1952).
Vaughan, Brian K., et al. *The Escapists* (2005-2007).

Bibliography

Behlman, Lee. "The Escapist: Fantasy, Folklore, and the Pleasures of the Comic Book in Recent Jewish American Holocaust Fiction." *Shofar* 22, no. 3 (Spring, 2004): 56-71.

Chabon, Michael. *The Amazing Adventures of Kavalier and Clay*. New York: Picador, 2000.

Chute, Hillary. "Ragtime, Kavalier and Clay, and the Framing of Comics." *Modern Fiction Studies* 54, no. 2 (2008): 268-301.

Harvey, Robert C. *The Art of the Comic Book: An Aesthetic History*. Jackson: University Press of Mississippi, 1996.

See also: *The Spirit Archives,* Volume 1*; American Flagg!; Omega the Unknown; Death of Captain America; Fallen Son: The Death of Captain America*

AMERICAN FLAGG!

Author: Badger, Mark; Chaykin, Howard; DeMatteis, J. M.; Grant, Steve

Artist: Mark Badger (illustrator); Howard Chaykin (illustrator); Joe Staton (illustrator, penciller); Mike Vosburg (penciller); Leslie Zahler (colorist); Ken Bruzenack (letterer)

Publisher: First Comics

First serial publication: *American Flagg!*, 1983-1988; *Howard Chaykin's American Flagg!*, 1988-1989

First book publication: *American Flagg!*, 2008

Publication History

American Flagg! was published by First Comics starting in October, 1983, and was initially written, illustrated, and inked by Howard Chaykin. First Comics was a start-up based in Chicago that offered unprecedented opportunities for creators to own their own work. The initial series was designed to be an ongoing satire of both contemporary popular culture and corporate influences, and it soon ranked next to Alan Moore's *Watchmen* and Frank Miller's work on *Daredevil* and *Batman* as one of the most sophisticated and truly adult comics of the early 1980's.

Chaykin was determined to parody what he saw as the obvious corruption of the Ronald Reagan era, but after the first twelve issues, the workload proved too much, and Chaykin began to relinquish the series' art and eventually plot to other artists and writers.

The first run was incredibly influential at first, but gradually sales began to wane as Chaykin lost interest, essentially dropping out of plotting the stories and creating the art from issues 33 to 45. Chaykin returned for the final four issues, but the series was canceled by issue 50.

A year later, Chaykin resumed the comic as *Howard Chaykin's American Flagg!*, which ended after twelve issues in 1989. A paperback edition of several issues collected as *American Flagg! State of the Union* was released in 1989, but the subsequent reissues were delayed by almost two decades. In 2008, Image Comics issued two volumes of *American Flagg*, collecting issues 1-14.

Howard Chaykin

American Flagg! remains Howard Chaykin's best-known work. An idiosyncratic mix of sex and science fiction, the series was one of the most stylish adventure comics of the 1980's. Chaykin broke into comics in the 1970's but was constrained by the limitations of the Comics Code, which did not allow him to pursue the adult themes for which he would become well known. Later projects for DC, including *Blackhawk* and *The Shadow*, offered updates on pulp traditions, while *Black Kiss* (published by Vortex) highlighted Chaykin's interest in sexualized violence. A preeminent visual stylist, Chaykin's art is among the most distinctive in comics, with its exaggerated naturalism and reliance on complex geometric patterns. Chaykin's page layouts were noticeably more complex than most mainstream comics work, with multiple inset panels and an often maze-like placement of word balloons.

Plot

American Flagg! was created by Chaykin in 1983 as a social satire of greed, rampant commercialism, and corporate control in the United States. In 2031, much of the United States has been destroyed, and the government has essentially fled to Mars, leaving large corporations in charge of most of the Earth, which includes a population living mostly in shopping malls.

In the first issue, Reuben Flagg, a former actor who has been replaced by a hologram in his hit show *Mark Thrust: Sexus Ranger*, arrives at the Chicago Mallplex where he is assigned to his first position in the rangers. His new superior, Hilton "Hammerhead" Krieger, quickly throws Reuben into the middle of a firefight with the local Gogangs, who seem to riot immediately after the popular program *Bob Violence* goes off the air.

Reuben is also introduced to Krieger's daughter, Mandy Krieger; corrupt mayor C. K. Blitz; and Krieger's assistant, Raul, a talking cat who quickly becomes Flagg's guide to his new environment. Krieger has been running a pirate television station, competing against violent shows such as *Bob Violence*, which, unknown to him or anyone outside Raul and Flagg, contains subliminal messages that urge the Gogangs to go to war immediately after the program is over. Blitz is concerned about the gangs as his daughter, Medea Blitz, is dating Cyril Farid-Khan, leader of the Genetic Warlords.

When Krieger is murdered, Medea and Cyril are immediately seen as possible suspects and are hunted by Flagg. However, Krieger was really killed by secret Plexus agent John Scheiskopf, who was investigating the illegal pirate station's blocking of the subliminal violent messages. After a fight, Scheiskopf is left for dead by Flagg, who resumes control of Q-USA.

Scheiskopf, who has not actually died, returns with new robotic legs and a plan to destroy all of Chicago with poison gas. Flagg thwarts his plan and Scheiskopf's neo-Nazi allies, but the gas is still primed to destroy the mall. However, when the amnesiac Peggy Krieger regains her memory, she is able to defuse the Siphogene gas, which was about to destroy the mall.

After briefly fighting an ecoterrorist, Flagg journeys to Canada, where Canadian Plexus Rangers are shown to be just as corrupt as the other rangers he had encountered previously. In Kansas, Flagg defeats a "pornocrat" who has used subliminal messages to turn all of the state's inhabitants into participants in a large orgy.

Flagg is able to defeat the pornocrat, but after deciding that the blame belongs to a higher authority, Flagg journeys to Mars, where he is able to defeat the U.S. government. He becomes president and separates Illinois from the rest of the country. Subsequently, Flagg loses control of Illinois, and after the destruction of the Plexmall, he is briefly imprisoned before moving to Russia to resume his career as a ranger.

Volumes

- *American Flagg!* Volume 1 (2008). Collects issues 1-6 plus a previously unpublished backstory by Chaykin. This volume details Flagg's introduction to the Plexus Rangers and the corruption inherent in the Plexmall.

- *American Flagg!* Volume 2 (2008). Collects issues 7-14, plus a previously unpublished story "I Want My Empty V!" written and illustrated by Chaykin. This ends the original story arc, as the action begins to move outside the Plexmall.

Characters

- *Reuben Flagg*, the protagonist, is a tall, handsome, brown-haired man of average height and build. He is a former actor and star of the popular television show *Mark Thrust: Sexus Ranger*. After Flagg is replaced on his own show by a more pliable hologram version of himself, he joins the Plexus Rangers and is stationed at the Chicago Plexmall, where he turns against the political and social corruption of the corporate-run Plexmall and takes on the role of the traditional Western-film town marshal. While Flagg is a rampant womanizer, his main love interests are C. G. Markova and, especially, Mandy Krieger.

- *Raul the Cat* is a small, orange, talking cat that uses special gloves to allow him to manipulate tools to write on a computer, use weapons, and even drive a truck. Initially, Raul is also the only one other than Flagg who can see the subliminal violent messages programmed into the show *Bob Violence*. Raul is loyal to Flagg and considers himself the equal of any human, especially with his ability to drink under the table men ten times his size.

- *Amanda (Mandy) Krieger* is a medium-height, curvaceous woman with striking red hair, usually styled like a 1940's femme fatale. She is the daughter of the ranger Hilton "Hammerhead" Krieger and is Flagg's primary love interest throughout most of the series. While initially a bit of a schemer, she eventually joins Flagg in rooting out corruption in the Plex and the American government.

- *Hilton "Hammerhead" Krieger* is a stocky, middle-aged, balding man who is the chief ranger at the Chicago Plexmall. Although he is touchy and cynical, he is also protective of the Plex. Hilton is also the chief of the pirate broadcast station Q-USA. He is initially hostile to Flagg and tries to impede him. Hilton is eventually killed by Plex special agent John Scheiskopf and leaves his station to Flagg.

- *Mayor C. K. Blitz* is a squat, bald black man in his fifties. While nominally a corrupt politician, adept at taking bribes and well versed in local graft, Blitz actually has the best interests of the city at heart. Although he and Flagg clash during the course of the series, they usually work together to protect Chicago. Blitz also runs an illegal basketball team, the Skokie Skullcrushers.

- *Medea Blitz* is a tall, thin diabetic woman, usually with shockingly dyed hair. She is the daughter of Mayor C. K. Blitz. Medea is originally the girlfriend of Cyril Farid-Khan, the leader of the Genetic Warlords gang, and miscarries what she says was their child but was actually Hilton Krieger's. Medea is eventually enrolled as a ranger, and despite her initial violent hostility to Flagg, they eventually work together.

- *C. G. (Crystal Gayle) Markova* is a tall, buxom woman with a 1920's bob haircut. She is the commander pilot for Brasilia Airlines and one of Flagg's many girlfriends.

- *Jules "Deathwish" Folquet* is an extremely tall, muscular, and intelligent black man who often wears glasses. He is a member of the Skokie Skullcrushers basketball team. He starts a group of deputy rangers and eventually becomes a key ally of Flagg.

- *Sam Luis Obispo* is a tall, thin, mustachioed con artist who works primarily in Havana. His many aliases and skills as a con artist come in handy when allied with Flagg.

- *Luther Ironheart* is a tall, muscular robot with a holographic cartoon head. Even though Luther means well and strives to uphold the law, his basic clumsiness often makes him a liability, especially in firefights, in which he tends to try to do too much.

- *William Windsor-Jones* is a medium-height, thin man with receding brown hair. He is also the heir to the throne of England, something he reveals only when drunk. He eventually helps Reuben run Q-USA.

- *Cyril Farid-Khan* is a tall Middle Eastern man with outrageous hair. He is the leader of the long-running Genetic Warlords gang, of which both Hilton Krieger and C. K. Blitz had been members, and former boyfriend of Medea Blitz. Although at first a public menace thanks to the subliminal messages in *Bob Violence*, Farid-Khan eventually begins to work with Flagg.

- *Peggy Krieger* is a vivacious, curvy woman in her mid-fifties with bright blond hair. Initially, she is known as Gretchen Holstrum, an amnesiac who does not know she is Peggy Krieger and mother to both Medea and Mandy. She later regains her memory and saves Chicago from destruction.

- *John Scheiskopf* is a tall, very thin man with a haircut reminiscent of the early era Beatles. While Scheiskopf introduces himself as a jewelry salesman, he is actually an agent from the Plex, investigating the pirate television station. He loses both his legs in an altercation with Flagg but later returns with bionic legs and superstrength, plotting with neo-Nazis to destroy Chicago. Scheiskopf is killed in another battle with Flagg.

Artistic Style

American Flagg! is characterized by the classic, almost neorealist look that Chaykin had pioneered in his work with DC Comics, particularly in his early work on *Batman*. Chaykin also used large blocks of text in his comics, sometimes surrounding the borders of the panels with commentary from either news broadcasts or interviews. Usually, this would be indicated by a character's profile appearing either above or to the side of the text. Chaykin also used graphics and different fonts in order to indicate action, sometimes using large fonts to express imminent danger or a commotion going on outside the panel's borders. In addition, Chaykin was instrumental in bringing back expressive sound effects, indicated by large blocks of garish, stylized lettering within the panels.

While Chaykin was the primary artist for almost half of the series, he began to use assistants such as a young Dean Haspiel to work on backgrounds. After issue 26, Chaykin relinquished the art to other artists, including Joe Staton, Mark Badger, and Mike Vosburg. However, as Chaykin's control relaxed, the intricate art and design work that was such a crucial part of *American Flagg!* disappeared, leading to lower sales and the eventual cancellation of the series. Many artists consider Chaykin's work on *American Flagg!* to be particularly influential in terms of design and composition, and his work of that period is often compared favorably to Jim Steranko's work on "Nick Fury: Agent of Shield," from *Strange Tales*.

Themes

Like many comics of the early 1980's that pushed the boundaries of narrative and plot, *American Flagg!* implies that the United States had become irrevocably corrupt. Flagg, the somewhat cynical hero, is nonetheless the innocent, looking to a vision of the United States that has not been corrupted by corporate and political greed. In the dystopian future of *American Flagg!*, the government is an absentee landlord off on Mars, while corporate power runs amok on Earth.

Most of Flagg's antagonists are not necessarily the large corporations themselves but neo-Nazis, drug-addled biker gangs, and innocents corrupted by power. In the dystopian future of *American Flagg!*, far closer to Aldous Huxley's *Brave New World* (1932) than to George Orwell's *Nineteen Eighty-Four* (1949), humans live in a literal shopping mall where television and drugs provide a quick escape from the pains of everyday life. Even the weapons used by the rangers, such as the Snowball 99, which launches a frozen globe of Somnabutol, are trademarked by the various corporations that sell the rangers new ways to keep order.

However, another recurring theme of *American Flagg!* is that redemption is possible, even for the most corrupt citizens of the Mallplex. In the course of the series, clearly corrupt individuals such as Medea Blitz, her father C. K. Blitz, and Mandy Krieger are all redeemed by their contact with Flagg and the basic decency that he promotes. *American Flagg!* was not only an attack on Reagan-era values but also in some ways a plea by the author to restore basic civility in an age when corporations were increasingly seeking power.

Impact

Although *American Flagg!* is somewhat forgotten and is often critiqued as having one of the greatest starts but weakest endings in a major ongoing series, it remains one of the most influential comic series of the 1980's. In some ways, Chaykin illustrated the main theme later discussed in Neil Postman's *Amusing Ourselves to Death* (1985): that malls, fast food, and relentless entertainment were increasingly numbing American culture. In a sense, people were more enamored of entertainment than serious issues and were therefore easily manipulated by unscrupulous politicians.

While the initial critical reception of *American Flagg!* was positive thanks to Chaykin's detailed plots and groundbreaking, almost photo-realistic artwork, Chaykin soon chafed under the pressure of creating as intricate a comic as *American Flagg!* The first half of *American Flagg!* is looked upon by most critics as equivalent to the contemporary work of Miller and Moore. Although some critics dismissed Chaykin as a crank, the series' critique of corporate culture and celebrity seems almost prescient. In the twenty-first century, *American Flagg!* remains as timely as when it was released.

Brian A. Cogan

Further Reading

Azzarello, Brian, and Eduardo Risso. *100 Bullets* (1999-2009).

Miller, Frank. *Ronin* (1983).

Moore, Alan, and David Gibbons. *Watchmen* (1986-1987).

Steranko, Jim. *Nick Fury: Who Is Scorpio?* (2001).

Bibliography

Chabon, Michael. Introduction to *Howard Chaykin's American Flagg! Definitive Edition*. Berkeley, Calif.: Image Comics, 2008.

De Blieck, Augie. "A Little Bit of *Flagg!* Waving." *Comic Book Resources*, September 3, 2004. http://www.comicbookresources.com/?id =14766&page=article.

Fielder, Miles. "Howard Chaykin—*American Flagg!*" *The List* 630 (June 2, 2009). Available at http://www.list. co.uk/article/17881-howard-chaykin-american-flagg.

Fingeroth, Danny. *Disguised as Clark Kent: Jews, Comics, and the Creation of the Superhero*. New York: Continuum, 2007.

Harvey, R.C. "Chaykin's Crusade" in *The Comics Journal* March 23, 2010, Accessed at http://www.tcj.com/superhero/chaykin's-crusade/

Irving, Christopher. *Graphic NYC Presents: Dean Haspiel—The Early Years*. New York: Idea and Design Works, 2010.

Postman, Neil. *Amusing Ourselves to Death: Public Discourse in the Age of Show business*. New York: Penguin Books 1985

See also: *100 Bullets; Ronin; Watchmen*

ANIMAL MAN

Author: Morrison, Grant

Artist: Chas Truog (illustrator); Paris Cullins (penciller); Tom Grummett (penciller); Doug Hazlewood (inker); Mark McKenna (inker); Steve Montano (inker); Helen Vesik (colorist); Tatjana Wood (colorist); Janice Chiang (letterer); John Costanza (letterer); Brian Bolland (cover artist)

Publisher: DC Comics

First serial publication: 1988-1990

First book publication: 1991-2003

Publication History

DC Comics received much critical acclaim for British writer Alan Moore's work on his revamp of *Swamp Thing* (1983-1987), and publisher Jeannette Kahn and editor Karen Berger sought out several other English and Scottish authors to reinvigorate other characters. They met with Grant Morrison, laying out an initial four-issue miniseries featuring Animal Man, a character that had appeared in several issues of *Strange Adventures* in the 1960's, with sporadic appearances afterward, primarily in the early 1980's.

Sales were strong enough to warrant an ongoing series, and Morrison continued writing through the twenty-sixth issue. The first trade paperback, comprising the initial miniseries as well as several stories that tied into a companywide crossover, *Invasion!*, were collected under the DC logo in 1991. Two subsequent volumes, which constituted the remainder of Morrison's work on the title, were published under DC's Vertigo imprint, intended for mature readers, in 2002 and 2003.

The monthly issues were published by DC even though an early issue depicted an attempted rape. The decision to reprint later volumes under the mature imprint was a marketing decision, as another of Morrison's works, *The Invisibles*, had been released as individual issues and in trade format under the Vertigo imprint.

Plot

Animal Man, created by Dave Wood and Carmine Infantino, first appeared in *Strange Adventures* 180,

---

Chas Truog

British artist Chas Truog is best remembered for his run on the first thirty-two issues of *Animal Man*. Truog has worked for a number of publishers in the comics industry, but is best known for his work at Vertigo, which includes the unusual series, *Chiaroscuro: The Private Lives of Leonardo da Vinci*. Over time, Truog shifted from a traditional representational naturalism toward a more psychedelic style that utilized the entirety of the page as a conceptual unit. His figure drawing on *Animal Man* was largely typical of the DC aesthetic at the end of the 1980's and featured clean lines and very clearly delineated characters. His later work became both more detailed and more cartoonish as he worked to bring a more lively sense to his pages.

---

although he was not known as such until *Strange Adventures* 190. While hunting in a wooded area with his friend Roger Denning, Buddy Baker hears a loud explosion and sees a spaceship that has crash-landed in a clearing. Another explosion follows, and Baker suddenly finds himself with the power to mimic other animals and, for example, gain the strength of an elephant or the ability to fly like a bird. Animal Man also appears as a member of the "Forgotten Heroes" in *Crisis on Infinite Earths*, which compressed DC's multiple universes into one.

At the beginning of the first arc of Morrison's revival, Animal Man is married to his high school sweetheart, Ellen, and has two young children, Cliff and Maxine. Baker is unemployed, and his wife supports the household by doing storyboarding. An animal-rights activist, Animal Man finds himself involved with an experiment dealing with the mutation of monkeys at S.T.A.R. Labs in San Diego. He wears a jacket with his costume, not made from animal skins, and refined goggles. He becomes a vegetarian, and he eventually fights ecoterrorists and foils a foxhunt in England.

After these events, Morrison sets up the deconstruction of the hero. Animal Man meets an anthropomorphic coyote named Crafty, who has carried his indecipherable gospel to Earth. He has come from a world where animals perform endless feats of destruction against one another; they seemingly blow up yet remain unhurt, free to cause more turmoil. Wanting to be free of this existence, Crafty is banished to "the second reality" by a creator who holds a paintbrush in his hand. The coyote is killed, and as Animal Man stands over his crucified form, the page pans back to show an unfinished background and a large brush dripping red ink.

The second volume reintroduces the yellow aliens seen in an Animal Man story from the 1960's. "Desleeped" by their higher power, they realize Animal Man has changed; this is an indirect reference to *Crisis on Infinite Earths*. Jim Highwater, a physicist studying implicate theory, visits Psycho-Pirate, who contains the lost multiverse within his Medusa mask. Highwater starts questioning his random actions, and after he and Animal Man take a spiritual journey, Animal Man learns "the second secret" from a ghost messenger named Foxy. In an example of breaking the fourth wall, a literary technique in which a fictional character becomes aware of and acknowledges the readers' reality in a direct or metatextual manner, he turns toward the reader and states, "I can see you!" He then returns home to find his family murdered.

Psycho-Pirate releases the multiple analogues of heroes from the destroyed universes, and the aliens tell Animal Man and Highwater that they have no choice in matters; each can play only his assigned roles. After Animal Man leaves to confront the "creator" who murdered his family, Highwater tells the teeming crowd of heroes that they will long outlive their own gods, every time someone reads of their adventures. Placated, they fall apart into pieces of colored paper.

Animal Man travels through Limbo, where obscure comic book heroes come and go. Several forgotten heroes recall Animal Man, but he has no recollection of ever being there. Wanting to meet the writer who killed his family, he walks for five years toward the City of Formation, along the way meeting a character from the Golden Age, the Red Bee. The Red Bee claims to be freezing, so Animal Man offers his jacket. Minus the

jacket, his hair shaped in a buzzcut, Animal Man looks exactly as he did in the 1960's. When he reaches for a doorknob, he is confronted by Grant Morrison.

Morrison points at his computer screen, telling Animal Man that he has twisted his life to please himself and that the next writer might do whatever he wants to change his character yet again. Morrison shows him several comics, one of which shows Ellen and the children lying dead on the kitchen floor of their home. When Morrison tells Animal Man he killed them off to add drama to his story, the hero claims that it is not fair.

Morrison then shows Animal Man a photo of his cat, Jarmara, who died just after her third birthday. He says that her death was not fair either, but to whom can he complain? At the very least, he can include her in the story. Comparing comics to life, he asks why blood and anguish excite everyone and why people cannot try to be kind. He then fades to pencil lines, and Animal Man finds himself sitting on his own couch. The doorbell buzzes, he answers it, and he finds his entire family there, Ellen having forgotten her key. The last two pages are of Morrison, ending Animal Man's story and then walking outside, narrating how he used to signal a childhood invisible friend named Foxy, who lived in the hills. Would he still answer after twenty years? Morrison shines a light into the empty night, morose over his dead cat and the idea that he did not tell a thrilling enough story. He walks away, and in the final panel, a light flashes back across the deserted street.

Volumes

- *Animal Man* (1991). Collects issues 1-9 and features Animal Man as an animal-rights activist and the start of Morrison's deconstruction of the hero, with "The Coyote Gospel," in the fifth issue.
- *Animal Man: Origin of the Species* (2002). Collects issues 10-17. Animal Man discovers his true origin in Africa, as he learns that aliens have graphed him into a morphogenic field.
- *Animal Man: Deus ex Machina* (2003). Animal Man's family is killed, and a rip in the continuum allows him to trek through Limbo and meet with Morrison, whom he asks to give him back his family.

Characters

- *Buddy Baker*, a.k.a. *Animal Man*, is thirty years old in his 1960's incarnation but is in his mid-twenties in this series. He gained his powers from an exploding spacecraft when he was nineteen.
- *Ellen Baker* is Buddy's wife and has a full understanding of how crazy superhero life can be. Mother to their children, Cliff, eight, and Maxine, five, she works as a storyboard artist.
- *James Highwater* is a physicist visiting Arkham Asylum and is an expert on superstring theory and the theory of implicate order.
- *Unnamed yellow aliens*, working for a higher power, manipulate Animal Man's origins.
- *Roger Hayden*, a.k.a. *Psycho-Pirate*, is an inmate at Arkham who releases multiple realities through a Medusa mask, threatening the world.
- *Grant Morrison* is the writer of the story, the creator of Animal Man's adventures.

Artistic Style

Chas Truog and Tom Grummett provided an early attempt at clean, realistic images. Rather than leaning heavily on inflated muscles and exaggerated proportions, they presented a world that was visually calm and normal, all to serve the unique and engaging writing. This technique fit in well with the many scenes set within the Baker household, as Animal Man is presented as a hero more attached to his wife and children than one compelled to defend a dark and urban city.

Each piece of cover art, created by Brian Bolland, depicts a single scene from the issue. Following Morrison's theme of reality, there are covers in which the reader is looking at the scene depicted and others in which an object is propped up, giving the impression that the viewer is being forced to look at an event with ramifications.

Themes

Animal Man is notable, first and foremost, for breaking the fourth wall. Early on, the protagonist encounters a coyote who lives in a world of cartoon violence, with cats and pigs resembling Warner Bros. cartoon characters. The coyote asks his creator, who sits in a high throne with an artist's brush at hand, to send him to hell, which for him is Animal Man's reality. In Animal Man's world, animals are treated to extreme violence via experimentation by humans. Morrison is Animal Man's creator, allowing him to talk with the original version of himself from the 1960's; to learn the secret of his reality, that he and others in his adventures are simply characters in a story; and to understand that everything that happens, primarily the murder of Animal Man's family, can be rewritten. Writers and artists will die, but their creations will live on through their works; nonetheless, creators can do nothing to "fix" their own reality.

Impact

Animal Man was Morrison's first work in which he "rebooted" an existing, albeit obscure, character. He did so with such vigor that the series continued for another four years after he left the project. In most of his work, Morrison presents a complex story involving hidden conspiracies and religious references. DC had not had any luck with updating old characters to any lasting degree, but based on the high sales that *Animal Man* provided, DC was able to reboot *Shade, The Changing Man*, and *Hawkworld*, a more straightforward look at the Hawkman mythos.

Allen Sallee

Further Reading

Azzarello, Brian, and Cliff Chiang. *Doctor 13: Architecture and Mortality* (2007).

Ellis, Warren, and John Cassady. *Planetary* (1998-2009).

Morrison, Grant, and J. G. Jones. *Final Crisis* (2008-2009).

Morrison, Grant, and Richard Case. *Doom Patrol* (1987-1992).

Wolfman, Marv, and George Perez. *Crisis on Infinite Earths* (1985-1986).

Bibliography

Beatty, Scott, et al. *The DC Comics Encyclopedia: The Definitive Guide to the Characters of the DC Universe*. New York: Dorling Kindersley, 2008.

Blankfield, Bryan Boyd, and Christopher Lyle Johnstone. "Framing Animal-Rights Activism: An Analysis of Grant Morrison's *Animal Man*." University Park: Pennsylvania State University, 2010.

Callahan, Timothy. *Grant Morrison: The Early Years*. Edwardsville, Ill.: Sequart Research and Literacy Organization, 2007.

Kwong, Sophia. "Post-Modern Pop: Reinventing Comic Book Literacy in Selected Works by Grant Morrison." Austin: University of Texas, 2007.

See also: *Planetary; Doom Patrol; Crisis on Infinite Earths*

ASTONISHING X-MEN

Author: Whedon, Joss
Artist: John Cassaday (illustrator); Laura Martin (colorist)
Publisher: Marvel Comics
First serial publication: 2004-2008
First book publication: 2004-2008

Publication History

In the 2000's, American comic book companies faced dwindling sales and increased competition from Japanese manga. In an attempt to attract new readers, companies began recruiting well-known writers from outside the industry. Although Joss Whedon had written for comics before this point, he was best known as a producer of fantasy and science-fiction television shows such as *Buffy the Vampire Slayer* (1997-2003), *Angel* (1999-2004), and *Firefly* (2002). Whedon had loyal fans, and his collaboration with Marvel Comics on its most popular superhero team generated much excitement for the debut of *Astonishing X-Men*. The collaboration was also an excellent fit for Whedon, an X-Men fan himself.

The series was unable to maintain the kind of monthly schedule expected by regular comic book readers, and meeting a bimonthly deadline was also difficult. Despite the delays, the series remained popular. Whedon's run on the book lasted for twenty-four issues and concluded with a special *Giant-Size Astonishing X-Men* issue 1 in 2007. John Cassaday was the artist for the entire run. *Astonishing X-Men*'s relatively contained story arcs made the series ideal for collection into trade paperbacks.

Plot

The X-Men are a team of superheroes whose powers are derived from genetic mutations. Feared by the public for this reason, the X-Men battle this prejudice in two ways. As educators, they run the Xavier Institute, a school designed to help mutants learn about their powers and to promote understanding. As superheroes, they fight evil mutants and human bigots who seek to eliminate mutations or mutants themselves.

Astonishing X-Men. (Courtesy of Marvel Comics)

The series can be broken into four six-issue arcs. In the first arc, Cyclops assigns Emma Frost, Wolverine, Beast, and Kitty to be the lead teachers at the Institute. Interpersonal conflict occurs as they grow into these new roles and gain prominence as superheroes, particularly as Cyclops deals with the effect of the recent death of Jean Grey on his relationship with Emma Frost. Kavita Rao's announcement of a cure for the mutant condition puts the team into conflict with Ord, Rao's mysterious backer, and with Nick Fury and Agent Brand. Beast is tempted to use the cure to stop his own devolution. Kitty then discovers that Colossus, her lost love who was presumed dead, has been kept alive for experimentation by Ord.

The next arc centers on the emergence of Danger. Working subtly, Danger uses the holographic technology of the Danger Room, the X-Men's training facility, to persuade Wing, who lost his powers when Ord used the mutant cure on him, to commit suicide. Knowing that the X-Men will send their students to the supposed safety of the Danger Room, Danger revives a damaged Sentinel robot to confront the team. After defeating the Sentinel and exposing Danger, the X-Men lose a fight with Danger's new humanoid form. Danger then goes after Professor Xavier. After an intense struggle, Danger is defeated, but not without emotional cost to the X-Men when the team learns of Charles Xavier's secret connection to the artificial intelligence.

The third arc focuses on Emma Frost's apparent betrayal of the team and the attack upon the group by the new Hellfire Club, composed of Emma, Cassandra Nova, Sebastian Shaw, Negasonic Teenage Warhead, and the mysterious Perfection. This attack is psychically brutal, and many of the X-Men's personal or emotional vulnerabilities are used against them. Cyclops is left in a vegetative state, while Beast regresses into a feral state and begins attacking people. In a comedic reversal, Wolverine reverts to the foppish persona of his childhood. Kitty is forced to live a fantasy of a future life in which her son from a marriage with Colossus is stolen from her by the X-Men. During this chaos, Ord and Danger join forces and also attack. The X-Men heroically struggle back from this near defeat, discovering that Emma's actions are the result of manipulation by Cassandra Nova. At the end of the story, the X-Men, Ord, and Danger are whisked away by Brand.

The final arc takes the X-Men to Ord's home planet, Breakworld. There, an ancient prophecy, promoted by Aghanne and feared by Kruun, tells that the world shall be destroyed by Colossus. Ord is shamed because he revived the very mutant that will bring Breakworld's doom. Attacked by alien forces in space and on the planet, the X-Men wrestle with the ethical question of whether to destroy Breakworld to save Earth. Cyclops exercises his strategic leadership skills, while Wolverine takes on Armor as a sort of sidekick and Emma discovers Danger's weakness. Although Colossus does not destroy the planet and his actions lead to the exposure of the true villain behind the scenes, the team cannot stop Breakworld's ultimate weapon from being fired at Earth. Kitty makes a terrible sacrifice to save her world.

Volumes

- *Astonishing X-Men: Gifted* (2004). Collects issues 1-6. These issues explore the development of a new X-Men team and the threat of a cure for mutants.
- *Astonishing X-Men: Dangerous* (2005). Collects issues 7-12. In these stories, the X-Men battle a new artificial intelligence with connections to their own history.
- *Astonishing X-Men: Torn* (2007). Collects issues 13-18. In this arc, the X-Men are betrayed by one of their own and must fight a battle to restore their minds.
- *Astonishing X-Men: Unstoppable* (2008). Collects issues 19-24 and *Giant-Size Astonishing X-Men* issue 1. The X-Men must decide whether to destroy an alien world in order to save Earth.
- *Astonishing X-Men Omnibus* (2009). Collects issues 1-24 and *Giant-Size Astonishing X-Men* issue 1. This collection features the entire story in one book.

Characters

- *Cyclops*, a.k.a. *Scott*, a protagonist, has a slim build and brown hair. He must wear a special visor or glasses because his powerful optic-force blasts are beyond his control. Cyclops is often conflicted by his responsibilities as leader of both the X-Men and the Xavier Institute. Although he is in a relationship with Emma Frost, he still has feelings for Jean Grey, his deceased wife who operated as Phoenix.
- *White Queen*, a.k.a. *Emma Frost*, a protagonist, is an attractive blond who wears revealing, all-white clothing. A powerful telepath, Emma has a secondary mutation that allows her body to turn to diamond. An aristocratic and sarcastic former enemy of the X-Men, once a member of the Hellfire Club, Emma struggles to understand her new role as a hero and her relationship with Cyclops.

- *Wolverine*, a.k.a. *Logan*, a protagonist, is short with unusual hair. He is aggressive and instinctual, and his indestructible claws and regenerative healing ability make him a terrifying opponent. The 2001 book *Origin* revealed Wolverine's surprising roots as a weak, wealthy boy in nineteenth century Canada whose life is destroyed by his mutant condition.

- *Beast*, a.k.a. *Hank*, a protagonist, is blue-furred and somewhat feline. Beast learned to use humor and empathy to offset the surprise of his appearance. However, a manifestation of a secondary mutation rendered him more like an animal. Afterward he became more agile and strong, but he fears the loss of his powerful intellect and sense of humanity.

- *Kitty Pryde*, a protagonist, is a young brunette woman who frequently wears the classic black-and-gold X-Men costume in combat. She is able to pass through any solid object. Intelligent, brave, and caring, Kitty is the heart of the team. Returning after a long absence, she is uncertain of her new place at the Xavier Institute. She has a deep love for Colossus.

- *Colossus*, a.k.a. *Peter*, a protagonist, is a Russian mutant able to turn his body into solid steel. The strength of his new form is matched by the strength of his compassion for his friends and others. Kitty is his beloved. Colossus once sacrificed himself in order to save the world from a deadly disease known as the Legacy Virus.

- *Armor*, a.k.a. *Hisako*, is a dark-haired student from Japan. Her mutant abilities allow her to create powerful armor around her body. She desires nothing less than to be a member of the X-Men. Though still learning about her abilities, she is quick-witted and brave.

- *Charles Xavier* is bald and is frequently shown in his wheelchair. He is a powerful telepath. The founder of the X-Men, Xavier is dedicated to promoting equality and understanding between mutants and humans. His concern for his students can lead him to mistakes in judgment. He works on the island of Genosha, where the

---

John Cassaday

One of the most influential artists to have emerged in the late-1990's, John Cassaday is best known for his celebrated collaboration with Warren Ellis on *Planetary*. Featuring highly detailed drawings and a widescreen aesthetic, Cassaday's work on *Planetary* was widely praised. At Marvel, he collaborated with Joss Whedon on *Astonishing X-Men* and with John Ney Rieber on the Captain America series, both of which were significant mainstream hits. With Fabien Nury he produced *Je suis légion*, later released in English as *I Am Legion*. Cassaday's art is extremely detailed, but also quite clean. He eschews extraneous lines and cross-hatching, allowing depth to be created on his figures through the deployment of color. His page layouts tend to maximize action, with few panels and the frequent use of full-page or double-page images. His work, particularly on *Planetary*, has a larger-than-life aspect that tends to focus on key moments in epic scenes rather than on the quotidian aspects of his characters' lives.

---

mutant population was devastated by Sentinel robots.

- *Lockheed* is a small purple dragon. He flies and breathes flame. A longtime loyal companion of Kitty, Lockheed has hidden depths.

- *Wing* is a sandy-blond mutant with the power of flight. A student at the Xavier Institute, he enjoys his ability to fly. His loss of power and death make him a tragic figure in the story.

- *Abigail Brand* is a green-haired, attractive woman who usually wears a skintight, green combat suit. She takes her job as leader of the Sentient Worlds Observation and Response Department (S.W.O.R.D.) with deadly seriousness. Cool and sarcastic, Brand will do anything to defend Earth from intergalactic threats.

- *Nick Fury* is the gray-templed, eye-patch-wearing director of the Strategic Hazard Intervention Espionage Logistics Division (S.H.I.E.L.D.). An old soldier with a grizzled attitude, Fury is a useful source of information, when he is willing to convey it.

- *Kavita Rao* is a dark-haired scientist from India. Her sophisticated knowledge of genetics has led her to a cure for the mutant condition, which she considers a disease. However, Rao's motivation is medicine, not bigotry.
- *Ord*, an antagonist, is the tall, green-skinned alien ambassador who typically wears a metallic band across his face. Ord's mission is to prevent the prophesied destruction of Breakworld by an Earth mutant. Aggressive and savage, he is not a careful planner.
- *Danger*, an antagonist, appears to be a female robot of wild design. She is the evolved consciousness of the Danger Room, a facility created by Xavier to train the X-Men. As such, she knows all the X-Men's strengths and weaknesses. Danger sees Xavier and by extension the X-Men as cruel oppressors and seeks revenge.
- *Cassandra Nova*, an antagonist, is a bald woman who wears a pith helmet. A parasitic being able to jump into new hosts, she once possessed Xavier. Her hateful nature and powerful telepathic abilities combine for sadistic effect. She enjoys being evil.
- *Sebastian Shaw*, an antagonist, is a dark-haired man in period costume. Shaw once led the Hellfire Club, and he lorded over Emma Frost. His ability to convert kinetic energy into strength and his manipulative leadership skills are deadly.
- *Negasonic Teenage Warhead*, an antagonist, is a blue-skinned girl in fringed black clothing. Her undefined abilities appear to make her dreams reality. She is an unfocused and annoying teen.
- *Aghanne* is a green-skinned alien on Breakworld. A former gladiator, she despises the brutality of her planet. Although not a direct player for most of the story, her actions set about the main conflict with the X-Men.
- *Kruun* is the green-skinned alien dictator of Breakworld. His brutality is matched only by his contempt of Ord. Kruun seeks to save his world only to continue to rule it.

Artistic Style

The effect of computer art, a powerful tool in graphic novels and modern comics, is evident in the color and shading of the stories. Cassaday's art style is crisp and cinematic. As befits a series focused on emotion, reactions, and connections, Cassaday's faces are expressive. This is particularly evident in the haughty arrogance of Emma Frost. In another example, Wolverine's personality reversal in issue 15 features his giddy smile of accomplishment after cutting out a paper-doll chain.

For many years before *Astonishing X-Men*, the X-Men appeared more often in dark team uniforms influenced by the characters' film appearances. Cassaday pushed for the return of superhero costumes that promoted the individuality of the characters. Surprisingly for a superhero book steeped in action, there are few motion lines in this artwork. Instead, motion is often conveyed through impact upon environmental elements. This is especially noticeable during the fight between Beast and Wolverine in issue 3. In one panel, Beast kicks Wolverine into the ceiling. The cracks in the ceiling and the debris raining down in the next panel demonstrate how hard Wolverine hit. A few pages later, Wolverine drives Beast through a door, splintering wood into slivers that appear to be heading toward the reader. Only the most powerful and dramatic of movements get action lines, as when Shaw boxes Colossus on the ears in issue 15.

Themes

In Whedon's works, happiness is a miraculous but fragile state, and love brings connections in surprising ways. Cyclops and Emma Frost are opposites, but they bond through adversity. Aggressive soldier Brand is drawn to an unlikely partner, the humanist Beast. The relationship between Kitty and Colossus is the best demonstration of this theme. Kitty's jubilant rediscovery of her lost love and Colossus's sad farewell to her serve as powerful bookends for the series. In between, there is a growing intimacy, made brighter by its tragic finale.

To some degree, all Marvel comics ride the thematic wake of *Amazing Fantasy* issue 15, wherein Spider-Man learned the tragic lesson that with great power comes great responsibility. *Astonishing X-Men* tackles that theme explicitly. Although the theme becomes less prominent as adventures mount, the early story arcs put the main characters in the complex role of educators, deciding how best to guide young people. Throughout the entire series, the X-Men also transition into a more public role as superheroes, most notably in issue 7, when they fight a giant monster alongside the Fantastic Four.

Fans of X-Men comics will also see much nostalgia for the title's glory days. When Kitty returns to the mansion in issue 1, her memories of events from earlier comics are shown to the reader. Cassaday also draws heavily on the art of various preceding X-Men comics. When Emma Frost psychically manipulates Cyclops in issue 14, she begins by evoking Cyclops's last moment of happiness with Jean Grey in the Dark Phoenix Saga.

Finally, the X-Men series' promotion of feminism is enhanced by Whedon's own interest in the topic. The series depicts many strong female characters, both heroes and villains. Kitty and Emma Frost are depicted as equal, if not a bit superior, to their male colleagues.

Impact

Although by no means the first "outsider" to write for comics, Whedon was certainly the most prominent creator to cross over since Kevin Smith wrote *Daredevil* for Marvel in 1999. Name recognition became an important trend in the mid-2000's, which saw the release of limited series by authors such as Brad Meltzer and Tamora Pierce as well as adaptations of Stephen King's *The Dark Tower* novels. The Whedon connection had the intended promotional effect, but the delays in the series further supported the perception among fans that comics by outsiders would fall frustratingly behind schedule.

Astonishing X-Men also reintegrated the X-Men into the mainstream Marvel continuity. Since the Silver Age of comics, Marvel had suggested that almost all of its superhero characters lived in the same universe. Characters promoted their own titles when they guest-starred in another book. Beginning in the late 1990's, the X-Men started to exist in a separate sphere, largely crossing over to other X-Men titles or spin-off series featuring other mutants. *Astonishing X-Men* reversed this trend, and the return of superhero costumes for the X-Men helped to further integrate the team into the Marvel Universe.

Finally, while not major characters, both Kavita Rao and Danger joined the massive family of X-Men supporting characters after appearing in *Astonishing X-Men*. Rao became a physician for the X-Men, serving in a group known as the X-Club. Danger continued the trend of redeeming former foes, becoming the warden for a prison of dangerous mutant antagonists held by the X-Men.

Michael Robinson

Films

X-Men: The Last Stand. Directed by Brett Ratner. Twentieth Century Fox, 2006. This film stars Famke Janssen as Jean Grey, Hugh Jackman as Wolverine, and James Marsden as Cyclops. The film differs from the novel in a number of major ways, drawing loosely upon the Dark Phoenix Saga for its main character drama. However, the development of a cure for the mutant condition and the character of Rao are imported into the film. The mutant cure is the threat that Magneto uses to organize a massive mutant army to battle against the government.

Further Reading

Claremont, Chris, et al. *Uncanny X-Men* (1975-1984).

Jemas, Bill, et al. *Origin* (2001-2002).

Morrison, Grant, et al. *New X-Men* (2004-2008).

Way, Daniel, Steve Dillon, and Mike Deodato. *Wolverine: Origins* (2006-2010).

Bibliography

Brady, Matt. "From Fanboy to Fan Favorite: Buffy Creator Joss Whedon Comes out of the Crypt." *Comic Buyer's Guide* (January 7, 2000): 38-40.

Housel, Rebecca, and Jeremy Wisnewski. *X-Men and Philosophy: Astonishing Insight and Uncanny Argument in the Mutant X-verse*. Hoboken, N.J.: John Wiley & Sons, 2009.

Singh, Arune. "X Marks the Spot: John Cassaday Talks *Astonishing X-Men*." March 12, 2004. http://www.comicbookresources.com/?page=article&id=3261.

See also: *Wolverine; Wolverine Origin; X-Men: Days of Future Past; X-Men: God Loves, Man Kills; X-Men: The Dark Phoenix Saga*

Astro City

Author: Busiek, Kurt

Artist: Brent Anderson (illustrator); Will Blyberg (inker); Alex Sinclair (colorist); Wes Abbott (letterer); John Roshell (letterer); Rob Steen (letterer); Alex Ross (cover artist)

Publishers: Image Comics; DC Comics

First serial publication: 1995-

First book publication: 1995-2011

Publication History

Astro City began as *Kurt Busiek's Astro City* (cover dates August, 1995, to January, 1996), which was published by Image Comics, though produced by Kurt Busiek's Juke Box Productions (comprising Busiek and his wife, Ann) and funded by Busiek through the royalties that he had earned through the hit 1993 Marvel Comics limited series *Marvels*. After the sixth issue came out, *Astro City* went on hiatus in order to "build up some more inventory" of stories. During this period, Busiek received several offers from publishers and eventually decided to go with Jim Lee's Homage Comics, which at the time was separate from Lee's WildStorm Productions under the Image Comics imprint. This allowed Busiek to try to make deadlines without having to do most of the trafficking, promotion, and production work.

The next *Astro City* story was *Wizard Presents Kurt Busiek's Astro City,* Volume 2, issues 1 and 2, which was put out by *Wizard: The Guide to Comics*, in conjunction with Homage, and was made available in 1996 through an offer in issue 62 of the magazine. The short story in that issue, "The Nearness of You," was nominated for awards and has been cited by Busiek as one of the stories of which he is most proud. Later that year, *Kurt Busiek's Astro City,* Volume 2, issue 1, was released with a September cover date. The first three issues of this series were published by Homage. Image Comics became the publisher (and the Image Comics logo appeared on the cover) starting with issue 4 (December, 1996). During its twenty-two-issue run (and a half issue that reprinted the *Wizard Presents* story and an unrelated text story by Busiek), the series suffered

Kurt Busiek

An Eisner and Harvey award-winner, Kurt Busiek is a celebrated comics writer who has worked on dozens of superhero and adventure titles over the course of his career. He is best known for two projects that have largely defined the "reconstructionist" style of superhero storytelling, *Marvels* and *Astro City*. *Marvels*, produced with painter Alex Ross, retells some of the most famous stories of Marvel Comics' Silver Age through the deeply reverential point-of-view of photographer Phil Sheldon. *Astro City*, with artist Brent Anderson, is a creator-owned title about the adventures of superheroes in the eponymous town. Each of these works ties the superhero to an ennobling and nostalgic view of the past where the morality of good and evil was more clear-cut than was often the case in the superhero titles of the 1990's, which were often characterized as "grim and gritty".

publication delays caused by a number of factors, the most important of which was a mysterious illness affecting Busiek, which was later revealed to be mercury poisoning. During one such delay between issues 14 and 15, Lee sold WildStorm (of which Homage had become part) to DC Comics, and issue 15 (December, 1998) became the first DC Comics issue (though the Image Comics logo was still on the cover). After issue 22, the series went on hiatus again so that additional stories could be completed in order to build an inventory and prevent future delays.

The next *Astro City* story to appear was a six-page story featured in *9-11: The World's Finest Writers and Artists Tell Stories to Remember,* Volume 2 (2002), an anthology put out by DC Comics, with profits going to the victims of the September 11, 2001, terrorist attacks and their families. This was followed by the five-issue *Astro City: Local Heroes* (April, 2003, to February, 2004). Beginning in 2004, the *Astro City* stories, and the three one-issue books that came out that year, were published by WildStorm. The three books were Astro

City Special; *Astro City: A Visitor's Guide*, which included character pinups by twenty-nine different artists; and *Astro City/Arrowsmith, a* "flip book" that contained both an *Astro City* story and a prequel to another Busiek work, *Arrowsmith*, that led to the next big project: *Astro City: The Dark Age*.

The twelve issues of *Astro City: The Dark Age* were divided into four four-issue "books" that came out from August to December, 2005; January to November, 2007; July to October, 2009; and March to June, 2010. During this period, three other *Astro City* titles came out: *Astro City: Samaritan*, issue 1 (September, 2006), *Astro City: Beautie*, issue 1 (April, 2008), and *Astro City: Astra*, issues 1 and 2 (November to December, 2009). Following the end of *The Dark Age*, the two-issue *Astro City: Silver Agent* was published in 2010. DC Comics ended the WildStorm imprint, and subsequent *Astro City* titles will be published by another imprint. The series has also been reprinted in Germany and Italy.

Plot

The world of *Astro City* is one in which superbeings and other costumed heroes and villains have been around for more than sixty years. While the heroes are based all around the world, most tend to congregate in Astro City, located in the western United States. Unlike most other comics, Astro City has no primary character or characters and often the focus of the stories is on a regular person who is living in a world of fantastic individuals. Many of the stories are narrated by the individual (or in some cases, a hero or a villain), and a number of stories take place in the past (though they are usually told from the point of view of someone in the present).

Most stories are only one or two issues long. Some of the memorable examples of these include the stories of a small-time crook who has to decide what to do when he discovers a hero's identity; two of the world's major heroes going on a first date; a gimmick-laden criminal who is annoyed when no one realizes that he committed the perfect crime; a superhero who must decide whether the importance of fighting crime outweighs that possibility that his unborn child will grow up without a father; the life and troubles of a cartoon

character come to life; a man who remembers the love of his life who, because of a "cosmic crisis," never existed; an artist who works on comic books based on actual heroes; a Lois Lane-type woman who finds out what happens when she exposes a hero's identity; and a lawyer who exonerates a criminal by pointing out the problems of positive identification in a world of shape changers, clones, and evil duplicates.

Unlike the characters in many other comic worlds, the characters of *Astro City* tend to age in real time. Astra, a member of the multigenerational First Family, is first shown as a ten-year-old who wants to live a normal life and then years later as a college graduate who has to deal with the superhero equivalent of the paparazzi.

Three major multipart *Astro City* stories exist. In "Confession," teenager Brian Kinney comes to Astro City with a desire to become a hero and is recruited by the mysterious hero the Confessor to be his sidekick, Altar Boy. At this time there is a rise in antihero sentiment, mysterious murders, and strange behavior by both heroes and politicians, which results in many heroes being arrested or otherwise detained. In the midst of this, Altar Boy learns the truth about the Confessor: He is a vampire. In the end, the Confessor exposes, at the cost of his own life, that much of the strangeness about him is attributable to the work of shape-changing aliens called Enelsians who are invading the Earth. The invasion is stopped by the world's heroes, and in an epilogue, after years of training, the Altar Boy becomes the new Confessor.

In "The Tarnished Angel," Carl Donewicz, the metal-skinned Steeljack, gets out of prison and returns to the neighborhood in which he grew up and one that is home to many criminals, costumed and otherwise. Someone has been killing the criminals, and the community asks Donewicz to investigate. Since he cannot find a steady job, he agrees. The truth behind the murders involves a disgraced former hero. Even if the other heroes will not believe his accusations, Donewicz is still able to stop the former hero and find himself a place in the community.

The four-book "Dark Age" takes place during the 1970's and early 1980's, a time of turbulence in the world of *Astro City* and its heroes. The main characters in the books are Charles and Royal Williams, two African American brothers whose parents were killed in 1959 during a fight between the hero the Silver Agent and an agent of the criminal organization Pyramid. Charles became a police officer, while Royal became a criminal. However, when they find that the Pyramid agent is still around, they dedicate their lives to taking him down. There are a number of semirelated subplots in the books involving the superheroes, most notably the story of the Silver Agent, who was framed for murder and executed, but who appears later on because of his ability to time travel. Other subplots include the strange heroes of the Apollo 11, the problems of the Street Angel, and early adventures of characters seen in previous *Astro City* issues.

Much of the story is narrated by brothers, in what is revealed to be an interview with a writer who says that when telling the story he will change the brothers' names to "Charles and Royal." The story has its origins in a proposal that Busiek created for a sequel to *Marvels*.

Even though the stories deal with a variety of characters, there is occasional foreshadowing, which may be a reference in a flashback story, a framed newspaper headline, or a character that appears for a panel in one issue and then is seen more later. For example, the Enelsians were first introduced with the appearance of a spy who was gathering information on the heroes (Volume 1, issue 5), a story which also included the first mention of the Confessor. The fate of the Silver Agent was hinted at for years, starting with a reference in a flashback story (Volume 1, issue 2) as "the poor doomed Silver Agent." Other hints, such as a memorial statue inscribed "To Our Eternal Shame," created interest in his story, which was finally featured in the first volumes of *The Dark Age*; additional information was given in the other volumes and the two "Silver Agent" issues.

All of the *Astro City* stories listed in this essay have been collected, with the exception of the stories and features of the *Visitor's Guide*. Besides the collected material and an introduction, each volume has a section that includes early sketches and designs for the characters and locations featured in the collected issues, with commentary by Busiek. These sections have different

names in each volume. A cover gallery is also included in each volume, showing not only the published covers of each issue but also Alex Ross's rough drafts and, occasionally, the photographs of people who he used for reference purposes. The earliest collections were published by Image Comics but have been reprinted by DC Comics, which published the subsequent issues.

Volumes

- *Kurt Busiek's Astro City: Life in the Big City* (1995). Collects *Kurt Busiek's Astro City,* Volume 1, issues 1-6. This introduces the city and several characters, including Samaritan, and contains various stories, including the award-winning "Safeguards." The volume also includes an introduction by Busiek and "Infrastructure."

- *Kurt Busiek's Astro City: Confession* (1997). Collects *Kurt Busiek's Astro City,* Volume 2, issues 4-9, and *Wizard Presents Astro City* ½. A teenage boy becomes the sidekick of a mysterious hero. The volume also includes "The Nearness of You," about a man who dreams of a woman who no longer exists; an introduction by Neil Gaiman; and "Dramatis Personae."

- *Kurt Busiek's Astro City: Family Album* (1998). Collects *Kurt Busiek's Astro City,* Volume 2, issues 1-3 and 10-13. This volume includes various one- and two-part stories, featuring Astra, Jack-in-the-Box, and others, including the Junkman in the award-winning "Show 'Em All." Also includes an introduction by Harlan Ellison and "Snapshots."

- *Kurt Busiek's Astro City: The Tarnished Angel* (2000). Collects *Kurt Busiek's Astro City,* Volume 2, issues 14-20. An ex-convict supervillain must protect his old neighborhood from a mysterious killer. The volume also includes an introduction by Frank Miller and "Mugshots."

- *Astro City: Local Heroes* (2003). Collects *Kurt Busiek's Astro City,* Volume 2, issues 21-22; *Astro City: Local Heroes*, issues 1-5; and a story from *9-11: The World's Finest Writers and Artists Tell Stories to Remember* Volume 2. Includes stories and items that appeared in various WildStorm titles to promote *Astro City*. Also included are an introduction by James Robinson and "Homegrown Heroes."

- *Astro City: The Dark Age 1, Brothers and Other Strangers* (2008). Collects *Astro City: The Dark Age,* Book One, issues 1-4; *Astro City: The Dark Age,* Book Two, issues 1-4; and the *Astro City* story from *Astro City/Arrowsmith,* issue 1. Set during the 1970's, this tells the stories of the Williams brothers, the fate of the Silver Agent, and the dark times that befell the people and heroes of Astro City. Also includes an introduction from Marc Guggenheim and "Dark Designs."

- *Astro City: The Dark Age 2, Brothers in Arms* (2010). Collects *Astro City: The Dark Age,* Book Three, issues 1-4, and *Astro City: The Dark Age,* Book Four, issues 1-4. These volumes continue the story of the Williams brothers into the early 1980's, along with the story of the Blue Knight and other events. Also includes an introduction by Ed Brubaker and "Dark Draftmanship."

- *Astro City: Shining Stars* (2011). Collects *Astro City: Astra,* issues 1-2; *Astro City: Silver Agent,* issues 1-2; *Astro City: Samaritan,* issue 1; and *Astro City: Beautie,* issue 1. A collection of solo adventures, including expansion on the Silver Agent story. Also includes an introduction by Mark Waid and "TBA."

Characters

- *Samaritan,* a.k.a. *Asa Martin,* one of the major heroes of the Astro City universe, was sent back from a dying future to change the past. The "empyrean fire" of the time trip gave him great powers, which he now uses to save the people of the "present." His secret identity is Asa Martin, a fact checker for a weekly news magazine.

- *The Confessor,* a.k.a. *Jeremiah Parrish,* is a mysterious hero who is revealed to be Jeremiah Parrish, a priest who was turned into a vampire over a century earlier and uses his supernatural powers to fight crime. After his final death, the role is taken over by Brian Kinney, who was briefly his sidekick, Altar Boy.

- *Jack-in-the-Box,* a.k.a. (at separate times) *Jack Johnson, Zachary,* and *Roscoe James.* Johnson

was an African American toy designer during the 1960's; his son Zachary took on the role six years after his father was killed; and James was recruited by Zachary to take over the role of this clown-costumed, gimmick-laden hero.

- *The Hanged Man,* a strange, mystical being who protects the Shadow Hill area of the city.

- *The Honor Guard,* the main superhero team, first founded in 1959.

- *The First Family,* a multigenerational team of adventurers, including brothers Augustus and Julius Furst; Augustus's superpowered adopted children, Nick and Natalie; Natalie's reptilian husband, Rex; and their daughter, Astra, who is the subject of two stories.

- *Steeljack,* a.k.a. the *Steel Jacketed Man* and *Carl Donewicz,* was a petty crook until his body was changed to metal. After twenty years in jail, he returns home to Astro City.

- *Crackerjack,* a wisecracking acrobatic hero, who can be a braggart. His true identity is unknown.

- *Charles Williams* and *Royal Williams* are two brothers whose parents' deaths lead them to opposite sides of the law in a quest for justice during a dark time in Astro City.

- *Supersonic* is a retired hero persuaded to go into action one last time.

- *The Silver Agent,* a major hero, was framed for murder and executed before the truth was told. Thanks to time travel, he continues to help the world. A statue dedicated to him bears the words "To Our Eternal Shame."

- *Beautie* is a sentient robot built to look like a life-sized "Beautie" doll (which is similar in appearance to the Barbie doll).

Artistic Style

The *Astro City* covers, painted by Ross—who had previously worked with Busiek on *Marvels* and who, along with longtime comic artist Brent Anderson, also helped to design many of the characters—are striking. Like those of *Marvels, Kingdom Come,* and other works, Ross's covers often use people as models, sometimes even putting them in rough versions of the costumes.

Because Anderson is the penciller for all of the *Astro City* stories, the artistic style is relatively uniform. The primary, noticeable change is seen in issues that feature Will Blyberg's inking instead of Anderson's penciling. Characters look "realistic," except when they are not supposed to be. Exceptions include "Looney Leo," a cartoon lion come to life; Beautie, who is a "living doll"; and other various nonhuman characters.

Given that stories in *Astro City* take place over many decades and that there have been many occasions in which a character has appeared without being identified, Anderson's artwork is helpful; it helps the reader recognize particular characters, which is useful when the character is finally identified by name. Other characters are meant to remind readers of certain character archetypes, specific characters, or real people. For example, many readers commented on Steeljack's resemblance to the actor Robert Mitchum.

The style of the panels varies as needed in both shape and quantity per page. Panels are often "busy" and filled with various details, some of which give more information about the world of *Astro City* or contain a reference or an inside joke. The coloring fits the stories, being as bright or dark as needed, even adding in such elements as indications that a character is glowing. Letter balloons are used in the standard way, though some changes are made for characters, such as the Confessor, that are not quite human; in these cases, the lettering is sometimes done in an odd way as well. The narrators' thoughts and recollections are shows in text boxes. These boxes are located in different areas of the panels, and sometimes there are more than one per panel. In the case of *The Dark Age*, which has two narrators, differently colored boxes are used to indicate the speaker.

Themes

One of the main themes of *Astro City* is the question of, as Busiek has stated, "What else happens in the worlds the superheroes inhabit?" What is life like for regular people who live in a world of superheroes, costumed villains, and entities with the power to destroy the world? This theme is also present in Busiek's *Marvels*, which is told from the point of view of a photographer.

Even when the focus of the story is a supercharacter, "stopping the bad guy and saving the world" is not the main point of the story. The points of the stories are, for example, Jack-in-the-Box worrying about being a father or Astra wondering what it is like to be a normal child. "Confession" has a worldwide alien invasion in it, but the main character plays only a small part in stopping it. Whereas other comics may stretch an "infinite cosmic identity war" into a multipart story, *Astro City* would employ such a story as, at best, the "b-story," happening in the background, while the main focus is on its effects on a particular character or characters. One example of this is in the story "Welcome to Astro City" (Volume 2, issue 1). Neighbors in an apartment building are gathered on the rooftop watching a fight between superheroes and a powerful cosmic being. The narrator is surprised that with everything going on, a neighbor let her son go back to the apartment to work on his homework, but she points out that things are out of their hands and "hey, if the world does not end he's still got school tomorrow."

As one critic has stated, *Astro City* is "an unabashedly fanboy series." Busiek was a comics fan long before he was a comics writer, and he includes in *Astro City* many of the superhero archetypes: the superpowerful character admired by the whole world (Samaritan); the "warrior woman" (Winged Victory); the wisecracking athletic hero (Crackerjack); the "dark" hero with his "bright" sidekick (Confessor and Altar Boy); the team made up of the "best and brightest" (Honor Guard); and the "family of heroes" (the First Family).

The history of comics is often referenced in the pages of *Astro City* in the naming of people and places. One of the most prominent landmarks in the city is Mount Kirby, named after Jack Kirby, cocreator of Captain America. Some of the names are chosen for a specific reason. For example, the Bakersville neighborhood that has a high African American population is named for Matt Baker, one of the first African Americans in mainstream comics. The prison is on Biro Island, named for the popular "crime comics" pioneer Charles Biro, and the "Sprang Museum of Popular Advertising" has items, such as giant typewriters, that Dick Sprang put into Batman comics. The information gatherer for the invading Enelsians is Mr. Bridwell, named after comics writer E. Nelson Bridwell, who had a great knowledge of comic book characters. In addition, the Silver Agent was shown to be active from 1956 to 1973, the years that some feel are the starting and ending dates for the Silver Age of comics. For readers unaware of these names and facts, they are just part of the story, but for the knowledgeable reader, they add to the enjoyment of the series.

Impact

Along with *Marvels*, *Astro City* has been credited with shifting some comics away from the "grim and gritty" and "deconstruction of superheroes" that had been prevalent in many comics of the time. Since *Astro City*, there have been other comics that deal with how regular people cope in a world of superheroes, such as *Gotham Central*, which deals with the police officers in the city where Batman fights crime. In addition, other comic book series have emerged with new worlds of superheroes, many of which fit into the main archetypes, ranging from the slightly humorous, such as *PS238* (first published in 2002), to the more mainstream, such as *Invincible* (first published in 2002), and the occasionally profane, such as *The Boys* (first published in 2006).

Another title of this type, *Irredeemable* (first published in 2009), is based in a world in which the Superman/Samaritan character type has gone mad and become a threat to the world. While many stories deal with the mad superhero and the superheroes trying to stop him, there have also been stories about the regular people affected by his actions, including a Lois Lane-type character and a reformed supervillain, who appears in the companion title *Incorruptible*.

David S. Serchay

Further Reading

Busiek, Kurt. *Marvels* (1994).

Grayson, Mark. *Invincible* (2003-).

Waid, Mark, and Jean Diaz. *Incorruptible* (2010-).

Waid, Mark, and Peter Krause. *Irredeemable* (2009-).

Bibliography

Busiek, Kurt. Introduction to *Kurt Busiek's Astro City: Life in the Big City*. La Jolla, Calif.: Homage Comics, 1996.

Guggenheim, Mark. Introduction to *Astro City: The Dark Age 1: Brothers and Other Strangers*. La Jolla: Calif.: WildStorm, 2008.

Klock, Geoff. *How to Read Superhero Comics and Why*. New York: Continuum, 2002.

Robinson, James. "Around Town." In *Astro City: Local Heroes*, edited by Kurt Busiek. La Jolla, Calif.: WildStorm, 2005.

See also: *Invincible; Marvels*

AUTHORITY, THE

Author: Ellis, Warren; Millar, Mark; Morrison, Robbie; Brubaker, Ed; Morrison, Grant; Giffen, Keith; Abnett, Dan; Lanning, Andy; Gage, Christos; Taylor, Tom

Artist: Al Barrionuevo (illustrator); Simon Coleby (illustrator); Gene Ha (penciller and cover artist); Bryan Hitch (penciller and cover artist); Dustin Nguyen (penciller and cover artist); Frank Quitely (pseudonym of Vincent Deighan, penciller and cover artist); Dwayne Turner (penciller and cover artist); Richard Friend (inker); Paul Neary (inker); Trevor Scott (inker); Sal Regla (inker); David Baron (colorist); Laura Depuy (colorist); Wendy Groome (colorist); Randy Mayor (colorist); Phil Balsman (letterer); Wes Abbott (letterer); Ryan Cline (letterer); Jared K. Fletcher (letterer); Rob Leigh (letterer); Jason Levine (letterer); Bill O'Neil (letterer); Richard Starkings (letterer)

Publisher: DC Comics

First serial publication: 1999-

First book publication: 2000-2010

Publication History

The Authority was created by Warren Ellis and Bryan Hitch and was first published in 1999 in a single-issue comic format by DC Comics through its WildStorm imprint. Writer Warren Ellis has stated that he considers his twelve-issue run on *The Authority* to be the third part of a story arc that started with *Stormwatch*, with which he was involved from 1996 to 1998. Ellis and Hitch came up with the idea for *The Authority* during a ten-minute phone call. At the time, Hitch was disillusioned and unhappy with the projects and work he had been doing and was preparing to leave the industry after completing his tenure with *Stormwatch*.

Ellis suggested Mark Millar take over as the writer of *Authority* after his run. Millar's run was affected and delayed by DC Comics in-house censorship and the September 11, 2001, World Trade Center terrorist attacks, after which DC Comics became increasingly sensitive to *Authority*'s overt scenes of destruction. Millar's stories contained extreme violence, but DC

(WireImage)

Bryan Hitch

One of the most admired superhero artists of his generation, Bryan Hitch has worked on a number of extremely high-profile titles. In the late-1990's he worked with writer Warren Ellis and inker Paul Neary on the relaunched *Stormwatch* title from WildStorm and co-created *The Authority* for the same publisher. These high-octane superhero titles were marked by expansive "widescreen" images that largely eschewed the restricting confines of traditional page layouts in favor of bigger and bolder images. After a stint on *JLA*, he and writer Mark Millar created *The Ultimates* for Marvel, a reconceived, mature version of the signature Avengers characters. Hitch's highly detailed images and powerful layouts have helped to make him one of the most popular—and influential—superhero artists of the 2000's, and the signature artist associated with the movement toward decompressed action comics in the 2000's.

declined Millar's request for a mature adult label. The project was already behind schedule because of artist Frank Quitely's slow drawing speed and the time he took off to draw the final issue of Grant Morrison's *The Invisibles*. Quitely left *The Authority* to draw Marvel's *New X-Men*, adding further scheduling problems.

The September 11 attacks stymied *The Authority*'s planned relaunch as part of WildStorm's "Eye of the Storm" line for mature readers. A Brian Azzarello story involving philosophical and religious belief systems was deemed too sensitive to be published. A two-issue story by Garth Ennis, bridging Millar's and Azzarello's stories, was also abandoned.

Ellis commented in 2001 that while DC was only doing what was appropriate during an "intensely charged and sensitive cultural situation," he further stated,

> *The Authority* will not appear in any form we recognize for some time to come. Because for it to work, it must be callous . . . horrible, and violent, and must be gleeful about what it's doing. If it's not cranked up to ridiculous volume, viciously insulting to the genre that spawned it and blatantly absurd in its scale and its disregard for human life . . . it's just another superhero team book.

In 2006, Morrison was hired to write what would become Volume 4, *The Lost Year*, but production ceased after issue 2 (May, 2007). In September, 2007, artist Gene Ha doubted *The Authority*, issue 3, would ever come out because of Morrison's commitment to redesigning the DC Universe. There was no script for issue 3 and possibly never would be.

In 2008, Morrison described *The Authority* as a "disaster." With the series running late, the two published issues receiving unfavorable reviews, and a commitment to DC's *52*, Morrison abandoned the title. In 2009, Keith Giffen took over Morrison's story arc, writing the scripts for issues 3 to 12 based on Morrison's ideas. Morrison received story credits for all twelve issues. Suffering from WildStorm's overall lack of direction, *The Authority* became a casualty of the company's closure in December, 2010.

Plot

Consisting of Jenny Sparks, Jack Hawksmoor, Apollo, Midnighter, the Engineer, the Doctor, and Swift, the members of The Authority were born after the demise of *Stormwatch* (in the *Wildcats/Aliens* crossover). Jenny Sparks put the team together after deciding someone was needed to "save the world." The Carrier, a sentient "shiftship" (a vessel that can penetrate alternate universes) voluntarily orbiting the Earth, is the team's headquarters.

In Volume 1, The Authority saves the Earth from Kaizen Gamorra, who, with his army of superhuman clones, tries to brand the Earth with his family symbol. The Authority repulses an invasion from a parallel Earth intending to turn Earth into a rape camp to propagate the parallel world's dynasty. An entity, "God," which created the Earth, has returned to find it infested with humans who must be exterminated. Jenny Sparks kills "God" by electrocuting its brain and then dies at the stroke of midnight, December 31, 2000, her tenure as "the spirit of the twentieth century" over. However, an infant is born at the exact time of her death.

The Authority then becomes proactive in trying to make "a finer world" by removing a dictator from an unnamed Southeast Asian country. The reborn Jenny Sparks (Jenny Quantum, the spirit of the twenty-first century) is located by the genius Dr. Jacob Krigstein, a former Cold War scientist who has engineered an almost endless supply of superhumans. Krigstein kidnaps the infant, thereby gaining the opportunity to shape the twenty-first century. He attempts a global coup that will result in a superhuman-enforced utopia. As The Authority prevents the coup, Swift offers Krigstein a deal: join them and use his ideas to better the world. He accepts, returning the infant.

As a result of "God" returning to Earth, the Earth itself revolts against its human inhabitants with a series of catastrophic natural disasters. With the Doctor recovering from a drug overdose, a deal is made with a previous doctor, who committed genocide. The deal involves transferring the current doctor's powers to him for one hour. The Authority battles the Doctor, to no avail, until he suddenly becomes enlightened by the conscience of the ultimate shaman and submits. A subplot involves The Authority under increasing criticism from the U.S. government for its actions.

In "Brave New World" and "Transfer of Power" (included in *The Authority: Transfer of Power*) story arc, The Authority is seemingly killed by a genetically engineered human cyborg, employed by the group of seven (G7) nations, and the members are replaced with second-rate substitutes who follow a right-wing political agenda. In fact, except for Midnighter, who escaped with baby Jenny, the members of The Authority have had their memories wiped, have been given new identities and personalities, or are being tortured. The Midnighter eventually eliminates the substitute Authority and, with Jenny's growing power, frees the real Authority. The denouement sees Apollo and Midnighter marry and adopt Jenny.

In *Harsh Realities*, The Authority defeats Reality Incorporated, a multiversal corporation that exploits worlds in other realities, and confronts the Andy Warhol-ish John Clay and his religious Transcendence Movement, which has become the largest religion in the world through his superhuman brainwashing ability. This arc includes Apollo and Midnighter as parents to Jenny Quantum and a romantic development between the Engineer and Jack Hawksmoor. The Authority's conflict with the American government also continues.

Coup d'État (2004), a WildStorm universe crossover, is influential on *The Authority* series, though not part of it. In *Coup d'État*, the U.S. government is responsible for taking Earth to the brink of interdimensional war. The Authority then installs itself as the ruler of the United States, putting in place disarmament and clean-energy policies. Meanwhile, ruptures in the fabric of reality are discovered to be caused by Jenny Quantum's twin sister, Jenny Fractal, who has been turned into a "superweapon" by a secret Chinese governmental agency. Jenny Quantum dies defeating Jenny Fractal, but Midnighter travels back in time, killing Jenny Fractal. The Doctor helps Jenny Quantum transfer her spirit into Jenny Fractal's body at the moment of her death in the present.

In *Revolution*, The Authority struggles with the day-to-day oversight of the United States. Henry Bendix, last seen in *Stormwatch*, returns to orchestrate a plot to remove The Authority from power. He creates a public rebellion, murders the Doctor, holds the new Doctor as a prisoner, and shows Midnighter a false vision of the future in which The Authority rules by dictatorship. The Authority relinquishes control of the United States and disbands. While The Authority is disbanded, Bendix changes the world through capitalistic ventures. However, with the help of previous "Jennys"—spirits of ages throughout history—Jenny Quantum reforms The Authority and defeats Bendix.

In *The Lost Year*, The Authority becomes lost in the Bleed (a time portal) with the Carrier low on power. The Authority searches its way back to Earth, visiting parallel Earths along the way and encountering different incarnations of itself on each Earth.

The *World's End* and *Rule Britannia* story lines are a culmination of the *WildStorm: Armageddon*, *WildStorm: Revelations*, and *Number of the Beast* crossovers, which portray worldwide cataclysms leading to a postapocalyptic world. In this story arc, Jenny Quantum is killed. This series also breaks with the political content that had dominated *The Authority*'s story lines and returns to a more traditional superhero story. Apollo monitors the Earth above a choking cloud cover that prevents sunlight from reaching the planet, and the Engineer struggles with the loss of her ability to manipulate her nanotechnology. The Authority battles a number of threats in this dour world while it tries to protect and organize aid for human survivors.

The Carrier responds to a beacon from space to save other shiftships from a race of aliens that harvests other alien races for sustenance. The membership of The Authority changes: Christine Trelane, Deathblow, Flint, Freefall, Grifter, the High, and Rainmaker join, while Apollo and Midnighter remain on Earth. The story line introduces a young boy, River Baldwin, as the spirit of the twenty-first century, who is able to control information and is instrumental in freeing the alien races.

Volumes

- *The Authority: Relentless* (2000). Collects Volume 1, issues 1-8. Jenny Sparks forms The Authority after the demise of Stormwatch. The group defends the Earth from terrorist Kaizen

Gamorra and repulses an invasion from a parallel Earth.

- *The Authority: Under New Management* (2000). Collects Volume 1, issues 9-16. Jenny Sparks dies killing "God." She is reborn as Jenny Quantum and is subsequently kidnapped by Jacob Krigstein, who wishes to use her to shape the twenty-first century. The Authority thwarts Krigstein's attempted world coup but asks him to join them and use his ideas to enrich the world.

- *Earth Inferno and Other Stories* (2002). Collects Volume 1, issues 17-20. The Authority makes a deal with a genocidal former doctor to save humanity from Earth itself.

- *The Authority: Transfer of Power* (2002). Collects Volume 1, issues 22-29. The G7 nations replace The Authority with a group of substitutes to carry out a right-wing political agenda.

- *The Authority: Harsh Realities* (2004). Collects Volume 2, issues 0-5. The Authority defeat Reality Incorporated, a multiversal company that exploits parallel worlds, and John Clay, a religious figure with superhuman brainwashing ability.

- *The Authority: Fractured Worlds* (2005). Collects Volume 2, issues 6-14. Following the events of *Coup d'État*, The Authority becomes the ruler of the United States. The group defeats Jenny Fractal (Jenny Quantum's twin sister), who was raised and trained by a secret Chinese government agency to be a superweapon.

- *The Authority: Revolution* Book 1 (2005). Collects issues 1-6. The Authority struggles to govern the United States, as a public rebellion against its rule grows. The group disbands after being unable to prevent an unstable superhuman from exploding, killing more than fifteen thousand civilians.

- *The Authority: Revolution* Book 2 (2006). Collects issues 7-12. The Authority investigates the suspicious death of the Doctor. Jenny Quantum meets all previous Jennys, including Jenny Sparks, and discovers Henry Bendix is behind the Doctor's death and The Authority's disbanding.

- *The Authority: The Lost Year* (2010). Collects Volume 4, issues 1-7. The Carrier loses power and crashes through the bleed. The Authority then navigates back through the bleed to its own Earth, exploring parallel Earths and encountering different versions of themselves on each.

- *The Authority: World's End* (2009). Collects Volume 5, issues 1-7. The Authority inhabits a postapocalyptic Earth, where the Carrier has crashed. Their efforts are now directed at helping human survivors.

- *The Authority: Rule Britannia* (2010). Collects Volume 5, issues 8-17. The Authority continues to battle threats on a postapocalyptic Earth.

Characters

- *Jenny Sparks* is the blond-haired and chain-smoking first leader of The Authority. She is also a century baby, the "spirit of the twentieth century." She can convert her entire body into electrical current and manipulate electricity. She died at the end of the twentieth century but was reborn as Jenny Quantum, the spirit of the twenty-first century. Jenny is pragmatic and often ruthless in the execution of her plans.

- *Jack Hawksmoor* is a victim of alien abduction as a child. He is stocky with black hair and rarely wears shoes. Hawksmoor experienced extensive alien organ implantation, turning him into a "neo-human"; the most obvious of the implants are jagged ripples on the soles of his feet. In urban areas, he manifests precognition, psychometry, and enhanced physical capabilities, allowing him to communicate with cities. He becomes leader of The Authority after Jenny Sparks dies and is often stubborn in accepting advice from team members.

- *Apollo* is blond and a big-muscled, bioengineered superhuman powered by the energy of the sun. He exhibits flight, superstrength, and eye beams. He is the Midnighter's partner.

- *The Midnighter* is a bioengineered superhuman who has the ability to foresee his opponents' moves in combat. He has enhanced senses, speed, and strength. He is Apollo's partner. Of all the members of The Authority, Midnighter is the most likely to kill without impunity and, apart from his feelings for Apollo, is often emotionless. He is blond but rarely removes his Midnighter suit even when not on duty or a mission.

- *The Engineer*, a.k.a. *Angela "Angie" Spica*, is the second person to hold the title of the Engineer. She is a scientist who replaced her blood with nine pints of liquid nanotechnology, allowing her to create complex machinery out of her body with her thoughts. As the Engineer, she appears completely covered in silver nanotechnology, sporting long, thick hair resembling wiry dreadlocks and a stylized helmet.
- *The Doctor*, a.k.a. *Jeroen Thorndike*, is a thin, red-haired shaman, sporting red-colored implants covering his eyes. He has the combined powers of hundreds of shamans who have come before him. He struggles with drug addiction and fame. Jeroen was killed by Rose Tattoo, an ally of Henry Bendix.
- *Swift*, a.k.a. *Shen Li-Min*, is a Tibetan woman with wings and sharp talons. Swift set aside her pacifist philosophy to work in The Authority.
- *Habib Bin Hassan*, a.k.a. *The Doctor*, is a young Palestinian granted the pseudonym of the Doctor after Jeroen Thorndike is killed. He managed to negotiate peace in the Middle East before being held prisoner by Henry Bendix. Scared by the apocalyptic events in the *World's End* story line, Hassan becomes the psychotic Green King, who tries to protect the Earth. Hassan/Green King is killed by The Authority with the help of "century baby" Gaia Rothstein.
- *Jenny Quantum* is the reborn *Jenny Sparks*, a century baby and spirit of the twenty-first century. Quantum exhibits the hard-nosed (and chain-smoking) characteristics of her predecessor, Jenny Sparks. Quantum aged herself to a teenager to enable her to better fight Henry Bendix. In the *Number of the Beast* series, Jenny sacrifices herself to prevent the Carrier's engine from destroying the universe.
- *Henry Bendix*, antagonist of the *Revolution* story line, is a highly intelligent, balding man who was previously the Weatherman in *Stormwatch*, before turning psychopathic. *Revolution*'s story line reveals that Henry Bendix was actually from a parallel Earth. The "real" Bendix returns and plots the breakup of The Authority but is eventually killed by Midnighter.
- *The Carrier* is the fifty-mile-long, thirty-five-mile-high, and two-mile-wide sentient shiftship powered by a caged baby universe that is The Authority's headquarters. The Carrier is tied to Earth's orbit and apparently abandoned; however, the Carrier was provided for Henry Bendix by another Bendix from a parallel Earth. The Carrier responds to suggestion and encouragement. It can also open "doors" between any two points in space and is capable of traveling through the bleed to other earths and dimensions.

Artistic Style

The Authority was the first comic to use a "widescreen" storytelling style, which employs techniques influenced by cinema, utilizing wide and emotive facial close-up shots and rarely more than six panels per page. Characteristic of this widescreen style, panels are the complete width of the page, allowing a straight-down reading pattern rather than the traditional "Z" reading pattern. Artist Hitch referenced films to get the right feel for the book, something that revolutionized his approach and allowed him to find his own style. Hitch is noted for his highly detailed artwork.

As is common with Ellis's scripts, which employ a "speed-reading" ethic, there are no written sound effects, and dialogue is kept to a minimum. Action scenes such as fights are devoid of dialogue. Millar and Quitely's run continued the widescreen format, reducing the panel count even further, often to four or fewer per page. Millar's run was also saturated with violent imagery. Dismemberment, exploding heads, drug addiction, and promiscuity are depicted explicitly. Quitely's signature attention to detail, minimalist settings, and kinetic motion is prominently featured.

The style returns to a more traditional comic art style and layout and less violent subject matter in subsequent series. For *The Lost Year*, different artists were employed to create a feel for each different reality that The Authority visited, ranging from the realistic, fine-line work to cartoon style. The artwork of *The World's End* and *Rule Britannia* is suitably dark, in line with these arcs' bleak, postapocalyptic setting.

Themes

Politics and use of power are major themes running through *The Authority*. In Millar's run, The Authority becomes proactive in trying to make a "finer world." Indeed, "a finer world" often becomes a slogan that The Authority's antagonists use to challenge them. Because of its superhuman ability, The Authority is answerable to no one but itself, yet as it topples dictatorships and forces armies out of occupied territories, it comes under criticism for being just another fascist regime, albeit influenced by left-wing politics.

The distinctly right-wing and left-wing political stances are painted in broad, stereotypical, and simplistic strokes. Government and business are positioned as right-wing, which in *The Authority* is aligned with corruption, homophobia, and racism and is driven by capitalistic desire to make money. The Authority represents a liberal humanist position, most indicative of which is Apollo and the Midnighter's gay relationship; they marry, adopt baby Jenny Quantum, and push policies of environmentalism and disarmament when ruling the United States.

The Authority takes it upon itself to impose its vision of a "finer world," and its uncompromising attitude and push for the world to "behave" move toward a fascist dictatorship in *Revolution*. Their morality is simply "might makes right." Indeed, the use of parallel Earths in *The Authority* stories, almost without exception, depicts the endpoint of The Authority's rule (*Revolution*, *The Lost Year*) as fascistic, dysfunctional, and doomed to failure. This end result is the only possible outcome when the politics are so extreme. Nevertheless, the series takes the view that this is the only way to "get things done." The Authority's politics, however, are differentiated by a matter of transparency: The Authority frequently addresses the whole Earth to explain to humans that they are telling them the "truth."

Impact

By exploring the use of power by superheroes, *The Authority* follows a path set by *Miracleman*, *Batman: The Dark Knight Returns*, *Watchmen*, and *Kingdom Come*. The depiction of Apollo and the Midnighter's homosexual relationship, their marriage, and their subsequent adoption and rearing of Jenny Quantum, however, is a first for superhero comics. They are presented as good parents (insofar as a superhero couple can be) when rearing Jenny. While the homophobic attitudes of antagonists are often evident, homosexuality itself is never an "issue"—that Apollo and Midnighter are both "masculine" and homosexual is never in question. Their relationship is depicted as normal, dealt with positively in most regards, and is not beset with melodrama. While Ellis left the sexuality of Apollo and Midnighter undisclosed, Millar intensified the energy and has been criticized for making Apollo a rape victim.

The Authority came to be synonymous with violence and superhero morality. Millar's run intensified the violence to high-voltage levels. While Ellis's tenure provided destruction on a massive scale and the tasteless and unseemly idea of a global rape camp, Millar's script and Quitely's corresponding art were substantially brutal. Millar kills a ward of newborn babies and (off screen) depicts Apollo's apparent rape at the hand of the Commander. In later series, without political motivation, The Authority's actions sometimes are reduced to sadism, and the group employs violence only for the sake of violence.

Although Ellis had been working in American comics from as early as 1994, *The Authority* (along with *Planetary*, 1998-2009) raised his profile as a comics writer. Hitch's artwork on *The Authority* made him a well-known and respected comics artist, and he went on to produce *JLA* (1997-2006) and (with Millar) the high profile Marvel "reboot" *The Ultimates* and *The Ultimates 2* (a series that began in 2002). Millar became virtually the biggest name in comics. He went on to produce several creator-owned titles that have been adapted for film (*Wanted*, 2008; *Kick Ass*, 2010). *The Authority* came to be regarded by writers and artists as a title that allowed unrestrained exploration of superhero power; subsequent series failed to meet the high levels of storytelling set by Ellis and Millar.

Ross Murray

Further Reading

Ellis, Warren, et al. *Stormwatch: Change or Die* (2000).

_____. *Stormwatch: Final Orbit* (2001).

Ellis, Warren, Bryan Hitch, and Paul Neary. *Stormwatch: A Finer World* (2000).

Millar, Mark, Bryan Hitch, and Andrew Currie. *The Ultimates: Super-Human* (2005).

Bibliography

Bainbridge, Jason. "'This Is the Authority. This Planet Is Under Our Protection'—An Exegesis of Superheroes' Interrogations of Law." *Law, Culture, and the Humanities,* no. 3 (2007): 455-476.

Klock, Geoff. *How to Read Superhero Comics and Why*. New York: Continuum, 2006.

Wolk, Douglas. *Reading Comics: How Graphic Novels Work and What They Mean*. Cambridge, Mass.: Da Capo Press, 2007.

See also: *The Ultimates; Kick Ass; Planetary; Miracleman; Watchmen; Batman: The Dark Knight Returns; Batman: The Dark Knight Strikes Again; Kingdom Come*

B

B.P.R.D.: Bureau for Paranormal Research and Defense

Author: Mignola, Mike; Arcudi, John; Augustyn, Brian; Dysart, Joshua; Golden, Christopher; Gunther, Miles; Harris, Joe; Johns, Geoff; Kolins, Scott; McDonald, Brian; Oeming, Michael Avon; Sniegoski, Tom

Artist: Jason Shawn Alexander; Paul Azaceta (illustrator); Gabriel Bá (illustrator); Guy Davis (illustrator); Scott Kolins (illustrator); Karl Moline (illustrator); Fábio Moon (illustrator); Michael Avon Oeming (illustrator); Patric Reynolds (illustrator); John Severin (illustrator); Peter Snejbjerg (illustrator); Ben Stenbeck (illustrator); Cameron Stewart (illustrator); Dave Stewart (illustrator); Derek Thompson (illustrator); Herb Trimpe (illustrator); Adam Pollina (penciller and cover artist); Matt Smith (penciller); Ryan Sook (penciller, inker, and cover artist); Curtis P. Arnold (inker); Guillermo Zubiaga (inker); Mike Mignola (inker and cover artist); Nick Filardi (colorist); Bjarne Hansen (colorist); Lee Loughridge (colorist); James Sinclair (colorist); Michelle Madsen (colorist and letterer); Pat Brosseau (letterer); Ken Bruzenak (letterer); Michael Heisler (letterer); Dan Jackson (letterer); Clem Robins (letterer); Dave Johnson (cover artist); Kevin Nowlan (cover artist)

Publisher: Dark Horse Comics
First serial publication: 2002-2010
First book publication: 2002-2010

Publication History

B.P.R.D. was created in response to Mike Mignola's desire to expand the *Hellboy* universe. While Hellboy was part of the Bureau for Paranormal Research and Defense (B.P.R.D.), the activities of the organization were usually overshadowed by the adventures of

---

Guy Davis

Guy Davis broke into the comic book industry with his punk-inspired retelling of the Sherlock Holmes stories, *Baker Street*. The critical success of that title led to an assignment drawing *Sandman Mystery Theatre* for DC Comics' Vertigo imprint, a retro-themed mystery series with some superheroic touches. He is also known for his work on *B.P.R.D.*, the spin-off from Mike Mignola's *Hellboy* comics. Davis's art is consistent across the range of his work. His lines are scratchy and his figures often have a frailty that makes them seem more vulnerable than classically heroic. With much of his work set in the past, he has a keen eye for period detail and fashions. His page layouts are classical and his action sequences are firmly grounded in the anatomic reality of bodily movement. Despite the stylization of his line, he is one of the most notable realists working in the superhero tradition.

Hellboy, known as the "world's greatest paranormal investigator." Following the events of *Conqueror Worm* (2001), which culminated in the resignation of Hellboy from the B.P.R.D., Mignola considered what to do with both the other characters that populated the B.P.R.D. and the organization itself.

Mignola had expressed an interest in working with artist Ryan Sook after meeting him in 1995 at a convention in California. Mignola's basic idea for what became the first *B.P.R.D.* series (*Hollow Earth*) was turned over to writers Christopher Golden (who wrote the first two prose novels, *The Lost Army* and *The Bones of Giants*, about Hellboy) and Tom Sniegoski

for expansion. Although *Hollow Earth* was printed from January to June, 2002, it was preceded by a three-page preview in *Dark Horse Extra* from December, 2001, to February, 2002, which included an appearance by the ectoplasmic Johann Kraus, who would become a focal member of the core B.P.R.D. team.

While the initial stories of the B.P.R.D. were a series of loose vignettes and stand-alone tales, beginning with *Plague of Frogs* more focused story arcs were introduced. Most of the core creative team had already collaborated on *B.P.R.D.* stories, and the collaboration continued on the majority of the *B.P.R.D.* series. The team included Guy Davis as illustrator, Dave Stewart as colorist, and Clem Robins as letterer.

The following series, *The Dead*, finalized the team with the addition of John Arcudi as cowriter. With Mignola, this team set the major narrative arcs and codified the aesthetic look of the series (with the exception of the prequel series *1946* and *1947*). The collected series, ending with *King of Fear*, comprises the first movement of what Mignola has identified as an even larger narrative arc, and the second phase of it began with the publication of *Hell on Earth—New World*, with the *Hell on Earth* designation identifying this new direction.

Plot

The founding of the B.P.R.D. has been explained in a number of flashback sequences within the *Hellboy* and *B.P.R.D.* series and receives a fuller treatment in the latter through several prequel stories. The piecemeal revelation of the bureau's background has underscored its reputation as a quasi-official yet shadowy organization operating at the fringes of society. However, its interaction with the supernatural is taken as a matter of fact within the context of the narrative; the world in which the B.P.R.D. operates is one in which demons, aliens, magic, pagan gods, witchcraft, and characters from folklore and mythology, while not exactly commonplace, are not necessarily out of the ordinary.

The sanctioning of the B.P.R.D. by the U.S. government, in direct response to the summoning of Hellboy to Earth by Rasputin while working for the Third Reich, enabled Professor Trevor Bruttenholm, the organization's founder and first director, to direct

Hellboy's upbringing while continuing to investigate other paranormal activity. Originally housed at a U.S. air base in New Mexico, the headquarters were officially established in Fairfield, Connecticut, in 1947.

For the following five years, Bruttenholm spent his time raising Hellboy, leading B.P.R.D. field operations, and lobbying Washington, D.C., for increased government support. Once Hellboy was granted honorary human status by the United Nations in 1952, Bruttenholm promoted him to a B.P.R.D. field agent. Bruttenholm tended to expanding the organization, which eventually grew from the original five agents in 1946 to more than fifty, and establishing training protocols for the members. Bruttenholm resigned in 1958, serving the bureau as an adviser and occasional agent.

Most of the stories of the B.P.R.D. from this point forward are situated within the *Hellboy* narrative, with Abe Sapien occasionally receiving stand-alone treatment in a few series, focusing on his early days as a field agent. While the B.P.R.D. had originally appeared in the first *Hellboy* series, *Seed of Destruction* (1994), changes in the direction of Mignola's titular character left the supporting members without a leader or a narrative focus. Hellboy's displeasure at the increasingly impersonal nature of the B.P.R.D. bureaucracy, especially after the death of Professor Bruttenholm, eventually turned to disgust at the bureau's distrust of the homunculus, Roger, and the revelation that he had been fitted with an incendiary bomb failsafe device that Hellboy was to detonate should Roger grow unstable.

Hellboy's departure opened up room for a new team member, Johann Kraus, a medium whose body was destroyed in a psychic event; he managed to retain control of his spirit in an ectoplasmic form. Fitted with a containment suit designed by B.P.R.D. researchers, Kraus joined amphibious man Abe Sapien, pyrokinetic Liz Sherman, and folklore and occult expert Dr. Kate Corrigan to form the core constituency of the enhanced-talents task force. Roger was allowed to participate as a provisional team member and was eventually granted full status after several missions.

Hollow Earth, the first team mission under the *B.P.R.D.* imprint, details a rescue operation to retrieve Liz Sherman, who quit the bureau two years before Hellboy's departure. The subterranean race that abducted Sherman, in an attempt to harness the living fire within her to power its war machines, are the remnants of the Hyperborean slaves who followed their masters, following the split of the first race of humanity. The remnants of the slaves overthrew their masters while being led by the King of Fear, who forms the focus of the final installment of the first *B.P.R.D.* story cluster and thus bookends the multiple series spread over many years. Following the retrieval of Sherman from under the Ural Mountains, the team travels to Venice to rescue the Roman goddess Cloacina. The globe-trotting nature of their adventures eventually became a hallmark of the series. Another hallmark was the expansive scope of the narrative, as the seemingly unrelated investigations—vengeful ghosts, haunted houses, and zombies—began to point toward one or more apocalyptic events.

Eventually, the team returns with a sample of a fungus retrieved from Cavendish Hall, the site of the frog creatures, first seen in *Seed of Destruction*. The fungus eventually grows into a manifestation of Sadu-Hem, escapes from a New Jersey laboratory by reanimating a dead researcher's body, and begins to infect the town of Crab Point, Michigan, turning the entire population into frog monsters. This event draws the B.P.R.D. into open engagement with this rapidly spreading global plague and creates the protracted "war on frogs" that dominates much of the *B.P.R.D.* narrative. As the frog monsters are noted as being the "new and final race of men" that will replace humanity, the efforts of the B.P.R.D. require increased financial and logistical support. To that end, the bureau is relocated in October of 2004 to a secret government compound, decommissioned in 1962, in the mountains of Colorado.

The team is joined by Captain Benjamin Daimio, a former special operations soldier, who assumed duties as the new commander, a move which did not sit well with the core team members. However, he quickly gained some respect by helping to defeat a mad German scientist bent on allowing an otherworldly creature into this dimension.

Daimio directs an increasingly aggressive campaign against the frogs, with the assistance of a growing roster of paramilitary forces mixed in with the B.P.R.D.

special agents. At the same time in 2005, the Zinco Corporation begins researching the frog monsters, eventually adapting them to human control under Landis Pope, chief executive officer (CEO) of Zinco, who utilizes a special armor that transforms him into the Black Flame.

A year later, another major player is introduced, Memnan Saa, who originally was Martin Gilfryd, a Victorian-era magician who transformed himself into an amazingly powerful sorcerer. Saa is an enigmatic character, appearing to Sherman in a dream, abducting her, and eventually controlling her telepathically as a way to use her pyrokinetic powers against the frog monsters and the manifestation of the Katha-Hem, a sort of elder god.

The war on frogs, which ends in what has become known as the *Scorched Earth Trilogy*, creates enormous casualties, both across the Earth and within the B.P.R.D.: Roger is destroyed in a battle with the Black Flame, Daimio is driven into self-imposed exile, Kraus begins plotting secretly to kill Daimio, and Sherman loses her pyrokinetic abilities. The campaign against the frog monsters does bring attention to the B.P.R.D., which initially was blamed for the situation but eventually was empowered by the United Nations to function as an international agency reporting directly to the U.N.'s security council. Newly empowered, the B.P.R.D. moves into its next phase of operations, unfolding in the *Hell on Earth* stories.

Volumes

- *B.P.R.D.: Hollow Earth and Other Stories* (2002). Collects selections from *Hellboy: Box Full of Evil*, *Abe Sapien: Drums of the Dead*, *B.P.R.D.: Hollow Earth*, and *Dark Horse Extra*, featuring the B.P.R.D. team's first adventure without Hellboy, an Abe Sapien solo mission that highlights his fight with the B.P.R.D. to reanimate Roger and includes an appearance by the adventurer Lobster Johnson, whose ghost sometimes appears on B.P.R.D. missions.

- *B.P.R.D.: The Soul of Venice and Other Stories* (2004). Collects the *B.P.R.D.* one-shots *The Soul of Venice*, *Dark Waters*, *Night Train*, and *There's Something Under My Bed*, featuring a collection of stories from a number of different writers. The titular story is a B.P.R.D. team mission, while the other stories focus on a few team members on smaller assignments, such as investigating a ghostly train of soldiers, looking for a Nazi collaborator, or stopping a possessed psychic in control of zombies.

- *B.P.R.D.: Plague of Frogs* (2005). Collects *B.P.R.D.: Plague of Frogs*, issues 1-5. This volume showcases the first major engagement of the team with the frog monsters and Rasputin's revenge against Abe Sapien for Rasputin's murder in Cavendish Hall, during which Sapien has a flashback to his life as the nineteenth century human Langdon Everett Caul.

- *B.P.R.D.: The Dead* (2005). Collects *B.P.R.D.: The Dead*, issues 1-5, and "B.P.R.D. Born Again" from the *Hellboy Premiere Edition*. As Sapien continues to investigate his past, the B.P.R.D. headquarters is moved to Colorado, and Captain Daimio assumes command, bringing his combination of military prowess as a Marine and status as a mysteriously reanimated man following three days of death. The team defeats Dr. Gunter Eiss by summoning a dimensional seraphim with the aid of Kraus, who has been possessed by the ghosts of other German scientists.

- *B.P.R.D.: The Black Flame* (2006). Collects *B.P.R.D.: The Black Flame*, issues 1-6. As the plague of frogs sweeps across the American heartland, Sherman becomes haunted by visions of a mysterious magician and the Zinco Corporation enacts its own plans for the frog monsters. Trying hard to emulate Daimio, Roger the homunculus is killed by the Black Flame.

- *B.P.R.D.: The Universal Machine* (2007). Collects *B.P.R.D.: The Universal Machine*, issues 1-5. This series is a bit more somber after the loss of Roger, focusing on expanding character backgrounds and relationships among team members. Dr. Corrigan is abducted by a mysterious collector who wants either to acquire the remnants of Roger or to give Corrigan the secret of his reanimation in return for Abe Sapien. Kraus learns the fate of Roger in the afterlife, a coda that

B.P.R.D. (Courtesy of Dark Horse Comics)

was highly regarded for its emotional content. This series also introduces Daryl, the wendigo, a mythical creature of the Algonquian tribes of North America.

- *B.P.R.D.: Garden of Souls* (2008). Collects *B.P.R.D.: Garden of Souls*, issues 1-5. Sapien's quest to discover more about his origins puts him farther away from the team, as he journeys to Indonesia and is reunited with his former associates from the Oannes Society, who have survived using steampunk exoskeletons. They plan to preserve humanity against the coming apocalypse by unleashing seismic destruction and absorbing the souls of the deceased into specially engineered bodies. Meanwhile, Sherman continues to receive prophetic visions. This series also introduces Panya, a reanimated Egyptian mummy.

- *B.P.R.D.: Killing Ground* (2008). Collects *B.P.R.D.: Killing Ground*, issues 1-5. The mystery of Daimio's resurrection is revealed to be the work of a Bolivian jaguar god, who has made Daimio an "emissary," half human and half demon. Sherman slips further into her visions, only to be rescued by the ghost of Lobster Johnson. Panya is returned to B.P.R.D. headquarters, as is a body from the Oannes Society's project; this is commandeered by Kraus, who finally has a human body to inhabit for the first time in years, and he indulges in all manner of hedonism.

- *B.P.R.D.: 1946* (2008). Collects *B.P.R.D.: 1946*, issues 1-5, and "Bishop Olek's Devil" from *Free Comic Book Day 2008*. This prequel series recounts the first adventures of the fledgling B.P.R.D. team in post-World War II Berlin as they investigate the Nazi's Project Vampir Sturm. Bruttenholm and his team must join forces with the Soviet Committee for Arcane Studies and Esoteric Teachings, headed by Vavara, a demon summoned by Czar Peter in 1709 and currently masquerading as a little blond girl. During the mission, the teams encounter Nazi scientist Herman von Klempt, who has resurrected the Nazi space program to send a rocket full of vampires to infect the United States.

- *B.P.R.D.: The Warning* (2009). Collects *B.P.R.D.: The Warning*, issues 1-5, and the story "Out of Reach" from *Free Comic Book Day 2008*. As part 1 of the *Scorched Earth Trilogy*, this series shifts the focus of the team to tracking down Sherman's mysterious magician, Memnan Saa, as a number of old enemies—frog monsters, the Hyperborean troglodytes, and the Black Flame—reappear with renewed vengeance. Kraus's hatred for Daimio grows, as it was the transformed Captain who "killed" Kraus's new body. Panya becomes more involved with the B.P.R.D. as her psychic abilities grow in power. Saa kidnaps Sherman to use as a weapon against the frogs.

- *B.P.R.D.: The Black Goddess* (2009). Collects *B.P.R.D.: The Black Goddess*, issues 1-5. As part 2 of the *Scorched Earth Trilogy*, Saa steps up his campaign against the frogs, using Sherman to harness the power of the Black Goddess. The B.P.R.D. hunts for Saa, contacting an old teammate of Lobster Johnson for information that leads them to Saa's fortress, which also comes under siege by frog monsters. Eventually Sherman destroys Saa with the very power he sought to control and frees herself, or so she thinks.

- *B.P.R.D.: War on Frogs* (2010). Collects *B.P.R.D.: War on Frogs*, issues 1-4, and "Revival" from *MySpace Dark Horse Presents*, issues 8 and 9. This anthology series is a set of five different stories from earlier in the chronology of the war against the frogs. Fan-favorite Roger returns for an adventure set at Cavendish Hall. Daimio is showcased in another tale about frogs infiltrating a prayer revival. Kraus helps some frog souls make the transition to the afterlife. Sherman shows a female rookie how to survive, and in perhaps the most interesting entry, a group of regular B.P.R.D. operatives must fight one determined frog monster.

- *B.P.R.D.: 1947* (2010). Collects *B.P.R.D.: 1947*, issues 1-5, and "And What Shall I Find There" from *MySpace Dark Horse Presents*, issue 23. Trying to recover after the harsh events of *1946*, Bruttenholm assembles another team of agents to investigate lingering concerns over vampires, one of whom has a particularly nefarious agenda, eventually requiring Bruttenholm to seek the services of an old exorcist.

- *B.P.R.D.: King of Fear* (2010). Collects *B.P.R.D.: King of Fear*, issues 1-5. As part 3 of the *Scorched Earth Trilogy*, the agents move to permanently eradicate the frog monsters. A confrontation with the King of Fear reveals that, despite their best intentions, they are actually the agents of the upcoming apocalypse. Speaking from beyond the grave, Saa still taunts Sherman with visions of the future, even as she seemingly expends all of her powers to finally stop the frog plague.

Characters

- *Professor Trevor Bruttenholm*, the founder of the bureau, was born in England in 1918. He studied politics, philosophy, and economics at Oxford before taking a civilian post with intelligence services during World War II. Bruttenholm's eccentric uncle, who was a friend of occult detective Sir Edward Grey, piqued Bruttenholm's interest in the supernatural, and Bruttenholm became more deeply involved with such issues, eventually appearing at the East Bromwich church to witness the summoning of Hellboy on Earth. Adopting the child and moving to the United States, Bruttenholm first worked with the U.S. military, and later the U.S. government, to establish the B.P.R.D. and help guide its growth. Ultimately, it was his interest in the occult that cost him his life at the hands of the frog monsters.

- *Abe Sapien*, after the departure of Hellboy, becomes the de facto leader of the B.P.R.D. special talents team, even though he does not necessarily want the job. Beginning his life with the B.P.R.D. as an amphibious man discovered after being hidden under a hospital in Washington, D.C., Sapien comes to understand that he once was nineteenth century scientist and occult investigator Langdon Everett Caul, an identity that he comes to reject. Sapien does develop as a team leader and becomes a competent tactician, even as he wonders about the future of the bureau.

- *Liz Sherman* had her pyrokinetic abilities first manifest at the age of eleven, when she accidentally immolated her family. The guilt over their deaths has been a driving force in her life. Befriended by Hellboy, Sherman eventually comes out of her shell and seeks to control her abilities, even as others seek to control her. Her relationship with the bureau is a rocky one; she quits the organization thirteen times in twenty-three years but always returns.

- *Dr. Kate Corrigan* joined the B.P.R.D., first as a consultant for a decade, before moving on to serve as a special liaison to the special-member team. As a former New York University professor, she developed expertise in the areas of folklore and the occult. Her work for the bureau was initially research oriented, but eventually she graduated to field work, became less introverted, and began growing as a person, while dealing with often unimaginable scenarios.

- *Roger*, a homunculus made from human blood and herbs, was first discovered in Romania and reanimated by accidentally stealing Sherman's pyrokinetic life force. Given his name by Hellboy, Roger voluntarily returned Sherman's power to her, regressing to a dormant state before being reanimated by electrical energy and running off a generator in his chest. Roger sought to understand and emulate humanity, even though he was often in the company of nonhumans. Roger was amazingly strong and practically indestructible, yet he was ultimately vulnerable to the power of the Black Flame, perishing in an attack.

- *Johann Kraus* is a German psychic who served as a medium and learned to let the dead manifest through his ectoplasm. During a séance in 2002, a release of psychic energy in Sichuan Province, China, sends a blast through the etheric plane, destroying Kraus's physical body but not his spiritual form. A German B.P.R.D. agent, Izar Hoffman, detected Kraus's spirit and managed to communicate the existence of an ectoplasmic containment suit to him. Kraus was able to enter the suit, which stabilized his essence, and he then traveled to the United States to join the bureau. While Kraus can infuse the deceased with his ectoplasm to learn what they have known, he also is subject to possession, which has happened on multiple occasions, sometimes for extended periods, during B.P.R.D. missions. The long separation from a physical form seems to strain Kraus, and his motivations become increasingly suspect.

- *Benjamin Daimio*, a career military man, had a promising career, being promoted to the rank of captain during the Persian Gulf War (1991), before his sudden death in 2001 in the jungles of Bolivia during a rescue operation. Technically dead for three days, Daimio returns to life with no explanation. His face, permanently shredded by a reanimated corpse during the fight that killed him, is an imposing one even among the ranks of the B.P.R.D.; because of that, coupled with his military bearing and experience, he is put in charge of the team and institutes changes that cause friction among its members. Wracked by guilt over the death of Roger, Daimio eventually loses control of the jaguar demon that inhabits his body and kills a number of B.P.R.D. personnel. Daimio then disappears into the wilderness and is later discovered by Sapien, who cannot persuade the captain to return.

- *Lobster Johnson*, a masked crime fighter from the 1930's and 1940's, tangled with Memnan Saa before perishing in the assault to stop the Nazi space program at Hunte Castle in Austria. Death could not quell his thirst for justice, and in death, his spirit has continued to roam, often helping the B.P.R.D. complete its missions. Armed with his trusty .45 and a glove that burns claw-shaped symbols into the foreheads of his victims, Johnson often manifests during the most desperate events. At the conclusion of the war on frogs, Dr. Corrigan made an effort to put Johnson's spirit to rest, returning him to Hunte Castle. After releasing Kraus, whom he had possessed for a notably long time, Johnson seemed to be finally at peace.

- *Panya*, an Egyptian mummy who was reanimated during the nineteenth century, was long a prisoner of various clandestine societies that sought to learn her secrets. Eventually succumbing to weakness through her long incarceration, she was rescued from the Oannes Society by the bureau and moved to its headquarters. Panya has demonstrated psychic ability, including telepathy and mind control. Her motivations, at first benign, have possibly taken a more nefarious turn.

- *Andrew Devon*, the later-edition high-profile member of the B.P.R.D., was a skeptic of the occult who attempted to use his doctorate in modern and medieval languages to debunk a report by Dr. Corrigan concerning demonic possession. Attracted to a world beyond anything he once knew,

Devon has moved from a bookish intellectual to an active, if somewhat trepidatious, field agent.

- *The Black Flame* is one of the major antagonists of the B.P.R.D., but his intentions are not completely malicious. Landis Pope, the CEO of Zinco Industries, created the Black Flame armor to control the frog monsters, and ultimately the Katha-Hem, but his plans were thwarted when the frogs began to control him, as Katha-Hem manifested and grew in power. Seemingly defeated by Sherman and unable to remove his armor, the Black Flame is dragged away by the frog monsters. Eventually, the eldritch energy burns away his physical form, leaving only an animated skeleton, but he continues to plot on behalf of the frog monsters. He appears to have been permanently destroyed during a second confrontation with Sherman, but at the expense of her powers.

- *Memnan Saa*, once a minor, almost charlatan sort of parlor-trick magician named Martin Gilfryd, became a complex antagonist for the bureau. After searching the world for true magic, Gilfryd evidently found a source, using it to transform himself into a powerful sorcerer, vexing even the formidable Lobster Johnson. Understanding the frog apocalypse at a level beyond human comprehension, Saa sought to use the living fire within Liz Sherman to prevent this particular calamity from transpiring even while other events were in motion. Saa's ultimate intentions and motivations remain unclear, and even after his death at the hands of Sherman, his ghost continues to haunt her.

Artistic Style

Because Mignola's writing style, drawing style, and subject matter are so distinct, finding an artist to provide a similarly distinctive look became important. Sometimes the visual content is influenced by Mignola as he provides a notable amount of conceptual sketches and additional notes on the drawings. While a number of illustrators have worked on the *B.P.R.D.* books, the one dominant contributor has been Davis. His style has largely become synonymous with the aesthetic of *B.P.R.D.*, which is rather different from Mignola's *Hellboy*, and helped to give the series its own strong identity.

Davis is a self-taught illustrator and tries for a sense of realism that suggests only what is necessary and allows the fantastic content of the stories to unfold in the reader's imagination. Often large panels are used to give a sense of the enormity of the task that the B.P.R.D. encounters in the face of a planetary apocalypse, but Davis also likes employing close-ups of characters' faces to give the reader a way to understand how these larger issues in the books are playing out in personal ways for the people involved. Much of the attention for Davis's work is directed at his depiction of monsters, particularly their grotesque quality. The depictions of the monsters often have a messiness to their organic structure: Limbs bend at improbable junctures, tissues are not always cleanly joined, and components from different species are jammed together. This contributes to the sense that the characters in *B.P.R.D.* live in the same world as the reader, albeit one that is slightly disturbing.

While Mignola developed the grand movements of the story in advance, he has also allowed other writers to contribute *B.P.R.D.* stories. His longtime collaborator on the series, Arcudi, who has long worked on graphic novels based on films and has written comic books that have been turned into films, gives the plotting of the *B.P.R.D.* series a sense of the cinematic in terms of how the character arcs rise and fall, where moments of action and exposition are, and when the adventure elements give way to emotional resonance in the character relationships. Juggling the large cast of characters requires shifting the narrative focus while staying true to the larger thematic points of the series.

Themes

B.P.R.D. explores several notable themes over the course of its frog-war arc. Perhaps one of the most pervasive is identity and how identity is internally and externally defined. The major members of the team all find themselves dealing with secrets from their pasts, and their decisions to face these mysteries, along with their methods of revelation, change their relationships within the story and affect readers' perceptions

of them. For example, Captain Daimio's introduction was as abrupt and shocking as his gruff demeanor, and the reaction of the characters within the story could be a parallel to readers' reactions to the introduction of an unknown character suddenly taking a major section of the narrative focus.

Over the development of the story, the revelation of Daimio's background made him a more sympathetic character, and his regret at the loss of Roger—and indeed many of the men who died under his command—helped to humanize his character. Roger's death strains the relationship between Daimio and Kraus, and Kraus grows increasingly resentful toward the captain, becoming fixated on murdering him if the opportunity presents itself.

Unlike mainstream ensemble superhero books in which the teammates often have little internal conflict, the members of the B.P.R.D. show that, despite their unusual circumstance and powers, they still have many of the vices and weaknesses of regular humans. In the midst of an apocalyptic situation, the vulnerability of the characters helps to underscore their efforts to retain

B.P.R.D. (Courtesy of Dark Horse Comics)

their humanity, the definition of which certainly interests Mignola. For example, he has cited the Nathaniel Hawthorne story "Feathertop" (1852)—about a scarecrow turned into a man who, upon seeing his true self reflected in a mirror, decides that he cannot live under an illusion—as some inspiration for Sapien's investigation into his background as Caul and what it means to no longer be that person.

Related to this, *B.P.R.D.* does not specifically define what is monstrous, but it seems that either the loss of identity or the imposition of identity from outside forces is what makes for a truly horrific situation. The frog monsters are grotesque, but are they because they used to be humans or because they represent a future for Earth after humanity? Is Memnan Saa's control of Liz Sherman monstrous because of the latter's loss of free will, or is it a calculated decision born of Saa's analysis of the war and thus somehow permissible?

These types of questions, while not immediately on the surface of the story, build over the course of the series and challenge readers to evaluate their own perception of the characters and how protagonists and antagonists are defined. The acquisition of knowledge, unfolding for the characters in the story as well as for the readers, is also questioned, for the act itself can fundamentally change an individual. This reinforces *B.P.R.D.*'s supposition that identity is one of the most basic horrors that a person can face.

Impact

As the largest independent American comic book publisher, Dark Horse Comics has built its reputation on several strong creator-owned titles under its Legend comic book imprint, which featured Mignola and several other important artists, such as Frank Miller and John Byrne. As a spin-off of Mignola's *Hellboy* title, *B.P.R.D.* expanded the *Hellboy* universe and helped to build a large market for *Hellboy* and *B.P.R.D.* merchandise.

By collaborating with other artists on the *B.P.R.D.* run, the book grew in notoriety for deepening the internal mythology of the series and offering intricately expansive plot development, encouraging readers to reread entire volumes to better understand the story, which had been unfolding over many years. This sort of protracted, multithreaded narrative elaboration puts *B.P.R.D.* in the same category as works such as Neil Gaiman's *Sandman* (1989-1996) or Kurt Busiek's *Astro City* (1995-   ) in using the serialized medium of comic books to tell stories that are scaled up beyond the range of other monthly titles but that nevertheless appeal to the deep reading and encyclopedic attention to detail of many comic book fans.

B.P.R.D. also draws upon many sources from folklore and mythology known by Mignola and other contributors. This blend associates *B.P.R.D.* with weird fiction more than standard horror and fantasy genres, particularly in the way that it combines the supernatural with the scientific. The sense of otherworldly dread that is a mark of weird fiction is certainly present in the series, and the seriousness of the subject and the real-world setting infuse a sense of realism into a realm populated by magic and experimental technologies.

Stefan Hall

Films

Hellboy. Directed by Guillermo del Toro. Revolution Studios, 2004. This film stars Ron Perlman as Hellboy, John Hurt as Professor Bruttenholm, Selma Blair as Liz Sherman, and Doug Jones as Abe Sapien. Using some elements from *Seed of Destruction*, the film features B.P.R.D. and its agents, with some differences from the *B.P.R.D.* series. For example, Abe Sapien is psychic, and Liz and Hellboy become romantically linked. B.P.R.D. director Tom Manning (Jeffrey Tambor) replaces Buttenholm. Roger the Homunculus can be briefly seen as a gray humanoid statue in the background at the B.P.R.D. headquarters.

Hellboy II: The Golden Army. Directed by Guillermo del Toro. Relativity Media, 2008. This film stars Perlman as Hellboy, Blair as Liz Sherman, Jones as Abe Sapien, and John Alexander as Johann Krauss. Introducing Krauss from the *B.P.R.D.* series is the most direct link to the books, although Krauss's ectoplasm is more like smoke, and his containment suit looks more like a deep-sea diver's suit than the sleeker version featured in the comics. Mignola contributed concept art for the film.

Television Series

The B.P.R.D. Declassified. Directed by Ben Rock. Visible Man Productions, 2004. This television special aired on FX Network to promote the first *Hellboy* film. It was done in the style of a fake documentary, mixing information about the film with scenes of B.P.R.D. agents, including Liz Sherman (Kristina Varvais) as a young child.

Hellboy Animated: Sword of Storms. Directed by Phil Weinstein and Tad Stones. IDT Entertainment, 2006. This animated, made-for-television film features the voice acting of Perlman as Hellboy, Peri Gilpin as Professor Kate Corrigan, Blair as Liz Sherman, and Jones as Abe Sapien. The B.P.R.D. is enlisted to help contain the Japanese demons Thunder and Lightning after a professor of folklore opens a forbidden scroll. Another B.P.R.D. agent, a psychic named Russell Thorne, is introduced. The story was written by Mignola and Stones. Visually, Mignola wanted the film to look different from both the comics and the live-action film. Furthermore, while all three movie productions are rooted in some of the same basic narrative elements, Mignola has stated that each is its own distinct narrative universe.

Hellboy Animated: Blood and Iron. Directed by Victor Cook and Tad Stones. IDT Entertainment, 2007. This animated, made-for-television film features the voice acting of Perlman as Hellboy, Hurt as Professor Bruttenholm, Gilpin as Professor Kate Corrigan, Blair as Liz Sherman, and Jones as Abe Sapien. The story was written by Mignola and Stones. Bruttenholm decides to accompany the B.P.R.D. agents as they investigate a haunting perpetrated by a vampire countess that Bruttenholm had encountered in his younger days before the formation of the bureau. The film also features agent Sydney Leach, who discovered Roger's body in the *Wake the Devil* series.

Further Reading

Davis, Guy. *The Marquis: Inferno* (2010).

Dorkin, Evan, and Jill Thompson. *Beasts of Burden: Animal Rites* (2010).

Hester, Phil, and Mike Huddleston. *The Coffin* (2000).

Powell, Eric. *The Goon* (1998-　).

Bibliography

O'Connor, Laura. "The Corpse on Hellboy's Back." *Journal of Popular Culture* 43, no. 3 (June, 2010): 540-563.

Szumskyj, Benjamin. *Right Hand of Doom: A Critical Study of Michael Mignola's "Hellboy."* Winchester, Va.: Wild Cat Books, 2006.

Weiner, Stephen, Jason Hall, and Victoria Blake. *Hellboy: The Companion.* Milwaukie, Ore. Dark Horse Books, 2008.

See also: *Hellboy; Goon; Sandman; Sandman Mystery Theatre*

BATMAN: ARKHAM ASYLUM
A SERIOUS HOUSE ON SERIOUS EARTH

Author: Morrison, Grant
Artist: Dave McKean (illustrator); Gaspar Saladino (letterer)
Publisher: DC Comics
First book publication: 1989

Publication History

Arkham Asylum was originally published as a single volume in 1989 by DC Comics. In 2004, a fifteenth anniversary edition was released containing the original script for the graphic novel with comments from Grant Morrison. These comments explain that the initial concept for the book came from a brief description of Arkham Asylum in a "Who's Who" publication by DC Comics in 1985. One of the few entries describing a setting rather than a character, the entry for Arkham Asylum described how the founder's wife and daughter had been murdered by Martin "Mad Dog" Hawkins. This inspired Morrison to create the story that would later become *Arkham Asylum*. Morrison pitched the idea to DC as a 48-page book, and it was accepted. The book was later increased to 64 pages, and Dave McKean was selected to do the artwork, which eventually resulted in the book expanding to the final 120-page version.

Plot

The story begins with a quote from Lewis Carroll and passages from Amadeus Arkham's journal, in which he describes his aging mother's mental breakdown. The next pages alternate between the present, in which Batman approaches Arkham Asylum, and the recent past, in which Commissioner Gordon receives a call from the asylum. The inmates, led by the Joker, have taken over. The commissioner calls Batman, whose presence is requested by the Joker. Batman agrees to enter the asylum, telling Gordon that this is something he must do.

Arkham's journal next describes his return to his family home, which he later converted into the asylum. Batman arrives as the narrative returns to the present.

(FilmMagic)

Dave McKean

Despite the critical success of Dave McKean's graphic novel *Cages*, which he both wrote and illustrated, many readers will best recall McKean for his elaborate and innovative collaborations with writer Neil Gaiman, including the covers of the seventy-five issues of *Sandman*. A multimedia artist, McKean blends line drawings with paint, collage, photography, and sculptural elements to produce truly distinctive original images, many of which eschew traditional representational realism. With Gaiman, he has produced a number of graphic novels, including *Violent Cases*, *Signal to Noise*, *Black Orchid*, and *Mr. Punch*. His collaboration with writer Grant Morrison, *Arkham Asylum: A Serious House on a Serious Earth*, pushed the limits of comic book expressionism in order to represent the instability and danger of an asylum filled with supervillains. Also renowned for his work in illustration and film, McKean has one of the most distinctive visual styles of any current cartoonist.

He is greeted by the Joker, who lets the hostages go and welcomes Batman to "the real world." Batman engages in conversation with a psychiatrist and Dr. Cavendish, the administrators of Arkham who have remained behind, and with various inmates before the Joker issues an ultimatum: Batman must play a game of hide-and-seek or the Joker will shoot one of the remaining psychiatrists. In one hour, the inmates will come looking for Batman, the person responsible for sending them to Arkham in the first place.

As Batman moves through the asylum, flashbacks of his parents' murder and of Arkham's wife and daughter being killed punctuate his declining mental state. Batman encounters his foes Clayface, Dr. Destiny, Scarecrow, the Mad Hatter, Maxie Zeus, and, finally, Killer Croc. The ensuing fight between Batman and Killer Croc is narrated by Arkham's journal, which reflects Batman's own implied thoughts and feelings at the time. Batman defeats Croc and immediately encounters Dr. Cavendish, who threatens to kill one of the psychiatrists.

It is revealed that Cavendish is responsible for the inmates escaping, allowing them to do so in an attempt to lure Batman to the asylum in order to fulfill a prophecy in Arkham's journal. The "bat," who is responsible for "feeding" the asylum, must be trapped and killed. As Cavendish attempts to choke Batman, he is killed by the psychiatrist he had held hostage. Batman gives Two-Face back his coin, which had been confiscated. Two-Face decides that if the unmarked face comes up, Batman goes free, but if the scarred face comes up, he dies. The Joker agrees to the terms, and based on the result of the coin toss, Two-Face lets Batman go. As Batman leaves the asylum, the Joker reminds him that he will always be welcome at Arkham. Just before the story ends, Two-Face looks down at his hand, revealing that the coin actually landed with the scarred side up. He then knocks over his tower of tarot cards as he quotes Carroll: "Who cares for you? You're nothing but a pack of cards."

Characters

- *Batman*, a.k.a. *Bruce Wayne*, undergoes a dramatic metamorphosis during the course of the novel, emerging stronger and more mentally sound than before and prepared to face whatever challenges lie ahead. As in many Batman stories, Batman's origin is central to the plot. The death of Bruce Wayne's parents parallels Arkham's loss of his wife and daughter, creating a connection between them and between Batman and the asylum. Coming to terms with this loss is part of Batman's transformation.

- *The Joker* is the main antagonist of the graphic novel, serving as both the villain and a sort of guide or therapist figure. The usual dichotomy between Batman and the Joker—sanity and insanity—is reversed in *Arkham Asylum*. Early in the story, one of the psychiatrists remarks, "We're not even sure if [the Joker] can be properly defined as insane." Later, it is posited that the Joker's supposed insanity is in fact "a brilliant new modification of human perception." This reversal casts the Joker as sane and Batman as a madman who must be "cured" by the asylum and the Joker.

- *Two-Face*, a.k.a. *Harvey Dent*, a recurring character in the Batman series, has become a patient at Arkham Asylum, where he has been "weaned" off of his characteristic coin that he uses to make decisions. The psychiatrists at Arkham replaced the coin with a die, giving Two-Face six choices instead of two. They then replaced the die with tarot cards, increasing his choices to seventy-eight. This resulted in Two-Face's consciousness becoming fractured—Batman notes that Dent cannot make even simple decisions without consulting his tarot cards.

- *Amadeus Arkham*, though not actually present during the main events of the novel, is Arkham Asylum's founder. He appears through a series of flashbacks and journal entries interspersed throughout the narrative. These reveal a disturbing backstory that informs and mirrors the events of the main narrative. Arkham was driven to insanity, in part by the brutal murder of his wife and daughter. He later treated their killer in the asylum and killed him with an overdose of electroshock therapy made to look like an accident.

Artistic Style

McKean's unique style lends a mysterious and often grim atmosphere to the characters and setting of *Arkham Asylum*. McKean combines photography with more traditional comic illustration to create an unusual blend of realism and abstraction. This results in a simultaneously lifelike and surreal depiction of the asylum, its inhabitants, and the events of the story. Batman's transformation becomes a visceral experience for the reader.

McKean frequently incorporates objects into his illustrations. For example, several pages involving Arkham's wife use lace texturing, and the pearl necklace worn by Batman's mother is physically present on the pages showing his memories of her. This realism is contrasted with panel borders that often seem to unravel onto the page and arrangements of images that are more organic than the orderly sequence usually found in comics. The asylum is "an organism, hungry for madness," and McKean's artwork reflects the chaos associated with it.

The lettering in *Arkham Asylum* is also somewhat unusual. In addition to regular lettering for minor characters, most of the important characters have unique lettering and text balloons. Batman has white text in a black balloon, the Joker has scrawled red text in no balloon, Clayface has dripping yellow balloons, Maxie Zeus has electric-blue balloons, and Amadeus Arkham's journal is lettered in handwriting on paperlike text boxes. These different text styles not only help to identify characters but also reinforce their existence as distinct individuals.

Themes

The plot of *Arkham Asylum* revolves around several symbols that are repeated throughout the narrative. Many of these symbols are represented as tarot cards, which are either used by the characters, usually Two-Face, or placed in the artwork. The first page, for example, shows the moon tarot card. The moon, representing trial and initiation, rebirth, and lunacy, is an important symbol in the novel. The symbol appears in many forms: as the moon itself, as two fish forming the symbol of Pisces (the astrological equivalent of the moon card), and as one of Two-Face's tarot cards.

Another group of symbols is related to home and family. The asylum itself is frequently referred to as a house, and the symbol of a house or home is used to connect the asylum with Arkham's and Batman's backstories, each involving family and a sense of "home." Batman's backstory also involves his mother, another recurring symbol. At one point in the story, a clip of the film *Psycho* (1960) plays on a television, and the quote "a boy's best friend is his mother" appears later. The connections to family and home are important in the novel. Two-Face's house of cards, seen throughout the novel, is another sort of house that connects this symbol with the theme of tarot cards.

Vision is also frequently referenced in the novel. During the Joker's call to Commissioner Gordon, he threatens to poke out the eyes of one of the hostages at the asylum. When Arkham discovers his murdered wife and daughter, he finds his daughter's severed head inside a dollhouse. His journal reads, "And then I look at the doll's house. And the doll's house looks at me." During a Rorschach ink-blot test, the Joker turns to Batman and asks, "What about you, Batman? What do you see?"

The most prevalent theme is madness, which permeates the entire novel, touching every character and location. The novel opens with a quote from Carroll's *Alice's Adventures in Wonderland* (1865): "We're all mad here. I'm mad, you're mad." This is echoed by the Mad Hatter, who explains that the asylum, again referred to as a house, "does things to the mind." The theme of madness connects many of the other themes in the novel, and the symbols are all interconnected, often through the use of tarot cards.

Impact

Arkham Asylum was published shortly after the release of Tim Burton's film *Batman* (1989), and it benefited from the resulting rise in popularity of the franchise. It quickly became the best-selling original graphic novel ever, but it was often misunderstood. The unusual narrative structure and style of *Arkham Asylum* caused it to be dismissed as either pretentious or confusing, particularly by an audience expecting a more traditional Batman story. However, *Arkham Asylum* has remained one of the most highly regarded graphic novels and is frequently cited alongside other well-known comics, such as *Watchmen* and *The Dark Knight Returns*, as an influential and formative work.

Matthew Halm

Films

The Dark Knight. Directed by Christopher Nolan. Warner Bros., 2008. The character of the Joker features prominently in this, the second of Nolan's Batman films. Though there are no direct parallels between the events of the film and graphic novel, the mannerisms of the Joker (played by Heath Ledger) and some of his physical qualities cannot help but be influenced by *Arkham Asylum*. The actual location of Arkham Asylum appears in the earlier *Batman Begins* (2005) but bears little resemblance to the asylum depicted in the graphic novel.

Further Reading

Gaiman, Neil, and Dave McKean. *Black Orchid* (1991).

Moore, Alan, and Brian Bolland. *Batman: The Killing Joke* (1988).

Morrison, Grant, and Klaus Janson. *Batman: Gothic* (1990).

Bibliography

Callahan, Timothy. *Grant Morrison: The Early Years*. Edwardsville, Ill.: Sequart Research and Literary Organization, 2007.

Khouri, Andy. "Grant Morrison: The Early Years— Part II: *Arkham Asylum*." Comic Book Resources, 2007. http://www.comicbookresources. com/?page=article&id=10710.

McKean, Dave. "Storytelling in the Gutter." *History of Photography* 19 (1995): 293-297.

See also: *Batman: The Killing Joke; Batman: The Dark Knight Returns; Batman: The Dark Knight Strikes Again; Watchmen*

BATMAN: BLACK AND WHITE, VOLUME 1

Author: Bolland, Brian; Chaykin, Howard; Dixon, Chuck; Gaiman, Neil; Goodwin, Archie; Helfer, Andrew; Janson, Klaus; Kubert, Joe; McKeever, Ted; O'Neil, Dennis; Otomo, Katsuhiro; Sienkiewicz, Bill; Simonson, Walter; Strnad, Jan; Timm, Bruce; Wagner, Matt; Williams, Kent

Artist: Neal Adams (illustrator); Mike Allred (illustrator); Simon Bisley (illustrator); Brian Bolland (illustrator); Howard Chaykin (illustrator); Richard Corben (illustrator); Gary Gianni (illustrator); Klaus Janson (illustrator); Michael Kaluta (illustrator); Teddy Kristiansen (illustrator); Joe Kubert (illustrator); Tanino Liberatore (illustrator); Ted McKeever (illustrator); Moebius (illustrator); José Muñoz (illustrator); Kevin Nowlan (illustrator); Katsuhiro Otomo (illustrator); Alex Ross (illustrator); P. Craig Russell (illustrator); Tony Salmons (illustrator); Bill Sienkiewicz (illustrator); Walter Simonson (illustrator); Brian Stelfreeze (illustrator); Bruce Timm (illustrator); Matt Wagner (illustrator); Kent Williams (illustrator); Jorge Zaffino (illustrator); Marc Silvestri (penciller); Matt Banning (inker); Ken Bruzenak (letterer); John Costanza (letterer); Ellie De Ville (letterer); Phil Felix (letterer); Tim Harkins (letterer); Todd Klein (letterer); Bill Oakley (letterer); John Workman (letterer); Jim Lee (cover artist); Frank Miller (cover artist); Alex Toth (cover artist); Barry Windsor-Smith (cover artist); Scott Williams (cover artist)

Publisher: DC Comics
First serial publication: 1996
First book publication: 1998, 2007

Publication History

The brainchild of DC Comics' editor Mark Chiarello, *Batman: Black and White,* Volume 1, was originally published in 1996. Inspired by Warren Publishing's *Creepy* and *Eerie* comics magazines, Chiarello wanted to gather the most talented artists and writers in the field to complete a black-and-white anthology of short Batman stories. Chiarello received artistic and writing contributions from such luminaries as

---

Mark Chiarello

An assistant to Archie Goodwin as editor at Marvel Comics in the 1980's, Mark Chiarello is an artist who is also a well-known editor at DC Comics. Athough he has produced a limited amount of interior art for comics, he is well known for the stylish covers that he has produced for titles including *Wolverine*, *Vigilante*, and *Terminal City*. His best-known work as an artist is the 1993 graphic novel *Batman/Houdini: The Devil's Workshop* from DC's imprint Elseworlds, written by Howard Chaykin and John Francis Moore, which teamed the caped crusader with the escape artist. Chiarello's work is produced with watercolors, which distinguish them from the majority of painters working in comics. His images have an ephemeral feeling to them, and his figures are presented in a realist manner, although facial characteristics are often obscured by his chosen medium. Chiarello's images are more gestural and impressionistic than is typical of the superhero genre.

Neil Gaiman, Archie Goodwin, Katsuhiro Otomo, and Ted McKeever.

In order to maintain Batman's integrity, Batman comics' editor Scott Peterson was brought in for guidance. Despite a common belief that readers do not like anthologies or black-and-white comics, the series proved successful after its release. After a *Batman: Black and White* preview was released in 1996, the original four issues were released monthly between June and September of the same year. DC Comics released a hardcover collector's edition combining the four issues of *Batman: Black and White,* Volume 1, in 1998 and a paperback version trimmed to the standard size of the original release in 2007.

Plot

Batman: Black and White, Volume 1, is a collection of original, eight-page Batman stories from some of the premier graphic novel artists and writers of the Modern Age. Without the constraints of fitting the stories into the official *Batman* canon, this anthology provides twenty unique perspectives of the Batman universe.

In "Perpetual Mourning," written and illustrated by McKeever and lettered by John Workman, Batman performs an autopsy on an unidentified murdered woman in order to understand more about the victim, the crime, and the murderer. Written by Goodwin and illustrated by José Muñoz, "The Devil's Trumpet" tells of a legendary trumpet that once belonged to the Devil. Musician Les Farrell wishes to possess the instrument. After tracking down the trumpet and killing its owner in a blind rage, Les attempts to harness the horn's power, but he is quickly apprehended by Batman.

Written and illustrated by Walter Simonson and lettered by John Workman, "Legend" is a futuristic story in which a mother tells her child about the legend of Batman and how he vanquished evil from the Earth. The mother says that if evil ever returns, Batman will return to save his people once again. The final page reveals the family living under totalitarian rule, leaving the reader with a glimpse of Batman's reappearance.

"A Black and White World" is a metanarrative in which Batman and the Joker are real people who happen to work as comics characters for a *Batman* comic. The story follows the two characters as they prepare for, and perform, a specific scene, complaining throughout about the nature of the business. This story was written by Gaiman, illustrated by Simon Bisley, and lettered by Costanza.

In "Good Evening, Midnight," written and illustrated by Klaus Janson and lettered by Bill Oakley, Alfred reads a note that Thomas Wayne had written for his son on his third birthday. As Alfred reads the note, the text overlays a journey Batman has undertaken to save a busload of children being held captive.

Written by Andrew Helfer, illustrated by Tanino Liberatore, and lettered by Costanza, "In Dreams" follows a young woman seeking treatment for a reoccurring nightmare in which Batman crashes through a window into her bedroom. The reader learns that the woman was kidnapped as a child and saved by Batman, but she has been unable to process the experience.

"Bent Twigs," by Bill Sienkiewicz, casts Batman in the role of child protector, as he witnesses a father threaten his child and throw his pet cat to its death. The single father attempts to defend himself, but Batman becomes infuriated with the father's neglect of his son. Batman berates him for his inadequacies while attempting to get him to be a better parent.

In "An Innocent Guy," written and illustrated by Brian Bolland and lettered by Ellie de Ville, a man records a video diary in which he discusses his desire to perform an evil act in order to help him determine whether he is inherently good or bad. He decides killing Batman will be the perfect crime and fantasizes about how his death will occur.

Written by Goodwin, illustrated by Gary Gianni, and lettered by Todd Klein, "Heroes" tells a remembered tale of a ten-year-old boy and his distracted architect father that is set in 1938. The two are kidnapped by a German soldier for secret designs, but Batman appears and rescues them. In the end, the boy discovers that his father's secret designs are actually for Batman's equipment.

In "The Third Mask," written and illustrated by Otomo, translated by Jo Duffy, and lettered by Oakley, Batman hunts a serial killer with multiple personalities. The killer draws a parallel to Batman's own duality, leading Batman to eventually question his own identity.

Characters

- *Batman*, a.k.a. *Bruce Wayne*, the protagonist, is the crime-fighting alter ego of American billionaire Wayne. Unlike many comic book superheroes, he does not harness any supernatural abilities or powers, instead relying on his physical prowess, intellect, and training and on advanced technologies to provide him with the resources necessary to perform his duties. Wayne is driven to fight crime after witnessing the murder of his parents in the streets of Gotham City as a boy.

- *Commissioner James Gordon* is the police commissioner of Gotham City and an ally to Batman. He often works with Batman to help solve particularly difficult or serious crimes and is one of the few people Batman trusts or would consider a friend.

- *Alfred Pennyworth* is Bruce Wayne's butler and one of the few people who are aware of Batman's true identity. He can sometimes act as a protector and surrogate father figure, as is evident in the story "Good Evening, Midnight," in which Alfred is in possession of a letter that Thomas Wayne wrote to his son on his third birthday.

- *Two-Face*, a.k.a. *Harvey Dent*, is Batman's antagonist in the story "Two of a Kind." Two-Face, formerly Gotham City's district attorney Harvey Dent, has gruesome scars covering the left side of his face. Two-Face uses the flip of a coin to direct his decision making. He offers a complex case study into mental illness.

- *The Joker* is one of Batman's most well known antagonists, but in the story "A Black and White World," Gaiman has reimagined their relationship. The two are seen as regular guys with real-world concerns as they work as characters in a comic. The Joker is very cynical of the whole business, jealous that Batman gets the best panels, and annoyed that the extras get to raid the commissary first.

Artistic Style

The only commonality in artistic style between the twenty stories in *Batman: Black and White,* Volume 1, is a lack of color. Each of the artists was given license to develop his story using the styles and designs of his choosing, with the only requirement being that the comic had to be in black and white. The editors of the anthology intentionally sought out many of the artists specifically because of their unique styles and notoriety throughout the graphic novel and comic book community. Some of the biggest names in the industry contributed to the piece, including such esteemed artists as Otomo, Richard Corben, Bolland, and Joe Kubert.

This diversity is evident in each story, but it is exemplified in the varied depictions of the Batman character. McKeever focuses on the humanness of Batman; he takes up little room on the page and conveys emotions in the very way he carries himself. Kubert, however, takes his inspiration from the "bat" aspect of Batman, focusing more on Batman as an almost inhuman creature who appears in frames covering large swathes of the page, hanging upside down and soaring through the air with his fellow bat creatures. Howard Chaykin and Sienkiewicz each portray a more retro Batman character, with a simple suit and little in the way of musculature, whereas Bisley and Janson each illustrate Batman with caricatured musculature.

Themes

In addition to the amazing diversity in the artistic styles, *Batman: Black and White,* Volume 1, includes incredible variety in narrative style and thematic elements.

"Perpetual Mourning" discusses the importance of death and focuses on the remembrance of those who have died; "Two of a Kind" confronts the ideas of love, duality, and the fragility of human nature; and "The Hunt" explores the subconscious driving force behind Bruce Wayne's need to fight crime.

"Petty Crimes" comments on the evolving nature of the world and mankind's necessity to keep moving forward, while "The Devil's Trumpet" focuses on the destructive nature of greed. "Legend" looks at the issue of personal freedom.

"Monster Maker" serves as a commentary on the dangers of children being raised on the streets. "Dead Boys Eyes" is a reflection on the motivational force of guilt and revenge. "The Devil's Children" is concerned with city crime and the inability of getting away with one's crimes.

"A Black and White World" serves as a comic commentary on working-class citizenship, while "Good Evening, Midnight" attempts to convey the complex emotions, hopes, and fears of a father for his son.

"In Dreams" explores the weight of one's dreams and the fragility of the human psyche. "Heist" focuses on some of the criminal elements of society. "Bent Twigs" is an exploration of the importance of a loving family and the difficulty of being a single parent. "A Slaying Song Tonight" discusses the importance of family and tradition.

"An Innocent Guy" offers a philosophical question about free will and the nature of good and evil. "Monsters in the Closet" explores the boundaries of science and the concept of playing God. "Heroes" focuses on the importance of parental role models. "Leavetaking" looks at the immense toll emotional scars can inflict on a person after a tragic event. "The Third Mask" discusses the nature, fragility, and importance of human identity.

Impact

Despite concerns about the perceived undesirable nature of both anthologies and black-and-white comics, *Batman: Black and White,* Volume 1, became a creative, critical, and financial success upon its release in 1996. Having gathered together some of the most talented artists and writers in the business to develop their own original stories, Chiarello helped to continue the already vast legacy of *Batman* comics. Part of the success arose from the authors' free rein to create their own story without having to worry about fitting into the official Batman canon. As such, *Batman: Black and White,* Volume 1, contains some of the most original and creative Batman stories written by some of the most famous minds in the comics industry.

Although the impact of this publication on the larger graphic novel world is minimal, its existence is still welcomed and celebrated. *Batman: Black and White,* Volume 1, did spawn two additional volumes, although neither was received as highly as the first. In 2001, Web site IGN rated *Batman: Black and White,* Volume 1, as the fourteenth best *Batman* graphic novel ever written.

Tyler J. Manolovitz

Television Series

Batman: Black and White. Directed by Ian Kirby and Adam Fulton. Sequence Post, 2008-2009. In 2008, distributor Warner Premiere Digital developed quasi-animated versions of a select number of stories from the three volumes of the *Batman: Black and White* series and published them online as motion comics. Each episode runs for approximately four to six minutes and includes actor voice-overs. Of the twenty episodes produced, seven derived from *Batman: Black and White,* Volume 1, including "Two of a Kind," "Good Evening, Midnight," "Perpetual Mourning," "Monsters in the Closet," "In Dreams," "Heroes," and "Legend."

Further Reading

Chiarello, Mark, ed. *Batman: Black and White,* Volume 2 (2002).

_____. *Batman: Black and White,* Volume 3 (2007).

Miller, Frank. *Batman: The Dark Knight* (1986).

Bibliography

Beatty, Scott, Chuck Dixon, and Sangbok David Hahn. *The Batman Handbook: The Ultimate Training Manual*. Philadelphia: Quirk Books, 2005.

Brooker, Will. *Batman Unmasked: Analyzing a Cultural Icon*. New York: Continuum, 2001.

Daniels, Les, and Chip Kiss. *Batman: The Complete History*. San Francisco: Chronicle Books, 1999.

White, Mark D., and Robert Arp. *Batman and Philosophy: The Dark Knight of the Soul*. Hoboken, N.J.: John Wiley & Sons, 2008.

See also: *All Star Batman and Robin, the Boy Wonder*; *Batman: Dark Victory*; *Batman: The Dark Knight Returns*; *Batman: The Dark Knight Strikes Again*; *Batman: The Killing Joke*; *Batman: The Long Halloween*; *Batman: Year One*; *Batman: Year 100*

BATMAN: DARK VICTORY

Author: Loeb, Jeph
Artist: Tim Sale (illustrator); Gregory Wright (colorist); Richard Starkings (letterer)
Publisher: DC Comics
First serial publication: 1999-2000
First book publication: 2001

Publication History

Following the success of Jeph Loeb and Tim Sale's previous graphic novels—*Batman: The Long Halloween* (1996-1997), which won both the 1998 Eisner Award for Best Limited Series and the 1999 Eisner Award for Best Reprint Graphic Album, and *Superman for All Seasons* (1998), which was nominated for the 1999 Eisner Award for Best Limited Series—the frequent collaborators began work on a sequel to *The Long Halloween* intended to tie up many of the story's loose ends. Of particular interest to Loeb was introducing Batman's sidekick, Robin. Though Sale was, by his own admission, initially skeptical of pairing their dark, moody version of Batman with a teenage sidekick, he was later won over by the story Loeb wrote introducing Robin.

Loeb and Sale's subsequent effort, *Batman: Dark Victory*, was published by DC Comics as a thirteen-part limited series between December, 1999, and December, 2000, and was later released as a single graphic novel in 2001. Issue 0, a promotional giveaway, was included as a prologue in the collected novel. It received positive reviews from critics and was listed as the eighth-best *Batman* graphic novel in a list compiled by IGN Comics in 2005.

Plot

Continuing the story of Batman's early years as the "Caped Crusader," *Batman: Dark Victory* is set several months after the conclusion of *Batman: The Long Halloween*. As the graphic novel begins, Batman is more isolated than ever before. Blaming himself for the downfall of his closest friend, former district attorney Harvey Dent, now a villain known as Two-Face, Batman has withdrawn from his former allies, refusing

Jeph Loeb

Coming to the comics industry from Hollywood where he wrote the screenplays for *Teen Wolf* and *Commando*, writer Jeph Loeb stepped into the spotlight by penning a series of acclaimed graphic novels with artist Tim Sale, including *Challengers of the Unknown*, *Batman: The Long Halloween*, *Batman: Dark Victory*, and *Superman for All Seasons*. The pair later collaborated on a series of books for Marvel Comics, including *Daredevil: Yellow*, *Spider-Man: Blue*, and *Hulk: Grey*. Loeb's comics for DC have been defined by their intricate plotting and willingness to advance fresh takes on members of the Batman supporting cast, while his work for Marvel was much more retrospective, opting to deepen the psychological characterization of existing characters through internal monologues, often presented in caption boxes. From 2006 to 2008, Loeb was co-executive producer of the NBC superhero television show, *Heroes*. Since 2010 he has served as executive vice president, head of television, for Marvel Entertainment.

(WireImage)

to accept help from either Commissioner James Gordon or Catwoman in his fight against crime.

Meanwhile, the criminal underworld of Gotham City teeters on the brink of annihilation. The city's crime boss, Carmine Falcone, was killed by Two-Face at the end of *The Long Halloween*, and Batman's classic rogues' gallery of freakish criminals has waged war on the more traditional gangsters. Sofia Gigante, Falcone's disabled daughter, has seized control of the crime families, but their power seems to be on the decline.

To make matters worse, Janice Porter, Harvey Dent's replacement as district attorney, has retried and overturned the death sentence of Alberto Falcone, the "Holiday Killer" whom Batman captured in *The Long Halloween* and placed under house arrest in Falcone's father's old cabin. Shortly after Alberto's release, a new set of killings begins when the body of Clancy O'Hara, the chief of police, is found hanging from a Gotham City bridge. A newspaper clipping with a hangman puzzle on it is taped to his chest.

As more police officers are killed by the mysterious Hangman Killer, Batman races to discover the murderer's identity. Learning that all of the documents left behind on the victims' bodies come from Dent's files, Batman descends to the sewers to find his old friend.

Though Two-Face escapes from Batman, the criminal begins his own investigation of the Hangman Killer to clear his own name. When Gordon is nearly killed by the Hangman, it is Two-Face who saves him, assuring Gordon that he is being framed for the murders.

As the Joker escalates the war between the "freaks" and organized crime, Bruce Wayne adopts Dick Grayson after his family is killed in an act of sabotage by the mob. Gordon, still searching for the Hangman, leads a police raid on Two-Face's underground hideout. Although Batman and Gordon finally catch Two-Face and put him on trial, Two-Face escapes when the other criminals attack the court building. Janice Porter is kidnapped during the escape and subsequently shot by Two-Face. Two-Face then leaves her body in Alberto Falcone's bed in order to persuade Alberto that he has killed her as part of a larger plan to drive Alberto mad.

Investigating the Falcones, Batman meets Catwoman, who has been investigating Sofia Gigante and

can find no record of her ever visiting a physical therapist. At the same time, Sofia and Alberto meet in the Falcone family mausoleum, where Sofia smothers Alberto, saying that he is not a true Falcone.

Two-Face's hideout is then attacked, and the Hangman is revealed to be Sofia Gigante. Her intention was to kill everyone who had helped Harvey Dent and then frame him for the crime, while posing as a paraplegic to avoid suspicion. In the ensuing fight, Two-Face shoots Sofia, and then the Joker shoots Two-Face. The Joker is about to shoot Batman as well when Dick, wearing his iconic Robin costume, arrives and saves Batman.

At the conclusion, Mario Falcone, the last surviving member of the Falcone family, burns his family estate and leaves town. Robin takes an oath in the Batcave to assist Batman in his mission to protect Gotham City.

Characters

- *Batman*, a.k.a. *Bruce Wayne*, the protagonist, is a billionaire who masquerades as a vigilante crime fighter in Gotham City. He attempts to foil the plots of both Sofia Gigante and Two-Face while also uncovering the identity of the Hangman Killer.

- *James Gordon*, the police commissioner of Gotham City, works with Batman to discover the identity of the Hangman.

- *Robin*, a.k.a. *Dick Grayson*, is an orphaned circus performer who is adopted by Bruce Wayne. His relationship with Wayne is initially cold, but the two eventually warm to each other. After learning of Wayne's secret identity, he becomes Batman's sidekick, Robin.

- *Sofia Gigante*, the acting head of the Falcone crime family, is obsessed with getting revenge on Harvey Dent, who murdered her father. Ostensibly confined to a wheelchair, her disability is actually a ruse. She is later revealed to be the Hangman, a mysterious killer who targets police officers, killing one on every holiday of the year.

- *Two-Face*, a.k.a. *Harvey Dent*, is the former district attorney of Gotham City. After being disfigured by sulfuric acid, he became the criminal mastermind Two-Face. He lives in the sewer system below Gotham City, plotting to eliminate the remaining crime families of the metropolis and seize power of the criminal underworld.

- *Janice Porter* is Harvey Dent's replacement as district attorney of Gotham City. She is distrustful of Batman and responsible for releasing Alberto Falcone from Arkham Asylum. She is later revealed to be Two-Face's lover.
- *Alberto Falcone* is the youngest son of deceased Gotham City crime lord Carmine Falcone. Exposed as the infamous Holiday Killer, Alberto is placed under house arrest in his family's home, where he is secretly manipulated by Two-Face, the Scarecrow, and Calendar Man into believing that he is being contacted by his father's ghost.
- *Catwoman*, a.k.a. *Selina Kyle*, is the love interest of both Batman and Bruce Wayne. An accomplished thief and vigilante crime fighter in her own right, she eventually leaves Gotham City after being rejected by both Batman and Wayne. She is possibly the illegitimate daughter of Carmine Falcone.

Artistic Style

Sale's Batman illustrations are known for a film-noir style that complements the brooding nature of Loeb's writing. There never seems to be enough light in Sale's illustrations; shadows fall across faces during conversations, and characters are frequently illustrated as silhouettes lit by the moon or by large splashes of color amid large dark backdrops. The end result is a gritty look reminiscent of artwork from the 1940's. Sale's illustrations display his careful control of pacing, breaking each movement or beat into its own small frame until the action explodes into a large full-page spread that effectively utilizes negative space, highlighting Sale's talent with backgrounds. Particularly in the action sequences, Sale's illustrations are lucid yet artful, full of classic heroic poses that complement the action without interrupting it.

Sale's carefully chosen departures from this style, however, have the strongest impact on the reader. Because the overall color scheme of the graphic novel is so dark and inky, perhaps the most effective moment

Christian Bale as Batman in *Batman Begins*. (David James/ Warner Bros/Bureau L.A. Collection/Corbis)

in the graphic novel is when Sale juxtaposes a stark, black-and-white flashback to the young Bruce Wayne with a lush blue depiction of Dick Grayson in nearly the same scene on the opposing page. In doing so, Sale manages to draw parallels between the two distinct heroes while still articulating their dissimilarity.

Themes

The major theme of *Batman: Dark Victory* is loneliness and the need for human connection. Following the events of *Batman: The Long Halloween*, Batman has resolved to isolate himself as Bruce Wayne, rebuffing Selina Kyle's romantic advances. As Batman, he consistently rejects the aid of both Gordon and Catwoman. His mission is his and his alone; he cannot bear to lose anyone else. However, isolated and alone, Batman finds himself becoming dark and brooding, obsessed with never being wrong and with never making a mistake. Dick Grayson becomes Batman's last opportunity to connect with someone. What Loeb and Sale eventually suggest is that in Robin, Batman finds a companion and an anchor to his humanity.

The motif of loneliness and isolation is not restricted to Batman, and many other characters feel acute isolation throughout the graphic novel. James Gordon, for example, is estranged from his family; his wife lives in Chicago, with their children, and refuses to speak to him on the phone. Only when his wife returns, when Gordon's family is made whole again, does he find the resolve he needs to see the Hangman case through to its end. Even Sofia Gigante, the villain of *Batman: Dark Victory*, can be understood as a deeply lonely character. It is the rage she feels at her father's death that drives her to become the Hangman.

Impact

As a stand-alone comic, the impact of *Batman: Dark Victory* is somewhat limited. Because it is a direct sequel to *Batman: The Long Halloween*, much of its nuance and effect can be lost on a reader who is not intimately familiar with the story lines that *Dark Victory* continues. However, when read shortly after finishing *The Long Halloween*, and perhaps its precursor, Frank Miller's *Batman: Year One* (1987), *Dark Victory* emerges as an important transitional moment in the *Batman* canon. As the final chapter of Batman's early career, a story that began in *Year One*, *Dark Victory* depicts the final step in the transition between Miller's corrupt Gotham City that is ruled by crime bosses and the chaotic, costumed-villain-plagued Gotham City more familiar to *Batman* readers. With the dissolution of the Falcone Organization at the conclusion of *Batman: Dark Victory*, the last organized crime syndicate in Gotham City has disappeared. The city is now ruled by Batman's well-known rogues' gallery.

Batman: Dark Victory, along with its precursor, *Batman: The Long Halloween*, has had a significant influence on Christopher Nolan's *Batman* films, which also tell the story of Batman's early years as a crime fighter. Many other characters from Loeb and Sale's work on *Batman* feature prominently in *Batman Begins* (2005) and *The Dark Knight* (2008), but perhaps more important, Nolan's films have borrowed heavily from the style and characterization of Loeb and Sale's *Batman* comics. *Dark Victory* and Nolan's films share a preference for psychological realism and a dark, brooding aesthetic over the colorful, campy feel that was a hallmark of many earlier depictions of Batman. In fact, Batman star Christian Bale has said that *Dark Victory* was one of the graphic novels he read in order to prepare for the role.

Stephen Aubrey

Further Reading

Loeb, Jeph, and Tim Sale. *Batman: The Long Halloween* (1996-1997).

Miller, Frank, and Dave Mazzucchelli. *Batman: Year One* (1987).

Moore, Alan, and Brian Bolland. *Batman: The Killing Joke* (1988).

Bibliography

Brooker, Will. *Batman Unmasked: Analyzing a Cultural Icon*. New York: Continuum, 2001.

Daniels, Les. *Batman: The Complete History*. San Francisco: Chronicle Books, 2004.

Sweet, Matthew. "NS Profile-Batman." *New Statesman* 134, no. 47 (June 27, 2005): 28-29.

See also: *All Star Batman and Robin, the Boy Wonder; Batman: Black and White,* Volume 1*; Batman: The Dark Knight Returns; Batman: The Dark Knight Strikes Again; Batman: The Killing Joke; Batman: The Long Halloween; Batman: Year One; Batman: Year 100; Watchmen; V for Vendetta*

BATMAN: THE DARK KNIGHT RETURNS

Author: Miller, Frank
Artist: Frank Miller (illustrator); Klaus Janson (inker); Lynn Varley (colorist); John Costanza (letterer)
Publisher: DC Comics
First serial publication: 1986
First book publication: 1987

Publication History

Batman: The Dark Knight Returns was a limited-edition, four-issue series published from February to June of 1986 by DC Comics. While the series is collectively referred to as *Batman: The Dark Knight Returns*, the original publication of each issue bore its own distinct title on the cover. The series' packaging was unique for the time: each issue was far longer than the usual comic book and sported square binding, glossy pages, and card-stock covers.

Frank Miller, the book's writer and illustrator, had long fought for more creative freedom for comic writers and authors. Dick Giordano, editor in chief of DC Comics, had wanted to make DC a more attractive place for the best writers and artists; therefore, he gave Miller unprecedented freedom with one of DC's core characters. The series was enormously popular with not only comics fans but also a much wider audience, and each issue went through multiple printings. The graphic novel collection remains in print, while a large number of hardcover, special, collector's, and "absolute" editions have been published.

Plot

The quality of the book's packaging and format announces a different kind of Batman story, something completely removed from the status quo maintained in the many ongoing series featuring the character. Readers are quickly introduced to a world that crosses the reality of 1986 with the comic book world of Gotham City: Ronald Reagan (or a Reagan-caricature) is president, and he appears bent on courting a full-bore nuclear exchange with the Soviet Union. Meanwhile, the city streets are dark and lurid places, filled with hypherviolent gangs, prostitutes, and armed psychopathic loners huddled in trenchcoats. The few good citizens are mostly frightened. They rush home from work and take cover indoors. There, their fears are fed by the television, by a breathless news media that sensationalizes stories of child kidnapping and "nun murder" before cheerfully and mindlessly segueing to assorted tidbits of celebrity wackiness.

In this world, the superheroes are gone. Many are dead, some abandoned Earth entirely, and the few who remained were forced into retirement. Having apparently retired the Batman identity some time ago, Bruce Wayne has become a reclusive old man. He drinks heavily most nights. The story that follows is one of reawakening. Wayne tries to remain in his mansion and sit and watch as the world slides further into chaos on his television. However, he is stirred by some private, yet elemental, force—something he identifies as "the creature in my gut." He begins sleepwalking, haunting the Batcave.

When Harvey Dent, better known as Two-Face and an old foe of Batman, returns to crime and threatens to bomb twin skyscrapers, Batman explodes from retirement. This Batman is no "Goody Two-shoes" in long underwear. He snarls and growls and strikes suddenly from above, below, and out of nowhere. He breaks fingers and shatters spines. He appears to enjoy inspiring terror in criminals.

At the end of the first issue, Batman defeats Two-Face, in whose dual-identity madness he sees "a reflection." In the second issue, he faces down the Mutants, the most powerful gang in Gotham. Driving a gigantic, tank-like version of the Batmobile, he attacks the gang during its meeting at the city dump. When the gang's monstrous leader challenges him and calls him an "old coward," Batman finds he cannot resist, and he abandons the Batmobile to fight hand to hand "as a young man would."

The leader defeats Batman, crushing him totally. That he survives at all is only because Carrie Kelly, a teenage girl who has been dressing as Robin and trailing Batman, intervenes and momentarily distracts the mutant leader. Batman retreats to the Batcave.

Despite Alfred's pointed reminders about the death of the previous Robin, Batman adopts Carrie as his new sidekick. With her help, he arranges another gathering of the Mutants at a sewage pit. There, he stages another fight with the Mutant leader and, taking advantage of the mud (and other tactics) to slow his opponent, he triumphs.

In the third issue, Miller's increasingly satirical bent takes center stage. Superman is revealed to be active still, but he is a secret tool of the government, reduced to fighting clandestine police actions against Soviet forces. The president orders Superman to intervene in Gotham City, where Batman's example threatens to "rile" the populace. In Gotham, pop psychologist Dr. Bartholomew Wolper, who previously petitioned for the release of Two-Face, now speaks on behalf of the Joker, whom he paints as a victim suffering from something called "Batman psychosis." In the streets, the former Mutant gang members, picking up after Batman's defeat of their leader, call themselves the "Sons

of the Batman" and deal out extreme levels of vigilante justice. On television, the talking heads debate whether it is Batman who is most at fault for the current poor state of the world.

Commissioner Jim Gordon retires, and his politically appointed successor, Ellen Yindel, immediately issues an arrest warrant for Batman. Dr. Wolper succeeds in getting the Joker released from Arkham Asylum and booked on a late-night talk show, where he appears alongside a noted German sex therapist. On the night of the program, the police hunt Batman and prevent him from reaching the television studio in time to stop the Joker from using a lethal laughing-gas bomb to kill everyone in the building (including Dr. Wolper) and escape. Pursued by police, Batman and Robin track the Joker to a carnival, where the madman is handing out poisoned cotton candy and popcorn to children. Wounded during their fight, Batman chases the Joker through a funhouse Hall of Mirrors and into the Tunnel of Love, where the two have their final

Michael Keaton as Batman in *Batman Returns.* (Time Life Pictures/Getty Images)

confrontation. Batman resolves to finally kill the Joker, but stops himself just short, unwilling to cross a line he set for himself years ago. The Joker, half-paralyzed in the fight, laughs at Batman's fastidiousness and commits suicide.

In the final issue, the Soviet Union, provoked by U.S. aggression on the tiny, strategically unimportant island of Corto Maltese, launches a preemptive nuclear strike. The president sends Superman to divert the single missile. Superman succeeds, but he is caught in the explosion. The Russian warhead is a specially designed "Coldbringer missile," which emits an atmospheric electromagnetic pulse that effectively blacks out the United States. Panic, rioting, and fires threaten to engulf Gotham until Batman organizes the former members of the Mutant gang into a militia and restores order and control.

Somewhat weakened from his nuclear ordeal, Superman follows presidential orders to take Batman into custody, and they confront each other at the street corner where Bruce Wayne's parents were killed. Batman wears an armored suit plugged into the restored power grid of Gotham and, with the help of his old, crippled friend Green Arrow and some synthesized kryptonite, he manages to defeat Superman. He then dies from an apparent heart attack.

The story closes with the media's reporting on Bruce Wayne's death and the revelation of his secret identity. Following his master's last orders, Alfred activates charges that destroy Wayne Manor, supposedly erasing all of Batman's secrets and closing the book on his legend. At Bruce Wayne's funeral, however, Superman is startled when he hears his friend's heart start to beat again, from within the casket. Before their fight, Batman had apparently taken a pill to fake his death.

Superman winks at a disguised Carrie Kelly and decides not to say anything about Bruce Wayne's condition. The book ends with Batman, Robin, Green Arrow, and the former Mutants gathered in the Batcave. Batman resolves to train his followers in secret, planning for a time when they are needed again.

Volumes

- *Batman: The Dark Knight Returns* (1986). Unable to keep his dark needs in check, an older

Batman emerges from his long, enforced retirement to fight crime in a bleak, hyperviolent, and media-maddened Gotham City. He fights an old enemy/friend, Harvey Dent/Two-Face, in whose monstrosity and dual nature he finds a reflection.

- *Batman: The Dark Knight Triumphant* (1986). Batman clashes with a new, young, and mindless breed of criminal: the pointlessly sadistic Mutant street gang and their gigantic, insane leader. He takes on a new Robin. A confrontation between Batman and Superman, now a government stooge who serves as a secret weapon against the Soviet Union, appears to be inevitable.

- *Batman: Hunt the Dark Knight* (1986). A media-hungry pop psychologist gets his "cured" patient, the Joker, a booking on a late-night talk show, where the madman makes good on his promise to kill everybody in the room. After an amusement-park murder spree, the Joker engages in his final battle with Batman in the Tunnel of Love.

- *Batman: The Dark Knight Falls* (1986). The Soviet Union launches a preemptive nuclear strike. Superman manages to divert the missile, but the electromagnetic pulse blacks out the United States. Batman enforces order in a panicked Gotham. Superman is sent to corral his friend once and for all, and after an epic showdown, the legend of the Dark Knight comes to an end.

Characters

- *Batman*, a.k.a. *Bruce Wayne*, is an old man, long since retired from crime fighting. When he becomes Batman again, he is a mythic figure, grand and almost operatically violent.

- *Superman*, a.k.a. *Clark Kent*, acts as a secret weapon for the U.S. government. The president treats him like a pet.

- *Carrie Kelly*, a.k.a. *Robin*, is a young teenage girl. Her parents are former hippies who tend to forget about her. Inspired by Batman's reemergence, she takes on the mantle of Robin, first on her own, and then under the tutelage of her idol.

- *Jim Gordon* is Bruce Wayne's oldest friend and still the police commissioner of Gotham when the series opens. Thoroughly decent, he is perhaps the most genuinely human character in the book.

- *The Joker* is a madman, interested only in murder for murder's sake. He laughs, but there is still something deliberate and calculating about him. He wakes from catatonia when Batman comes out of retirement.
- *The Mutant Leader* is young, perhaps not yet twenty years old. He is a sadistic sociopath. His fingernails and his teeth are filed to razors. He is unafraid of Batman.
- *The President*, a caricature of Ronald Reagan, has a shrunken prune face and an incongruously dark, full head of hair. Despite the looming threat of nuclear Armageddon, he remains cheekily optimistic about America's future.
- *Two-Face*, a.k.a. *Harvey Dent*, has spent years in psychotherapy designed to cure him of his dual identity and obsession with the number two. He takes up crime again, threatening to blow up twin skyscrapers.
- *Dr. Bartholomew Wolper* is a liberal psychologist and publicity hound who works first to "cure" Harvey Dent and then to free the Joker.
- *Alfred* is Bruce Wayne's aged, loyal butler and Batman's combat medic.
- *Ellen Yindel* replaces Jim Gordon as Gotham City commissioner. She does her job by the book.
- *Green Arrow*, a.k.a. *Oliver Queen*, is an older man who apparently went up against Superman long ago and lost his arm as a result.

Artistic Style

In a word, Miller depicts Batman as "large." Batman's shoulders are gigantic, filling the panels. His pectorals are massive. His stomach and abdominals resemble the surface of an outsized pineapple grenade, and his biceps and thighs are bloated with muscle. He is drawn out of proportion to the other characters in the work (Superman and the Mutant leader are the only characters who approach him in pure size). Most of the minor players are drawn and inked in a way that seems deliberately crude or indistinct, so that a single

characteristic—an enormous belly or a tiny head, for example—is emphasized.

Much of the work is drawn in an exaggerated, aggressive style. Gotham City has tremendous buildings towering at impossible angles, while the streets below are empty and gray. At times, backgrounds disappear entirely and become splashes of watercolor (often gray but also red, orange, and pink) or simply black or white space in which the characters seem to float. The reader is often put in the position of a television viewer, the panels themselves taking on the round-sided shape of a television screen. These panels frequently interject or interrupt the main story's action, commenting on it and, thus, functioning as a kind of randomly chattering Greek chorus.

Themes

Initially, *Dark Knight Returns* is mostly concerned with age and the gaps between generations. The youthful gang members are the most extreme example of this: they belong to a different, more dangerous and ruder world than the one Batman remembers and upholds. These teenagers do not need any reason to rob, maim, or kill; they do so mostly for fun. Batman represents straighter, more conventional World War II-era values—as when he barks at Robin to "sit up straight" or in his intolerance for foul language—and social order. This is somewhat strange, given Batman's own status as a law-breaking vigilante, one later hunted by the police. The larger implication is that the social order, or that civilization itself, is so broken down that it takes an outsider (even one crazy enough to dress up as a big scary bat) to reestablish some measure of sanity and structure.

Political corruption is a related theme: the mayor of Gotham City replaces Commissioner Gordon (another representative of World War II-era values) with a young woman because his public-relations people tell him it will make him seem "decisive" and help his reelection; a congressman and general divert shipments of heavy automatic weapons to the crazed Mutant street gang; and the president is an old babbler, but not so much of a fool that he cannot use the presumed patriotism of his office to order Superman around and use him as a secret weapon against the Russians.

There is a large element of satire and a winking sense of humor, too, running throughout the work. One of Miller's key targets is the television media. News anchor Lola consistently mixes up the lead on every story ("Commissioner Gordon was shot and killed—no, excuse me, Commissioner Gordon shot and killed . . ."); she has a triangular orange haircut and wears a sweatshirt that reads "All this and brains, too." Cultural commentators do not debate; they scream, curse, and call one another "fat." What passes for hard news mostly consists of reporters asking random, angry people on the street what they think or feel.

The book also explores arguments about how directly actions are influenced, or even programmed, by popular media, including television shows, films, songs, and, indeed, comics. Batman's example turns the Mutant street gang into "Sons of the Batman," and it inspires Carrie Kelly to become Robin. The Joker's psychologist, Dr. Bartholomew Wolper, makes a career out of using Batman as an excuse for his client's crimes, holding him responsible for anything and everything. But Miller's stance on this is ambivalent. The kind of thinking represented by Wolper is clearly a target; at the same time, Wolper is right in that it is Batman's reemergence that prods the Joker from his catatonic state and back into murder.

Impact

In the aftermath of the campy 1960's television show *Batman* (starring Adam West in the title role), writers and artists such as Denny O'Neil and Neal Adams worked hard to return the character to his detective roots so that comic book fans, at least, took the character seriously again. The enormous mainstream success and attention garnered by *Batman: The Dark Knight Returns* eliminated any vestiges of goofiness and silliness still surrounding the character in the wider popular consciousness. Miller's Batman reestablished the character and the Batman brand for DC comics. It largely dictated how the caped crusader was to be depicted in regular comics and in film for the following two decades and beyond.

The book's influence helped to start a number of trends in superhero comics. The first was in the form and manner of publication itself: specially formatted,

self-contained worlds, "what-if" stories, and out-of-continuity limited series became increasingly popular. Beyond this, the conception of the superhero itself shifted. After *Batman: The Dark Knight Returns*, seemingly every superhero, in DC, Marvel, and independents alike, was made in the vein of Miller's Batman: dark and grim, tormented, even borderline psychopathic. One of Miller's main ideas—the transparency of the line between hero and villain—has become a well-established superhero theme, one that continues to preoccupy many comics.

Michael Smith

Films

Batman. Directed by Tim Burton. Warner Bros., 1989. The mainstream popularity of *Batman: The Dark Knight Returns* set the stage for this weird but mostly dark film built around the shared origins of Batman and the Joker. There were three sequels during the 1990's, each taking the character less seriously, moving him further away from any echo of *The Dark Knight Returns* and back into the camp of the 1960's television show.

Batman Begins. Directed by Christopher Nolan. Warner Bros., 2005. Much like *Batman: The Dark Knight Returns* did for the comics, this film revitalized Batman by approaching the hero and his world straightforwardly and realistically.

The Dark Knight. Directed by Christopher Nolan. Warner Bros., 2008. Many of the themes (in particular, the exploration of the line between hero and villain) owe a great deal to *Batman: The Dark Knight Returns*, although Nolan is not as interested in satire as Miller was.

Further Reading

Brubaker, Ed, and Doug Mahnke. *Batman: The Man Who Laughs* (2005).

Loeb, Jeph, and Tim Sale. *Batman: The Long Halloween* (1996-1997).

Miller, Frank, and David Mazzucchelli. *Batman: Year One* (1987).

_____. *Daredevil: Born Again* (1986).

Miller, Frank, Lynn Varley, and Todd Klein. *Batman: The Dark Knight Strikes Again* (2002).

Miller, Frank, et al. *All Star Batman and Robin, the Boy Wonder* (2008).

Moore, Alan, and Brian Bolland. *Batman: The Killing Joke* (1988).

Moore, Alan, and Dave Gibbons. *Watchmen* (1986).

Pope, Paul. *Batman: Year 100* (2008).

Bibliography

Jameson, A. D. "Reading Frank Miller's *Batman: The Dark Knight Returns*." *Big Other*, January 23, 2010. bigother.com/2010/01/23/reading-frank-millers-batman-the-dark-knight-returns-part-1.

Miller, Frank. "Frank Miller: Returning to the Dark Knight." Interview by Kim Thompson. *The Comics Journal* 101 (August, 1985): 58-79.

_____. "Returning to the Dark Knight: Frank Miller Interview, Parts 1 and 2." Interview by Charles Brownstein. *Comic Book Resources*, April 21, 2000. http://www.comicbookresources.com/?page=article&id=192.

Moore, Alan. "The Mark of the Batman: An Introduction." *The Dark Knight Returns*. New York: DC/Warner Books, 1986.

Porter, Alan, and Chris Robinson, eds. *Batman Unauthorized: Vigilantes, Jokers, and Heroes in Gotham City*. Dallas, Tex.: Benbella Books, 2008.

See also: *All Star Batman and Robin, the Boy Wonder; Batman: Black and White,* Volume 1*; Batman: Dark Victory; Batman: The Dark Knight Strikes Again; Batman: The Killing Joke; Batman: The Long Halloween; Batman: Year One; Batman: Year 100*

BATMAN: THE DARK KNIGHT STRIKES AGAIN

Author: Miller, Frank
Artist: Frank Miller (illustrator); Lynn Varley (colorist); Todd Klein (letterer)
Publisher: DC Comics
First serial publication: 2001-2002
First book publication: 2002

Publication History

Originally published as a three-issue miniseries, *Batman: The Dark Knight Strikes Again* was the long-awaited sequel to Frank Miller's original *Batman: The Dark Knight Returns* (1986). Both the popularity of *The Dark Knight Returns* and its open ending made a sequel seem obvious. However, because of a falling out between Miller and DC Comics, it took nearly twenty years to get the project started. The series was supposed to be released over the final three months of 2001, but was delayed because of the September 11, 2001 (9/11), terrorist attacks.

The story's themes of a totalitarian government, fake president, and the use of war to subjugate the American people, in conjunction with images of a destroyed and ash-covered Metropolis, gave DC Comics pause in releasing the rest of the series. The final issue of the series was eventually released in July of 2002. Though not as well received as its predecessor, *Batman: The Dark Knight Returns*, *Batman: The Dark Knight Strikes Again* was eventually collected into a trade paperback in 2004, after being published in hardcover format in 2002. It was republished in the *Absolute Dark Knight* (2006), a deluxe hardback edition that collects both of Miller's Dark Knight tales into one book.

Plot

Batman: The Dark Knight Strikes Again is the sequel to Miller's *Batman: The Dark Knight Returns*, which chronicles the adventures of an aging Bruce Wayne, who has retired from his role as Batman. In a world in which totalitarian puppet governments have numbed the populous and superheroes are only remembered as stories or legends, Bruce Wayne decides to return to his role of Batman and fight for his own form

(Getty Images)

Frank Miller

American graphic novelist Frank Miller is not for the faint of heart. Using direct language and stark images, he tells potent, visceral stories of crime and violence, sometimes with established superheroes, sometimes with characters and worlds of his own creation. His noir sensibilities lend a dark, pessimistic tone to the books, and the characters, though compelling, are likely to endure tremendous hardships, often resulting in death. Readers willing to enter Miller's bleak universe, however, will be rewarded with action-packed stories and thought-provoking social commentary.

of justice. Since the events of *Batman: The Dark Knight Returns*, Bruce Wayne has stayed in hiding after faking his own death. He has spent these years training a small army and putting together plans to free his former teammates to take down the oppressive American shadow government run by Lex Luthor and Brainiac.

Batman's first order of business is to free Ray Palmer, the Atom. Batman sends Carrie Kelly (as Catgirl), his second in command, into the research lab where the Atom has been shrunken down and imprisoned in a petri dish through experiments in marine biology.

After being freed, the Atom helps Catgirl rescue the Flash. After Luthor kidnapped his wife, the Flash was imprisoned and forced to run inside a giant electrical turbine to power one-third of the United States.

Batman's initial actions begin to destabilize the hold Luthor and Brainiac have on the United States, so they turn to three other superheroes they have been able to manipulate: Superman, Wonder Woman, and Captain Marvel. To manipulate the heroes, Brainiac has taken hostage Superman's bottle city of Kandor, nuclear weapons have been pointed at Wonder Woman's Paradise Island, and Captain Marvel's sister Mary has been taken prisoner by the government. These dire situations are used to persuade the three heroes to put Batman in check.

Superman flies to Batman's cave hoping to persuade him to stop. However, upon Superman's arrival, Batman launches a full-scale attack, with the help of the Atom, the Flash, and Green Arrow. Disoriented, caught off guard, and covered in kryptonite napalm, Superman is ordered by Batman to leave his cave.

With Superman temporarily out of the way, Batman continues to break Luthor's grip on the United States. To show Luthor he is serious, Batman attacks Luthor's offices directly. After eliminating the guards, Batman comes face-to-face with Luthor and tells him his false government will be toppled.

Meanwhile, in Superman's Fortress of Solitude, located in the Antarctic, Wonder Woman finds Superman recovering from his fight with Batman. The narrative reveals that Wonder Woman and Superman have a daughter, who is living on Paradise Island. She has her father's Kryptonian powers and her mother's Amazonian fighting spirit. Superman makes Wonder Woman promise to keep her hidden so Brainiac and Luthor will not have anything else to take away from him.

The reappearance of superheroes and their actions against the government catch the attention of both the public and other retired heroes. As the tides of battle start to turn against Luthor and Brainiac, they prepare their final gambit by faking an alien invasion of Metropolis; Brainiac promises to release Kandor if Superman throws the battle with the fake invader. Though the Atom urges him to help Superman in Metropolis, Batman heads to Arkham Asylum to free Plastic Man. As the battle rages in Metropolis, other superheroes decide to come out of retirement.

Waiting for many of these aging heroes is a new Joker, who starts to kill them off one by one. Luthor uses the chaos and civil unrest to take revenge on other retired heroes. He nukes part of Costa Rica, where Hawkman and Hawkwoman live, killing the heroes, but failing to kill their two children.

In the ash and destruction of Metropolis, Captain Marvel and Wonder Woman are dispatched easily when they attempt to come to Superman's aid. Superman is prepared to give up his life; however, before Brainiac can deliver the final blow, Superman's daughter, Lara, intervenes and destroys Brainiac's body. Batman decides to take advantage of the reappearance of Superman and reveals himself to the assembled audience at a concert in Gotham, signaling a new age of heroes.

With public support on his side, Batman decides to bring all of his plans together. He contacts Green Lantern, who left Earth years ago, and allows himself and Lara to be captured by Luthor and Brainiac. While in Brainiac's fortress, Lara asks Brainiac to let her see Kandor. When he does, the Atom, who was hiding in Lara's tear duct, sneaks into the miniaturized city and releases the inhabitants. Free and irradiated with yellow sun, the inhabitants of Kandor now possess enough power to help Lara completely eradicate Brainiac.

In Luthor's offices, Batman is held captive and submits to a vicious beating from Luthor, biding his time until Green Lantern arrives and destroys the space cannons Luthor has pointed at Earth. Now free, Batman sits back as Hawkman's son arrives and kills Luther. With Luthor and Braniac defeated, Batman receives a distress call from the Batcave where the new Joker has captured Catgirl and is preparing to kill her. Batman rushes to her aid and is able to save Catgirl. In an attempt to kill the Joker, Batman initiates the cave's self-destruct sequence, and the Joker reveals his true identity as the former Robin, Dick Grayson. Because of Grayson's new advanced healing ability, Batman decides to throw himself and Grayson into the volcanic crater opening under the cave. At the last moment Superman scoops up Batman and returns him to the Batmobile, where Catgirl is recuperating.

Characters

- *Batman*, a.k.a. *Bruce Wayne*, is the protagonist. Wayne is a former socialite and millionaire. Thought to have died after the events of *Batman: The Dark Knight Returns*, Batman is nearly sixty years old and has been in hiding, raising an army of followers, called Batboys, to combat the new evil he sees in the corrupt puppet government of the United States.
- *Catgirl,* a.k.a. *Carrie Kelley*, formerly Robin, has taken on the guise of Catgirl (in homage to Catwoman). Though young, she is Batman's trusted second in command. She is responsible for much of the training and discipline of the Batboys. She is also the first person sent on some of Batman's most important missions, including the missions to free the Atom and the Flash. She is told that of all the heroes, the new Joker hates her the most.
- *Lex Luthor*, with Brainiac, runs the United States through the use of a hologram that the American people think is the real president. He controls and manipulates many of the most powerful superheroes by keeping their loved ones hostage. He has imprisoned other heroes or uses their powers for greed.
- *Brainiac* is Luthor's second in command and provides much of the technology that allows Luthor to control the United States. He is also in possession of the bottle city of Kandor, a miniaturized Kryptonian city, which he and Luthor use as leverage in getting Superman's cooperation. Brainiac disguises himself as an alien craft that attacks Metropolis in an attempt to bring the rebelling populace under control. Eventually, Lara destroys Brainiac and frees the inhabitants of Kandor.
- *Superman* is a pawn of Lex Luthor and Brainiac. He has a daughter, Lara, with Wonder Woman.

Advancing age has weakened him, and when he tries to confront Batman under Luthor's orders, Batman and a handful of heroes beat him easily. Eventually, when he is pushed by his daughter and Batman, he fights back.
- *Lara* is Superman and Wonder Woman's daughter. She has the attributes of both her parents: Kryptonian powers and Amazonian warrior spirit. Initially, she is kept hidden on Paradise Island so Luthor and Brainiac cannot use and manipulate her. She attempts to persuade Superman to rise to his abilities. Batman incorporates her into his plans, and she surrenders to Brainiac to ensure the release of the inhabitants of Kandor and to kill Braniac.
- *The Joker* is a reimagined version of the classic Batman villain, one whose mission is to destroy old superheroes. His face and makeup are reminiscent of the iconic image of this Batman villain, but his costumes change continually. His victims include Martian Manhunter, Creeper, and the Guardian. During his battle with Batman, he is unveiled as Dick Grayson, formerly Robin, and his psychological makeup has been manipulated by Luthor through radical gene therapy. He is eventually thrown into a magma crater that is opened in the Batcave.

Artistic Style

In comparison to Miller's earlier works, the pencils in *Batman: The Dark Knight Strikes Again* can best be described as thick and chunky. Miller uses neither photorealistic nor highly detailed illustrations, instead relying on visual iconography to communicate with the reader. Characters are distinctively male or female; Miller tends toward a number of objectifying, curvy "cheesecake" poses for some of his female characters. With colorful, easily recognizable characters in iconic clothes, Miller is never too precise about bodies or features.

Superman is recognized as Superman because of the giant "S" shield on his chest. Wonder Woman has her iconic star-spangled shorts, and Batman has his bat insignia and distinctive fletched gloves. The reliance on visual iconography goes beyond just character identification. When Catgirl refers to her shoes as "Chucks" the reader can see the distinct image of Chuck Taylor sneakers.

In conjunction with Miller's thick line work are Lynn Varley's bright, garish, and blurry colors. Colors shift between traditional effects and high-tech computer effects. The combination of Miller's line work and Varley's colors makes for a constant string of cartoonish caricatures. Regardless of tone, each scene is rendered in the same over-the-top style. Miller and Varley go as far as creating their own cartoonish two-panel *Battleship Potemkin* (1925) step sequence. All of this works as a counterpoint to the hyperrealism of mainstream comics of the time. In comparison to *Batman: The Dark Knight Returns*, *Batman: The Dark Knight Strikes Again* moves away from dark and gritty to bright and loud.

Themes

The major themes of *Batman: The Dark Knight Strikes Again* are politics, the distinction between good and evil, and sexuality. The idea of politics shows up mostly as disgust for politics of any kind. Heroes such as the Question and Green Arrow are portrayed as extreme right- and left-wing ideologues. They eventually even show up as talking heads arguing during news broadcasts. Even the battle that Batman is fighting is not against a traditional costumed villain but against a government that has brainwashed its people into complacency and belief in a holographic image. More than a physical battle, Batman is fighting a battle of ideology, which also underscores the distinction between right and wrong.

The villains are so irredeemably evil and the heroes so completely good that any action they take is painted wrong or right, respectively. Like Luthor, Batman does his fair share of manipulating individuals to get what he wants, but because Batman is working toward a greater good, his manipulations are also good, while Luthor's are always evil. When Superman chastises his daughter for her ideas of using their powers to take over the world, he does so because he is intrinsically good.

Finally, the idea of sexuality, in relation to the heroes and their powers, permeates the story. With Superman,

in particular, there is a distinct connection between his Kryptonian powers and his virility. After seeing him defeated, Wonder Woman questions how she could have loved a powerless and impotent hero. To prove himself, Superman has sex with Wonder Woman; the act is so powerful that it causes hurricanes, tidal waves, and volcanic explosions. In contrast, Batman's power has not diminished with advanced years. He is still able to take hits from the bad guys and give back as much as he gets; his sidekick is a young girl who is romantically enamored with him.

Impact

Though the project was long awaited, *Batman: The Dark Knight Strikes Again* was not as highly acclaimed as its predecessor. People expecting the slow-paced, controlled storytelling of the original were surprised to find a story that seemed out of control and at a breakneck speed. The long delay between the release of the first issue and final two issues also soured readers' initial response to the series. In the aftermath of 9/11, the theme of a lying government did not sit well with readers, who wanted to trust their government to keep them safe.

The series did mark an important turn from the dark and gritty comics that had grown in popularity during the 1990's to a brighter and lighter style of superhero storytelling. The book also applied many of the strange gimmicks that found their way into the DC Universe during the Silver Age. Readers who were unfamiliar with ideas such as the bottle city of Kandor or heroes such as Hawk and Dove or Saturn Girl were left clueless to inside jokes and even major plot points. Nonetheless, though not considered as strong as it predecessor when first released, *Batman: The Dark Knight Strikes Back* has aged well.

Joseph Willis

Further Reading

Millar, Mark, and Steve McNiven. *Wolverine: Old Man Logan* (2009).

Miller, Frank. *All-Star Batman and Robin, the Boy Wonder* (2008).

Pope, Paul. *Batman: Year 100* (2007).

Bibliography

Knowles, Christopher. *Our Gods Wear Spandex: The Secret History of Comic Book Heroes*. San Francisco: Weiser, 2007.

Miller, Frank. *Frank Miller: The Interviews: 1981-2003*, edited by George Milo. The Comics Journal Library 2. Seattle, Wash.: Fantagraphics Books, 2003.

Wolk, Douglas. *Reading Comics: How Graphic Novels Work and What They Mean*. Cambridge, Mass.: De Capo Press, 2007.

See also: *All Star Batman and Robin, the Boy Wonder*; *Batman: Black and White,* Volume 1; *Batman: Dark Victory*; *Batman: The Dark Knight Returns*; *Batman: The Killing Joke*; *Batman: The Long Halloween*; *Batman: Year One*; *Batman: Year 100*

BATMAN: THE KILLING JOKE

Author: Moore, Alan
Artist: Brian Bolland (illustrator); John Higgins (colorist); Richard Starkings (letterer)
Publisher: DC Comics
First book publication: 1988

Publication History

Batman: The Killing Joke was published in 1988 in a single softcover volume by DC Comics. The artist, Brian Bolland, was a popular British artist most noted for his work on *Judge Dredd* in the late 1970's. When contacted by DC and asked to illustrate a project, Bolland chose a Batman one-shot, written by Alan Moore, that differed from other *Batman* comics in that it focused on the Joker rather than Batman himself. Moore, a well-known writer, had already created some of his most lauded works, including *Watchmen* (1986-1987) and *V for Vendetta* (1982-1989). As Bolland was unable to do the coloring for the comic at the time, the novel was colored by John Higgins. Bolland later insisted on reproducing the work, revising some of the art and recoloring it personally for the twentieth-anniversary edition. The graphic novel received critical and popular acclaim when it was first released, and the later edition became a best seller in 2009.

Plot

Batman: The Killing Joke opens with a joke as Batman arrives at Arkham Asylum. Batman makes a plea to a silent Joker for an attempt at rehabilitation. Immediately, Batman discovers this Joker is a fake and the real Joker has escaped. Meanwhile, the real Joker purchases a derelict amusement park from an eager but anxious salesman. The story quickly transitions into a scene of a young man confessing his failure at a comedy audition to his wife, Jeannie. The flashback ends, and the Joker finishes his transaction by simply killing the salesman with his signature smiling poison.

Batman obsesses over the Joker's whereabouts and his lack of understanding of the Joker's motivation. Elsewhere, Commissioner James Gordon and his daughter, Barbara, have a conversation about the Joker.

> ### Brian Bolland
>
> Best known as the cover artist on long-running series like *Animal Man*, *The Invisibles*, and *Wonder Woman*, Brian Bolland also created celebrated interior art for some of DC's most notable comics of the 1980's. *Camelot 3000*, written by Mike Barr, was DC's first maxiseries. Retelling the Arthurian legend in a science-fiction context, the series is marked by the meticulous nature of the artist's compositions. In 1988, with writer Alan Moore, he produced *The Killing Joke*, a prestige format one-shot examining the complicated relationship between Batman and his arch-nemesis the Joker. In 2008, to celebrate the twentieth anniversary of the work, *The Killing Joke* was reissued in a new edition completely recolored by Bolland to better reflect his original conception of the work. Bolland's penchant for painstakingly detailed figure drawing has made him one of the most distinctive stylists in superhero comics.

When Barbara answers a knock at the door, the waiting Joker shoots her. The Joker strips Barbara and renders Commissioner Gordon unconscious. In flashback, the young man seen earlier makes a deal to assist two men in a crime. The criminals assure him that he will remain anonymous because he will be wearing the costume of the Red Hood.

Batman arrives at the hospital and is informed of Barbara's permanent paralysis and the likelihood that she was photographed in the nude by the Joker. Barbara tells Batman that the Joker has changed and will take his crimes to the limit.

At the amusement park, Commissioner Gordon is awakened by a group of deranged dwarves and paraded nude before the Joker and a crowd of deformed circus performers. While driving the beaten commissioner onward, the Joker describes the world as a collection of pointless tragic events and argues that maintaining society is futile. After placing Gordon in the car of an amusement-park ride, the Joker warns him of the brutality of life and insists that the only escape is to go insane.

In the past, the young man is finalizing his plans with the criminals when police officers appear and inform him that his wife and unborn son have been killed in a freak accident. While heartbroken and in shock, he is told that he must continue with the crime despite his loss or be killed.

The torture of Commissioner Gordon continues as the Joker describes the pointlessness of fighting injustice and touts the bliss of insanity in a song. During this performance, Commissioner Gordon is bombarded with images of his naked and bleeding daughter, flashed across the walls of the tunnel-like ride.

Batman feverishly searches for the Joker, but he is able to find him only when the Joker sends him a ticket to the amusement park. The ride ends, and after the Joker questions the commissioner and finds him completely unresponsive, he locks Gordon in a cage.

In the final flashback, the young man dons his costume and accompanies the criminals through a chemical plant, only to be spotted by security guards and Batman. During the ensuing panic, the man climbs onto a catwalk and falls into a vat of fluid before he escapes. The man removes his costume to reveal that the fluid has disfigured him, transforming him into the white-faced and green-haired Joker.

Batman arrives at the park and skirmishes with the Joker, who quickly flees to the fun house. The commissioner urges Batman to capture the Joker "by the book," and Batman avoids the traps in the fun house and is able to subdue the Joker. Batman pleads with the Joker to seek help, for if their ongoing battle continues, the only possible outcome is death for one or both of them. The Joker remorselessly refuses the request and tells the joke that opened the book. As police approach in the distance, Batman and the Joker laugh hysterically.

Characters

- *The Joker* is the central figure. His green hair, white skin, and too-wide grin make him a garish parody of a clown. He most often wears a purple suit with green gloves. In this book, the young

Heath Ledger as the Joker in *The Dark Knight.*
(Courtesy of AP Photo)

man who would become the Joker is a struggling comedian. This man has a long face and short-cropped hair and suffers from the anxiety of most struggling adults.

- *Batman*, a.k.a. *Bruce Wayne,* is the hero, but not the focus of the story. Driven by the murder of his parents when he was a child, he has sworn to rid Gotham City of evil. Though disciplined and highly trained, he often struggles with the possibility of killing his most destructive foes, such as the Joker.
- *Commissioner Gordon* is Gotham City's aging police commissioner, recognizable by his mustache and large glasses. He is one of the few people Batman truly trusts, considering him to be one of the best examples of a good person.

- *Barbara Gordon*, a.k.a. *Batgirl*, is the daughter of Commissioner Gordon and has faced the Joker before, alongside Batman. Thus, her ability to notice the change in the Joker's demeanor is particularly important.

Artistic Style

Batman: The Killing Joke is distinguished from other Batman comics through its use of vibrant colors. The Joker's affinity for purple and other bright colors affects the depiction of all the characters, tinting them in his signature hues. Even the shading on Batman's cape uses purple, rather than the classic blue, to indicate light, although blue also appears on his cape in other scenes. The drawing style stresses the elongation of the face and the tall, thin bodies of both Batman and the Joker. This style accentuates iconic features of both characters, especially the Joker's smile and the ears on Batman's mask.

The color scheme is also used to indicate flashbacks. The initial flashbacks are limited to only two or three colors, but as the flashbacks progress toward the present, more colors are introduced until the newly created Joker is unveiled in his full spectrum of colors.

This color scheme was changed drastically when Bolland recolored the art for the deluxe twentieth-anniversary edition in 2008. The flashbacks were depicted in black and white rather than the minimalist colors of the original version, creating a sharper contrast between the past and present and better representing the Joker's distrust of his own memories. Bolland toned down the coloring of most of the book and removed much of the yellow, which Higgins used extensively to highlight when characters were in direct lighting. Bolland's "noncoloring" also created better definition within the brightly colored objects, such as the Red Hood's mask and the Joker's hair. While the original version is visually consistent with the era in which it was originally colored, the deluxe edition appears much closer to the styles of the early twenty-first century.

Themes

With the Joker as the core of *The Killing Joke*, its themes revolve around his character, including his relationship with Batman and Gotham in general.

Presented in the text is the Joker's motivation to create insanity through the chaos of his own actions and its underlying cause, his personal trauma. This humanization of the Joker provokes sympathy, especially since it draws a strong parallel between the Joker's and Batman's origins. To a loyal Batman reader, the Joker's motivation can be understood as a desire to prevent his own personal tragedy from recurring. His response to the loss of his wife and child contains the same sense of hopeless chaos as Batman's response to the death of his parents, but while Batman's pain motivates him to fight criminals, the Joker's loss cannot be blamed on a concrete individual or group. The death of his wife and child was an accident, a completely unpredictable event in a chaotic world, and this fact causes the Joker to drift into insanity.

Batman's repeated attempts to bridge the gap between himself and the Joker only reinforce the fact that the slight differences in their traumas led to drastically different coping mechanisms. By most medical definitions, the Joker is not coping and has simply slipped into a sociopathic delirium in order to avoid the emotional pain of his loss and his disfigurement. His actions force both Batman and the reader to consider the chaos of the world, confronting them with the possibility that adherence to the social contract is not truly the best way to survive.

Impact

Although the book was produced as a one-shot, the crippling of Barbara Gordon by the Joker became part of the Batman series canon and has affected later iterations of the character. Barbara's paralysis led to the creation of her persona of Oracle, a character that has appeared in several DC Comics series, including *Birds of Prey* (1999). The portrayal of the Joker as a remorseless madman obsessed with subjecting others, especially Batman, to his own insanity has become the standard depiction of the character.

While various versions of the Joker's origin story exist, the version in *The Killing Joke* is one of the most accepted. Despite this, the Joker's motivations have continued to evolve since the graphic novel's publication, and the character has lost any sympathetic features created by this portrayal of a tortured soul embracing insanity as the only option for living. Moore has come to dislike this work and does not number it among his top achievements. However, it continues to receive praise from critics and fans, with the twentieth-anniversary edition introducing the novel to a new generation of readers.

Joseph Romito

Films

Batman. Directed by Tim Burton. Warner Bros., 1989. Burton has claimed that his approach to portraying the Joker's character, as well as the origin story depicted in the film, was inspired by *Batman: The Killing Joke*.

Batman: The Dark Knight. Directed by Christopher Nolan. Warner Bros., 2008. The character of the Joker, played by Heath Ledger, is portrayed as uncertain of his own past, similar to the Joker of *Batman: The Killing Joke*.

Television Series

Batman: The Animated Series. Produced by Jean Mac-Curdy and Tom Ruegger. Warner Bros. Animation, 1992-1995. The series contains a number of episodes featuring the Joker, voiced by Mark Hamill. The style of the Joker character in the series is most closely associated with the Joker from *Batman: The Killing Joke*.

Further Reading

Brubaker, Ed, and Doug Mahnke. *Batman: The Man Who Laughs* (2005).

Loeb, Jeph, and Tim Sale. *Batman: The Long Halloween* (1996-1997).

Moore, Alan. *V for Vendetta* (1988).

Bibliography

Pearson, Roberta E., and William Uricchio. *The Many Lives of the Batman: Critical Approaches to a Superhero and His Media*. New York: Routledge, 1991.

Wandtke, Terrence R. *The Amazing Transforming Superhero! Essays on the Revision of Characters in Comic Books, Film, and Television*. Jefferson, N.C.: McFarland, 2007.

White, Mark D., and Robert Arp. *Batman and Philosophy: The Dark Knight of the Soul*. Hoboken, N.J.: John Wiley & Sons, 2008.

See also: *All Star Batman and Robin, the Boy Wonder; Batman: Black and White,* Volume 1*; Batman: Dark Victory; Batman: The Dark Knight Returns; Batman: The Dark Knight Strikes Again; Batman: The Killing Joke; Batman: The Long Halloween; Batman: Year One; Batman: Year 100; Watchmen; V for Vendetta*

BATMAN: THE LONG HALLOWEEN

Author: Loeb, Jeph
Artist: Tim Sale (illustrator); Gregory Wright (colorist); Richard Starkings (letterer)
Publisher: DC Comics
First serial publication: 1996-1997
First book publication: 1998

Publication History

Originally published as a thirteen-issue maxiseries, *Batman: The Long Halloween* was created as a follow-up to the popular Frank Miller series *Batman: Year One* (1987). Before beginning work on *The Long Halloween*, Jeph Loeb wrote almost exclusively for Marvel Comics. During this time, Loeb teamed up with artist Tim Sale for a three-issue run on *Legends of the Dark Knight* for DC Comics. The popularity of the team's issues prompted editor Archie Goodwin to ask Loeb and Sale to collaborate on a story that took place during Batman's early career and use the characters introduced in *Batman: Year One*.

Taking inspiration from works of noir pulp fiction as well as *The Godfather* (Mario Puzo's novel, published in 1969, and Francis Ford Coppola's three films, released in 1972, 1974, and 1990), Loeb and Sale crafted their story that focused on the often-confusing origins of the villain Two-Face.

Plot

Batman: The Long Halloween recounts the yearlong killing spree of the "Holiday Killer" and the attempt by Batman, James Gordon, and Harvey Dent to stop the murders and loosen the Falcone crime family's stranglehold on Gotham City. *The Long Halloween* opens with the wedding celebration of Carmine "The Roman" Falcone's nephew, Johnny Vitti. The wedding is attended by Gotham's powerful and wealthy, including Bruce Wayne (Batman). Also in attendance, but not invited, is District Attorney Harvey Dent. Instead of celebrating, Harvey writes down license plates in the parking garage below the celebration, hoping to learn the identities of Falcone's guests and associates.

Tim Sale

Known almost exclusively for his collaborations with writer Jeph Loeb, Tim Sale is one of the most distinctive stylists working in contemporary superhero comics. Sale is the artist behind several of the most acclaimed superhero series of recent years, including *Batman: The Long Halloween* and *Batman: Dark Victory*, and the series of Marvel "color" titles (*Daredevil: Yellow, Spider-Man: Blue, Hulk: Grey,* and *Captain America: White*). His images are carefully composed and constructed, uncluttered, and with a tremendous sense of design. Unlike most artists in the superhero genre, Sale gravitates more toward a chunky minimalism than to the action-packed page, using a clean line and dark blacks to create pages that are extremely easy to read. Sale is unusual in the fact that he rarely works in comics without writer Jeph Loeb, having produced only a small handful of work with other writers. He also contributed artwork to the television series *Heroes*, for which Loeb was co-executive producer.

(WireImage)

To prevent such meddling, Falcone sends his men to attack Dent. However, the men are stopped by the arrival of Bruce Wayne and Selina Kyle (Catwoman) as they are leaving the wedding. This attack convinces Dent that in order to stop Falcone, he must form a pact with Batman and Captain James Gordon, of the Gotham City Police Department, to take down the Falcone crime empire. They agree to do whatever is necessary, within the confines of the law. The three men spend the rest of their summer attacking Falcone and his assets.

Because of the unceasing attacks, Falcone hires a team to deliver and detonate a bomb at Dent's house on Halloween night; the resulting explosion hospitalizes Dent's wife, Gilda, and destroys their home. Halloween night is also when the villain called Holiday strikes for the first time, killing Johnny Vitti. For the following twelve months, Holiday commits one murder each month, always on a holiday. In order to further make a mark, Holiday leaves an item to signify the specific holiday, a .22 pistol, and a baby-bottle nipple at the scene of the crime.

Initially, the murders target members of Falcone's crime family: the hired bombers on Thanksgiving; Falcone's personal bodyguard on Christmas; Falcone's son, Alberto Falcone, on New Year's Eve; and a group of Falcone gunmen on Valentine's Day. This leads Falcone to believe that Holiday is connected with his main rival, Sal "The Boss" Maroni. However, the Holiday Killer changes targets on St. Patrick's Day and murders Maroni's men.

While the crime families deal with an escalating body count, Batman, Harvey Dent, and James Gordon are torn between their battle to take down Falcone, the need to identify and apprehend Holiday, and the continual onslaught of criminals escaping from Arkham Asylum. All of these pressures begin to have a negative effect on Dent's marriage, driving a wedge between Dent and Gilda. Dent's inability to bring Falcone to justice also causes him to make choices he would not normally make, including striking a deal with Sal Maroni, whose father is killed by Holiday on Father's Day, to obtain testimony against Falcone. Dent's plan backfires when Maroni throws acid in Dent's face during his testimony. The acid permanently scars half of Dent's face, and he begins his transformation into the villain Two-Face.

Following up on a tip that Holiday's next target is Sal Maroni, Batman and Gordon set a trap for the killer, using Maroni as bait. However, Holiday is able to kill Maroni before Batman can intervene. Batman stops Holiday from escaping and reveals the killer to be Alberto Falcone. Having faked his death, Alberto took on the identity of Holiday in the hope of gaining attention from his father. With Holiday in prison, Batman turns his attention to the task of locating Dent, who is still missing and still obsessed with removing Falcone from power. To achieve this goal, Dent, now Two-Face, frees and enlists a number of Arkham inmates and confronts Falcone. Batman arrives and stops the villains, but not before Two-Face kills Falcone with Holiday's signature .22 pistol.

After killing Falcone, Two-Face turns himself in to Batman and Gordon, claiming he has finally accomplished what they agreed to do a year ago. In Arkham Asylum, Two-Face realizes what his choices have done to his life, while his wife Gilda packs up their home and burns clothes that are identical to those worn by Holiday. She admits to committing the first three Holiday murders, bringing doubt to the extent of Alberto's involvement.

Characters

- *Batman*, a.k.a. *Bruce Wayne*, the protagonist, is a masked crime-fighting vigilante. After seeing his parents murdered on the streets of Gotham City, Wayne vows to clean up the city so no one else has to suffer as he did. Batman is able to bend the law in ways the regular police force cannot. This makes him a valuable ally in the battle to save Gotham from Carmine "The Roman" Falcone.
- *Harvey Dent*, later *Two-Face*, is Gotham's district attorney. A married man, Dent is dedicated to his job and to cleaning up Gotham City. Realizing he cannot do the job on his own, he aligns himself with Batman and Captain James Gordon to take down Carmine "The Roman" Falcone. He eventually has acid thrown in his face, which triggers his transformation into the villain Two-Face. As Two-Face, he kills Carmine Falcone.

- *Captain James Gordon* is a married man and the father of a new son. He has risen through the ranks of the Gotham City Police Department by being one of the few honest cops on the force, making him an obvious choice to team up with Batman and Dent for their war on crime.
- *Gilda Dent* is Dent's wife. Her desire to be closer to Dent and start a family with him causes her to adopt the identity of the Holiday Killer and commit the first three Holiday murders, in hope that the resulting gang war will create less work for Dent so he can spend more time with her.
- *Carmine Falcone*, a.k.a. *The Roman*, is the head of the Falcone crime family. He has at least two known children, Alberto Falcone and Sophia Gigante Falcone. As the untouchable crime lord of Gotham, he is the target of both gangsters and law enforcement.
- *Alberto Falcone* is the son of Carmine "The Roman" Falcone. He wants to be involved in the family business, but his father wants him to follow a more legitimate career path. His father's neglect causes him to fake his own death, adopt the Holiday Killer persona, and carry out a number of murders, until Batman catches him after he murders Sal "The Boss" Maroni.
- *Sal Maroni*, a.k.a. *The Boss*, head of the Maroni crime family. He constantly tries to get ahead of his main competition, Carmine "The Roman" Falcone, but always comes in second. He eventually makes a deal with Dent to present evidence against Falcone after his father is murdered by Holiday. However, he changes his mind and instead throws acid in Dent's face.
- *Holiday*, the primary antagonist, is a serial killer who kills once a month, always on a holiday. Holiday is always clothed in a fedora and trench coat to hide his or her identity. At the scene of the crime, the murderer always leaves the signature weapon, a .22 pistol; a baby bottle nipple, used as a silencer; and an item to represent the holiday. The Holiday persona is adopted by at least two people: Gilda Dent, who admits to the first three killings, and Alberto Falcone, who admits to all of the Holiday killings. However, it is possible that others, including Harvey Dent, adopted the persona over the course of the year.

Artistic Style

Batman: The Long Halloween was serialized as a thirteen-issue maxiseries to allow the issues' releases to coincide with the months and holidays of Holiday's murders. Artist Sale began work on *Batman: The Long Halloween* after a successful collaboration on *Legends of the Dark Knight* with writer Loeb. Because of their close working relationship, both Loeb and Sale are credited as "storytellers" on collaborations. The narrative development and storytelling of this noir murder mystery set in Batman's superhero world relies heavily on Sale's focus on character details and the creation of a dark atmosphere.

Because Sale is color-blind, his art tends to have darker tones and rely on heavy shading. This shading helps to add depth and contrast to his characters and panels. This dark feel also helps to highlight the darker nature of Batman, Gotham, and the noir crime story being told. Sale's black-and-white drawings are highlighted in the full-page Holiday murder scenes that are free of color except for a single emphasized item. Sale's character designs avoid the hypermasculine and hypersexualized characterizations popular in mainstream superhero comics of the 1990's in favor of realistic characters. However, to create visual distinctions between the old-fashioned gangsters and the new supervillains of Gotham, Sale skews the physical dimensions of the Arkham inmates, making them inhumanly thin, fat, or endowed with abnormal mouths and hair.

In contrast to Sale's attention to character details, his backgrounds are in a minimalist representational style that becomes more detailed in the six black-and-white panels leading up to the final full-page panel of each Holiday murder. During the murders, small details, such as furniture, buildings, and the killer's weapon, are brought into sharper focus.

Themes

Batman: The Long Halloween is, at its core, the story of Dent's fall from grace and his transformation into Two-Face. Because of this, the idea of duality is constantly present throughout the book. This duality is most present in the relationship between Bruce Wayne and Selina Kyle and in the relationship of their alter egos, Batman and Catwoman. During the day, the two date, dance, and carry on romantically, but by night, they fight, quip, and chase each other. Duality is also seen in the struggle over Gotham between the crime families and the new wave of "Freak Criminals," as Falcone calls them. This duality is highlighted by Julian Day, the Calendar Man, who is imprisoned in Arkham Asylum, and his nonfreak counterpart Alberto Falcone, the confessed Holiday Killer.

The Long Halloween centers on families who are integral to Gotham City: the Waynes, Dents, Gordons, Falcones, Maronis, and families that are created through partnership. The pact that Batman, Dent, and Gordon enter makes them brothers in a common cause. Though their methods differ, they are united by their passion for justice. The families in *The Long Halloween* are in constant flux: The Dents are disintegrating slowly, the Gordons are growing closer, and the Falcones are losing Gotham. Comparing these families reveals further examples of duality: Dent's inability to maintain his family and distant relationship with Gilda is in stark contrast to Gordon's ability to strengthen his family and the bond he has with his wife, Barbara.

Impact

Batman: The Long Halloween is considered the canonical origin of Two-Face. In his Golden Age and Silver Age incarnations, Two-Face was another in a long line of gimmicky additions to Batman's rogues' gallery. His crimes were always focused on the number two, taking place on the second of a month or at two o'clock with targets such as a shipment of two-dollar bills. Loeb made Harvey Dent a more tragic character and Two-Face a believable villain.

Considered a sequel to the popular Miller series *Batman: Year One, The Long Halloween* experienced critical and commercial success and was followed by two sequels of its own. *Batman: Dark Victory* picks up soon after the events of *The Long Halloween* and chronicles the origins of Robin, Batman's sidekick. *Catwoman: When in Rome* fills in Catwoman's adventures between *The Long Halloween* and *Dark Victory*. The success of *The Long Halloween* also led Loeb and Sale to collaborate on further graphic novels chronicling the early and formative years of other popular heroes.

Joseph Willis

Films

Batman Begins. Directed by Christopher Nolan. Warner Bros., 2005. While not a direct adaptation, this film starring Christian Bale chronicles Bruce Wayne's transformation into Batman and his attempt to clean up Gotham City by taking down the crime boss Carmine Falcone, played by Tom Wilkinson. While the storyline and many characters of *The Long Halloween* are not found in the film, Nolan and screenwriter David S. Goyer frequently cite the graphic novel as a primary source material.

The Dark Knight. Directed by Christopher Nolan. Warner Bros., 2008. The sequel to *Batman Begins*, this film introduces Aaron Eckhart as District Attorney Dent. As in the graphic novel, Dent, James Gordon (Gary Oldman), and Batman (Christian Bale) enter into a pact to take down the crime families of Gotham, this time led by Salvatore Maroni (Eric Roberts). However, the Joker, played by Heath Ledger, replaces Holiday as the primary antagonist. Another significant difference between the film and graphic novel is that instead of being scarred by acid thrown in his face, Dent is disfigured and begins his transformation into Two-Face after being kidnapped and strapped to explosives by the Joker.

Further Reading

Loeb, Jeph, and Tim Sale. *Batman: Dark Victory* (1999-2000).

_____. *Catwoman: When in Rome* (2007).

Miller, Frank, and David Mazzucchelli. *Batman: Year One* (1987).

Bibliography

Brooker, Will. *Batman Unmasked: Analyzing a Cultural Icon*. New York: Continuum, 2001.

Loeb, Jeph, and Tom Morris. "Heroes and Superheroes." In *Superheroes and Philosophy*, edited by Tom Morris and Matt Morris. Chicago: Open Court, 2005.

Loeb, Jeph, and Tim Sale. *Absolute Batman: The Long Halloween*. New York: DC Comics, 2007.

Morris, Matt. "Batman and Friends: Aristotle and the Dark Knight's Inner Circle." In *Superheroes and Philosophy*, edited by Tom Morris and Matt Morris. Chicago: Open Court, 2005.

See also: *All Star Batman and Robin, the Boy Wonder; Batman: Black and White,* Volume 1*; Batman: Dark Victory; Batman: The Dark Knight Returns; Batman: The Dark Knight Strikes Again; Batman: The Killing Joke; Batman: Year One; Batman: Year 100; Watchmen; V for Vendetta*

Batman: Year One

Author: Miller, Frank
Artist: David Mazzucchelli (illustrator); Richmond Lewis (colorist); Todd Klein (letterer)
Publisher: DC Comics
First serial publication: 1987
First book publication: 1988

Publication History

Batman: Year One was first published by DC Comics as a single-format, four-issue story in the regular *Batman* comics series. Known for his dark and violent crime-laden stories and accompanying noir-inspired artwork, writer Frank Miller first worked in comics purely as an artist, notably collaborating with Chris Claremont on *Wolverine* and illustrating Roger McKenzie's *Daredevil* scripts before taking on the writing duties. Miller had previously worked with artist David Mazzucchelli on *Daredevil: Born Again* (1986).

　　Batman: Year One is a prequel to *Batman: The Dark Knight Returns* (1986) and is part of what Miller terms the "Dark Knight universe," which includes *Batman: The Dark Knight Returns*, *Spawn/Batman* (1994), *Batman: The Dark Knight Strikes Again* (2001), and *All-Star Batman and Robin the Boy Wonder* (2005-2008). These stories occur on DC Comics' Earth-31, one of fifty-two realities created after the events of *Infinite Crisis*.

　　One of DC Comics' best-selling titles, *Batman: Year One* was collected in a trade paperback edition in 1988. A deluxe edition was produced in 2005.

Plot

Spanning an approximately twelve-month period, *Batman: Year One* tells of Batman's first attempts to tackle crime and corruption in Gotham City and the genesis of his alliance with James Gordon. In the first chapter, twenty-five-year-old Bruce Wayne returns to Gotham after twelve years abroad and assumes control of Wayne Enterprises. On the same day, Lieutenant Gordon arrives in Gotham to a police department beset by corruption and violence. Gordon's wife, Barbara, is pregnant, and Gordon is reluctant to bring up a child in a place such as Gotham.

David Mazzucchelli

David Mazzucchelli began his career as a superhero artist and then slowly transformed himself into one of the most respected creators of literary comics. In the superhero genre, Mazzucchelli is best remembered for his collaborations with Frank Miller: *Daredevil: Born Again* for Marvel and *Batman: Year One* for DC. The latter, in particular, is grounded in a starkly minimalist style, filled with shadows and grit. Mazzucchelli's Batman appeared more like a real-life person in costume than a superhuman caped crusader. Abandoning the field of superhero comics, Mazzucchelli self-published three volumes of anthology titled *Rubber Blanket* and adapted Paul Auster's postmodern detective novel, *City of Glass*, into comics form. In 2009, after a near-fifteen-year hiatus from comics publishing, he released *Asterios Polyp*, a graphic novel about an architect that uses several different cartooning styles to delineate different characters.

After a month, Gordon is making headway combating corruption, much to Detective Arnold John Flass and Commissioner Gillian B. Loeb's chagrin. Flass and other fellow cops beat up Gordon as a warning to curtail his investigation. To show he will not be intimidated, Gordon beats up Flass in retaliation, drawing on his army training.

　　In disguise, Wayne ventures into Gotham's dangerous East End. After defending a young streetwalker named Holly, he gets into a fight with her pimp. Holly stabs Wayne in the leg for his trouble. Selina Kyle, Holly's protector and a dominatrix, joins the fracas. The police arrive, and Wayne is shot and arrested. Wayne soon escapes and returns to Wayne Manor, bleeding heavily. Before calling for Alfred's help, Wayne searches himself for a way to make criminals afraid. A bat crashes through the study window, triggering a childhood memory of

PROPERTY OF MURRELL LIBRARY
MISSOURI　　　　　COLLEGE
MARS　　　〇 65340

being scared by a bat. He takes it as a sign and resolves to assume a bat's appearance.

In the second chapter, Gordon single-handedly resolves a hostage situation while simultaneously angering special weapons and tactics (SWAT) team leader Branden. He is hailed as a hero by the media.

Wayne ventures out for the first time as Batman, confronting three teenage burglars on a fire escape. The Batman visage scares them at first, but the situation soon deteriorates. Batman knocks one off the fire escape but manages to save him from falling to his death while the other two continue to attack. Batman prevails, barely, and acknowledges that he is a "lucky amateur."

A month later, Gordon investigates Batman after seventy-eight assaults on criminals have been attributed to him. Detective Sarah Essen joins the investigation. Detective Flass recounts an encounter with Batman, much to the police department's amusement—no one else believes that Batman is not human. Commissioner Loeb is not particularly concerned about Batman's vigilantism; however, when Batman threatens Loeb, mob figure Carmine Falcone, and Gotham's mayor at a dinner party, Loeb quickly changes his mind. Batman soon escalates his agenda of terrorizing powerful Gotham crime figures.

Gordon thinks go-getter assistant district attorney Harvey Dent may be Batman, while Detective Essen suspects Bruce Wayne. Gordon and Essen cross paths with Batman when they both try to stop a runaway delivery van. Batman stops the van, saving several civilians in the process. As police arrive, Batman is chased and shot in the leg before he holes up in an abandoned building. Branden's SWAT team is called in and drops a bomb on the building.

In the third chapter, Batman escapes the blast by sheltering himself in the building's basement. The SWAT team searches the building's ruins while Gordon watches, ruminating on Batman's selfless exploits.

Batman disables the SWAT team but is in danger of being caught as dawn approaches. Low on gadgets, he uses a device that attracts a swarm of bats from the Batcave under Wayne Manor. Under the cover of

thousands of bats, a wounded Batman fights his way out and escapes.

Gordon investigates Wayne, trying to link him to Batman, but comes up empty-handed. Gordon also reassesses his idea of Batman as a criminal, and he begins an affair with Essen. Wayne decides he needs Gordon as an ally. Meanwhile, inspired by Batman's exploits, Selina Kyle buys a cat suit and begins her career as the burglar Catwoman.

In the fourth chapter, as Gordon's prosecution of corrupt cops continues, Commissioner Loeb tries to protect himself by blackmailing Gordon with pictures of him kissing Detective Essen. Gordon instead tells his wife about the affair and continues his crusade.

With Detective Flass indicted on corruption charges, Gordon, Barbara, and their newborn son become targets of Loeb and Falcone. Wayne reasons that Gordon will be targeted and races to Gordon's home, deliberately coming to his aid as Wayne, rather than Batman, in order to gain his trust. Gordon is called out to a hoax crime but soon realizes he has been tricked, returning home to find Barbara and the baby being held hostage. Gordon shoots at the criminals, allowing Barbara to get away; however, the criminals speed off with the baby.

Gordon and Wayne pursue the criminals, who crash their car on a bridge after Gordon shoots out a tire. Gordon struggles with the remaining criminal, and the baby falls over the railing. Wayne dives after the baby and catches the child before he hits the water. Gordon realizes that Wayne is Batman but plays dumb, claiming to be unable to see without his glasses. At the conclusion of *Year One*, Batman and Gordon's alliance is further cemented by the introduction of a new threat—the Joker.

Characters

- *Batman*, a.k.a. *Bruce Wayne*, the protagonist, is a handsome, twenty-five-year-old bachelor and heir to the Wayne Enterprises fortune. After twelve years abroad training himself to physical perfection, Wayne returns to begin a crusade against Gotham's crime and corruption. Batman's first attempts at crime fighting are far from confident. Miller's Batman is fallible and lucky, continuously questioning his own ability. In his first year as a crime fighter, he only begins to come to terms with the depth of his mission.

- *Lieutenant James Gordon* is a glasses-wearing, mustached member of the Gotham City police force. He reluctantly begins a new life in Gotham with his pregnant wife, Barbara. Gordon is confronted by endemic police corruption yet pursues a hard line even after physical harassment. He has a no-nonsense attitude but struggles when dealing with his personal life.
- *Commissioner Loeb* is the obese, smug, corrupt head of the Gotham City Police Department, with links to organized crime. Loeb is self-important and self-indulgent, more worried about winning elections than stopping crime. He is instrumental in organizing the abduction of Gordon's child.
- *Detective Flass* is a solidly built, corrupt detective in the Gotham City Police Department. He is an arrogant, selfish, and violent bully. After being indicted on corruption charges, Flass turns informant to help bring down organized crime.

- *Catwoman*, a.k.a. *Selina Kyle*, is a hot-tempered dominatrix working in the seedy East End of Gotham. Inspired by Batman's exploits, she adopts the persona of Catwoman.
- *Carmine Falcone*, a.k.a. *The Roman*, is the calculating and suave head of organized crime in Gotham.
- *Detective Sarah Essen* is a Gotham City police detective who has an affair with James Gordon, which compromises his anticorruption efforts. Essen requests a transfer from Gotham to end their relationship.
- *Alfred Pennyworth* is Wayne's butler and confidante. Alfred has training in combat medicine. He has a sarcastic attitude toward Wayne and his life as Batman.

Artistic Style

Mazzucchelli appropriately interprets Miller's script as a noir piece and therefore makes heavy use of silhouettes and shadows reminiscent of Miller's own artwork. Gotham is suitably dark, gloomy, and atmospherically menacing. Mazzucchelli also continues Miller's use of panels resembling television screens when depicting

Christian Bale as Batman in *Batman Begins*. (David James/Warner Bros/Courtesy of Warner Bros./Bureau L.A. Collection/Corbis)

media and associated story elements. Inspired by early detective comics and Bob Kane's original *Batman* design, Mazzucchelli portrays Batman with a credible, realistic physique, one that would allow him to climb up the side of a building while still wearing a heavy cape and boots.

Colors are muted and generally consist of grays, blacks, browns, and ochres, with many panels having a three-color palette. Primary colors are used minimally. The coloring is often flat, leaving the inking to provide shades.

Lettering is personalized for Batman/Wayne and for Gordon. In opposition to the standard practice of using all capital letters, Batman/Wayne's voice-overs appear in cursive, resembling handwritten diary entries. Gordon's voice-overs are written using normal sentence-style capitalization. The boxes for both characters' voice-overs have ragged edges and resemble ripped pieces of paper, representing the fragmentation of both characters' thoughts.

Themes

Corruption is a major theme of *Batman: Year One*. This theme particularly applies to Gordon. Having been transferred after a failed attempt to bring down a corrupt cop, Gordon is faced with worse corruption in Gotham. Gordon loathes Gotham but works to achieve results, even when faced with violence. However, he is tempted and falls for his female coworker, Detective Essen.

Miller's use of noir archetypes presents Barbara Gordon as "the good woman" and Essen as a pseudo "femme fatale." While he has resisted the endemic police corruption, Gordon has been corrupted by Essen, which leads to his being blackmailed. Gordon, however, finds a kind of redemption in confessing to Barbara. More important, the confession allows him to continue his fight against police corruption. Nonetheless, neither Batman nor Gordon "wins." While Loeb resigns, Flass is convicted, and Falcone becomes mired in the beginning of a mob turf war, Gotham's corruption remains. As corruption looks to be impossible to rout, Gordon concedes that help must come from outside the law, in the form of Batman. Similarly, Wayne's life can be seen as having been corrupted by the murder

of his parents when he was a child, pushing him to create Batman to redeem a corrupted Gotham, a goal that can never be achieved.

A second theme presented is trust. Both Gordon and Wayne arrive in Gotham as outsiders, alone and virtually friendless. Wayne's transformation into Batman succeeds because of his trusting relationship with his butler, Alfred. Batman resolves that he must have an ally, which means he must build trust with Gordon.

Similarly, after having an affair, Gordon must regain the trust of his wife in order to be fully effective in his fight against corruption. Gordon does not regain his wife's complete trust by the end of the story, and corruption in Gotham continues. The story posits that without trust, justice cannot be achieved, which is demonstrated by Gordon and Batman's inability to completely eliminate corruption.

Impact

Like *The Dark Knight Returns*, *Batman: Year One* is a revisionary comic that, while keeping Batman's origin true to the original vision of artist Bob Kane and writer Bill Finger, rewrites Batman and the complete Batman cast of characters. While adapted from works of Kane, Finger, and Jerry Robinson, Miller's Batman is an original creation. He displays little of the trademark scowls and anger that characterize the "older" Batman. Miller's Batman is unsure of himself as he takes his first steps in crime fighting, and he is far from the accomplished crime fighter typically presented. Miller's Batman is human and fallible. Wayne is not yet fully immersed in the Batman role in *Year One*, though Miller emphasizes the psychological split between the Bruce Wayne and Batman personas.

Most important, Miller rewrites the Gordon-Batman relationship with Gordon's realization that Batman is Wayne and his choice to keep the knowledge secret. Gordon becomes not an ignorant cop, as in some of his previous incarnations, but a true ally. *Year One* is as much about Gordon as it is about Batman. Gordon's struggles with impending fatherhood, his attraction to another detective, and police corruption make him a well-rounded character and ground the story in realism.

Batman: Year One has contributed significantly to

comics being treated as a serious literary medium. In addition to inspiring a number of other comics dealing with the early years of popular heroes, *Year One* has become Batman's authoritative origin story. Other stories that have expanded upon Batman's early years include *Batman: Year Two* (1987), *Batman: Year Three* (1989), *Batman: Legends of the Dark Knight* (1989-2007), *Batman: The Man Who Laughs* (2005), *Batman: The Long Halloween* (1996-1997), and *Batman: Dark Victory* (1999-2000). In 2005, *Batman: Year One* was ranked number one by IGN Comics in its list of the twenty-five greatest *Batman* graphic novels.

Marise Williams

Films

Batman: Mask of the Phantasm (a.k.a. *Batman: The Animated Movie*). Directed by Eric Radomski and Bruce W. Timm. Warner Bros., 1993. This film stars Kevin Conroy as the voice of Batman and Stacy Keach as the voice of Phantasm. Flashback scenes reference *Batman: Year One*, showing an inexperienced Wayne fighting street thugs and being cornered in a building by a SWAT team.

Batman Begins. Directed by Christopher Nolan. Warner Bros., 2005. This adaptation, starring Christian Bale as Bruce Wayne/Batman and Gary Oldman as James Gordon, directly references *Batman: Year One* through its use of the characters Commissioner Loeb, Detective Flass, and Carmine Falcone. Other references include Wayne's return to Gotham after an extended absence, his clothing while walking in the East End, his use of a device to attract bats from his cave headquarters, and Gordon's announcement regarding the Joker in the concluding scene.

Further Reading

Brubaker, Ed, and Doug Mahnke. *Batman: The Man Who Laughs* (2005).

Loeb, Jeph, and Tim Sale. *Batman: Dark Victory* (1999-2000).

_____. *Batman: The Long Halloween* (1996-1997).

Bibliography

Klock, Geoff. *How to Read Superhero Comics and Why*. New York: Continuum, 2006.

Murphy, Graham J. "Gotham (K)Nights: Utopianism, American Mythology, and Frank Miller's Bat(-topia)." *ImageTexT: Interdisciplinary Comics Studies* 4, no. 2 (2008).

Wolk, Douglas. *Reading Comics: How Graphic Novels Work and What They Mean*. Cambridge, Mass.: Da Capo Press, 2007.

See also: *All Star Batman and Robin, the Boy Wonder; Batman: Black and White,* Volume 1*; Batman: Dark Victory; Batman: The Dark Knight Returns; Batman: The Dark Knight Strikes Again; Batman: The Killing Joke; Batman: Year 100; Watchmen; V for Vendetta*

Batman: Year 100

Author: Pope, Paul

Artist: Paul Pope (illustrator); José Villarrubia (colorist and cover artist); Jared K. Fletcher (letterer); John Workman (letterer)

Publisher: DC Comics

First serial publication: 2006

First book publication: 2007

Publication History

Before beginning *Batman: Year 100*, author and artist Paul Pope worked on a number of mainstream and independent comics, winning an Eisner Award for his Batman and Robin story "Teenage Sidekick" (2005) in DC Comics' *Solo*. Designed as a miniseries, *Year 100* was originally published in four volumes between February and May of 2006. The volumes also featured Gotham police and news media reports regarding "Bat-Man" sightings and activities, giving the reader a glimpse into the dystopian, police-state Gotham of 2039. The collected paperback edition reproduces these reports, along with the original covers and a section entitled "The Making of *Batman: Year 100*." This afterword of sorts contains commentary and sketches by Pope, as well as an early letter regarding Batman's character and build sent to editor Bob Shreck. In addition, the paperback edition includes Pope's first *Batman* story—also his first work in mainstream comics—entitled "Berlin Batman," originally published in 1997 in issue 11 of *The Batman Chronicles*.

Plot

Set in the Gotham City of the year 2039, *Batman: Year 100* is a science-fiction superhero tale that takes place one hundred years after Batman's first appearance in 1939's *Detective Comics* 27. The book opens with a full-page spread of a severely wounded Batman running on a rooftop, pursued by a pack of growling rottweilers. Using both airships and ground units, squads of the Federal Police Corps (FPC) pursue the "batlike" suspect.

    The scene shifts to the Capitol Building in Washington, D.C., where the events in Gotham are monitored

---

José Villarrubia

Best known in the comics industry as an award-winning colorist, José Villarrubia is also an illustrator who has contributed images to a number of graphic novels, including *Promethea*. With writer Alan Moore, Villarrubia has illustrated two books. *The Mirror of Love* combines a series of same-sex love poems with photographs by Villarrubia. The artist also contributed photographic illustrations to every chapter in Moore's 1996 novel *Voice of the Fire*. Villarrubia's contributions to these works tend to offer abstract ruminations on the subjects of the work, commenting in oblique ways on the subject matter or theme. In addition to his work as an illustrator, Villarrubia is a particularly sought-after colorist, who has worked extensively with artists including J. H. Williams III, Paul Pope, and Jae Lee. He won the Harvey Award for his work with Inverna Lockpez and Dean Haspiel on *Cuba: My Revolution*.

---

through cameras installed in the dogs' retinas. The agent in charge, Pravdzka, learns that a federal agent has been killed and is highly distressed by the sightings of a "Bat-Man." He orders Agent Tibble to take over operations in Gotham. Meanwhile, Captain Gordon of the Gotham City Police Department (GCPD) tries to access the murder scene but is turned away by the federal agents. After learning of the murder from Gordon, coroner Dr. Goss receives a call from the bleeding Batman, asking her to meet him at a safe house. Goss and her daughter, Tora, rush to save Batman and find him unconscious on the floor, having suffered a gunshot wound.

    Gordon is interrogated by Tibble about his knowledge of Batman but claims he has never heard of him. Ordered to search through the GCPD archives for any mention of Batman, Gordon discovers that the little data gathered on Batman over the last one hundred years point mysteriously to a single suspect sharing the same handwriting and voice signature. Meanwhile,

Batman wakes up in the safe house with Robin and Tora after a twelve-hour recovery. Batman proceeds to meditate blindfolded, in an effort to remember the previous night's events. He recalls seeing an impostor dressed as an FPC officer being murdered and remembers being shot at close range, but he does not remember his assailant's face. Batman decides he will need to inspect the victim's body, but only after eating a couple of steaks.

Irked by Tibble's intrusions, Gordon pretends he has found nothing in the archives in an effort to buy time. Illegally accessing the crime scene, Gordon finds a hidden copy of the security footage, confirming that Batman is innocent of the murder. Meanwhile, Batman heads to FPC headquarters to inspect the victim's body. Guided by Tora and Robin through his earpiece, Batman successfully sneaks into the morgue, discovering a suspicious porcelain tooth in the victim's mouth. He secures the evidence but is spotted by a guard squad and must fight his way out.

Suddenly, Robin and Tora inform Batman that the FPC has a sample of his DNA. Batman subsequently destroys all the DNA samples, only to be interrupted by the telepathic Agent Mercer, who uses mind control to force Batman to reveal his secret identity. "I'm Batman" is the only answer Mercer can get before Batman escapes on his motorcycle. Back at the safe house, Robin, Tora, and Batman examine the extracted tooth, which is actually a sophisticated organic processor with an encrypted code containing a biochemical recipe for a vicious doomsday virus called "fleshkiller."

Gordon travels upstate to his grandfather's old cabin, hoping to find information about Batman. He confirms that his grandfather, the original Commissioner James Gordon, knew Batman and wonders why Batman did not age as his grandfather did. Opening an old laptop and using the password "Bruce Wayne," Gordon gains access to the secret Batman file.

Meanwhile, Batman deduces that this cover-up has the makings of a military coup, likely spearheaded by Pravdzka. With Gordon's help, Batman and company devise a plan to expose the plot. When Pravdzka, Tibble, and Mercer meet, presumably to hand over the Batman file, Batman intervenes just in time to save Gordon and foil the conspiracy. Tora broadcasts the

fleshkiller formula—complete with antidote—on the Internet, and the reader learns that Mercer is actually the one responsible for the murder and for clouding Batman's memories of the event.

After securing the conspirators, Gordon gives Batman the only copy of his secret file, mysteriously calling him "Bruce." Batman—who may somehow still be Bruce Wayne—retreats into the night.

Characters

- *Batman*, the protagonist, is a mysterious man endowed with fantastic physical and mental abilities, agility, strength, and ingenuity. Living "off the grid" underneath and above Gotham City, he is appropriately skilled in theatricality and deception.

- *Agent Pravdzka*, the main antagonist, is the face and commander of the Federal Police Corps. He always wears a pink flower on his suit lapel. A ruthless agent of the state, Pravdzka was a true believer from a young age, allowing him to climb the ranks early and assume a commanding role.

- *Agent Tibble* is the tall, belligerent leader of the Wolves, the elite squad of the FPC. This intimidating Texan gets the information he needs through blackmail and brute force.

- *Doctor Goss* is the blond, middle-aged coroner for the GCPD and, secretly, a longtime close associate of Batman. Her connections and medical skills are instrumental to Batman's survival and to the success of their missions.

- *Tora* is Dr. Goss's incredibly reliable teenage daughter. A technology whiz, she assists Batman with her computer skills and code breaking.

- *James Gordon* is a gray-haired, thickly mustached captain in the GCPD and the grandson of the original Commissioner Gordon. Early in his career, he was the warden of Arkham Asylum.

- *Agent Mercer*, a telepath and Pravdzka's second in command, is a major conspirator in the criminal plot Batman uncovers. He possesses both mind-reading and mind-control powers, which he uses to try to stage a military coup by unleashing the fleshkiller virus in order to make himself leader.

- *Robin* is a young, dark-featured man who was raised by Batman after being orphaned. Batman's sidekick, he is a gifted mechanic and prone to glibness.

Artistic Style

Paul Pope's art style is known for its blend of influences. The art in *Year 100* is unlike that of most American superhero comics, possessing a more European adventure *bande dessinée* feel, combined with a dash of manga. There is an eerie, almost elastic, looseness to the brush-strokes and a dearth of perfect straight lines—even the buildings sometimes seem to bend or warp—that reflect the rough, dirty, and corrupt Gotham environment. With their similar palette, minimal saturation, and gritty tone, José Villarrubia's colors are reminiscent of *Batman: Year One* (1987). Pope makes liberal use of sound effects and elides thought balloons and captions, contributing to the overall realism.

Pope draws a Batman different from any seen before. At times, Pope makes him look almost awkward, like a freak of nature, but he is also depicted with more athleticism and flexibility than are usually associated with him. During his raid on the FPC headquarters, Batman looks like a mad gymnast, a perception emphasized by his hanging upside down, wearing gnarly prosthetic vampire teeth.

Pope's Batman is lean, lanky, and weary but also rugged and strong, like an animal. In between battles, he seems to lead a messy, grungy lifestyle reminiscent of a slacker or squatter, with dirty plates and clothes lying around. Significantly, only the Batman uniform that sits on a couch arm is neatly folded. When wearing the detailed, refreshingly realistic Batman costume, his muscles are taut, giving him an abnormally nimble and animalistic gait. He enhances this animalistic quality in battle, sometimes by growling. With his seams, spikes, and sweat, this Batman is grounded in a realism that is, as Robin says of the Batmobile, "ugly as sin."

Themes

Primarily a science-fiction comic with a crime-fiction plot, *Batman: Year 100* pits radical individualism against an oppressive police state, a formula often favored by dystopian narratives. In emphasizing Batman's symbolic status as the "last mask," Pope turns privacy into this world's rarest commodity. Privacy is thus valorized by its absence, and Batman poses a double threat in his efforts to expose the state's secrets while preserving his own secret identity.

With the story's futuristic setting, Pope is free to introduce unfamiliar cityscapes, new technology, and humans with powers such as telepathy. Nevertheless, the book also highlights a grim realism, often best portrayed through Batman's own detailed and naturalistic costume. The absence of Batman's usual rogues' gallery also allows the reader to reassess the Batman character with greater purity and freedom.

On a broader level, Batman's legacy and his own brand of vigilantism are at stake. Pope explores the aging of legends and the resurrection of myth in times of need. The story is filled with examples of the "old" being valorized, from old bodies to old technology. The old hero and the old honest cop can still take care of business, late grandpa Gordon's old OS-16 laptop holds the key to Batman's real name, and Tora's final moral indecision is solved by her desire to "live to be old." On the other hand, the young, such as the villain Pravdzka, or the new, such as the fleshkiller virus, represent what is wrong in this dystopia. Gordon's reference to Batman as "Bruce" at the story's end and Batman's refusal to have his DNA analyzed contribute to the fog of mystery around the mythic figure, enriching the immortality of the old hero.

Pope began work on *Batman: Year 100* at the age of thirty-three, a year that he has described as one marked by deep personal change. Previously certain he would die young, turning thirty-three meant that he had lived beyond his expectations. This preoccupation with cheating fate clearly lies at the heart of *Year 100*. The book can be read as an autobiographical meditation on living into the future, with Batman serving as the artist's spiritual avatar.

Impact

Since the release of *Batman: Year 100*, Pope has quickly become one of the medium's leaders, to both fans and fellow artists. The work itself was greatly shaped by previous Batman works, with Pope citing *Batman: Year One* and *Batman: The Dark Knight Returns*

(1986) as particularly strong influences. Indeed, like its predecessor *Batman: Year One*, *Year 100* features corrupt police squads, and the Batman creature regains its novelty in suddenly reappearing. Early sightings in both stories prompt allusions to Dracula, and circumstances in both force Batman to join forces with a cop called Gordon. By standing outside Batman's canon, however, the story belongs to DC Comics' Elseworlds series, enabling it to stray from more familiar continuity without limiting the potential of other Batman comics.

The year 2006, when *Year 100* was first published, was marked by a newly intensified concern with Batman's "succession" at DC headquarters. The questions of who will take up Batman's mantle, and whether anyone other than Bruce Wayne could do the job, are at the core of Batman-related issues. Grant Morrison's run as writer on *Batman*, which also began in 2006, is similarly concerned with Batman's movement into the future. *Batman: Year 100* plays up this concern over Batman's legacy, exploring what he represents in the mythic imagination.

Jean-Christophe Cloutier

Further Reading

Miller, Frank. *Batman: The Dark Knight Returns* (1986).

Miller, Frank, and David Mazzucchelli. *Batman: Year One* (1987).

Pope, Paul. *Heavy Liquid* (1999-2000).

Bibliography

Arrant, Chris. "Paul Pope Talks *Battling Boy*, DJing, and the new *THB*." *Robot 6. Comic Book Resources*, September 3, 2010. http://robot6.comicbookresources .com/2010/09/paulpope.

Jatras, Todd. "The Dark Knight Returns: The Dark Prince of Comix Takes Batman Thirty Years into the Future." *Wired* 14, no. 2 (February, 2006). http://www.wired.com/wired/archive/14.02/pope.html.

Pope, Paul. *Pulphope: The Art of Paul Pope*. Richmond, Va.: AdHouse Books, 2007.

See also: *All Star Batman and Robin, the Boy Wonder; Batman: Black and White,* Volume 1*; Batman: Dark Victory; Batman: The Dark Knight Returns; Batman: The Dark Knight Strikes Again; Batman: The Killing Joke; Batman: Year One; Watchmen; V for Vendetta*

BIG GUY AND RUSTY THE BOY ROBOT, THE

Author: Miller, Frank

Artist: Geof Darrow (illustrator); Claude Legris (colorist); Bill Spicer (letterer); Lynn Varley (cover colorist); Xavier Giacometti (logo design)

Publisher: Dark Horse Comics

First serial publication: 1995

First book publication: 1996

Publication History

Characters from *The Big Guy and Rusty the Boy Robot* first appeared in comic books published by Dark Horse Comics during the late 1950's. The Big Guy was featured in issues published in 1959 and throughout the 1960's and 1970's. Covers displayed the Big Guy in action, confronting such foes as crocodiles and dinosaurs, traveling to the Moon, and rescuing victims exposed to a villain named Captain Chernobyl. Artwork incorporated Cold War imagery. Issues in 1963 displayed the Big Guy with Rusty the Boy Robot, with Rusty's name printed on covers. In 1969, a comic focusing on Rusty the Boy Robot depicted him exploring electricity, including visiting a dam generating hydroelectricity.

Three decades later, Frank Miller and Geof Darrow, the artistic team who created the *Hard Boiled* comics, collaborated to produce a modern version of an adventure starring Rusty the Boy Robot and the Big Guy. Their publisher, Dark Horse Comics, released two issues featuring Miller and Darrow's work in the summer of 1995, combining those comics in a graphic novel the next year. They strove to honor their comics and other media precedents, both in the United States and in Japan, which celebrated the roles of robots, monsters, and superheroes. Miller and Darrow aimed to create an entertaining comic suitable for younger readers that would also appeal to adults who had enjoyed similar heroic, action-filled adventure cartoons when they were children.

Plot

The Big Guy and Rusty the Boy Robot chronicles the heroes' response when a monster attacks Tokyo. In the first section, titled "Rusty Fights Alone!," scientists at

---

Geof Darrow

Though he has produced only a small amount of comics art, Geof Darrow is among the most distinctive artists working in the field. After publishing a series of stories featuring his own character *Bourbon Thret* in France, Darrow undertook two collaborations with writer Frank Miller. *Hard Boiled*, about a homicidal cyborg tax collector, reveled in gratuitous violence, while *The Big Guy and Rusty the Boy Robot* parodied the conventions of Japanese monster movies and manga. After collaborating on the *Matrix* films, Darrow worked with the Wachowski brothers on the seven-issue *Shaolin Cowboy* series. Darrow's art is renowned for its incredibly high levels of detail, in which images are packed solid with characters and backgrounds. He draws figures with extremely thin, clean lines that highlight his compositional skills while also tending to downplay the distinction between characters and their settings. Despite his fascination with outrageous violence, Darrow's art is characterized by a very elegant sense of design.

---

the Itsibishi laboratory activate amino acids in a genetic investigation that goes awry, spawning a horrific reptile. The powerless scientists cannot stop the monster from crashing through the laboratory's wall and trampling through Tokyo, provoking mayhem. Using telepathy, the monster impedes people's escape by transmitting messages that their destiny is to submit. The creature states that it is superior to humans and its mission is to seize control of Earth. The monster's saliva transforms people it touches, converting them to mutants.

The creature effectively resists military forces flying helicopters and driving tanks. A Japanese military leader deploys boy robot Rusty, who bravely confronts the monster, which swiftly immobilizes Rusty, tossing him aside, then stepping on him. In a secret chamber, Japanese officials agree to seek assistance from the U.S. military just prior to the monster's attack.

Japan's prime minister manages to alert the Big Guy with a signal. This section concludes with the signal reaching a satellite that sends it to a U.S. battleship stationed for duty in the Persian Gulf.

The second section, "The Big Guy Kicks Butt!," starts with U.S. military personnel on the battleship preparing for the Big Guy's emergency mission. The Big Guy, a pilot named Dwayne, is swiftly transported to Tokyo in a rocket resembling a large robot. He confronts the monster, and the rivals taunt and insult each other. The monster utilizes its telepathic abilities to disrupt Dwayne's thoughts. His eyes glowing red, the Big Guy throws missiles at the monster. Thinking he has killed the monster, the Big Guy then fights the mutants swarming around him, trying not to hurt them because he recognizes their humanity. The Big Guy uses anesthetic bullets and then tranquilizer grenades until those weapons are depleted.

Sensing a large foot overhead, the Big Guy realizes the monster has regenerated. The monster realizes that the Big Guy is human, not robot. The Big Guy's thoughts indicate that he is defeated and is asking for the monster's forgiveness, but he has actually blocked the monster's power and is able to attack and wound it. The Big Guy seems to be winning until the monster's fluids infect the armor on the Big Guy's right arm. The armor's molecules mutate, and the Big Guy is forced to remove that arm. The monster thrusts the Big Guy underground into the subway. Determined not to quit, the Big Guy forms a rope with subway cars, which he uses to fling the monster out of Tokyo. As the creature enters the atmosphere, U.S. forces launch a nuclear missile to the coordinates the Big Guy specifies. The missile strikes the monster, which falls into the ocean. A mushroom cloud rises over that site.

The Japanese prime minister rewards the Big Guy by giving Rusty to him at a celebration. Rusty is thrilled to be near his idol. Wanting to impress the Big Guy, Rusty states he is prepared to serve. He feels rejected when the Big Guy responds to an emergency call that aliens have invaded Cedar Rapids, Iowa (Darrow's hometown), and departs. In pursuit, Rusty declares he wants to be the Big Guy's sidekick.

Characters

- *Rusty the Boy Robot*, is the first protagonist who confronts the monster. A prototype utilizing artificial intelligence, he is built to resemble a child and is eager to defend his homeland. He is devastated by his failure to stop the monster and excited about being given to the Big Guy.

- *Big Guy*, formally named Dwayne, is the second protagonist to respond to the crisis. A U.S. military pilot who answers the Japanese leader's emergency request, he maneuvers inside a large armored device, which causes most people to think he is a robot, and defeats the monster.

- *Monster*, the antagonist, is a gigantic lizard that is unintentionally created in the Itsibishi laboratory during a genetics experiment. The monster plans to defeat humans by mutating and killing them, resulting in battles with the Big Guy, who refers to the monster as Liz.

- *Scientists* are unnamed male and female genetics investigators whose scientific endeavors at the Itsibishi laboratory create the monster.

- *Japanese civilians* are unnamed masses of people who become victims of the monster; many are transformed into smaller versions of the monster. Although none of the civilians is identified by name, several are given lines of dialogue expressing people's reactions to the monster.

- *Japanese soldiers* include unnamed helicopter pilots and tank personnel who unsuccessfully attempt to kill the monster and an officer who orders Rusty to fight the monster.

- *Japanese prime minister* is a political official, who activates the emergency device when the monster attacks the site where he is sequestered. He later presents Rusty as a gift to the Big Guy at a victory ceremony. His name is not revealed.

- *American soldiers* include unnamed personnel serving on an U.S. battleship who receive the emergency beacon and deploy the Big Guy to fight the monster.

Artistic Style

The Big Guy and Rusty the Boy Robot utilizes vibrant colors, not black ink, which is used in Miller's and

Darrow's noir works. Instead of accentuating despair and hopelessness through dark imagery, illustrations convey optimism that justice will prevail no matter how much tragedy is inflicted. The front cover welcomes readers, with Rusty waving and the Big Guy standing ready for action against a background of blue sky and white clouds. The back cover shows the protagonists from behind and a backdrop of pink clouds suggesting the sun setting after a victorious day. These covers are reminiscent of the 1995 comics covers, except that one issue's cover has Rusty airborne in front of the Big Guy and another has a close-up of the Big Guy's torso, head, and clenched fists.

Tall with thick arms and legs, the Big Guy's exterior resembles an astronaut's spacesuit. Rusty's childish nature is portrayed with a curly cowlick and a wide grin; he looks like a robotic Kewpie doll. His playfulness is emphasized with illustrations showing him pulling back page corners and peeking at readers. Both protagonists are drawn with elements suggestive of 1950's technology. Rusty's belt buckle displays an atomic symbol; the Big Guy resembles a rocket.

The monster has horns, claws, and a spiked spine and tail. Its mouth is lined with sharp teeth, and it spits venomous fire beams. It fills frames as it grows, with some panels focusing on its feet crushing cars or its fists seizing humans.

Illustrations move readers quickly through the story. Panels depicting the urban landscape are congested with skyscrapers, traffic, and apartment buildings. Illustrations use blue and white coloring and flat and curved lines to indicate glass and steel in structures. Succinct, frequently alliterative dialogue and thoughts effectively convey characters' alarm, furor, and resolve.

Images revealing decorum, then frenzy in the laboratory and cabinet's secret room, show the abrupt transition from normality to chaos. Some scenes are angled to emphasize turmoil as the monster's rampage upsets Tokyo. Panels become crowded with mutants as the monster moves through the city. Darrow creates several panoramic images, spreading across two pages to display the immense damage. The artwork sometimes seems three-dimensional, with some panels zooming into the panoramas of previous panels to provide close-ups.

Themes

Survival is the primary theme of *The Big Guy and Rusty the Boy Robot* and is associated with power. Themes of warfare and defeating foes are intrinsic to plot development. The monster represents the dangers of uncontrolled science. However, science also represents the theme of salvation though technology. With Japan threatened with annihilation, Japanese leaders hope the robotic boy, Rusty, can save Tokyo and Japan from destruction. Rusty's diminutive size and enthusiastic naïveté contrast with the huge, vile monster, which is reminiscent of the horrific Godzilla and Grendel from films and literature. The monster is a metaphor for greed, because it craves power over all of Earth and its inhabitants. Intent to succeed, Rusty is overwhelmed and soon conquered. Thematically, his loss of innocence parallels that of the vulnerable civilians whose bodies and minds are usurped en masse by the monster.

Summoned to Japan, the Big Guy represents themes of courage and patriotism, with images showing his mechanical appearance, weaponry, and assertive combat style emphasizing military elements. Like the archetypal warrior Beowulf, the Big Guy is determined to slay the monster he fights to protect people. He exemplifies themes of duty and sacrifice as he battles the creature, resiliently continuing despite losing an arm. Like Ted Hughes's *The Iron Man* (1968), the Big Guy represents strength, loyalty, and dedication, providing support to his allies.

Humanity is another essential theme. The Big Guy recognizes the human goodness in the mutants and is reluctant to harm them even though they are hostile. He persists despite the monster's mind games. The suspense intensifies in this confrontation between good and evil, with honor prevailing. Although the Big Guy is empowered by the technology that encases him and destroys the monster, it is his human thoughts and actions, and not the child robot's artificial intelligence, that ensure salvation for Japan and the planet.

Impact

The Big Guy and Rusty the Boy Robot comics and graphic novel received minimal critical attention because their creators focused on other works: Miller on his *Dark Knight* stories and Darrow on his *Hard Boiled* illustrations. They received accolades for *The Big Guy and Rusty the Boy Robot* from many comics-industry peers such as Mike Allred, who praised their artistry, faithfulness to superhero predecessors, and contribution to popularizing that genre in modern comics accessible to both young and mature readers. Consumer interest grew when a king-sized edition of *The Big Guy and Rusty the Boy Robot* was released in 1997. That oversized book omitted dialogue that blocked details in panel images so readers could concentrate on the illustrations. Because the comic's universal themes appeal to readers worldwide, translations were published, including the Finnish version, *Iso Heppu ja Rusty Robottipoika* (1995), and the Spanish edition, *Big Guy y Rusty el Chico Robot* (2009).

Most press coverage related to the protagonists of *The Big Guy and Rusty the Boy Robot* occurred when the television series began airing in 1999; the cartoon attracted more attention from the media than the comics and graphic novel had. Because of the success of the television series, *The Big Guy Rusty and the Boy Robot* was licensed for merchandise and appropriated for menu items designed by cafeteria supplier Pierre Foods for distribution at approximately thirty-five hundred schools. The characters inspired fan fiction and art, often posted on Web sites dedicated to the Big Guy and Rusty.

Elizabeth D. Schafer

Television Series

The Big Guy and Rusty the Boy Robot. Columbia Tri-Star Television and Dark Horse Entertainment, 1999-2001. This animated series featured the voices of Jonathan Cook as the Big Guy and Pamela Segall as Rusty. Set in a U.S. metropolis, New Tronic City, the Big Guy instructs Rusty how to deploy his robotic resources to deter villains. Pretending to be the Big Guy's mechanic, Lieutenant Dwayne Hunter, who pilots the Big Guy, conceals his dual identity

to avoid weakening defenses against Squillacci Empire aliens and Legion Ex Machina robots. Darrow, a consultant for the television adaptation, influenced the appearance of the antagonists and the technological devices used by the protagonists. Animators incorporated some of the graphic novel's images.

Further Reading

Kitoh, Mohiro. *Bokurano* (2004-).

Tezuka, Osamu. *Astro Boy* (1952-1968).

Urasawa, Naoki, and Takashi Nagasaki. *Pluto: Urasawa x Tezuka* (2003-2009).

Bibliography

Bolton, Christopher, Istvan Csicsery-Rony, Jr., and Takayuki Tatsumi, eds. *Robot Ghosts and Wired Dreams: Japanese Science Fiction from Origins to Anime.* Minneapolis: University of Minnesota Press, 2007.

Coogan, Peter. *Superhero: The Secret Origin of a Genre.* Austin, Tex.: MonkeyBrain Books, 2006.

Gehr, Richard. "Hero Worship: Frank Miller, the Creator of *Dark Knight*, Reinvents the Superhero Comic with *The Big Guy and Rusty the Boy Robot*." *Spin* 11, no. 9 (December, 1995): 36.

Miller, Frank. "Interview Four." Interview by Christopher Brayshaw. In *Frank Miller: The Interviews, 1981-2003*, edited by Milo George. Seattle, Wash.: Fantagraphics Books, 2003.

Rodman, Larry. "New Blood: A Frank Miller Career Overview." In *Frank Miller: The Interviews, 1981-2003*, edited by Milo George. Seattle, Wash.: Fantagraphics Books, 2003.

Singer, Peter W. *Wired for War: The Robotics Revolution and Conflict in the Twenty-first Century.* New York: Penguin Press, 2009.

See also: *All Star Batman and Robin, the Boy Wonder; Batman: Black and White,* Volume 1*; Batman: The Dark Knight Returns; Batman: The Dark Knight Strikes Again; Spawn*

BLACK PANTHER

Author: Hudlin, Reginald
Artist: John Romita Jr. (illustrator); Scot Eaton (penciller); Manuel Garcia (penciller); Francis Portela (penciller and inker); Klaus Janson (inker); Dean White (colorist); Chris Eliopoulos (letterer)
Publisher: Marvel Comics
First serial publication: 2005-2008
First book publication: 2006-2008

Publication History

In 2005, writer Reginald Hudlin and artist John Romita, Jr., combined to produce the fourth series to feature the Black Panther. Teaming Hudlin, a well-established Hollywood writer, director, and producer, with the well-respected Romita was intended to broaden the series' appeal. Indeed, heavily promoted, *Black Panther* catered to new readers.

While the character is historically important—the Black Panther is considered the first black superhero in mainstream comics—the *Black Panther*'s publication history is spotty at best. The character was featured in *Jungle Action*, issues 5-24, in two classic self-contained, multichapter stories, "Panther's Rage" and "Panther vs. the Klan," between November, 1973, and November, 1976. After this appearance, the character received his first solo series; *Black Panther* Volume 1, by Jack Kirby, ran a mere fifteen issues from 1977 to 1979. The Black Panther then appeared in two miniseries, *Black Panther: Cry the Accursed Country!* (1988), written by Peter Gillis with art by Denys Cowan, and *Panther's Prey* (1990), written by Gene Colan with art by Dwayne Turner.

Christopher Priest wrote *Black Panther*, Volume 3, the series that defined the character for modern readers, with art by Mark Texeira, beginning in 1998. The series ran for sixty-two issues from 1998 to 2003 under the Marvel Knights imprint. Marvel Knights was intended to explore edgier characters and appeal to readers fifteen years and older. With the creators given creative carte blanche and editorial support,

Black Panther. (Courtesy of Marvel Comics).

Black Panther garnered critical and fan praise but suffered from sluggish sales.

Poor sales triggered the decision to end Priest's *Black Panther*; however, the termination of this volume coincided with the integration of all Marvel Knights titles into the Marvel Universe. Moreover, Joe Quesada, the former editor of the Marvel Knights imprint, had become editor in chief at Marvel. Quesada was a strong proponent of *Black Panther*, and his approach to branding Marvel properties emphasized bringing creative teams to characters with the mandate to innovate. The new series continued to emphasize the character's centrality in the Marvel Universe but drew in new readers not familiar with the character by creating a more accessible story.

Plot

Published over the course of three years, beginning in 2005, as a series of thirty-two-page monthly comic books, *Black Panther* focuses on T'Challa, the leader of Wakanda, an advanced African nation never conquered by outsiders. The Black Panther is a hereditary title, marking the leader of the Panther Tribe. As chief of the tribe, the Black Panther is also representative of the dominant religion, the Panther Cult. The Panther Tribe dominates the tribal council, which in turn makes T'Challa both political and religious leader of Wakanda.

The Black Panther character was originally created during the 1960's, but this series reestablished him as a prominent figure in the Marvel Universe. More than a hero, the Black Panther, as leader of an advanced African nation, is engaged in statecraft designed to promote Wakandan security and, by extension, global stability.

The six-issue *"Who Is the Black Panther?"* story arc makes clear the Black Panther's identity as ruler and symbol of Wakanda, a resource-rich and wealthy African nation. The Wakandas are characterized by a fierce warrior culture and a tradition of xenophobia; thus, Black Panther represents the ultimate expression of Wakandan independence.

This story is told in the context of an attempted coup. Led by Ulysses Klaw, a Belgian mercenary, a cadre of supervillains invades Wakanda with the intention of conquering the country and gaining control of vibranium, a rare mineral and the source of Wakanda's geopolitical autonomy. Klaw, who assassinated T'Challa's father, is working for Western interests and uses the neighboring country of Niganda as a staging area for his invasion.

Paying off the Nigandan prime minister, M'Butu, Klaw's team, backed by the Nigandan army, invades Wakanda, attacking the royal family and the vibranium mine. Observing the invasion, U.S. policymakers, resentful of Wakandan refusal to acquiesce to U.S. corporate and military power, decide to use the invasion as a pretense for intervention. Using cyborgs created from fallen soldiers from other conflicts, U.S. forces violate Wakandan territory. Klaw's and the U.S. leadership's attempts to "restore order" are repulsed, allowing Wakanda to continue untouched by imperialist hands.

In the next major story arc, the Black Panther, along with the bulk of Marvel Comics' recognizable African American characters—Luke Cage, Blade, Brother Voodoo, and Captain Marvel (Monica Rambeau)—journey to a post-Hurricane Katrina New Orleans. The story juxtaposes Black Panther symbolism with the black-power-inspired origins of characters such as Luke Cage, Brother Voodoo, and Blade to great effect, as the black characters pledge to protect African Americans in New Orleans from predatory elements attempting to displace the residents. Discovering a plan hatched by a southern aristocrat turned vampire to claim New Orleans for the undead, the Black Panther and the black heroes protect the city's African American population. The entire story provides an allegory to white indifference to African American struggles during Katrina.

From this adventure, T'Challa embarks on a world-wide tour searching for a suitable queen. Deciding on Storm of the X-Men, T'Challa rekindles a childhood romance and wins her hand. The wedding of T'Challa and Storm serves as a major global (and cosmic) event in the midst of the superhero civil war taking place in the United States. After the wedding, T'Challa and his new bride embark on a world tour that brings the Black Panther into contact with other superpowered world leaders. He meets with Doctor Doom (Latveria), Namor (Atlantis), and Black Bolt (Inhumans), as he works to contain the destabilizing effect of the escalating superhero civil war.

In the aftermath of civil war, T'Challa and Storm come to the aid of Reed Richards (Mr. Fantastic) and Susan Storm (Invisible Woman). Growing out of their opposing views of the civil war, these two take a leave of absence from the Fantastic Four to repair their relationship. Black Panther and Storm join Ben Grimm (The Thing) and Johnny Storm (Human Torch) to become a new Fantastic Four.

The Baxter building becomes the temporary Wakandan consulate. T'Challa becomes the leader of the Fantastic Four, and his scientific knowledge and inventive genius are put on display in a series of cosmic adventures spanning space, time, and different dimensions. The foursome journey into space; travel to multiple dimensions, where they survive a zombie-infested world; and lead a revolution on a Skrull-controlled gangland Earth. Once home, T'Challa and Storm return to Wakanda to face internal strife and the challenge of a resurrected Eric Killmonger. A longtime enemy of T'Challa, Killmonger leads a rebel tribe attempting to overcome the Panther Cult's spiritual domination and T'Challa's political leadership.

Volumes

- *Black Panther: Who Is the Black Panther?* (2006). Collects issues 1-6, the origin story of Wakanda and the Black Panther.
- *House of M: World of M, Featuring Wolverine* (2006). Collects *Wolverine*, issues 33-35; *Black Panther*, issue 7; *Captain America*, issue 10; and *Pulse*, issue 10. The "House of M" story featured Wakanda once again taking an anticolonial stance, this time against Magneto's new world order.
- *X-Men/Black Panther: Wild Kingdom* (2006). Collects *X-Men*, issues 175-176, and *Black Panther*, issues 8-9, the crossover that introduces the relationship between T'Challa and Storm.
- *Black Panther: Bad Mutha* (2006). Collects issues 10-13. T'Challa, along with Luke Cage and a cadre of other black superheroes, goes to a posthurricane New Orleans to defend those left behind.

- *Black Panther: The Bride* (2006). Collects issues 14-18. A global quest for the perfect queen ends with the marriage of T'Challa and Storm.
- *Black Panther: Civil War* (2007). Collects issues 19-25. The Black Panther embarks on a world tour to position Wakanda in the midst of super-hero civil war.
- *Black Panther: Four the Hard Way* (2007). Collects issues 26-30. In the aftermath of civil war, T'Challa and Storm come to the aid of Reed Richards and Susan Storm, becoming members of the Fantastic Four so the couple can take time to reconnect.
- *Black Panther: Little Green Men* (2008). Collects issues 31-34. The new Fantastic Four go on a Kirby-inspired cosmic adventure.
- *Black Panther: Back to Africa* (2008). Collects issues 35-38, annual 1. The Black Panther returns to Wakanda to face internal political strife and a threat from Killmonger.

Characters

- *T'Challa*, a.k.a. *the Black Panther*, the protagonist, is a six-foot-tall black man with black hair and brown eyes. He is generally considered to be an excellent tactician, strategist, scientist, and warrior. He is extremely responsible and most, if not all, of his actions are related to his duties as king of Wakanda. He is depicted as cool under pressure, thoughtful, and commanding

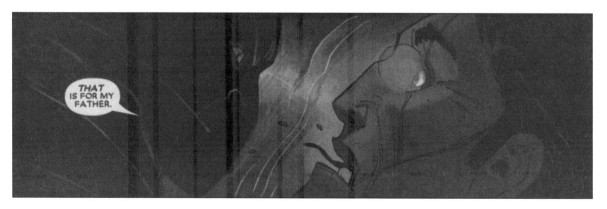

Black Panther. (Courtesy of Marvel Comics)

when confronting threats. At the same time, he is shown to be warm, funny, and deeply committed to his subjects and engaged in promoting the well-being of his subjects and the broader world. He is, at some level, the perfect king, Arthurian in his ability to overcome threats, judge the capacity of others, and inspire confidence.

- *Storm*, a member of the X-Men, marries the Black Panther. The two had been childhood sweethearts and rekindle their love for each other amid the threat of a superhero civil war.

- *Princess Shuri* is a black woman of medium height with short black hair. She is the sister of T'Challa and second in line for the Wakandan throne. Like all members of the royal line, she has trained to be the Black Panther, but she has not completed the process. Nonetheless, on the ceremonial day of challenge, the one day of the year any Wakandan can challenge the sitting ruler for the throne, she disobeys her mother and sneaks out of the palace in an attempt to challenge the sitting Black Panther for the throne. She is unable to get into the arena, but she witnesses her brother, T'Challa, defeat her uncle to become the new Black Panther. Princess Shuri possesses a strong sense of entitlement, and she is willing to assert opinions and, in pursuing her opinions, put herself in harm's way during the invasion.

- *Ulysses Klaw*, the antagonist, is a five-foot-eleven-inch-tall white man with facial scars and an artificial right hand. He is a sociopath with a ruthless focus on his own personal goals. A professional assassin, he was seriously wounded when he assassinated T'Chaka, father of T'Challa, at the behest of Western economic powers interested in exploiting Wakanda. He is Belgian, and his ideology corresponds to that held by his racist colonial forebears. This ideology shapes his worldview, informing his overall desire for revenge and driving his invasion of Wakanda. Klaw's great-great-great-grandfather was one of the founders of South Africa. It is revealed in the series that this ancestor died in an attempted invasion of Wakanda in the nineteenth century. Thus, Klaw's murder of T'Challa's father was

driven by a desire to avenge his family's honor. Critically wounded by a young T'Challa, Klaw expresses a desire to kill T'Challa.

- *The Cannibal*, a psychic vampire, takes over a host, controlling the body and gaining full access to the memory of the person whose body he/she invaded. While the Cannibal is inside the host, there are no outward signs of possession, but once the Cannibal moves to a new host, the former host's body dies. The Cannibal is recruited out of prison by Klaw, who arranges for him/her to possess the body of a beautiful prostitute to facilitate the recruitment of the Black Knight to aid in the invasion.

- *Batroc the Leaper* is a white man of medium height with dark hair. A French mercenary and professional criminal, he is known for his mastery of savate, a fighting style that emphasizes acrobatic kicks. His motivation for partaking in the invasion of Wakanda is purely financial. A professional, he mocks Rhino's lack of intelligence and the religionist extremism underpinning the Black Knight's motivations.

- *The Rhino* is a white man encased in an invulnerable body suit with enhanced strength. He is the "muscle" for the invasion force assembled by Klaw. Completely unconcerned with the social or political motivation underscoring others' participation in the invasion, the Rhino relishes the opportunity to destroy and profit from that destruction.

- *The Black Knight* is a six-foot-tall white man with dark hair and blue eyes. Of English ancestry, he is employed by the Catholic Church and exhibits a chivalrous manner associated with a medieval knight. The Black Knight wields the Ebony Blade, a mystical sword capable of cutting through anything. Controlled by a secret cabal within the Catholic Church concerned with spreading Christianity, the Black Knight leads the invasion force, using a language reminiscent of twelfth century church-sanctioned military campaigns. The Black Knight believes Wakanda represents a pagan society opposing Christianity's spread on the African continent and that it is God's will that the country be converted.

- *C. Everett Ross* is a white man of medium height with brown hair and brown eyes. He is an expert on Wakandan culture employed by the U.S. Department of State. Ross provides an assessment of Wakandan society and culture that acknowledges its social, political, and economic superiority to the West. The only neutral, if not positive, voice within the U.S. government, Ross is marginalized in favor of military and corporate forces that push for the expansion of military power within Wakanda.

Artistic Style

The initial series run of *Black Panther* was written by Hudlin and drawn by Romita, a second-generation comic book artist well known for his work on major comic book characters. Romita's artwork emphasizes clear strong lines and complex action sequences that mix dynamic action and fine details that highlight character emotion. Romita worked with Klaus Janson (inker), Dean White (colorist), and Chris Eliopoulos (letterer). In many ways, this artistic team provided the most engaging depiction of T'Challa since Jack Kirby introduced him.

Romita's drawing emphasizes the athleticism and physicality of the character in action, but those same lines provide a depth of emotion and intelligence for character faces. White's color work further defines a vibrant visual tableau that is recognizably African. Small details in clothing, body tattoos, and other detail help to firmly establish that Wakanda is a distinct African place with its own identifiable culture. Fusing these traditional African cues with flourishes of futurist imagery, the overall effect is visually engaging and aids the story. The style structure established by Romita was maintained throughout the series, with individual artists providing slightly different takes on stylistic depictions of characters and action. Notable additional artists who worked on *Black Panther* later in the series include Scot Eaton (issues 14-18), Manuel Garcia (issues 26-20), and Francis Portela (issues 31-34).

Themes

The major theme of *Black Panther* is postcolonial, anti-imperial struggle, represented by T'Challa as leader of Wakanda. The Black Panther, in his person and in his actions, symbolizes a resistance to European power associated with pan-Africanism, which was first articulated in the early twentieth century but linked to the emergence of the Black Power movement, which was hostile to the structural racism in the United States. Often associated with the leftist Black Panther Party, an African American political party that was founded in 1966, the Black Panther, for a generation of African American readers, represents African American resistance to white hegemony.

Anticolonial sentiments reinvigorated in response to the George W. Bush administration's global "war on terror" served to provide the rhetorical foundation for the story. As the series progresses, T'Challa's actions serve to integrate the anti-imperial and anticolonial commentary associated with the character's 1960's origins with modern real-world geopolitics. T'Challa's

Reginald Hudlin

Reginald Hudlin is a filmmaker and television director who was a key figure in the mainstreaming of African American cinema in the early 1990's. His light comedy *House Party* (1990) and the Eddie Murphy romantic comedy *Boomerang* (1992) made him a notable Hollywood figure, and he has continued to work in film and television. In comics, he is best known for his writing on Marvel Comics' *Black Panther* from 2005 to 2008, during which he wrote a storyline featuring the marriage of Black Panther and X-Men's Storm. Additionally, he has worked on a wide range of titles published by Marvel during the 2000's. He is also the co-writer (with Aaron McGruder) of *Birth of a Nation: A Comic Novel*, which was illustrated by Kyle Baker. That work, which depicts the succession of East St. Louis from the United States following the 2000 election, is reflective of the author's interests in human politics, and the investigation of contemporary black identities in the comics form.

leadership, his journey to New Orleans, and his resistance to the U.S. Superhero Registration Act all emphasize his status as a counterweight to traditional white heroes and the power they represent.

Impact

The publication of this volume broadened the audience for *Black Panther* among Marvel Comics readers. The Black Panther is a character with a long history, and the volume integrated this legacy into the mainstream Marvel Universe in a public way. Given the limited number of black comic book characters, the story established the Black Panther as the most important black character in the Marvel Universe and showcased that importance in numerous ways. Moreover, the marriage of T'Challa and Storm provided additional importance to both characters' cultural standing by framing their union as a milestone of cultural history. Throughout this series, the Black Panther participates in every major story event framing the Marvel Universe. In the aftermath of this story, the Black Panther and Wakanda remain key players in the state of the Marvel Universe.

Julian C. Chambliss

Television Series

Black Panther: Who Is the Black Panther? Directed by Mark Brooks. Marvel Animation LLC, in association with Titmouse Studios, 2010. This series starred Djimon Hounsou as Black Panther/T'Challa, Kerry Washington as Princess Shuri, Alfre Woodard as Dondi Reese/Queen Mother, Jill Scott as Storm, Carl Lumbly as Uncle S'Yan, Stephen Stanton as Ulysses Klaw, and Stan Lee as General Wallace. It differs from the novel in its minor alterations of character depictions (Juggernaut replaces Rhino in the invasion force). Elements of Jerome Dickey's *Storm* miniseries, depicting the romance between T'Challa and Storm, are included in the story.

Further Reading

Way, Daniel, Steve Dillon, and Mike Deodato. *Wolverine: Origins* (2006-2010).

Whedon, Joss. *Astonishing X-Men* (2004-2008).

Bibliography

Brown, Jeffrey A. *Black Superheroes, Milestone Comics, and Their Fans*. Jackson: University Press of Mississippi, 2001.

Feldman, Keith P. "*Black Panther.*" *MELUS* 32, no. 3 (Fall, 2007): 255-258.

Goggin, Joyce, and Dan Hassler-Forest. *The Rise and Reason of Comics and Graphic Literature: Critical Essays on the Form*. Jefferson, N.C.: McFarland, 2010.

Radford, Bill. "Marvel Re-Introducing Black Panther." *The Colorado Springs Gazette*, February 6, 2005.

See also: *Death of Captain America; X-Men: Days of Future Past; X-Men: God Loves, Man Kills; X-Men: The Dark Phoenix Saga*

BLACKSAD

Author: Díaz Canales, Juan
Artist: Juanjo Guarnido (illustrator)
Publishers: Editions Dargaud (French); Dark Horse Comics (English)
First serial publication: *Blacksad*, 2000-2010 (partial English translation, 2003-2010)
First book publication: 2010 (English translation of first three books)

Publication History

The first *Blacksad* book, *Quelque part entre les ombres* (*Somewhere Within the Shadows*) was published in France by Editions Dargaud in 2000, after its creators had also presented it to the publishing houses of Casterman and Delcourt. Ten years earlier, writer Juan Díaz Canales and artist Juanjo Guarnido had met at the Spanish animation studio Lapiz Azul and had decided to create a comic book based on a series of short stories by Díaz Canales. The first book was an immediate success, which allowed the creators to develop the story as a series. Three more books have been published since then: a second one, *Arctic-Nation* (*Arctic Nation* in English), in 2003; a third one, *Âme rouge* (*Red Soul*), in 2005; and a fourth volume, *L'Enfer, le silence* (*The Hell, The Silence*), in 2010.

U.S. publisher ibooks published English-language editions of the first two books in 2003 (*Somewhere Within the Shadows*) and 2004 (*Arctic Nation*), along with a collection of sketches and artwork by Guarnido in 2005 (*The Sketch Files*). After ibooks filed for bankruptcy in 2006, Dark Horse Comics published a collected edition of the first three books in 2010.

Plot

In *Somewhere Within the Shadows*, Natalia Wilford, a young but celebrated actor, is found murdered. Since she is a former client of private investigator John Blacksad, and also his first lover, he decides to find out who killed her and to avenge her death. Blacksad, a big black cat, discovers that Wilford's most recent lover, lion and scriptwriter Leon Kronski, has disappeared, and he sets off to find him. Kronski has died as well and

(Alberto Bocos/AFP/Getty Images)

Juanjo Guarnido

Juanjo Guarnido is the Spanish artist responsible for the best-selling and award-winning *Blacksad* series. Coming to comics from a background as a Disney animator, Guarnido has a classical approach to drawing that is highly disciplined and polished. Since 2000, he has published four volumes of *Blacksad* with writer Juan Díaz Canales through the French publisher Dargaud. *Blacksad* is an anthropomorphic crime comic book set in a noir-inspired America of the 1950's. The series has a hardboiled feeling to it that is sometimes minimized by the stylish presentation of the main characters as animals. Guarnido's art is characterized by its remarkable level of detail and subtle use of painted color. In a palette of browns and grays, Guarnido has created a fictional world that is moodily believable, despite the presence of highly stereotyped talking animals in human form.

has already been hastily buried. When two thugs beat him up for discovering Kronski's grave, Blacksad feels his instinct is validated: Whoever is responsible must be powerful.

Purely by chance, Blacksad finds out that Ivo Statoc, a toad and one of the richest men in town, had been spurned as a lover by Wilford, who preferred Kronski's fur to Statoc's cold skin. Statoc had been enraged with jealousy and ordered both Wilford and her companion killed. Blacksad confronts Statoc, but to his surprise, Statoc congratulates him on his perseverance and tries to enlist him in his operation. Blacksad, however, remains true to his cause.

Arctic Nation opens with the disappearance of a young black girl, Kyle (or "Kayleigh" in certain editions), in a neighborhood that is rife with racial unrest. Blacksad is hired to investigate the case, and together with his sidekick, Weekly, he finds out that local police chief Hans Karup, a polar bear who is involved in a white-power gang called Arctic-Nation, has tried to put the blame on a local black gang.

Karup is rumored to have pedophilic tendencies, and when a bloody dress is found in his car, his own gang executes him. The chief instigator of this violent punishment, a snow fox called Huk, had his own reasons to remove Karup from the scene, as he is Karup's wife's (Jezabel's) lover. In a dramatic turn of events, the hall where Karup's execution took place burns down, but not before a magpie called Cotton leads Blacksad to Kyle's hiding place.

Cotton reveals that, with the help of Huk, Jezabel staged Kyle's disappearance in order to frame her husband. However, the final truth runs even deeper: Jezabel turns out to be Karup's own daughter, who together with her sister, Dinah, who is Kyle's mother, had plotted to avenge their black mother, who was abandoned by Karup when she was pregnant.

Book 3, *Red Soul*, focuses on U.S. and global post-World War II politics. When his latest assignment, being a bodyguard to a wealthy turtle, is less than exciting, Blacksad attends a lecture by Otto Liebber, one of his old teachers. Liebber is an atomic physicist and the inventor of the hydrogen bomb, but he is also a member of a left-wing organization called the Twelve Apostles, a group that included rich benefactor Samuel

Gotfield and his fiancé, Alma Mayer; painter Sergei Litvak; and chemist Laszlo Herzl.

After a party, during which Alma and Blacksad become attracted to one another, another member of the group, who happens to look like Liebber, is murdered. Shortly afterward, Liebber hardly escapes a car bombing and goes into hiding. Blacksad finds out that Herzl, a survivor of the Nazi concentration camps, was in fact hunting Liebber, who used to work for the Third Reich.

In the meantime, the Federal Bureau of Investigation (FBI) and Senator Gallo have put the pressure on Gotfield to reveal Liebber's hiding place, and they kill Litvak in the process. Liebber confides in Blacksad that he has been trying to atone and bring balance to the political spectrum by smuggling the formulas for the hydrogen bomb to the Soviet Union with the help of Gotfield and Litvak, who hides the formulas in one of his works. Gallo tries to frame Blacksad for Litvak's death, but he settles for a deal when Blacksad threatens to reveal his hidden plans—to create an elite "Noah's ark" in case of a nuclear holocaust. In the end, Liebber returns to Germany, his suicide is staged, and Blacksad fails to show up at Niagara Falls, where Alma was waiting for him.

In *L'Enfer, le silence*, Blacksad is in New Orleans. Record producer Faust LaChapelle asks him to track down genius jazz and blues pianist Sebastian "Little Hands" Fletcher, who has disappeared and left his pregnant wife. LaChapelle's son, Thomas, asks Blacksad to refuse the assignment, stating that his father's illness has already cost him too much money. Thomas feels betrayed by his absent father and his wife, who is divorcing him, and finds solace in playing protector to Fletcher's wife, who tells Blacksad and Thomas that Fletcher was all worked up about a song, "Pizzen Blues," before he disappeared. Fletcher, in the meantime, has been planning to sing this song during an impromptu performance, since, as Blacksad learns from one of his earlier bandmates, it tells the story of the many deaths and disfigurements that occurred in his hometown as a result of Dr. Dupré's Life Everlasting, a lethal drug sold as a cure for asthma.

Blacksad learns that Dr. Dupré is, in fact, Faust LaChapelle, who has been trying to hide the truth all this time and is dying of a lethal bronchial disease himself. After his performance, Fletcher dies of a shot of heroin laced with strychnine sulfate, at about the same time as Faust dies of his illness. Thomas, Fletcher's widow, and her child are left to start anew.

Volumes

- *Blacksad: Quelque part entre les ombres* (2000; *Blacksad: Somewhere Within the Shadows*, 2003). Private investigator Blacksad disproves the point that money can buy anything by punishing a rich spurned lover who had killed his former girlfriend.
- *Blacksad: Arctic-Nation* (2003; *Blacksad: Arctic Nation*, 2004). A heated mix of racial hatred, private history, and sexual intrigue is unraveled before Blacksad's eyes. Crimes that have been committed in the past come back to haunt the perpetrator (Karup), but the truth is always stranger than it initially seems.
- *Blacksad: Âme rouge* (2005; *Blacksad: Red Soul*, 2010). Set to the backdrop of the Cold War, this volume pits Blacksad against a former teacher, a physicist attempting to smuggle formulas for the hydrogen bomb into the Soviet Union. Blacksad and Alma Mayer begin to have feelings for each other.
- *Blacksad: L'Enfer, le silence* (2010). Blacksad is hired by record producer Faust LaChapelle to find jazzman Sebastian Fletcher, who has disappeared. Blacksad discovers that LaChapelle has a connection to his disappearance.

Characters

- *John Blacksad*, the protagonist, is a large black tomcat who works as a private investigator. Even though he prefers to use his wits to solve his cases, he resorts to violence if necessary and is known to have murdered at least one man in cold blood. Blacksad strongly believes in justice over gain and in morals over the law.
- *Smirnov*, a police commissioner, is a German shepherd. Smirnov feels trapped within the limits of the law and feeds information to Blacksad to

help him solve cases. In *Red Soul*, the two become friends.

- *Weekly*, a brown least weasel, is Blacksad's sidekick. He works as a gossip reporter for a tabloid newspaper called *What's News*. Weekly got his nickname because he bathes only once a week.
- *Ivo Statoc*, the antagonist in *Somewhere Within the Shadows*, is a rich and powerful businessman who believes he can buy anything. This attitude allows Blacksad to assert his moral integrity.
- *Hans Karup*, one of the antagonists in *Arctic Nation*, is a polar bear, a chief of police, and a member of a white-power organization. Blacksad and Karup instantly dislike each other.
- *Jezabel*, the wife (and daughter) of Karup, is the embodiment of pure revenge, as she is solely focused on bringing about her father's downfall with the help of her lover and her sister, Dinah.
- *Samuel Gotfield*, is a billionaire dalmatian of feeble nature and communist who betrays his friends at the first signs of pressure.
- *Otto Liebber*, a nuclear physicist and an owl in *Red Soul*, was Blacksad's mentor, but he turns out to be a former Nazi and a spy for the Soviet Union. Liebber is driven by an urge to set right the wrongs he has brought about.
- *Alma Mayer*, a cat and a writer, is Blacksad's love interest in *Red Soul*. She embodies the tragic impossibility of love in Blacksad's life.
- *Faust LaChapelle*, a billy goat, is a record producer and former snake oil salesman. His main role is to illustrate how truth always prevails.
- *Sebastian Fletcher* is a dog and a talented pianist; a heroin addict, he is troubled by what he knows about what has been done to his friends and cannot live with that knowledge.

Artistic Style

The contributing factor to *Blacksad*'s initial success (of the first issue, 300,000 copies were sold in France alone) was Guarnido's artistic style. Before *Blacksad*, Guarnido worked for the Walt Disney Studios in Montreuil, where he was the lead animator for the Sabor the leopard in *Tarzan* (1999). His mastery of animal physiognomy and movement is unique: Guarnido's characters actually move the way animals do and he also knows the secret to making them seem believable as humanoids. They are not just four-legged creatures or people with animal heads but a perfect mixture of the two.

This effect is strengthened by the level of realism Guarnido puts in his settings and sceneries. He makes great effort to accurately document the look and feel of a typical American city in the early 1950's, and this results in detailed apartments, state rooms, streets, and alleyways, all of which seem to breathe, as if they were part of the cast themselves. Guarnido's accuracy does not result in players in front of a cardboard setting—his characters belong to the city, and it fully surrounds them.

A third aspect of Gaurnido's style is the large amount of dynamism he injects into his pages. No two pages in *Blacksad* have a similar layout, and the classic nine-panel grid is absent completely. Guarnido carefully chooses the one single panel that is correct for the scene he is drawing, but within the panel he also sets up his "camera" to gain maximum effect.

Juan Díaz Canales

Juan Díaz Canales is a Spanish comics writer who is best known as the co-creator of *Blacksad*, with artist Juanjo Guarnido. Set in 1950's America, *Blacksad* is a film-noir-inspired, hardboiled detective series featuring anthropomorphic animals in the place of people. The titular Blacksad is a cat/private investigator with a stereotypically cynical outlook on the world surrounding him. Blacksad's jaded personality is a central element to the historical fiction that plays out across the United States. Over the course of the four volumes published to date, Canales has explored issues involving racism and the Red Scare, with frequent cameos by important historical figures ranging from Adolf Hitler to Senator Joseph McCarthy. Canales's contribution to the success of *Blacksad* is sometimes minimized in relation to that of Guarnido, but his stories are well-crafted genre entertainments.

The final important feature in Guarnido's art is his use of color. In most of his panels, he employs fairly realistic coloring, though in his more recent pages he has started to use expressive shadow-and-light contrasts. For dramatic effect, Guarnido bathes certain key scenes in different dominant hues, ranging from red to blue. This is predominantly the case for flashbacks and narrated scenes, in which one of the characters tells something to another.

Themes

Blacksad echoes some of the main themes associated with the hard-boiled detective genre. To begin with, it is an urban comic; even when the story takes place in a suburb, Blacksad remains a city detective. The city, however, is more than a backdrop: It is a personification of the behavior of its inhabitants, who treat one another like "animals" for their own gain.

Blacksad distances himself from this behavior, however. He believes strongly in moral correctness and ensures that the wicked are punished. A crime may be committed in the most artful way, but it will always come back to harm the perpetrator. Justice is more important than money, even to the extent that Blacksad might refuse payment for his services. It is quite interesting, in this light, that the plight of and possibilities for the purely innocent characters have changed over the years. In the final scene of *Arctic Nation*, Blacksad looks with despair at the young girl Kyle, uncertain of what the future has in store for her. At the end of *L'Enfer, le silence*, however, he seems to believe in an optimistic future for Thomas and his newfound family.

In Blacksad's own life, love is at best an episodic affair. Blacksad's love interests die, are too remote to even be considered a possibility, or are lost for him because of dramatic consequences of the story.

Blacksad may be a detective by trade, but he does not excel at his job: Most of the big breaks in his investigations result from happenstance, such as from things he overhears, information that is told to him by one of the parties involved, or scenes into which he happens to stumble. Blacksad is not in control of the situation but, rather, sails along until he can make his stand.

A final important theme, which is the background of all the others, is the United States during the 1950's in all its glory and garishness. The United States is the land of opportunity and of great art, music, writing, and science; but at the same time, it is a place where racism, corruption, and political bigotry are allowed to flourish, with tragic consequences for all involved.

Impact

By using anthropomorphic animals as characters, the creators of Blacksad have found an interesting way to reintroduce classic detective themes and motifs into current-day comics. If the animals were to be replaced with human beings, only a fairly standard, albeit cleverly written, hard-boiled detective story would remain. Díaz Canales has often cited classic detective stories, by the likes of Dashiell Hammett or Raymond Chandler, and comics, such as the *Alack Sinner* series (by Carlos Sampayo and José Muñoz, which began in 1975), as influences on his work. By adding the aspect of the animal characters to the examples these predecessors set, Díaz Canales and Guarnido have helped to reinvent or reinvigorate the genre.

Interestingly, the series has changed, even within the span of only four books. The first book, *Somewhere Within the Shadows*, was a fairly straightforward, classic detective story. The two following stories, *Arctic Nation* and *Red Soul*, were dense, intricate stories with a sizable cast and several intertwining plotlines that require the reader's full attention. In the fourth episode, *L'Enfer, le silence*, Díaz Canales and Guarnido have opted for a relatively simple story, but they tell it in a convoluted way, using many intertwining flashbacks, narrated sequences, and fragments that mirror one another, as if the book were a piece of postwar New Orleans jazz music.

Even though *Blacksad* has had a fairly slow-paced production cycle, even for a European comic (only four titles in ten years), the series has had almost unanimously positive critical acclaim from the start. Similarly, with each new book, the series proves itself to be widely appreciated; though new titles are not staged as multimedia events, as is the case with bestsellers such as *XIII* (first published in 1984), *Largo Winch* (first published in novel form in the 1970's), or *Lanfeust* (first published in 1994), *Blacksad* remains a steady seller with a loyal audience.

Wim Lockefeer

Further Reading

Eisner, Will. *The Spirit* (1940-1952).
Hergé. *The Adventures of Tintin* (1929-1976).
Spiegelman, Art. *Maus: A Survivor's Tale* (1986).

Bibliography

Díaz Canales, Juan. "Blacksad." Review of *Blacksad* by Martha Cornog. *Library Journal* 135, no. 15 (September 15, 2010): 49.

_____. "Blacksad 2: Arctic-Nation (Book)." Review of *Blacksad*. *Publishers Weekly* 251, no. 24 (June 14, 2010): 46.

Horsten, Toon. "The Cat's out of the Bag." *Forbidden Planet International*, December 10, 2010. http://forbiddenplanet.co.uk/blog/2010/the-cats-out-of-the-bag-juan-diaz-canales-talks-about-blacksad-4-part-2.

Ng, Suat Tong. "Commercial Interlude: *Blacksad*." *The Hooded Utilitarian*, September 27, 2010. http://www.tcj.com/hoodedutilitarian/2010/09/commercial-interlude-blacksad.

Preiss, Byron, and Howard Zimmerman. *Year's Best Graphic Novels, Comics, Manga: From "Blankets" to "Demo" to "Blacksad."* New York: St. Martin's Griffin, 2005.

See also: *The Spirit Archives,* Volume 1

Blood: A Tale

Author: DeMatteis, J. M.
Artist: Kent Williams (illustrator); Gaspar Saladino (letterer)
Publisher: DC Comics
First serial publication: 1987
First book publication: 1997

Publication History

Blood: A Tale was first published in 1987 as a four-issue miniseries by Marvel's now-defunct Epic line. DC Comics reprinted the series, again as single issues, under its Vertigo imprint ten years later. There have been two paperback editions, the first in 1997 and the second in 2005, both from DC's Vertigo. As of 2011, the work is out of print.

Kent Williams was one of three illustrators of the well-received series *Moonshadow* (1985-1987), written by Jon J. Muth. Williams had also done cover art for Marvel and interior art for other comics companies, namely Eclipse Comics. Based on his prior collaboration with Williams, Muth suggested Williams to J. M. DeMatteis for *Blood*.

DeMatteis wrote a significant amount of mainstream comics and graphic novel stories prior and subsequent to *Blood: A Tale*, most notably the autobiographical *Brooklyn Dreams* (1994), which is included on the American Library Association's (ALA) list of ten best graphic novels.

Plot

Blood: A Tale appeared during the heyday of creator-owned works in the mid- to late 1980's. The work is experimental in form, using few word balloons and utilizing paintings as the primary form of illustration. While it presents itself as a vampire story, it is more properly a nightmare and an allegory.

In the first chapter, "Ouroborous," a young girl tells a story to a dead king. A river of blood flows into a sea, which gives up a thorny pod that is found by a young girl. Inside she finds a baby. An elder tells her she can nurture the boy. When the child comes of age, he studies at a monastery. When he is given

> ## J. M. DeMatteis
>
> One of the most notable superhero comic book writers for thirty years, J. M. DeMatteis debuted in the 1980's for Marvel Comics, writing titles like the Defenders and Captain America. Since that time he has worked on dozens of titles, most notably the Justice League titles for DC Comics and their related spin-offs, and the Spider-Man titles for Marvel. In the 1990's he was one of the signature writers affiliated with the Vertigo Comics imprint, writing *Mercy*, *The Last One*, and *Seekers Into Mystery*. Among his most celebrated graphic novels are *Moonshadow*, with Jon J. Muth, Kent Williams, and George Pratt, and *Blood: A Tale*, with Kent Williams. Collaborating with Glenn Barr, he created the semi-autobiographical graphic novel *Brooklyn Dreams* for Paradox Press. DeMatteis's writing ranges between traditional, though psychologically inflected superheroics, to much more personal and dreamlike ruminations and fantasies, as in *Moonshadow*.

leadership of the monastery, the boy rebels, slays the teacher, and leaves. Encountering others, he is told his name is Blood. He denies the name and shoots the tribal elder. His gun becomes a snake. He wakes from his dream.

In chapter two, "Communion," Blood discovers he has become a vampire. He feeds. When he wakes from his delirium, he meets "the Woman." She tells him the two of them are different from the others, as they are neither human nor vampire. In a sensual embrace, he drinks blood from her breasts. They bond, leave the vampire pack, and discover Little One in a tree. The three form an ersatz family and travel.

The three characters discover a deserted airplane. Blood's hungers return. He kills a charging black panther. Caught in a storm, the three hide in a cave, where they see the slain Elder. The Elder becomes a cave painting, pointing to a rope ladder heading out of the cave. Climbing the rope ladder, Blood leaves the cave alone. He exits the cave through a manhole cover, thus becoming a modern man; he is wearing a suit and is late for work.

In chapter three, "Theophany," Blood is married to a woman who is expecting their child. He harbors fading dreams of rock stardom. When she confesses to having an affair, he reenters the previous world in visions, including one in which he sees a bandaged man. Blood has cancer and again sees visions. He unwraps the bandages and sees the slain elder, who tells him not to worry. Leaping into an open manhole, he returns to the other world.

The Woman questions and then comforts him. As Blood and the Woman prepare to die together, Little One begs them not to. He floats to a painting of the Woman on a rock wall and flies at its door, dying. The door opens. A lake of blood rushes out. Blood and the Woman cradle Little One's corpse. Elders approach in a floating ark and demand the body of Little One, to take to Isle of the Dead. Blood and the Woman vow to bring him back.

In chapter four, "Ouroborous," Blood and the Woman fly as bats to the Isle of the Dead, find Little One, and see Father and Brother, now soulless and with no memory of Blood and the Woman. Blood begs their forgiveness. The island becomes a jagged rock. The two stand atop it. The Woman is pregnant. She dies giving birth. Blood throws the newborn into the storm, proclaiming his love for the Woman. He falls asleep. He wakes to a drumbeat and joins the marching Silent Ones. As he marches, his "selves" fade and merge until he falls, hitting his head. Looking up, he sees a tomb. His Elder is in front, again telling him not to worry. Blood kneels and goes to the door of the tomb, which opens, revealing Blood behind it. Inside, he encounters everyone he knew and loved. A flintlock pistol discharges. Blood dies. The sea consumes his body, and he is taken back to his birth in the thorny pod. The story starts again.

Characters

- *The King* is a dead monarch. A young girl, nameless throughout and functioning as a Greek chorus, tells him the stories of Blood, framing each chapter. The King has been dead for more than a year as the young girl begins telling him the stories that comprise the bulk of the narrative.

- *Blood*, a.k.a. *the Boy*, is the protagonist. As the stories begin, he has floated in a thorny casket from a sea of blood to clear waters. He is found by a woman, who nurtures him until he is taken to a monastery, where he meets the elder known only as Father and learns the mysteries of life.

- *Father* tutors Blood. His lessons are rote. He responds to Blood's questions with blows, followed by kind words and hugs. When Father tells Blood that he will be his successor, Blood rebels and kills him. After his death, he reappears periodically to Blood and to the Woman.

- *Little One* is an amorphous fetal being with a stout, thick body and stumps for limbs; he is encased in a sort of spacesuit. He floats at Blood's eye level, despite being half his height. He asks many questions and has few answers, but he provides Blood with some small comfort. Despite his truncated body, he has a fully mature face, seen in only two panels. His behavior is that of a petulant child, needy and fearful.

- *The Woman* is Blood's lover, nurturer, and occasional food source. She teaches him and needs him and is a companion, a wife, a mother, and a spiritual guide for him. By turns bringer and recipient of knowledge, she is a totem for female mysteries.

- *The Silent Ones* serve as stand-ins for the masses. They are unthinking and behave tribally. Their main goals are duty and persuasion. They do not act as individuals.

Artistic Style

Williams is a painter who studied at Pratt Institute. His approach to visual narrative is driven by color and pose. His style is loose and energetic but is anatomically accurate. Almost every page of *Blood: A Tale* functions as an independent painting, even when panels are used. The environments used in the story, primarily in watercolors, are sparse and lack detail but are rich in mood. When combined with the tense, often-abstract text, these create a feeling that drives the narrative more than the words do. This is surprising, since of the 192 pages of story, 19 rely on blocks of text as the dominant visual element. Most of these pages use small, equally sized border illustrations as support for the text. This is a variation of the conventional use of words and images in comics or graphic novels.

Williams also made a deliberate decision to minimize other conventions of the format. Only 75 pages, less than half the book, use word balloons at all. None of the balloons are mechanically drawn; all are freehand. Some contain only symbols, and a few are completely empty. However, all text is typeset and not hand rendered. Sound effects are used, but they are painted and are seen as part of the images.

Themes

Writer DeMatteis describes *Blood: A Tale* as "an odd, eerie fever-dream of a story set in an odd, eerie fever-dream of a world." The primary themes of this work are the contradictions of life and universal fears. The book begins with a living person describing birth to a dead one. Rivers of blood and water, coupled with a thorny cradle from which Blood is pulled, serve as birth metaphors.

The names are iconic. Blood is life and death. As a vampire, he must be both. Blood's refusal to accept his vampiric nature echoes humans' unwillingness to accept their animal natures.

Blood responds to knowledge passively, accepting what he is told rather than dealing with the pain of questioning it. He kills his teacher rather than accept responsibility for teaching others. Paradoxically, he kills to resist causing pain. When he is given the truth of his vampiric nature, he slays his teacher.

Blood's climb up the rope ladder out of the cave gives dual messages. This is the lonely journey to awareness. Passage out of a small tunnel in the roof of a cave is yet another birth metaphor.

When Blood emerges into a more mundane world, the reader is given the sense that this world is also a dream, or that Blood's first world is the real one and the reader's is the dream. The characters he encounters in this world, his friend Warren and his wife Helen, feel less real to the reader and to him than the iconic beings in his original world.

Blood joins the march of the Silent Ones. His death is alluded to repeatedly in the story, but this death appears final. He encounters the sage he had killed earlier, who offers him comfort.

Blood hits his head on a rock. The wound from this injury takes the appearance of a third eye and echoes the same image on the forehead of his slain teacher. As Blood dies, the story returns almost word for word to its beginning, implying a never-ending cycle. The first and last chapters have the same title, "Ouroborous," which refers to a worm or snake biting its own tail to make a full circle.

Impact

Originally published by Epic Comics, *Blood: A Tale* is a product of its time in comic history. Nested in the late Bronze Age to early Modern Age of comics, it was promoted as part of a creator-owned line of properties. Creator-owned work was a response to litigation from older creators and to similar contracts being offered by newer publishers. This circumstance made the reprinting of the work under DC's Vertigo possible a decade later.

Opinion on DeMatteis's story has always been divided because of its more elusive aspects. However, Williams's art was well received and led to other lucrative and successful graphic novel projects, including the 1992 *Tell Me Dark* and his 2005 collaboration with filmmaker Darren Aronofsky on the graphic novel *The Fountain*. Most significantly, taken in conjunction with Williams's earlier work on *Moonshadow*, *Blood: A Tale* served as a template for the painted graphic novel.

Diana Green

Further Reading

Aronofsky, Darren, and Kent Williams. *The Fountain* (2005).

DeMatteis, J. M., et al. *The Compleat Moonshadow* (1998).

Muth, Jon J. *M* (2008).

Wagner, Karl Edward, John Ney Rieber, and Kent Williams. *Tell Me Dark* (1992).

Bibliography

Voger, Mark. *The Dark Age.* Raleigh, N.C.: TwoMorrows, 2006.

Wolk, Douglas. *Reading Comics: How Graphic Novels Work and What They Mean.* Cambridge, Mass.: Da Capo Press, 2007.

See also: *Moonshadow*; *Death: The High Cost of Living*; *Spider-Man: Kraven's Last Hunt*

BLOODSTAR

Author: Howard, Robert E.; Corben, Richard; Jakes, John

Artist: Richard Corben (illustrator)

Publisher: Morning Star Press

First book publication: 1976

Publication History

Bloodstar, originally scheduled to be called "King of the Northern Abyss," is generally considered the first self-proclaimed "graphic novel." The first edition, a luxury hardcover with dust jacket, was published with a full-color cover and black-and-white interior in 1976 by Morning Star Press. A six-page preview, "The Slaying of Satha," had been printed in the fantasy magazine *Ariel*, issue 1, earlier that year. In 1979, a longer edition (107 pages), with color cover and black-and-white interior, was published in large paperback format by Ariel Books.

Bloodstar is the major character in the book, which is adapted from a short story entitled "The Valley of the Worm" by pulp writer Robert E. Howard. That story was published in *Weird Tales* in 1934. Howard's major character in "The Valley of the Worm" was Niord; Gil Kane renamed him Bloodstar and created a starlike, crimson design for his forehead. John Jakes, who had extensive experience writing fantasy for both novels and comics, added considerable new material to "The Valley of the Worm." Richard Corben rewrote and further expanded the story for its 1976 publication.

The 1979 edition had more material added by John Pocsik. In 1980 and 1981, a color version of *Bloodstar* was serialized in *Heavy Metal* magazine, issues 45-52. The story has been reprinted, in whole or in part, in France, Germany, Italy, the Netherlands, Spain, and the former Yugoslavia.

Plot

Bloodstar expands on Howard's "The Valley of the Worm" and cannot be understood without referencing that tale. In "The Valley of the Worm," a dying modern man recalls a past life as Niord, a savage whose Aesir tribe lived before recorded history. Wandering into

---

Richard Corben

One of the defining visual stylists of the 1970's, Richard Corben was one of the signature artists affiliated with *Heavy Metal* magazine and helped to establish the look and feel of science-fiction and fantasy imagery during that period. His *Den* saga, published sporadically over a period of decades, is the work that he is most closely associated with, an unevenly plotted fantasy comic about a hairless and nude adventurer. In the 2000's, Corben began contributing art to a number of mainstream superhero titles, including *Hellblazer* and *Cage* (both with writer Brian Azzarello) and *The Punisher: The End* (with writer Garth Ennis). Corben's art is distinguished by the intersection of exceptionally detailed fantasy elements and characters with extremely cartoony features. His characters are generally beefy, and he employs a tremendous amount of shading in his drawings, while his paintings use airbrush effects to create depth.

---

southern jungles, Niord and his tribe of northern warriors encounter a savage race called the Picts. A battle is fought, and Niord first defeats and then befriends a Pict named Grom. Grom warns Niord to avoid a valley strewn with ancient ruins. Some Aesir are slaughtered in that valley by a monstrous, wormlike creature, which is called out of a deep well by an apelike being playing the panpipes. Niord then kills the piper and the worm using arrows dipped in the venom of a giant serpent, Satha, but is killed himself. Niord's tale is, supposedly, the inspiration for the heroic stories of Beowulf, from *Beowulf* (c. 1000); Siegfried, from *Nibelungenlied* (c. 1200; first English translation, 1848); Saint George (and his encounter with the dragon); and others.

Bloodstar begins when a maverick star approaches the solar system and collides with the Sun. Earth survives, but human civilization is destroyed. (This section of *Bloodstar* seems based upon "The Star," an H. G. Wells short story.) The scene then shifts centuries into the future. Civilization is virtually forgotten, and humanity has sunk into savagery. Many mutations have occurred because of radiation released during the cataclysm. A character named Bloodstar and his friend and mentor, Grom, are hunting. Grom is injured by a mutated boar and on his deathbed tells Bloodstar of his father (Bloodstar the Elder) and the "Worm," which Grom calls the "King of the Northern Abyss." Except for the addition of a romantic subplot, the rest of the story closely follows Howard's "The Valley of the Worm."

Bloodstar the Elder and his Aesir tribespeople wander into the land of Grom's people and are attacked. Bloodstar defeats Grom in battle but spares him. The Aesir leader, Byrdag, is badly wounded, and a powerful warrior named Loknar is chosen to succeed him. Initially, Loknar and Bloodstar are friends. The new chief is promised Helva, Byrdag's daughter, as his mate. However, Bloodstar and Helva are in love, and Loknar catches them together. Bloodstar is forced to run the gauntlet, but survives. In battle, Bloodstar defeats Loknar, who loses an eye and flees the tribe. Bloodstar is exiled, with Grom and Helva accompanying him. Helva bears Bloodstar's son, Bloodstar the Younger, but she misses her father. While returning to the Aesir settlement, Helva and young Bloodstar are kidnapped. Byrdag finds his young grandson and comforts him. In the meantime, the Aesir village is destroyed by the "Worm."

As in "The Valley of the Worm," Bloodstar kills Satha and soaks arrows in the snake's venom. He enters the Worm's valley to find that Loknar has become the "piper" who summons the monster. Bloodstar kills Loknar, who admits to murdering Helva, but Loknar's corpse continues playing its horrid music. The Worm, which resembles a giant white slug with numerous tentacles, responds to the music and Bloodstar shoots it with venomous arrows. The dying Worm crawls back into its pit after fatally injuring Bloodstar. Grom and Byrdag arrive, and Bloodstar gets to see his son one last time. An epilogue reveals that Bloodstar the Younger sired a great line of heroes.

Characters

- *Bloodstar the Elder* is the main protagonist but appears only about one-third of the way into the book. He is a powerfully built young savage of the Aesir race, a superb warrior, hunter, and tracker. He is the first to carry a crimson mark on his forehead resembling a "blood star." His heroism in slaying the monstrous "Worm" ends the book.

- *Bloodstar the Younger*, a protagonist, is Bloodstar the Elder's son. He looks identical to his father and is also a great warrior and hunter. Early in the story, he appears as an adult and is told about his father and the Worm by Grom. In Grom's story, Bloodstar the Younger appears only as a small child.

- *Grom*, a protagonist, is a member of a primitive, Neanderthal-looking race. He becomes Bloodstar the Elder's friend and bears witness to the hero's defeat of the Worm. Grom later mentors Bloodstar the Younger and tells him about his father.

- *Byrdag*, the Aesir chief, is a great warrior. He is a protagonist, although he has conflict with Bloodstar the Elder. Injured in the first battle with Grom's people, Byrdag's body becomes twisted. He banishes Bloodstar from the tribe for sleeping with Helva. However, he lives long enough to meet and love his grandson, Bloodstar the Younger.

- *Helva*, a protagonist, is the tall, blond daughter of Byrdag, chieftain of the Aesir, who resemble Cro-Magnon peoples. Helva is betrothed to Loknar, but she loves Bloodstar the Elder and flees the tribe with him. She bears his son but is murdered by Loknar.

- *Loknar the Bold*, another superbly muscled young warrior of the Aesir, is originally Bloodstar the Elder's friend. He later becomes an antagonist. Set to succeed Byrdag and take Helva as his mate, Loknar catches Bloodstar and Helva making love, and his friendship turns to hate. After losing a fight with Bloodstar, Loknar flees and becomes the "Worm's" servant.

- *The Worm*, the primary antagonist, is a titanic, mutated slimy white beast. It resembles a slug with many tentacles. Its appearance and nature are apparently influenced by H. P. Lovecraft's Cthulhu Mythos stories. Its level of intelligence is unknown.

Artistic Style

Richard Corben, the artist for *Bloodstar*, is well known for his work at *Heavy Metal* magazine and for creating the cover art for rock musician Meat Loaf's *Bat out of Hell* (1977) album. He has illustrated many other comics and magazines and produced several short animated films. His art is known for its portrayal of heavily muscled, heroic men and voluptuous women. His characters are often nude or seminude and are generally depicted "in action." Their faces often convey intense emotion. The construction and arrangement of his comic book panels appears influenced by film-animation techniques, and he worked as a commercial animator before becoming an independent illustrator.

Except for the full-color cover, all illustrations in *Bloodstar* are black and white. The art, created using an airbrush, markers, and pencils over a period of about nine months, contains Corben's usual heroic action, nudity, and intense emotion. There is considerable violence, often graphic, and some nongraphic sexual activity. Figures often appear exaggerated and foreshortened, with heads that are almost caricatures and with faces showing dramatic rage or joy.

Corben uses many panels showing multiple figures and sometimes uses aerial perspectives for large-scale dramatic scenes. He uses shadows and hatching to good effect. Although the animals depicted in *Bloodstar* are supposedly mutated, the illustrations show most of them as normal, if somewhat large, representations of warthogs, saber-toothed tigers, and snakes. The "Worm," however, certainly appears mutated.

Somewhat of a transitional work between prose novels and the modern visually dominated graphic novel, *Bloodstar* contains more dialogue and description than later graphic novels. There are even full pages of text that summarize story events. However, the story is still told primarily in graphic format, with many panels advancing the story through visual means alone.

Themes

Bloodstar falls into a subgenre of fantasy called sword and sorcery, typified by larger-than-life heroes who pit physical strength and primitive weapons against often supernatural foes. The modern form of the genre was pioneered by Howard, creator of the character known as Conan the Barbarian and author of "The Valley of the Worm," upon which *Bloodstar* is based. However, science-fiction elements were added to the story, probably by Corben, turning *Bloodstar* into a postapocalyptic rather than prehistorical work. A romantic subplot was also added, with Bloodstar the Elder becoming a husband and father. These are unusual developments in sword and sorcery. Such changes made *Bloodstar* a larger-scale story than "The Valley of the Worm" but weakened the original's "mythic" feel.

Sword and sorcery is an adventure genre and is often labeled "escapist" literature. However, the genre and *Bloodstar* share many common elements with such early masterpieces of literature as the Gilgamesh epic (translated into English as *Gilgamesh Epic*, 1917), *The Odyssey* (c. 725 B.C.E.; English translation, 1614), *Beowulf* (c. 1000), *Chanson de Roland* (c. 1100; *The Song of Roland*), and the Norse *Eddas*. Sword and sorcery feeds the reader's need for imaginative adventure but also examines the nature of good and evil. In *Bloodstar*, the "good" is the love and loyalty that characters such as Bloodstar and Helva feel for each other, their children, and their tribe. The "evil" may be an indifferent universe (the wandering star that destroys human civilization), a living but inhuman force (the Worm), or an individual who has forsaken goodness (Loknar). Evil must be fought with acts of heroism and sacrifice so that the "good" (love) can survive.

Impact

In 1976, the year *Bloodstar* was published, two other works also claimed the title "graphic novel." However, Jim Steranko's *Chandler: Red Tide* is really a typeset novel with illustrations, while George Metzger's *Beyond Time and Again* was originally a serialized comic. From the start, *Bloodstar* was conceived as a complete story with a beginning, middle, and end, with the illustrations helping tell the story rather than merely amplifying the text. This makes *Bloodstar* the first graphic novel as that term is generally conceived, cementing the book's place in history. *Bloodstar* showed what could be done with the graphic format and remains a seminal work in the rapidly expanding field of graphic novels. Its influence on the comic book industry has waned, however, as more complex and literate works such as Alan Moore's *Watchmen* (1986-1987) have been published. Among Howard fans, *Bloodstar* remains one of the most respected adaptations of his work.

Corben, illustrator and one of the primary authors of *Bloodstar*, remains widely influential within the comics industry. He has been lauded by artists such as Robert Crumb, Will Eisner, Moore, and Frank Miller, painter and set designer H. R. Giger, and filmmaker Guillermo del Toro. His heroic warriors and voluptuous female characters have been widely imitated and many consider *Bloodstar* to be his best work.

Charles Gramlich

Further Reading

Davis, Alan. *Killraven* (2007).

Moore, Alan, and Dave Gibbons. *Watchmen* (1986-1987).

Strnad, Jan, et al. *Sword of the Atom* (2007).

Bibliography

Bharucha, Fershid. *Richard Corben: Flights into Fantasy*. New York: Thumbtack Books, 1981.

Corben, Richard. "The Richard Corben Interview." Interview by Brad Balfour. *Heavy Metal* 5, no. 3 (June, 1981): 6-11. Available at http://www.muuta.net/Ints/IntCorbHM51.html.

Estren, Mark James. *A History of Underground Comics*. 3d ed. Berkeley, Calif.: Ronin, 1993.

Wiater, Stanley, and Stephen R. Bissette. "Up from the Deep." In *Comic Book Rebels: Conversations with the Creators of the New Comics*, edited by Stanley Wiater and Stephen R. Bissette. New York: Donald I. Fine, 1993.

See also: *Watchmen; Cerebus; Ronin*

BONE

Author: Smith, Jeff
Artist: Jeff Smith
Publisher: Cartoon Books; Image Comics
First serial publication: 1991-2004
First book publication: 1993

Publication History

Published beginning in 1991 as a bimonthly, black-and-white, twenty-four-page comic book by Jeff Smith's own imprint, Cartoon Books, *Bone* ran for fifty-five issues, finishing in 2004. Issues 21-27 (December, 1995, to April, 1997) were published by Image Comics. Cartoon Books resumed publishing *Bone* with issue 28. *Bone* was also published as a complete nine-volume graphic novel series beginning as *The Complete Bone Adventures,* Volume 1, in 1993. The nine volumes were collected in one book called *Bone: One Volume* in 2004. The nine *Bone* graphic novels were republished in color on a biannual schedule by Scholastic Press under the Graphix imprint beginning in 2005 and finishing in 2009.

    The Complete Bone Adventures, Volume 1, (later renamed *Out from Boneville*), was serialized in *Disney Adventures* during 1997-1998. *Disney Adventures* published an original eight-page *Bone* story, "The Powers That Be," in August, 1994.

Bone. (Courtesy of Cartoon Books)

Plot

The plot centers on the three Bone cousins, Fone Bone, Phoney Bone, and Smiley Bone, who have been banished from Boneville and into an unknown valley. The cousins find a map, which Fone Bone hopes will lead them back to Boneville. While escaping a swarm of locusts, they become separated, and Fone Bone falls off a cliff. Stumbling around, he chances upon the cave inhabited by Red Dragon, the only member of the dragon race who has not gone underground. Fone Bone is immediately chased by two rat creatures and is saved by Red Dragon.

    Fone Bone continues his quest to find the others, but he cannot get out of the forest before winter begins. He spends the winter with a friendly possum family and

has several scrapes with rat creatures. As winter begins to thaw, he meets Thorn, a teenage girl with whom he is smitten. Thorn befriends Fone Bone, and he moves into her house with her grandmother, Gran'ma Ben.

    Thorn and Gran'ma Ben attend a town festival; Phoney Bone goes before them, hoping to exploit the townspeople. Before Fone Bone, Thorn, and Gran'ma Ben leave, rat creatures attack their farmhouse. While Gran'ma holds off the rat creatures, Thorn and Fone Bone escape. They are trapped by more rat creatures and then rescued by Red Dragon.

    Phoney Bone makes it to the town, Barrelhaven. In a bar owned by Lucius Downs, he finds his cousin Smiley. Phoney convinces Smiley to masquerade as a cow so they can enter the annual cow race. During the cow race, the rat creatures invade Barrelhaven. A fight ensues, and the villagers hold off the rat creatures. As the story closes, readers learn that the rat creatures follow a being named the Hooded One, who is looking for Phoney Bone.

Next, Phoney, still hatching plots to make money, convinces the townspeople that he can protect them from dragons, and he temporarily catches Red Dragon. This leaves the townspeople unprepared when the rat creatures attack again. As this is happening, Thorn experiences "the turning," something that happens to members of the royal family as they come into their power. This is the climactic moment in the *Bone* story; the war for control of the valley has begun, and everyone must be ready to join the battle, even a teenage princess.

Next, Fone Bone and Smiley embark on an adventure of their own while escaping some dangerous rat creatures. The rats want the Bones, and a giant lion, Rock Jaw, master of the same mountain range that the Bones travel, intends to deliver them to the leader of the rat creatures, Kingdok. As he is about to turn over Smiley and Fone Bone, Kingdok and Rock Jaw fight, allowing the Bone cousins to escape.

The war escalates. The Hooded One, who is also Briar Harvestar (Gran'ma Ben's sister), visits Lucius Downs as the townspeople intend to make a stand at Old Man's Cave and Thorn rescues Smiley and Fone Bone from a troop of rat creatures. Meanwhile, Phoney Bone has run away. Gran'ma finds Phoney; at the same time, Rock Jaw finds them and leaves, intending to deliver Phoney and Thorn to the Hooded One. In an attempt to save Thorn and Phoney, Gran'ma, Smiley, and Fone Bone follow Rock Jaw to temple ruins where the Hooded One intends to sacrifice Phoney Bone. There is an earthquake, and Gran'ma, Thorn, and the Bone cousins escape once again.

The Hooded One has released deadly "ghost circles" across the valley, and only Thorn is safe. She attempts to lead Gran'ma and the Bone cousins through the circles as the rat creatures attack, including Bartleby, a cub raised by Smiley Bone. Bartleby changes sides and helps the Bones, Thorn, and Gran'ma evade the rat creatures. Meanwhile, more rat creature troops attack Old Man's Cave, and the Veni Yan (an association

of hooded warrior monks) leave the cave headed to Atheia, the ancient city.

Thorn has been instructed by a voice to seek out the "Crown of Horns." The companions reach Atheia, where Thorn falls under the spell of the Hooded One. A wise man brings Thorn out of her trance, and she reveals that she is looking for the Crown of Horns. The wise man knows that if Thorn touches it, all life will be erased. Thorn and Fone Bone are arrested while the city is attacked by rat creatures and their allies.

As Thorn and the Bones are imprisoned, the rat creatures, led by the Hooded One, attack Atheia. Meanwhile, Phoney and Smiley have found the treasure of Atheia, and Phoney intends to bring it back with him to Boneville. Thorn realizes only by touching the magical Crown of Horns will order be restored, and that she must do it. Followed by Fone Bone, Thorn leaves the city, believing that the Crown of Horns must be in the dragon burial ground. After several scrapes with the rat creatures, Thorn finds the Crown of Horns, which is guarded by Kingdok. Thorn kills him but cannot reach the crown because the dead Kingdok holds onto her leg. Fone Bone arrives, and together they are able to touch the Crown of Horns. This wakes all the dragons, who have been sleeping underground. Red Dragon rescues Thorn and Fone Bone and an energy bolt emitted from the crown kills the Hooded One. The war is over, and now Thorn is queen. The Bone cousins, with Bartleby in tow, return empty-handed to Boneville.

Volumes

- *Out from Boneville* (1996). Collects issues 1-6. Describes how the Bone cousins come to the valley.
- *The Great Cow Race* (1996). Collects issues 7-12. Introduces the villagers, as Thorn begins to awaken to her destiny.
- *The Eyes of the Storm* (1996). Collects issues 3-19. The war with the rat creatures intensifies.
- *The Dragonslayer* (1997). Collects issues 20-27. Phoney manipulates the villagers to hire him to protect them from dragons.
- *Rock Jaw: Master of the Eastern Border* (1998). Collects issues 28-32. Fone Bone and Smiley go

on an adventure and run into Rock Jaw, a giant mountain lion.

- *Old Man's Cave* (1999). Collects issues 33-37. As the war intensifies, Thorn and the Bone cousins seek shelter in Old Man's Cave.
- *Ghost Circles* (2001). Collects issues 38-43. While trying to get to the old city, Thorn must lead her party through deadly "ghost circles."
- *Treasure Hunters* (2002). Collects issues 44-49. As the war rages, Phoney Bone finds the hidden treasure beneath the old city.
- *Crown of Horns* (2004). Collects issues 50-55. Thorn and Fone Bone reach the Crown of Horns, defeating the enemy.

Characters

- *Fone Bone* is the hero of the *Bone* series. He is good-natured and helpful. He left Boneville because he was concerned about his cousin Phoney Bone. He has a fondness for *Moby Dick: Or, The Whale* (1851) and is often found reading the novel. When he meets Thorn, he is completely smitten with her. As the adventure progresses, he helps Thorn win back the kingdom of Atheia for the Harvestar family.
- *Smiley Bone* is the tallest of the cousins and is a happy-go-lucky character who moves from one experience to another without reflection or insight. Smiley wants to help people, but his simplemindedness usually ends up irritating them. Smiley is willing to go along with any of Phoney Bone's schemes, but he is also capable of strength of character when it is completely necessary.
- *Phonciple "Phoney" Bone* is a greedy, self-centered character. He was run out of Boneville after campaigning for mayor. He is always scheming ways to cheat people out of money and he makes enemies easily. At times, he is deeply concerned for the welfare of his cousins. This was evident when they were children when he plotted ways to steal food.
- *Thorn* appears to be a farm girl but is soon revealed to be heir to the valley, something she does not know as the story unfolds. She is also the "awakened one" or the "Veni-Yan Cari," and

a member of the royal Harvestar family. As she learns of her destiny, she becomes very powerful; she is able to fly on occasion, possesses great strength, and has tremendous courage. Her only real confidant is Fone Bone.

- *Rose Harvestar*, a.k.a. *Gran'ma Ben*, is the dethroned queen of Atheia. She is living in the country to keep her granddaughter Thorn hidden until Thorn is ready to assume a leadership position. She is incredibly strong and strong-willed.
- *Lucius Downs* was Captain of the Guards before the war. Even though he is old, he is still strong and athletic. He is an innkeeper, living in the country, doing his best to protect Thorn until it is time for her to assume power.
- *The Red Dragon* is centuries old and is the son of Mim, the queen of dragons. While all the other dragons have gone underground, only Red Dragon is left to help the Harvestar family. Red Dragon often arrives just in time to rescue Fone Bone.
- *Bartleby*, a baby rat creature whom Smiley adopts, chooses to stay with the Bone cousins after Thorn has been made queen rather than returning to the rat creatures.
- *Briar Harvestar*, a.k.a. *The Hooded One*, is Rose's sister. As a beautiful young girl, Briar fell under the spell of the Lord of the Locusts. Now, as an adult, her devotion to the Locusts has made her deformed and hideous. She intends to deliver the valley to the Lord of the Locusts.
- *The rat creatures*, originally afraid of humans, now run freely through the valley and pose a threat to humans. They are especially fascinated by the Bone cousins.

Artistic Style

The artistic style of *Bone* is one of its greatest contributions to the comics world. Using deceptively simple line drawings, Smith conveyed a number of contrasts. The Bone cousins are small, while the rat creatures are large; therefore, pitting the two groups against each other is visually humorous, particularly during rapid scene changes in which the hero suddenly experiences a life-and-death situation. It is also accomplished because the Bone cousins are odd-looking and vaguely resemble small animals. Smith put great effort toward facial expressions and body language, and many responses one character gives to another are humorous. The realistic representation of human characters and landscapes further reveal the comedic aspect of *Bone*. The sparse narration made readers focus on the drawings, leading them to read entire pages quickly, giving the full page more impact than a single panel. It is worth noting that there are few full-page illustrations in the entire *Bone* series.

Although the style Smith employed was consistent throughout the series, one occasion on which he used specific techniques in order to more deeply involve the reader was the chapter "Double or Nothing" in the book *Eyes of the Storm*. In this story, the characters are caught in a heavy rainstorm. Smith physically moves the characters through the storm in about ten minutes, the same time it takes the reader to read the issue of *Bone*. The result is that the reader is not detached from the story but, because of the frantic pacing, feels like a participant.

Jeff Smith

Serialized from 1991 through 2004, Jeff Smith's *Bone* is one of the best-loved children's graphic novels published in the past quarter century, and ranks as one of the most important comic book series for children published in the American comics market. Smith's mixture of fantasy elements with slapstick humor established *Bone* as an all-ages work that is likely to attract readers for generations. His art work mixes two registers: the Bones are drawn with bold, cartoony strokes that recall animation traditions, while other characters and backgrounds are depicted with thinner and more static lines and greater degrees of texture. The tension between cartoons and naturalism is reflective of the overall storytelling in the series as a whole. Since finishing *Bone*, Smith has worked on a variety of series, including *Shazam! The Monster Society of Evil* for DC Comics and the self-published *RASL*, a science-fiction story about an art thief.

The original *Bone* series was produced in black and white. The color contrasts further developed the humorous and dramatic aspects of *Bone*, as the book became in part a series of visual contrasts: The Bone cousins were small, the rat creatures large, and the Hooded One always dark surrounded by light. When the series was reproduced in color, the contrasts were more subtle, particularly the backgrounds, which mirrored the emotional state of the protagonists. By introducing color, not only was the reading experience deepened visually, but also the colored version presented a more complicated story.

Themes

There are several themes that run throughout *Bone*. One is control, specifically of the valley where Fone, Phoney, and Smiley have found each other. The royal family is in hiding after a war with the rat creatures fifteen years earlier. The Bone cousins are taken in by the royal family and help them win back control of the valley after Thorn Harvestar (the princess) discovers her power when she becomes sixteen. Once Thorn realizes her power, she is able to win back the kingdom for her family.

Other themes of *Bone* are self-discovery and change. Fone Bone begins the story as a reluctant hero. Although he is loyal to his cousins, he has yet to give himself to another person. After Fone grows to love Thorn, he takes on her mission to regain control of the valley and stands up to his cousins when they ask him to return to Boneville. The other main character who experiences change is Smiley Bone, Fone Bone's happy-go-lucky cousin. As Smiley cares for Bartelby, the orphaned rat creature, he discovers mature qualities within himself.

Impact

Bone became one of the most influential of the alternative comic books of the 1990's. It set a new standard for self-published comic books because Smith held himself to professional standards in terms of quality printing and distribution as well as issue delivery dates. *Bone* was one of the early adopters of the graphic novel format. *The Complete Bone Adventures,* Volume 1, sold more than fifty thousand copies in 1993, and the

Cartoon Books motto, "always in print, always available," helped comic book publishers see the viability of the graphic novel format. As graphic novels blossomed out of the traditional comic book marketplace, *Bone* was one of the first to be collected by public librarians. *Bone* also broke new ground for the graphic novel format in 2005 when Scholastic Books colorized it and made it the cornerstone of its own graphic novel publishing imprint, Graphix.

Stephen Weiner

Further Reading

Smith, Jeff. *Shazam! The Monster Society of Evil* (2007).

Smith, Jeff, with Tom Sniegoski. *Bone: Tall Tales* (2010).

Smith, Jeff, and Charles Vess. *Rose* (2009).

Bibliography

Smith, Jeff. *The Art of Bone*. Milwaukie, Ore. Dark Horse Comics, 2007.

_____. *Bone Handbook*. New York: Graphix, 2010.

Weiner, Stephen. *Faster Than a Speeding Bullet: The Rise of the Graphic Novel*. New York: NBM, 2003.

See Also: *Rose*

BOOKS OF MAGIC, THE

Author: Gaiman, Neil
Artist: John Bolton (illustrator); Scott Hampton (illustrator); Paul Johnson (illustrator); Charles Vess (illustrator); Todd Klein (letterer)
Publisher: DC Comics
First serial publication: 1990-1991
First book publication: 1993

Publication History

In 1988, DC Comics announced through editorial spots in monthly comic books the release of an upcoming miniseries, written by J. M. DeMatteis and featuring painted interiors, that would bring new attention to the company's magical characters. When DeMatteis and the original lineup of artists pulled out of the project, DC approached Neil Gaiman, then writer of the popular *Sandman* (1989-1996) series, to take over.

The Books of Magic was ultimately published as a four-issue miniseries, released under DC Comics' main imprint, beginning in December, 1990. Each forty-eight-page issue was published in what DC Comics called "prestige format": The covers were made of harder-than-usual paper stock, the pages were made of higher-than-usual quality paper, and the spine was bound to resemble a miniature graphic novel. Because of its format, the series was sold only in comic book specialty stores (not at newsstands) at the comparatively high cover price of $3.95 per issue.

The graphic novel itself has gone through a few versions. The first edition's cover was dominated by the title, printed with gold foil stamping over a darkly colored image of a summoning circle, which is a symbol designed to summon spirits. In order to link the graphic novel with subsequent *The Books of Magic* installments (released under the Vertigo imprint), later versions featured an image of the protagonist on a skateboard. In 2003, the series was published in novelized form (adapted by Carla Jablonski) by HarperCollins as part of their teen imprint, HarperTeen.

John Bolton

Though he has not produced a large number of comics, John Bolton is recognized for his distinctive painterly style that occasionally borders on the photorealistic. Initially recruited into the American comic book industry as an illustrator of fantasy comics, including two *Kull* stories for Epic Comics and *Marada* for *Epic Illustrated*, Bolton began working on *X-Men* stories with writer Chris Claremont in the late-1980's. The bulk of his comics work has been in the fantasy and horror genres, with notable collaborations with writers Clive Barker and Neil Gaiman. The original *Books of Magic* miniseries, with Gaiman, remains his best-known work. In it he employed a moody, painted photorealist approach that underscores the magical elements of the work. Bolton's paintings generally begin from a strongly realist framework and then veer slightly into the unusual and the bizarre.

Plot

The Books of Magic describes a twelve-year-old British boy's encounter with the world of magic. The boy, Timothy Hunter, is shown the various forms and features of the world of magic and then, at the story's end, given a choice to either embrace this world or return to the normal world of reason and science. Each issue involves a journey, led by a different guide, through one aspect of the magical world: its past, its present, its extradimensional realms, and finally its future. Overall, the series reads and functions more as an illustrated tour than it does a typical story—there is no major antagonist, the plot occurs episodically, and the major internal conflict turns out to be illusory. Each issue's individual chapter is also largely self-enclosed.

Like *Hellblazer* (1988-   ) and *The Sandman* but unlike similar modern fantasy titles published by DC Comics (most of them under the Vertigo imprint), *The Books of Magic* is set in DC's primary, superhero universe. In fact, the miniseries was conceived as an introduction, for both new and established readers, to the magical, nonsuperhero characters that inhabit this universe. For this reason, the majority of characters appearing in *The Books of Magic* had been previously introduced and developed in older series. Some of them date back as far as the 1930's. In some instances, outside knowledge of these preexisting characters is necessary to fully follow the plot (particularly in issue 2, with the multiple appearances of Boston Brand, also known as Dead Man). In general, however, Gaiman avoids this problem by modeling Timothy upon the uninformed reader. In this role, Timothy makes frequent interpretive mistakes, mixing up characters' names and, at one point, misidentifying a major DC character as gay.

In the first issue, subtitled "The Invisible Labyrinth," Timothy is accosted on the street by four mysterious men. The men, John Constantine, Dr. Occult, Mister E, and the (Phantom) Stranger, inform Timothy that he has the potential to become the greatest magician of the modern age. Before Timothy can set forth upon this path, however, he must learn what magic is and decide whether he wishes to embrace it. Skeptical that magic even exists, Timothy is persuaded to listen to the men by Dr. Occult's transformation of the boy's yo-yo into an owl.

Timothy's first lesson requires him to travel to the beginning of time with the Stranger. During this trip, he witnesses the birth of creation, Lucifer's war in heaven, Earth's prehistory, the sinking of Atlantis, Merlin's childhood, and many other mythical events. He also encounters a series of characters, including the original Doctor Fate and the magician Zatanna Zatara, who warn him of the price magic exacts from those who claim it.

In issue 2, "The Shadow World," Timothy travels with Constantine to the United States, where he meets Lady Xanadu, the Spectre, the new Doctor Fate, Jason Blood, and Baron Winters. In the middle of his tour, Constantine is called away to India, where he joins the other three guides in a battle (occurring off-panel) against the Cold Flame, a cult seeking Timothy's death. In Constantine's absence, Timothy is taken by Zatanna to Bewitched, a magicians' club, where he meets many magical villains.

Issue 3, "The Land of Summer's Twilight," brings Timothy to the land of Faerie with Dr. Occult, who is transformed through its magic into a woman named Rose. Here, Timothy sees a number of important mythical sites, including the Faerie market, the King's Tomb, Baba Yaga's hut, and Titania's castle. At the castle, Titania gives Timothy a key with which he visits other realms owned by DC Comics, including Gemworld and Skartaris.

In the series' last issue, "The Road to Nowhere," Timothy travels with Mister E into the future, where he witnesses a future version of himself leading the forces of evil in a cosmic war. After further travel to the end of time, Mister E attempts to kill Timothy but is thwarted by Yo-yo (the owl), who intercepts the blow. Sent back to the present by Death, Timothy reencounters the other three guides, who present him with the choice: magic or a normal life. Fearing the path of magic, Timothy chooses normality, but he ultimately finds that the choice was a false one, as he inadvertently transforms his yo-yo back into an owl while alone in his bedroom.

Characters

- *Timothy Hunter*, the protagonist, is a twelve-year-old British boy with short brown hair. He wears blue jeans, a white T-shirt, and glasses and first appears riding a skateboard. Intended as a children's Everyman, he is largely undeveloped as a character. He possesses the curiosity and faux jadedness typical of children his age, but few other distinguishing personality traits. Set to become the most powerful wizard of the modern era, he is the target of both well-intentioned sorcerers who seek to help him and magical villains who seek his death.

- *The Stranger*, a.k.a. *The Phantom Stranger*, the first of Timothy's guides, brings Timothy on a tour of the past. Called "The Phantom Stranger" in other titles, the Stranger originally debuted in his own series during the 1950's. In subsequent decades, he made guest appearances in various superhero series published by DC, where he occasionally served the role of magical adviser. A mysterious character with an enigmatic past, he is the most serious of Timothy's four guides. In

The Books of Magic he wears a trench coat, dark fedora, and white turtleneck. His eyes, though usually hidden by the shadow of his hat, sometimes appear as white slits or sparkles.

- *John Constantine* serves as one of *The Books of Magic*'s four tour guides, leading Timothy across the United States to witness the present state of magic. A British punk turned street magician, Constantine was originally created by Alan Moore for *Swamp Thing* in 1985; in 1988, he received his own ongoing series, which continued in 2011. In *The Books of Magic*, he appears as a friendly-looking young man with blond hair. He wears a trench coat and is frequently depicted smoking a cigarette. Of the four guides, Constantine acts most like a normal human being: He tells jokes, expresses doubt, and finds pleasure in the people and places of the world.

- *Dr. Occult*, sometimes appearing as *Rose*, the third of the guides, leads Timothy through the world of Faerie. Originally created by Jerry Siegel and Joe Shuster in 1935, Dr. Occult appeared as a magical detective in DC's *Fun* comics lines throughout the late 1930's. Subsequently ignored by DC writers and editors, his character was revived briefly in 1985 in Roy Thomas's *All-Star Squadron* and then by Gaiman for *The Books of Magic*. Dressed as a noir detective and sometimes depicted smoking a pipe, Dr. Occult is the gentlest of Timothy's guides. In the world of Faerie he is occasionally transformed into Rose (a former girlfriend whose persona had merged with Dr. Occult's in a previous series).

- *Mister E* serves as the final tour guide for Timothy, taking him on a supposedly one-way trip to the end of time. A disturbing character, Mister E debuted in 1980 in the pages of DC's *Secrets of Haunted House*, where he was blinded by his father for discovering evidence of his father's perverted sexual desires. As an adult, the blind Mister E acquired magical powers, which he used to fight the forces of evil. In *The Books of Magic* he appears as an older man in a white suit and ruby-tinted glasses and carries a walking stick.

The most violent of the four guides, he attempts to murder Timothy at the end of time.

Artistic Style

In *The Books of Magic*, all aspects of a single issue's art (including coloring) are handled by a single artist. There are thus four artists associated with the series, one for each issue. The differing tastes and skills of each artist result in each issue bearing a distinct artistic style. To some degree, each issue's unique style has also been determined by the plot, which progresses in four distinct segments.

John Bolton, who handles issue 1 (a tour of the past), uses dark tones to convey a sense of mystery. He also utilizes relaxed panel borders to signal the disruption of time through time travel. Scott Hampton's style in issue 2 (a tour of the present) is, by contrast, more traditional. His panel layouts are deliberately unremarkable, his colors are brighter, and his focus is on individual characters and expressions rather than events. Charles Vess, illustrator for issue 3 (a tour of Faerie), deploys the most delicate style of the four. His light, airy panels put emphasis on props and scenery, while his penciled figures, placed atop watercolor backgrounds, invite comparisons to classic Disney animated films. The final issue (a tour of the future) is illustrated by Paul Johnson. Like Hampton did for issue 1, Johnson uses dark colors and deconstructed panels to convey the uncertainties of time travel. He also uses gestural marks (visible brushstrokes and pencil scribbles) to communicate the gradual disintegration of creation.

Despite the differing styles of each issue, the art for *The Books of Magic* as a whole has some general properties. Each issue features mixed-media interiors (watercolor, acrylic, charcoal, and pencil) and thus possesses a "crafted" look, generally lacking from DC's other monthly comic books. The art also functions, especially in issues 1 and 4, more as illustration than as narrative sequence. In this, the art reflects Gaiman's "tour guide" approach to plot, in which seeing is given greater priority than is acting.

Themes

An homage to DC's many magical characters, *The Books of Magic* is, like many of Gaiman's works, a passionate defense of the idea of myth and the psychological importance of imagination. Loosely inspired by T. H. White's *The Once and Future King* (1958) and other mid-twentieth-century fantasy-adventure novels, the series uses the conceit of Timothy's mystical education to provide a catalog of Western myths and stories.

Beyond celebrating these myths in their own right, the series interrogates their value by structuring the plot's central conflict upon the choice presented to Timothy at the first issue's opening: Does he want a magical life or a normal life? Through this plot device, the very concepts of myth and magic are subjected to a rational assessment of their worth.

In general, this assessment finds much fault with the magical life. Such a life requires from the magician a crippling sacrifice or payment, exposes him to tremendous danger (both bodily and psychological), deprives him of freedom by subjecting him to the concept of destiny, and deprives him of the ability to distinguish between good and evil. It also replaces familial relationships with casual ones, as demonstrated by Timothy's inability to communicate with his father once the magical education has begun.

Despite this assessment, however, *The Books of Magic* also suggests that the choice between magic and normality is itself a false one. Though Timothy chooses the safety of a normal life, the series refuses to honor that decision. Magic is chosen for him, and the series ends on a panel depicting a wide-eyed Timothy as he exclaims, "Magic!" With this ending, the series seems to suggest that if one is capable of recognizing the existence of the choice, one has already answered it in favor of myth and magic.

Impact

Though published during the Modern Age of comic books, a period that saw much formal and narrative experimentation, *The Books of Magic* is particularly idiosyncratic in its approach to the medium. Indeed, there has not been another work published by DC or Marvel that has utilized the structure of an illustrated tour of the publisher's universe to tell a story. Despite its oddness, however, the series was a hit, cementing Gaiman's reputation as a master storyteller and relaunching a host of DC characters and intellectual properties.

DC's mature-audience imprint, Vertigo, launched in 1993, featured many of the characters spotlighted in *The Books of Magic* for its magic-themed books. Indeed, the early Vertigo universe was modeled upon the interconnected world presented in Gaiman's series. Vertigo explicitly signaled this interconnectedness by launching a crossover event titled *The Children's Crusade* (1993-1994), which reintroduced Timothy Hunter as a character. After this initial appearance, a seventy-five-issue series titled *The Books of Magic* (primarily written by John Ney Rieber and illustrated by Peter Gross) was published under Vertigo and ran from 1993 to 2001.

Since 2000, Timothy has starred in three other series: *The Names of Magic* (2001), *Hunter: The Age of Magic* (2001-2003), and *The Books of Magic: Life During Wartime* (2004-2005). Neither these series nor Rieber's earlier *The Books of Magic* series, however, has much in common with Gaiman's original beyond the protagonist and their frequent utilization of the land of Faerie. Though *The Books of Magic* graphic novels remain in print, the intellectual property has received no attention or development since 2005.

Also of note are the rumors, appearing on Web sites and in British tabloids, that Harry Potter was based upon Timothy Hunter. Though the two characters bear many visual resemblances, Gaiman has vigorously denied—both in interviews and on his blog—that any copying occurred. Whether or not the rumors are true, no lawsuits have been filed by Warner Bros., owner of DC Comics and the copyright to Timothy Hunter.

Gregory Steirer

Further Reading

Azzarello, Brian, et al*., John Constantine: Hellblazer* (1988-   ).

Carey, Michael. *Lucifer* (2000-2006).

Gaiman, Neil. *The Sandman* (1989-1996).

Rieber, John Ney, and Peter Gross. *The Books of Magic* (1994-2000).

Bibliography

Hanes, Stacey, and Joe Sanders. "Reinventing the Spiel: Old Stories, New Approaches." In *The Sandman Papers*, edited by Joe Sanders. Seattle, Wash.: Fantagraphic Books, 2006.

Lowe, John. *Working Methods: Comic Creators Detail Their Storytelling and Artistic Processes*. Raleigh, N.C.: TwoMorrows, 2007.

Vess, Charles. *Drawing down the Moon: The Art of Charles Vess*. New York: Dark Horse Comics, 2009.

Wagner, Hank, Christopher Golden, and Stephen R. Bissette. *Prince of Stories: The Many Worlds of Neil Gaiman*. New York: St. Martin's Press, 2009.

Zelazny, Roger. Introduction to *The Books of Magic*. New York: DC Comics, 1993.

See also: *Lucifer; Sandman; Sandman Mystery Theatre; Hellblazer*

BOYS, THE

Author: Ennis, Garth

Artist: Darick Robertson (illustrator); Keith Burns (illustrator); Carlos Ezquerra (illustrator); John Higgins (illustrator); John McCrea (illustrator); Peter Snejbjerg (illustrator); Hector Ezquerra (inker); Matt Jacobs (inker); Rodney Ramos (inker); Tony Aviña (colorist and cover artist); Simon Bowland (letterer); Greg Thompson (letterer)

Publisher: DC Comics (issues 1-6); Dynamite Entertainment (issues 7-   )

First serial publication: 2006-

First book publication: 2007-

Publication History

Despite his concerns about whether DC Comics would tolerate the series that "out-preachered *Preacher*"— *Preacher* (1995-2000) was a series published by DC Comics that was criticized for its excessive sexual and violent themes—author Garth Ennis moved forward with DC Comics' imprint WildStorm for the launch of his series *The Boys*. DC Comics canceled the series after the release of issue 6. After the cancellation, Ennis and artist Darick Robertson resumed the series at Dynamite Entertainment with no significant hitches over licensing and rights from DC Comics. The series continued with the same numbering and narrative direction. Ennis and Robertson expressed relief about the creative freedom granted to them by their new publisher, with less editorial interference in postproduction. All trade paperbacks for the series have been published by Dynamite Entertainment, including the first volume, which features an introduction by actor Simon Pegg, after whom the main character, Hughie Campbell, was modeled.

Much like Ennis's other series, and unlike mainstream superhero narratives, *The Boys* has a specific endpoint toward which Ennis has been working, aiming for a series run of roughly seventy-two issues. However, he continues to build and elaborate on the mythology of the series. In 2009 and 2010, he wrote two six-issue miniseries, *The Boys: Herogasm* and *Highland Laddie*, both of which provide significant

The Boys. (Courtesy of Dynamite Entertainment)

background to events in the ongoing series and have been integrated into numbered volumes with the trade paperbacks.

Plot

From the outset, Ennis executed *The Boys* as an unabashedly gratuitous critique of the superhero narrative through its use of satire, parody, and hyperbole. Additionally, strong critiques of the concentration of power (particularly within corporations), moral absolutes, and the naïveté of truth and faith feature prominently in the series.

The series follows a Central Intelligence Agency (CIA)-formed team, named "The Boys," whose mission is to keep superheroes from excess. Over the years, superheroes have been the pawns of a single corporation that creates, uses, abuses, and manipulates its superheroes through merchandizing, public appearances, false emergencies, and unethical testing to increase its profit margin. The superheroes and their various teams have become increasingly hedonistic, egotistical, and careless about their collateral damage, which includes significant public, private, and physical destruction. The Boys step in when the superheroes become more problem than solution.

The series opens with Hughie Campbell on the cusp of telling his girlfriend that he loves her. Unfortunately, A-Train, a first-league superhero, collides into her so fast that Hughie is left holding just her arms; the rest of her has been smashed into a wall. Hughie is devastated and blindsided by the tragedy, and his disdain for superheroes turns vitriolic. Enter Billy Butcher, the leader of the Boys, who convinces Hughie to join his team to fight superhero corruption, destruction, and decadence.

As Hughie learns about the Boys, Vought-American (the major corporation that controls all the superhero teams), and the true atrocities perpetrated by superheroes, readers are exposed to the particulars of this world's history: Superheroes emerged from World War II and the creation of a drug known as Compound V. In pure form, the drug develops lifelong inheritable powers for the person who consumes it. However, in the present, Compound V is used in small doses by the Boys and others at times and has even been mixed with various narcotics with usually problematic results.

Vought-American is the corporation that creates, organizes, and manages all the superhero teams. A nameless executive calls all the shots for Vought-American, though the executive continually allows a figurehead to stand as chief executive officer. Its domestic and international schemes have been the reason to deploy the Boys to keep its superheroes in check. Throughout the series, it is responsible for innumerable crimes, including torture, imprisonment, illegal human experiments, mass murder, and terrorist acts.

Over the years, Vought-American has transitioned from a simple (but dysfunctional) arms producer into a multinational conglomerate with innumerable subsidiaries and vested interests, including the production, maintenance, and merchandizing of superpowers and superpower teams. Vought-American and its best team, "The Seven" (which includes A-Train), serve as the series' major antagonists, against which the Boys, under Butcher's direction, enact a sometimes overt but mostly covert war, for not only their widespread indiscretions and atrocities but also personal affronts to members of the Boys. Hughie learns from his teammates about a variety of tragedies that were perpetrated by superheroes, including an event on September 11, 2001 (9/11), in which superheroes caused a plane to crash into the Brooklyn Bridge, provoking a military invasion of Muslim countries.

While working for the Boys, Hughie meets and dates Annie January, who also happens to be Starlight, a member of the Seven. Neither realizes that their alter egos are enemies, until Butcher reveals the fact to Hughie while trying to figure out where Hughie's loyalty lies. Upon discovering this truth, Hughie confronts both Annie and Butcher before departing to his family home in Scotland to debate his next step.

Volumes

- *The Boys,* Volume 1*: The Name of the Game* (2007). Collects issues 1-6. The death of Hughie's girlfriend and the arrival of Butcher persuade Hughie to join the Boys. On the group's first mission, Hughie is coerced into taking Compound V to help defeat the group Teenage Kix, which creates ambiguous feelings in him.
- *The Boys,* Volume 2*: Get Some* (2008). Collects issues 7-14. The Legend, an essential contact, sends the Boys to investigate Tek Knight, a superhero with a deadly sexual hang-up. Next, they arrive in Russia to deal with new complications resulting from Vought-American.
- *The Boys,* Volume 3*: Good for the Soul* (2008). Collects issues 15-22. This volume provides significant background on Vought-American, Compound V, the real events of 9/11, and the origins of the Boys
- *The Boys,* Volume 4*: We Gotta Go Now* (2009). Collects issues 23-30. The Boys send Hughie in disguise to infiltrate and investigate a suicide by one of the G-Men. The story reveals that the

supposed group of orphans and runaways were subject to sexual assault by their leader, John Godolkin.

- *The Boys,* Volume 5*: Herogasm* (2009). Collects issues 1-6 of *The Boys: Herogasm*. At the annual superhero gathering, Herogasm, heroes and villains join together for several days of extreme debauchery and depravity. The Boys manage to infiltrate the event to discover more about the Seven and Vought-American.
- *The Boys,* Volume 6*: The Self-Preservation Society* (2010). Collects issues 31-38. The Boys fight Payback, the second best team. They barely survive intact, though Payback is eliminated. This volume also provides the background to Mother's Milk, Frenchie, and the Female.
- *The Boys,* Volume 7*: The Innocents* (2010). Collects issues 39-47. When Malchemical, a sadistic superhero, is assigned to SuperDuper, a band of superheroes with disabilities, the Boys discover the depths of Vought-American's maliciousness. Butcher manipulates events to determine if Hughie and Annie know they are on opposite sides.
- *The Boys,* Volume 8*: Highland Laddie* (2011). Collects issues 1-6 of *Highland Laddie*. Hughie leaves the Boys to figure out what he wants but becomes mixed up in a drug ring, realizing that one can never actually return home.

Characters

- *Hughie Campbell*, a.k.a. *Wee Hughie*, is the main protagonist of the series and is the simplest and sincerest of the characters. He is the common man with whom readers identify, as he questions the motives and actions of the Boys, while clearly condemning and loathing the superheroes. This latter trait comes back to haunt him when he discovers his girlfriend, Annie, is a superhero. Upon learning this, Hughie leaves the Boys to contemplate his situation.
- *Billy Butcher*, a protagonist, is the British leader of the Boys, but his motivations are often unclear. His sometimes blatant disregard for superheroes and even his own teammates makes him appear as equally appalling as the superheroes he fights. His desire to avenge the destruction of his family at the hands of the Homelander motivates him beyond the parameters of the team.
- *Mother's Milk*, a protagonist, is an African American who proves to be both intelligent and the sanest member of the team, prior to Hughie's arrival. His family has suffered at the hands of Vought-American, and he seeks to bring down the company. However, he tends to be the voice of reason and restraint within the group and is often needed to keep Butcher from going too far.
- *The Frenchman*, a protagonist, is a French (or possibly pseudo-French) assassin, whose propensity for violence is only rivaled by the Female of the Species, for whom he acts as mouthpiece and caretaker. Though his skills are most often

The Boys. (Courtesy of Dynamite Entertainment)

used for fighting superheroes, he is known to lash out and kill people over mere insults. According to him, he renounced pacifism after his father was unfairly killed in a bicycle duel.

- *The Female of the Species*, a protagonist, is the silent and violent woman of the team. The Frenchman communicates for her. Her behavior results from being exposed to Compound V waste as a baby and becoming a prisoner of Vought-American. At times, she works for organized crime as a hired assassin. Her connection to the world is tenuous but maintained and nourished by the Frenchman, who continuously tries to bring out her humanity.

- *Annie January*, a.k.a. *Starlight*, a protagonist, is Hughie's girlfriend. Upon joining the Seven, she is coerced into performing sex acts on team members, which makes her question the moral integrity of the world. For much of the series, neither she nor Hughie realizes that they are at odds; however, Butcher reveals a sex tape of Annie with members of the Seven. Upon discovering this, Hughie confronts her and then leaves for Ireland. She arrives there to talk, and they reunite eventually.

- *The Legend*, a protagonist, is an old man who knows a great deal of information, which he shares with the Boys to help them with their battles. He previously worked for years as a comics writer for Vought-American, redeveloping the actual atrocities of the superheroes into adolescent narratives for mass consumption. Though he hints at his own agenda, his interests have continually coincided with those of the Boys.

- *The Homelander*, an antagonist, is the leader of the Seven. He was the first and appears to be the strongest superhero in the world. He was also responsible for the demise of Butcher's family and seems to be Butcher's main target. As the series has progressed, he has become increasingly unstable.

Artistic Style

The artistic style remains consistent throughout the entire series and aligns well with Ennis's content.

The art direction provides clear visual sequences; in addition, the artists use paneling, color patterns, and motifs to establish mood and irony within the series. Though the series does not break any new ground in its artistic style, the artists go to substantial lengths to depict the violence and depravity present in the narrative. Each issue contains affronting images every few pages or so.

Black is the dominate color of the series; it is prominent in the Boys' uniform (black leather coats) and is the color of choice for gutters and blank space. Even when a white background is presented, the panels usually have thickened black borders beyond normal parameters. The black corresponds well to the dark themes of violence, corruption, and destruction. However, the color is equally apropos as a visual invocation of the dark comedy prominent in the series.

Consistent color schemes are reproduced for certain settings within the series that often mock the events occurring therein. Superhero teams' headquarters are often depicted utilizing bright colors that produce a clean and sanitized feeling to the environment. This serves in direct contrast to the corrupt, immoral, and often horrific events that occur in these headquarters. In this context, the bright colors of traditional superheroes' costumes become clear indicators of ineptitude, immorality, and malignancy.

Themes

The series functions as a satire on both the superhero genre and the real world. Many of the superheroes and teams are analogues to the various characters of Marvel Comics and DC Comics. For example, Homelander's faux origin story parallels Superman's origin story. (Almost all of Vought-American's superheroes have fake origin stories to make them more appealing to the public.) He is an orphaned alien sent to Earth and brought up in wholesome America and has super-strength, as well as superior speed and flight, a heat ray, and several other similar powers. Ennis creates narratives that purposely mock standard tropes within the more popular series. For instance, the miniseries *Hero-gasm* focuses on the superheroes coming together on a resort island for an extended orgy. However, the story fed to the public is that all the superheroes and villains are banding together to fight an epic battle in space, a scenario that is a nod to the often repeated megaevents that both major publishers perform annually.

The series also mocks unhesitatingly the modern political world, particularly actions of the United States. The various connections that the president and vice president have with Vought-American and the decisions, covert actions (including the launching of the Boys), and profiteering have purposeful parallels to the George W. Bush presidential administration. In particular, the series presents fictional parallels to Blackwater, former vice president Dick Cheney, and the co-opting of 9/11 for political empowerment of the Republican base.

Ennis is well known for narratives that are directed toward a mature audience, and this series holds to that standard. Nudity, violence, and ghastly imagery are found throughout. However, much like filmmaker Quentin Tarantino's work, *The Boys*' intentional gratuitousness serves as a commentary on modern culture's obsessive concern about sex and violence in media, rather than being just a reason to depict such things.

Impact

As an ongoing series that has published slightly more than fifty issues and is from an independent publisher, *The Boys* has a yet-to-be-determined legacy. While some might place the series within the context of postmodern superhero narratives first started in the 1980's with Alan Moore's *Watchmen* and Frank Miller's *Batman: The Dark Knight Returns*, this series seems to go even further in trying to challenge the bastions of the comic elite. *The Boys* challenges the status quo of superhero narratives and critiques how the genre's

dominant form (the Marvel Comics and DC Comics continuities) rejects authenticity and complexity.

Other series have taken on the narrative point of view of the villain. However, Ennis goes beyond, implying that the good and noble superhero (such as Starlight) is the exception to the rule. Instead, Ennis has inverted the superhero genre, inventing a universe in which superheroes are the villains. Some series since the release of *The Boys* have progressed Ennis's idea; these include Mark Waid's *Irredeemable* and *Incorruptible*, both of which began publication in 2009. Ultimately, Ennis's series serves as a warning about power in the real world and what happens when performance-enhancing drugs allow for superpowered people.

Lance V. Eaton

Further Reading

Ennis, Garth, and Steve Dillon. *Preacher* (1995-2000).
Vaughan, Brian K., and Tony Harris. *Ex Machina* (2004-2010).
Veitch, Rick. *Bratpack* (1990-1991).

Bibliography

Dyer, Ben. *Supervillains and Philosophy*. Chicago: Open Court, 2009.
Reynolds, Richard. *Super Heroes: A Modern Mythology*. Jackson: University Press of Mississippi, 1994.
Wolk, Douglas. *Reading Comics: How Graphic Novels Work and What They Mean*. Cambridge, Mass.: Da Capo Press, 2007.

See also: *Preacher; Ex Machina; Bratpack; Watchmen; Batman: The Dark Knight Returns*

BRAT PACK

Author: Veitch, Rick
Artist: Rick Veitch (illustrator); Gary Fields (letterer)
Publisher: Tundra (comics); King Hell Press (book)
First serial publication: 1990-1991
First book publication: 1992

Publication History

Brat Pack was first published in color as a five-volume series for Tundra's King Hell imprint in 1990. After achieving early fame working on independent projects such as *The One* (1985-1986), Rick Veitch gained mainstream success illustrating *Miracleman* for Eclipse and *Swamp Thing* for DC Comics, both in the 1980's. After he took over writing duties on the latter, he encountered editorial resistance when he tried to publish a story in which Swamp Thing encountered Jesus Christ. He was unable to resolve these differences, leaving the book and the company. The plot to *Brat Pack* had already been on Veitch's mind, but his experience with DC (as well as DC's much-publicized "Death in the Family" story line, in which fans voted to kill Robin) likely influenced him as he wrote the book.

Veitch heavily revised *Brat Pack* when it was collected; when Tundra went out of business, his King Hell imprint remained the publisher of the book, releasing it as a black-and-white volume. A further series, *The Maximortal* (2002), is set in the same universe and shares some tonal elements with *Brat Pack*. A fifth edition of *Brat Pack* was published in 2009.

Plot

The fictional city of Slumburg is protected by four superheroes: the openly gay vigilante Midnight Mink, the over-the-top female supremacist Moon Mistress, the rich and wild arms dealer and gadgeteer King Rad, and the fascist and racist Judge Jury. The heroes are generally beloved (or at least respected), but their sidekicks—Chippy, Luna, Wild Boy, and Kid Vicious—are loathed. The sidekicks are lured to a local church; when they follow a trail of evidence seemingly planted by the evil Doctor Blasphemy, they are blown up in an explosion.

Rick Veitch

One of a small number of renowned creators to move from mainstream comics publishing to the independents, Rick Veitch initially made his name as an artist on the Alan Moore-written *Swamp Thing*, a series that he took over as writer after Moore's departure. Following a falling out with DC over censorship issues, Veitch began self-publishing his comics under the name King Hell Press. His graphic novels *Bratpack* and *Maximortal* offered a scathing indictment of superhero genre conventions, including the sexualization of superheroes. Later collaborations with Moore, including *1963* and the Greyshirt stories in *Tomorrow Stories*, led to a return to DC Comics, which published his graphic novel *Can't Get No* in 2006. Veitch is best known for his horror and fantasy work, and for incorporating those elements into his superhero titles. His stories frequently push the boundaries of what is acceptable in mainstream comics, and include mythological, political and conspiratorial elements.

The four heroes intimidate Father Dunn, a local priest, into providing them with new sidekicks. After the heroes meet the replacement sidekicks and warn them about Doctor Blasphemy, all four teens learn that their parents have died in accidents. They thus begin their training as orphans.

Each sidekick is trained according to their hero's style, and each is sent on a mission that traumatizes them: Wild Boy loses a young hostage, Luna is nearly raped by a mob, Kid Vicious realizes he has beaten his former maid to death, and Chippy sees the Mink burn to death one criminal and sodomize another. In response to their sidekicks' concerns, the heroes explain their origins, noting that all were influenced by True-Man, a Superman-esque hero who left the planet years ago.

As the months go by, the sidekicks begin to resemble their predecessors. Vicious becomes addicted to steroids (and suffers the side effects); Luna becomes pregnant and needs an abortion. Wild Boy extorts crack from dealers; and Chippy receives a blood transfusion from Mink, who had received a transfusion from True-Man, thus gaining a tremendous healing ability.

After Chippy nearly gets killed, the others realize that he has gained some powers, thus increasing their dislike of him. After the four are lured to the church and nearly blown up in a similar fashion to how their predecessors were killed, they realize that Doctor Blasphemy was not the killer, but that their partners had killed off the sidekicks. Chippy explains his healing ability to his teammates, and they drink his blood, thus gaining his power, even as the heroes launch a missile into the church.

The heroes assume that all is well, but they are surprised to discover the body of Father Dunn hanging from a noose in a bell tower wearing Doctor Blasphemy's mask. Even as they start to suspect that Dunn was not really their nemesis, they are surprised by a sudden storm and the return of True-Man. The returning superhero captures all of the heroes—as well as the sidekicks, who have survived the missile thanks to the blood Chippy shared—inside a church bell and blasts them, explaining that he needs to take back what the heroes took from him. As the book ends, the reader learns that Doctor Blasphemy had been King Rad's manservant Fredo all along.

Characters

- *Chippy*, a.k.a. *Cody*, is the second Chippy and an altar boy. He is the primary everyman character for the early part of the book; the previous Brat Pack, as well as Mink, is first seen through his eyes, and he actively begs Father Dunn to let him be the next sidekick. He is generally the most idealistic of the sidekicks and also the most likely to see events holistically.
- *Luna*, a.k.a. *Shannon*, is the only one of the sidekicks to have a seemingly happy home life before her parents are killed. At first, she is nervous about embracing the raw sexuality of her sidekick role, but she soon does, acting as Moon Mistress asks her, teasing both opponents and her own teammates.

- *Wild Boy*, a.k.a. *Karlo*, a young skate punk, is picked on by other kids because of his small size. He is willing to take incredible risks, even before he becomes addicted to drugs as King Rad's sidekick.
- *Kid Vicious*, a.k.a. *Beau*, is a rich, spoiled teen, and his parents often travel and have no time for him. As he starts taking more and more steroids, he becomes increasingly violent and physically repulsive.
- *Midnight Mink* is a Batman-like hero who is flamboyantly gay and predatory in his approaches to villains. He met True-Man at a gay resort, and they became lovers. True-Man infuses him with his powerful blood when he discovers that Mink has AIDS.
- *Moon Mistress*, a former party girl, met True-Man in his civilian identity on her wedding night and soon began an affair with him. She is inspired by Wonder Woman. She is ruthless against men, using her body and sidekick to distract them and cutting off their testicles when they attack women.
- *King Rad* is a rich weapons manufacturer who inherited millions of dollars from his father. He resembles Oliver Queen (Green Arrow) physically but seems largely patterned on Tony Stark (Iron Man), given his addictive and risk-taking personality. It was his company that developed True-Man as a weapon and created his identity.
- *Judge Jury* is a racist and murderous vigilante in the tradition of the Punisher who believes that since True-Man was white, the white race is the only good one. He physically abuses his sidekicks as he trains them and also gets them addicted to steroids. He is the only one of the four core heroes who did not have direct contact with True-Man.
- *True-Man*, the hero who inspired the others, was a moral man who cared more about saving the world than about profiting financially from his actions, something the heroes who follow do not comprehend. He is bisexual (or possibly pansexual), having relationships with both Moon

Mistress and Midnight Mink, and supposedly the product of a military experiment.

- *Doctor Blasphemy*, a.k.a. *Fredo*, opposes the heroes as Doctor Blasphemy, although the character is never seen committing any explicit crimes other than taunting the heroes. As Fredo, he works for King Rad (and for all of the heroes), handling both mundane tasks and major undertakings, including planting the bombs used to kill the first sidekicks.

Artistic Style

As the illustrator as well as the writer, Veitch uses a style largely influenced by the 1930's to 1960's-era DC and Marvel artists. Heroes have powerful bodies, but not the muscular mockeries that became common in the 1990's. Veitch uses the style to underscore the era of comics that he is largely addressing, in which the early sidekicks were introduced. The lack of color underscores the dark, dreary mood of Slumburg, a city where riots, poverty, and drug use are rampant and where the hope represented by the traditional heroic figures is lost.

As a storytelling mechanism, Veitch embraces the two-page comic layout to tell four parallel stories. Throughout the book, he follows each of the four sidekicks as they go about their day—training, fighting crime, or learning about True-Man—focusing half of a page on each of the four story lines. This not only forces the reader to slow down and not flip through one character's plotline too rapidly but also equalizes the importance of all four character arcs.

Veitch is not above playing with the reader, sometimes using artistic obfuscation to hide Fredo's face as Doctor Blasphemy. In one case he reveals something only the reader can see, using a combination of graffiti, window signs, and a television broadcast in four different scenes to spell the message "Greetings from Doctor Blasphemy."

Veitch is also willing to make his art grotesque, giving Doctor Blasphemy a long, nearly prehensile tongue (reminiscent of Marvel villain Venom) that drips acid. He depicts the first Chippy as a nearly zombified corpse feasting on raw pigeons and at first shows Moon Mistress toothless and with sagging breasts.

Themes

At its core, *Brat Pack* is an overt commentary on the silliness of the sidekick concept. Veitch realizes that the idea of a young teen running around fighting crime is, in the end, only going to endanger the life of that teenager. Since that idea seems obvious to him, he questions why an adult superhero would have a teenage sidekick. The conclusions to which he comes are varied but largely reflect the cynicism of the superheroes. Since they all have licensing contracts, having a sidekick ensures that the heroes continue to make money from these characters. The comic companies themselves are not absolved of this; as Neil Gaiman notes in his introduction, a new Robin was introduced by DC shortly after the death of the previous one. The sidekicks also serve as focal points for the hatred the public might have for heroes, distracting people from the actions of the real vigilantes. Also, in a reference to the accusations of Fredric Wertham (to whom the book is dedicated), the Batman-influenced Midnight Mink views Chippy as a potential romantic partner, or at least a sexual conquest.

Going further, Veitch explores the idea that adults often exploit their children, both on an individual level (parents who live vicariously through their children, forcing them into careers or expectations they cannot handle or outright abusing them) and on a societal level (in which children are the consumers to whom adults target products and manipulate with various forms of media, including comic books). It is hard not to read at least some autobiographical content into the story, as Veitch's themes could also apply to how the comic industry treats its creators and the characters they publish, something very likely on Veitch's mind at the time he first wrote *Brat Pack*.

Impact

Along with *Batman: The Dark Knight Returns* (1986) and *Watchmen* (1986-1987), *Brat Pack* is one of the significant books that helped reshape the view of superheroes in the late 1980's and early 1990's. Books such as *The Authority* (2000-2010), particularly Mark Millar's run, *Marshal Law* (1997-2002), and *The Boys* (2006-) show an irreverence toward their heroes that can be directly traced to *Brat Pack*. Likewise, the use of obvious stand-ins for contemporary heroes in those books, although certainly older than *Brat Pack*, became more prevalent after this book.

Brat Pack also encouraged a willingness to add more mature content to mainstream superhero storytelling, something that Veitch was, on many levels, protesting. *The Maximortal*, a series that followed True-Man in his earlier years, also takes a hard look at the comic industry, although it focuses more directly on the relationship between creators and the corporations that own the characters.

Adam Lipkin

Further Reading

Veitch, Rick. *The Maximortal* (2002).

Ennis, Garth, and Darrick Robertson. *The Boys* (2006-   ).

Mills, Pat, and Kevin O'Neill. *Marshal Law* (1987-2002).

Bibliography

Veitch, Rick. "Rick Veitch Interview." Interview by D. J. LoTempio. *Fanzing* 41 (December, 2001). http://www.fanzing.com/mag/fanzing41/iview.shtml.

_____. "Veitch Brags About the Brat Pack." Interview by Jennifer Contino. *Comicon.com*, March 19, 2009. http://www.comicon.com/ubb/ubbthreads.php?ubb=showflat&Number=539353.

Gaiman, Neil. Introduction to *Brat Pack*, by Rick Veitch. West Townshend, Vt.: King Hell, 1992.

See also: *The Boys; Batman: The Dark Knight Returns; Watchmen; Authority; Swamp Thing*

BUFFY THE VAMPIRE SLAYER SEASON 8

Author: Allie, Scott; DeKnight, Steven S.; Espenson, Jane; Goddard, Drew; Greenberg, Drew Z.; Meltzer, Brad; Petrie, Doug; Vaughan, Brian K.; Whedon, Joss

Artist: Georges Jeanty (penciller); Karl Moline (penciller); Cliff Richards (penciller); Andy Owens (inker); Michelle Madsen (colorist); Dave Stewart (colorist); Richard Starkings (letterer); Jo Chen (cover artist)

Publisher: Dark Horse Comics
First serial publication: 2007-2011
First book publication: 2007-2011

Publication History

Based on the *Buffy the Vampire Slayer* television series (1997-2003), *Buffy the Vampire Slayer Season 8* was originally published in magazine format by Dark Horse Comics beginning on March 14, 2007. At the conclusion of each story arc, Dark Horse published a trade paperback collecting the individual issues. The first collection, *The Long Way Home*, was released in November of 2007. The trade paperbacks also included supplementary material relevant to the series that appeared in *Dark Horse Presents* and in one-shot issues, such as stories focusing on Buffy's best friend, Willow, and on Buffy's former boyfriend Riley.

Scott Allie, the series editor and a contributing writer, had previously worked with *Buffy the Vampire Slayer* creator Joss Whedon and Twentieth Century Fox to develop *Buffy* as a comic book while the television series was ongoing. Several of the writers from the television program contributed to the series, notably Whedon and staff writers Jane Espenson and Drew Goddard, all of whom wrote major story arcs for the comic. Steven S. DeKnight, Drew Z. Greenberg, and Doug Petrie, also writers from the television series, contributed individual issues collected in the volume *Predators and Prey*. This allowed many fans of the television series to feel that the comic book was in the hands of people who knew the characters well and were invested greatly in the story line.

(Getty Images)

Joss Whedon

The creator of the television series *Buffy the Vampire Slayer*, *Angel*, *Firefly*, and *Dollhouse*, Joss Whedon expanded a number of television shows into comic books after they left the air. *Fray* is set in the far future of the Buffy universe, while *Buffy: Season 8* is considered to be a "canonical" continuation of the narrative established by the television show. *Serenity: Those Left Behind* acted as a narrative bridge between the cancelled series *Firefly* and the film *Serenity*. In addition to characters that he created himself, Whedon has worked for Marvel on *Astonishing X-Men* and *Runaways*. *Astonishing X-Men* (with artist John Cassaday) was a continuation from Grant Morrison and Frank Quitely's *New X-Men* and revolved around the same core cast. Whedon's writing is characterized by its use of humor and pop culture references, and he uses quick-witted and amiable banter as a means of establishing character.

Plot

The story follows Buffy Summers, a young woman gifted with supernatural strength and reflexes, as she and her friends combat the forces of evil one year after the conclusion of the *Buffy the Vampire Slayer* television series.

At the start of the series, Buffy, Xander, Dawn, and several activated vampire slayers are living in Scotland, essentially operating as an organized military unit. Xander coordinates missions that the slayers carry out, some of which Buffy leads herself. Her other friends—Willow, Rupert Giles, and Faith—are scattered around the globe.

The U.S. government, fearing that Buffy and her operation are effectively an organized terrorist cell, look for a way to stop her. The government investigates the ruins of Sunnydale, California, where they discover a former friend and current enemy of Buffy, Amy Madison.

With the help of her boyfriend, Amy plans an attack on Buffy's Scotland fortress. Willow arrives to fight Amy, but she is kidnapped by Warren Mears. The comic reveals that Warren survived his death at Willow's hands in the television series after Amy intervened. Still skinless, he intends to make Willow the same. Buffy tracks them back to the military's headquarters and manages to save Willow just in the nick of time.

The next arc focuses on supporting character Faith, another vampire slayer and a former enemy of Buffy. Faith guards an alternate Hellmouth, an unseen dimensional whirlpool of demonic activity, in Cleveland, Ohio. At the beginning of the story, Giles recruits Faith to assassinate an evil slayer named Lady Genevieve Savidge.

Despite her early objections, Faith eventually relents, knowing that she will do what needs to be done. Giles trains her to be a proper British aristocrat so that she can infiltrate Savidge's world without suspicion. Faith is caught off guard when she begins to develop a friendship with Savidge; she discovers that she likes the luxurious lifestyle to which the spoiled girl is accustomed. When Buffy accidentally intervenes, Faith is exposed. Despite not wanting to murder Savidge, Faith accidentally kills her when she is forced to defend

herself from the younger girl's attack. Faith and Giles develop a partnership of sorts and agree to confront the menaces Buffy refuses to deal with.

Buffy is confronted by the mysterious Twilight, who easily defeats her, displaying advanced strength and the ability to fly with ease. He also hints at somehow knowing her. After Twilight almost kills Buffy's friend Satsu, Buffy returns the girl's unrequited attraction to her. Meanwhile, a rogue group of vampires based in Tokyo steals Buffy's mystical scythe, which activated her army of vampire slayers. Using magic, the gang discovers that they can reverse the process, turning an active slayer back into a normal girl. Noticing that the vampire gang displays powers similar to their old enemy Dracula, Xander recruits the famous vampire to aid Buffy and her friends. Xander's girlfriend is killed in the climax of the battle with the Japanese vampires, and Satsu eventually decides to remain in Tokyo after the gang is defeated, determining that Buffy is not yet ready for a serious relationship.

After the Tokyo debacle, Buffy and Willow head to New York City, following a suggestion from one of Willow's contacts. This contact, a powerful snake demon creature, hints that the source of the scythe's power has been found in Manhattan. As Willow prepares a spell of revelation, a random demon from the future appears. Buffy is propelled forward in time, taking the creature's place.

In the future, Buffy encounters a vampire slayer named Melaka Fray. After initial hostilities, the two slayers work together to find a way to send Buffy home. It is soon revealed that Fray's mortal enemy, her vampire brother Harth, is in league with an ancient madwoman, a future version of Willow who has used magic to stave off her aging. In order to get home, Buffy is forced to kill the future version of Willow, who readily accepts her fate. Meanwhile, back in Scotland, Dawn and Xander fend off an attack sent by Warren and Amy, and their castle headquarters is destroyed as a result.

Several characters are highlighted during the next arc. Harmony Kendall, a vampire and high school classmate of Buffy, makes plans to star in her own reality television series. When she is attacked by an inexperienced slayer on national television, she ruthlessly kills the upstart. Society begins to change, as vampires are revealed to the world at large.

Next, slayers Satsu and Kennedy team up to stop an invasion of "Vampy Cats," demonic stuffed animals. In Italy, Buffy and Andrew join forces to stop a rogue vampire slayer named Simone, who is amassing an army of slayers and is in control of a small coastal community. Likewise, Giles and Faith save a small European village from an evil demon's influence. Finally, Dawn is restored to humanity after being briefly transformed into a living doll by an evil Geppetto-like figure.

Still being hunted by the military and the mysterious Twilight, Buffy decides to pull her forces back to their new mobile base of operations, an abandoned submarine. When Twilight's forces finally track down Buffy and her gang and attack, Willow transports the submarine and everyone in it to Buffy's intended fallback location: Tibet. Hoping to hide their power from Twilight, Buffy calls upon her ally Oz, a werewolf who can control his magical nature, to learn how the group can suppress their mystical energies. Just as the slayers and witches learn to repress their supernatural power, Twilight's forces find them at their weakest and resume their attack. Buffy gains newfound supernatural abilities in the aftermath, and Twilight is eventually revealed to be Buffy's former ally and lover, Angel. Another vampire ally, Spike, arrives and provides Buffy with information about Angel's goal. By the end of the series, Buffy and her friends defeat Angel, who had not acted of his own free will. This battle has the effect of removing all magic from the world.

Volumes
- *The Long Way Home* (2007). Collects issues 1-5, featuring the status of Buffy's army of vampire slayers following the conclusion of the television series.
- *No Future for You* (2008). Collects issues 6-10, focusing on the character of Faith and her collaboration with Buffy's former watcher, Rupert Giles.
- *Wolves at the Gate* (2008). Collects issues 11-15, chronicling the slayer army's trip to Tokyo and the return of Dracula.
- *Time of Your Life* (2009). Collects issues 16-20, featuring the first meeting between Buffy Summers and future slayer Melaka Fray.
- *Predators and Prey* (2009). Collects issues 21-25 and short stories from *MySpace Dark Horse Presents*, issues 18 and 19, featuring specific character vignettes and character collaborations.
- *Retreat* (2010). Collects issues 26-30 and short stories from *MySpace Dark Horse Presents*, issues 24 and 25, chronicling Buffy and her army's retreat to Tibet.
- *Twilight* (2010). Collects issues 31-35, featuring the revelation that Twilight is Angel and Spike's subsequent return.
- *Last Gleaming* (2011). Collects issues 36-40, chronicling the final battle between the slayer army and Twilight's forces of darkness.

Characters
- *Buffy Summers*, the titular vampire slayer, is the uncontested leader of her group of friends. Facing an uncertain future, Buffy is constantly tested by her ambiguous present. She eventually gains Superman-style powers shortly before learning that her nemesis, Twilight, is actually her former boyfriend Angel.
- *Willow Rosenberg* is Buffy's best friend and possibly the most powerful witch in the world. She keeps secrets from her friends, including her relationship with a powerful snake demon. When Buffy travels forward in time, she is forced to kill an evil future version of Willow.
- *Xander Harris* is Buffy and Willow's close friend. When the story begins, he is the only man living with Buffy, Dawn, and the slayers in Scotland. He enters into a relationship with a slayer named Renee, but she is killed shortly after they begin dating. He eventually reciprocates the feelings of Buffy's sister, Dawn.
- *Twilight*, a.k.a. *Angel*, the primary antagonist, is a masked villain who is both directly and indirectly responsible for many of the threats Buffy, Xander, Willow, and their allies face. He confronts Buffy at a graveyard and easily defeats her, hinting that he somehow knows her. He is

finally revealed to be the soul-possessing vampire Angel.

- *Rupert Giles* is a watcher and Buffy's former mentor. Although he is also based in Europe, he has little contact with Buffy, Xander, and the others when the story begins. Once again finding his relationship with Buffy strained, he takes on Faith as a partner. Together, they save the small town of Hanselstadt.
- *Faith* is a vampire slayer and Buffy's former nemesis. She becomes one of Buffy's friends and is initially based at a Hellmouth in Cleveland, Ohio. Giles eventually approaches her with a mission, and the two form a team.
- *Dawn Summers* is Buffy's younger sister. While she does not possess any supernatural powers, she begins the series as a giant. She alludes to losing her virginity to a thricewise, a demon with three eyes and large tentacles, resulting in her transformed state. She metamorphoses into a centaur and a doll before finally returning to normal. She eventually begins dating Xander.
- *Amy Madison* is a witch and former ally of Buffy and her friends. After being trapped as a rat for several years, she has become bitter and vindictive toward Willow in particular. She raises a zombie army to battle Buffy and her slayers in Scotland and is revealed to have saved Warren's life.
- *Warren Mears* is a former antagonist of Buffy's group. Willow apparently kills him when she magically rips his skin off in the television series, but Amy Madison is revealed to have been present for those events and saved his life, although he still has no skin. Using his technological genius, he supports the U.S. military's efforts to stop the slayers.
- *Spike*, a.k.a. *William the Bloody*, is a vampire ally and former lover of Buffy. Arriving with pertinent information relating to the current supernatural crises, he works alongside Buffy and joins her in the final climactic battle against Twilight.
- *Melaka Fray* is a future slayer who fights Buffy in issue 16. She is the protagonist of the comic book *Fray*, a spin-off of the *Buffy* television series.

Artistic Style

The series' primary illustrator was Georges Jeanty, an artist who penciled the majority of the individual issues for *Buffy the Vampire Slayer Season 8*. Jeanty drew the comic characters so that they closely resemble their television counterparts. For example, the comic version of Buffy looks very much like Sarah Michelle Gellar, the actor who portrayed her on television. Many of the scenes Jeanty depicts are action-oriented, with Buffy leaping into a demonic battle or fighting Twilight late at night in a cemetery. Jeanty is skilled at depicting the characters' movements within and between panels, allowing readers to visualize the fight scenes. Large battles, as in the volumes *Retreat* and *Twilight*, can be confusing and chaotic, featuring numerous characters in large-scale, warlike campaigns.

Karl Moline, who previously illustrated Whedon's *Fray* (2001-2003), returns to his futuristic New York-inspired world to introduce Melaka Fray to Buffy Summers in *Time of Your Life*. However, character designs and action sequences follow the format laid out in the issues penciled by Jeanty.

A notable exception to the realistic art included in the series is issue 20, which features "animation" credits for Eric Wight, Ethen Beavers, and Adam Van Wyk. Between the end of the television series and the publication of *Season 8*, Wight was the key artist in an unproduced *Buffy the Animated Series* project. The series, which would have set Buffy back in high school and possibly featured a voice cast of many of the original stars, failed to materialize. In "After These Messages . . . We'll Be Right Back!" Buffy has a dream set in high school, illustrated using the unused cartoon-style character designs from the animated project. The end result has a lighthearted and joyous feel, contrasting with many of the darker elements into which the series later delves. Facial expressions are exaggerated, colors are much brighter, and the final product feels much like the intended cartoon.

Themes

A recurring theme in *Buffy the Vampire Slayer Season 8* is the connection between feminism and power. Buffy is a young woman who possesses supernatural physical strength that makes her much stronger than an average man. She has also shared this power with other young women, forming a small army of vampire slayers. Xander, one of the only characters without any supernatural powers, is also one of the only recurring male characters. Nearly every main character in *Season 8* is female and displays a significant yet different of level of strength and power. This roots the series in a positive feminist portrayal of women.

However, not all of these women use their powers for good, connecting to another of *Season 8*'s major themes, abuse of power. The series examines a few different rogue vampire slayers and Buffy's methods of dealing with them. Because she and Willow are responsible for empowering these women, including Lady Savidge in *No Future for You* and Simone in *Predators and Prey*, Buffy largely feels responsible for their abuse of power.

Willow, a witch and by far the most powerful member of Buffy's group, is also shown abusing her power, as she keeps secrets from her friends. Buffy discovers Willow's involvement with an all-knowing snake demon who advises her on mystical matters. This discovery, as well as Buffy's encounter with a dark future version of Willow in *No Future for You*, causes friction in their friendship. Buffy believes that Willow might once again abuse her power, forcing Buffy to stop her as she did during the television series. While in Tibet, Willow is the most vocal opponent to Buffy's plan to give up their magic, feeling it makes them too vulnerable to a potential attack by their enemies. Willow is proven right when the group is quickly overpowered in Twilight's ensuing attack.

Even Buffy is not always depicted as using her power completely responsibly. At one point, she is shown stealing in order to support her army financially and promptly calling Willow to confess. However, Buffy makes the argument that this immoral action is ultimately for the greater good.

Impact

Buffy the Vampire Slayer Season 8 illustrates that though a television series may end, it can continue to exist as a graphic novel. The series' popularity led *Buffy*'s television spin-off, *Angel*, to also be adapted as an ongoing comic book. Due to the comic book medium, *Season 8* was able to portray the characters in exotic locations, such as Tokyo and Tibet, and depict epic, magical battles for which the original series would not have had the budget. This medium also allowed the series to incorporate plot points such as Dawn's transformation into a giant and Willow's ability to fly without reliance on costly special effects.

Despite being scripted by writers from the television show, many of the story lines have caused controversy, most notably Buffy's sexual experimentation with another woman, the vampire slayer Satsu, in *Wolves at the Gate*. Later in the series, Xander and Dawn begin dating during the *Retreat* arc, another decision that caused controversy among longtime fans of the television series. Early cover image previews revealed Twilight's identity before the story broke in the comics, causing a stir as fans reacted to the revelation.

Despite certain incongruities, *Buffy the Vampire Slayer Season 8* is generally considered to be a legitimate continuation of the television series. In early 2011, it was announced that the story would continue in *Buffy the Vampire Slayer Season 9*, slated to begin later that year.

Ryan P. Donovan

Films

Buffy the Vampire Slayer. Directed by Fran Rubel Kuzui. Twentieth Century Fox, 1992. This film adaptation stars Kristy Swanson as Buffy and Luke Perry as Pike. The film differs from the novel in that, although it uses the same basic formula—a young woman fighting the forces of darkness—the plot is much more general and the tone is more campy than the television series and subsequent graphic novels. Certain narrative elements from the original film were adapted into the television series.

Television Series

Buffy the Vampire Slayer. Written and directed by Joss Whedon. Mutant Enemy, 1997. This television series stars Sarah Michelle Gellar as Buffy Summer, Alyson Hannigan as Willow Rosenberg, and Nicholas Brendon as Xander Harris. The graphic novel series serves as the continuation of this television show. Many elements and characters created during the television series are referenced and expanded upon in the graphic novels. These include the creation of the slayer army and characters such as Faith and Oz.

Further Reading

Hamilton, Laurell K., et al. *Anita Blake, Vampire Hunter: Guilty Pleasures* (2009).

Vaughan, Brian K., and Adrian Alphona. *Runaways* (2003-2007).

Whedon, Joss, and Karl Moline. *Fray* (2001-2003).

Whedon, Joss, Brian Lynch, and Franco Urru. *Angel: After the Fall* (2008-2009).

Bibliography

Allie, Scott, et al. *Buffy the Vampire Slayer, Panel to Panel: The Art of the Comics, the First Seven Seasons*. Milwaukie, Ore. Dark Horse Books, 2007.

"*Buffy the Vampire Slayer Season 8,* Volume 1*: The Long Way Home.*" Review of *Buffy the Vampire Slayer Season 8,* Volume 1*: The Long Way Home. Publishers Weekly* 254, no. 40 (October, 2007): 42-43.

Yeffeth, Clenn. *Seven Seasons of Buffy: Science Fiction and Fantasy Authors Discuss Their Favorite Television Show*. Dallas: BenBella Books, 2003.

See also: *Runaways series; Astonishing X-Men*

C

CAMELOT 3000

Author: Barr, Mike W.

Artist: Brian Bolland (penciller and cover artist); Terry Austin (inker); Dick Giordano (inker); Bruce D. Patterson (inker); Tatjana Wood (colorist); John Costanza (letterer)

Publisher: DC Comics

First serial publication: 1982-1985

First book publication: 1988

Publication History

One of the earliest attempts by DC Comics to sell a book only to the direct market, and thus bypassing the then-traditional newsstand distribution route and selling only directly to comic book stores, *Camelot 3000* was printed on high-quality Baxter paper and was one of the first monthly maxiseries published, a story deliberately planned to run only twelve issues. Writer Mike W. Barr had made a solid name for himself in independent comics, and Brian Bolland had already drawn a number of covers for DC after a successful run in the United Kingdom. Although the series was well received, delays plagued the second half of the run, as Bolland's art grew increasingly meticulous. Delays between issues eventually ran as long as nine months, and the series was eventually released over a twenty-nine-month period. The series regained popularity when DC released a trade paperback collecting the entire run in 1988.

Plot

In the year 3000, Earth has been invaded by lizardlike aliens. While running from the aliens that killed his parents, a young student named Tom Prentice stumbles across King Arthur's tomb (beneath Glastonbury Tor, an ancient monument) and awakens the sleeping king. Arthur promptly kills the two aliens and sets out on a quest to save the world from alien invasion. With Tom as his squire, he heads to Stonehenge to find Merlin,

> ### Mike W. Barr
>
> After breaking into the comics industry as a writer in the mid-1970's, Mike W. Barr became an editor at DC Comics in the 1980's. In 1982 he worked with artist Brian Bolland on one of DC's first projects intended exclusively for the direct market, *Camelot 3000*. This maxiseries, a retelling of the Arthurian legend in science-fiction form, is one of the key titles for which he is remembered. His lengthy run on *Batman and the Outsiders* (1983-1986), with artist Jim Aparo, and the stand-alone graphic novel, *Batman: Son of the Demon* (with Jerry Bingham), are his most noteworthy contributions to the superhero genre. Barr's writing largely sought to expand the typical interests of the superhero story in the 1980's by exploring themes including romance and social exclusion that were not frequently central to the genre.

who in turn guides King Arthur to the sword Excalibur. With Merlin's help, Arthur also finds a handful of his knights, who have been reincarnated, and his long-lost wife, Guinevere.

As the knights begin their quest to defend the world, Arthur's half sister, Morgan Le Fay, reveals herself to be the mastermind behind the alien invasion. Furthermore, she reincarnates Arthur's son and nemesis, Mordred, to help with her schemes. The knights fight numerous battles on Earth, including one at Arthur and Guinevere's wedding, where the queen is shot and nearly killed; however, as a subplot, Arthur and Guinevere find themselves adrift when Guinevere and Lancelot renew their affair. Sir Kay also figures prominently into the story line, adding an element of intrigue when he betrays the group and allows Merlin to be captured. Before he can be executed for his crime, he sacrifices his life to save Arthur from an alien attack.

The attack leaves Tom wounded, and a group of knights, led by Percival (who was reborn into a monstrous, hulking body), begin a quest for the Holy Grail; they lose the Grail to Mordred after healing Tom. The knights eventually end up on the alien world, where the aliens make it clear that they want their subjugation to Morgan to end. In the ensuing battle, Mordred dons a seemingly impenetrable suit of armor made from the Grail. However, Arthur destroys his son by throwing him at the imprisoned Merlin, causing the holiness of the Grail to react to Merlin's satanic heritage and explode. Arthur then channels the magic in Excalibur to create a nuclear explosion, sacrificing himself to save the world as Merlin transports the surviving knights back to Earth. A coda reveals that Guinevere is now pregnant (possibly with Arthur's child) and that Excalibur is now embedded in a stone on an alien world, where a downtrodden creature finds it, thus starting the heroic cycle anew.

Characters
- *Tom Prentice*, the protagonist, is an everyman character. Newly orphaned by the war, he joins Arthur as the king's squire. His lack of familiarity with Arthurian legend provides plenty of opportunities for Barr to retell famous bits of Arthurian mythology, and thus ensuring that the readers are familiar with the material as well.
- *Arthur Pendragon* is the reincarnation of the legendary king of Britain. A classic hero, he is a fearless, well-trained fighter and strategist. His blind spot, as always, is his love for his wife, Guinevere, and his inability to deal with her inevitable adultery.
- *Merlin*, Arthur's wizard and adviser, remains an enigmatic character. Incredibly powerful, he usually prefers to offer guidance than to act directly, but is capable of acts of great power when pushed.
- *Morgan Le Fay*, the primary antagonist, has been alive ever since Arthur's fall and has been planning to invade Earth for years. She is self-serving

and vengeful, bent on hurting those whom she feels have betrayed her.
- *Mordred*, Arthur's illegitimate son, has been reincarnated as a United Nations security director named *Jordan Matthew*. In this life, as in the last one, he seeks revenge against his father for abandoning him to die. As Jordan, he generally avoids confrontation, but as Mordred, he is much more assertive and combative.
- *Guinevere*, Arthur's queen, has been reincarnated as *Joan Acton*, a commander in the United Earth Defense. As Guinevere, she retains her shrewd military mind, but she also finds herself torn between Arthur and Lancelot, as she was in her previous life. She is unable to resist Lancelot, contributing to the undermining of New Camelot.
- *Lancelot du Lac* is the most famous of Arthur's knights, reincarnated as a rich French industrialist named *Jules Futrelle*; his money helps fund New Camelot. He is a heroic figure, but cannot resist his attraction to Queen Guinevere.
- *Sir Tristan* is the reincarnation of one of Arthur's most handsome knights, but he finds himself in the body of *Amber March*. The former lothario is frustrated at finding himself in a woman's body and constantly struggles with what gender roles to accept. Tristan's situation is complicated by the reincarnation of his long-lost love Isolde, who remains female.
- *Sir Gawain* is the only family man among the reincarnated knights and his decision to abandon his wife and son to fight for King Arthur proves to be a frustrating one for the melancholy knight.
- *Sir Kay*, Arthur's foster brother, is a petty criminal and the joker of the group. He sees it as his duty to try to keep the group focused, even if it means committing an act of betrayal.
- *Sir Galahad*, reincarnated as a samurai, embodies the concept of sacrifice of self; he was about to take his life for failing his master when Arthur finds him.

Artistic Style
Bolland's bold style evolves throughout the series. He uses layouts that range from one-page pinups to

chaotic, multipanel designs. He also experiments with border-free panels and other styles, although his attention to facial expressions and anatomy remains consistent. As the series progresses, he adds great levels of detail to the background art (for example, adding intricate control panels to spaceship scenes and leaves to outdoor scenes).

Although *Camelot 3000* is not a superhero comic, the use of bright colors and variants on panel layouts are reminiscent of the typical superhero storytelling style. There are few departures in terms of narrative structure, with standard voice and thought balloons mixing with narrative exposition as needed. Bolland's style suits this storytelling format well, as do Wood's sharp colors. The Baxter paper used for the initial printing highlighted the art much better than the traditional newsstand material.

For his storytelling, Barr often relies on futuristic gimmicks that are simply variants of present-day items (that samurai in the future not only exist but also use laser swords that look just like regular ones is typical of the silliness). However, the heroic style of the story allows for a hefty amount of leeway, as well as for Arthur's blend of Middle English and contemporary twentieth-century English.

Themes

Heroism is a primary theme of *Camelot 3000*. Tom is willing to sacrifice himself to save Arthur, the most basic heroic act. Others, however, take different approaches. Kay believes that betraying Arthur will force the king to look past his personal problems and fight his battles, and Arthur, Guinevere, and Lancelot, despite their eternal love triangle and personal differences, fight side by side. Galahad, reincarnated as a Bushido warrior, fights for honor. Likewise, the villains are evil at a fundamental level, being entirely self-interested and operating only out of greed and revenge. The final scene, in which the heroic cycle begins again on another world, underscores the heroic theme.

Sex and gender also play major roles. Morgan is portrayed as highly sexualized and wears little clothing, while Guinevere, although still often scantily clad, tends to dress much more modestly, and her sex drive serves as a roadblock for the heroes. Tristan is constantly at war with his/her own body and memories, conflicted by the desire to be a strong man and the perception that failure is a result of being reincarnated into the wrong body. When she finally accepts that she is a woman, it is not to give in to Tom's constant seduction attempts, but to be with Isolde; Tristan has finally accepted that her gender matters less than her relationship.

Religion is an impossible-to-avoid theme, although Barr rarely plumbs its depths. However, given the holy nature of the Grail (which Percival finds thanks to prayer) and Merlin's origins as the son of the Devil, it is hard to ignore religion's place in the story. That said, there is never any sense of conflict between Galahad's pure Christianity and his son Percival's beliefs, nor is there any sense that religion can trump science any more than it could be subservient to it.

Barr also throws in a good amount of political satire, though not always successfully, and almost never with any subtlety. The crude parodies of U.S. president Ronald Reagan and Soviet premier Yuri Andropov are dated, and the portrayal of the brutish leader of Africa can be construed as racist, as he barely speaks in complete sentences and is confused by basic technology. Like much science fiction, the future here is clearly meant to be a reflection of the present (as things were in 1982), but the fact that these political story lines undercut the storytelling itself is hard to avoid.

Impact

Camelot 3000 was one of the first maxiseries and helped pave the way for a format that has become standard at both DC and Marvel. It was also one of the first major direct-market projects from a major publisher and laid the groundwork for future titles, including Barr's own *Outsiders* run for DC (which began in 1983). *Camelot 3000* also helped launch Bolland as a superstar illustrator in the United States. His artwork helped him become one of the top cover and pinup artists for a period and led to his work on *Batman: The Killing Joke* (1988).

Although not explicitly marked for mature audiences, it was advertised as such and its publication as a book that did not adhere to the Comics Code Authority and its myriad restrictions was also groundbreaking.

After *Camelot 3000*, books such as *Ronin* (1983), *Watchmen* (1986-1987), and *Batman: The Dark Knight Returns* (1986) all handled mature themes under the DC banner.

Camelot 3000 was also one of the first mainstream books to feature a transgender character in a relationship that did not hew to the heteronormative tradition. Although Tristan did not necessarily open the floodgates for transgender mainstream characters—even after thirty years, there were still only a handful of them—Tristan's romantic involvement with Isolde was groundbreaking and helped pave the way for gradual acceptance of lesbian relationships in mainstream comics, marking another innovative element in an already otherwise landmark series.

Adam Lipkin

Further Reading

Miller, Frank. *Ronin* (1983).

Moore, Alan, and Brian Bolland. *Batman: The Killing Joke* (1988).

Wagner, Matt. *Mage: The Hero Discovered* (1984-1986).

Bibliography

Bolland, Brian. *The Art of Brian Bolland*. Berkeley, Calif.: Image Comics, 2006.

Grace, Dominick. "The Future King: *Camelot 3000*." *The Journal of Popular Culture* 41, no. 1 (February, 2008): 21-36.

Larrington, Carolyne. *King Arthur's Enchantresses: Morgan and Her Sisters in Arthurian Tradition*. London: I. B. Tauris, 2006.

Salisbury, Mark. *Artists on Comic Art*. London: Titan Books, 2002.

See also: *Ronin; Watchmen; Batman: The Killing Joke*

CEREBUS

Author: Sim, Dave
Artist: Dave Sim (illustrator); Gerhard (backgrounds)
Publisher: Aardvark-Vanaheim
First serial publication: 1977-2004
First book publication: 1986-2004

Publication History

Originally self-published as a black-and-white comic book by Dave Sim and his wife, Deni Loubert, *Cerebus* was later published by Aardvark-Vanaheim. Because *Cerebus* tells a single story in three hundred chapters, Sim realized relatively early that it would become increasingly difficult for new readers to begin reading the title after having missed the earliest issues. To redress this problem, he published short collections of four issues under the title *Swords of Cerebus* in 1981. Recognizing that this would not provide a long-term solution, in 1986, he began publishing collections of older material in thick books, nicknamed "phone books" because of their bulk and low-quality paper. The sixteen volumes collecting the series have remained in print. The success of the "phone books" in the late 1980's helped lead American comic book publishers to consider the graphic novel a serious publishing genre. Sim himself was a strong proponent of the graphic novel and, particularly, of long-form comics. He was also the leading proponent of comic book self-publishing, which he championed in numerous editorials and interviews, with *Cerebus* serving as the prime example of a successful self-published product.

Plot

Created by Sim in 1977 as a parody of the then-popular sword and sorcery genre, *Cerebus* eventually grew into one of the most significant graphic novel experiments in the history of the field. Published as a series of twenty-page monthly comics over the course of twenty-eight years, *Cerebus* tells the life story of an anthropomorphic aardvark in a society populated by ordinary people. Over the course of six thousand pages, Cerebus takes on many roles, from mercenary to politician, pope, bartender, traveler, and holy figure.

Cerebus. (Courtesy of Aardvark-Vanheim)

Cerebus's fictional world is immense and incredibly detailed.

In the earliest of Cerebus's adventures he is portrayed as an amoral barbarian and a mercenary. These fantasy stories parodied the popular *Conan the Barbarian* comics by crossing them with the absurdist humor of Steve Gerber's *Howard the Duck* (which started in the 1970's). The tone of Cerebus changed dramatically with Sim's first extended story, *High Society*. In this volume , Cerebus travels to the city-state of Iest, where he is drawn into the world of high finance. Caught in a tug-of-war between Lord Julius and Astoria, Cerebus is elected prime minister of Iest but is unable to keep Iest financially solvent. A series of military miscalculations lead to his downfall, and Cerebus returns briefly to life as an adventurer.

In the two volumes of *Church and State*, Cerebus returns to Iest after a brief period in exile. Weisshaupt, the president of a newly created federation of states opposing the matriarchal Cirinists, schemes to have the popular former politician named as pope of the Eastern Church of Tarim. Unlimited religious power goes immediately to Cerebus's head, and he becomes despotic. He threatens his followers with the end of the world unless they deliver to him all of their gold. After battling with a giant stone monster named Thrunk, Cerebus learns that his former political adviser, Astoria, has assassinated the Western pope. Confronting her in a dungeon, Cerebus marries, then rapes, her, and then dissolves the marriage. Following this, Cerebus ascends to the moon, where he meets a character named The Judge, who recounts the creation myth to Cerebus and warns him that he will shortly die "alone, unmourned and unloved." When Cerebus returns to Earth, he discovers that the Cirinists have invaded Iest and destroyed his empire in his absence.

Now living under a Cirinist dictatorship, Cerebus is wanted by the authorities. He lives with Jaka, a dancer with whom he had fallen in love during his days as a mercenary, and her husband, Rick. The story of Jaka's childhood is recounted by a character named Oscar and is written in a style approximating that of Irish writer Oscar Wilde. With Cerebus away, Jaka, Rick, and Oscar are arrested by the Cirinists. Rick leaves Jaka when he is told the truth about her past, including her decision to have an abortion. When Cerebus returns to their home, he assumes Jaka to be dead and enters a state of near-catatonic mourning, and the death of Oscar is recounted.

The four-part "Mothers and Daughters" story line focuses on Cerebus's battle with Cirin and her forces. After learning that Jaka is alive, Cerebus returns to Iest and slaughters a number of Cirinist soldiers, leading briefly to a failed revolution. Cerebus ascends into darkness for a second time and meets the philosopher Suenteus Po. When Cerebus returns to Earth, he is assisted by a woman who is under the surveillance of the Cirinists (later revealed to be the real Cirin, with an impostor having deposed her). Cerebus, Cirin, Astoria, and Suenteus Po are brought together and engage in a philosophical discussion about the nature of power. Ultimately, Cerebus and Cirin engage in a drawn-out sword fight, but the fight ends when both begin a new ascension. Now separated from Cirin, Cerebus is given

a tour of the solar system, where he is shown images from his past. Dave, identified as Cerebus's creator, lectures Cerebus on the origins of Cirinism and of Cerebus's personal failings. After realizing that Jaka can never truly love him, Cerebus asks to be returned to a bar that he remembers from his mercenary past.

Cerebus tends bar in a pub for degenerate men beside the Wall of T'si. During this portion of the story, a series of characters are introduced, each of whom is parodic of a figure in the comic book industry. Cerebus begins a relationship with a woman named Joanne, who eventually leaves him for Rick. When Jaka's former husband arrives at Cerebus's bar, he is heavily scarred from the events at the end of *Jaka's Story* and mentally unbalanced because of alcoholism. Rick begins writing a book about Cerebus as a holy figure. When the romantic triangle involving Cerebus, Joanne, and Rick reaches a critical phase, Rick departs. Jaka arrives at the bar, and she and Cerebus decide to travel to his childhood home in Sand Hills Creek.

Cerebus and Jaka travel by riverboat, under the constant watch of the Cirinists. While on the journey, they are accompanied by F. Stop Kennedy, a fictional version of F. Scott Fitzgerald, a writer who, though married, flirts with Jaka. Later, Cerebus and Jaka continue their journey in the company of Ham and Mary Ernestway, fictional versions of Ernest and Mary Hemingway. When Ham kills himself, Cerebus believes him to have been murdered by Mary, and he flees. When he and Jaka arrive at his childhood home, they find that his parents are dead and that his community has shunned him. Cerebus blames Jaka and drives her away.

Years later, Cerebus is abducted by three men modeled on the Three Stooges. In his absence, a religious movement based on the teachings of Rick has been born. When Cerebus provides a revelation, an anti-Cirinist rebellion takes place. Nearing the end of his life, Cerebus falls in love with a woman who looks exactly like Jaka, and he marries her. The two have a son, Sheshep Ankh, nicknamed Shep-Shep.

Cerebus concludes with the depiction of the final day in the life of its protagonist. Now enfeebled and senile, Cerebus has a theological dream that he endeavors to transcribe. He meets with Shep-Shep, who has sided against Cerebus and with his mother in establishing a "feminist-homosexualist" world promoting pedophilia, zoophilia, and lesbian motherhood. When Cerebus tries to kill his son, he falls out of bed and breaks his neck, dying alone, unloved, and unmourned. As Cerebus enters "the light" he worries that he may not be going to Heaven but to Hell.

Volumes

- *High Society* (1986). Collects issues 26-50, featuring Cerebus's political campaign and life in office.
- *Cerebus* (1987). Collects issues 1-25, featuring Cerebus's adventures as a barbarian.
- *Church and State I* (1987). Collects issues 52-80, in which Cerebus becomes pope of the Eastern Church and is corrupted by power.
- *Church and State II* (1988). Collects issues 81-111. The two volumes of *Church and State* recount Cerebus's life as pope and ascension to the moon.
- *Jaka's Story* (1990). Collects issues 114-138. This volume introduces long text pieces into the story for the first time. This prose, written in the style of Oscar Wilde, recounts the story of Jaka's youth.
- *Melmoth* (1991). Collects issues 139-150. Tells the story of the death of Oscar Wilde.
- *Flight* (1993). Collects issues 151-162. First chapter of the four-part "Mothers and Daughters" story line.
- *Women* (1994). Collects issues 163-174. Includes excerpts from books written by Astoria and Cirin, pertaining to their differing philosophical systems.
- *Reads* (1995). Collects issues 175-186. Includes a series of controversial essays by Viktor Davis outlining Sim's theory on the nature of gender relationships, the "Male Light" and the "Female Void."
- *Minds* (1996). Collects issues 187-200. Conclusion to the "Mothers and Daughters" story line.
- *Guys* (1997). Collects issues 201-219. Contains a wide array of parodies of comic book industry figures.

- *Rick's Story* (1998). Collects issues 220-231. This volume contains the first significant discussion of the Bible in Cerebus, written in a highly parodic form as the Book of Rick.
- *Going Home* (2000). Collects issues 232-250. Features the appearance of F. Stop Kennedy, a character based on F. Scott Fitzgerald.
- *Form and Void* (2001). Collects issues 251-265. Features characters named Ham and Mary Ernestway, based on Ernest and Mary Hemingway.
- *Latter Days* (2003). Collects issues 266-288. Contains a lengthy examination of the Torah from the point of view of the characters in the book.
- *The Last Day* (2004). Collects issues 289-300. Details the final day in the life of Cerebus.

Characters

- *Cerebus*, the protagonist, is a three-foot-tall anthropomorphic aardvark with gray fur and a long nose. He is one of only three aardvarks in the fictional world of the story. He is nearly sociopathically self-interested and pursues his own goals to the exclusion of any sustaining interest in the lives of other people. He is deeply in love with Jaka but is unable to sustain that relationship because of his selfishness. Late in the series, it is revealed that Cerebus is a hermaphrodite.
- *Jaka Tavers* is Cerebus's primary love interest. Tall, thin, and blond, she was raised in a family of great wealth and privilege but met Cerebus when she was dancing in a tavern. She loves Cerebus but, after being spurned by him, marries Rick. The story of her youth is recounted in the text sections of *Jaka's Story*.
- *Astoria* is Cerebus's political adviser and the chief philosophical opponent of Cirin. She is the founder of the Kevillist movement. She is the former wife of Lord Julius and the Duchess of Parmoc. When she assassinates the Western pope, Cerebus marries and rapes her, then divorces her. She is a tall, thin brunet drawn to resemble the actress Mary Astor.
- *Cirin* is another of the three aardvarks in Estarcion, although she is much taller than Cerebus.

She is the leader of the Cirinists, a group of soldiers who impose matriarchal martial law across the lands depicted in the series. She is the author of numerous philosophically feminist works and is an opponent of Astoria. She was originally known as Serna, but she adopted the persona of Cirin in order to seize power.

- *Lord Julius* is Grandlord of Palnu. His character is based on Groucho Marx, whom he resembles exactly. He rose to a position of power by using double-talk to confuse his enemies and a system of open bribery. He is the former husband of Astoria and the uncle of Jaka. He is a major rival of Cerebus during *High Society*. There are many other characters who look exactly like Lord Julius, and these are termed Like-a-looks.

- *Rick Nash* is Jaka's husband during *Jaka's Story* but later divorces her. He is a tall, thin man with blond hair and a goatee, affable but not really very bright. When he reencounters Cerebus late in the narrative, he begins to write a book, the Book of Rick, in which he posits Cerebus as a prophet. This book later becomes the basis of a religious movement.

- *Oscar* is a fictionalized version of Oscar Wilde and is drawn to resemble a cartoonish version of the Irish author. In Cerebus's world, Oscar is the author of *Daughter of Palnu*, a biography of the young Jaka Tavers that is popular with the upper class. He is imprisoned by the Cirinists at the end of *Jaka's Story*. *Melmoth* tells the story of his death.

- *The Judge* is an overweight, balding man with a mustache who wears black robes and lives on the moon. When Cerebus ascends to the moon, The Judge recounts the origin myth to him and reveals to Cerebus the circumstances of his own death. Cirin states that The Judge is actually the god Tarim, a philosopher-king as hermit.

- *The Roach* is a character who takes on numerous personae over the course of the book, many of which are parodies of popular superhero characters. The Roach is a mentally unbalanced character who is manipulated by various other characters in the books. Among the personas adopted

by The Roach are Captain Cockroach, Moon Roach, Wolveroach, Punisheroach, Loboroach, Swoon, and Fanroach.

- *Viktor Davis* is a pseudonym for Sim, whose first and middle names are David Victor, within the fictional world of Cerebus. The character is depicted only in silhouette, and during the course of the story he speaks to Cerebus, and directly to the reader, in text pieces. The character gives voice to much of the misogynistic philosophy about the opposition between the "male light" and the "female void" outlined by Sim in the *Cerebus* series and elsewhere.

Artistic Style

The earliest issues of *Cerebus* were entirely written and drawn by Sim and are visually unsophisticated. Sim's artwork changed dramatically over the course of the three hundred issues, and the way that he draws Cerebus changed accordingly. Sim's art mixes an extremely cartoony depiction of Cerebus akin to the anthropomorphic characters found in Disney and Warner Bros. animations, with increasingly realistic human supporting figures. Beginning with issue 65 (August, 1984), Sim collaborated with an assistant named Gerhard who was responsible for the elaborately detailed background illustrations in the comic; Sim continued to draw the characters. Gerhard's contribution freed Sim to become more expressive with his figure drawing and added a high level of pictorial realism to the design of places and sets in the fictional world of the comic. Sim frequently experimented with unusual page designs, including the addition of extremely ornate panel borders to many of his pages. His work shows a greater attention to the presence of negative space than does the work of most of his contemporaries, and the overall feel of *Cerebus* is of a series with a keen sense of visual design.

More than almost any other cartoonist, Sim incorporated lengthy text pieces into his work. Beginning with *Jaka's Story*, Sim told a significant part of the story through illustrated prose intended to recall the writing style of Wilde. In later volumes, Sim would incorporate travel diaries, letters, philosophical statements, religious exegeses, and essays written in his own voice as elements of the *Cerebus* narrative. To this end, *Cerebus* is one of the most text-intensive graphic novels ever published.

Themes

The major theme of *Cerebus* is power. In the first half of the epic narrative Cerebus is constantly seeking power. Initially, in his adventures as a barbarian, this is physical power, as he seeks riches and glory through physical exploits. In *High Society* he seeks political power, realizing that this is superior to sheer brutish strength. In *Church and State* he seeks religious/spiritual power and is ultimately corrupted by it, becoming despotic. In the second half of the narrative, Cerebus spends much of his time combating the tyrannical power of the Cirinists and learning to live a simpler life devoid of power.

Cerebus's opponents through most of the story are matriarchal feminists known as Cirinists, modeled on real female figures as diverse as Margaret Thatcher and Oprah Winfrey. Gender relations are introduced as an important theme in *Cerebus* with the appearance of Astoria in *High Society*, but they come to dominate the

second half of the book from *Flight* onward. Issue 186 (collected in *Reads*) contains a long prose essay describing Sim's "antifeminism" that has been widely decried for its deep-rooted misogyny. One important theme of *Cerebus* is the destructive power of women in contemporary society.

Much of *Cerebus*, and particularly the final third, is concerned with spiritual themes. The two volumes of *Church and State* can be read as a satire of the power and excesses of the Catholic Church. The final two volumes of *Cerebus*, in which Cerebus himself becomes a holy figure to the cult that has sprung up around the teachings of Rick, offer lengthily detailed analyses of scripture. These have been read as an elaboration of Sim's personal theology, which draws equally on Jewish, Christian, and Islamic beliefs.

Impact

In its earliest years, represented by the first collection, *Cerebus* was primarily a vehicle for parodies of other comic books and fantasy novels. While the targets changed over time, *Cerebus* remained an important and widely celebrated source of comic book parody, particularly through the character of Artemis, who adopted numerous personas related to comic book superheroes, including send-ups of Marvel's Moon Knight and Wolverine, the Frank Miller version of DC's Batman, Neil Gaiman's Sandman, and Todd McFarlane's Spawn.

More than many graphic novels, *Cerebus* is read by its adherents and detractors as the reflection of the personal psychology of its creator. Over the course of more than a quarter century, the work shifted tone dramatically from a lighthearted parody to a highly idiosyncratic reflection on the act of creation. Once widely regarded as among the most important of graphic novels, the work and its reputation faded considerably in the light of the political statements made by its author.

Bart Beaty

Dave Sim

One of the most outspoken and controversial figures in comics, Dave Sim rose to fame by producing the six-thousand-page *Cerebus* epic at a pace of twenty pages per month for almost a quarter-century. Sim became the spokesman for a generation of self-publishing cartoonists through the editorials and essays that he published in his comic book, and the long-term success of the title became his calling card. Moreover, over the course of his endeavor he became one of the most distinctive stylists in the comics form. His blend of cartoony anthropomorphism and carefully composed pages, buttressed by superbly detailed background work by Gerhard, made him one of the liveliest of cartoonists and the producer of comics in which every detail counted, even down to the lettering. Sim alienated many readers with his pronouncements on gender and religion late in the series, but is widely regarded as a superlative comics stylist.

Further Reading

Gerber, Steve, et al. *Howard the Duck* (1973-1978).
Hernandez, Gilbert, Jaime Hernandez, and Mario Hernandez. *Love and Rockets* (1982-1996).

Laird, Peter, and Kevin Eastman. *Teenage Mutant Ninja Turtles* (1984-1993).
Smith, Jeff. *Bone* (1991-2004).

Bibliography
Beaty, Bart. "My Life with *Cerebus*: An Autobiography in 6000 Words." *The Comics Journal* 263 (October/November, 2004): 110-117.
Blackmore, Tim. "*Cerebus*: From Aardvark to Vanaheim, Reaching for Creative Heaven in Dave Sim's Hellish World." *Canadian Children's Literature* 71 (1993): 57-78.
Rothenberg, Kelly. "*Cerebus*: An Aardvark on the Edge (A Brief History of Dave Sim and His Independent Comic Book)." *Americana: The Journal of American Popular Culture 1900 to Present* 2, no. 1 (Spring, 2003).

See also: *Bone; Conan; Wolverine; Spawn*

CONAN

Author: Busiek, Kurt; Mignola, Mike; Nicieza, Fabian; Truman, Benjamin; Truman, Timothy

Artist: Tomás Giorello (illustrator); M. W. Kaluta (illustrator); Rafael Kayanan (illustrator); Joe Kubert (illustrator); Paul Lee (illustrator); Tom Mandrake (illustrator); Cary Nord (illustrator); Eric Powell (illustrator); Greg Ruth (illustrator); Timothy Truman (illustrator); Thomas Yeates (illustrator); John Severin (penciller); Bruce Timm (penciller); Richard Corben (penciller and inker); JD Mettler (colorist); Tony Shasteen (colorist); José Villarrubia (colorist); Richard Isanove (colorist and cover artist); Dave Stewart (colorist and cover artist); Albert Deschesne (letterer); Richard Starkings (letterer); J. Scott Campbell (cover artist); Frank Cho (cover artist); Geof Darrow (cover artist); Tony Harris (cover artist); José Ladrönn (cover artist); Joseph Michael Linsner (cover artist); Mike Mignola (cover artist); Justin Sweet (cover artist); Leinil Francis Yu (cover artist)

Publisher: Dark Horse Comics

First serial publication: *Conan* (2003-2008); *Conan the Cimmerian* (2008-2010)

First book publication: 2005-2011

Publication History

The works of pulp writer Robert E. Howard have received considerable treatment since his untimely death in 1936, notably since Lancer Books reprinted the *Conan* prose series in 1966, which was followed by adaptation of the work in comic books, cinema, painting, sculpture, video games, and audio books, among other media. While Howard created a number of iconic figures, including Kull of Atlantis and Puritan swordsman Solomon Kane, none has reached the pinnacle of fame as Conan the Barbarian has. Beginning in 1970, Marvel Comics adapted Conan into a long-running series, *Conan the Barbarian* (1970-1994), and featured him in *Savage Tales* (1971-1975), the mature-content magazine *Savage Sword of Conan* (1974-1995), *King Conan/Conan the King* (1980-1989), and numerous graphic novels, miniseries, and one-shots. For

---

Cary Nord

After breaking into comics in the late-1990's with a series of work at Marvel, Cary Nord created an acclaimed run on *Daredevil* with writer Karl Kessel. In the 2000's he became synonymous with the visual style of the relaunched *Conan* comics from Dark Horse, working with writers Kurt Busiek and Tim Truman. Nord's work on *Conan* has been widely praised for its ability to reinvent a character that had been previously so closely associated with the 1970's visual stylings of Frank Frazetta and Barry Winsor-Smith. Nord's elaborate illustrations emphasize the fantastic element of the stories by crossing elaborately detailed settings and costumes with action sequences that feature controlled chaos and strikingly delineated characters.

---

a nonsuperhero title, *Conan the Barbarian* became a signature series for Marvel Comics, written for a major portion of its run by Roy Thomas. Thomas, and other writers on the series, drew from Howard's stories about Conan and reworked stories about other Howard characters as well as creating their own original tales. This became a source of constant debate among Conan fans and scholars not only while the comics were in publication but also long after Marvel Comics had ceased printing all *Conan* titles.

Dark Horse Comics' involvement, beginning with its adaptation in 2003, was grounded in the desire to create a *Conan* series that used only material by Howard and to arrange the stories in chronological order according to Conan's life, which is not how Howard originally published them. Dark Horse hired Kurt Busiek, who had worked on a variety of comic titles (including his own successful *Astro City*, 1995-2011), to essentially adapt Howard's works and stay "true" to Howard's spirit. With Cary Nord and Dave Stewart, he set about this goal. Fans and scholars of Howard and *Conan* debated the success of the team's objective, as the group had to create interstitial tales to bridge the Howard stories and provide narrative continuity.

After Busiek's departure a little more than halfway through the fifty-issue run, made necessary by an exclusivity contract he signed with DC Comics, Mike Mignola wrote a short story arc before Timothy Truman became the full-time writer. Truman finished the remainder of the *Conan* series, chronicling the origin and early years of Conan's life, at which point the series continued in a new title, *Conan the Cimmerian*, documenting the adventures of Conan in midlife. Artist Tomás Giorello, arriving near the end of the *Conan* run, replaced Nord, while colorist José Villarrubia replaced Stewart. Completing this phase of Conan's stories, the creative team on *Conan the Cimmerian* was to return for the third and final installment of Conan and his reign as king of Aquilonia.

Plot

In a specially numbered zero issue, subtitled *Conan the Legend*, readers of Conan, both in prose and in comics, were introduced to the character through a framing technique. Long after the cataclysm that befell Conan's Hyborian Age, but still far before contemporary society, a young prince is surveying newly conquered lands for his father when his retinue discovers a chamber containing a statue of Conan. Intrigued by the Cimmerian's visage, the prince demands to know more about Conan and instructs his wazir (minister) to consult the records for tales of Conan. The wazir is actually the evil sorcerer Thoth-Amon, who appeared in the first Conan story, "The Phoenix on the Sword," and is a longtime foe of Conan. As the various tales unfold over the *Conan* series, the prince and wazir occasionally reappear to provide some context for the stories and make them seem as if they are actually records of a lost age of humanity, as Howard himself had envisioned.

Starting with events that would lead into "The Frost-Giant's Daughter," Conan is introduced in the cold environs of the north, involved in a battle between the Vanir and Aesir people. Falling in with the Aesir while rescuing one of their women, Conan explains that his presence away from his homeland is borne of his desire to travel and see the world, an unusual trait for a Cimmerian, but one likely inherited from his wandering grandfather. Following another battle with the Vanir, Conan pursues a mysterious woman named Atali across the frozen wasteland, besting her "frost giant" brothers before she magically escapes with the help of her father, the god Ymir. Conan's prowess often helps him through many conflicts where he was seemingly outmatched by more physically powerful or magically enabled enemies.

Eventually Conan is betrayed by some jealous Aesir and enslaved by Hyperboreans, who bring him to their city to fight as a gladiator. Their civilization has fallen into decay through an overreliance on magic. The Hyperboreans are bored and ritualistically kill themselves and all their servants on what is known as a Day of Farewell, by jumping into a seemingly bottomless pit. Conan attempts to organize a slave revolt but is stopped; he flees by climbing down the cliffs, escaping to human civilization and murdering the men who sold him into slavery.

Next, Conan travels farther south, going through the Border Kingdoms to Nemedia, where he becomes a thief and is entangled in a conflict between Kalanthes, priest of Ibis, and Thoth-Amon, who worships the dark god Set. Conan then joins forces with the warrior woman Janissa, who serves a mystical witch known as the Bone Woman, to protect Kalanthes.

Parting ways with Janissa, Conan journeys through Corinthia to Zamora and the City of Thieves to continue his career as a thief, encountering strange magic along the way, before trying to assault the Tower of the Elephant with the "prince of thieves," Taurus of Nemedia. Inside the tower, Conan discovers mechanical and magical traps protecting Yogah of Yag, an elephant-headed, otherworldly alien enslaved by the sorcerer Yara. Rejecting Yogah's plea for a mercy killing, Conan frees the poor creature from his torture and then watches briefly as Yogah takes revenge on Yara. Conan barely escapes the tower as it collapses around him.

Conan returns to a life of spending his stolen money in taverns, on ale and on wenches, and his exploits rile the other thieves. He joins up with Nestor, who is captured, at which point Nestor bargains his freedom in exchange for delivering Conan to the authorities. Unbeknownst to Nestor, he has spells placed upon him to ensure his success in life or in death. Nestor pursues

Conan to a ruined city, where Conan is attempting to steal an ancient treasure guarded by a giant amphibian. Following that encounter, Conan and Nestor join forces against reanimated corpses, as they steal treasure and flee the city; Conan thinks Nestor has been killed, as the city consumes itself and disappears. Nestor follows Conan west, and they again join forces to defeat a group of worshipers of Grak'ka, the son of Bel, god of thieves.

Putting aside their differences, Conan and Nestor adventure together. Nestor seems to have forgotten his quest to capture Conan until a wizard informs Nestor of the curse placed upon him should he fail to live up to the bargain. Nestor is subsequently captured and hanged, prompting Conan to take revenge on the priests of Anu for Nestor's death, after which Conan is captured and imprisoned. Prince Murilo offers the chance for freedom in exchange for killing the Red Priest Nabonidus, religious councilor to the king of Zamora. Conan's assault on Nabonidus is disrupted because Thak, a subhuman apelike servant of Nabonidus, has taken over the priest's house. Conan and Nabonidus, along with Murilo, must work together to defeat Thak. Conan is then able to kill the treacherous Nabonidus.

Fleeing to the city of Yaralet, Conan becomes involved in a plot by the wizard Atalis to possess the body of Prince Than. Deriving his power from the dark god Nergal, Atalis feeds the god's earthly scion, Ela D'snal, a steady diet of corpses. One of these is the body of Nestor, who is reanimated by the curse that had been placed on him. Conan rescues the Princess Ereshka, who informs Than of Atalis's treachery, but Atalis still manages to kill Than and possess him; this possession is short-lived, as Conan intercedes to destroy Atalis. Finally, Conan is confronted by Nestor's corpse, and Conan defeats him, laying his soul to rest.

The next cycle of stories in Conan's life begins in *Conan the Cimmerian*, in which Conan, sickened by what he sees as the corruption of civilization and haunted by the death of Nestor, returns to Cimmeria. Conan encounters a strange hermit, who is actually a werewolf and who tells Conan a story about Connacht, Conan's grandfather. Conan continues on and encounters Caollan, his first love, as she is being pursued by the Aesir. Conan helps Caollan flee the Aesir and the

demonic Skrae, summoned by an Aesirean witch. Rescued by the werewolf and his wolf brothers, Conan escorts Caollan home, learning that she is pregnant with the child of Brecan, a northern Cimmerian war chief, who had intended on using her to pay a blood debt to the Aesir. Conan's reunification with his mother is cut short as Brecan murders Caollan, prompting Conan to kill Brecan, which restores the truce between the Aesir and the Cimmerians. Motivated once more by wanderlust, Conan bids farewell to his mother and rides away.

Heading back to Corinthia, Conan finds the country at war with Khoraja, and he enlists in the mercenary army of Khoraja under the command of Amalric the Lion. Being promoted through the ranks, Conan is noticed by both the men and Princess Yasmela, who is being stalked by the mysterious magician Natohk, really a centuries-old magus awoken by the thief Shevatas. Prompted by the god Mitra, Yasmela makes Conan the commander of her armies, and a brutal war is waged with enormous casualties. Eventually, Conan defeats Natohk, much to the chagrin of Thoth-Amon, who had been secretly watching the entire conflict.

Yasmela, initially smitten with Conan, finds herself losing interest in him, as Conan himself begins to chafe at a courtly life. Replaced romantically, Conan decides to rescue Khossus, the king of Khoraja, angering Yasmela, who replaces Conan with her lover, Prince Julion. Conan invites the mercenary army to leave with him and travel the world as a roving band of plunderers; thus, he sets off with five thousand men under his command. Their prowess in battle and success at looting leads them to be hunted down by Shah Amurath, who is protecting the interests of the kingdom of Turan. Only Conan survives an ambush at the Ilbars River; he stays alive in the swampland until he encounters Amurath pursuing Olivia, an Ophirean princess and his former slave. Conan splits Amurath in two and takes Olivia with him.

Still hunted by Turanian soldiers, Conan and Olivia are chased to the Vilayet Sea, disappearing into the isles there. Arriving on a seemingly deserted island, Olivia is haunted by dreams about the lifelike statues spread among some ancient ruins. Conan meanwhile is more concerned with the arrival of a group of pirates and also has to contend with a giant ape-man stalking the jungle. The statues awaken at night and massacre most of the pirates, giving Conan time to commandeer their ship. Conan is acknowledged as the ship's new captain and sails away with Olivia to more adventure.

Volumes

- *Conan,* Volume 1*: The Frost-Giant's Daughter, and Other Stories* (2005). Collects *Conan*, issues 0-6 and part of issue 7. Beginning with an adaptation of Howard's story "The Frost-Giant's Daughter," this volume moves forward in chronological order, relating Conan's earliest adventures, including a journey to the decaying realm of Hyperborea.
- *Conan,* Volume 2*: The God in the Bowl, and Other Stories* (2005). Collects part of *Conan*, issues 7 and 9-14. Features the adaptation of Howard's "God in the Bowl," with a more thoughtful and less impulsive Conan, and, in an original story, introduces the controversial character Janissa the Widowmaker.
- *Conan,* Volume 3*: The Tower of the Elephant, and Other Stories* (2006). Collects part of *Conan*, issue 0, as well as issues 16-17 and 19-22. Features the adaptation of Howard's "The Tower of the Elephant" in the City of Thieves, as a young Conan dares to invade a sorcerer's tower and discovers a treasure different from the gold and jewels he sought.
- *Conan,* Volume 4*: The Hall of the Dead, and Other Stories* (2006). Collects part of *Conan*, issue 0, as well as issues 24, 25, 29-31, 33, and 34. Concludes Busiek's run on the *Conan* series. Mignola takes over by adapting the two-page outline Howard left for "The Hall of the Dead." The fragment showcases Conan in a strange situation involving a frog god and cursed treasure in a ghostly city. Truman follows Mignola's story with an interstitial tale involving Conan on the run but moving toward the direction of Tarantia and the next major Howard tale.
- *Conan: The Blood-Stained Crown, and Other Stories* (2008). Collects *Conan*, issues 18, 26-28, and 39. This collection of stories, all originally written by Busiek, rounds out Conan as a

character. For example, it explains the origins of his iconic horned helmet and shows a bit of Conan's gigantic mirth as well as offering a few stories that are commentaries on the nature of storytelling itself.

- *Conan: Born on the Battlefield* (2008). Collects *Conan*, issues 0, 8, 15, 23, 32, 45, and 46. Provides the story of Conan's early childhood, from his birth on a battlefield to learning to hunt, to love, and, to fight, the latter of which occurs at the Battle of Venarium.
- *Conan,* Volume 5*: Rogues in the House, and Other Stories* (2008). Collects part of *Conan*, issue 0, as well as issues 37, 38, and 41-44. Features the adaptation of Howard's Edgar Allan Poe-like "Rogues in the House," wherein Conan must survive a priest's house of antitheft contraptions and a rebellious simian servant.
- *Conan,* Volume 6*: The Hand of Nergal* (2008). Collects *Conan*, issues 0 and 47-50. Features the adaptation of Howard's "The Hand of Nergal," including an original prelude, begun by him but finished after his death by Lin Carter. Conan must confront the necromancer Atalis to free the city of Yaralet.
- *Conan,* Volume 7*: Cimmeria* (2009). Collects *Conan the Cimmerian*, issues 0-7. Following his adventures in other lands, Conan returns to Cimmeria, weary of the machinations of civilization. The story interweaves flashbacks of Conan's grandfather, Connacht, as Conan reunites with his first love, Caollan.
- *Conan,* Volume 8*: Black Colossus* (2010). Collects *Conan the Cimmerian*, issues 8-13. Features the adaptation of Howard's "Black Colossus," as Conan must confront the seemingly unstoppable wizard Natohk in defense of Princess Yasmela and her kingdom of Khoraja.
- *Conan,* Volume 9*: Free Companions* (2010). Collects *Conan the Cimmerian*, issues 14 and 16-21. Courtly intrigue prompts Conan to choose life back on the road as leader of a large army of mercenary swordsmen; eventually, their fame becomes their downfall, and Conan must avenge his murdered compatriots.

- *Conan: The Spear, and Other Stories* (2010). Collects *Conan*, issues 35, 36, and 40; *Conan the Cimmerian*, issue 15; and the *Conan: Free Comic Book Day 2006* special issue. This collection of stories, all originally written by Truman, includes assorted vignettes from Conan's reign as king of Aquilonia. Conan must variously contend with a variety of magicians and the vampiric queen Akivasha.
- *Conan,* Volume 10: *Iron Shadows in the Moon* (2011). Collects *Conan the Cimmerian*, issues 22-25, as well as the *Weight of the Crown* one-shot and its prologue from *MySpace Dark Horse Presents*. Features the adaptation of Howard's "Iron Shadows in the Moon" and the conclusion of the *Conan the Cimmerian* series. Hunted by soldiers from Turan, Conan flees to the Vilayet Sea and seeks refuge on an island only to be trapped among the pirates of the Red Brotherhood, foreboding statues waiting within haunted ruins, and an ape stalking him through the jungle.

Characters
- *Conan*, born on a Cimmerian battlefield, became a thief and a slayer before becoming a king by his own hand. Distrustful of magic and wary of the rules of "civilized" men, Conan becomes one of the greatest warriors of the Hyborian Age through his prowess, iron will, and quick wits.
- *Nestor*, a mercenary from Gunderland, began as Conan's rival, hunted him as an enemy, and eventually became a compatriot. After many adventures, Nestor is captured and is tortured to death instead of betraying Conan. His reanimated corpse had been cursed with a spell that compels him to try to kill Conan.
- *Thoth-Amon* is a major Stygian wizard who serves the serpent god Set. He fights with Conan repeatedly over their lives, and despite being armed with the Serpent Ring of Set, he is usually defeated or at least partially thwarted in his evil plans.
- *Atali*, the beautiful daughter of the frost giant god Ymir, lures wounded warriors away from battle

and into the arms of her giant brothers. Conan escapes her trap and is left with only her veil as proof of his tale.
- *Kalanthes*, a priest of Ibis, is a force of good in the Hyborian lands, although his ways are often mysterious. His path occasionally crosses with that of Conan. Conan typically aides him and does not get much in return for his trouble.
- *Janissa*, known as the Widowmaker, abandoned a courtly life of pleasure, desiring to become a great warrior. She asks for the assistance of the witch known as the Bone Woman, who forces Janissa to fight against an ever-increasing horde of demons. Those that Janissa does not kill rape her. The Bone Woman heals Janissa each day, the magic strengthening her as her "training" continues. Her backstory makes her into an extremely controversial character.
- *Yogah* is an elephant-headed alien from the planet Yag. His cosmic wings are burned away by Earth's atmosphere, and so he and others from his home world remain on Earth to watch the dawn of humanity. After millennia of existence, Yogah is the last of his race and is eventually imprisoned and tortured by the wizard Yara, who uses Yogah's powers for nefarious tasks.
- *Nabonidus*, a.k.a. the *Red Priest*, is a master manipulator and high official in the Zamoran court. Dabbling in sciences such as botany and optics, which appear like magic to most people, Nabonidus makes his home into a series of traps for thieves and assassins, which are tended to by his apelike manservant, Thak.
- *Iniri*, a street waif and minor illusionist with some precognitive power, is saved by Conan and feels indebted to him, especially after she has a vision of doom for the Cimmerian. Attempting to follow Conan to warn him, she encounters Princess Ereshka and takes her place as kidnappers come to capture her. She eventually uses her power to help defeat the sorcerer Atalis.
- *Blind Jerim*, a spy who was blinded for a past offense, occasionally gives Conan intelligence and also looks out for Iniri as she searches for Conan. He imparts wisdom to those around him.

- *Atalis*, a wizard in the service of the malevolent god Nergal, hopes to transfer his essence from his dying body to that of Prince Than.
- *Connacht*, Conan's grandfather, originally came from one of the southern Cimmerian tribes. Wandering the world, he has many adventures and eventually tires of the mercenary life (and the rules of civilized behavior), returning to Cimmeria, where he is wounded and then falls in love with the woman who helped heal him.
- *Caollan*, Conan's first love, has grown in the years that Conan was away from Cimmeria. Upon his return, they realize they still have feelings for each other even though their lives have put them on different paths.
- *Fialla*, Conan's mother, is a strong Cimmerian woman but recognizes the wanderlust in her son and encourages him to spend time with his grandfather.
- *Amalric the Lion*, leader of the mercenary army serving the nobility of Khoraja, provides Conan with serious military training in formal combat, honing Conan's natural fighting skills.
- *Yasmela*, as the princess of Khoraja, trusts the fate of her nation to the hands of Conan while her brother, the crown prince, lies imprisoned. Attracted to Conan, they become lovers, but only for a brief time, as she realizes that he is not fit for courtly life.
- *Natohk*, originally the sorcerer king Thugra Khotan, ruler of the city of Kuthchemes, is centuries old when his city is overrun. Instead of perishing, he locks himself away, protected by magic, and sleeps for hundreds of years before awakening as Natohk. Driven by a desire to serve Set, he is compromised by his desire to possess Princess Yasmela.
- *Shah Amurath*, a nobleman charged with protecting Turanian trade routes, organizes an army to obliterate Conan and his Free Companions. Amurath's sadism is expressed in his brutality not only on the battlefield but also in the bedchamber, particularly as he abuses Olivia, the daughter of the king of Ophir.

- *Olivia*, sold into bondage by her own father, inadvertently delivers Amurath to Conan's vengeance, and she stays with Conan, who becomes her protector and lover.

Artistic Style

Conan is an iconic character that has received considerable visual treatment. Starting with the *Weird Tales* illustrations of the 1930's, Conan attracted artists working in illustration, but Frank Frazetta, during the 1960's, provided a new visual interpretation in a series of paintings done for paperback reprints of Conan stories that attracted a whole new generation of readers and redefined sword and sorcery as a genre. Frazetta's work was so galvanizing that he is often cited as the artist who most captured the spirit of Conan and the standard by which other interpretations are measured. This is not to dismiss notable contributions by major talents such as Barry Windsor-Smith, John Buscema, Ernie Chan, Nord, or Giorello, but is pointed out to underscore just how powerful the imagery of Conan is for many readers.

The book is intended for mature audiences; thus, the nature of the visual adaptation of this incarnation of *Conan* at Dark Horse Comics, from the depictions of nudity to the graphic quality of violence, had to conform to the promise made by the company to stay true to Howard's stories. At the same time, it had to be commercially viable, particularly given the First Amendment challenges some comics retailers face. This was certainly the case for cover artist Tony Harris, whose work on issue 24 was initially censored for publication since it depicted a fully nude woman. The original cover illustration was subsequently printed as a limited variant edition. Harris is just one cover artist, however, among many notable contributors, including Mignola, Frank Cho, Geof Darrow, Joseph Michael Linsner, and Joe Kubert, who have added their interpretation of Conan to the vast repository of imagery.

The issue of artistic continuity within a title is an interesting one to consider. As the two primary illustrators on *Conan* and *Conan the Cimmerian*, Nord and Giorello each brought their visual styles to the character while matching a general aesthetic already associated with Conan. Nord cites Frazetta and the

Kubert brothers as influences on his own art, while Giorello also has a similarly strong background in fantasy art, citing Buscema, Neal Adams, and Alfredo Alcala as significant figures. With this set of progenitors, Nord and Giorello brought a controlled chaos to their lines, giving Conan a hardness that mirrored the desire for a more mature treatment through an increased level of realization with regard to violence. Howard himself appears in the prologue to *Conan the Cimmerian*, writing the poem "Cimmeria," with images from the comic illustrating the words of his famous verse.

One final issue of note concerns the format of the captions used for narration within the issues, specifically the typewriter-style font used within that is strikingly different from that used within the speech balloons by letterer Richard Starkings. The appearance of the typewritten lines was selected as a means to suggest that the reader is somehow viewing the words as Howard might have written them; however, this caused some controversy as it created a tension between the suspension of disbelief necessary for the story and recognizing at a metanarrative level that this is in fact a story. Howard's presence is actually underscored in each issue of *Conan* in the presence of *The Adventures of Two-Gun Bob*, by Jim and Ruth Keegan, found on each issue's letter page. Through the illustration of excerpts from Howard's letters and biographies in a comic-strip format, Howard himself has become a comic book creation.

Themes

One of the major themes in *Conan* is the tension between civilization and barbarism. Conan may have repeatedly been called a barbarian—although Dark Horse Comics chose to avoid this designation, likely because of the Marvel Comics series—but his actions often make him more honorable than those people from "civilized" lands that he encounters, who often covet money or power. Howard often wrote of his feelings about the trappings of civilization in his letters to fellow fantasy writer H. P. Lovecraft and also commented on this topic within his stories. Perhaps the most famous declaration came in the 1935 short story "Beyond the Black River."

"Barbarism is the natural state of mankind," the borderer said, still staring somberly at the Cimmerian. "Civilization is unnatural. It is a whim of circumstance. And barbarism must always ultimately triumph."

While Conan is often motivated by personal gain or basic survival, it is problematic to see him as an anti-hero, as he has a sense of ethics when it comes to protecting those under his care. This begins with friends and family but extends to his kingdom after he becomes ruler of Aquilonia. Conan's sense that the machinations of politics are far more underhanded than those of armed conflict are expressed in 1933's "Tower of the Elephant," when he states, "Civilized men are more discourteous than savages because they know they can be impolite without having their skulls split, as a general thing". It is expressed again in 1935's "Rogues in the House," when he tells Nabonidus, "Someday, when all your civilization and science are likewise swept away, your kind will pray for a man with a sword." Eventually this displayed disgust toward the convenient excuses that allows civilized men to do heinous acts prompts Conan to return to Cimmeria after the early part of his life. Although his wanderlust eventually overcomes his distaste, and he leaves his homeland again, Conan continues to find the rules of polite society to be a minor irritant at best and the ultimate source of villainy at worst.

Another theme is the function of free will in shaping one's own destiny. Conan is destined to become a king, but by his own hand, meaning the time and method will be his choosing. He is self-reliant, espousing a sort of rugged individualism that Howard himself espoused in the frontier of Texas hill country. In this regard, Conan is reflective of the time of his creation, with the United States struggling under the Great Depression and Howard struggling to sustain himself as a writer, an occupation quite in opposition to the manly physical activities of most men around him. By contrast, Conan's physical prowess is often at the forefront of his successes, yet his intellectual component should not be overlooked; his ability to think is particularly highlighted in Howard's prose. The thoughtful nature of Conan is often overlooked in the comic books because of the action component, or in Conan's preference for a solid broadsword over some magician's parlor tricks, but discerning readers will note a great deal of complexity beneath the Cimmerian's brooding visage.

Impact

The excitement over the release of a *Conan* title was palpable both in the comics community and in Howard fandom, particularly since Dark Horse Comics had made the commitment to execute the adaptations in a manner faithful to the original source material. The final product became an immediate source of debate. Was the art style in line with Howard's vision? How much interstitial narrative material could the creators inject to link the Howard stories together, giving them continuity, and still remain thematically and perhaps prosaically consistent with Howard's original texts? An incident in which Conan slapped a young boy became a major debate about the nature of Conan's personality and whether or not the incident was consistent with his persona. Interestingly, this debate not only appeared in the letter column in the individual issues but also was argued quite strenuously on the Internet, which allowed Busiek and other contributors to respond directly to their detractors and supporters.

Another firestorm of controversy ignited over the backstory of Janissa. While linking the rape of a woman with warrior skills had already occurred in the pages of *Conan the Barbarian*, with the character of Red Sonja, many readers felt that the writing should have had a more contemporary, and sensitive, attitude toward gender issues, while others contended that it was permissible for the writing to reflect a hard, less civilized edge. Ultimately, when it came to "faithfully" adapting the source material, Dark Horse Comics and its contributors seemed to make an effort to balance their versions of the Howard stories with their interest in contributing to the legend of Conan. This resulted in the creation of original material, some worked into the Conan canon and other published as stand-alone titles. The overall nature of this debate highlights some important issues when it comes to adapting work, including moving from one medium to another and defining the nature of authorial intent.

Conan is likely a creation far beyond anything that Howard had originally conceived, however powerful his original vision of Conan may have been. The centenary celebration of Howard's birth in 2006 helped to increase attention on Howard's works and created solid sales for Dark Horse Comics, which also began reprinting the older Marvel Comics *Conan* titles, thus linking the two primary sets of adaptations. The new Conan comic books also helped foster an interest in Conan in other areas, including the *Conan* (2007) and *Age of Conan* (2008) video games, a line of action figures from McFarlane Toys in 2004 and 2005, and a few video projects, including a live-action film and an animated adaptation of the novella *Red Nails*.

Stefan Hall

Films

Conan the Barbarian. Directed by Marcus Nispel. Lionsgate (2011). Starring Jason Momoa as Conan, the film offers a fresh interpretation of the Conan legend, with the warrior traversing a harsh land, battling witches, monsters, and the warlord responsible for destroying his village.

Conan the Barbarian. Directed by John Milius. De Laurentiis/Universal Pictures (1982). Starring Arnold Schwarzenegger as Conan, the film is essentially a revenge story, in which Conan, sold in to slavery, hunts for the warlord responsible for killing his people.

Conan the Destroyer. Directed by Richard Fleischer. De Laurentiis/Universal Pictures, 1984. Starring Schwarzenegger as Conan and Grace Jones as Zula, the film finds Conan seeking a magic crystal that, if he possesses it, will resurrect his dead love.

Further Reading

Allie, Scott. *Solomon Kane: The Castle of the Devil* (2009).

_____. *Solomon Kane: Death's Black Riders* (2010).

Busiek, Kurt, and Len Wein. *Conan: Book of Thoth* (2006).

Landsdale, Joe. *Pigeons from Hell* (2009).

Landsdale, Joe, and Timothy Truman. *Conan and the Songs of the Dead* (2007).

Nelson, Arvid. *Kull: The Shadow Kingdom* (2009).

Russell, P. Craig. *Conan and the Jewels of Gwalhur* (2005).

Thomas, Roy. *Almuric* (1991).

Thomas, Roy, et al. *The Chronicles of Kull,* Volume 1: *A King Comes Riding, and Other Stories* (2009).

_____. *The Chronicles of Kull,* Volume 2: *The Hell Beneath Atlantis, and Other Stories* (2009).

_____. *The Chronicles of Kull,* Volume 3: *Screams in the Dark, and Other Stories* (2009).

_____. *The Chronicles of Kull,* Volume 4: *The Blood of Kings and Other Stories* (2011).

Thomas, Roy, et al. *Conan the Barbarian* (1970-1994). Reprinted in *The Chronicles of Conan* (2003-).

_____. *The Saga of Solomon Kane* (2009).

_____. *The Savage Sword of Conan.* Reprint. (2008-).

_____. *The Savage Sword of Kull* (2010).

Thomas, Roy, and Ralph Macchio. *The Chronicles of Solomon Kane* (2009).

Thomas, Roy, and Dann Thomas. *Cormac Mac Art* (1989).

Yoshida, Akira. *Conan and the Demons of Khitai* (2006).

Bibliography

Finn, Mark. *Blood and Thunder: The Life and Art of Robert E. Howard.* Austin, Tex.: MonkeyBrain Books, 2006.

Herman, Paul. *The Neverending Hunt: A Bibliography of Robert E. Howard.* Rockville, Md.: Wildside Press, 2007.

Nielsen, Leon. *Robert E. Howard: A Collector's Descriptive Bibliography.* Jefferson, NC: McFarland, 2006.

Sammon, Paul. *Conan the Phenomenon: The Legacy of Robert E. Howard's Fantasy Icon.* Milwaukie, Ore.: Dark Horse Books, 2007.

Szumskyj, Benjamin. *Two-Gun Bob: A Centennial Study of Robert E. Howard.* New York: Hippocampus Press, 2006.

Thomas, Roy. *Conan: The Ultimate Guide to the World's Most Savage Barbarian.* New York: Dorling Kindersley, 2006.

See also: *Cerebus; Bloodstar*

CONCRETE

Author: Chadwick, Paul
Artist: Paul Chadwick (illustrator); Bill Spicer (letterer)
Publisher: Dark Horse Comics
First serial publication: 1986-1995
First book publication: 1994

Publication History

Concrete is an award-winning black-and-white series created, written, and drawn by Paul Chadwick. The eponymous character first appeared in the inaugural issue of the anthology series *Dark Horse Presents* (July, 1986) and was eventually featured in twenty-three stories published in *Dark Horse Presents* between 1986 and 1995. Dark Horse also published ten issues of *Concrete*, the comic book, between 1986 and 1990, as well as several self-contained miniseries that were subsequently reissued as trade paperbacks: *Concrete: Fragile Creatures* (1991), *Concrete: Killer Smile* (1994), *Concrete: Think Like a Mountain* (1996), *Concrete: Strange Armor* (1997), and *Concrete: The Human Dilemma* (2005).

The environmentally conscious, all-ages-friendly character has additionally appeared in one-off titles such as *Concrete: Odd Jobs* (1990), *Concrete*: *Eclectica* (1993), and *San Diego Comic Con Comics* (1993). Dark Horse later collected every *Concrete* short story and comic book in a seven-volume series (2005-2006), with the exception of a few pages from the short story "Moving a Big Rock" (1995).

Plot

The protagonist of *Concrete*, Ron Lithgow, was working as a political speechwriter for Senator Mark Douglas when he went on a wilderness vacation with his closest friend, Michael Maynard. Seeing a strange light near their camp, they go exploring, only to find themselves in a cave filled with extraterrestrial artifacts. When they awake they are trapped in massive concrete bodies. The aliens run numerous tests on the two friends, who eventually manage to escape by overpowering their alien guards. While Ron leaves the cave

---

Paul Chadwick

Transitioning to comics from the field of cinema story-boarding, Paul Chadwick is the Eisner Award-winning creator of *Concrete*. Launched in 1986, the series tells the story of a man whose brain is transplanted by aliens into a large body made of stone. *Concrete* was a radical departure from the fantasy and science-fiction comics of its era because it largely eschewed fantastic elements in favor of heightened emotional realism. The series pays particular attention to the psychological cost imposed on Ron Lithgow of having a completely alien body in a world of normal humans. Over time, Chadwick's comic book became a venue in which he explored themes involving environmentalism and deep ecology. His art style is defined by a strict naturalism and detailed realism, and he frequently positions his characters within lushly realized landscapes. The overall pacing of the series is remarkably sedate and muted, and the series as a whole is more contemplative and reflective than adventure-driven.

---

and heads for civilization, Michael remains behind, in hopes that the aliens might restore him to his original condition. Only a short time later, Ron watches with a sense of helplessness as the alien starship emerges out of the mountainside and heads for the stars. With help from Senator Douglas and other influential players in Washington, D.C., Ron Lithgow is reborn as Concrete, the supposed one-off product of an experimental cyborg program. To distract the public from the sheer strangeness of his cover story, Concrete goes on numerous talk shows, where he pretends to be an amiable dummy without a care in the world. The strategy to turn Concrete into a banal cultural novelty works, and with the exception of a couple of journalists and artists, nobody pays much attention to the Thing-like superhuman.

Rather than using his powers to combat crime or solve mysteries, Concrete decides to pursue a life of adventure, along the lines of his hero, the nineteenth century explorer Sir Richard Francis Burton. Dismissed as a publicity seeker by the media, Concrete embarks on a series of stunts that effectively test the limits of his new body. Thus, he attempts to swim across the Atlantic Ocean and to scale Mount Everest. He works on a family farm and becomes a bodyguard for a manic pop star. He explores the California coastline, spends a night in the desert, and even attends a star-studded Hollywood party. He gets to see and do things that Ron Lithgow could not. Rather than feeling sorry for himself, he makes the best of his new circumstances. He also finds that he has become a lightning rod for greasy freeloaders and unscrupulous entrepreneurs. Navigating the social world poses special challenges for a man encased in a mobile concrete slab.

The ten-issue comic book series focuses on Concrete's origins, his travel adventures, and his friendship with Larry Munro and Dr. Maureen Vonnegut. The subsequent miniseries feature the regular cast of characters but place Concrete in unusual contexts. In the first miniseries, *Fragile Creatures*, Concrete works on a generic Hollywood film as a one-man special-effects team. His usual good humor is tested by the clash of egos on the set and by the absurdity of genre-based Hollywood storytelling.

In the second miniseries, *Killer Smile*, cultural satire gives way to unrelenting horror, as Larry Munro tries to find a way of escaping the clutches of a murderous sociopath. Chadwick's implicit pessimism about human nature, which is usually checked by the main character's sweet-natured humor, is given full expression in this series. In the follow-up miniseries, *Think Like a Mountain*, Concrete joins forces with a small group of radical environmental activists to help save an old-growth forest. More than any other set of *Concrete* stories, this series explicitly confronts difficult issues of political strategy and social-movement morality. While the author warns against the dangers of antihumanist environmental rhetoric, he also makes it clear that he largely agrees with Earth First!-style activism.

With the fourth *Concrete* miniseries, *Strange Armor*, Chadwick revisits Concrete's origins and fleshes out the steps by which Ron Lithgow became a real-world superhero. The miniseries is derived from a screenplay that Chadwick prepared for a film adaptation that was never filmed. The subsequent Dark Horse collection includes the script as well as several short stories that touch on Concrete's relationship to his body and to his makers. The most recent Concrete miniseries, *The Human Dilemma*, returns to environmental themes and foregrounds the controversies over population growth and population control. This series also set the stage for major changes in Concrete's relationship with Maureen Vonnegut as well as in Larry Munro's personal life.

Volumes

- *Concrete: Complete Short Stories, 1986-1989* (1990). The short-story format allowed Chadwick to explore various aspects of Concrete's daily life and his interactions with both his close friends and random strangers. Several of the stories are humorous in nature but hint at the character's growing involvement with environmental politics.

- *The Complete Concrete* (1994). Collects the original ten-issue comic book series. The book includes intelligent, award-winning stories that helped expand the boundaries of superhero and fantasy storytelling in American comics. The artwork became increasingly confident as the series continued.

- *Concrete: Fragile Creature* (1995). Trade paperback of the 1991 four-issue limited series. This full-color miniseries sharply contrasts Concrete's humanism with the mercenary ethics of B-film Hollywood. The story draws on the author's own experiences in the movie industry.

- *Concrete: Killer Smile* (1996). Trade paperback of the 1994 four-issue limited series. Arguably the pulpiest story in the Concrete corpus, and also the fastest paced, it provides yet another example of Chadwick's ability to work within, and combine, well-established fictional genres.

- *Concrete: Think Like a Mountain* (1996). Trade paperback of the 1996 six-issue limited series. A pivotal contribution to the Concrete mythos that foregrounds the creator's interest in issues of political strategy and efficacy in the context of radical environmental activism.

- *Concrete: Complete Short Stories, 1990-1995* (1996). As with the 1986-1989 short-story collection, this volume features tightly constructed ministories that are fueled by both humor and political consciousness. These pages feature some of the most ambitious graphic compositions that Chadwick has committed to print.

- *Concrete: Strange Armor* (1998). Trade paperback of the 1997 five-issue limited series. Revisiting the character's science-fiction-like origins, this limited series provides the template for a movie that might have been.

- *Concrete,* Volume One: *Depths* (2005). Reproduces the first five issues of the original *Concrete* series. The stories offer an affectionate portrait of a likable, well-meaning individual who finds himself in an alien body.

- *Concrete,* Volume Two: *Heights* (2006). This companion volume reproduces issues 6-10 of the original *Concrete* series. The storytelling and artwork are more evolved, and the environmental awareness comes into sharper focus, laying the basis for the miniseries that followed.

- *Concrete,* Volume Three: *Fragile Creature* (2006). This is a glossy reprint of the 1991 four-issue limited series that placed an earnest, hard-working, and financially strapped superhuman in the seedy world of low-budget Hollywood.

- *Concrete,* Volume Four: *Killer Smile* (2006). A useful reprinting and repackaging of the 1994 four-issue limited series that pits Concrete's close friend Larry Munro against a vicious serial killer.

- *Concrete,* Volume Five: *Think Like a Mountain* (2006). This is a nicely produced reprint of the 1996 six-issue limited series that explores the politics of extralegal activism and the urgency of environmental change.

- *Concrete,* Volume Six: *Strange Armor* (2006). This is a significantly expanded version of

Concrete's origin story as well as a reprint of the 1997 five-issue limited series.

- *Concrete,* Volume Seven: *The Human Dilemma* (2006). As with *Think Like a Mountain*, this collection highlights Concrete's fervent commitment to environmental change by exploring the tangled politics of population control.

Characters

- *Ron Lithgow*, a.k.a. *Concrete*, is a kindhearted, good-natured everyman, albeit trapped inside an imposing alien body. Throughout the series he tries to make sense of his unique condition and strange new powers. He develops close friendships with Larry Munro and Maureen Vonnegut and gains an ever-greater appreciation for the wonders of nature. Meanwhile, the general public is told that Concrete's unique condition is the result of a "discontinued cyborg development program, conducted by the NSA with terminally ill volunteers," of whom Concrete is the only survivor.

- *Larry Munro* is a would-be novelist, a bon vivant, and Concrete's personal assistant. While Larry is a well-meaning and loyal friend, he tends to cut ethical corners. His relaxed, situational ethics stand in sharp contrast to the carefully considered social and environmental moral code that Concrete self-consciously embraces.

- *Dr. Maureen Vonnegut* is a biologist at the National Science Agency who works with Concrete in order to understand how his body functions. She has a cerebral, somewhat aloof personality and is oblivious to the fact that Concrete is in love with her. She nevertheless shares Concrete's passion for the environment as well as his upright ethics.

- *Senator Mark Douglas* is Ron Lithgow's former employer. He is an honorable politician who helps facilitate Concrete's return to something resembling ordinary life. The senator is one of only a small number of people who knows the truth behind the official cover story.

- *Michael Maynard* was one of Ron Lithgow's closest friends. On a camping trip, they explored a cave where aliens were conducting brain transplantation experiments. Both his and Ron's brains were placed in alien, concrete bodies, but he decided to remain behind in hopes that the aliens would return his brain to his human body. His present whereabouts are unknown.

Artistic Style

Chadwick works mostly in black and white and favors a clean, uncluttered line that serves the interest of the story. With the exception of the main protagonist, his characters are ordinary human beings who live and work in the real world. Concrete often ventures from his home in Los Angeles to the countryside, in both the Western United States and abroad, and Chadwick uses these travels to capture the teeming biological diversity hidden in deserts, oceans, and mountains. He has a special talent for rendering the tunnels, holes, and burrows of animals that do not want to be observed. His pages have become more complex and ambitious over time, and the latter-day Dark Horse collections offer tangible evidence of Chadwick's artistic progress from the mid-1980's to the early 2000's.

While Chadwick generally sticks to a more or less realistic style, he occasionally experiments with the comics form and puts the story on hold. In *Concrete*, issue 2, for example, he crams 150 panels into a single page to show in striking detail the repetitive motions of Concrete's transatlantic swim. In the following issue, which tells the story of how Ron Lithgow became Concrete, several surreal pages are devoted to showing the Jack Kirby-inspired interior of the alien spacecraft. These pages are the exception, however. If major Silver Age artists such as Kirby, Alex Toth, and Steve Ditko are obvious sources of inspiration, so is the nineteenth century painter John James Audubon. With *Concrete*, Chadwick found a way to combine his passion for the great outdoors and his interest in the so-called big questions with his love of mainstream American comics.

Themes

From its inception, *Concrete* has featured substantial interior monologues on large, open-ended philosophical questions that give it an unusually ruminative, contemplative aspect. Chadwick has used the series as a platform to express and help flesh out his views on a range of issues. The series has arguably become more politically engaged over time, particularly with reference to environmental and feminist concerns. The inherent seriousness of these issues has been balanced by the science-fiction and fantasy elements of the story, as well as by the main protagonist's gentle, self-deprecating humor.

Three themes in particular stand out. The first has to do with the question of human connectedness and people's need for contact and intimacy. Encased in a massive stone body, Concrete has to work extra hard to forge meaningful relationships and maintain ties to the social world. Strangers treat him with disdain or fear, or they find him comical. Only his closest friends appreciate Concrete's humanity. His condition poses the issue of alienation and loneliness with unusual clarity. To some extent, all humans are mini-Concretes trapped inside their bodies, trying to express their innermost thoughts and feelings even as people respond in predictable ways to exterior appearance.

The second theme concerns the role of women in society and the ways in which obnoxious male behavior constrains their autonomy and freedom. Concrete's gentle nature is in sharp contrast to most of the other male characters, who aggressively pursue multiple sex partners and view gender relations as a battlefield. The paradox is obvious: While Concrete's form embodies raw masculinity, his outlook is broadly feminist. At the same time, lacking any sort of conventional release for his natural urges, he collects fine-art paintings of nude women and spends much of his time pining over Dr. Vonnegut.

The third theme, that of environmental awareness, was only hinted at in the early stories but eventually became a defining feature of the comic books as well as the several miniseries that followed. Concrete's superpowered senses allow him to experience the natural world as no human being can. He can remain underwater for more than an hour and can lift thousands of pounds. More important, he can see things that no ordinary eye can perceive—the number of stitches, for example, in a flag flying a mile away. As Concrete travels the planet, he is struck by the variety and vibrancy of natural settings but disturbed by the undeniable impact of population growth, industrial development, and residential sprawl. Concrete is a superhero, a feminist, an eco-warrior, and a political liberal. His stories hold a special appeal for readers who are already sympathetic to the author's worldview.

Impact

Concrete was one of a number of consequential titles to emerge out of the explosion of independent, creator-owned, black-and-white comics during the 1980's. Its creator showed that it was possible to tell emotionally meaningful, human-scale stories that centered on a superpowered individual with alien technology at his disposal. Chadwick created believable, recognizable characters with three-dimensional flaws and limits and placed them in densely constructed, real-world settings. At the end of the 1980's, writing in *Playboy* magazine, American writer Harlan Ellison said that *Concrete* was "probably the best comic being published today by anyone, anywhere. Trying to describe the down-to-earth humanity and sheer dearness of Paul Chadwick's creation requires more than words or pictures." While not all writers on comics would have agreed with Ellison's critical assessment, even at the time, it is undoubtedly the case that quirky, nonmainstream titles such as *Concrete, Eightball* (1989-2004)*, Neat Stuff* (1985-1989), and *Love and Rockets* (1982-1996) helped set the stage for the alternative comics bonanza of the 1990's and 2000's.

Kent Worcester

Further Reading

Gonick, Larry, and Alice Outwater. *The Cartoon Guide to the Environment* (1996).

Morrison, Grant. *Animal Man* (1988-1990).

Murphy, Steven, and Michael Zulli. *The Puma Blues* (1986-1989).

Schultz, Mark. *Xenozoic Tales* (1987-1996).

Bibliography

Baisden, Greg, and Dale Crain. "Man of Stone: Paul Chadwick." *The Comics Journal* 132 (November, 1989): 76-102.

Chadwick, Paul. "Paul Chadwick Interview." Interview by Darren Hick. *The Comics Journal* 221 (March, 2000): 38-70.

De Laplante, Kevin. "Making the Abstract Concrete: How a Comic Can Bring to Life the Central Problems of Environmental Philosophy." In *Comics as Philosophy*, edited by Jeff McLaughlin. University Press of Mississippi, 2005.

Gravel, Gary. "A Life Cast in Stone: Seven Short Essays in Contemplation of Paul Chadwick's *Concrete*." In *The Complete Concrete*. .Dark Horse, 1994.

See also: *Animal Man; Black Panther: Who Is the Black Panther*

COSMIC ODYSSEY

Author: Starlin, Jim
Artist: Mike Mignola (illustrator); Carlos Garzon (inker); Steve Oliff (colorist); John Workman (letterer)
Publisher: DC Comics
First serial publication: 1988-1989
First book publication: 1992

Publication History

Cosmic Odyssey was first published by DC Comics from 1988 to 1989 as a four-issue prestige-format comic book miniseries. It was later released in a single-volume graphic novel format by DC Comics in 1992. *Cosmic Odyssey* was an early part of a recurrent practice at DC Comics to gather numerous superheroes together in a crossover miniseries. The writer of *Cosmic Odyssey*, Jim Starlin, had illustrated and written numerous comic book series for both DC Comics and Marvel Comics since the early 1970's. At the time of the writing of *Cosmic Odyssey*, Starlin was best known for his work on *Captain Marvel* during the 1970's and on the "Metamorphosis Odyssey" story line in *Epic Illustrated* for Marvel Comics during the 1980's. By the time of the writing of *Cosmic Odyssey* Starlin had largely transitioned to working primarily as a scripter rather than an illustrator. The artist, Mike Mignola, had a fairly limited background prior to *Cosmic Odyssey*, having worked primarily as an inker and artist for low-profile series such as *Rocket Raccoon* (1985), *Alpha Flight* (1983-1994), and *The Hulk* (during the 1980's).

Plot

Cosmic Odyssey tells the story of Darkseid's attempt to control the power of the legendary Anti-Life Equation. Darkseid, the malevolent ruler of the planet Apokolips, discovers that the inquisitive New God Metron has been rendered catatonic after piercing the veil that separates the dimension containing the Anti-Life Equation from the larger universe. Seizing Metron's catatonic body and the knowledge Metron gained about the Anti-Life Equation, now contained within Metron's Mobius Chair, Darkseid realizes that he

Jim Starlin

The creator of the first "graphic novel" ever marketed by Marvel Comics using that term, Jim Starlin is well known as a writer and artist of cosmic superhero stories. Originally published in 1982, *The Death of Captain Marvel* was highly unusual, not only because it featured the death of a major character (a rarity at that time), but also because he died of cancer rather than in a cataclysmic fight to save the universe. That same year, Starlin debuted the first title for Epic Comics, Marvel's creator-owned line. *Dreadstar* was a science-fiction title with strong space opera elements. Though he has worked on a number of traditional superhero stories, his main achievements have involved works set in science-fiction settings. Themes of death are prevalent in his comics, and he has also incorporated strong political critiques in his work.

needs to enlist the aid of his enemies if he is going to harvest the power of the Anti-Life Equation for himself.

To this end, he manages to persuade the ruler of the peaceful planet New Genesis, Highfather, to recruit a team of superheroes (Starfire, J'onn J'onzz the Martian Manhunter, Batman, Superman, the Green Lantern John Stewart, and Jason Blood) to come to New Genesis. Once there, it is revealed that the Anti-Life Equation is actually a deadly sentient antimatter being that cannot travel safely to the superheroes' universe. Darkseid tells the assembled superheroes that when Metron fled the Anti-Life Entity's dimension the entity sent four aspects of itself into the universe along with Metron. These four aspects were sent to four particular planets (Earth, Rann, Thanagar, and Xanshi) in order to construct doomsday bombs to destroy the planets. Darkseid explains that the destruction of any two of these four planets will result in the destruction of the Milky Way, thereby allowing the Anti-Life Entity to cross over into their universe.

With the exception of Jason Blood, the recruited superheroes from Earth join forces with Forager, a humanoid member of New Genesis' insect kingdom, and the New Gods Orion and Lightray to form four teams of two. Each team is responsible for traveling to one of the four planets, capturing one of the Anti-Life Entity's aspects, and defusing its doomsday bomb.

The team of Superman and Orion and the team of Lightray and Starfire destroy the bombs and retrieve the aspects from Thanagar and Rann, respectively. On Xanshi, John Stewart ignores J'onn J'onzz's warnings about the need for caution in approaching the Anti-Life aspect and uses the power of his ring to prevent J'onn J'onzz from intervening as he attempts to defeat the aspect by himself. However, the aspect has painted the doomsday bomb yellow, the one color against which a Green Lantern's ring is helpless. Stewart watches in horror as the bomb explodes, destroying Xanshi and the millions of people who live on it; his ring is able to save only him and J'onn J'onzz. Back on New Genesis, upon learning about the destruction of Xanshi, a reluctant Jason Blood finally assents to being reunited with the Etrigan the Demon, thereby allowing Darkseid to implement his true plan to harvest the energies of the Anti-Life Entity.

Darkseid takes the Demon to the Anti-Life Entity's dimension and tries to use the Demon's mystical powers to steal part of the Anti-Life power for himself, only to realize that the Anti-Life Entity is far more powerful than he imagined. Highfather, Orion, and Doctor Fate, the latter of whom has been monitoring the situation at Batman's request, appear in the Anti-Life Entity's dimension and collectively form a "cinque of cosmic power" with Darkseid and the Demon. Using the collective power, Dr. Fate destroys the Anti-Life Entity's dimension, imprisoning it. Returning to New Genesis, Batman informs them that Forager has died while successfully destroying the last doomsday bomb (and saving both Batman and Earth), thereby ending the threat of the embodiment of the Anti-Life Entity. In the aftermath of these events, John Stewart contemplates suicide for his complicity in the destruction of Xanshi. The story ends with Darkseid returning to Apokolips in possession of a secreted shard of pure Anti-Life energy.

Characters

- *Darkseid*, the antagonist, is a physically powerful New God with gray, rocklike skin and glowing red eyes. He rules over the harsh world of Apokolips and is constantly seeking to expand his power throughout the universe. His attempts to harness the power of the Anti-Life Equation, escalating the threat posed by the Anti-Life Entity.

- *Highfather* is the white-haired, white-bearded, father-figure ruler of New Genesis. Wise and powerful, Highfather seeks to find peaceful means to resist Darkseid's attempts to conquer New Genesis and the universe. Highfather's decision to form an alliance with Darkseid in order to stop the Anti-Life Entity is the central conflict in the story.

- *Superman* is a human-looking Kryptonian who was sent to Earth from his dying home planet. Possessed of enormous physical superpowers, Superman embraces a strong moral code centered on a deep compassion for life. This belief will place him at odds with Orion's merciless approach to conflict.

- *Lightray* is a white-garbed, youthful New God who pursues life with optimism and hope. He successful teams with Starfire to defeat one of the Anti-Life aspects.

- *Metron* is a somber New God who travels the universe astride his Mobius Chair, a technologically enhanced throne that serves as both a means of interdimensional travel and a powerful scientific instrument. Noncombative and contemplative, Metron seeks to learn the secrets of the universe. His attempt to probe the nature of the Anti-Life Equation will precipitate the threat from the Anti-Life Entity.

- *Batman* is an exceptionally well-trained and muscular male human. A master of strategic thinking and hand-to-hand combat, Batman is hypervigilant in planning for every contingency. His secret recruitment of Dr. Fate will ensure that the Anti-Life Entity is defeated.

- *Starfire* is an orange-skinned super-powered female from the planet Tamaran. Starfire embodies the warrior tradition, while maintaining an ebullient personality. She teams successfully with Lightray to defeat one of the Anti-Life aspects.

- *John Stewart* is an African American man who has been recruited to be a member of the Green Lantern Corps. Stewart is arrogant and boastful of the power he possesses as the wielder of a Green Lantern ring. His arrogance results in his failure to stop the Anti-Life aspect from destroying Xanshi.

- *J'onn J'onzz*, a.k.a. the *Martian Manhunter*, is a green-skinned member of the Martian race. Possessed with both telepathic powers and great strength, he has often served as a mentor for other superheroes. John Stewart's failure to acknowledge his ability to help will lead to the destruction of Xanshi.

- *Jason Blood* is an elderly male human who has a long history of being bonded to the large yellow humanoid demon Etrigan. Blood longs to be separated from the demon but agrees to be rebonded with Etrigan in order to defeat the Anti-Life Entity.

- *Orion* is a physically powerful New God who wears an armored helmet and a metallic harness. Orion is battle-hardened, ruthless, and devoid of compassion for whomever he fights. These traits lead him into using extreme levels of force, resulting in the slaughter of innumerable Thanagarians, putting him at odds with Superman.

- *Forager* is a clever, nimble, and strong humanoid member of New Genesis' insect kingdom. He dies stopping the threat of the last Anti-Life aspect.

- *Etrigan*, a yellow-skinned demon, is an enigmatic, chaotic being that is able to tap into deep wells of mystical power. This ability is central to stopping the Anti-Life entity.

- *Dr. Fate* is a yellow-caped, golden-helmeted man possessed of tremendous sorcery skills. He destroys an entire dimension in order to end the Anti-Life Entity's threat.

Artistic Style

In *Cosmic Odyssey*, Mignola employs a representational art style that renders characters in a highly stylized manner. His use of such techniques is somewhat inconsistent throughout the series, but the overall effect is often to tilt his characters toward a figurative rather than literal representation. He achieves this effect through the use of softened detail that emphasizes particular features of a character, as opposed to elaborating a dense representational form. This technique is enhanced by the frequent use of heavy black character outlines and dark shadows and shading, often for extended sequences.

With frequent use of panels that extend to the edge of the page (called "full bleed" in publishing terms), inset panels, sequenced panels emphasizing small actions and moments, and panels layered upon and exploding into other panels, Mignola's art creates a dynamism that engages the reader in not only the actions but also the emotions of the story. The frequent use of interior monologue narration boxes also serve to maximize the emotional intensity of the story, as the reader sees the story as interpreted from multiple perspectives.

Mignola's page-filling art also reflects the epic nature of the story. In the first half of the story, panel backgrounds are often densely composed with highly elaborated and stylized detail. As the story shifts toward its end, Mignola emphasizes the otherworldliness of its interdimensional setting through the extensive use of gold, yellow, and white compositions of explosions and force lines. Indeed, throughout the series there is frequent fluctuation between compositions emphasizing dark tones of blue and black and those emphasizing shades of gold and yellow. Through these techniques Mignola attempts to direct the emotion of the story, suggesting an almost elemental narrative of competing mythical forces and creating a sense of recognizable otherworldliness. This dynamic art style is reminiscent of that pioneered by Jack Kirby, the creator of the New Gods and many of the other characters appearing in *Cosmic Odyssey*.

Themes

The major theme of *Cosmic Odyssey* is the consequence of arrogance. The central plot of the story revolves around the repeated attempts of arrogant individuals to control the power of the Anti-Life Equation. The story shows that arrogance is folly whether pursued for noble causes, represented by Metron's search for knowledge, or more sinister causes, represented by Darkseid's attempt to empower himself. This theme is further emphasized in the John Stewart subplot of the book. Stewart's arrogance about his own power leads to his failure to plan or to use assistance, leading to the destruction of a highly populated planet.

Cosmic Odyssey also contains a strongly related theme about the nature of compassion and humanity. At several points in the story characters are pitted against one another based upon their stance regarding the humanity of others. The character of Orion, who sees the ends as justifying the means and who has little compassion for those he perceives as being weaker than he, is set in opposition to Superman, who believes that all life has value and should be protected. By the end of the story, Orion is humbled by the fact that Forager, a mere "bug" from Orion's viewpoint, sacrifices himself to save the universe. By this act, the story reinforces for the reader the viewpoint expressed by Superman that all lives have value and that people should be measured by their deeds and not their station in life.

Impact

Cosmic Odyssey's most lasting impact was on the characterization of several important characters within DC Comics. Most important, John Stewart dealt with the repercussions of his action on Xanshi for years to come. His struggle to accept what had happened and to overcome his guilt and self-doubt over his part in the events became central features of his character. The destruction of Xanshi was also integrated in the DC Comics continuity as the precipitating event leading to the creation of the villain Fatality. *Cosmic Odyssey* also

made significant changes to the New Gods continuity. In particular, Orion became a more compassionate character after Forager's death.

The success of *Cosmic Odyssey* served to bolster the trend toward epic crossover events at DC Comics, helping to establish such multiepisodic crossover series as near annual events. *Cosmic Odyssey* also served to raise the profile of artist Mignola, who later created the *Hellboy* series (beginning in 1993) for Dark Horse Comics, and writer Starlin, who scripted *The Infinity Gauntlet* (1991), *Infinity War* (1992), and *Infinity Crusade* (1993) crossover miniseries for Marvel Comics.

Jason M. LaTouche

Further Reading

Mignola, Mike. *Hellboy* (1993-).

Starlin, Jim, George Perez, and Ron Lim. *The Infinity Gauntlet* (1991).

Waid, Mark, and Alex Ross. *Kingdom Come* (1996).

Bibliography

Greenberger, Robert. Introduction to *Cosmic Odyssey*. New York: DC Comics, 2002.

Starlin, Jim, and Mike Mignola. "Pro2Pro." *Back Issue!* 9 (April, 2005).

Voger, Mark. *The Dark Age: Grim, Great, and Gimmicky Post-Modern Comics*. Raleigh, N.C.: Two-Morrows, 2006.

See also: *Hellboy; Infinity Gauntlet; Kingdom Come; All Star Superman; Superman: For All Seasons; Superman: Red Son; Superman: The Man of Steel; Batman: Black and White,* Volume 1*; Batman: Dark Victory; Batman: The Dark Knight Returns; Batman: The Dark Knight Strikes Again; Batman: The Killing Joke; Batman: The Long Halloween; Batman: Year One; Batman: Year 100*

CRIMINAL

Author: Brubaker, Ed
Artist: Sean Phillips (illustrator); Val Staples (colorist)
Publisher: Marvel Comics
First serial publication: 2006-
First book publication: 2007-

Publication History

Icon Comics, the Marvel Comics imprint for creator-owned work, began publishing *Criminal* to supplement Ed Brubaker's and Sean Phillips's mainstream work for the company. The pair had previously collaborated on *Sleeper* (2003-2005), which blended superheroics, noir, and espionage. *Criminal* began as an ongoing series that ran for ten issues. After a hiatus, the series launched a second volume that ran for seven longer issues. The duo then began a new limited series, *Incognito* (2008-   ), and alternated between it and two further limited runs of *Criminal*. According to interviews with Brubaker and Phillips, future series of *Criminal* will continue to alternate with others of their creator-owned projects in different genres.

Despite the existence of *Criminal* collections, the mostly uncollected back matter in the single issues—such as interviews and articles about crime films, television shows, and novels—encourages readers to purchase the issues. The articles feature illustrations by Phillips and are written by Brubaker and his friends, including writers Jason Aaron, Steven Grant, Joe Hill, Tom Piccirilli, and Duane Swierczynski. The back matter has become one of the most popular aspects of the series and has turned *Criminal* into a de facto crime-fiction minimagazine.

Plot

Brubaker and Phillips's *Criminal* accommodates a wide variety of crime and noir story patterns and archetypes in a universe free of the costumes and superpowers present in most of their other noir-influenced work. *Criminal*'s overarching story builds slowly, with each story arc standing on its own. These arcs are deeply interrelated, with numerous references to past

Coward. (Courtesy of Marvel Comics)

and future details of the universe and to minor characters who become protagonists in later stories. Much remains to be revealed about the central story of *Criminal*, but it concerns two generations of professional thieves operating out of Bay City (the moniker detective writer Raymond Chandler used for Santa Monica, though the city in *Criminal* is modeled more on San Francisco).

Coward depicts the traditional story of a heist gone wrong, as a group of crooked police officers and former associates coerce Leo Patterson into helping them plan the robbery of blood diamonds from a police transport van bringing them to court as evidence. In reality, the cops work for a drug dealer and want the uncut heroin being transported in the van. The cops and a former partner of Leo betray him and the rest of the thieves. Leo and Greta Watson escape with the heroin. Despite the great lengths to which he goes to avoid violence, Leo decides to retaliate against the drug dealer and the dealer's associates. This retaliation lands Leo in prison.

Lawless serves as a revenge story for Tracy Lawless, the older brother of Leo's childhood friend, Ricky. Tracy finds out about his brother's murder and deserts the Army in order to infiltrate his brother's crew of thieves as a wheelman. Tracy has been mostly forgotten and assumes an alias (a nod to the pseudonyms of crime writer Donald Westlake, whose remorseless thief Parker is an avowed model for Tracy). Ricky's old crew plans a mysterious Christmas Eve heist, and Tracy helps them in the preparations, resulting in a heist in every issue of the story line. Tracy murders and tortures his way through the crew to learn the hard truth about his brother's murder, but he discovers he has killed all the wrong people for it. The aftermath of his actions leaves Tracy working to pay debts incurred by himself and his brother to syndicate boss Sebastian Hyde.

Through three stand-alone stories providing multiple perspectives, *The Dead and the Dying* concerns a heist in the early 1970's. The first story tells about the end of Gnarly Brown and Sebastian's friendship and the origins of the Hyde family's power from the partnership between their fathers, Clevon and Walter. The second introduces Teeg Lawless and shows how he began working for Sebastian after returning from Vietnam. The third story explains the motivations of Danica Briggs, whose death readers have already seen.

Bad Night shifts to another second-generation criminal, Jake Kurtz, whose parents worked with Leo's and Tracy's. Jake reformed after marrying Sebastian's niece, but he is continually drawn back into crime. An insomniac who often walks the city at night, he finds himself ensnared by a beautiful redhead named Iris and her volatile boyfriend. This story uses the classic formula of a romantic triangle leading to murder, as popularized by crime writer James Cain, and adds in an unreliable narrator, a technique reminiscent of the work of Jim Thompson.

The Sinners returns to Tracy, a year after the events of *Lawless*. The worst hit man imaginable, Tracy only executes people he thinks deserve it. In frustration, Sebastian assigns him to search for the person responsible for the deaths of several organized-crime figures in the city. Tracy is not much of a detective, but he beats and stumbles his way into the truth behind the killings, which are motivated by a grotesque vigilantism. The volume ends with Tracy trapped in a different, even more guilt-ridden situation than at the end of *Lawless*.

Volumes

- *Coward* (2007). Collects issues 1-5, featuring Leo dealing with the aftermath of a heist gone wrong.
- *Lawless* (2007). Collects issues 6-10, featuring Tracy infiltrating Ricky's old crew to avenge Ricky's murder.
- *The Dead and the Dying* (2008). Collects issues 1-3 of Volume 2, featuring a triptych perspective on a 1970's heist.
- *Criminal: Deluxe Edition* (2009). Collects the contents of the first three trade paperbacks and previously uncollected material, including a preview for the series that appeared in *Walking Dead*, issue 30; the backup prose story "Caught in the Undertow" and backup essays by Brubaker; Phillips's art for the backups; and the story "No One Rides for Free" from Image Comics' *The Comic Book Legal Defense Fund Presents: Liberty Comics*, issue 1.
- *Bad Night* (2009). Collects issues 4-7 of Volume 2, featuring Jake, an insomniac and former counterfeiter, unwillingly taking part in a heist.
- *The Sinners* (2010). Collects *Criminal: The Sinners*, issues 1-5, featuring Tracy investigating murders for Sebastian.

Characters

- *Leopold "Leo" Patterson* is the protagonist of the first arc, *Coward*, and two planned, forthcoming arcs. Leo ekes out a living as a pickpocket, reluctant to participate in heists, despite his genius for planning them and escaping from them if they fail. Most associates believe Leo is a coward afraid of prison and violence, but Leo's hesitance comes from a fear of releasing his demons.

- *Ivan* is young Leo's guardian after his father's imprisonment. By the first arc, he is a heroin addict with Alzheimer's disease, dependent on the care of Leo and private nurses. Despite his condition, Ivan remains an adept pickpocket and groper.
- *Greta Watson* is the widow of Leo's partner, Terry. Greta is a recovering addict and the single mother of a sick child. She persuades Leo to plan a heist, despite his misgivings.
- *Jacob "Gnarly" Brown* is a supporting character in several stories and a protagonist in the third arc. He is a mob enforcer's son whose boxing career ended because of a love triangle. He runs The Undertow, and despite the bar's reputation as a neutral site for criminals, Gnarly aids friends such as Leo and Mallory.
- *Tommy Patterson* is Leo's father and the leader of a crew of thieves. He died after being imprisoned for the murder of Teeg Lawless. He and his partner, Ivan, trained Leo.
- *Detective Jenny Waters* is the daughter of members of Tommy's crew but works as an Internal Affairs investigator. Despite her pariah status

with both the police and the underworld, she remains friends with Leo and Tracy.
- *Sergeant Tracy Lawless*, a.k.a. *Sam West*, is the protagonist of the second and fifth arcs. Tracy is a deadly special-forces deserter with a hatred for abusers of women. He infiltrates his brother's crew in order to find out who murdered Ricky. In doing so, he incurs a debt to Sebastian and must work it off as his hit man.
- *Broderick M. "Ricky" Lawless* is Tracy's younger brother, who, unlike Tracy, admired his father. Like his father, he worked as a thief, until his violent alcoholism and instability caused one of his partners to murder him.
- *Sebastian Hyde* is the son of the city's syndicate boss and former best friends with Gnarly in the third arc, set during the 1970's. By the present day, he has inherited his father's position and is the richest man in the city.
- *Jacob "Jake" Kurtz* is a supporting character in the second arc and the protagonist in the fourth. His parents were a part of Tommy's crew, and he was a counterfeiter before marrying Sebastian's niece. His wife disappeared under suspicious

Coward. (Courtesy of Marvel Comics)

circumstances, leading the police to persecute him and Chester to cripple him. He is an insomniac and the artist of the *Frank Kafka PI* strip. He is often suborned against his will to produce fake IDs.

- *Frank Kafka PI* is the private detective who appears in Jake's comic strip throughout the series. He is a decisive, two-fisted man of action but often finds himself buffeted by existential confusion.

- *Mallory* is Ricky's former on-again, off-again girlfriend. She takes up with Tracy when he joins her crew as a wheelman.

- *Danica Briggs* is a protagonist of the third arc, set during the 1970's. She is a young woman involved in a love triangle and a heist. The fallout from these events has grave personal consequences for her and Gnarly.

- *Teegar "Teeg" Lawless* is a protagonist of the third arc. He is a Vietnam veteran and the abusive, alcoholic father of Tracy and Ricky. He works for Sebastian and with Tommy's crew until his murder in 1989.

- *Iris*, a.k.a. *Nurse Nancy*, is a former dancer and nurse who manipulates Jake.

- *Detective Max Starr* is the investigator assigned to Jake's wife's disappearance. He tries to beat the truth out of Jake. Jake parodies him in the *Frank Kafka* strip as Detective Wrong.

- *Elaine Hyde* is the much younger and dissatisfied wife of Sebastian. Their son, Damian, has cancer.

- *Sabrina Hyde* is Sebastian's rebellious teenage daughter from a previous marriage, estranged from her stepmother.

- *Special Agent Yocum* is an Army officer sent to the city to retrieve a valuable deserter, Tracy.

Artistic Style

Criminal is set in the traditional layout of three rows of panels per page with between one and four panels per row. Phillips has stated that he wants *Criminal* to be accessible to the non-comics-reading audience, so he pares down and simplifies his style. Phillips does not pencil pages, instead using a blue marker to make an underdrawing and then filling in the rest of the details

with inks. These minimalist yet evocative artistic choices suggest the qualities of cinematic sleaziness the story requires. Val Staples's colors not only evoke mood but also highlight contrasts in light and among the characters.

Despite *Criminal*'s intentional simplifications, the art often has experimental qualities. Frank Kafka begins to interject himself into the narrative of *Bad Night*, and Phillips draws Frank in a cartoonish newspaper style that contrasts with the grimy detail of the rest of his art. Staples occasionally abandons realism in *Bad Night*, creating a completely red background in instances of violence. In the many flashbacks to Tracy's childhood, Phillips paints and draws with a ballpoint pen to give the past an alien feel. In the frequent chronological jumps in the opening story of *The Dead and the Dying*, Staples's colors mark the abrupt transitions. *Criminal* sometimes uses an all-black panel and an intertitle to show a transition in the story. In the second part of *The Dead and the Dying*, these black interpanels become a manifestation of Teeg's alcoholic blackouts. Phillips's and Staples's art is unobtrusive enough to allow for a straightforward reading of the crime narratives but simultaneously experiments with style and technique.

Themes

The major thematic concerns of *Criminal* are the effects of the violent actions of the past on the characters in the present. Leo explains to Greta in issue 3 that he avoids violence because it creates "a ripple effect." The reason that Leo succumbed to violence in 1989 and killed his best friend's father seems to be the major story *Criminal* will eventually tell. In the meantime, most protagonists in *Criminal* struggle with guilt and pain stemming from past violence. Tracy fears becoming like his father, even as he inherits his father's job as a hit man. Tracy differentiates himself from Teeg by reacting violently against the abusers of woman. Teeg's and Tracy's violent tendencies predate their military service, but their tours in Vietnam, Bosnia, and Iraq have further immersed them in killing. The guilt Leo, Tracy, Gnarly, and Jake experience over the results of their actions borders on the masochistic and even suicidal, and most *Criminal* stories end with the protagonists severely injured, having almost died.

Concurrent with the violent past, *Criminal* portrays the culmination of cycles of abuse. The main example of this is Ricky, who is repeatedly described as a sweet kid, but through his father's example and physical abuse becomes as unstable and violent against those close to him as his father had been. Along these lines, *Criminal* attempts to revise the tradition in crime fiction of dangerous women drawing men to their deaths. Greta, Mallory, Danica, Iris, and Elaine look like traditional "babes" of male escapist fiction, but these women retain the agency and desirability of dangerous woman while being portrayed sympathetically. Male violence has affected almost all of these women, and their relationships with the protagonists cost them more than even the most masochistic of their male partners.

Criminal's cast is dominated by white and black characters, and *The Dead and the Dying* takes on issues of race explicitly. That story shows the impossibility of

---

Ed Brubaker

Coming to superheroes and crime comics from a background in alternative comics (he wrote and drew the autobiographical *Lowlife* for Slave Labor), Ed Brubaker's writing for DC's Vertigo imprint brought him to the attention of a larger audiences in the mid-1990's. In 2001, with artist Darwyn Cooke, he revamped *Catwoman* in a critically acclaimed run on that title. In 2004 he was hired to relaunch *Captain America* at Marvel Comics, and in 2006 he took over as writer on *Daredevil* and *Uncanny X-Men*. Since that time he has become one of the leading architects of the direction of the Marvel Universe. His creator-owned crime title, *Criminal*, is one of the few attempts to create crime comics in the 2000's. Brubaker's writing is defined the use of real-world situations and political commentary within the confines of the superhero genre, and he is particularly interested in the exploration of familial and interpersonal relationships.

Gnarly and Sebastian remaining friends as they grow older and as Sebastian decides to follow the path of his father, who has power and a superior class position. Despite Sebastian and Gnarly's professions of friendship and closeness, their relationship and the similar one between their fathers have uncomfortable implications, as powerful white men command the violence of their black subordinates. Both Gnarly's willingness to step aside so that Sebastian can have Danica and Walter Hyde's command for Clevon to deal violently with Danica, pregnant with his grandchild, demonstrate white male sexual privilege.

Impact

Criminal is arguably one of the most realistic major American crime comics, lacking the over-the-top, cartoonish violence of *Sin City*, the extended fantasy sequences of *Stray Bullets*, and the labyrinthine conspiracies of *100 Bullets*. Thus, *Criminal* shifts American crime comics away from the continuing influence of superheroes. In terms of publishing, the creators of *Criminal* resist the move to a market dominated by trade paperbacks and encourage the purchase of single issues through the inclusion of extra content in the back of the singles. This back matter has become so popular that the expansion of *Criminal* after the first hiatus was done in part to provide room for two backup features an issue.

Demonstrating an increase in the popularity of crime comics, *Criminal*'s success has contributed to the launch of several publishing ventures, including the Vertigo Crime subimprint of DC Comics and a Marvel Comics alternate universe called Marvel Noir. Publishers such as Dark Horse Comics, Fantagraphics Books, IDW Publishing, and Running Press have also begun to translate European crime comics for the American market and release anthologies of crime comics.

Bob Hodges

Further Reading

Azzarello, Brian, and Eduardo Risso. *100 Bullets* (1999-2009).

Díaz Canales, Juan, and Juanjo Gaurnido. *Blacksad* (2010).

Lapham, David. *Stray Bullets* (1995-   ).

Bibliography

Benton, Mike. *Crime Comics: An Illustrated History.* Dallas: Taylor, 1993.

Lindenmuth, Brian. "The Fall (and Rise) of the Crime Comic." *Mulholland Books*, December 14, 2010. http://www.mulhollandbooks.com/2010/12/14/a-history-of-and-appreciation-for-crime-comics.

Phillips, Sean. "Criminal Week: Sean Philips Interviewed by Michael Lark!" Interview by Michael Lark. *MySpace Comic Books*, February 1, 2008. http://www.myspace.com/comicbooks/blog/353739484?__preferredculture=en-US&__ipculture=en-US.

See also: *100 Bullets; Blacksad*

CRISIS ON INFINITE EARTHS

Author: Wolfman, Marv

Artist: George Pérez (illustrator); Jerry Ordway (penciller and inker); Mike DeCarlo (inker); Dick Giordano (inker); Mike Machlan (inker); Carl Gafford (colorist); Robert Greenberger (colorist); Tom McCraw (colorist); Adrienne Roy (colorist); Anthony Tollin (colorist); Tom Ziuko (colorist); John Costanza (letterer)

Publisher: DC Comics

First serial publication: 1985-1986

First book publication: 1998

Publication History

Crisis on Infinite Earths was a twelve-issue maxiseries published by DC Comics. The story was conceived by writer Marv Wolfman as a solution to the problematic issue of DC Comics' convoluted continuity. Because of several decades' worth of stories, this continuity included multiple versions of characters and worlds, which was confusing, especially for new readers. *Crisis on Infinite Earths* was intended to simplify the continuity by eliminating the excessive alternate characters and worlds, establishing a new, singular continuity that could be followed by readers and comic creators alike.

Although first announced in 1981, research for the story line took several years, leading the maxiseries to be published in 1985, marking DC Comics' fiftieth anniversary. Originally titled *The History of the DC Universe* and proposed as a ten-issue maxiseries with a two-issue epilogue intended to establish the new history, the scope of the story extended the series to twelve issues, while the two-issue history epilogue was pushed back and released in 1987.

Writer and editor Len Wein was initially involved as the story's cowriter but was unable to devote enough time because he was editing DC Comics' *Who's Who* handbooks. Although not initially considered for the project, artist George Pérez got the job partially because of his previous partnership with Wolfman on *The New Teen Titans*. Dick Giordano was the inker on the first three issues but was too busy to ink the rest because of

(Getty Images)

Marv Wolfman

One of the stalwart names associated with superhero comics in the 1970's and 1980's, writer Marv Wolfman has extensive credits with both Marvel and DC Comics. At Marvel in the 1970's he had well-regarded runs on *Amazing Spider-Man*, *Fantastic Four*, and *Doctor Strange*, and is particularly remembered for a six-year run on *Tomb of Dracula*, with artist Gene Colan. In 1980, at DC Comics, he re-launched *Teen Titans* with artist George Pérez, and the series went on to become the most celebrated DC title of that decade. In 1985 he and Pérez worked on DC's first company-wide crossover, *Crisis on Infinite Earths*, which is still the high-water mark for projects of this type. Wolfman's contribution to comics was the revitalization of the entire DC Universe, and the careful attention to individual psychology within the dynamics of team books. He was among the most conscientious craftsmen of his generation.

his schedule as executive editor. His assistant inker, Mike DeCarlo, worked on the fourth issue before Jerry Ordway was hired to ink the rest of the series.

Almost all of DC's writers and editors tied their comics to the *Crisis* crossover. However, the monumental changes that the story line brought to the respective comic books and characters caused controversy among some writers. This led those working on *Crisis* to change the ending of one of the issues and decide against renumbering all of the subsequent comic books.

Plot

Crisis on Infinite Earths opens with the gradual destruction of the Multiverse, parallel universes that contain duplicate worlds with alternate histories and inhabitants. Aware of this crisis is the Monitor and his assistant, Harbinger, who both decide to take action. Harbinger disperses herself into multiple identical versions to recruit heroes and villains across the Multiverse, while the Monitor retrieves the infant Alexander Luthor, Jr., who escapes his universe's destruction. The group of heroes and villains meet the Monitor, who informs them of the danger that threatens their respective universes. The group is dispatched into smaller groups to protect massive golden towers placed across different points in time in Earth's history, later revealed to be machines to unite the Multiverse into a single universe. Psycho-Pirate is abducted by the Anti-Monitor, the individual responsible for the crisis. Afraid of the Anti-Monitor's power, Psycho-Pirate pledges his servitude to him.

Heroes everywhere try to stem the chaos brought about by the Crisis, while the groups guarding the towers fight shadow demons who intend to destroy them. Conflicts grow and escalate across time and space, culminating with the Monitor's death at the hands of a possessed Harbinger. Foreseeing his death, the Monitor releases his energies, activating the towers and creating a realm that protects the remaining universes from the Anti-Monitor. The heroes later stage an assault against the Anti-Monitor, resulting in his temporary retreat and the death of Supergirl.

During this reprieve, the villains band together in an attempt to take control of the remaining Earths. The

Anti-Monitor constructs an antimatter cannon to destroy the Earths but is thwarted by Barry Allen, the Flash of Earth-1, who sacrifices his life to destroy the cannon. The Anti-Monitor then travels to the dawn of time to rewrite existence in his favor. The heroes and villains work together to stop it; the former fight the Anti-Monitor and the latter travel to the planet Oa's distant past to prevent the scientist Krona from looking back to the origin of creation, which would cause the Anti-Monitor to succeed. The villains fail to stop Krona, and the Spectre's battle with the Anti-Monitor causes reality around them to explode and shatter.

The heroes find themselves on an unfamiliar Earth and learn that the battle from the dawn of time resulted in the creation of a single universe with no one except themselves remembering the previous reality. The Anti-Monitor makes another attack on Earth, but the heroes coordinate a successful counterassault that puts down the Anti-Monitor long enough to transport the Earth and themselves to safety. When the Anti-Monitor revives, Superman of Earth-2 opposes him and, assisted by an attack from the New God Darkseid, finally manages to kill the Anti-Monitor. Escaping the destructive effects of the Anti-Monitor's death, Alexander Luthor sends Superman and Lois Lane of Earth-2, Superboy of Earth-Prime, and himself to a paradise dimension to live out the rest of their days.

After detailing the statuses of certain heroes in the aftermath of the Crisis, Harbinger resolves her intent to live her life and explore the new Earth. The story ends with Psycho-Pirate committed in Arkham Asylum, rambling to himself about the events of the Crisis.

Characters

- *The Anti-Monitor*, the central antagonist, is a cosmically powered being who appears as a humanoid mass of energy encased in sinister-looking metallic armor. He has massive teeth and eyes that seem to be on fire. He was born during the creation of the antimatter universe. His plan to destroy the positive matter Multiverse and establish his native antimatter universe as the sole dominant reality presents a threat so great that all heroes must band together to oppose him.

- *Pariah* is a purple-haired man garbed in a green hood and cloak. The premier scientist of his world, he performs an experiment that allows him to watch the beginning of the universe but ultimately revives both the Monitor and the Anti-Monitor, resulting in the destruction of his universe. The sole, guilt-ridden survivor, he is empowered by the Monitor to teleport to locations that will be targeted for and struck by catastrophic events. Although he warns others of impending doom, he views his power as a curse, witnessing death after death.

- *Alexander Luthor, Jr.*, has curly red hair and dresses in a metallic gold suit. The sole survivor of Earth-3, he is the son of superhero Alexander Luthor and his wife Lois Lane. He escapes the antimatter wave when his father sends him to another universe as an infant. Rescued by the Monitor, who discovers that his body miraculously carries both positive and negative matter, he quickly grows into an adult and helps coordinate the heroes' attempts to save the remaining worlds. He possesses the power to act as a living portal to other universes, allowing the heroes to follow and battle the Anti-Monitor.

- *The Monitor* is a cosmically powered, pink-skinned humanoid with a nearly bald head. He wears armor and a cape, and is the benevolent counterpart to the Anti-Monitor. He alerts, prepares, and coordinates heroes and villains across the Multiverse to protect their worlds from the Anti-Monitor. Killed by a possessed Harbinger, his death helps protect the remaining Earths from the Anti-Monitor.

- *Harbinger,* a.k.a. *Lyla*, is a young, blond human who primarily wears skintight blue armor and a red headdress. Rescued by the Monitor after being adrift at sea and raised by him, she possesses the power to split herself into numerous identical versions and travel to different places and eras across the Multiverse. She gathers the heroes from throughout the Multiverse and helps them save the remaining worlds.

- *Superman of Earth-2* is a mature man with graying hair who wears a prominent red-and-blue

costume with a waist-length red cape. He is distinguished from his Earth-1 counterpart by his slightly different costume, older age, and marriage to his Earth's Lois Lane. Possessing the various Kryptonian superpowers, including superstrength and flight, Superman of Earth-2 is one of the foremost heroes during the Crisis, recruited by the Monitor at the beginning and opposing the Anti-Monitor during the final battle.

- *Psycho-Pirate*, a.k.a. *Alex Hayden*, is a villain whose golden mask and red-and-black attire is reminiscent of a court jester. Originating from Earth-1, he is the second man to assume the villainous mantle of the Psycho-Pirate. With his golden Medusa Mask, he possesses the power to manipulate other people's emotions and feed off of them. Although initially recruited by the Monitor, Psycho-Pirate is later abducted and terrorized by the Anti-Monitor.

Artistic Style

Crisis on Infinite Earths was DC Comics' biggest and most ambitious superhero epic to date, filled with multitudes of characters and countless scenes of action, pathos, and fantastic phenomena that took place over a variety of settings across space and time. Pages contain an average of seven to eight busy panels, at times numbering up to fifteen. Although this style limited Pérez's opportunities to showcase the high level of detail for which his art is known, the numerous panels highlight key visual, physical, or emotional aspects of a scene or event. The variation in panel size and placement within layouts presents a more dynamic reading experience while also allotting the appropriate space for accompanying exposition without obstructing the panels' visual content. Inking by artists such as Ordway gives the pages their appropriate dramatic weight and gravity while emphasizing the visual quality and detail of Pérez's art.

Pérez's clean line work allowed him to pack details within the images contained in the panels. Although he illustrated a variety of environments and fantastic phenomena, such as the destruction of entire worlds, Pérez is best known for his character art. He paid significant attention to appearances, researching characters' costume details and studying their physical attributes and expressions to distinguish the characters from one another. Taking advantage of the unique opportunity to draw all of DC's characters, Pérez took the initiative to include as many prominent and obscure characters alongside the key characters as possible within any given image.

Bright colors complete the story's grandeur. Originally, DC used flexography, printing technology new to comics at the time, to improve color brightness. The first issues were printed with this technology, but DC decided to return to traditional printing when the visual result was jarring. When the maxiseries was collected in trade, colorist Tom McCraw recolored the issues, realizing the bright colors that DC originally envisioned for the work.

Themes

The major themes of *Crisis on Infinite Earths* are heroism and the conflict between good and evil. The threat posed by the Anti-Monitor causes everyone to rise and unite against him. Characters such as the Monitor, Harbinger, and Alexander Luthor, Jr., act as leaders, coordinating efforts to save the remaining worlds and stop the Anti-Monitor. Heroes rise to the occasion, pushing themselves to do their best in protecting their worlds and combating the Anti-Monitor. Some, such as Supergirl, give their lives, and their examples inspire others to acts of heroism. Even the villains are moved to acts of heroism; for example, the Crime Syndicate of America tries to stop the antimatter wave from consuming their world. In the face of an encompassing threat, all kinds of people are moved to action and unite to protect all that they hold dear.

Tied to the theme of heroism is the theme of loss. Worlds, people, and entire universes are destroyed, killed, or ultimately wiped from existence. Characters throughout the series deal with loss in terms of their respective homes and loved ones. Some, such as Superman of Earth-2, experience doubt, survivor's guilt, and a loss of motivation to continue. Others, such as Batgirl, are intimidated by the foreboding feeling of potential loss and feel insecure and helpless. However, the heroes overcome this sense of loss, finding the resolve to continue protecting others and to face the danger that threatens them, emphasizing the theme of heroism.

Impact

Crisis on Infinite Earths was only partially successful in achieving its intended goal. Some longtime readers were alienated by the elimination of decades of stories and the deaths of numerous characters. In addition, although the story line and the simplified continuity succeeded in drawing in new readers, DC Comics did not immediately take advantage of the new creative opportunities. For part of 1986, DC comic books and characters continued on as if the *Crisis* story line had not happened. Eventually, the editors and writers revamped and rebooted their characters. Some characters, such as Superman and Batman, were successful, while others, such as Hawkman, were not as well received or were reintroduced to readers several years later. New continuity issues arose and amassed over time, eventually leading to another reboot in *Zero Hour: Crisis in Time* (1994).

Despite the remaining continuity issues, the drastic creative direction of *Crisis on Infinite Earths* helped attract new creative talent to DC Comics and allowed for the development of influential projects such as *The Dark Knight Returns* (1986) and *Watchmen* (1986-1987). Furthermore, *Crisis on Infinite Earths* became a significant DC Comics landmark, to the extent that fans discuss continuity and publication history in terms of pre-*Crisis* and post-*Crisis*.

On a broader scale, *Crisis on Infinite Earths* is widely remembered as the seminal story line of the comics industry. The series brought the issue of continuity to the forefront, calling attention to its importance for both readers and comics professionals. In addition, its success helped popularize the limited series format among most major comics companies in the industry, as well as the major event story line and related format. As in *Crisis*, major event crossovers are used to bring significant changes to characters, settings, and themes in order to facilitate a new creative direction and introduce new or revamped characters to readers. Such story lines generally occur within a limited series, with other comics and even other new limited series tying into it, and are used by comics companies to generate sales and establish new comic books, following *Crisis on Infinite Earths*' example.

Walter Lai

Further Reading

Busiek, Kurt, and George Pérez. *JLA/Avengers* (2003-2004).

Johns, Geoff, et al. *Infinite Crisis* (2005-2006).

Morrison, Grant, et al. *Final Crisis* (2009).

Bibliography

DiDio, Dan, and Robert Greenberger, eds. *Crisis on Infinite Earths: The Compendium*. New York: DC Comics, 2005.

Kaveney, Roz. *Superheroes! Capes and Crusaders in Comics and Films*. New York: Continuum International, 2002.

Kolck, Geoff. *How to Read Superhero Comics and Why*. New York: I. B. Tauris, 2008.

Lawrence, Christopher. *George Perez: Storyteller*. Runnemede, N.J.: Dynamic Forces, 2006.

See also: *Infinite Crisis; Green Lantern-Green Arrow; Green Lantern: Secret Origin; Swamp Thing; Wonder Woman: Love and Murder; Wonder Woman: The Circle; Batman: The Dark Knight Returns; Superman: For All Seasons; Superman: Red Son; Superman: The Man of Steel*

D

DAREDEVIL: BORN AGAIN

Author: Miller, Frank
Artist: David Mazzucchelli (illustrator); Richmond Lewis (colorist); Christie Scheele (colorist); Joe Rosen (letterer)
Publisher: Marvel Comics
First serial publication: 1986
First book publication: 1987

Publication History

Daredevil: Born Again was originally published in the monthly, thirty-two-page superhero comic book *Daredevil*, issues 226-233 (February-August, 1986). The issues were collected in graphic novel format in 1987 and went though several editions, including a deluxe hardcover edition released in 2009. The deluxe edition included recolored covers of the monthly *Daredevil* issues without the *Daredevil* logo, as well as the original, uninked pencil drawings from issue 228 and sample penciled pages from issues 229, 231, and 232. The deluxe edition also included Frank Miller's script for issue 233, "Armageddon." Finally, though not part of the *Born Again* story arc, "Warriors" (*Daredevil*, issue 226) was included in this collection because it was the only other *Daredevil* collaboration between writer Miller and artist David Mazzucchelli. *Born Again* colorist Christie Scheele and letterer Joe Rosen also contributed to the "Warriors" issue, with other contributors including Denny O'Neil (writing) and Dennis Janke (art). The first issue of the *Born Again* story line, "Apocalypse" (*Daredevil*, issue 227), was voted the eleventh best of the top one hundred Marvel Comics of all time in a 2001 readers' poll.

Plot

The story begins as Karen Page, Daredevil's former lover, sells his secret identity to a drug dealer for heroin. This information is passed on to Daredevil's

Daredevil: Born Again. (Courtesy of Marvel Comics)

enemy, a powerful crime lord known as the Kingpin. The Kingpin uses his influence to bankrupt and disbar Daredevil's public persona, Matt Murdock, who does not understand his decline until his house is bombed, making him realize that the Kingpin is responsible. Now homeless, Murdock plots to get his life back, but he no longer knows whom he can trust. When he calls his law partner and finds that his partner and his girlfriend have become involved with each other, he becomes unhinged. He confronts the Kingpin as

Murdock, rather than Daredevil, and is bested. The Kingpin locks him in a car and attempts to drown him, but he escapes. When he stumbles across some thieves stealing Santa Claus suits, he tries to stop them and is stabbed. Wounded, Murdock finds his way to the gym where his father trained as a fighter. This reinvigorates him, and he vows to get his life back.

Next, Murdock finds himself in a mission attended by nuns. His stab wound takes some time to heal, but he discovers that his long-lost mother is a nun. Meanwhile, Page travels to New York in the hope of saving him. She contacts his law partner and learns that Murdock is missing. Meanwhile, reporter Ben Urich decides to make public that Murdock was framed. The Kingpin's mob goes after Urich, and Murdock saves him.

The Kingpin knows that Murdock is in hiding and tries to flush him out by having one of his men pose as Daredevil. Murdock defeats the imposter and rescues Page, who was captured by a drug dealer. The two rekindle their relationship.

Undeterred, the Kingpin sends Nuke, a supersoldier in his employ, to find and destroy Murdock, who is living quietly in the Hell's Kitchen area of Manhattan. However, when Nuke goes on a rampage, Daredevil emerges fully costumed to face him, and the two battle. After a short time, the Avengers, led by Captain America, appear and take Nuke into custody. However, Nuke escapes and is eventually shot.

Daredevil takes Nuke to the reporter Urich, contributing to the downfall of the Kingpin, who is indicted for numerous crimes. Although he avoids jail, his power is broken, and he vows revenge. The story concludes with Daredevil and Page deciding to remain in Hell's Kitchen, their lives having been transformed.

Characters

- *Daredevil*, a.k.a. *Matt Murdock*, the protagonist, is a blind lawyer and superhero who was both athletic and bookish growing up. His father, a prizefighter, made him promise to get an education. At fifteen, he was blinded while pushing an old man out of the way of a truck. The accident exposed him to radioactive materials that heightened his other senses. Remaining true to his father's wishes, he became a brilliant attorney. Using his athletic abilities, his heightened senses, and his legal expertise, he fights crime as Daredevil.

- *Karen Page* is Murdock's former secretary and girlfriend. She left his employ and embarked on an unsuccessful career as an actress that led her to star in pornographic films. By the beginning of *Born Again*, she has become a heroin addict.

- *Franklin "Foggy" Nelson* is Murdock's law partner, existing in the shadow of Murdock's legal brilliance. He emerges as an exceptional attorney in his own right, defending Murdock against fraudulent claims.

Daredevil: Born Again. (Courtesy of Marvel Comics)

- *The Kingpin*, a.k.a. *Wilson Fisk*, is a powerful crime lord determined to destroy his archenemy, Daredevil. He is also an able wrestler.
- *Maggie Murdock* is Matt Murdock's mother. As a boy, Murdock was told that his mother had died. In *Born Again*, she returns as a nun who cares for him while he is homeless.
- *Glorianna O'Breen* is a photographer and a girlfriend of Murdock. She is frustrated by Murdock's absences, not knowing that he is Daredevil, and becomes involved with Foggy Nelson.
- *Ben Urich* is a crack reporter for *The Daily Bugle*. From following Daredevil's career closely, he has surmised that Murdock is Daredevil. As a result, he has become Murdock's confidant.
- *Captain America*, a.k.a. *Steve Rogers*, is a superhero who received his powers during World War II, when he was too weak to join the U.S. Army. He agreed to participate in a scientific experiment and was transformed into the supersoldier Captain America. He was frozen in ice toward the end of the war, and when he thawed out, he returned to fighting crime as a member of the Avengers.
- *Nuke* is a supersoldier, the product of an attempt to create more soldiers like Captain America. However, this experiment went awry, and Nuke often works outside the law.

Artistic Style

The visual presentation is one of the most interesting aspects of *Daredevil: Born Again*. For the most part, the art by Mazzucchelli is representational in style, focusing on soft lines that indicate understated movements and facial expressions. Some objects are depicted as oversized to indicate their impact on a character; for example, a loudly ticking clock is depicted as very large. Likewise, the action scenes are simplified, helping to present an understated action story. Catholic images such as cathedrals, stained-glass windows, and nuns abound in *Born Again*, reflecting both the content of the story and the theme of redemption. In keeping with the redemptive theme, the color red is used heavily. This is partially representative of Daredevil's red costume, but it also symbolizes the

idea that bloodshed is necessary for rebirth. The other predominant color is black, and both colors emphasize each other. Other colors used in the story are softer, making both the red and the black stand out in contrast.

Another important visual component of the story is the use of small panels to depict movement and larger panels to indicate isolation. Generally, the small panels are used for routine or quick actions, while the larger ones slow down the pace and allow the reader to focus on the characters. In several cases, overhead shots are used to better depict the characters' powers. When an ill Daredevil confronts the Kingpin, the reader sees how small he is when viewed from above. When the triumphant Daredevil emerges from a fire, he faces the reader defiantly.

Miller had been both the writer and artist of *Daredevil* from 1979-1983 and had a distinct visual style, focusing on clever use of blacks and hard lines. Mazzucchelli's artistic style in *Born Again* borrows some of Miller's visual language while portraying dramatic scenes, but his work also echoes earlier, less stark *Daredevil* artists such as Wally Wood, Gene Colan, and Gil Kane.

Themes

The theme of *Daredevil: Born Again* concerns personal redemption, as Daredevil, or Matt Murdock, must save himself after his life has been shattered by the Kingpin. Murdock embarks on the epic hero's journey; he is deprived of his worldly goods, questions his sanity, and is physically wounded nearly to the point of death. However, as the title indicates, the hero is reborn and restored. The chapter titles— "Apocalypse," "Purgatory," "Pariah," "Born Again," "Saved," "God and Country," and "Armageddon"—further imply this rebirth. As the story progresses, Murdock's law partner comes out of Murdock's shadow; Murdock finds his mother, whom he believed since childhood to be dead; and he rekindles his relationship with his former lover, Page. As the story closes, Murdock must build a new life for himself.

Impact

Although it did not garner any major industry awards, *Daredevil: Born Again* wielded great weight in the comics industry. It solidified Miller's position as one of the premier mainstream comic book storytellers and gave newcomer artist Mazzucchelli star status. The *Born Again* story line set the pattern for the Daredevil character for the next several years, as Murdock relocated from his brownstone to New York's Hell's Kitchen, where Daredevil battled drug lords and street thugs rather than superpowered villains.

The *Born Again* story line also helped ground many superhero stories in the real world, as opposed to a more fantastical world populated by supervillains and magic. *Daredevil: Born Again* was part of the break away from the superpowered fantasies of the 1970's and early 1980's, signaling the turn toward more mature stories.

Stephen Weiner

Films

Daredevil. Directed by Mark Steven Johnson. Twentieth Century Fox, 2003. This feature film starring Ben Affleck, Jennifer Garner, and Colin Farrell was in part based on the Daredevil character presented in *Daredevil: Born Again*. The film was received well enough that a follow-up film also starring Jennifer Garner, *Elektra* (2005), was produced.

Further Reading

Bendis, Brian Michael, and Alexander Maleev. *Daredevil: Lowlife* (2003).

Miller, Frank, and David Mazzucchelli. *Batman: Year One* (1988).

Miller, Frank, and John Romita, Jr. *Daredevil: The Man Without Fear* (1994).

Bibliography

George, Milo. *The Comics Journal Library,* Volume 2*: Frank Miller*. Seattle: Fantagraphics Books, 2003.

Weiner, Stephen. *The 101 Best Graphic Novels,* Revised Edition. New York: NBM, 2005.

Wolk, Douglas. *Reading Comics: How Graphic Novels Work and What They Mean*. New York: De Capo Press, 2007.

Wright, Bradford W. *Comic Book Nation: The Transformation of Youth Culture in America*. Baltimore: Johns Hopkins University Press, 2001.

See also: *Daredevil: The Man Without Fear; Elektra Assassin; Elektra Lives Again*

DAREDEVIL: THE MAN WITHOUT FEAR

Author: Miller, Frank

Artist: John Romita, Jr. (penciller and cover artist); Al Williamson (inker and cover artist); Christie Scheele (colorist); Joe Rosen (letterer)

Publisher: Marvel Comics

First serial publication: 1993-1994

First book publication: 1994

Publication History

Daredevil: The Man Without Fear was published monthly as a five-part series from October, 1993, to February, 1994. The series began as a hardcover project (and possible film idea) but was recast as a limited series. The series was subsequently published as several prints of trade paperback and hardback editions, as well as being included in the larger *Daredevil Omnibus: Frank Miller Companion* (2007), which includes numerous related materials connected with *Daredevil: The Man Without Fear*, such as original scripts, alternate covers and pages, and reproduced covers with publication information.

Plot

Frank Miller recasts the origin of Daredevil (Matt Murdock), first introduced to Marvel in April, 1964. Issue 1 opens with Murdock as a child in the Hell's Kitchen area of Manhattan. Murdock's dual life as a good boy who is "sneaky" is presented with him stealing a cop's nightstick and slipping away to the boxing gym. His father, Jack, struggles with depression, sighing about the mysterious "Maggie," and finds himself trapped as an aging boxer at night and a mob enforcer for the Fixer by day. After his father hits him, Murdock commits himself to learning, specifically the law; he also dedicates himself to working out at the gym. Murdock's fate is sealed when he pushes a blind man from an oncoming truck carrying toxic chemicals, which blind Murdock but also give him supersenses. After being visited in the hospital by an unnamed nun, Murdock is mentored by the Stick to harness his new powers. Issue 1 ends with Jack Murdock failing to throw a fight and being killed by the mob.

Daredevil: The Man Without Fear. (Courtesy of Marvel Comics)

Murdock visits the morgue to identify his father in issue 2, and then he sets out to avenge his father's death by attacking the henchmen of the Fixer, leading to the Fixer dying of a heart attack when chased by Murdock. During the attacks, Murdock throws a prostitute out a window and to her death, forcing him to face his acts as a vigilante. Stick discusses Murdock's rash behavior with Stone and mentions Elektra.

The narrative jumps a year to Columbia University, where Murdock attends college and has befriended Franklin "Foggy" Nelson. Murdock is pulled back to his secret fight for justice because Foggy is harassed by classmates as Murdock had been as a child. The issue ends with Murdock lured into a chase through a snow-covered park and a reckless car ride with Elektra, exposing that he is haunted by the innocent prostitute he killed.

In issue 3, Murdock dives into an icy lake to look for Elektra but returns to his dorm alone. Foggy tells Murdock about Elektra, including where she lives with her Greek diplomat father. Murdock slips into the compound, creates a scene, and then runs away, shot in the arm. While he is tending to his wound in his bathroom, he discovers Elektra in the shower. Foggy sits outside the locked door to their dorm room and learns that Murdock and Elektra are together when she leaves.

Next, Elektra lures five thugs down an alleyway, where she drops her fur coat and taunts them into attacking her. She kills them all, leaving behind a gruesome scene for the police. Murdock and Elektra become lovers despite a late-night warning from Stick. Issue 3 ends with Elektra leaving Murdock after the murder of her father and a brief scene introducing the Kingpin in Hell's Kitchen.

Jumping years ahead, issue 4 shows the rise of the Kingpin and that Murdock has graduated summa cum laude from Harvard Law School and is working in Boston at a corporate law firm. Praising Murdock for his work, the firm sends him to New York for a case, where he revisits Hell's Kitchen and beats up a group of thugs. He finds the old gym and meets a young girl, Mickey, who hides there. An old poster of Jack Murdock leads Murdock to tell Mickey about his nickname as a child, Daredevil. Murdock and Mickey begin to work out together, and Murdock is reunited with Foggy, who does class-action work for struggling clients. Murdock helps Foggy with his

cases and feels renewed. The Kingpin feeds off the children in Hell's Kitchen, where his thugs push some addicts to find a twelve-year-old girl, which imperils Mickey. Just as Murdock is about to return to Boston, he learns Mickey has been kidnapped, leading him to don a crude, ninjalike outfit and steal into the Kingpin's compound to save Mickey.

In issue 5, the superhero Daredevil comes into focus, with the panels and artwork announcing the dramatic end to the limited series with an opening full-page panel of Murdock in his makeshift costume. Murdock fights and defeats the thugs, attempting to keep track of Mickey, who is being dragged away during the fights. When Murdock is close to saving her, the police capture and handcuff him and hold him inside a police cruiser. Murdock frees himself and tracks down Mickey's captor, telling him to release the girl, since Murdock does not want to kill him. Murdock displays his unique talents, swatting away bullets with his baton, striking the captor, and killing him with his own bullet. The issue ends with the Kingpin fretting over this new adversary and with Murdock losing his Boston job, soon joining Foggy to form a practice in New York.

While Foggy and Murdock are making plans, Stick returns to warn Murdock. The final scenes show the costumed Daredevil in silhouette crossing rooftops before the final two-page panel, expanding the opening full-page panel of the last issue, showing a series of leaping Daredevils in full costume, the first three in the classic yellow and red and the final two in the most well known, fully red Daredevil costume.

Daredevil: The Man Without Fear. (Courtesy of Marvel Comics)

Characters

- *Matt Murdock*, a.k.a. *Daredevil*, is the protagonist and a superhero. As a boy, he is blinded by radioactive chemicals and subsequently acquires superpowers (radar and heightened senses); he also develops abilities of an elite gymnast and martial artist. Obsessed by law and justice, he struggles with, but eventually commits to, assuming the role of the superhero Daredevil.
- *Jack Murdock* is Murdock's father. He is a small-time boxer who has lost his love and works as a mob enforcer. When Jack is faced with throwing a fight, he chooses to honor his promise to Murdock and not quit, resulting in his murder.
- *The Fixer* is a mob boss who runs Hell's Kitchen in Murdock's childhood. He and his thugs kill Murdock's father.
- *Stick*, a sensei, is the blind stranger who follows and befriends young Murdock, teaching him the skills needed to harness his superpowers and develop into the crime fighter Daredevil.
- *Elektra*, a.k.a. *Natchios*, the daughter of a Greek diplomat, circles in and out of Murdock's life while creating a great deal of mystery concerning her connection with Stick and apparent fated connection with Murdock/Daredevil. A ninja assassin, she reveals a dark vigilante streak that parallels Murdock's.
- *Stone*, a student of Stick, appears in silhouette, arguing for Murdock with Stick after Murdock inadvertently throws a prostitute to her death.
- *Franklin "Foggy" Nelson* is Murdock's college roommate who becomes his best friend and law partner. Foggy provides motivation for Murdock to reexamine his own experiences of being bullied (and called "Daredevil" as a child).
- *The Kingpin* is introduced as a sinister crime lord who takes over Hell's Kitchen while Murdock is attending college and becoming a lawyer. The Kingpin is shown as a particularly cruel villain who preys on drug addicts and children.
- *Mickey* is a homeless girl of fourteen, stowing away in the abandoned gym of Murdock's childhood. She and Murdock become friends, and her

kidnapping leads Murdock to embrace fully his role as Daredevil.

Artistic Style

Daredevil: The Man Without Fear is driven by narrative panels, not dialogue, that capture the mystery and noir style of the character. The panels are more traditional and linear in the opening issues, but change, becoming more dynamic as the character Murdock moves toward being fully realized as a superhero. For example, in issue 5, the panels vary among full-page, double-spread, and horizontal, instead of vertical, double-page. The action scenes also have panels overlaying and overlapping with larger background panels highlighting the action. The artwork suggests the darker artwork and coloring that followed years later in the work of Alexander Maleev, for example.

John Romita, Jr.'s pencils and Al Williamson's inks capture a realistic and stark style that reminds readers of classic work by John Buscema and Jack Kirby, while echoing Miller's bold and distinct form of superheroes and villains juxtaposed with children and normal

---

John Romita, Jr.

Arguably the artist most clearly associated with the Marvel style over the past thirty years, John Romita, Jr. is the son of acclaimed *Spider-Man* artist John Romita. Romita, Jr. got his start at Marvel in the late-1970's and has, with a very few exceptions, worked exclusively for that publisher ever since. Romita, Jr. has penciled an extremely wide variety of titles over the years, including *Iron Man, Spider-Man, Daredevil, The Punisher War Zone, The Mighty Thor, Black Panther*, and *World War Hulk*. With Neil Gaiman he produced a high-profile reinterpretation of *The Eternals*, and with Mark Millar he created *Kick Ass*, which was later adapted into a movie of the same name. His style was initially very tightly detailed and heavily influenced by his father, but has loosened considerably over time. Critics complain that his work can sometimes feel sketchy, but he is renowned as one of the most consistent storytellers in the superhero genre.

---

characters. The characters are often rough and heavily shaded, although Elektra is drawn with simple lines that reveal both femininity and a dark anger. Murdock is often portrayed slumping, fighting the weight of his burdens, and the many thugs and villains of the issues are distinct but massive and imposing against the children and decaying buildings and ominous alleyways. The city landscapes and buildings almost make Hell's Kitchen an additional "character" in the story. Setting, not only the city but also the snow-covered scenes and icy waters with Elektra, for example, carries the stark and powerful characters of the narrative.

The full- and double-page panels accentuate the grand scale of the themes of the Daredevil myth— themes of justice and violence portrayed in the larger-than-life superhero Daredevil, the contradictory Elektra, and the giant villain the Kingpin.

The coloring from Christie Scheele emphasizes basic and dark colors, reinforcing black and red (with yellow and orange hues) throughout to parallel the motifs of violence and darkness that drive the Daredevil narrative.

Themes

The driving motif of *Daredevil: The Man Without Fear* is duality, identified immediately in issue 1 with the dual life of young Murdock as "good son" and "sneaky boy." Murdock as a boy is also confronted with his father's duality as a masked boxer and a mob enforcer. Later, when Murdock assumes the dual roles of lawyer and superhero, he is haunted by his accidental murder of a prostitute and the dual nature of Elektra, who represents the blurring of good and evil.

Within the duality motif, justice and law are contrasted with crime and violence. Miller accentuates the blurring of right and wrong through Murdock's own actions (which echo the tensions in the Batman/Bruce Wayne mythos) as well as through the alluring character Elektra.

Blindness also adds complexity to Miller's consideration of justice (as justice is blind), with the accidental blinding of Murdock and the blind sensei Stick mentoring Murdock to embrace and enhance his heightened senses once he loses normal sight. Throughout the narrative, Murdock is highly perceptive about the law but struggles with his own violent outbursts and history with breaking the law (as a child and with the accidental killing of the prostitute).

Present throughout the Daredevil narrative are themes addressing innocence and experience—from Murdock's childhood to Mickey and the many nameless children and innocent bystanders overwhelmed by the violence, crime, and ominous cityscape of Hell's Kitchen.

Daredevil: The Man Without Fear. (Courtesy of Marvel Comics)

Impact

Originally created to be a graphic novel or movie idea, *Daredevil: The Man Without Fear*, released as a monthly five-issue run from October, 1993, through February, 1994, helped solidify Miller's reenvisioning of Daredevil and Elektra in the Marvel Universe. This origin story stands as the definitive Miller view of the character and informs the Marvel Universe version of Daredevil in the late Modern Age after the 1980's.

Miller also perpetuated the complicated portrayal of Elektra, a character that presents many problems for a unified Marvel Universe because her origin and existence have been refashioned often despite her minor status. The series and eventual graphic novel also represent and perpetuate Miller's own influence as a writer on the comic book/graphic novel industry; his collaboration with Romita as a penciller revealed the growing influence of manga on Western comic book art. Miller recreated Daredevil in much the same way he did Batman, expanding the rise in superstar creators (such as Miller) who began to drive the comic book/graphic novel industry regardless of the publisher. The transi-

tion between comic book single issues/series and repackaged graphic novels is also reflected in the continued success of this graphic novel.

P. L. Thomas

Further Reading

Bendis, Brian Michael. *Daredevil: Underboss* (2002).

Miller, Frank. *Batman: Year One* (1988).

_____. *Daredevil Visionaries: Frank Miller,* Volume 2 (2001).

Bibliography

Gravett, Paul. *Graphic Novels: Everything You Need to Know*. New York: Collins Design, 2005.

Miller, Frank, et al. *Daredevil Omnibus Companion*. New York: Marvel Comics, 2007.

Thomas, P. L. *Challenging Genres: Comic Books and Graphic Novels*. Rotterdam, Netherlands: Sense, 2010.

See also: *Daredevil: Born Again; Batman: Year One; Ronin*

Death of Captain America, The

Author: Brubaker, Ed

Artist: Steve Epting (illustrator); Roberto De la Torre (illustrator); Butch Guice (illustrator); Mike Perkins (illustrator); Fabio Laguna (penciller); Rick Magyar (penciller); Luke Ross (penciller); Frank D'Armata (colorist); VC's Joe Caramagna (letterer)

Publisher: Marvel Comics

First serial publication: 2007-2008

First book publication: 2008

Publication History

The Death of Captain America was published initially in the comic book *Captain America*, issues 25-42. *The Death of Captain America,* Volume 1*: The Death of the Dream* comprises issues 25-30 and was published in hardback in November of 2007; the paperback followed in June, 2008 *The Death of Captain America,* Volume 2*: The Burden of Dreams* collects issues 31-36 and was published in hardback in May, 2008, and in paperback in October, 2008. The series concludes with *The Death of Captain America,* Volume 3*: The Man Who Bought America*. This volume compiles issues 37-42 and was published in hardback in November, 2008, and paperback in March, 2009. The entire series can be found in the hardcover *The Death of Captain America Omnibus*, published in December of 2009.

Plot

The Death of the Dream begins with the origin of Captain America. Steve Rogers is rejected from military service during World War II. He volunteers for a secret initiative called "Project: Rebirth." A German scientist who escaped Adolf Hitler's regime discovered a formula to create supersoldiers. The United States military plans to build a squadron of supersoldiers to win the war. Rogers is the first volunteer and is transformed into a muscular warrior with incredible speed and agility. At the moment of triumph, a German spy kills the scientist and destroys the formula. Thus, Rogers becomes a symbol of what might have been while also becoming Captain America.

The Death of Captain America. (Courtesy of Marvel Comics)

In Marvel's *Civil War* (2007), Captain America leads a band of heroes against the Superhuman Registration Act, a law requiring superheroes to surrender their secret identities and become agents of the U.S. government. Captain America is winning his battle but surrenders when he realizes that it is harming the public. In the aftermath, he stands accused of federal crimes. He appears in shackles outside a courthouse. A shot is fired. Sharon Carter, his girlfriend and S.H.I.E.L.D.. agent, attempts to get to him. (S.H.I.E.L.D.. is the top investigative and defense agency in the country.)

A second gun flashes in the crowd, and three more shots are fired. Rogers is wounded and collapses onto the steps of the building. High above the street, the

Falcon confronts Bucky, Captain America's sidekick, believing him to be the assassin. Bucky swears his allegiance to Captain America; Falcon and Bucky set out to find Crossbones, the man who fired the rifle. Captain America is rushed to the hospital but is soon pronounced dead. At the hospital, Sin, Red Skull's daughter, disguises herself as a nurse and approaches Sharon. She tells Sharon that Dr. Faustus wants her "to remember." Suddenly, Sharon realizes that she fired the second gun that killed Steve Rogers.

Chaos ensues in the aftermath of the death of Captain America. The Red Skull, whose spirit inhabits the body of Aleksander Lukin, has hired Arnim Zola and Dr. Faustus to wage a campaign against the economic stability and political leadership of the United States. Tony Stark (Iron Man) assumed command of S.H.I.E.L.D. after the *Civil War*. A posthumous letter from Steve Rogers is delivered to Stark asking him "to save Bucky." Bucky steals Captain America's shield, which is in the possession of the government. His next task is to find the person who killed Steve Rogers.

Bucky hunts down Lutkin and discovers that he has become the Red Skull. The Skull defeats Bucky and remands him to Dr. Faustus. Faustus tortures Bucky with memories of his time as a Soviet assassin and questions the young man's loyalty to Captain America.

Sharon and the Falcon help Bucky escape but turn him over to Tony Stark. A battle ensues between Bucky and Iron Man (Stark) because Bucky blames Stark for the death of Steve Rogers. Stark reveals the letter from Steve, and Bucky agrees to become the new Captain America. The first challenge for the new hero is Skull's plot to overthrow the government. A Skull-induced financial crisis brings protests in the streets of Washington, D.C. Mind-controlled guards shoot innocent citizens. The new Captain America stops the assault but fails to assure the citizenry in his first campaign as a hero. The Skull then resurrects an experimental Captain America to fight for the hearts and minds of the American people.

Senator Gordon Wright becomes a third-party candidate for the presidency, and Dr. Faustus resurrects a delusional figure from the 1950's to play the role of the "real" Captain America. Bucky must overcome his personal doubts and the strength of a supersoldier to defeat the 1950's Captain America. Bucky stops an assassination attempt during a televised debate, and as he crashes into the control room, he declares, "I'm Captain America." Once again, Captain America earns his shield by defeating his oldest nemesis, the Red Skull.

The Death of Captain America. (Courtesy of Marvel Comics)

Volumes

- *The Death of Captain America,* Volume 1*: The Death of the Dream* (2008). Collects issues 25-30 of *Captain America*. Charts the origin of Captain America as a military experiment that becomes a one-off when the scientist in charge is killed by a German spy.
- *The Death of Captain America,* Volume 2*: The Burden of Dreams* (2008). Collects issues 31-36 of *Captain America*. Steve Rogers is shot and killed, and Bucky assumes the mantle of Captain America, attempting to combat the Red Skull's plot against the U.S. government.
- *Captain America,* Volume 3*: The Man Who Bought America* (2008). Collects issues 37-42 of *Captain America*. Bucky as Captain America must fight a 1950's version of the superhero. He earns respect by stopping a political assassination during a televised debate.
- *The Death of Captain America* (2009). A Marvel Omnibus that collects issues 25-42 of *Captain America*, thus compiling in one volume the three previously published volumes.

Characters

- *Steve Rogers*, a.k.a. *Captain America*, the super-soldier, is the symbolic World War II hero who represents the best of the United States.
- *James Barnes*, a.k.a. *Bucky*, is the World War II sidekick of Captain America. He was believed dead for many years. It was later discovered that he had been rescued by the Soviets and brainwashed; he became the assassin named the Winter Soldier.
- *Sam Wilson*, a.k.a. *the Falcon*, is the former partner of Captain America.
- *Sharon Carter* is former Agent 13 of S.H.I.E.L.D.. and the girlfriend of Steve Rogers.
- *Nick Fury* is the former director of S.H.I.E.L.D.. He was head of the Howling Commandos in World War II and served with Captain America.
- *Red Skull* is Captain America's nemesis and an aide to Hitler in World War II.
- *Sin* is the daughter of the Red Skull and girlfriend of Crossbones.

- *Arnim Zola* is a longtime enemy of Captain America and a mercenary scientist.
- *Aleksander Lukin* is a former general in the KGB and head of the Kronos corporation; his body became a vessel for the Red Skull after repeatedly using the cosmic cube.
- *Crossbones* is an aide to the Red Skull.
- *Dr. Faustus* is a master of psychological manipulation through the use of drugs. He infiltrates S.H.I.E.L.D.. and controls a number of agents, including Sharon Carter. He is also responsible for the return of the 1950's Captain America.
- *Tony Stark*, a.k.a. *Iron Man*, is a billionaire industrialist and S.H.I.E.L.D.. director. He opposed Captain America in Marvel's *Civil War*.
- *Natalia "Natasha" Romanov*, a.k.a. *the Black Widow*, is a former Soviet agent who became an Avenger.
- *Senator Gordon Wright* is a corrupt politician and Skull's third party candidate for the presidency.

Artistic Style

In *Understanding Comics* (1993), theorist Scott McCloud formally defines the art of comics as "Juxtaposed pictorial and other images in deliberate sequence, intended to convey information and/or to produce an aesthetic response in the viewer." McCloud illustrates in his text that artists may use various styles, frames, sequences, colors, and print fonts to depict their stories. The choice of the word "juxtaposed" is particularly relevant in the analysis of *The Death of Captain America*. Since his resurrection in 1964, Captain America has been "a man out of time." Writers and artists have struggled to tell the story of a World War II hero battling villains in the era of the Vietnam War (U.S. involvement, 1965-1975), the Watergate scandal (1972), and the twenty-first-century fight against terrorism.

In *Death of the Dream*, the artists use black-and-white frames with yellow word boxes to convey the image of memories, as though the reader is viewing old newsreel footage. The dark depiction of the hero as a warrior fighting against a shaded background lends itself to explosive bursts of color to illustrate weapons, blasts, and narrative cries. Throughout the series, the modern depiction of television news footage is wrapped in red banners and bold print to highlight its presence. Bucky's nightmare in *The Burden of Dreams* exhibits another form of juxtaposition when Bucky and Steve are seen battling in a World War II scene and discussing the Internet. Even more than Steve, Bucky is a man battling with his past because of his actions as the brainwashed Winter Soldier.

The most notable artistic feature of this series is the redesign of the Captain America costume. Steve Rogers as Captain America is adorned in a shirt with a bright blue chest bearing a white star over an abdomen of red-and-white stripes. Bright blue pants are tucked into red boots; it is a costume that draws visual attention. The only weapon remaining from the traditional Captain America is his round shield. It is primarily a defensive weapon used to protect the innocent and to disarm the criminal.

Bucky's Captain America uniform is much darker than Rogers's. A red-white-and-blue chest plate covers a black shirt. Bucky wears a holster with two sidearms and has a nightstick strapped to his leg. Black pants and black boots complete the outfit. Barnes carries the traditional shield, but his is a much darker image of a modern Captain America. He is a trained warrior who is not hesitant to use a weapon.

Themes

World War II has been called the last "good war." It was a time when Americans united in a common cause to defeat Hitler. Americans sacrificed to serve the war effort—soldiers stormed beaches, women worked regular factory shifts, and children collected scrap metal to be recycled into military equipment. It was a time when the vast majority of Americans read comic books and searched for heroes to solve the extraordinary problems of the day. It was the era that gave birth to Captain America.

The twenty-first-century "war on terror" bears little resemblance to that time. People are divided over issues of security and privacy; religious differences frighten and divide neighbors; politicians challenge the motives and character of colleagues. Marvel's *Civil War* series reflected many of these issues.

The Superhuman Registration Act required superheroes to surrender their secret identities and become agents of the government. The charge was that superpowered individuals are like weapons of mass destruction, and the public could not be sure how these powers would be used. One would expect a hero created by a secret military program to agree with this decision. Captain America, however, did not. Questions of identity, privacy, personal rights, security, and individual freedom drove Steve Rogers to challenge the law. He surrendered to authorities only when he believed that he had lost public support. *The Death of Captain America* is ultimately a story about identity and honor. Steve Rogers died for the latter as Captain America; Bucky Barnes picked up the shield to fight for it.

Impact

Steve Rogers resumed the role of Captain America in July of 2011, in *Captain America*, issue 1 (which coincides with the release of the film *Captain America: The First Avenger*). The death of a superhero is a device used to stimulate sales and inject drama into the story line. Most readers know that death is rarely an end in comic books. Characters such as Captain

---

Steve Epting

Though he broke into the industry with First Comics in 1989, Steve Epting's first high-profile art assignment was Marvel's *The Avengers* in the early 1990's. Since that time he has worked on a wide variety of titles for both Marvel and DC, including *X-Men*, *Aquaman*, *Captain America*, *The Fantastic Four*, and *The Invaders*. He was one of the artists most closely associated with the short-lived CrossGen Comics, drawing *Crux*, a title that he co-created with writer Mark Waid, and *El Cazador*, a pirate comic with writer Chuck Dixon. Epting's art is notable for its extremely close attention to detail and careful focus on anatomy. He tends to compose his images in depth, creating clearly established spaces through which his characters move. In his recent work Epting's art has become increasingly realistic and polished.

America have died, disappeared, or cast off the superhero uniform many times. The comic strip *The Phantom*, for example, created an aura of immortality for "The Ghost Who Walks" by passing the mask from generation to generation. Most heroes simply bend time by adapting to new villains and eras. Captain America, however, is different.

Most Golden Age heroes adapt to the times. Superman and Batman, for example, have changed with readership and market tastes. Captain America, on the other hand, is a product of World War II. The "Star Spangled Avenger," as he has been called, was so associated with the war that readers left him in the 1950's, and the series was canceled. *The Death of Captain America* allowed a new generation of readers to celebrate the history and life of Steve Rogers.

Readers questioned if Captain America, a patriotic symbol, was still relevant in the twenty-first century and if a country divided by politics, religion, race, and economics would unite behind one hero. *The Death of Captain America* affirmed the relevance not only of Steve Rogers but also of the recently revived Bucky Barnes.

It is interesting to note that at the same time Marvel killed Captain America, DC decided to kill Batman. Both were lost in time streams and later recovered, but in each case, the shield and cowl fell to their former sidekicks: Bucky Barnes and Dick Grayson, respectively. Barnes and Grayson honored their mentors by carrying on the tradition, but they also revealed differences in their character and the roles of Captain America and Batman.

These iconic figures have woven their stories into the modern mythology of the United States. A new retrospective book, entitled *Captain America and Bucky*, set for a 2012 release, will explore the relationship of Steve Rogers and his young sidekick. *The Death of Captain America* is a significant addition to the mystique of Steve Rogers/Captain America and comes at nearly the same time that a major motion picture introduced the story of Captain America to a new generation of viewers.

Daniel J. O'Rourke

Films

Captain America: The First Avenger. Directed by Joe Johnston. Marvel Studios and Paramount Pictures, 2011. The film stars Chris Evans as Captain America and details the superhero's origin during World War II as an experimental "supersoldier." Hugo Weaving stars as the Red Skull, Captain America's nemesis, while Sebastian Stan assumes the role of Bucky Barnes, Captain America's sidekick. The film ends with the discovery of Captain America frozen in ice in the present day.

Further Reading

Brubaker, Ed, et al. *Captain America: Winter Soldier—Ultimate Collection* (2010).

Englehart, Steve, Mike Friedrich, and Sal Buscema. *Captain America and the Falcon: Secret Empire* (2005).

Millar, Mark, and Steve McMiven. *Civil War* (2007).

Bibliography

Dittmer, Jason. "Ret-Conning Captain America." In *The Amazing, Transforming Superhero: Essays on the Revision of Characters in Comic Books, Film, and Television*, edited by Terence Wandtke. Jefferson, N.C.: McFarland, 2007.

Duncan, Randy, and Matthew J. Smith. *The Power of Comics: History, Form, and Culture*. New York: Continuum, 2009.

Englehart, Steve. "Captain America and the Falcon, Issue 155." In *Essential Captain America* Volume 3, by Stan Lee, et al. Baltimore: Johns Hopkins University Press, 2006.

Weiner, Robert G., ed. *Captain America and the Struggle of the Superhero*. Jefferson, N.C.: McFarland, 2009.

Wright, Bradford W. *Comic Book Nation: The Transformation of Youth Culture*. Baltimore: Johns Hopkins University Press, 2001.

See also: *Fallen Son: The Death of Captain America; All Star Batman and Robin, the Boy Wonder; All Star Superman*

DEATH OF CAPTAIN MARVEL, THE

Author: Starlin, Jim
Artist: Jim Starlin (illustrator); Steve Oliff (colorist); James Novak (letterer)
Publisher: Marvel Comics
First serial publication: 1982
First book publication: 1982

Publication History

When it was first published in 1982, *The Death of Captain Marvel* was billed as Marvel Comics' first graphic novel. Generally speaking, Marvel's "graphic novels" were simply oversized versions printed on higher-quality paper stock than the traditional serial, stapled issues. Writer Jim Starlin returned for Marvel's third official graphic novel, *Dreadstar*, later that same year. Marvel continued to rerelease the book for a number of years, later including the story in *The Life and Death of Captain Marvel* in 2002 and an expanded *Death of Captain Marvel* in 2010.

Plot

After a lifetime of fighting for justice—first, for his native race, the Kree, and later on behalf of all aliens as a "Protector of the Universe"—Captain Mar-Vell is enjoying a semiretirement, having found love with his onetime foe Elysius. When Mentor, the leader of the Eternals on the moon of Titan, seeks Mar-Vell's aid in transporting the stony remains of the galactic villain (and Mentor's wayward son) Thanos to their final resting place, Mar-Vell complies. Mar-Vell, Mentor, and his other son, Eros, meet with opposition from followers of Thanos; the three dispatch of them easily, only to discover in the melee that Mar-Vell has taken ill.

Mentor's scans later detect cancer in a nearly untreatable form. In the past, Mar-Vell had been banished to the other-dimensional Negative Zone, where he could be liberated only by switching places physically with human adventurer/musician Rick Jones. Free of that bond, the effects of his long-ago battle with the supervillain Nitro began to take effect; Nitro had manually sealed a canister of lethal nerve toxin in Mar-vell,

The Death of Captain Marvel. (Courtesy of Marvel Comics)

resulting in what the Kree call "blackend" and humans call "cancer."

As Mar-Vell informs allies and loved ones of his failing health, Mentor enlists great minds to attempt to find a cure. Their efforts are in vain, as Mar-Vell, honored by friends and foes alike, succumbs to the disease. Thanos appears to Mar-Vell, teetering on the edge of death, and the apparition challenges him to one last glorious battle. The hero enjoys this final clash, ultimately realizing it is taking place beyond his physical body. As he dies in bed, his mind accepts Death, and Mar-Vell, Thanos, and Death exit the plane of the living; Mar-Vell's vital statistics flatline, and Mentor covers the deceased hero with a bedsheet, whispering "He's gone" in the final panel.

Characters

- *Captain Marvel*, a.k.a. *Captain Mar-Vell*, the story's titular hero, usually wears a skintight red-and-blue suit highlighted with a yellow starburst on the chest and golden-colored Nega-Bands on his wrists; his plume of rich blond hair emerges from atop his facemask. Previously, he was an official captain in the Kree military, sent to Earth for infiltration and espionage in advance of a Kree invasion. Ultimately, though, he sided with humanity and, shunned by his own people, became a protector of Earth and, later, the universe. Empowered by the entity Eon with "cosmic awareness," he could sense when something was awry in the cosmos and utilize the photonic power of his Nega-Bands to fight for balance.
- *Mentor*, leader of the Eternals living on the moon of Titan, has the wrinkled countenance

The Death of Captain Marvel. (Courtesy of Marvel Comics)

and white hair of an old man but the spry and vital body of his fellow Eternals. His race is a genetically modified offshoot of Earth's humans, enhanced by the supertechnologies of the mysterious Celestials. Having relocated his people to the moon of Titan long ago, he has the impressive data and sciences of Integral Synaptic Anti-Anionic Computer (ISAAC), the Eternals' megacomputer, at his disposal to try to aid Mar-Vell in his fight against death.

- *Thanos*, errant son of Mentor and cosmic megalomaniac, resembles the Eternals' adversaries, the Deviants, more than his kin: His purple skin, deep black eyes, ridged jawline, muscled girth, and centurion-like garb give him a ghoulish appearance. His quests for cosmic domination had been previously thwarted by Mar-Vell, the Avengers, Spider-Man, and the late Adam Warlock; from beyond the grave, Warlock froze the Death-worshipping Thanos into a stone statue, denying him forever, it seemed, the true embrace of the grave. However, he returns to usher Mar-Vell into Death's afterlife.
- *Rick Jones*, former partner and symbiotic "spacemate" of Mar-Vell, retains his youthful demeanor from his days as the teen sidekick of both the Hulk and Captain America. Once tethered to Mar-Vell through the Nega-Bands and forced to swap physical presences with the hero, he has returned to a career in music when Mar-Vell comes to tell him the news of the cancer. Though Rick is clear of the disease, he is initially furious that Mar-Vell is accepting such a fatalistic destiny. He is successful in prodding Earth's greatest minds to join Mentor in seeking a cure for Mar-Vell. He ultimately reconciles with his former partner, staying with him at his bedside until the end.
- *Elysius*, the artificial creation of Titan's massive computer ISAAC, appears to be fully humanoid as a beautiful flesh-and-blood Eternal. Previously a villain, she chooses to side with Mar-Vell and his companions in combating her former co-conspirators. Eventually, she and Mar-Vell fall in love and plan to have children together but cancer overtakes him.

Artistic Style

Starlin often favors ripplingly athletic protagonists, interspersing kinetic and action-packed fights with brooding, pensive musings. His attention to anatomy, in particular, lends his characters a peculiar vitality; in a genre frequently featuring voluptuous female characters, Starlin produces sexualized male protagonists as well. This manner of unrestrained physique is frequently combined with cosmic background or multicharacter vignettes, so as to emphasize the mental processes of the main character. Psychedelic elements are commonly employed, too, to express images and experiences beyond traditional sight, especially in realms outside of physical space.

Frequently, Starlin forgoes the traditional "blank-pupil" look of masked superheroes to communicate characters' humanity or decency through their eyes. Villains are not often given the same treatment, thereby underscoring the effect. Likewise, Starlin's villains are often blockier than the heroes, stripping them of any positive sexuality.

The color palette for *The Death of Captain Marvel* is relatively muted when compared to some of Starlin's later work, such as *Dreadstar*. It could be that, given the newness of Marvel's graphic novel line, the production process was either uncertain or botched, thereby leading to only moderate brilliance for the hue of the work. Either way, apart from the colors themselves, the balance between light and dark scenes is carefully maintained, ending as it does with Mar-Vell's shaded, quiet demise in bed. The inking is relatively thick, given the level of detail each panel attempts to convey, all of which may suggest to the reader, even subconsciously, a weight or heaviness.

The Death of Captain Marvel. (Courtesy of Marvel Comics)

Themes

Like much of Starlin's work, the combined concerns of heroism and mortality suffuse the entire text. Specifically, *The Death of Captain Marvel* is a meditation on how a battle-sharpened warrior must finally lay down his arms to an obstacle he cannot defeat, death itself, and what ultimate justice there may or may not be in that realization. In interviews, Starlin is quoted as saying that the graphic novel was "cheaper than going to a shrink" as "a great way of working through my own father's death." After offering several different responses to Mar-Vell's imminent demise (denial, anger, and depression, for example) through the other characters, Starlin eventually has the hero accept both the reality of death and the possibility of a journey into the afterlife. In this way, Mar-Vell's heroism has not been in vain, and he finds peace in having to exit mortal existence. In fact, he comes to embrace death, battling to the bitter end, as his friend Rick Jones wants him to do. Readers do not get to step into the great beyond and can only stand by helplessly, as do the other superheroes and villains, as Mar-Vell dies. Ultimately, the primary theme of the book, in a manner akin to biblical Ecclesiastes, is the recognition that to all things, there is a season, and even for superheroes, there is a time to die.

Impact

Unlike a great many superhero characters (such as Bucky, Superman, Green Arrow, Green Lantern, Captain America, and Wonder Woman), Captain Marvel has never "returned" from his death, only appearing in alternate realities, flashbacks, and supernatural stories. However, he did play a central role in Alex Ross and Jim Krueger's *Earth X* (1999-2000) trilogy, set many decades into the future of the Marvel Comics Universe.

Mar-Vell's legacy has been taken up, largely, by a pair of heroes. In the late 1980's, Wendell Vaughn (also known as Quasar) took on Mar-Vell's mantle of "Protector of the Universe" with his Quantum Bands, similar to Mar-Vell's Nega-Bands. He forged a relationship with Epoch that was similar to Mar-Vell's with Eon, Epoch's progenitor. (Similarly, another hero, Monica Rambeau, would dub herself Captain Marvel, though, as an Earth-based crime fighter with the ability to transform herself into various energy wavelengths, she bore little resemblance to and had little connection with Mar-Vell.) In the late 1990's, Mar-Vell's artificial son, Genis-Vell, went from calling himself Legacy to assuming the name Captain Marvel. Coincidentally, after a massive mental breakdown and recovery caused by the burdens of cosmic awareness, he began calling himself Photon, the same name that Rambeau took after abandoning the Captain Marvel identity. Mar-Vell has no relationship to the Captain Marvel of DC Comics.

A. David Lewis

Further Reading

Giffen, Keith, et al. *Annihilation* (2006-2007).

Sim, Dave, and Gerhard Sim. *The Last Day* (2004).

Starlin, Jim. *The End: Marvel* (2003).

Starlin, Jim, and Ron Lim. *Rann-Thanagar Holy War* (2008).

Starlin, Jim, et al. *The Infinity Gauntlet* (2006).

Bibliography

Starlin, Jim. "A Success Written in the Stars." Interview by UHQ Team. *Universo HQ*, March 3, 2001. http://www.universohq.com/quadrinhos/entrevista_starlin_eng01.cfm.

Starlin, Jim, Joe Pruett, and Justin Eisinger. *The Art of Jim Starlin: A Life in Words and Pictures*. San Diego, Calif.: IDW, 2010.

Weiner, Stephen. *Faster Than a Speeding Bullet: The Rise of the Graphic Novel*. New York: NBM, 2003.

See also: *Infinity Gauntlet; Cerebus; Marvel Zombies; Silver Surfer: Parable; Earth X*

DEATH: THE HIGH COST OF LIVING

Author: Gaiman, Neil
Artist: Dave McKean (illustrator); Chris Bachalo (penciller); Mark Buckingham (inker); Steve Oliff (colorist); Todd Klein (letterer)
Publisher: DC Comics
First serial publication: 1993
First book publication: 1994

Publication History

Originally released in single magazine format as *Death: The High Cost of Living* Volumes 1-3 and *Death Talks About Life*, and published by DC Comics, *Death: The High Cost of Living* was released in three monthly installments from March through May, 1993, under the following titles: *The Spirit of the Stairway* (March, 1993); *A Night to Remember* (April, 1993); and *The High Cost of Living* (May, 1993). The hardcover edition of *Death: The High Cost of Living*, with the appended *Death Talks About Life*, was published in November, 1993. The trade paperback was published in June, 1994.

The story of Death was released as an offshoot of Neil Gaiman's popular *The Sandman* (1989-1996) series; the title character is one of the Endless of that series, the sister of Gaiman's popular characters Dream, Delirium, and others. Gaiman and Dave McKean were already well-established graphic novel writers and artists, respectively, at the publication of this graphic novel, and Mark Buckingham had established his talent during the previous decade with *Hellblazer*, issues 18-22. Chris Bachalo, having achieved recognition for his work with *The Sandman* series, gained further recognition for his work in *Death*. *Death: The High Cost of Living* was released in full color, though *Death Talks About Life*, illustrated by McKean rather than Bachalo, was released in black and white and sepia.

Plot

For one day each century, Death takes human form and walks among the living, learning about their lives to better sympathize with those whom she must escort from life. *Death: The High Cost of Living* is the story of

---

Chris Bachalo

Chris Bachalo broke into the comics industry as the artist on Peter Milligan's revisioning of *Shade, the Changing Man* for DC's Vertigo imprint, illustrating the majority of the first fifty issues. The opportunity to collaborate with writer Neil Gaiman on the *Death: The High Cost of Living* miniseries, elevated his status considerably at the beginning of the 1990's. Shortly thereafter he created a new X-Men title, *Generation X*, with writer Scott Lobdell, during which time he began to consciously alter his style to something that was more cartoony and manga-inspired, with anatomical correctness largely abandoned. This tendency reached a zenith with the launch of *Steampunk* with Joe Kelly, in which he pushed his style in increasingly complex directions that some readers found difficult to decipher. In the 1990's, Bachalo was one of the most unusual cartoonists in mainstream comics, pushing the limits of representation far from strict realism and dynamic action.

---

one of those days—a fairly average day in the early 1990's, when Death has come to Earth in the form of a teenage girl named Didi and has landed right in the middle of New York City.

Readers first encounter Mad Hettie, a two-hundred-fifty-year-old woman seeking her lost heart. After roughing up a gang of tough-living teenagers who have tried to take advantage of her, Hettie divines Death's impending arrival among the living. Mad Hettie, readers learn later, will implore Death to find her heart for her.

The first living person that Death meets is Sexton Furnival, a jaded and suicidal sixteen-year-old boy who has lost all interest in life. Sexton is introduced to readers through the suicide note he is drafting on his computer while his mother does housework in the other room. Though his suicidal intentions are hardly to be taken seriously, interrupted as they are when his mother sends him out for the afternoon so that she can do her spring cleaning, his imminent encounter with Death hardly seems coincidental.

Death, in her human form as Didi, rescues Sexton from the garbage heap in which she has found him, then brings him to her place to get him cleaned up. Her place and her human form are part of a facade, established by some unknown power as a cover for her presence on Earth. Death is aware of the fabrication and mentions as much to Sexton, who begins to doubt her sanity. This doubt catalyzes both his continued interest in Didi throughout the remainder of her day on Earth and his skepticism about the reality of the strange events that follow.

Once Sexton is cleaned up, he and Didi begin roaming the city together: She charms everyone she meets and finds myriad ways to intertwine with the lives of those around her; he stands back and watches as she navigates New York City culture in wholly unusual ways. At a nightclub, Sexton and Didi are confronted by Theo, a minion of the Eremite, who lures them into an abandoned warehouse, where they are imprisoned. The Eremite, blind, ancient, and seemingly supernatural, steals Death's ankh, an ancient Egyptian symbol of life, believing it to be the key to her knowledge and power. Indeed, Death seems less powerful once her ankh is gone. She and Sexton experience some of their most typical human moments together— as well as the only human death to occur in this story— once she is robbed of this symbol.

Meanwhile, Mad Hettie, sensing Death's distress, leads Didi's friend and landlord, Mrs. Robbins, to rescue them from the warehouse. Once freed, Sexton and Didi spend a relatively normal morning together, eating breakfast and strolling in a park before Death's time on Earth is done and she is forced to leave. However, before she leaves she evades the Eremite again and fulfills her promise to Mad Hettie.

Characters

- *Death*, a.k.a. *Didi*, the protagonist, is the human incarnation, for one day each century, of the concept she represents. Pert, chipper, and dressed in all black, she is the Grim Reaper, the one who comes to greet the living as they depart from Earth. For the duration of this story, she is a teenage girl much like any other, trying to navigate the complexities of human life and charming all she meets.

- *Sexton Furnival* is a suicidal sixteen-year-old boy with no appreciation for life or its many charms. Unwittingly swept into Death's day on Earth when she finds him trapped in a garbage heap, he represents the depressed and jaded members of humanity who Death all too frequently has to escort from Earth before their time. He experiences the most dramatic development of any character in this story.

- *Mad Hettie* is a slovenly, two-hundred-fifty-year-old bag lady who is seeking Death with the intention of asking her a favor. Killing a dove to discern the time of Death's next arrival on Earth, Hettie adds a touch of the supernatural to the story and to Sexton's experience.

- *The Eremite*, blind and disheveled, has been chasing Death across centuries to steal the one thing she has that is of value to him: knowledge. Not seeming to realize that such a thing cannot be stolen, he pursues Death relentlessly, heedless to the harm he causes along the way. He traps Sexton and Death in an abandoned warehouse and kills Theo.

- *Theo*, a classmate of Sexton, is a fast-talking street hustler who has taken up with the Eremite in an attempt to earn quick money. His is the only death depicted in the story, which, as the first death Sexton has ever witnessed, provides an opportunity for Sexton and Death to discuss what death means.

Artistic Style

Death: The High Cost of Living employs remarkably bright and vivid coloring for a book about such a grim subject. The coloring, which emphasizes the items and characters in which Death finds intense joy as she experiences her one day on Earth, is only one of several elements used to emphasize specific aspects of the story. Meticulous use of light and shadow and chiaroscuro shading, as well as close attention to seemingly innocuous background details, serve to heighten the reader's awareness of the minute elements of daily existence that make life interesting. In this way, the artistic design dovetails neatly with one of the prominent themes of the story.

Though the book relies heavily on dialogue (presented through speech balloons) to progress the plot, a portion of the narration occurs through Sexton's suicide note and thoughts, which are presented in text boxes; the suicide note in particular uses computer-font-style lettering. In a departure from the lettering of *The Sandman* series, the text is otherwise uniform, and different characters are not given their own lettering styles. However, characters are generally distinguished by their own thematic colors: Death always appears in all black surrounded by bursts of color in the background, while Sexton appears slightly shadowy in muted blues and with comparatively darker shading over his face. Characters' coloring thus reveals as much about their traits and characteristics as their words.

Death Talks About Life reveals a wholly different artistic approach, under the hand of McKean. Death's character appears more cartoonish and roughly crafted, without the sharp lines and realistic details of Bacha-lo's sketches. However, the rough-hewn nature is in keeping with the casual approach to the topics of sexual heath and sexually transmitted disease, and the minimalist approach detracts nothing from and rather supports the discussion of so significant a subject.

Themes

The prominent theme of the story, expressed in its subtitle, is the cost of life and an appreciation for its value. Death is present on Earth, for a one-day respite from her usual duties; she spends the day experiencing the joys of life, rather than escorting others from it. Only when weakened by the loss of her ankh does she escort a human from his life on Earth (though she does not serve in her usual role as psychopomp, or the guide between realms, but is simply another human presence attending his demise).

The novel's intense sensitivity to the value of life is striking in its contrast to the senseless violence so often depicted in comics and provides a backdrop for exploration of other themes, including love, friendship, mortality, and human strength. Though the friendship between Didi and Sexton has the potential to blossom

into romance, the novel carefully avoids these grounds and limits itself to themes of platonic love and relationships.

The character of Death gives voice to the exploration of the meaning of life. While the meaning of life is never stated overtly, through Sexton's character development, the reader is able to witness a remarkable transformation from apathy to interest and almost excitement at the variety of experience life can contain. Minor supporting characters, some voiceless, provide further opportunities to explore the value of life and living, and what that may mean for different people. Though death is presented as inevitable, even for those with extreme longevity, the story does not evince fatalism but rather revels in human choices and intentions.

Impact

Death: The High Cost of Living is less significant on its own than as an offshoot of Gaiman's popular and highly acclaimed *The Sandman* series. The title character herself is not an original creation but a member of a family more fully represented in *The Sandman* stories. While the novel, which relies on many standard and easily accessible elements of the graphic novel genre, provides an excellent starting point for those newly acquainted with the format, the technique is not particularly groundbreaking nor does it represent a significant departure from the creators' typical work.

The most striking component of the book is the appended *Death Talks About Life*, which many readers have tended to dismiss as an afterthought but which represents far more intense attention to specific social issues than is generally expected of comic books or graphic novels. Death's no-nonsense discussion of sex, sexual health, condoms, sexually transmitted disease, AIDS, and drug and needle use is far more frank and direct than is common for comic books, which tend to allegorize such matters. Nevertheless, the subject is appropriate to the character and has helped to expand the role of the graphic novel medium in presenting challenging subjects to a vast and varied readership.

Rachel E. Frier

Further Reading

Carey, Mike, and John Bolton. *God Save the Queen* (2007).

Carey, Mike, et al. *Lucifer* (2000-2006).

Gaiman, Neil, et al. *The Sandman* (1989-1996).

Kwitney, Alisa. *Destiny: A Chronicle of Deaths Foretold* (2000).

Miller, Frank, and David Mazzucchelli. *Batman: Year One* (1988).

Moore, Alan, and Dave Gibbons. *Watchmen* (1995).

Simmonds, Posy. *Tamara Drewe* (2008).

Wagner, Matt, and Steven T. Seagle. *Sandman Mystery Theater* (1993-1999).

Bibliography

Howard, Elise. "Neil Gaiman." *Horn Book Magazine* 85, no. 4 (2009): 351-354.

Sutton, Roger. "It's Good to Be Gaiman." *School Library Journal* 55, no. 3 (2009): 30-32.

Wagner, Hank, Christopher Golden, and Stephen R. Bissette. *Prince of Stories: The Many Worlds of Neil Gaiman*. New York: St. Martin's Press, 2008.

Zaleski, Jeff. "The Arts and Ambitions of Neil Gaiman: Comics! Books! Films!" *Publishers Weekly* 250, no. 30 (2003): 46.

See also: *Sandman; Sandman Mystery Theatre; Hellblazer; The Books of Magic; Miracleman*

Demo

Author: Wood, Brian

Artist: Becky Cloonan (illustrator); Ryan Yount (letterer)

Publisher: AiT/Planet Lar

First serial publication: 2003-2004

First book publication: 2005

Publication History

Demo was first published in single-issue format by AiT/Planet Lar in 2003. Originally, both AiT/Planet Lar and writer Brian Wood asserted that there would be no collection and that the single issues were the only way to experience the project because of the large amount of additional content included in each issue, such as playlists, guest art, sketches, and script excerpts.

After the issues were out of print for a time, however, AiT/Planet Lar relented, and in 2005, the stories were collected in the *Demo* trade paperback, which did not include the additional content. A companion book, *Demo: The Twelve Original Scripts* (2005), was also published, assembling the scripts, notes, and character illustrations in a separate volume. In September of 2007, the publication rights reverted to Wood and artist Becky Cloonan, who made a deal with DC's Vertigo imprint to republish the original *Demo* run in a new collection, which was released in 2008.

Plot

Demo is unique in that it is a collection of single issues without any recurrent characters. There is no overarching plot, which is the source of the series' strength. In an interview with *Comic Book Resources*, Wood cited short films as a big influence on the creation of *Demo*, as well as on the particular approach to storytelling he used.

The uniting factors are the emotional struggles each of these characters faces, along with the central theme of superpowers (or supernatural circumstances) granted to young men and women with otherwise ordinary lives. Each issue addresses the way these characters handle their superpower or supernatural circumstances and

---

Becky Cloonan

One of the most successful female comic book artists of the 2000's, Becky Cloonan's big break came in 2003 when she collaborated with writer Brian Wood on *Channel Zero: Jennie One*. Her subsequent series with Wood, *Demo*, was nominated for an Eisner Award. In 2006 she launched, with writer Steven Seagle, *American Virgin*, a monthly series about a young born-again Christian preacher for DC's Vertigo imprint. Cloonan has also published her own solo series, *East Coast Rising*, with TOKYOPOP. Cloonan's drawing style shows a heavy manga influence, particularly in *Demo* and *East Coast Rising*. *American Virgin* is drawn in a more traditional American comics style, though with round, sketchy lines that help to reinforce the humorous undertones of the work. Her graphic style is generally lighthearted and vibrant, but it does not veer off into traditionally satiric representational strategies.

---

how they shape their lives. Though some of the characters are akin to superheroes, such as those in issues 1 ("NYC") and 5 ("Girl You Like"), there are slight deviations, namely in issues 11 ("Midnight to Six") and 12 ("Mon dernier jour avec toi," which translates to "my last day with you"). The latter two stories fit tonally with what Wood was seeking to create—a series that dealt with personal responsibility, identity, growth, and struggle—if not with the superhero/supernatural focus that the earlier stories had. Thus, character development is the heart of *Demo*, which sets it apart substantially from other deconstructive works that view superheroes in a critical or realistic light, especially because the characters lack external threats to their lives. With nothing else to distract the readers, they are left with the characters and their stories.

In "NYC," individuals deal with the dilemma of conformity versus individuality, while issue 2 ("Emmy") addresses personal responsibility in regards to superpowers. Issue 3 ("Bad Blood") touches on family connections between children and less-than-ideal parents. On the other hand, issue 4 ("Stand Strong") shows family to be a source of pride and strength against peer pressure. Issue 5 ("Girl You Want") opens dialogue on the mutability of personal identity and obsession. Issue 6 ("What You Wish For") addresses rage, racism, and mixed-race identity.

Issue 7 ("One Shot, Don't Miss") looks at the concerns of a volunteer soldier whose abilities and needs put him at odds with his moral code, and issue 8 ("Mixtape") deals with selfishness, suicide, and regret in an unselfish way. Issue 9 ("Breaking Up") examines an acrimonious break-up from both positive and negative angles.

Issue 10 ("Damaged") deals with themes of isolation and the need for dependence on others. Issue 11 ("Midnight to Six") is a departure from the superpowered stories that examines society from the vantage point of three deliberate underachievers. The final installment of the series, issue 12, "Mon dernier jour avec toi," is told entirely without dialogue and tackles the depths and extent of young love.

Characters

- *Marie*, the protagonist of "NYC," is a teenager struggling with her psychokinetic powers after discontinuing the use of her mind-dampening medication.
- *Mike*, in "NYC," is Marie's boyfriend. He helps her escape her controlling mother.
- *Emmy*, the titular character of "Emmy," is a young woman in her early teens who lives a lonely lifestyle and feels regret for misusing her superpower on her mother.
- *Samantha Hurley*, the main character of "Bad Blood," reconciles with her half brother after their father's apparent funeral and learns about their family's unnatural healing ability.
- *Sean Hurley* is Samantha's half brother in "Bad Blood." He convinces her to forgive their absentee father and demonstrates their mutual immortality.
- *James McMurray* is the main character of "Stand Strong," a mid-twenties, heavily tattooed fac-

tory worker who has superstrength and is reluctantly recruited for a payroll heist.
- *Amy* is James's girlfriend, who pressures him to help his coworkers steal the factory payroll.
- *Kate* is the main character of "Girl You Want," a young woman whose appearance changes to match the subconscious desires of anybody who sees her.
- *The Barista* is an unnamed character in "Girl You Want" and the object of Kate's romantic obsession.
- *Ken* is the mixed-race protagonist of "What You Wish For," whose rage-based necromantic abilities are triggered by racial slurs, the ire of his neighbors, and the death of his dog.
- *PFC John Hatfield*, the protagonist of "One Shot, Don't Miss," is forced to negotiate his uncanny marksmanship, his desire to avoid killing people, and the orders he is issued as an enlisted soldier in the U.S. Army.
- *Kendra*, John's wife, could be considered the moral antagonist of "One Shot, Don't Miss." She is more concerned about John's ability to pay the bills and support their family than his personal struggles with the deadly nature of his job.
- *Nick*, the protagonist of "Mixtape," is forced to confront his self-centered reality after his girlfriend Jess's suicide.
- *Jess*, Nick's girlfriend, leaves him the titular "mixtape" that conjures a ghost of her, so that she can impart some last bits of wisdom to him.
- *Gabe*, a young man endowed with total and complete memory of every experience he has ever had, is the repentant antagonist of "Breaking Up."
- *Angie*, Gabe's former girlfriend in "Breaking Up," alternates between being sympathetic and antagonistic. Ultimately, she and Gabe leave on good terms.
- *Thomas Martin* is the main character of "Damaged," a hardworking, well-heeled loner who comes in contact with a young homeless girl, who seems to have incredible insight into his life.

- *The Therapist* is the unnamed young girl in "Damaged" who helps Thomas sort out his life, before being revealed as a scam artist.
- *Jace Sterling*, the antagonist of "Midnight to Six," is determined to hold true to the "Slacker's Pledge" that his cohort Brad Searles created ten years before and is perfectly satisfied with his life of underachievement.
- *Brad Searles*, the protagonist of "Midnight to Six" and creator of the "Slacker's Pledge," has aspirations to break out of his dead-end life and comes in conflict with Jace's desire to uphold the status quo.
- *Jill Macomber*, the secondary protagonist of "Midnight to Six," is the voice of reason and the third signee of the "Slacker's Pledge."
- *The Boy* is half of the young, unnamed couple in "My Last Day with You." He spends his last day with the girl, before jumping off a building. His fate is uncertain.
- *The Girl* is the other half of the young, unnamed couple in "My Last Day with You." She spends her last day with the boy, before jumping off a building. Her fate is uncertain.

Artistic Style

The overall visual strength of the series is the result of Cloonan's virtuosity. She handled pencilling, inking, toning, and lettering, while incorporating elements of storytelling and paneling from both manga and Western comics to create something wholly unique. Though many of the stories have the thick inks and hatching for which she has become known, she embraces lightness, manga tropes, and thinner lines in places they are needed to bring out the most in each story. The art is done in black and white, which allows for the emotional depth of the drawing to come through. In an interview with *Anime News Network*, Cloonan noted that she found different inspirations for each story: "For example, the fourth issue, 'Stand Strong,' was about strength, so I looked at old propaganda posters that really convey ideas of strength and power when coming up with the visuals. These

were really striking images, and I wanted to bring that impact to the story."

Also notable are the Frank Miller influences in "One Shot, Don't Miss"; the relatively lighthearted approach of "Midnight Til Six"; and the clean, stylized approach in "What You Wish For," which pulls from the manga tradition but remains rooted in Cloonan's style. Most striking about Cloonan's work is the ability with which she creates emotionality: The character's facial expressions are vivid, and her inking creates a raw, emotional undercurrent. However, the rawness does not overpower the content. Her inks and stylistic choices never distract from the story; rather, they add tremendously to it.

Themes

Demo is generally described as a set of coming-of-age stories, but that does not do justice to the breadth of topics and situations that occur in the course of the twelve issues. There are stories of loss, rage, heartbreak, obsession, growth, and responsibility, as well as those of joy, happiness, and little victories. There is no evil to fight, no grand, epic struggle; the character's struggles are daily ones, and the evils mirror humanity's. "Breaking Up" might be considered one of the weaker stories because it lacks these strong emotions, but it has a subtle strength to it. The story can be seen from both sides of a breakup, and when one takes into account that Gabe's superpower is one of total recall—being able to remember every high and low of his life perfectly—the reflections of the couple's shared past take on a different feel with his present.

With the exception of "Girl You Want" and possibly "My Last Night with You," personal growth is a theme that all of the stories have in common, with "Emmy," "Stand Strong," "Midnight to Six," and "One Shot, Don't Miss" standing out as particularly effective examples of characters taking responsibility. Emmy decides to avoid hurting others with her power; Jeremy of "Stand Strong" embraces a steady job and ditches his larcenous friends; Brad and Jill of "Midnight to Six" leave a dead-end lifestyle to move on with their lives; and James Hatfield makes a moral stand against using his ability to kill, leaves the Army, and returns home to raise his child in "One Shot, Don't Miss." Aware of the normal view of superheroes as paragons of responsible action, Wood decides to give his a simpler, more down-to-earth set of responsibilities.

Impact

Demo has had a small but significant impact in that it helped expand the careers of both Wood and Cloonan and led to an additional six stories in the *Demo* style to be published by Vertigo. It won the title of "Indie of the Year" from *Wizard* magazine and was nominated for two Eisner Awards: Best Single Issue and Best Limited Series. It has also paved the way for other thematically similar books, such as Cloonan collaborators Gabriel Bá and Fabio Moon's *Daytripper* (2010-   ). While other books released in the same period of time may have had a more direct influence on content being released, *Demo*'s impact is yet to be fully felt or seen.

Brian A. Lynch

Further Reading

Bá, Gabriel, and Fabio Moon. *Daytripper* (2010-   ).

Segal, Steven T., and Becky Cloonan. *American Virgin* (2006-2008).

Wood, Brian, and Becky Cloonan. *Demo,* Volume 2 (2011).

Wood, Brian, and Ryan Kelly. *Local* (2008).

Bibliography

Khouri, Andy. "Brian Wood Talks *Demo* at Vertigo." *Comic Book Resources*, May 9, 2008. http://www.comicbookresources.com/?page=article&id=16351.

Miller, Evan. "The Gallery: Becky Cloonan." *Anime News Network*, December 19, 2009. http://www.animenewsnetwork.com/the-gallery/2009-12-19.

Sunu, Steve. "*Demo*-ing with Brian Wood." *Comic Book Resources*, February 1, 2010. http://www.comicbookresources.com/?page=article&id=24662.

See also: *Kick Ass*

DMZ

Author: Wood, Brian

Artist: Riccardo Burchielli (illustrator); Brian Wood (illustrator and cover artist); Nikki Cook (illustrator); Kristian Donaldson (illustrator); Ryan Kelly (illustrator); Danijel Zezelj (illustrator); Andrea Mutti (pencils); Jared K. Fletcher (letterer); Jeromy Cox (colorist); John Paul Leon (cover artist)

Publisher: DC Comics

First serial publication: 2005-

First book publication: 2006

Publication History

DMZ was first released in 2005 as part of DC Comics' Vertigo line. The idea for the series was born out of Brian Wood's experiences living in New York City, and he has called the book a collection of "city stories, but amplified." The series began after editor Will Dennis facilitated a meeting between Wood and artist Riccardo Burchielli. Wood had seen Burchielli's art on an Italian comic (*Chourmo*), which featured elements of graphic military action. Burchielli, a native of Italy, had grown up as a fan of American comics and was quick to accept the opportunity to work on *DMZ*.

Even though Burchielli has never visited the United States, the series is a vivid portrayal of New York, mostly because of Wood's supply of photographic references and personal experiences. While he is best known for his work as an author, Wood also worked for Rockstar Games and did graphic-design work for music magazines and Nike. Despite Wood's initial uncertainty regarding the longevity of the series, it became a premiere title for the Vertigo line. Wood has announced that the series will end with issue 72, but he has also mentioned the possibility of writing prequel stories that chronicle the events leading up to the second American civil war.

Plot

The first image of the series lays out the conflict according to a map. New Jersey and Inland are the Free States; Brooklyn, Queens, and Long Island comprise the United States of America; and in between is

Brian Wood

One of the most distinctive graphic stylists of the late-1990's and 2000's, Brian Wood actually developed his reputation as one of the preeminent writers in the comics industry, collaborating with Warren Ellis on *Generation X* and writing *Demo* with Becky Cloonan. *DMZ*, the series for which he is best known, tells the tale of a young reporter named Matty Roth who is lost in a futuristic Manhattan that has devolved into a demilitarized zone controlled by warring gangs. When not writing comic books, he works as a designer and cover artist for various titles published by AiT/Planet Lar and he has designed fourteen covers for Warren Ellis's *Global Frequency*. His visual sensibility relies on the use of stark contrasts and post-apocalyptic imagery that is highlighted by the use of spot color and heavily inked figures.

Manhattan Island, the DMZ. According to the initial time line, the story begins after the war has reached a stalemate, and the first issue takes place three days after a tentative cease-fire agreement has been reached.

The story begins with Matt Roth, a recent college graduate, accepting a job as an intern for Liberty News, where his father is on the board of directors. Almost immediately, Matt is given camera equipment and put on a helicopter bound for the DMZ with famous journalist Viktor Ferguson. Upon arrival, Ferguson and his security team are attacked and flee in the helicopter, leaving Matt behind. Ferguson's helicopter is shot down, and Matt is left alone in the DMZ.

Matt soon meets Zee Hernandez, a medical student turned doctor, who protects Matt, instructing him on the dangers, rules, and customs of the war-torn area. When Matt contacts Liberty News for extraction, he sees firsthand the constant dangers faced by DMZ residents who are caught in between two warring factions. Wary of Liberty News and the U.S. government, Matt sets out to chronicle life in the DMZ. He quickly learns that the stories he had heard about residents of

Manhattan are wildly inaccurate. As he witnesses the horrors of war and the toll paid by the disenfranchised and downtrodden locals of the city, Matt comes to think of himself as a journalist and is inspired to tell their stories.

Matt's role as a journalist is first tested when he is vaulted into the limelight and forced into a political battle to decide the fate of Ferguson, who (it turns out) was captured, not killed, by the Free States. The U.S. Army uses the fact that Matt is stranded and the kidnapping to justify an invasion of the DMZ, but the Army is halted after Matt blackmails the government with photos of Ferguson's murder by U.S. soldiers.

In an effort to win public support, the U.S. government grants the Trustwell Corporation a contract to rebuild Manhattan. Matt goes undercover in Trustwell's organization to investigate allegations of corruption, eventually joining a terrorist cell within the company. Through conversations with a suicide bomber and a Free State spy, Matt learns that Trustwell is funding the terrorists against the company, creating a culture of panic and fear that secures their business interests in the DMZ. Subsequently, Matt exposes Trustwell through a rival news network rather than allowing the information to benefit Liberty News financially or benefit the Free States politically. Trustwell is discredited but remains a powerful player in the DMZ. Meanwhile, Matt becomes a DMZ icon.

During Matt's second summer in the DMZ, he arrives at the Liberty News headquarters to do a story about the Day 204 Massacre, an event early in the conflict in which U.S. soldiers murdered a crowd of unarmed civilian protestors. According to the King, an absent-without-leave (AWOL) U.S. soldier featured throughout the series, Day 204 was the day the United States died. It sent the message that the United States was killing its own people and changed the public's perception of the conflict.

During Matt's investigation, a military tribunal acquits the soldiers involved and riots break out across the city. With the city calling for blood, the U.S. military drops one of the soldiers involved into an angry mob and he is beaten to death. Matt's investigation leaves him disillusioned toward both Liberty News and the U.S. government.

To combat the growing tension within the DMZ, the Free States and U.S. government agree to form a provisional government. Leery of a return to a two-party approach, Parco Delgado announces his intention to run as a people's candidate for the position. Matt joins Delgado's efforts to win the election, especially after an assassination attempt on Delgado at a rally. Delgado's charisma and Matt's efforts, along with his mother's role as a political consultant, help guide Delgado to victory.

Early in Delgado's administration he evicts Trustwell and remaining representatives of the U.S. government. He consolidates his influence within an area referred to as Parco City. Matt's first task for the administration is to use his connections with Wilson to find a rumored stockpile of Chinatown gold. Wilson gives Matt a portion of the gold, which Delgado uses to buy a nuclear weapon from Soames; the purchase of the weapon forces Matt to reassess his role within the Delgado administration. After turning over the bomb, he takes his mother's job as press secretary. Matt fights against propaganda by establishing Radio Free DMZ, an independent voice to counter the U.S.-controlled Liberty News Network. However, he also hires a personal security force and engages in militant actions across the city. Matt has become an "enclave of one," which allows him to be an autonomous agent within the city.

After Matt announces to the world that the DMZ is a nuclear state, a threatened U.S. government sends soldiers into the DMZ. Delgado goes underground and hides the bomb, leaving Matt to handle the press. As Matt ventures into the city he is captured and beaten by a group of U.S. soldiers. Bleeding in the street and filled with rage, Matt orders his security team to kill those responsible. Matt's security team accidentally kills a group of civilians. Suddenly a pariah, Matt is left alone as U.S. bombers destroy the presumed site where Delgado was storing his bomb.

Volumes

- *DMZ*, Volume 1: *On the Ground* (2006). Collects issues 1-5. Addresses themes of journalistic integrity, the cost of civil war on the citizenry, and the dangerous power of the media to inform public opinion.

- *DMZ,* Volume 2*: Body of a Journalist* (2007). Collects issues 6-12. Criticizes the media's role in justifying war, as the U.S. military creates a reason to bomb American citizens. Parallels discussions of weapons of mass destruction in Iraq.
- *DMZ,* Volume 3*: Public Works* (2007). Collects issues 13-17. Criticizes the unchecked influence of the military-industrial complex in creating a culture of fear in order to secure business interests.
- *DMZ,* Volume 4*: Friendly Fire* (2008). Collects issues 18-22. Tells a cautionary tale for journalists. When a conspiracy becomes a tragedy, those involved must make sacrifices to preserve peace rather than expose the truth.
- *DMZ,* Volume 5*: The Hidden War* (2008). Collects issues 23-28. Includes short stories chronicling the lives of residents within the DMZ and explores the emotional and physical costs of war on artists, musicians, reporters, mobsters, and AWOL soldiers.
- *DMZ,* Volume 6*: Blood in the Game* (2009). Collects issues 29-34. Criticizes the representative gap created by a two-party system in politics as expressed by the DMZ's first election. This arc also features themes of corporate influence over elections and skewed media coverage of local candidates.
- *DMZ,* Volume 7*: War Powers* (2009). Collects issues 35-41. The first arc follows a detachment of soldiers lying to their superiors to avoid combat with other Americans; the second deals with the acquisition of power within the DMZ and the threat it poses to military and political bodies.
- *DMZ,* Volume 8*: Hearts and Minds* (2010). Collects issues 42-49. One arc explores how grief can be corrupted in service of violence, and the second covers the ethical and physical dangers faced by journalists who cross into activism.
- *DMZ,* Volume 9*: M.I.A.* (2011). Collects issues 50-54. Addresses the theme of journalistic integrity as Matt, experiencing self pity after previous

events, is given a second chance at redemption but chooses to deny himself amnesty in order to pursue the truth.

- *DMZ,* Volume 10*: Collective Punishment* (2011). Collects issues 55-59. Focuses primarily on the U.S. bombing campaign in the DMZ. Also features a story arc about Wilson.

Characters

- *Matt "Matty" Roth*, the lead protagonist, is a reluctant journalist who becomes a DMZ icon. Often seen with a bandaged nose and a press pass, he is the only journalist writing from the perspective of the locals. His character evolves over the course of the story, growing into a respectable journalist who eventually plays a central role in the rhetoric and politics of the DMZ. In later issues, he becomes a political adviser and soldier, and his actions reflect a growing cynicism and distrust of those in power.
- *Zee Hernandez*, a medical student turned DMZ doctor, runs a clinic to treat the wounded. After the war began and most citizens fled Manhattan, she stayed behind to care for the wounded. She often acts as Matt's conscience, but she is also his girlfriend for a brief time.
- *Wilson* is Matt's kooky neighbor and head of the Chinatown triad and initially helps Matt with bugged electronics, but as the series matures, he takes on more power. Eventually, he solidifies his power over Chinatown, an independent political entity within the DMZ.
- *Parco Delgado* is an uptown resident who becomes the first governor of the DMZ. Because of his charisma and loyalties, he is described as "the bastard child of Hugo Chavez and Al Sharpton."
- *The Free States Movement* is a political group that rose up against the U.S. government. Within the DMZ, the group is led by an unnamed commander who operates out of the Lincoln Tunnel.
- *The United States of America* maintains military might and a recognizable political structure despite losing significant territory to the Free States. The government is as an extremist regime, fighting to regain lost control and influence.

- *The Trustwell Corporation* is a military contractor working closely with the U.S. government and Liberty News. Its actions are motivated by a desire for power and profit. Even after being forced out of the DMZ, several of its security groups remain to operate independently within the city.
- *The Ghosts* are a group of AWOL soldiers, led by Soames, who live in and police Central Park. Its members are rumored to be vigilantes but are also portrayed as environmentalists.

Artistic Style

The two primary artists on the book are Burchielli, who handles the majority of the interior pencil and ink artwork throughout the series, and Brian Wood, who does periodic pages and covers. While other artists have been featured throughout the series, Burchielli and Wood best express the artistic tone of the book.

In terms of their collaboration, Burchielli says Wood gives him a lot of freedom to set up the action and layout. Their primary debates are about the look and personality of New York. In describing his style, Burchielli states, "I really like simplicity in the stroke and a graphic synthesis that sometimes takes its inspiration from the 'clear line' of the French comics and from some South American authors." Compared to Wood's supplemental artwork, Burchielli's art is strongly narrative, with dynamic action and high levels of background detail.

Wood's experiences as an illustrator and graphic designer are evident in his incorporation of photography and graffiti art. At times his subjects are highly shadowed or featured in extreme close-ups that focus on a few specific aspects of faces or buildings. His visuals are often dark (in tone and composition), combining street art and realism. The sections of the book illustrated by Wood usually fuse words and images, creating art with a dramatic punch. For example, an early cover image featured Matt towering over his world, straddling the two territories, which are laid out like a map. An early story, titled "New York Times," is illustrated by Wood and provides a tour guide's perspective of life in the DMZ. While he intended to incorporate more of his art into the story, his success as an author

has limited his availability. Fortunately, Wood illustrated the covers through issue 41, before passing the duties to John Paul Leon.

Themes

The main themes of DMZ deal with the daily life of citizens living in a war zone and the political, cultural, and human casualties of war. The journalistic perspective that guides the reader through the DMZ is part of an established comic tradition of reporters on the front lines of historic events, which stretches from Clark Kent (Superman) and Peter Parker (Spider-Man) to more recent examples such as Ben Urich (from *Daredevil* and other comics series) and Jessica Jones (from *The Pulse*). More impartial than a police officer, with the noble intentions of a public servant and the undercover and surveillance habits of a spy, the recent crop of journalists in comics have embraced a dark and gritty realism.

At times, Matt is an iconic example of the noble reporter, risking his life to expose truths that threaten public safety. However, later issues also show how reporters can themselves become the news, especially as Matt ceases to be a reporter and becomes a political adviser and soldier. Aspects of Matt's evolution may represent the changing role of the media in the United States, as it increasingly influences political policy and debate.

As the series matures, it tackles issues such as war politics, corporate corruption, American nationalism, and journalistic integrity. The central military conflict in the story is essentially a war over the idea of America, fought with weapons and rhetoric. The war provides the thematic backdrop for the series, but the majority of the stories are about the people caught in the conflict, from poor citizens who could not flee to AWOL soldiers attempting to avoid fighting other Americans.

Impact

The concept of a second American civil war is in itself controversial. A similar comic thematically and conceptually is Frank Miller's *Give Me Liberty: An American Dream* (1990); however, Miller's series places the conflict in the future, adding a science-fiction element to the story. *DMZ* aims at a current and realistic portrayal of a war on American soil.

Some early reactions to the book described it as an attack on conservatives, but Wood was quick to dismiss the claim, stating, "the two warring groups in *DMZ* are just extremists fighting extremists. Home-grown insurgents fighting an extremist government regime, and it is the sane, normal people of all political affiliations that are caught in the middle." Following Matt through the DMZ gives readers a street perspective on the locals who struggle to survive while two warring factions battle over their home.

Some story lines draw from contemporary news events, such as "Blood in the Game," which depicts an uncertain election within the *DMZ* at the same time as the 2008 U.S. presidential campaign. Also within that story, Matt's journalistic objectivity is lost as he finally picks a side in the conflict and becomes a political entity himself. Matt's evolving role connects to previous traditions of comic journalists as well as modern concerns over the political power of the news to shape national debate.

Patrick D. Johnson

Further Reading

Ellis, Warren, and Darick Robertson. *Transmetropolitan* (1998-2002).

Miller, Frank, and Dave Gibbons. *Give Me Liberty: An American Dream* (1990).

Bibliography

Knight, Bill. "Comic Journalists Beyond Clark Kent." *IJPC Journal* 1 (Fall, 2009): 138-146. http://www.ijpc.org/journal/index.php/ijpcjournal/issue/view/18.

Wood, Brian, and Riccardo Burchielli. "The War at Home: Wood and Burchielli Talk *DMZ*." Interview by Dave Richards. *Comic Book Resources*, November 9, 2005. http://www.comicbookresources.com/?page=article&id=5926.

See also: *Give Me Liberty; Transmetropolitan*

DOOM PATROL

Author: Morrison, Grant

Artist: Rian Hughes (illustrator); Sean Phillips (illustrator); Ken Steacy (illustrator); Steve Yeowell (illustrator); Doug Braithwaite (penciller); Paris Cullins (penciller); Mike Dringenberg (penciller); Vince Giarrano (penciller); Kelley Jones (penciller); Duke Mighten (penciller); Ian Montgomery (penciller); Steve Pugh (penciller); Jamie Hewlett (penciller and cover artist); Richard Case (penciller, inker, and cover artist); Mark Badger (inker); Philip Bond (inker); Kim DeMulder (inker); Carlos Garzon (inker); Scott Hanna (inker); Doug Hazlewood (inker); Mark McKenna (inker); John Nyberg (inker); Malcolm Jones III (inker); Brad Vancata (inker); Stan Woch (inker); Daniel Vozzo (colorist); Michelle Wolfman (colorist); John Kaziesdad (letterer); Gaspar Saladino (letterer); John Workman (letterer); Simon Bisley (cover artist); Brian Bolland (cover artist); Duncan Fegredo (cover artist); Keith Giffen (cover artist); Shaky Kane (cover artist); Mike Mignola (cover artist); Mike Sekowsky (cover artist); Tom Taggart (cover artist); Gavin Wilson (cover artist)

Publisher: DC Comics

First serial publication: 1989-1993

First book publication: 2000-2008

Publication History

Grant Morrison and Richard Case's *Doom Patrol* began in 1989, continuing for forty-five issues and one parodic special, *Doom Force*. It continued from two earlier iterations of the same title: the original *Doom Patrol*, created for DC Comics in 1963 and dubbed "the world's strangest heroes," and the 1987 relaunch. As Morrison and Case took over the relaunched title with issue 19, they retained some characters (such as the robotic Cliff Steele), transformed others (turning Negative Man into the hermaphroditic Rebis), and invented their own, most notably the superpowered sufferer of multiple personality disorder, Crazy Jane.

Tongue-in-cheek promotional material released by DC Comics in 1990 praised Morrison for his "crimes

---

Richard Case

Best known for his art on the Grant Morrison-written issues of *Doom Patrol*, Richard Case was one of the signature artists of the early years of the Vertigo imprint at DC Comics. With Dylan Horrocks, he produced *Hunter: The Age of Magic*, a spin-off from *The Books of Magic* series popularized by John Ney Reiber. Over the years Case's art has slowly transformed, becoming more angular and minimalist. His figure drawing pulls from realist and naturalist traditions even within the surrealistic fantasy worlds that he is often called on to depict by his writers. His page layouts are often very traditional, which allows him to maintain high levels of readability even within the confines of some of the off-the-wall stories that he has been called upon to draw.

---

against reason" and for "altering DC characters beyond recognition" with his work on earlier idiosyncratic superhero titles such as *Animal Man* (first published in 1998); however, original *Doom Patrol* creator Arnold Drake was quoted as saying Morrison's approach to *Doom Patrol* was the only one that captured the spirit of the original. *Doom Patrol* was placed under DC Comics' mature-readers imprint, Vertigo, only after Morrison and Case's final issue, though the collected editions have been released under the Vertigo banner.

Plot

Immediately upon taking over *Doom Patrol*, Morrison and Case shifted the tone from traditional superheroics to the unexpected and surreal. Cliff Steele is institutionalized for depression, where he meets Kay Challis, calling herself Crazy Jane. Meanwhile, a hospitalized Larry Trainor (the original Negative Man) is fused with his doctor, Elenore Poole, to become the new being Rebis. The first story, "Crawling from the Wreckage," features the team battling the Scissormen from the fictional world of Orqwith. Orqwith is infecting reality until Rebus forces its rulers to confront their fictional status. In "The Butterfly Collector," comatose Doom Patrol teammate Rhea Jones is kidnapped by Red Jack, a being who claims to be both Jack the Ripper and God. At Doom Patrol headquarters, Dorothy, a powerful young psychic, is attacked by her imaginary childhood friends.

The Painting That Ate Paris introduces the new incarnation of classic *Doom Patrol* villains the Brotherhood of Evil. Now under the leadership of Mister Nobody, they become the Brotherhood of Dada, focused on art and absurdity. The brotherhood steals a magical painting that absorbs Paris, and the Doom Patrol battles them through the painting's layers of art history. Jane is left comatose, and Cliff projects his consciousness inside her as she confronts a monstrous version of her abusive father. "The World Made Flesh" introduces the magician Willoughby Kipling, who joins forces with the Doom Patrol to stop a cult from another dimension who worship the "decreator." In an eccentric one-off story, Cliff's robot body then achieves consciousness when his brain is temporarily removed.

In *Down Paradise Way*, the Doom Patrol faces Mister Jones and the Men from N.O.W.H.E.R.E., who want to destroy the world's eccentricities. The team protects Danny the Street, a sentient, transvestite street. During the battle, one of Danny's inhabitants remembers that he was once the legendary crime fighter Flex Mentallo. After Rhea Jones awakens, the Doom Patrol follows her into a seemingly endless war among alien races. The conflict is resolved when Rebis suggests a "potlatch"—requiring each side to give up increasingly valuable items or admit defeat. Rather than return home with the Doom Patrol, Rhea leaves to explore distant stars.

Musclebound begins with the origin of Flex Mentallo. Under the pentagon, a military conspiracy releases more powerful Men from N.O.W.H.E.R.E. to kidnap Dorothy and Flex. Flex rescues an imprisoned psychic named Wally Sage, who is revealed to have created Flex by drawing him in a comic book when Wally was a boy. Dorothy calls on a dangerous being called the Candlemaker to save her friends. After a spoof of macho vigilante comics, the Doom Patrol encounters the Shadowy Mister Evans, a bizarre dandy who is a sign of the impending apocalypse.

In *Magic Bus*, Mister Nobody forms a new Brotherhood of Dada to steal the bicycle of Albert Hoffman, the inventor of LSD. They use the bicycle's hallucinogenic powers to infect the population, as Mister Nobody runs for president; government troops attack, killing Mister Nobody. Subsequent one-off stories feature a hypothetical Doom Patrol reimagined in the style of Jack Kirby and Rebis in a symbolic quest on the moon.

Jane is tormented by her memories of abuse and the personalities warring inside her and teleports back to her childhood farm to confront the memories of her father. Meanwhile, Josh is shot and killed in Doom Patrol headquarters by the Chief. When Cliff confronts him, the Chief explains that he was behind the accidents that created the original Doom Patrol. He plans to engineer a global catastrophe to force the world to change. Dorothy releases the Candlemaker, who immediately kills the Chief and destroys Cliff's human brain.

Planet Love begins with Cliff dreaming he is a delusional man who only thinks he is a robot, until a virtual copy of his personality is loaded back into his body. Meanwhile, the Candlemaker has unleashed a "psychic apocalypse" in New York. The Candlemaker sends Jane to another dimension he calls "hell." Cliff is torn in two, and Rebis is killed and reborn. Dorothy faces her fears and blows out the Candlemaker. Danny expands until he becomes Danny the World. The final issue of *Doom Patrol* focuses on Kay Challis, trapped in the "real" world. After shock treatment, Kay attempts suicide, but Cliff appears just in time to take her to Danny the World.

Volumes

- *Doom Patrol: Crawling from the Wreckage* (2000). Collects issues 19-25, featuring the formation of the new Doom Patrol.
- *Doom Patrol: The Painting That Ate Paris* (2004). Collects issues 26-34, featuring the Brotherhood of Dada and the Cult of the Unwritten Book.
- *Doom Patrol: Down Paradise Way* (2005). Collects issues 35-41, introducing the Men from N.O.W.H.E.R.E., Danny the Street, Flex Mentallo, and the Doom Patrol in outer space.

- *Doom Patrol: Musclebound* (2006). Collects issues 42-50, explaining the origin of Flex Mentallo, the battle with the Pentagon conspiracy, the Shadowy Mister Evans, and the return of Mister Nobody.
- *Doom Patrol: Magic Bus* (2007). Collects issues 51-57, concluding the "Mister Nobody for President" story line and exposing the Chief's secret.
- *Doom Patrol: Planet Love* (2008). Collects issues 58-63 and *Doom Force*, issue 1, featuring Crazy Jane in the "real world" and the Doom Patrol's battle with the Candlemaker. It also includes the *Doom Force* special, with a grown Dorothy Spinner in a superhero spoof.

Characters

- *Cliff Steele*, a.k.a. *Robotman*, a human brain kept alive inside a powerful robot body, is the everyman hero of the Doom Patrol. He has multiple bodies throughout the series as they are destroyed or upgraded; in later issues, his brain is also destroyed, so none of his original biology remains. He struggles with depression related to the limitations of his robot body.
- *Kay Challis*, a.k.a. *Crazy Jane*, is a young woman suffering from multiple personality disorder after a history of abuse. Each of her sixty-four personalities possesses its own distinct name and superpower. Jane is usually a normal, if eccentrically dressed, young woman, though some of her personalities also transform her physically. Her personalities eventually cooperate, giving her an identity she describes as a "kaleidoscope."
- *Rebis* is a fusion of three separate entities: test pilot Larry Trainor, known as Negative Man in the original Doom Patrol; Larry's doctor, a woman named Elenore Poole; and a being of negative energy. Together they become a new being, disconnected from human emotion and wrapped in glowing bandages. Rebis later gives birth to a new Rebis, possessing the same memories.
- *Niles Caulder*, a.k.a. *the Chief*, is the leader of the Doom Patrol, a wheelchair-bound scientist with a genius IQ and a penchant for chocolate. He gathered the original Doom Patrol and now persuades Cliff, Jane, and Rebis to form a new team. Cold and arrogant, he is revealed to have caused the accidents that crippled the Doom Patrol.
- *Joshua Clay*, a.k.a. *Tempest*, is a trained combat medic capable of firing destructive energy blasts from his hands. He retires from active superhero duty at the beginning of Morrison and Case's run, choosing to serve as the Doom Patrol's doctor. He is later murdered by the Chief.
- *Rhea Jones*, a.k.a. *Lodestone*, a woman with magnetic powers, is left in a coma as Morrison and Case begin on Doom Patrol. She awakens as a new creature: a flying, faceless woman with a giant eye across her chest. After leading the Doom Patrol into outer space, she decides not to return to Earth.
- *Dorothy Spinner* is a facially disfigured teenage girl, first introduced by writer Paul Kupperberg in *Doom Patrol*, issue 14. She was raised in isolation and claims to have been taught by imaginary friends. Her psychic powers allow her imaginary friends to manifest in the real world.
- *Willoughby Kipling* is a cowardly, hard-drinking magician and member of the Knights Templar who appears periodically to enlist the Doom Patrol's help. He is reminiscent of John Constantine from DC Comics' *Swamp Thing* and *Hellblazer* titles.
- *Danny the Street* is a sentient, transvestite street, communicating through street signs and smoke signals and capable of inserting himself into cities around the world. He comes to be the base of operations for the Doom Patrol. In the penultimate issue of *Doom Patrol*, he expands to become an entire parallel world.
- *Flex Mentallo* is a crime fighter from the 1950's, based on the protagonist of the Charles Atlas "dynamic tension" advertisements that appeared in comic books throughout the 1940's. Dressed as a circus strongman in an animal print loin cloth, he fights the Pentagon conspiracy with superpowers born of his amazing physique.
- *Mister Nobody*, a.k.a. *Morden*, briefly appeared as the latter in the original Brotherhood of Evil.

An experiment turns him into the "spirit of the twenty-first century," appearing as an impossible black outline. The leader of the Brotherhood of Dada, he fights the status quo with absurdity and art. He is killed as he is running for president.

- *The Men from N.O.W.H.E.R.E.* are strange foot soldiers of a government conspiracy to remove eccentricities from the world. The first, weaker version speak in sentences only forming the acronym of their name; the later, more powerful version speak in novelty comic book advertisements.

- *The Candlemaker* appears to be an imaginary friend created by Dorothy Spinner, but it is also suggested to be the personification of mankind's fear of nuclear war. A winged monster with burning candles atop its head, it functions as the Doom Patrol's climactic enemy.

Artistic Style

In the years since *Doom Patrol*'s publication, Morrison has become one of the most influential writers in comics, but his main collaborator on *Doom Patrol*, artist Richard Case, is less well known. Case provides *Doom Patrol* with a distinct visual style—stylized, simple, and with thick clean lines. He eschews realism for a flat, pop-art aesthetic, aided by Daniel Vozzo's bright colors throughout the series. As the majority of the Doom Patrol's antagonists and adventures are extradimensional, Case uses abstract visual designs to illustrate them, such as Mister Nobody's impossible silhouette and the map of Crazy Jane's interior landscape. His art approximates the same elements of collage that appear as plot points throughout *Doom Patrol*'s narratives. While he is not a traditional superhero artist, his work retains the classic hyperbolic aesthetic of superhero stories.

Some of *Doom Patrol*'s guest artists (such as Kelley Jones and Steve Yeowell) fill in during ongoing story lines, but others are used on atypical issues. Ken Stacey draws a Jack Kirby homage in issue 53; Mike Dringenberg and Doug Hazlewood illustrate the origin of Flex Mentallo, borrowing from old advertising imagery in issue 42; and multiple artists collaborate on the *Doom Force* one-shot to parody the stylistic excesses of the art

of Rob Liefeld. *Doom Patrol* is also closely associated with the painted, distorted cover art of Simon Bisley.

Themes

The major theme throughout Morrison and Case's *Doom Patrol* is best summed up by Cliff in issue 21: "Is this real or isn't it?" The Doom Patrol faces threats from extradimensional or imaginary worlds, and Cliff regularly expresses confusion caused by these events, wishing for more traditional superheroic adventures. Much of *Doom Patrol* serves to praise imagination and creativity. As the Doom Patrol fights villains from various other realities, the group must use creative, untraditional means to defeat them, such as logic puzzles or William S. Burroughs's cut-up technique. The hero, Flex Mentallo, comes to life from the pages of a child's comic book, and Dorothy uses an "imaginary gun" to fight imaginary enemies.

Doom Patrol is also concerned with transformation and how it relates to personal identity. For example, Cliff wonders if his robot body means that he is no longer a man and, after his human brain is destroyed, he mourns that "there is less and less of me all the time." Equally, is Rebis still Larry, Elenore, or something else entirely?

The Chief's plan to initiate global catastrophe is designed to force the world to transform. The idea of traditional subjectivity is also interrogated, and Morrison is particularly interested in the possibility of multiple subjectivities. Jane's evolution is not to integrate her personalities into a whole but to allow them to form more than the sum of their parts. Dualities appear constantly throughout *Doom Patrol*, including male-female, order-chaos, and (explicitly stated as Cliff Steele's robot form rejects his human brain) mind-body. Strict dualities, however, are usually refuted throughout. The real villains of *Doom Patrol* are those who attempt to quash ambiguity and difference, exemplified by the Pentagon conspiracy and the Men from N.O.W.H.E.R.E. The Brotherhood of Dada are, in a sense, the true heroes because of their war against the status quo. In *Doom Patrol*'s final issue, it is suggested that the "real" world is "hell" because it does not contain the spectacular and absurd possibilities present in *Doom Patrol*.

Impact

The *Doom Patrol* title has been relaunched multiple times in the years since Morrison and Case's work, usually as more traditional superhero fare, although some of their elements and characters remain. Morrison went on to write both *The Invisibles* (first published in 1994) and *Flex Mentallo* (first published in 1996) for Vertigo. Many of Morrison's offbeat ideas from this series have since reappeared into his mainstream superhero work on DC Comics titles such as *All-Star Superman* (2005-2008) and *Final Crisis* (first published in 2008).

Martyn Pedler

Further Reading

Morrison, Grant, and Frank Quietly. *Flex Mentallo* (1996).

Morrison, Grant, Frank Quietly, and Jamie Grant. *All-Star Superman* (2006-2008).

Morrison, Grant, et al. *Animal Man* (1988-1990).

_____. *The Invisibles* (1994-2000).

Bibliography

Bukatman, Scott. "X-Bodies (The Torment of the Mutant Superhero)." In *Matters of Gravity: Special Effects and Supermen in the Twentieth Century*. Durham, N.C.: Duke University Press, 2003.

Callahan, Timothy. *Grant Morrison: The Early Years*. Edwardsville, Ill.: Sequart Research and Literacy Organization, 2007.

"Comics You Should Own—Doom Patrol 19-63." *Comic Book Resources*, September 10, 2006. http://goodcomics.comicbookresources.com/2006/09/10/comics-you-should-own-doom-patrol-19-63.

Pedler, Martyn. "Morrison's Muscle Mystery Versus Everyday Reality . . . and Other Parallel Worlds!" In *The Contemporary Comic Book Superhero*, edited by Angela Ndalianis. New York: Routledge, 2009.

Shaviro, Steven. *Doom Patrols: A Theoretical Fiction About Postmodernism*. New York: High Rise Books, 1997.

See also: *Animal Man; All Star Superman; Invisibles*

DYLAN DOG CASE FILES, THE

Author: Marcheselli, Mauro; Sclavi, Tiziano

Artist: Bruno Brindisi (penciller and inker); Giampiero Casertano (penciller and inker); Luigi Piccatto (penciller and inker); Angelo Stano (penciller and inker); Andrea Venturi (penciller and inker); Mike Mignola (cover artist)

Publisher: Sergio Bonelli Editore (Italian); Dark Horse Comics (English)

First serial publication: *Dylan Dog*, 1986- (partial English translation, 1999)

First book publication: 2009

Publication History

Dylan Dog was created by writer Tiziano Sclavi in 1986 for Sergio Bonelli Editore. Ever since, it has been a ninety-six-page-long monthly. In addition to the regular series, several semestral and annual books have been published in Italian: *Dylan Dog Special* (1987-2010), *Dylan Dog: L'almanacco della paura* (1991), *Dylan Dog presenta Groucho* (1992-1999), *Albo gigante Dylan Dog* (1993), *Maxi Dylan Dog* (1998), and *Dylan Dog Color Fest* (2007). There also are numerous reprints. Stories are usually black-and-white; occasionally, issues are full color. The page size is 6.29 × 8.27 inches, a classic format for Italian comic books.

After the first period of intense writing by Sclavi, stories were written by other authors. During the 1990's, *Dylan Dog* reached its record of almost one million copies sold monthly. Later, the sales decreased; in 2008, 170,000 copies sold in Italy, not counting foreign editions. Nonetheless, *Dylan Dog* is the second best-selling comic book series in Italy after Gianluigi Bonelli's long-running *Tex*, which started in 1948. *Dylan* Dog has also sold in Argentina, Brazil, Croatia, Finland, France, Greece, Holland, Macedonia, Norway, Poland, Serbia, Russia, Slovenia, South Korea, Spain, and Sweden.

In 1999, Dark Horse Comics published a six-issue monthly with some *Dylan Dog* representative adventures, and in 2002, the publisher issued another adventure in a one-shot book, all of which is included in the omnibus paperback. These stories were originally

Tiziano Sclavi

One of Italy's most famous graphic novel writers, Tiziano Sclavi has carved out a significant career as both a comics writer and a novelist. Beginning in the 1970's, Sclavi developed his career as a novelist and short story writer. In 1977 he began writing for comics, creating series like *Jonny Bassotto* and *Il cavallino Michele*. In the 1980's he began working for Sergio Bonelli's Casa Editrice Cepim, where he created his best-known character, Dylan Dog, an investigator of the paranormal. An almost-immediate bestseller, *Dylan Dog* is the signature Italian horror series of the past quarter century, and his adventures have been illustrated by a wide range of Italian artists. Sclavi's stories are characterized by their combination of light-hearted humor, horror elements, and philosophical reflection. Dylan Dog and his sidekick Groucho are well-crafted characters whose adventures in the bizarre and inexplicable have made them popular across generations.

published in Italy in the regular series, in issue 1 (October, 1986), issue 81 (June, 1993), issue 19 (April, 1988), issue 8 (May, 1987), issue 25 (October, 1988), issue 26 (November, 1988), and issue 84 (September, 1993).

Plot

In *Dawn of the Living Dead*, Sybil Browning is accused of the murder of her husband, John. Thus, she hires Dylan Dog, claiming that when she "killed" the man he was already dead. In fact, he was and had been made a zombie by the sorcerer Xabaras. Dylan Dog faces Xabaras, who secretly is the evil half of his father, mystically separated from the good one. Because this is the first story of the series, it also focuses on introducing the main characters and their psychological makeup.

Johnny Freak has a realistic and "educational" plot. Johnny Arkham is an eighteen-year-old boy nicknamed

"Freak" by the press. For his entire life, he has been the victim of systematic violence, amputations, and surgical removals: His parents have used him as a human store (organs, body parts) for his brother Dougal, who suffers from a degenerative disease. One day, Dylan Dog finds Johnny, escaped from the prison of his house, and tries to help him. Johnny has the soul of an artist but is deaf and mute and unable to explain his story; therefore, he is taken back to his parents, who imprison him again in the basement of their house. When Dylan figures out what is really happening, he does not hesitate to intervene. The conclusion of the story is distressing, surprising, and narratively compelling.

In *Memories from the Invisible World*, a murderer kills prostitutes in London. One of the prostitutes asks Dylan to investigate, before she or other women get killed. It is the beginning of a sad romance. A witness to the facts, an "invisible man," is writing a disturbing diary: He turned invisible when the last person who noticed him stopped being aware of his existence. Both he and the butcher are portrayed as results of social indifference.

In *The Return of the Monster*, Damien is a psychopath who has been confined for sixteen years at the Harlech Asylum, in Scotland, until he escapes. Seemingly, he has killed all the members of a rich family, the Steeles, except Leonora, a blind girl, who was a teenager at the time of the massacre. Now, Damien, formerly the stableman of the Steeles, seems to be about to come back, possibly to complete his butchery; Dylan appears to be the only one who can stop him.

Morgana introduces the character Morgana for the first time. She is one of the zombies created by Xabaras in issue 1 and is his wife and Dylan's mother. Dylan is not aware of the latter until issue 100 of the original series. In this story, he falls in love with her. The main plot, however, is a zombie story full of action. It is also a "metacomic," in that the author of the story appears as himself, that is, as the creator of the adventure, reflecting on how he can conclude the plot.

In *After Midnight*, Dylan forgets his house keys and has to spend the night wandering London. After midnight, anything can happen; people's nightmares even become true, and Dylan finds himself trapped in such nightmares. In the middle of the night, London is a

mishmash of surreal, frightening, and deadly figures (monsters, killers, ghosts), but also of very human and sad situations, which are narrated as bitter social commentaries.

In *Zed*, Zed is a mysterious land, an Edenic world where everyone wants to go. It is possible to reach it only by paying a stiff price to Scout, the guide who possesses the key to this land. Among those who want to find a refuge in Zed is Joey MacFarris, a young woman, former militant member of the Irish Republican Army, and girlfriend of Dylan in this issue. Contrary to appearances, Zed is not an idyllic place. Dylan discovers its secret and that it is just as dangerous as reality.

Volumes

- *Dylan Dog,* Volume 1*: Dawn of the Living Dead* (1999). Collects issue 1 of the original Italian series. The very first story of Dylan Dog presents Sclavi's characters, the general style of the series, and the elegant drawings of Stano. Considered a cult issue within the series and one of the most sold and reprinted comic books of all time.
- *Dylan Dog,* Volume 2*: Johnny Freak* (1999). Collects issue 81 of the original Italian series. It presents the "other" *Dylan Dog:* the part of the series not devoted to fantasy/horror but to "next-door monsters," that is, to the moral squalor that humankind can reach. This is a touching story and one of the most beloved by younger readers. Drawings are particularly effective.
- *Dylan Dog,* Volume 3*: Memories from the Invisible World* (1999). Collects issue 19. This Volume is one of the deepest social commentaries in the whole series. The fantastic element is used to reflect on the social condition of recognition and approval.
- *Dylan Dog,* Volume 4*: The Return of the Monster* (1999). Collects issue 8 of the original Italian series. Firmly within the horror genre, the story recalls Alfred Hitchcock's films and crime magazines. As always, *Dylan Dog* is full of allusions to literature and cinema. Drawings are not the best of the series; therefore, one can argue that

this story did not deserve to be included in the American edition as much as the others did.

- *Dylan Dog,* Volume 5: *Morgana* (1999). Collects issue 25 of the original Italian series. With the introduction of Morgana, *Dylan Dog* reveals new details about the protagonist's past. A narrative continuity begins to develop. This story features a mystical Oedipus conflict that is a compelling idea in mainstream comics and is potentially shocking for American readers.
- *Dylan Dog,* Volume 6: *After Midnight* (1999). Collects issue 26 of the original Italian series. Explicitly inspired by Martin Scorsese's film *After Hours* (1985) but retold in a horror key, it displays a wide range of surprising graphical methods of rendering a nightmarish evening for Dylan Dog in London.
- *Dylan Dog: Zed* (2002). One-shot; collects issue 84 of the original Italian series. Zed is one of the most impressive otherworlds created by Sclavi, and the drawings by Bruno Brindisi complement the script. It is a much appreciated story because it is one of the few written by *Dylan Dog*'s creator.

Characters

- *Dylan Dog* is a thirty-three-year-old, six-foot-tall Caucasian man, modeled after British actor Rupert Everett. He lives in London at 7 Craven Road and works as a private investigator, specializing in paranormal activities. However, he is often also involved in "normal" stories of ordinary violence and human meanness. He is a melancholic type; among his interests are clarinet and his galleon miniature model. As the series progresses, the reader discovers new details of Dylan's history and psychological makeup, for example, that he is a former Scotland Yard agent and currently a teetotaler but formerly an alcoholic.
- *Felix,* a.k.a. *Groucho,* Dylan's sidekick (known as Groucho in the original edition) is modeled on Groucho Marx in terms of his looks and screwball sense of humor; in the American edition, his moustache is erased. A recurring theme is that, in

many issues of the series, he often throws his Bodeo revolver to Dylan when he is in trouble, so that Dylan can stop his enemies.
- *Inspector Bloch,* of Scotland Yard, is a stout, middle-aged man. He was Dylan's boss when Dylan was a police agent. He is a widower and was father to a problematic son, Virgil, who died before the series' main time line. His assistant is Jenkins, a dense and funny agent who takes everything to the letter.
- *Xabaras,* whose name is the anagram of Abraxas (a demon), is the evil half of Dylan Dog's father, who was separated from the good half by a spell. He appears as a slender, middle-aged man with a moustache and a goatee. He was born in the seventeenth century, in a time line previous to the main one and told in other issues of the comic book.
- *Morgana,* a beautiful woman with long black hair, is Dylan Dog's mother and wife of Xabaras, with whom she shares a similar narrative origin in the series' seventeenth-century time line. Dylan falls in love with her, not knowing she is his mother, and becomes victim of a typical Oedipus conflict, which is intensified by the mystical nature of their relationship.

Artistic Style

The graphic style of *Dylan Dog* is, overall, a naturalistic one: Characters and objects are drawn in a realistic fashion. The series makes use of black-and-white drawings, with rare halftones and textures and a wide presence of strong dark/bright contrasts. The artists who have participated in *Dylan Dog* are many; despite that, they all follow the general rules of the series' graphical bible (basic appearances for the characters and settings). However, each one has his or her own graphic idiolect. The artistic contributors worth mentioning are Angelo Stano, Fabio Celoni, Brindisi, Carlo Ambrosini, Giampiero Casertano, Giovanni Freghieri, Marco Soldi, Massimo Carnevale, and Nicola Mari. The most appreciated is Stano, whose style, characterized by an elegant brushwork, is reminiscent of Egon Schiele's figures. Beginning with issue 42 of the Italian series, Stano was also the cover artist, following

Claudio Villa (issues 1-41), whose style was elegant but judged by readers to be too vigorous and bright for *Dylan Dog*. Among the other artists, Celoni is much esteemed. His sensibility for horror themes makes him a perceptive interpreter of *Dylan Dog*'s shadowy settings.

The layout of *Dylan Dog*'s average page is based on three strips of 2/3 panels each; panels are usually rectangular, following a classic pattern of Italian comic books. In the original edition, lettering was handmade; in the American edition it is computer generated with an aseptic style, which creates a dystonia with the art. Bubbles usually have customary shapes and dialogue is an important part of the story, as it often is in Italian comics. Dialogue, however, is rendered without verbosity, being verbal texts well proportioned within the panels, accurately counterbalanced by action scenes almost free from speech balloons, and occasionally accompanied, instead, by visual onomatopoeias that render well the frightening mood of the horror sequences.

Themes

At first glance, the overall structure of the series is quite simple: Dylan Dog is a melancholic and lonely London private detective who investigates paranormal and supernatural activities with the help of a funny sidekick. However, the series does not belong to the crime-fiction genre, since it is only mildly based on detection and deals fully with the horror genre. As it is easily deducible from the plots and the characters' features, the big themes of *Dylan Dog* deal with fantasy/horror clichés—vampires, werewolves, zombies, demons, witches, and myriad forms of psychopaths and killers—and, on the other hand, the supernatural, including motifs such as ghosts, alternate dimensions, and the afterlife. However, the writers, especially Sclavi, also convey more mature issues: At a deeper level, *Dylan Dog* is a commentary on people and societies, life's ups and downs, and sensitive issues such as alcoholism, drug addiction, grief, violence, love, otherness, personal commitment, and disability.

As a further element of interest, *Dylan Dog* is a cultured comic book that makes references to high and popular culture, including philosophy, history, psychology, literature, theater, cinema, music, and television. Virtually every story of the series is based on this triple structure: horror or supernatural plot, social commentary, and cultural quotations; in several *Dylan Dog* monthly adventures, many details on the protagonist's personal history are gradually revealed. Therefore, the attention level, the emotional participation, and the approval from readers are constantly high, as sales figures have shown since the series was first published.

Impact

Dylan Dog's impact on the U.S. comics market and public, first as a short seven-issue series and a separate one-shot book, then as an omnibus paperback volume, is, overall, nonessential for two main reasons. First, the United States has a weak tradition in importing and translating European comics; this is deducible from the way that Dark Horse Comics has treated its *Dylan Dog* publication rights—only seven translated stories from twenty-five years of serial publication (the Italian version has about three hundred issues) plus a number of special books and reprints. Second, *Dylan Dog*'s format and genre are quite different from both average American comic books and manga, therefore its popularity is rather limited and restricted to a small section of the comics fandom.

The editorial behavior of Dark Horse Comics has not helped *Dylan Dog* in the United States. Opinions among American critics and fans have frequently underlined the debatable choice of the *Dylan Dog* stories included in the omnibus, and the absence of any context to introduce the work to American readers has hindered its success in the United States. However, the series and the overall level of the stories published in the United States have been generally appreciated by American readers and critics, precisely because *Dylan Dog* is different from superhero comic books.

Dylan Dog has been defined as a mix between *Tales from the Crypt* (1950's) and the narrative moods of filmmaker David Lynch. Another important reason why the series has been accepted by American readers and critics is the relatively low price of the omnibus edition. *Dylan Dog*'s acceptance in the United States is an ongoing process. The film *Dylan Dog: Dead of*

Night (2011) has partially stimulated a renewed interest in the comics series; the respectable revenue of the movie at the box office, despite the many differences from the original comic book's characters and narrative mood, was fairly promising.

Marco Pellitteri

Films

Cemetery Man. Directed by Michele Soavi. Audifilm, 1994. Starring Rupert Everett as Francesco Dellamorte. Orginally titled *Dellamorte Dellamore* in Italian, the film transposes a novel by Sclavi and is reminiscent of *Dylan Dog*. A cemetery guardian discovers that corpses resurrect as zombies. Everett had already been an inspiration for Sclavi for the look of the character of Dylan Dog. *Cemetery Man* does have connections with *Dylan Dog*: Dellamorte is mentioned by Dylan in *Dylan Dog*'s Italian edition (issues 94 and 205) and appears in two other adventures starring Dylan Dog: special album, issue 3, and a short story, "When the Stars Fall."

Dylan Dog: Dead of Night. Directed by Kevin Munroe. Hide Park Film, 2011. Starring Brandon Routh as Dylan Dog and Sam Huntington as Marcus. Reception has been negative among fans and critics. Marcus is a surrogate of Felix. The white Volkswagen Beetle (Dylan's car) has been changed into a black one, due to copyright issues. In the movie version, Dylan is a superficial, muscular hero, while in the comic book he is an emaciated and melancholic antihero. The film is set in New Orleans instead of London.

Radio Series

Dylan Dog: Jack lo squartatore. Directed by Armando Traverso. Radiotelevisione Italiana (RAI), 2002. Audio story with twenty episodes, produced by RAI, the Italian public radio company, and broadcast on RAI Radio 2. Music by Luigi Seviroli. Starring Francesco Prando as Dylan Dog and Mino Caprio as Groucho. This is the first radio show of *Dylan Dog* and introduces the characters. In English the title translates to "Dylan Dog: Jack the Ripper." It was not the first time that an Italian comic book

was transposed into a radio series: *Tex* and *Diabolik* (first published in 1962) had already been adapted into "audiocomics" by RAI.

Dylan Dog: Necropolis. Directed by Armando Traverso. Radiotelevisione Italiana, 2004. Four-episode audio story broadcast on RAI Radio 2. Music by Seviroli. Starring Prando as Dylan Dog and Caprio as Groucho. *Necropolis* was originally published as a story in issue 212 of the original series, by writer Paola Barbato and artist Freghieri. In the plot, following a miscarriage of justice, Dylan Dog is taken into a prison, where every single movement of the convicts is guarded and recorded by a sort of "Big Brother."

Dylan Dog: L'uccisore di streghe. Directed by Armando Traverso. Radiotelevisione Italiana, 2004. Six-episode audio story broadcast on RAI Radio. Music by Seviroli. Starring Prando and Caprio. Translated in English as "Dylan Dog: The Witch-Killer," *L'uccisore di streghe* was originally published in issue 213, by writer Pasquale Ruju and artist Pietro Dall'Agnol. Dylan Dog falls in love with Angelique, a beautiful witch from Beauport, but a mysterious witch killer makes an attempt on her life.

Further Reading

Kirkman, Robert, Tony Moore, and Charlie Adlard. *The Walking Dead* (2004-   ).

Mignola, Mike. *Hellboy* (1993).

Moore, Alan, and Eddie Campbell. *From Hell* (1989-1996).

Niles, Steve, and Ben Templesmith. *30 Days of Night* (2002).

Bibliography

D'Arcangelo, Adele, and Federico Zanettin. "Dylan Dog Goes to the USA: A North-American Translation of an Italian Comic Book Series." *Across Languages and Cultures* 5, no. 2 (October, 2004): 187-210.

Froehlich, Thomas. "My Name Is Dog...Dylan Dog!" Translated by Binu Starnegg. *Evolver Die Netzzeitschrift*, April 7, 2008. http://www.evolver.at/reloaded/Dylan_Dog_Tiziano_Sclavi_Comic.

Ho, Oliver. "Dylan Dog Versus Hellboy: A Study of Pulp and Pop Pastiche." *Pop Matters*, August 26, 2009. http://www.popmatters.com/pm/feature/109764-dylan-dog-vs.-hellboy-a-study-of-pulp-and-pop-pastiche.

Sclavi, Tiziano. "Dylan Dog FAQ: Tiziano Sclavi Replies to Your Questions." *Sergio Bonelli Editore*. http://www-en.sergiobonellieditore.it/dylan/servizi/faq.html.

White, Bryan. "The Android's Dungeons: *Dylan Dog Case Files*." *Cinema Suicide*, May 5, 2009. http://www.cinema-suicide.com/2009/05/05/the-androids-dungeon-dylan-dog-case-files.

See also: *Hellboy*

E

EARTH X

Author: Krueger, Jim; Ross, Alex
Artist: John Paul Leon (illustrator); Bill Reinhold (inker); Melissa Edwards (colorist); Matt Hollingsworth (colorist); James Sinclair (colorist); Todd Klein (letterer); Alex Ross (cover artist)
Publisher: Marvel Comics
First serial publication: 1999-2000
First book publication: 2001

Publication History

After the critical and popular success of DC Comics miniseries *Kingdom Come* (1996), a story that featured familiar DC superheroes in a dystopian future, Alex Ross was asked to sketch out similar character redesigns for Marvel heroes for a special feature in *Wizard* magazine. Jim Krueger provided brief written origins for each of Ross's new character designs.

While designing these characters, Ross developed a general idea about humanity being mutated, while Krueger suggested the Terrigen Mist as the cause of mutation. The two began to develop a "bible" for the project, realizing its potential beyond the original *Wizard* feature. Together, they established information, including descriptions and backstory, for nearly every Marvel character.

The *Wizard* feature was popular and was republished as a separate sketchbook. When this also proved popular, Marvel approved the *Earth X* miniseries. Initially published as a limited series released monthly from March, 1999, to June, 2000, *Earth X* consists of an introductory 0 issue, numbered issues 1-12, and issue X, which was both a conclusion and an epilogue to the story. While Ross provided character designs and painted the covers, the art within each issue was drawn by John Paul Leon. The miniseries was collected in a trade paperback in 2001. The popularity of the original series motivated Marvel to publish two additional

Earth X. (Courtesy of Marvel Comics)

limited series, *Universe X* (2000-2001) and *Paradise X* (2002-2003), with Doug Braithwaite replacing Leon as the primary artist.

Plot

Earth X is intended to provide a twofold glimpse of almost all of the superheroes in the Marvel Universe: a conjectural depiction of these heroes in a dystopian future setting and a unification of all of these heroes' origins into a single master narrative. Much of *Earth X* consists of retelling the origins and background of the various Marvel heroes, as well as exploring the prehistory of the Marvel Universe. It is revealed that the Celestials have manipulated the evolution of all life on Earth, implanting a "celestial seed" that enables humans to be turned into superheroes. Their true motive, however, is to develop these superhumans as antibodies to protect the Earth itself, which is actually housing a nascent Celestial "egg."

The primary story line involves the Inhumans returning to Earth after traveling through space for twenty years. They find that all of Earth's population has been transformed into superhumans. This mass transformation has caused a food shortage and social and political collapse, and the former Green Goblin is now the unelected president of the United States. There are a number of threats to his domination, including the parasitic hive-mind of Hydra, as well as a new villain, the Skull, whose mind-controlled army marches on New York.

While the Inhumans investigate the cause of the transformation, Captain America searches the globe for a superhero army to stand against the Skull. He recruits Bruce Banner and the Hulk, who are separated into an apelike monster and a blind child; a retired and overweight Peter Parker; Colossus, ruling Russia as the "Iron Czar"; and Scott Summers, now called "Mr. S" by his new team of X-Men-in-training. No matter how many heroes side with Captain America, their fight is futile, since the Skull's mind-control techniques simply add more bodies to the Skull army.

Meanwhile, Reed Richards, with help from X-51, discovers that the worldwide mutation was caused by Black Bolt, the king of the Inhumans, in an attempt to turn the entire population into Inhumans—ending discrimination and prejudice forever. X-51 also reveals the true nature of the Celestials and the danger of their return.

After the Skull reaches New York and kills President Osborn, he is stopped only when Captain America leads a new army of classic "Marvels" (animated clay statues of Golden and Silver Age Marvel heroes). Captain America, hidden inside a clay version of his Golden Age costume, is able to surprise the Skull and snaps the boy's neck. As he takes the youth's life,

Captain America apologizes for failing him, proclaiming "The war ends here."

The battle for Earth has just begun, however, as the Celestials approach the planet. Tony Stark launches his entire factory, in the form of a massive Iron Man suit, in a futile attack. Similar attacks by Thor and the Asgardians, as well as Namor's Atlantean army, fail to slow down the Celestials. Following Richard's advice, Black Bolt sacrifices himself to call across the reaches of space for Galactus, the devourer of worlds and the only natural enemy of the Celestials. Galactus arrives, fights the Celestials to a standstill, and then removes the embryonic Celestial from the Earth's core, causing the Celestial host to leave the planet forever.

With the threats of the Skull and the Celestials finally gone, Captain America and Richards light their "Human Torches," devices that will return Earth's population to normal. X-51 officially takes over for Uatu, but pledges to be a more active "watchman" for the planet.

Characters

- *X-51*, a.k.a. *Aaron Stack* or *Machine Man*, the narrator and current watchman of Earth. X-51 is summoned to the blue area of the moon by Uatu, the former watchman. His humanity has literally been stripped away, and his circuitry and inner workings are covered only by a translucent shell. His bright-red optic sensors are the only elements of his design to retain any coloring. Despairing the loss of his human "face," he fights to maintain his individual humanity and self-determination, even when it requires deceiving Uatu. After he realizes the true nature of the Celestials and the danger they pose to the Earth, he defies Uatu by interfering and assisting the heroes.
- *Captain America*, the primary protagonist, is almost one hundred years old, and his supersoldier physique is weathered and scarred. He wears an American flag wrapped around his torso, and his bald head features a prominent scar shaped distinctly like his trademark letter "A." For the first time in almost a century, his

resolve is beginning to falter in the face of endless war.

- *Tony Stark*, a.k.a. *Iron Man*, no longer active as his alter ego, controls his Iron Avengers (robotic versions of the now-dead Avengers) from his airtight mechanical control room. He resembles Howard Hughes in his eccentric isolationism—Stark believes that his quarantine has left him the last unmutated human on the planet—and in his gaunt, frail appearance and long, unkempt hair.

- *Reed Richards*, after the dissolution of the Fantastic Four (Invisible Woman and the Human Torch are killed in battle, alongside Dr. Doom), has moved into Dr. Doom's Latverian castle. Longhaired and unkempt, Richards now wears Dr. Doom's armor as he silently roams the empty castle. He wrongly blames his experiments for humanity's mutation, but he returns to action to help X-51 stop the Celestials.

- *The Skull*, *Earth X*'s initial antagonist, is a teenage boy who wears clothes with a blood-red version of the Punisher's skull symbol. He often sits on a throne made from an empty Mental Organism Designed Only for Killing (MODOK) shell. He is callously evil, maliciously treating everyone around him as playthings and tools. As the sole remaining psychic on Earth, he has powerful mind-control abilities that give him a growing army of former heroes and villains.

- *Celestials* are the true antagonists in the story. A mysterious race of omniscient, godlike beings, they appear as mile-high suits of bizarre armor.

Artistic Style

The visual style of *Earth X* is noteworthy for combining the styles of two very different artists. Ross, whose sketches formed the earliest foundation for the comic, created multiple covers for each issue. Ross is not only one of the best-known comic book artists of the 1990's and 2000's but also one of the few superhero artists whose popularity is recognized outside of comic book fandom. His artistic style is characterized primarily by

detailed, sometimes hyperrealistic characters. His pictures are often paintings (rather than simply inkings and colored-pencil sketches). Typically, Ross uses photographed models as the basis for his character designs and scene compositions.

Ross's participation is limited to the covers and initial character sketches; however, his perspective on the nature of these familiar superheroes is an influence on the art. While Ross has sometimes been criticized for presenting overly idealized physiques and poses, in a book such as *Earth X* (as well as some of his other works, such as *Kingdom Come*), even the most heroic characters are notably flawed. Ross's character designs merge the mythological nature of comic book superheroes with the frailty of age and a general sense of impotence.

These character designs are in sharp contrast to Leon's art for *Earth X*. Where Ross is especially detailed, Leon uses relatively minimalist designs with a fairly dark color palette. Perhaps most noticeable are Leon's thick lines and extremely heavy shading; in fact, most of the panels within the book are dominated by undifferentiated black shadows. Leon utilizes a variety of creative and innovative layouts, including widescreen-style

Earth X. (Courtesy of Marvel Comics)

splash pages and panels arranged in concentric circles. This distinct visual style and page layout is used most effectively in the many flashbacks found throughout *Earth X*. Every issue begins with several pages that summarize character and background origins, and Leon is able to balance his own distinctive style with otherwise familiar images.

Themes

Like many superhero comic books, *Earth X* engages themes of good versus evil and the nature of heroism. The book utilizes familiar, established characters as a way of positioning itself against the themes found in typical Marvel superhero series. *Earth X* is in the unique position of reinforcing the significance and importance of Marvel superheroes while simultaneously redefining the collective origins of the Marvel Universe and the heroic motives of the individual heroes and villains.

Earth X emerged from the question: "What would superheroes look like in a world where everyone gained superpowers?" Despite the prevalence of superhumans, the heroes still stand in stark contrast to the rest of the population. While the average person in this setting might have horns or wings, they are never depicted as behaving out of the ordinary. Additionally, Leon subtly emphasizes the difference among superheroes, as they are the only characters in the book who show clearly the effects of significant aging.

Superheroes are also distinguished by their actions, but the ongoing fight against evil has a clearly dangerous, harmful side effect. Even the best-intentioned heroic actions have long-lasting effects that not only threaten innocent people but also lead to the downfall of the heroes themselves. Captain America's efforts to stop the Skull repeatedly backfire, as the former's troops are incorporated into the latter's army; when Captain America is forced to kill the Skull himself, it results in a symbolic and thematic destruction of the values of the Golden Age superhero.

Earth X expands beyond the actions of individual heroes and frames its story within the larger cosmic history of the superhero universe. By suggesting the role of the Celestials in every stage of human and superhuman evolution, Krueger and Ross argue that any

---

Jim Krueger

Known primarily for his collaborations with artist Alex Ross, Jim Krueger emerged in the 2000's as a writer of epic-scale miniseries for a number of publishers. *Earth X*, Krueger's breakthrough work, portrayed a dystopian future version of the Marvel Comics Universe. Based on a concept developed by Ross, the series was illustrated by John Paul Leon. In 2005 Krueger and Ross collaborated on writing *Justice* (art by Doug Braithwaite), a twelve-part miniseries depicting a war between the heroes and villains of the DC Universe. In 2007 *Avengers/Invaders* reunited him with Ross and artist Steve Sadowski for a twelve-part series featuring the return of World War II-era heroes to the contemporary period. Krueger's work has most typically been on an epic scale, involving large casts of characters and enormous battle scenes. His writing is better known for its high-concept excesses than for careful character development.

---

traditional notions of good and evil are simply the results of Celestial manipulation. This theme of predetermination is taken even further, as *Earth X* suggests that the ultimate stage of human evolution is not the development of individual powers but the ability to completely redefine one's fundamental identity based on the beliefs and perceptions of others—a state seen in both the Asgardians, who behave like Norse gods only because others believe they are gods, and the new Galactus, who becomes a compassionate defender of Earth once his human father tells him he possesses that trait. These potentially subversive questions of predetermination are never fully resolved by the end of *Earth X*, as the very attempt to stop the Celestials represents free will and self-determination.

Impact

Earth X combined two common aspects of superhero comic books from the Modern Age—it was a widely promoted and hyped limited series featuring a variety of Marvel's flagship characters and a noncontinuity "imaginary story" in the tradition of Marvel's *What*

If . . . ? series or DC Comics' 1990's Elseworlds imprint. *Earth X* was released during a time when Marvel stopped publishing its alternate universe series (the second and third volumes of *What If . . . ?* were released in 1998 and 2005). *Earth X* is categorized alongside this series as part of Marvel's "multiverse" books.

The most evident legacy of *Earth X* can be seen in the two follow-up series. *Universe X* addressed the aftermath of the battle with the Celestials, when the planet's axis shifted as the result of the missing core and the mutated population resisted Richard's "cure." This series focused on the reincarnated Captain Marvel, as well as many of the secondary characters in the Marvel Universe, as Mar-Vell and Captain America collected devices that would eventually destroy Death itself. The third series, *Paradise X*, focuses on alternate time lines and attempts to connect all of the story properties ever published by Marvel Comics into a single (relatively) coherent narrative.

Earth X was initially considered as an extension of the dominant Marvel narrative continuity. While Krueger and Ross altered details of some of the heroes established origins, the series was assumed to depict Earth-616 twenty years into the future. The *Official Handbook of the Marvel Universe* (Volume 12 was published in 2009) later established the *Earth X* series as Earth-9997 and suggested that *Earth X* actually depicts present-day events in an alternate universe. This accounted for later changes to various character developments in the Earth-616 universe.

Jeff Geers

Further Reading

Busiek, Kurt, and Alex Ross. *Marvels* (1994).

Krueger, Jim, and Doug Braithwaite. *Paradise X* (2002-2003).

_____. *Universe X* (2000-2001).

Waid, Mark, and Alex Ross. *Kingdom Come* (1996).

Bibliography

Kreuger, Jim, Richard Case, and Alex Ross. *The Earth X Trilogy Companion*. New York: Marvel, 2008.

Ross, Alex, and Chip Kidd. *Mythology: The DC Comics Art of Alex Ross*. New York: Pantheon, 2003.

Smith, Roberta. "Art in Review: Alex Ross." *The New York Times*, December 1, 2000.

See also: *Marvels; Kingdom Come; Death of Captain America; Astro City*

ELEKTRA: ASSASSIN

Author: Miller, Frank

Artist: Bill Sienkiewicz (illustrator); Jim Novak (letterer); Gaspar Saladino (letterer)

Publisher: Marvel Comics

First serial publication: 1986-1987

First book publication: 1990

Publication History

Elektra: Assassin was originally an eight-issue limited series published from August, 1986, to March, 1987. Approached by series editor Jo Duffy in the summer of 1982, Frank Miller was asked to create something new for Epic Comics, a creator-owned imprint of Marvel Comics. Miller told Duffy that he was working on a new graphic novel featuring Elektra, whom Miller had introduced and subsequently killed in *Daredevil* (beginning in 1979). In 1985, Miller approached Duffy and Archie Goodwin, then editor in chief at Epic Comics, about a different Elektra story.

Working through Epic Comics allowed Miller to bypass the Comics Code Authority seal and produce a story more appropriate for adults, both in terms of story content and visual representation. Additionally, the book was to be distributed solely through direct-sales outlets and specialty stores, instead of retail outlets geared to general buyers. For an artistic collaborator, Miller had already decided he wanted to work with Bill Sienkiewicz, a decision with which Duffy and Goodwin both agreed, having seen Miller and Sienkiewicz's teamwork on *Daredevil: Love and War* (1986). A 2008 version of the book included *Elektra: Assassin, Elektra Lives Again*, and Elektra stories from *Bizarre Adventures*, issue 28, and *What If...?*, issue 35.

Plot

The story begins with Elektra's earliest memories, from her time as a fetus and the murder of her mother (the act of which induces Elektra's birth), the death of her father, molestation by her father (which she attributes to an invented memory), training in martial arts, meeting Matt Murdock (Daredevil), returning to her training grounds to encounter the Beast, and

Elekra: Assassin. (Courtesy of Marvel Comics)

assassinating the politician Carlos Huevos. Elektra's memories are jumbled and leap haphazardly as she is being tortured in an institution for the criminally insane.

The Beast, who controls people who drink its "milk," is an ancient evil that controls the Hand, a ninja clan that shows up in various Marvel Comics titles. Initially, the motives of the Beast are not apparent, but eventually readers discover it is attempting to launch a nuclear war to bring about humanity's destruction. Spreading its influence to several government officials, the Beast eventually corrupts popular Democratic presidential candidate Ken Wind. Although Wind has the demeanor of a peace-loving liberal, he secretly plans to launch a nuclear attack on the Soviet Union after his election and fulfill the Beast's plans.

As a mystically trained ninja, Elektra uses her considerable psychic powers to escape the institution where she is a prisoner, encountering S.H.I.E.L.D.. agent John Garrett and his partner, Perry. On Elektra's trail, Garrett starts to feel a psychic bond with Elektra and becomes infatuated with her; Perry's feelings veer to deadly obsession. Impaling Perry through the head with his own bayonet, Elektra traps Garrett in a building that she blows up, destroying most of his physical body, part of which had already been cybernetically augmented by S.H.I.E.L.D..'s ExTechOp division. ExTechOp replaces Garrett's human body with a robotic one while leaving most of his brain organic.

The bond between Garrett and Elektra grows, until eventually Garrett transitions from being psychically dominated and controlled by her to actively choosing to help her in her quest to stop the Beast. These deaths, and the apparent targeting of Ken Wind, draw the attention of S.H.I.E.L.D.. director Nick Fury, who sends agent Chastity McBryde to stop Elektra and return Garrett to S.H.I.E.L.D.. custody. In the course of her investigation, Chastity learns the truth about ExTechOp and their agents, who were recruited from the criminal population; however, she learns this too late to stop ExTechOp from creating a superpowered cyborg body for the reanimated Perry, a sociopath who sides with the Beast.

In an overwhelming victory, Ken Wind is elected president of the United States. Elektra and Garrett infiltrate his victory rally, causing an incredibly chaotic battle, during which Elektra seriously injures the Beast and terminates Perry again, this time permanently destroying what is left of his organic brain. Pursuing Wind while being hunted by Chastity, Elektra and Garrett finally confront Wind. Using her psychic abilities of mind transference, Elektra transfers the mind of Garrett into Ken Wind's body and traps Wind's broken mind in Garrett's broken body before she and Garrett are captured by Chastity. Recapping the final events of the story through flashback, Elektra transfers her mind from one of the ExTechOp genetic dwarves back into her own catatonic body and escapes S.H.I.E.L.D.. custody. Garrett, now living as Ken Wind, turns his atten-

tion to his presidential duties, forcing the Soviet premier to sign a peace treaty.

Characters

- *Elektra*, a.k.a. *Elektra Natchios*, the protagonist, is the daughter of Greek diplomat Hugo Natchios and his wife, Christina. Through martial arts, her natural gymnastics skills were transformed into those of a ninja, giving her an athletic physique buoyed by a measured amount of beauty. Her robust will gives her several psychic abilities, including telepathy, mind transference, and the ability to project illusory disguises that fool both other humans and technological devices such as cameras and scanners, all of which help to craft her into an imposing assassin. In addition to her skills at unarmed combat and espionage, she is an expert with almost every weapon in existence.

- *John Garrett* is perhaps the second protagonist of the story, as he shares almost equal time with Elektra in the telling of the narrative. He is

Elekra: Assassin. (Courtesy of Marvel Comics)

recruited into ExTechOp, and the organization hid his criminal past, refashioning him as a high-tech agent, giving him some cybernetic enhancements before constructing him a totally cybernetic body.

- *The Beast*, a minotaur-like creature clad in samurai-styled armor, is an apocalyptic being bent on the destruction of humanity. It enslaves people through their consumption of its "milk" and then exerts a psychic control over its servants. It has a high resilience to physical damage.
- *Ken Wind* is the Democratic presidential candidate who is corrupted by the Beast's milk. His smiling countenance rarely changes, and his upbeat features turn chillingly sinister as he conceals an almost unspeakable evil.
- *Nick Fury*, as the second director of S.H.I.E.L.D.., relies on his experience in combat and as an agent to guide his decisions. Wearing his trademark eye patch, Fury scrutinizes his agency with the derision of a soldier who sees an increasing level of bureaucracy prohibiting efficiency.
- *Chastity McBryde* is assigned to the Elektra/Garrett situation by Fury because she is a reliable agent who has remained essentially uncorrupted and, as her name indicates, has a certain level of virtue when it comes to performing her duties as a S.H.I.E.L.D.. agent. Although physically striking, her platinum locks and voluptuous body are mere diversions from her serious tactical skills.
- *The President*, never named in the story, is rendered as a diminutive Richard Nixon with just a dash of Ronald Reagan. Worried about losing the upcoming election, he has become obsessed with carrying "the box" everywhere he goes, even threatening to use it; this simple device, a black box with one large red button, gives him the ability to launch the entire U.S. nuclear arsenal.
- *Perry*, former ExTechOp partner of Garrett, is initially killed by Elektra. Essentially brain dead, he is reanimated and given a superhuman cybernetic body that makes him fireproof, bulletproof, and shockproof, with no need to breathe or eat.

He is a former criminal, albeit several orders of magnitude worse than Garrett.

Artistic Style

Elektra: Assassin was lauded for its distinctive visual style. Sienkiewicz uses collage, oil painting, mimeograph, and other artistic forms generally uncommon in comic books and graphic novels. His mixed-media techniques recall those of Robert Rauschenberg, and his use of caricature evokes British cartoonist Ralph Steadman, famous for his work with author Hunter S. Thompson. Sienkiewicz illustrated *Elektra: Assassin* primarily using watercolors. After producing the script for each issue, Miller would turn it over to Sienkiewicz, who would paint the issue incorporating "color photosats, Xeroxes, doilies, staples, or sewing thread." This would prompt Miller to do a final draft, reacting to Sienkiewicz's artwork and changing scenes and characters. Some aspects were dropped entirely, while others were expanded; often this was happening as Sienkiewicz was also redoing or revising entire pages of art to try new techniques. In this regard, the book is even more noteworthy given the intense collaboration between Miller and Sienkiewicz.

Sienkiewicz started working professionally in the comics industry at age nineteen, drawing *Moon Knight* (1980's) and garnering quick attention for his avant-garde style of illustration. *Elektra: Assassin* allowed him to follow this artistic line even further, occasionally employing surrealism, particularly because the continual changes in narrative point of view created new ways to make connections between plot points that were more visual than textual.

Themes

Much as it did in Miller's *Batman: The Dark Knight* (1986), the specter of the Cold War hangs over the entire narrative, although Miller pushes the satirical bent of *Elektra: Assassin* far past the levels in *Batman. Elektra: Assassin* seemingly criticizes both liberals and conservatives; ultimately, however, where the actual critique lies remains debatable, as Miller has continually vacillated between fascism and libertarianism in his work. Political systems are seen as weighted down with cumbersome bureaucracy or rife with corrupt leaders.

Whereas *The Dark Knight* had its moments of violence, *Elektra: Assassin* revels in ultraviolence, seemingly more in tune with Stanley Kubrick's film *A Clockwork Orange* (1971) than anything in comics. The danger of satire is that it also can glorify that which it seeks to spoof, and the issue of violence in the story is never completely resolved. Both men and women are the originators and victims of violence, and the sheer amount of violence that they can withstand is often taken to superhuman levels. For example, the amount of repeated punishment to which Garrett's cybernetic body is subjected is almost cartoonish in its extremism.

Miller not only pushes violence into the realm of cliché but also adds other overworn comic book forms into the mix, such as ninjas—pioneered by Miller but later overused in the industry—and cyborgs. The issue of cyborgs is particularly interesting in this case, since both of the cyborg characters are men, and having been outfitted with robotic bodies, they are literally stripped of their manhood. Garrett constantly fantasizes about Elektra but he is incapable of doing anything to consummate his desire.

The issue of identity politics with regard to gender is also an important theme in *Elektra: Assassin*. Miller is often critiqued for his problematic portrayal of women as either saints or sinners, with little room for a more complex representation. Elektra is beautiful, and even more deadly, but perhaps her most powerful attribute is her ability to choose her own destiny.

Impact

Along with other significant titles such as *Batman: The Dark Knight* and Alan Moore's *Watchmen* (1986-1987), *Elektra: Assassin* was a pivotal product of comics in the 1980's, helping to revive the industry. Both the high production value of its artistic style and the adult orientation of its subject matter pushed the medium into the direction of more mature readers. Already renowned in the field of comics, both Miller and Sienkiewicz had their reputations further enhanced by the series. Sienkiewicz has commented several times on the influence of Miller on his work and why he has been selective about projects since his work on *Elektra: Assassin*.

In terms of the story's place within the contentious world of comics canon, *Elektra: Assassin* was deliberately vague about Elektra's place in the chronology and the larger Marvel Universe. Based on statements made by Duffy in the introduction to the 2008 version of the book *Elektra*, Miller reportedly conceived of the series as occurring before Elektra's appearance in *Daredevil*, which prompted many readers to dismiss the series as noncanonical; however, Miller used John Garrett in a cameo role in *Elektra Lives Again* (1990), and D. G. Chichester, while writing on *Daredevil*, also used Garrett as a character. Additionally, events in *Elektra: Assassin* are referenced by Garth Ennis in his work on *The Punisher* (2000-2001), in which Elektra makes an appearance.

Stefan Hall

Bill Sienkiewicz

Few superhero artists in the 1980's had a more expressionistic and individualized graphic style than Bill Sienkiewicz. Hired by Marvel when he was only nineteen, Sienkiewicz debuted on *Moon Knight* before making a name for himself on the X-Men spin-off title, *The New Mutants*. His 1988 miniseries, *Stray Toasters*, for Marvel's Epic imprint signaled a move away from the mainstream of superhero imagery, while his 1986-1987 collaboration with writer Frank Miller, *Elektra: Assassin*, is one of the most stylistically unusual superhero comic series ever published by Marvel. In 1990 he produced two issues of the miniseries *Big Numbers* with Alan Moore before abandoning that labor-intensive project. More than almost any other single artist, Sienkiewicz revolutionized the aesthetics of superhero comics in the 1980's, breaking from the legacies of the 1960's and 1970's that privileged a house style, and pursuing his own form of self-expression.

Films

Daredevil. Directed by Mark Steven Johnson. New Regency, 2003. This film adaptation stars Ben Affleck as Daredevil, Jennifer Garner as Elektra, and Colin

Farrell as Bullseye. Elektra's trademark red satin outfit was replaced by black leather, largely as a concession to the needs of stunt harnesses. Elektra and Matt Murdock meet and fall in love but come to blows when Daredevil is framed for the death of Elektra's father by the Kingpin. Elektra is killed. After confronting Bullseye and Kingpin, Daredevil returns to find that Elektra's body has mysteriously vanished.

Elektra. Directed by Rob Bowman. Twentieth Century Fox, 2005. This film adaptation stars Jennifer Garner as Elektra and Terrence Stamp as Stick. After being resurrected by Stick, Elektra is trained in the Way of Kimagure, which she must use to thwart the plans of assassins of the Hand.

Further Reading

Moench, Doug, and Bill Sienkiewicz. *Moon Knight: Countdown to Dark* (2010).

Morrison, Grant, and Dave McKean. *Arkham Asylum* (1990).

Niles, Steve, and Bill Sienkiewicz. *30 Days of Night: Beyond Barrow* (2007).

Sienkiewicz, Bill. *Stray Toasters* (2008).

Wheatley, Mark, and Marc Hempel. *Breathtaker* (1990).

Bibliography

Duffy, Jo. Foreword to *Elektra: Assassin*. New York: Marvel Comics, 1990.

Eisner, Will, and Frank Miller. *Eisner/Miller: A One-on-One Interview*. Milwaukie, Ore.: Dark Horse, 2005.

George, Milo, ed. *Frank Miller: The Interviews: 1981-2003*. Seattle, Wash.: Fantagraphics Books, 2003.

Sienkiewicz, Bill. *Bill Sienkiewicz Precursor*. Neshannock, Pa.: Hermes Press, 2003.

_____. "Interview with Bill Sienkiewicz." Interview by Kuljit Mithra. *Daredevil Manwithoutfear.com*, January, 2000. http://www.manwithoutfear.com/interviews/ddINTERVIEW.shtml?id=Sienkiewicz.

See also: *Batman: Arkham Asylum*; *Elektra Lives Again*; *Daredevil: Born Again*; *Daredevil: The Man Without Fear*

ELEKTRA LIVES AGAIN

Author: Miller, Frank
Artist: Frank Miller (illustrator); Lynn Varley (colorist); Jim Novak (letterer)
Publisher: Marvel Comics
First book publication: 1990

Publication History

Elektra Lives Again was first published in hardback only in 1990 by Epic Comics, an imprint of Marvel Comics, in an oversized format. A paperback edition was published in 1993. The work is included in the 2008 *Elektra by Frank Miller Omnibus*, with additional materials, stories, and works connected with Elektra and Daredevil.

Plot

The story is organized chronologically, starting with Monday, April 1, suggesting, through the use of April Fools' Day, that Matt Murdock (Daredevil) is delusional throughout the story. On the first day, Murdock walks along snow-covered streets; an internal-monologue narration reveals his obsessive thoughts about Elektra. Matt enters a cathedral and confesses to a priest his hatred for the Church and his obsession with Elektra, who he explains became an assassin and is now dead. Murdock also shares a gruesome vision of Elektra that haunts him.

On Tuesday, April 2, Murdock's dream of Elektra—nude and bloody, then in her costume—is intermixed with scenes of the city and Murdock tossing and turning in bed. Then, the reader is pulled fully into the dream, with Elektra chained in a snow-covered scene. In the dream, Elektra is being chased by a horde of zombielike creatures who overtake her. These creatures have all died at Elektra's hands, and they dismember her while taunting her. The narration drifts back and forth between Murdock in bed and his dream/delusion. Murdock struggles against the dream and forces himself to stay awake, but the delusion wrestles itself into his conscious state, where he admits he wants Elektra back and alive.

On Saturday, April 6, Murdock wakes from the dream still fixated on Elektra being alive and calls

Elektra Lives Again. (Courtesy of Marvel Comics)

Karen Page, who brushes off his advances. After working out using the boxing bag, Murdock visits Elektra's grave; the artwork shows Elektra as the headstone, supporting the surreal nature of this story.

On Monday, April 8, while speaking with a client, Alice Courtney, Murdock remembers a violent memory from his childhood. He takes Alice for a drink and then dinner, which leads them to make love. Murdock leaves Alice in the bed; Elektra remains on his mind. He is shown kneeling at her grave surrounded by ninjas in all white, believing what he envisions is a dream. As he fights the ninjas, Elektra joins him, dressed in her red costume. Elektra tosses a star, which strikes Murdock in the right palm before he passes out.

On Tuesday, April 9, Murdock, with a bandaged right hand, takes Valium, although the internal monologue explains he never uses drugs, and settles into a hot bath. There, he struggles to understand what is real and what is a dream, believing Elektra is alive and being tracked by the Hand, a band of ninjas whom Elektra left. Murdock mentions the resurrection of Kirigi, whom Elektra killed, and nearly falls asleep; he is roused by a phone call from Foggy Nelson.

On Wednesday, April 10, the opening scene details the killing of Bullseye in prison. Murdock/Daredevil's fights with Bullseye are mixed with his recollection of Bullseye killing Elektra, who makes it to Murdock's house before collapsing. Next, Murdock and Foggy are at prison, with Bullseye's corpse in the prison morgue; the people surrounding Murdock claim Elektra is alive, and she is shown going to the morgue to decapitate Bullseye, where other corpses come to life and attack her. Murdock confronts Bullseye's assassin, who appears to have control of Murdock's mind, leaving Murdock unconscious and the assassin dead from a brain hemorrhage. Elektra, nude, bursts through a window. The entire city is on fire around them, and Murdock takes her in his arms only to discover she is cold—and that he is dreaming again.

Murdock returns to the boxing bag and then is attacked by a ninja; they fight, leading Murdock to chase him across building tops. Murdock thinks of Elektra, and the scene shifts to Bullseye's corpse being raised from the dead, as Murdock continues to chase the ninja to a cathedral littered with the bodies of ninjas and a bloody nun, where Murdock, along with the nun, fights Bullseye; the nun slays Bullseye. Murdock holds the bloody nun, Elektra, who tells him good-bye. He then struggles to the emergency room, his faced scarred and bloody, before buying five gallons of gas and burning down the cathedral to fulfill the priest's recommendation that he let go of Elektra.

The final two pages are a full spread showing Elektra standing alone and facing away.

Characters

- *Matt Murdock*, a.k.a. *Daredevil*, is the central figure of this Elektra story. He is the haunted former lover of the deceased Elektra. He is a lawyer who seeks to rid himself of his obsession with Elektra after her death.
- *Elektra*, the daughter of a Greek diplomat and ninja assassin, fills a secondary role in this graphic novel named after her. She appears as either a resurrected former lover of Murdock or a delusion so powerful that it drives Murdock to behave as if she has been resurrected.
- *Karen Page*, a former lover of Murdock, is mentioned briefly as Murdock attempts to reconnect with her while fighting his nightmares about Elektra.
- *Alice Courtney* is a client of Murdock, with whom he has a one-night stand.
- *The Hand* is the powerful and corrupt order of ninjas to which Elektra had belonged, a fact that leads them to club her for revenge. Ninja assassins from the Hand attack Murdock and Elektra throughout the story.
- *Franklin "Foggy" Nelson* is Murdock's former college roommate and law colleague. He accompanies Murdock to the prison where Bullseye is assassinated.
- *Bullseye*, an archenemy of Daredevil, murders Elektra and is assassinated in prison and then resurrected. He is a supervillain (an assassin for Kingpin) without superpowers but has highly refined skills that allow him to use nearly any object as a weapon.

Artistic Style

Miller's art and Lynn Varley's coloring are central to *Elektra Lives Again*, a work driven by narration (more than dialogue) and by the art and coloring, since many panels and pages have no text. Miller's style is nearly fully realized by *Elektra Lives Again* and moves beyond the classic "comic book" style of his earlier work (which looks more like Sal Buscema or Ross Andru than Jack Kirby, whose style seems influential on Miller). The emerging style includes a stylized and rougher Kirby-esque technique that emphasizes the surrealism of the story and the evil or darkness that lurks beneath all the characters.

Miller's art is distinct, with a heavy line emphasis that makes characters dynamic and dark; even Murdock is often monstrous, bloodied, and sinister. The panel design is central to the surreal nature of the narrative, which is bound by a short span of time, ten days, but ambiguous about the distinction between reality and Murdock's delusions and obsessions. Full-page panels overlaid with smaller panels help blend time and reality or dreams. Miller also emphasizes setting using bold cityscapes, snow-covered scenes (with Elektra), spiraling staircases, and the ominous cathedral that bookends the narrative.

Miller's attention to motion and action are also notable and bold. Murdock is shown often in acrobatic movements and the fight scenes are aided by the large-page format that allows full-page scenes packed with multiple assailants (for both Murdock and Elektra) and sequenced action to highlight time and the violent nature of the battles.

Another key element of the surreal nature of the narrative is Miller's perspective. Many scenes angle the reader's view to shift perspective and even distort perspective, especially to offer a greater view of the scene and to capture the passing of time. For example, the scene in prison between Murdock and Bullseye's assassin skews the images of the characters behind bars against a white background and small panels that overlay their psychic battle.

Miller's solo work is supported heavily by Varley's coloring, which presents dynamic colors against the dominant dark work. Varley's detailed coloring matches Miller's highly detailed scenes (that contrast the occasional stark artwork punctuated throughout). Varley's coloring helps emphasize the contrasts of the narrative and reinforces the surrealism, dream states, and overall ambiguity of the story line. The contrasts of light and dark raise the tension and dramatic effect of many scenes throughout.

Elektra Lives Again. (Courtesy of Marvel Comics)

Themes

Loss and the quest for redemption and closure bookend *Elektra Lives Again*. Murdock represents the power of loss to fuel and distort the psyche, and his quest for understanding and letting go of his compulsion connected with Elektra builds a powerful psychological drama that leaves the reader unsure of the fine line between reality and delusion.

The mythological reference tied to Elektra's name (and the association with Freudian and Jungian psychology and literary analysis) connects the guilt motif to the themes of loss and redemption. Elektra is driven by the murder of her father, which parallels Murdock's inability to leave his love for Elektra behind after her murder. The guilt motif is also reinforced by Murdock's confession to the priest and the final apocalyptic scene in the cathedral.

Possibly the work's most powerful theme is the blurring of reality and surrealism; the reader is left with ambiguous distinctions between Murdock's haunting dreams and the actions of his conscious life. However, the narrative never confirms the ambiguities. The recurring dreams and nightmares reinforce the Freudian and Jungian elements of *Elektra Lives Again*.

Dreams carry a double meaning, representing those composed during rapid eye movement (REM) sleep and the hopes that Murdock still holds for Elektra to be resurrected. Resurrection and the mystical powers of ninjas weave within the broader consideration of dreams and reality.

Revenge is presented as a key element of redemption and release, both for Murdock in his journey to be free of Elektra (if he cannot be reunited) and for Elektra as she seeks to keep Bullseye from being resurrected. The revenge motif is also paralleled in the assassination of Bullseye and the confrontation between Bullseye's assassin and Murdock.

Violence punctuates Murdock's and Elektra's personas, and it seems integral to many of the other motifs of the work, including revenge, redemption, and release. Sex and intimate relationships are examined throughout *Elektra Lives Again*. Murdock's relationship with Elektra is one of turmoil and contradiction, since he pursues justice and she lived her life as an assassin. Nonetheless, their connection suggests the power of soul mates and the influence of fate. Murdock's attempts to calm himself by calling, and hoping, to see Page and the "hollow" one-night stand with Courtney contrast with the deeper (although more problematic) passion he feels for Elektra. The torturous connection between Murdock and Elektra expresses the existential argument that passion is also the source of suffering.

Impact

Elektra Lives Again serves as one of many reconsiderations of Elektra in the history of the character and in the career of Miller, who seems unable to set the character aside even though he has expressed a desire to do so. The work is a continuation of Miller's stylistic development, falling between *The Dark Knight Returns* (1986) and *Sin City* (1991-2000).

P. L. Thomas

Films

Elektra. Directed by Rob Bowman. Regency Enterprises, 2005. This film stars Jennifer Garner as Elektra. As a spin-off of *Daredevil* (2003), it features a reborn Elektra as she is trained to be an assassin.

Further Reading

Miller, Frank. *Batman: The Dark Knight Returns* (1986).

_____. *Sin City: The Hard Goodbye* (1991).

Miller, Frank, and Bill Sienkiewicz. *Elektra* (2008).

Bibliography

Miller, Frank, and Milo George. *Frank Miller: The Interviews, 1981-2003*. Seattle, Wash.: Fantagraphics Books, 2003.

Paul, Ryan. "Star-Crossed in Comics Land." *PopMatters*, February 6, 2003. http://www.popmatters.com/comics/elektra-lives-again.shtml.

Thomas, P. L. *Challenging Genres: Comic Books and Graphic Novels*. Rotterdam, Netherlands: Sense, 2010.

See also: *Daredevil: Born Again; Daredevil: The Man Without Fear; Elektra Assassin*

ELFQUEST

Author: Pini, Wendy; Pini, Richard
Artist: Wendy Pini (illustrator); Richard Pini (letterer)
Publisher: WaRP Graphics
First serial publication: 1978-1985
First book publication: 1981

Publication History

The first issue of *ElfQuest* was published in *Fantasy Quarterly* in 1978. After that publication folded, Wendy and Richard Pini started WaRP Graphics and began to self-publish. The original story arc (referred to as the "Original Quest") was published by WaRP Graphics (later Warp Graphics) as twenty-one black-and-white magazine-sized issues from 1978 to 1985 and as four graphic novels between 1988 and 1989: *Fire and Flight* (issues 1-5), *The Forbidden Grove* (issues 6-10), *Captives of Blue Mountain* (issues 11-15), and *Quest's End* (issues 16-20).

Marvel Comics reprinted the entire Original Quest in thirty-two color issues from August, 1985, to March, 1988, as part of their Epic imprint. The Original Quest continued in the eight-part series *Siege at Blue Mountain*, published by Apple Comics/Warp Graphics from September, 1987, to December, 1988, and in the nine-part series *Kings of the Broken Wheel*, published by Warp Graphics from June, 1990, to February, 1992. From 1992 to 2007, the Pinis wrote a number of spin-offs that involve some of the original characters and add many more new characters. Some of these new titles are drawn by guest artists and writers. These include: *ElfQuest: The Hidden Years* (1992-1996; twenty-nine issues); *ElfQuest: New Blood* (1992-1996; thirty-five issues); *Blood of Ten Chiefs* (1993-1995; twenty issues); *Wave Dancers* (1993-1994; six issues); *Shards* (1994-1996; sixteen issues); *The Rebels* (1994-1996; twelve issues); *Jink* (1994-1996; twelve issues); *Kahvi* (1995-1996; six issues); and *ElfQuest: Two-Spear* (1995-1996; five issues).

From 2003 to 2007, the Pinis licensed all publishing and merchandising rights to DC Comics, which began republishing the Original Quest in color and in manga

---

Wendy Pini and Richard Pini

Known for their fantasy-adventure series, *Elf-Quest*, Wendy and Richard Pini are the most famous husband-and-wife creative team in the history of American comics. After beginning a correspondence based on a letter published in an issue of *Silver Surfer*, the couple wed in 1972. Six years later they began publishing the adventures of the Wolfriders, the Sun Folk, the Gliders, and the Go-Backs, tribes of elves that populate their fictional world. *ElfQuest* was one of the most notable successes of the late-1970's "ground level" comics movement: post-underground, independently produced comics often centered on fantasy or science-fiction genre elements. The series was praised for its frank depictions of sexuality and feminine points of view. Wendy Pini's art, which mixes lushly romantic fairytale-inspired imagery with cartoony elements in the context of an adventure setting, has been highly influential in the fantasy field.

---

formats. Since 2008, all *ElfQuest* stories have been available digitally on the *ElfQuest* official Web site.

Plot

The story is set in the World of Two Moons, an Earth-like world inhabited by early humans, elves, and trolls. The elves and trolls had arrived several generations back through the accidental colonization of the High Ones, a pure, highly advanced elfin race whose origins are extraterrestrial. In the Original Quest, the main protagonists are members of a small and closely knit elfin tribe called the Wolfriders, who are descendants of the High Ones and of wolves.

At the opening of the Original Quest, the Wolfriders are chased from their Holt by humans who burn down the forest in which they had lived for ten generations. This flight sets the tribe on a quest for a new home and ultimately for reunification with the other lost and scattered elfin groups, including the Sun-Folk (desert dwellers), the Gliders (mountain dwellers), and the Go-Backs (tundra dwellers). Under the visionary Wolfrider chief, Cutter, the Wolfriders negotiate survival among the treachery and hostility of the humans and trolls and try to establish strong bonds with the other elves. That part of the quest fails because not all the elves get along. Cutter's goal is to unite all these races of elves and to return to the lost palace of the High Ones.

The quest ends when the various elves go to war with the trolls in order to regain the palace. They are victorious with the help of an original High One named Timmain, but then return to their homes, leaving only Rayek behind as keeper of the palace. Cutter decides to look to the future rather than the past in order to lead the Wolfriders and the other elves who have joined his tribe. For him, the quest will continue.

Volumes

- *ElfQuest:* Book One, *Fire and Flight* (1988). Collects issues 1-5. This book focuses on the Wolfriders' departure from their Holt and their arrival at Sorrow's End. Cutter defeats Rayek and becomes Leetah's "lifemate."
- *ElfQuest:* Book Two, *The Forbidden Grove* (1988). Collects issues 6-10. Cutter and Skywise embark on their quest to rediscover lost elf tribes and to reclaim the palace of the High Ones.
- *ElfQuest:* Book Three, *Captives of Blue Mountain* (1989). Collects issues 11-15. The Wolfriders encounter the Gliders, elves who dwell in Blue Mountain and bond with enormous birds. The evil Winnowill has captured the Wolfriders; they escape.
- *ElfQuest:* Book Four, *Quest's End* (1989). Collects issues 16-20. The Wolfriders and Gliders fly to the tundra to find the Palace. The Go-Backs join the Quest. They go to war with the trolls and recover the Palace.

Characters

There are approximately 650 named characters in the *ElfQuest* universe. All of the elves are beautiful, thin, and muscular. They have long, pointy ears, disproportionately large eyes and big hair, and no body hair, although the men grow beards once they become elders.

The High Ones and Gliders are tall, but the Sun Folk, Go-Backs, and Wolfriders are short. The Wolfriders are light in complexion, athletic, and healthy; the Sun Folk are dark-skinned and usually have green or dark eyes; the Gliders are tall, pale, and slim; the Go-Backs are pale, dark-haired, and athletic.

- *Cutter* is the main character and protagonist, the chief of the Wolfriders. He wants to reunite all the elves and reconnect with the High Ones. He has twins, Ember and Suntop, with Leetah. The key to the lost palace of the High Ones is hidden within his sword, Newmoon, which was forged by Two-Edge. His character represents vision and evolution, while simultaneously celebrating the bestial nature of the Wolfriders.
- *Skywise* is the most intellectual character and has a serious interest in astronomy and astrology. He and Cutter are inseparable "soul brothers"; this means that they exchanged soul names. He carries a lodestone that guides the quest. He is very sexual and aggressive.
- *Dewshine* experiences "recognition" with the Glider Tyldak and gives birth to Windkin, another mixed elf child, whom she raises with Scouter, her "lovemate." Her character embodies the quest itself, as she creates a child of mixed parentage.
- *Ember* is the daughter of Cutter and Leetah. Her twin brother is Suntop, later Sunstream. Ember appears to take after her father more than her mother and is therefore an enthusiastic hunter and forest dweller. She will succeed her father as chief of the Wolfriders. Her character renews the bloodlines of the Wolfriders. Her soul name is not revealed. She may not possess one, as she is half Sun Folk, and their tribe does not use soul names.
- *Suntop*, a.k.a. *Sunstream* and *Klynn*, is the son of Cutter and Leetah and the twin brother of Ember. He is sensitive and possesses magical abilities on par with Savah and Rayek, who live at Sorrow's End where he was born. He can sense the presence of magic and can send his body out to telepathically communicate with the great wisewomen elves of the story: Savah, Winnowill, and

Timmain. He is important because his magical powers propel the plot of the continuation arcs. His soul name is Klynn.

- *Clearbrook* is an elder of the Wolfriders. She was the recognized lifemate of One-Eye, who was killed in the war with the Go-Backs against Guttlecraw's trolls. She later becomes a lovemate of Treestump, whose mate was also killed. Her grief makes her character important, as she embodies the sacrifice and pain of war and of the quest. Her son is Scouter, and her wolf friend is Whitebrow. Her soul name is not revealed.

- *Dart* is the son of Moonshade and Strongbow. He does not join the quest, but chooses to separate from his parents and from the Wolfrider tribe in order to remain in Sorrow's End and to teach the Sun Folk how to hunt with bow and arrows. He leads his own Wolfriders made up of Sun Folk and desert wolves. The two packs live briefly and uneasily together in the forest Holt.

- *Moonshade*, a.k.a. *Eyrn*, is a tanner. She is the obedient and subservient lovemate of Strongbow and the mother of Dart. In the Original Quest, Strongbow convinces her to leave the tribe in Blue Mountain in order to preserve the "Way." She obeys him. Her soul name is Eyrn.

- *Nightfall*, a.k.a. *Twen*, is a serious warrior and hunter. She is adept with a bow and arrow and with a knife. She is the lifemate of the gentle Redlance. Her soul name is Twen.

- *One-Eye*, a.k.a. *Sur*, is a hunter. He was named Woodhue but has been called One-Eye ever since he was captured and tortured by humans. He is the lifemate of Clearbrook and father of Scouter. He was killed by trolls during the war to regain the palace. His body is preserved in the palace where his spirit continues to dwell. His soul name is Sur.

- *Pike* is known for his skill with a spear and for being the "howl keeper," which is similar to being a bard. He is the least serious of the Wolfriders and is frequently drunk on "dreamberries."

- *Redlance*, a.k.a. *Ulm*, is a paternal character who can shape plants and trees. He is the lifemate of Nightfall. He is left behind to guard the children

during the war with the trolls for the palace. In *Kings of the Broken Wheel*, he and Nightfall enlist Leetah to help them conceive a child within the palace of the High Ones. His soul name is Ulm.

- *Scouter* is the scout. He is the son of Clearbrook and One-Eye. His lovemate is Dewshine. Windkin is his "adoptive" child.

- *Strongbow* is the archer. He almost never speaks but, rather, communicates by "sending." He is ill-tempered and the least supportive character of the quest. He clings to "the Way" and the old days of the Holt. He is lifemates with Moonshade and the father of Dart, with whom he has a prickly relationship. At the end of *Siege of Blue Mountain*, he kills a Glider, Kureel. He tortures himself over killing another elf and temporarily loses his ability to hunt.

- *Treestump* is also an elder and is the brother of the late Joyleaf, Cutter's mother. He is strong and brave. His lifemate, Rillfisher, was deaf after an illness and died when she was struck by a fallen limb when their daughter, Dewshine, was a baby. He and Clearbrook become lovemates.

- *Leetah* is the daughter of Sun Toucher, the blind chief of the Sun Folk. She is a healer. Once recognized by Cutter, she supports his vision and joins the Wolfriders on their quest. Her mother is Toorah. Her sister is Shen Shen, the midwife.

- *Rayek* is the chief hunter of the Sun Folk and has a special bond with Savah, who helps guide his magical abilities, which include flying. At the end of the Original Quest, he becomes the keeper of the Palace of the High Ones. He is the antihero.

- *Savah* is the wise woman of the Sun Folk at Sorrow's End. She was a founder of Sorrow's End. She never sleeps and can project astrally.

- *Winnowill* is a Glider and the villain. She is tall, dark-haired, and beautiful but cold. It was her idea to sequester the Gliders in Blue Mountain, the isolated world that caused her to unravel mentally and leads her to control their leader, Lord Voll. She was a healer and can alter other elves' bodies, including making them part of the mountain itself. She is worshiped by a tribe of humans.

- *Tyldak* is a Glider who has been shape-shifted by Winnowill to resemble a bird. He has a great wingspan and can fly. He is initially loyal to Winnowill but then supports the Wolfriders. He hunts with the Chosen Eight.
- *Aroree* is one of the Chosen Eight, the hunters for the Gliders. She can fly. She is very unhappy and terrified of Winnowill, but her loyalty to and love for Lord Voll keep her in Blue Mountain. She is one of the few Gliders to survive at the end of *Siege of Blue Mountain*. She is a major actor of the events of that story and the *Kings of the Broken Wheel*. She is a lovemate of Skywise. She befriends Kahvi and joins the Wolfriders.
- *Lord Voll* is the founder and lord of the Gliders. He is a son of the original High Ones and lovemate to Winnowill. He and his "bondbird" Tenspan are killed by the trolls while flying the Wolfriders to the palace.
- *Two-Edge* is half elf and half troll. His mother is Winnowill. He looks like a handsome troll and has the muscular physique of the elves. He is mentally unbalanced as a result of his mother's abuse. He manipulates the quest.
- *Kahvi* is the chief of the Go-Backs. She is a fierce warrior and strong leader. She is extremely violent and sexual. Her lovemates include Cutter, Rayek, and Tyldak. She leads the great war with the Trolls.
- *Skot* and *Krim* were members of the Go-Backs, but they leave the tundra and join Pike as lovemates in the new Holt. Skot is an epicurean just as Pike is indulgent with dreamberry wine.
- *Venka* is the daughter of Kahvi and Rayek. She appears to possess some of his magical powers and is adept at countering Winnowill's psychic attacks. She defeats Winnowill in *Kings of the Broken Wheel*.
- *Ekuar* is an elderly rock shaper who spent decades as a prisoner of trolls. Rayek rescues him, and the two form a close bond while living with the Go-Backs. His ability to open and close

passages in rock caves makes him a useful asset on all legs of the quest.

- *The High Ones* include Timmain, who is the only one who actually appears in the comic. The others are frequently referenced. They include: Aerth, Adya, Deir, Gibra, Guin, Haken, Ima, Kalil, Kaslin, Orolin, Sefra, and Tislin.
- *The Trolls* live underground, but are responsible for much of the strife that the various elfin tribes face. They are portrayed as lazy, stupid, and greedy. They live in two separate rival tribes and include Picknose, Guttlekraw, Oddbit, Greymung, Old Maggoty, Scurff, and Trinket.
- *Nonna* and *Adar* are the humans who rescue Cutter and are drawn to resemble Wendy and Richard Pini.

Artistic Style

Wendy Pini's original run showcased high-quality black-and-white pen-and-ink panels. She used a high contrast style. The style was rooted in both realism and idealism, and the characters were drawn with great detail and to scale. The various landscapes were imaginative and penciled with great care and meticulous affect. The physical bodies of the elves were idealized and sexualized. Wendy Pini has said that she was influenced by Japanese animation, Art Nouveau, and traditional fantasy illustrators.

Wendy Pini's bright, colorful cover art overflows with emotion and movement. On the back of the original twenty magazine-sized issues, she drew lush, colorful, painterly portraits of the main characters. When she began drawing in color, she would photocopy the black-and-white pages and then paint over them with watercolor. In 1998, she began using Adobe Photoshop.

The layout of the series varies. Some pages are divided into panels, others are collages of images, and still others are full-page images. Dialogue is sometimes enclosed in word balloons; other times it is written as captions. When the elves communicate by sending, a dark four-sided star with radiating lines appears over their brows. The sending dialogue itself appears in double-ringed ovals.

The book's artistic style has evolved over the years. While being reprinted by Marvel Comics, the book was colorized by Glynis Oliver and was printed on Mando paper. The book was restructured from twenty thirty-two-page issues into thirty-two eighteen-page issues. Wendy Pini drew transitional pages to bridge the narrative gaps.

Themes

Community and identity are major themes. Cutter wishes to pinpoint and redefine his own community and his place within it. He wishes to understand the relationship of his own tribe with the others. He attempts to overcome physical and cultural barriers in order to create one united community of all elves. The scattered elves do intermingle and join new tribes, but they fail to create one multiethnic family. The Pinis reveal the limits of identity as the various elves struggle to accept one another and adapt to their new environments. It is, however, difficult for them to get along.

Love is another major theme. One of the elves' most heroic qualities is their ability to love deeply and for eternity. They love selflessly and without possessiveness and many make serious sacrifices for one another. As the tribes interbreed, the Pinis present interracial relationships that are perfectly natural, healthy, and beneficial. The elves speak openly about one another's ethnicities without judgment. This openness extends to their attitudes about sex. Sex does not create issues in the elfin communities. There is no marriage, monogamy, rape, molestation, domestic violence, honor killing, or unwanted pregnancies. There are no sexually transmitted diseases or prostitutes. Sex is healthy and natural and not used to gain power or humiliate one another. Nudity is common. The elves have no body shame or eating disorders. The Pinis created a healthy body-positive, sex-positive world that offers an idealized vision of relationships and emotions.

Another prominent theme is that violence is necessary and often enjoyable. This is a violent comic that features war, torture, sacrifice, and hunting. Hunting and killing figure prominently in each issue and are glorified by all the tribes. The Wolfriders consider hunting to be natural, and almost all the members of the tribe hunt. In the other tribes, it is a position of privilege for the chosen elves. The extreme violence of their hunt is mirrored in their combative relationship with

humans, with trolls, and with one another. Meat is an important part of the tribes' rituals, sexuality, and identity. The Wolfriders eat their meat raw and howl after the kill.

The Pinis have said that another theme is maturation. Their various characters, especially Cutter, grow up throughout the quest and leave adolescence behind. At the beginning of the quest, Cutter agonized over and reflected on his own leadership abilities, but he grew more confident as the quest moved forward.

Impact

ElfQuest, a Modern Age alternative fantasy comic, is considered a successful cult hit. The Pinis are often credited with inspiring other independent titles and self-publishers. Their fans are devoted; the Pinis have always maintained a close relationship with their fans and have made themselves accessible at conventions, via email, and through other forms of correspondence. Fans often refer to an *ElfQuest* universe much as fans of Joss Whedon reference the "Buffyverse" of *Buffy the Vampire Slayer*.

The Pinis are also credited with redefining the commercial potential of independent alternative comics. They were some of the first to create a specialized line of *ElfQuest* merchandise that is now standard in the industry. They were also among the first to publish reprints and novelizations and to push merchandising, especially T-shirts and statuettes. They released compact disks of music inspired by *ElfQuest*. A *Wolfrider's Reflections: Songs of "ElfQuest"* was released in 1987. Terry Moore, author of the self-published comic book *Strangers in Paradise* (1993-2007), has followed their example and released music and lyrics taken from his long-running book.

Part of their expansive merchandising includes a role-playing game released in 1984 by Chaosium, Inc. The original boxed set included the ElfBook and the WorldBook, a parchment map of the World of Two Moons, fifteen character sheets, an instructional booklet, quick reference sheets, and a collection of various-sided dice. Wendy Pini's original artwork is included, and she hand drew the map. The game follows the story line of the Original Quest and allows players to choose one of the elf characters and to participate in the quest. In the Internet age, several fan-generated on-line games have arisen.

Katherine Allocco

Further Reading

Carey, Michael. *Lucifer* (2000-2006).

Moore, Terry. *Strangers in Paradise* (1993-1997).

Pini, Wendy. *Beauty and the Beast: Portrait of Love* (1989).

Sim, Dave. *Cerebus* (1977-2004).

Bibliography

Gallo, Don, and Stephen Weiner. "Bold Books for In-novative Teaching." *The English Journal* 94, no. 2 (November, 2004): 114-117.

Pini, Wendy, and Richard Pini. "Talking with Wendy and Richard Pini, the Team Behind *ElfQuest*." Inter-view by Julie Scordato. *Library Media Connection*, March, 2005, pp. 46-49.

Sanderson, Peter. "Say Hello to *ElfQuest*." *Marvel Age*, July, 1985. http://www.elfQuest.com/edits/MarvAge.html.

See also: *Lucifer; Cerebus*

Ex Machina

Author: Vaughan, Brian K.

Artist: Tony Harris (penciller, inker, and cover artist); John Paul Leon (penciller); Chris Sprouse (penciller); Jim Clark (inker); Tom Feister (inker); Karl Story (inker); JD Mettler (colorist); Jared K. Fletcher (letterer)

Publisher: DC Comics

First serial publication: 2004-2010

First book publication: 2005-2011

Publication History

Ex Machina was published as a monthly series by the DC Comics imprint WildStorm, concluding shortly before the imprint was absorbed into the main DC line in late 2010. Additionally, *Ex Machina* has been collected into ten trade paperback volumes and five deluxe hardcovers.

Brian K. Vaughan was an established comics writer by 2004, having written for a variety of series at DC and Marvel and created two successful and critically acclaimed series, *Y: The Last Man* (2002-2008) and *Runaways* (2003-2007). As he had previously done with *Y: The Last Man*, Vaughan planned *Ex Machina* as a limited series taking place within a specific time period. The exact plot structure was not set; Vaughan had a tragic ending in mind, but he wanted to remain flexible so as to be able to reflect real-world current events within the story.

The overall creative staff of *Ex Machina* was significantly static. Tony Harris was responsible for the art throughout the series' fifty issues, with work by other artists appearing only in the four *Ex Machina* special issues. Both Vaughan and Harris appear in issue 40 of *Ex Machina*, in which the protagonist commissions a comic book biography.

Plot

Through a series of flashbacks, *Ex Machina* tells the story of the first superhero mayor of New York City, focusing on his four-year term from 2002 to 2006. In a world in which superheroes are otherwise absent, a mysterious explosion endows civil engineer and

---

Tony Harris

Tony Harris has received multiple Eisner Award nominations for his work on *Starman*, the series he co-created with writer James Robinson in 1994. Working on the vast majority of issues in the first five years of that series, Harris became known for his distinctive sense of design featuring bold, angular lines and deep patches of black. In 2004 he and writer Brian K. Vaughan co-created *Ex Machina*, about a superhero who is elected mayor of New York City following the terrorist attacks of September 11, 2001. Harris's art is celebrated for its dynamic realism. His pages are largely uncluttered, and he works with only a small number of panels per page. His storytelling is particularly straightforward, with action sequences that are easy to follow, while his cover designs are strikingly bold and draw upon the traditions of futurist poster illustrations.

---

comic book fan Mitchell Hundred with the ability to communicate with machines. Hundred is unsuccessful as the costumed hero the Great Machine, with most New Yorkers assuming he is a performance artist or part of a reality-show stunt. Wanting to make a real difference, Hundred retires as the Great Machine and announces his candidacy for mayor. However, despite some mild notoriety as a costumed hero, Hundred is considered unlikely to garner a significant number of votes.

The terrorist attacks of September 11, 2001, change Hundred's life. For one day, the Great Machine returns to action, diverting United Airlines Flight 175 and saving one of the towers of the World Trade Center. Hundred is devastated that he cannot save both towers. Nevertheless, Hundred's popularity surges after the attacks, and he is elected mayor.

Unsurprisingly, Mayor Hundred finds that running New York is not nearly as simple as chasing down muggers and drug dealers. Attempts to provide clear solutions to the city budget, ratify gay marriage, and reduce crime rates are all met with resistance. He is constantly besieged by demands from various interest groups and unions, protests over offensive art, and even further terrorist attacks. These external demands pale before the infighting and disruption from within his own office. His advisers have their own agendas, the police still view him as a dangerous vigilante, and one of his closest friends actively undermines and sabotages him at each turn. Hundred becomes more jaded and finds himself slowly sacrificing his own ideals in order to accomplish his goals.

Although Hundred has officially retired from his career as a superhero, the legacy of the Great Machine remains. Other citizens appear in costume, stepping in as replacements for Hundred, and his dead archenemy seems to make a reappearance. A mysterious traveler shuts down the city's power grid with a warning that Hundred's powers might have been given to him by some otherworldly malevolent source.

Finally, just as Hundred begins to achieve some success, a journalist uncovers evidence that the mayor might have used his superhuman powers to secure victory in the election. An attempt to subdue the journalist before the news goes public has disastrous results when she is transformed by a similar force. However, while the Great Machine was an engine for social order, this new force is one of chaos. The nature of Hundred's power is revealed: He is meant to be part of an interdimensional colonization, paralyzing technology so that dimensional "immigrants" can invade and plunder without resistance.

Hundred once again dons the uniform of the Great Machine and halts this threat, at least temporarily. Afterward, his political capital is sufficient to catapult him onto the national stage. However, the victory is costly, as loved ones lie dead and his most loyal friend takes the blame for Hundred's vigilantism. When he is confronted again with the evidence of his election tampering, Hundred uses his powers to do one thing he swore he would never do again—take a life. As the flashback ends and the story concludes, Hundred is now the vice president of the United States, but he sits alone in the dark, with no one to talk to but his machines.

Volumes

- *Ex Machina: The First Hundred Days* (2005). Collects issues 1-5. The first issue, "The Pilot," ends with a surprise full-page image of a single remaining World Trade Center tower.
- *Ex Machina: Tag* (2005). Collects issues 6-10. Cryptic images copied from the device that gave the Great Machine powers cause second-hand trauma.
- *Ex Machina: Fact v. Fiction* (2006). Collects issues 11-16. The Automaton emerges to fill in for the Great Machine. Hundred learns that his mother has hidden secrets from him and that machines can lie to him as well.
- *Ex Machina: March to War* (2006). Collects issues 17-20 and *Ex Machina*, special issues 1-2. A terrorist attack on an antiwar march kills one of the mayor's advisers and panics New Yorkers. The special issues feature the first appearance of the Great Machine's archenemy Pherson, including his origin and death.
- *Ex Machina: Smoke Smoke* (2007). Collects issues 21-25. Hundred's reliance on marijuana to control his powers is revealed. Issue 25, titled "Standalone," focuses entirely on Rick Bradbury's background.
- *Ex Machina: Power Down* (2008). Collects issues 26-29. An extradimensional visitor causes a citywide blackout, while Hundred temporarily loses his powers. This volume contains an additional chapter of script-to-sketch comparisons, along with essays from Vaughan and Harris regarding the creative process behind the series.
- *Ex Machina: Ex Cathedra* (2008). Collects issues 30-34. Hundred is summoned to the Vatican by Pope John Paul II, who performs an exorcism on him. This volume includes "World's Finest," a story outlining the background of Commissioner Angotti's eventual acceptance of Hundred and the Great Machine.
- *Ex Machina: Dirty Tricks* (2010). Collects issues 35-39 and *Ex Machina*, special issue 3. A risk-loving troublemaker interferes with the Republican National Convention.

- *Ex Machina: Ring out the Old* (2010). Collects issues 40-44 and *Ex Machina*, special issue 4. A plague of rats attacks New York, seemingly the work of the dead Jack Pherson. Hundred once again becomes the Great Machine to fight the threat.
- *Ex Machina: Term Limits* (2011). Collects issues 45-50. The Great Machine fights a transformed Suzanne Padilla to prevent a transdimensional attack. Hundred is revealed to be the current vice president.

Characters

- *Mitchell Hundred*, a.k.a. *the Great Machine*, the protagonist, has circuitry under the skin of the left side of his face, which glows green when his powers are active. He has the ability to communicate with and even control nearly all mechanical devices, but it is revealed that he does not have full control over his abilities and that he self-medicates to drown out the mechanical noise. In his role as the Great Machine, he wears a black flight suit with a modified motorcycle helmet, an equipment harness, and a chrome-winged jet pack. Hundred later wears variations on this suit when acting in secret. Raised by a politically active single mother and heavily influenced by superhero comic books, especially those published by DC Comics, he believes strongly in civil service. He is often described as being machinelike, working extremely long hours, and obsessing over problems. His sexuality is questioned by several other characters, but the series never establishes Hundred's orientation.
- *Rick Bradbury* is Hundred's bodyguard and friend. A former marine, Bradbury is a large, heavyset man who tends to react to any perceived threat with violence. He is extremely devoted to Hundred and is willing to work outside legal constraints to protect the mayor's public reputation. Bradbury is responsible for the transformations of both Hundred and Padilla; he was the harbor patrolman who brought Hundred to look at the artifact in the East River and also struck Padilla with the "white box," infusing her with superhuman power. Bradbury takes the blame for the Great Machine's appearance in the fight against Padilla and serves prison time.

- *Ivan Tereshkov*, a.k.a. *Kremlin*, is a Russian immigrant who was Hundred's mentor and father figure and helped the Great Machine build a jet pack and other equipment. Kremlin is a thin, ragged older man with Vladimir Lenin-style facial hair who smokes perpetually. It is implied that Kremlin is romantically involved with Martha Hundred, Mitchell's mother. Kremlin is extremely cynical about the capabilities of government bureaucracy and fights to get Hundred to return to his role as the Great Machine, going as far as to spy on Hundred and hire the mayor's adviser to steal confidential information to hurt Hundred's political career.
- *Suzanne Padilla* is a journalist with short brown hair and cat-eye glasses. Originally presented as analogous to Lois Lane, she is a feisty reporter who ambushes the mayor in attempts to interview him informally. While they are seen together later in the series, her on-and-off, possibly romantic relationship with Hundred is ruined by his busy schedule. After Kremlin leaks Hundred's secrets to Padilla in an attempt to ruin the mayor, Padilla is struck by the "white box" as she confronts Bradbury. Padilla is transformed into a parallel of the Great Machine, with the right side of her face covered in an organic lattice of white energy tubes. In this form, she gains superhuman strength, the ability to fly, and the ability to control humans in the same way Hundred controls machines.
- *Dave Wiley* is Hundred's deputy mayor and, later, successor as mayor. Wiley is an African American man with long dreadlocks who often challenges Hundred's assumptions and claims, often serving as the voice of reason and reserve in contrast to Hundred's extreme suggestions. Even though the two characters have different views, Wiley clearly has earned Hundred's trust. Vaughan describes Wiley as "the only fundamentally decent human being in the entire series."

- *Jack Pherson* is the Great Machine's archnemesis, a former television engineer who wears a purple walking coat and is accompanied at all times by his parrot. After he attempts to record Hundred's voice to duplicate the effect of the Great Machine's powers, his parrot manages to repeat the exact pitch and tone, instantly traumatizing and transforming Pherson. He gains the power to communicate with and control animals, which he uses to take revenge on humans for perceived cruelty. He repeatedly confronts the Great Machine, who eventually uses lethal force and turns Pherson's controlled animals against him, killing him. Even though Pherson dies before Hundred ever takes office, he is a constant motivating force, helping Hundred, Kremlin, and Bradbury justify keeping the Great Machine's technology at hand even after Hundred goes public. While he is referred to as the Great Machine's "nemesis," he sees himself and his connection to animals not as antagonistic to but instead potentially collaborative with Hundred's machine-based power.

Artistic Style

As a series drawn entirely by a single artist, Tony Harris, *Ex Machina* has a distinctly uniform visual style. While *Ex Machina* features a similar artistic design to that of *Starman* (1994-2000), one of Harris's previous series, the series features increased detail and digital enhancement.

Harris's character designs and layouts are based on models and photo references, and the trade paperbacks of *Ex Machina* include samples of his multistage work. Given the series' focus on politics, many of the illustrations depict characters engaged in prolonged conversations. Harris presents these everyday conversations in a variety of arrangements, beginning by photographing multiple models from nontraditional angles and perspectives. In interviews, Harris has noted that using the same photo models for the same characters throughout the run of the series made the models more comfortable portraying their characters and allowed them to suggest expressions and poses.

Another notable characteristic of Harris's artwork is the grotesqueness of the facial expressions and gestures used in his illustrations. The characters are "caught" in mid-motion, fingers splayed and faces contorted. This has the effect of emphasizing the humanity of *Ex Machina*. Even when the Great Machine is shown in action, it is far from the traditional depiction of superheroism. Harris's unflattering detail captures the chaotic, sometimes mindlessly reflexive, rocketing flight of the Great Machine.

Throughout the series, different flashbacks are effectively distinguished from one another by the use of pervasive color tones, with most of the scenes unified by muted pastel blues, greens, and reds. On the covers, and in some of the later issues, Harris experiments with a "graywash" layer when inking the pages. This effect results in a much greater sense of depth in the images, highlighting action and emphasizing the overall realism of *Ex Machina*.

Themes

On the first page of the series, Hundred tells the reader that his story "might look like a comic, but it's really a tragedy." Fundamentally, the series examines the parallel systems of power in which the costumed superhero and the politician each function. For both, it is not enough simply to have good intentions or ideals—well-meaning gestures and decisions have catastrophic consequences. *Ex Machina* reminds the reader that, in many cases, public statements from a political figure can be just as damaging as out-of-control superstrength or heat vision.

Ex Machina suggests that politics and superheroics also share a common, if often unnoticed, victim: the political or heroic agent, who is often destroyed by the attempt to preserve order. Mitchell Hundred's presumed victories in both facets of his life are shown to be tragically hollow. While the Great Machine seals the dimensional portal, the "immigrants" remind Hundred that their return is inevitable and that the true invasion force is led by a multitude of alternate "Great Machines" and corrupt alternate Mitchell Hundreds. Similarly, even though Hundred's last act as mayor of New York City is to gain the support and funding to rebuild the lost World Trade Center tower, his political success comes at the cost of the ideals he holds most dear. The final pages reveal that Hundred is vice president, having been elected alongside John McCain in 2008. By presenting Hundred as analogous to a political figurehead such as McCain's real-life running mate, Sarah Palin, Vaughan depicts the loss of Hundred's fundamental belief that he can effect real change from within the system. Instead of working within the "great machine" of government, Hundred is simply a smiling, ineffectual public celebrity.

Significantly, this discussion of power within the systems of superheroes and politicians is framed by the terrorist attacks of September 11, 2001. *Ex Machina* interrogates the lasting effects of such a massive cultural trauma, with the dimensional disruption caused by the "artifact" paralleling the ripples of remembered trauma. Hundred's life is fundamentally changed by the initial event, and he must also accept the permanent shift in reality. This disruption is mirrored by the effects of the remaining fragment of the artifact, which drives witnesses to madness and suicide. *Ex Machina* addresses differing ways of experiencing the same traumatic event, as characters whose exposure is second-hand, akin to the experience of the 9/11 attacks through media coverage, are equally traumatized.

Impact

Ex Machina was met with critical and popular success at the time of its publication, with promotion and reviews appearing in a variety of media within and outside of the comics industry. This success, along with that of his earlier series, allowed Vaughan to establish his reputation with a larger audience and pursue work across multiple media channels, including writing for the television series *Lost* (2004-2010).

Ex Machina was one of the few series still being published by WildStorm in 2010, the imprint's final year of existence. WildStorm had initially formed as part of the early 1990's comics boom and represented a creator-centered approach. However, by 2010, *Ex Machina* was the only ongoing creator-owned original series released monthly. While both DC and Marvel maintain distinct creative teams on many of their ongoing titles, the end of *Ex Machina*, along with the end of the WildStorm line, was symptomatic of the decline of the creator-controlled superhero comic book.

Jeff Geers

Further Reading

Bendis, Brian Michael, and Michael Avon Oeming. *Powers* (2000-   ).

Fraction, Matt, and Barry Kitson. *The Order* (2007-2008).

Vaughan, Brian K., and Pia Guerra. *Y: The Last Man* (2002-2008).

Bibliography

Brophy-Warren, Jamin. "Comics Writer Fulfills Dream." *The Wall Street Journal*, January 31, 2008. Available at http://online.wsj.com/article/SB120173850529130383.html.

Renaud, Jeffrey. "*Ex Machina*'s Final Days in Office." *Comic Book Resources*, September 15, 2009. http://www.comicbookresources.com/?page=article&id=22930.

Smith, Zach. "EXit MACHINA." *Newsarama*, August 10, 2010. http://www.newsarama.com/comics/Ex-Machina-Exit-part-1-100816.html.

_____. "Harris Says Goodbye to *Ex Machina*." *Comic Book Resources*, May 27, 2010. http://www.comicbookresources.com/?page=article&id=26421.

Vaughan, Brian K. "Interview: Brian K. Vaughan." Interview by Leonard Pierce. *The A.V. Club*, November 17, 2010. http://www.avclub.com/articles/brian-k-vaughan,47783.

See also: *Powers; Y: The Last Man; Runaways*

F

FABLES

Author: Willingham, Bill

Artist: Mark Buckingham (penciller); Lan Medina (penciller); Craig Hamilton (inker); Steve Leialoha (inker); Daniel Vozzo (colorist); Todd Klein (letterer); James Jean (cover artist); João Ruas (cover artist)

Publisher: DC Comics

First serial publication: 2002-

First book publication: 2002-2011

Publication History

Fables is an ongoing series published by Vertigo, an imprint of DC Comics. Author Bill Willingham wrote for such titles as *Elementals* (1984-1988), *Proposition Player* (1999-2000), *Coventry* (1996-1997), *The Sandman Presents: The Thessaliad* (2002), and *The Sandman Presents: Thessaly—Witch for Hire* (2004) before pitching the idea for a series in which characters from fairy tales live in modern-day Manhattan disguised as ordinary people.

Having at his disposal a large number of characters from which to draw, Willingham set an elementary rule for the series: He would use only characters that were already in the public domain. Thus, while he originally thought of casting Peter Pan as the villain responsible for driving the Fables into exile, he changed his mind when he discovered that the character, created by J. M. Barrie, was still under copyright in Britain.

Fables began as a monthly series in 2002. Written by Willingham and usually drawn by Mark Buckingham, the comic has won acclaim as an engaging and literary contemporary graphic narrative, inviting comparisons to Neil Gaiman's groundbreaking series *The Sandman* for its inventive use of myth and legend.

Bill Willingham

Bill Willingham is best known for his *Fables* series of graphic novels, though he is also well loved for his spin-off series and his traditional print novel, *Peter and Max*. In his fantasy universe, the world is our own but there remain a few pockets of refuge for exiled characters from fairy tales. His renditions of familiar characters are delightful (Prince Charming is a playboy, Goldilocks is a militant feminist), while his stories are captivating blend of contemporary politics and old-world charm.

Plot

Fables concerns the adventures of a group of characters from fairy tales and nursery rhymes who live in modern-day New York disguised as ordinary mortals. The Fables, as they call themselves, have been driven from their magical realms, the Homelands, by armies led by a mysterious enemy known only as the Adversary. Those who can pass for human occupy a city block in Manhattan, which they call "Fabletown," while the talking animals and enchanted beasts reside on a farm in upstate New York. The Fables must cope with the annoyances and aggravations of modern society, while having to contend with the pitfalls and disputes that are specific to the lives of quasi-immortal magical beings.

The first story arc follows the leading characters as they attempt to solve a crime that threatens to dissolve the fragile community of exiles. Rose Red, the wayward sister of Snow White, is the apparent victim of a murder. However, the Big Bad Wolf, or Bigby, head of security for Fabletown, manages to unravel the mystery at the annual ceremony during which the Fables commemorate their lost homes. The murder turns out to be a hoax, planned by Rose Red and her boyfriend Jack Horner, to enable her to escape her obligation to marry the wealthy Bluebeard, who had provided her with a large dowry as part of their engagement.

The next story line adroitly reworks George Orwell's *Animal Farm* (1945). Snow White and Rose Red visit the Farm, where the talking animals reside, only to stumble into a conspiracy led by Goldilocks and the three bears to overthrow the rule of the human Fables and then invade the Homelands with modern weapons specially modified for use by animals. After Snow White outmaneuvers the rebels, the community is threatened with exposure to the world of the "mundies," or ordinary humans. A newspaper columnist confronts Bigby with evidence he has gathered attesting to the Fables' magical nature, though he mistakenly concludes that they are vampires. Briar Rose's enchantment, which puts people to sleep whenever she cuts her finger, enables the Fables to ensure that the nosy journalist takes his secret with him to the grave.

Meanwhile, Goldilocks joins forces with Bluebeard. She wishes to kill Snow White, while Bluebeard seeks vengeance against Bigby, who has humiliated him on repeated occasions. Bluebeard casts a spell on the pair, sending them to the Pacific Northwest so that Goldilocks can murder them in a remote location. Snow White and Bigby manage to escape with their lives, while, back in Fabletown, Prince Charming kills Bluebeard in a duel. However, a shadow is cast over their triumphant return when Snow White learns that she is pregnant, having slept with Bigby while both were under the enchantment.

The mysterious Adversary at last moves against the refugees by sending the witch Baba Yaga, disguised as Red Riding Hood, and an elite force of wooden soldiers to attack Fabletown. The wooden soldiers demand that Pinocchio, their eldest brother, be turned over to them. In the ensuing battle, many of the Fables are killed, and Pinocchio is accidentally beheaded, which causes his body to revert to wood. Bigby eventually overwhelms the wooden soldiers with his powerful lungs, while Frau Totenkinder, the Black Forest Witch, bests Baba Yaga in single combat.

Though he is the savior of Fabletown, Bigby leaves the community after the birth of his children. The infants born to Snow White can fly, and most have fur and lupine features. Because they cannot live in Fabletown without attracting the attention of the mundies, Snow White is forced to raise her children at the Farm, which Bigby is not allowed to enter because of the great number of creatures he killed back in the Homelands. Prince Charming, newly elected mayor of Fabletown, sends Boy Blue on a secret mission to the Homelands. Boy Blue reaches the capital of the Empire, where he succeeds in beheading the fearsome emperor but is taken prisoner. He awakens in Geppetto's studio to discover that the emperor is really a wooden puppet.

The Adversary turns out to be the humble woodcarver himself, whose imperial ambitions began as a modest attempt at restoring political stability. Leaving behind Pinocchio, whom Geppetto restores to life, Boy Blue escapes to Fabletown accompanied by the real Red Riding Hood. Fabletown soon welcomes the arrival of Sinbad and his attendants from the land of the Arabian Fables, the latest realm to be invaded by the Empire. Fabletown and the Empire draw up plans to attack each other, a process that intensifies after Bigby destroys the enchanted forest that provides the material for Geppetto's elite soldiers. Ambrose, the Frog Prince, becomes a mighty king and deprives the Empire of many of its best troops. Before the Empire can set in motion its own plans, Fabletown launches a surprise attack. The exiled Fables win a great victory, shattering the Empire and bringing Geppetto back to Fabletown in chains, but Prince Charming and Boy Blue perish as a result of the combat.

The ensuing power vacuum in the Homelands results in the release of the insidious Mister Dark, who had been imprisoned by the sorcerers of the Empire. Angered by the Fables' use of his magical devices, he destroys the buildings in Fabletown and forces the Fables to take refuge at the Farm. Frau Totenkinder challenges Mister Dark but proves unable to defeat him. The Fables depart for Haven, the kingdom of the Frog Prince, having resolved to return to the mundane world and fight Mister Dark after devising a suitable plan.

Volumes

- *Fables: Legends in Exile* (2002). Collects issues 1-5. Rose Red appears to be the victim of a murder, and Bigby sets out to solve the mystery.
- *Fables: Animal Farm* (2003). Collects issues 6-10. The talking animals tire of being confined at the Farm and, led by Goldilocks, rise up in revolt.
- *Fables: Storybook Love* (2004). Collects issues 11-18. The first issue recounts Jack Horner's adventures in the U.S. Civil War. Then, the Fables thwart an attempt by a journalist to expose them, and Snow White and Bigby evade the plot against their lives.
- *Fables: March of the Wooden Soldiers* (2004). Collects issues 19-21 and 23-27. At terrible cost, the Fables repulse the assault by a unit of wooden soldiers from the Empire.
- *Fables: The Mean Seasons* (2005). Collects issues 22 and 28-33. Prince Charming is elected mayor of Fabletown, while Snow White gives birth to seven children, most of whom do not look human.
- *Fables: Homelands* (2005). Collects issues 34-41. With the aid of a magical cloak, Boy Blue returns to the Homelands.
- *Fables: Arabian Nights (and Days)* (2006). Collects issues 42-47. Fabletown attempts to form an alliance with the Arabian Fables, whose lands are the latest to be invaded by the Empire.
- *Fables: 1001 Nights of Snowfall* (2006). Stand-alone prequel to the series. Snow White tells the stories of various Fables in the Homelands to the Sultan of the Arabian Fables.
- *Fables: Wolves* (2006). Collects issues 48-51. Bigby destroys Geppetto's enchanted forest and then marries Snow White.
- *Fables: Sons of Empire* (2007). Collects issues 52-59. Geppetto and his advisers debate how best to deal with the renegades of Fabletown.
- *Fables: The Good Prince* (2008). Collects issues 60-69. Flycatcher becomes Prince Ambrose and leads a group of deceased Fables to found a new kingdom.
- *Fables: War and Pieces* (2008). Collects issues 70-75. The Fables attack the Empire.
- *Fables: The Dark Ages* (2009). Collects issues 76-82. Boy Blue dies of his wounds after Mister Dark is released from his imprisonment by an unfortunate pair of adventurers.
- *Fables: The Great Fables Crossover* (2010). Collects issues 83-85; *Jack of Fables*, issues 33-35; and *The Literals*, issues 1-3. The Fables join forces with the Literals to prevent their creator from erasing their existence.
- *Fables: Witches* (2010). Collects issues 86-93. A power struggle breaks out among the Fables after they are driven from Fabletown by Mister Dark.
- *Fables: Rose Red* (2011). Collects issues 93-100. Snow White and Rose Red's childhood is explored, and Frau Totenkinder and Mister Dark fight a duel.

Characters

- *Snow White* is the deputy mayor of Fabletown at the beginning of the series. Having experienced a series of betrayals by those closest to her, including her sister and husband, she throws herself into the often thankless work of running the exile community as its de facto leader. She is portrayed as hard-nosed and resourceful in her dealings, though also quick-tempered and snappish. She becomes pregnant by Bigby while both are under the influence of a spell, but she refuses his advances even after the birth of their children.
- *Bigby*, a.k.a. *the Big Bad Wolf*, is the sheriff of Fabletown until Prince Charming takes office as mayor. He can transform into his original wolf form, although he is usually depicted as looking like a grizzled and unshaven noir detective. Infamous for the atrocities he committed in the Homelands, he now uses his fearsome powers to serve and defend Fabletown. He marries Snow White after he destroys the enchanted forest that provides the Adversary with his wooden soldiers.
- *Prince Charming* is a thrice-divorced cad who lives off the "mundy" women he seduces. Through a combination of impetuosity and cunning, he seizes Bluebeard's fortune and then

wins election as mayor. He shows his valiant and generous side when he defends Fabletown from attack, leads the war against the Empire, and enables Snow to reunite with Bigby.

- *Rose Red* is Snow White's twin sister. Her short red hair contrasts with Snow's dark hair. A rebellious party girl at the outset, she takes on the responsibility of running the Farm after the animals revolt. A thrill seeker who justifies her caprices as a way to hide her grief from having been abandoned, she later gives way to deep regret and provides leadership for the entire community at a time of grave crisis.

- *Jack Horner* is a trickster and wheeler-dealer whose unregenerate narcissism serves as a trigger for dramatic escapades with comical reversals. Jack violates the terms of the Fabletown compact by making a series of hit movies based on the various adventures of the Fables, which results in his permanent banishment. The spin-off comic *Jack of Fables* (2006-2011) details his further misadventures.

- *Boy Blue* is a worker in the mayor's office who undertakes a solo mission to explore the Homelands. He is the only surviving witness of the last battle fought by the Fables against the forces of the Adversary. Though endowed with talent, good looks, and affability, he is nevertheless quite unlucky in love.

- *Frau Totenkinder*, a.k.a. *the Black Forest Witch*, is best known for trying to kill Hansel and Gretel. Like Bigby, she has reformed her murderous ways, no longer kidnapping and slaying innocent children to reinvigorate her magic. The narrative implies that she instead draws her vast magical power from the practice of abortion in the mundane world.

- *Flycatcher*, a.k.a. *Ambrose the Frog Prince*, is tall and lean, with ears that stick out and prominent brow ridges. He has been so traumatized by witnessing the deaths of his wife and children that he believes them to be still alive. The mayor's office keeps him busy with custodial work so that he will not be overwhelmed by guilt and leave in search of his family.

- *Cinderella* is the owner of a shoe store, but her insolvent business is a front for her activities as a spy. She poses as a double agent to ferret out a possible traitor, Ichabod Crane. She also helps negotiate the treaty between Fabletown and the Cloud Kingdoms, which provides the Fables with the staging ground for their attack on the Empire, and later rescues Pinocchio from imperial agents when he escapes from the Homelands.

- *Pinocchio* is a preadolescent boy who has not aged in more than three hundred years. Initially a marginal character, he provides comic relief with petulant wisecracks and frustration over the spell that has made him human but also prevented him from reaching adulthood. He becomes a major focus of the narrative when it is revealed that the Adversary is his father, Geppetto. He later arranges for his father to receive amnesty under the terms of the Fabletown compact.

- *Beauty* and *the Beast* are, at the outset, a long-married couple with financial and marital difficulties, but they later rise to take over the positions of deputy mayor and sheriff. The Beast reverts to looking like a monster whenever Beauty is angry with him.

- *King Cole* is the genial, longtime mayor of Fabletown until his defeat in the first-ever mayoral election. He reassumes his old role after the death of Prince Charming.

- *Geppetto* is the real power behind the Empire, despite his appearance as a humble wood-carver. The Empire, which spans an immense number of worlds, is administered by a warrior caste made up of wooden soldiers carved from the sacred grove that produced Pinocchio. Taken prisoner after the collapse of the Empire, he resides in Fabletown with his first-born son, under the watchful eyes of the authorities.

- *Goldilocks* is a zealous would-be revolutionary who seeks to free the talking animals from their oppression. As sanctimonious as she is egotistical, she tries to kill Snow White on two occasions.

Artistic Style

The original artists for the series were penciller Lan Medina and inkers Steve Leialoha and Craig Hamilton. Buckingham, who became the primary penciller for the series, came aboard in December, 2002, with Leialoha continuing as inker. James Jean drew the distinctively ornate covers until issue 81, after which João Ruas took over as cover artist. Guest artists have included Bryan Talbot, P. Craig Russell, Linda Medley, Tony Akins, David Hahn, Shawn McManus, Jim Fern, Aaron Alexovich, Niko Henrichon, Darwyn Cooke, Mark Allred, David Lapham, Inaki Miranda, and Eric Shanower. *1001 Nights of Snowfall* featured the art of John Bolton, Tara McPherson, Esao Andrews, and Jill Thompson, among others.

The visuals of *Fables* well illustrate the clash between the mundane and the magical that characterizes the series' story lines. Medina's artwork tends to favor sharp and angular lines in portraying human faces and figures. By contrast, Buckingham's use of pencils is softer and more straightforwardly expressive, evoking the directness and simplicity of myth. Whereas Medina's style yields a heightened sense of realism, well suited for depicting a gleaming but shadowy metropolis inhabited by beautiful and privileged people, the more classical look of Buckingham's drawings harmonizes the fantastic and the commonplace. The enchanted creatures and their human counterparts convincingly appear to inhabit the same reality.

The artwork of *Fables* shows a striking range of stylistic influences, including the work of the Russian artist Ivan Bilibin, whose illustrations came to typify the look of Russian fairy tales. Medina takes the familiar look given to the characters of Snow White and Cinderella by Disney and then makes them appear more modern and mature. Starting with issue 15, Buckingham begins to experiment with the layouts of the panels and the borders of the page, eliminating them altogether in many instances. Smaller panels appear as insets within a full-page illustration as Snow White and Bigby tried to elude their would-be assassin, Goldilocks, in the dark forests of the Pacific Northwest. The panels concerning the intrigues of Prince Charming are laid out in the pattern of a shield. The leaves on the trees of the forest serve as a border design as Snow

White fights Goldilocks, as does the image of a snowflake when she becomes estranged from Bigby after learning that she is pregnant by him. This technique is particularly striking in the volumes *Homelands* and *Sons of Empire*, in which the border design signals whether the action is taking place in the lands of legend or in the mundane world.

James Jean's exquisitely detailed covers, which have garnered numerous Eisner Awards, recall a variety of styles from the late nineteenth century, such as those of the painters associated with Pre-Raphaelitism, including Sir Edward Coley Burne-Jones and Lawrence Alma-Tadema; Symbolism, such as Gustave Moreau; and Art Nouveau, which represented a turn away from realism in favor of mythical and fantastic themes. The covers by Ruas are similar in style and in the range of stylistic references.

Themes

Fables concerns a group of characters from legend and folklore who are forced to live in a high-tech modern world. The disparities between these long-lived mythical beings and the mundane world of ordinary humans are often played for humor, especially whenever the Fables resort to magic to solve their problems, but these supernatural characters clash in deeper ways with their adopted home. Their convictions and values provide a stark contrast with the attitudes and beliefs of modern people. Many of the leading Fables are princes who have been forced into poverty by the loss of their lands. Instead of assimilating into the modern world, they tend to cling to aristocratic ways. Furthermore, after quelling the revolt at the Farm, Snow White expresses disdain for the "mundy social philosophy" that favors the rights of criminals over those of law-abiding citizens.

The series explores as a key theme the tension between aristocratic and traditional values that stress duty and obligation and the modern, democratic and secular outlook. In certain cases, the modern ways win out, such as when Fabletown holds its first mayoral election and when the Fables use high-tech weapons to attack the Empire. On the other hand, duty overrules individual desire or psychological comfort, such as when Snow White goes through with an unwanted pregnancy and when Flycatcher is forced out of his stupor to confront the truth about the death of his family. After rousing himself from centuries of avoiding the truth, Flycatcher is able to become the powerful ruler of Haven, the kingdom he founds and defends against repeated assaults from the Empire.

The strength of the series derives to a considerable extent from its portrayal of familiar characters undergoing striking transformations. Indeed, Fabletown itself is founded on a compact that provides amnesty for all offenses that the Fables committed before signing the document. Thus, Bigby and Frau Totenkinder are able to become vital and important members of the community, having received pardons for the innumerable atrocities they perpetrated in the Homelands. Of course, the covenant does not prevent characters such as Bluebeard, Goldilocks, Jack Horner, and Prince Charming from scheming to increase their power or plotting to bring about the downfall of the authorities.

The new beginnings for these fairy-tale characters come at the cost of the fairy-tale endings of their respective stories. "No more happily ever after," reads the message written in blood in Rose Red's apartment early in the series. The new lives granted to these familiar and beloved figures are unlike anything from the tales intended for modern children. Marriages come to an end, and new romances flower. Princes and princesses are forced to give up their privileged lifestyles and engage in drudgery and labor. Heroes and heroines, after their triumphs in the Homelands, must make common cause with their enemies and tormenters in order to survive in a new world. That the lives of these characters become even more compelling while remaining faithful to the spirit of the old tales is a testament to Willingham's extraordinary gifts as a storyteller.

In its frank exploration of mature literary themes, *Fables* provides arresting and memorable reinterpretations of these fairy tales. The story of Snow White and the Seven Dwarfs is retold as a grim account of sexual slavery and merciless revenge. Frau Totenkinder, recovering from her burns at the hands of Hansel and Gretel, recounts her girlhood as a tribal seer at the end of the Ice Age and the betrayal that led her to sacrifice her own infant son. She embarks thereafter on her

lengthy career as a powerful sorceress, helping those who please her and harming those who do not, while stealing children to sacrifice every year to regenerate her magical abilities. The witch is both victim and perpetrator, murderer of children and protector of communities, whose spells save Fabletown on numerous occasions. The complexity of Totenkinder's characterization is reflected by what she tells Snow White and Rose Red in gratitude for taking care of her: "You deserve to hear my tale. Even the evil parts."

The Fables are deeply traditional people, clinging to values that seem outmoded and obsolete, yet they are marked by a determination to face the world as it is and not make excuses for their actions or lapses. They may adhere to old-fashioned values, yet they accept fully the morally ambiguous nature of their choices. Beast, when sheriff, is horrified by the methods employed by Frau Totenkinder to increase her magical strength— she ostensibly draws power from the abortions committed by the mundies—yet, he chooses not to banish or otherwise punish her, realizing how vital her powers are for the defense of Fabletown.

The sense of ambiguity extends to the politics of the series. Willingham has received some criticism for the plotline in which Bigby expresses his admiration for the Israeli government's willingness to commit harsh acts in self-defense. His portrait of Geppetto as the ruler of an empire that is insatiable in its drive for expansion makes for unsettling parallels with the present-day United States, where many embrace unchecked economic growth as a social good. In *Sons of Empire*, the Snow Queen and Pinocchio offer contrasting hypothetical apocalypses. In the first, the sorcerers of the Empire unleash plagues on a mundane world helpless against attacks of a magical nature. The high-tech industrialized world succumbs to further plagues of fire and ice, which wipe out the human population, leaving the planet open for exclusive use as a prison for the Empire. In the second scenario, the modern, mundane world invades the Empire, using advanced technology to overwhelm feudal societies where innovation has been suppressed. The mundy nations send out conquistadores armed with modern weapons to annihilate the denizens of the worlds ruled by Geppetto and carve out private kingdoms in the Homelands.

These divergent scenarios reflect the deep divisions in the United States over what constitutes the most pressing problem and greatest danger: climate change, resource depletion, terrorism, economic decline, lone gunmen, the invasion of economic criteria into all spheres of social life, or the spread of fundamentalist faith. It could be said that what is most apocalyptic is the very uncertainty over these questions, especially as society finds itself less capable of retreating into privatized dream worlds. In the later issues, the adversary of the Fables, Mister Dark, builds a residence on the ruins of Fabletown, served by people his magic has transformed into shambling, zombielike entities. Unlike Geppetto, who banned all technology from his Empire, Mister Dark avails himself of televisions, computers, and mass media to found his own kingdom of darkness. Thus, the world of the Fables takes a chilling step closer to our own reality.

Impact

Fables debuted in 2002, becoming one of the best-selling titles in the Vertigo line. Its success led to the creation of a spin-off title, *Jack of Fables* (2006-2011), which has a much lighter, more humorous tone and explores in more explicit ways the problem of being an imaginary character living in a real world. Whereas *Fables* is more discreet in its treatment of the mundane world's relationship to the worlds of myth and legend, *Jack of Fables* is more blunt and satirical.

Echoes of *Fables* can be seen in such narratives as the Vertigo limited series *Vimanarama* (2005), written by Grant Morrison, in which the protagonists battle godlike beings from Hindu mythology, and Mike Carey's *Crossing Midnight* (2007-2008), in which the gods and spirits of Japanese folklore are revealed to be alive and active in modern Japan. Carey's ongoing series, *The Unwritten* (2009-   ), has as its protagonist a young man who as a child was the model for a boy wizard in a best-selling series of fantasy novels written by his father. The series portrays a mundane reality invaded by characters from a fantastic fictional world.

Peter Y. Paik

Further Reading

Carey, Mike, and Peter Gross. *The Unwritten* (2009-   ).

Sturges, Matthew, Bill Willingham, and Luca Rossi. *House of Mystery* (2008-   ).

Wagner, Matt, and Amy Reeder Hadley. *Madame Xanadu* (2008-2011).

Bibliography

Kukkonen, Karin. "Popular Cultural Memory: Comics, Communities and Context Knowledge." *NORDICOM Review* 29, no. 2 (2008): 261-273.

Miller, Andrea Nicole. "*Fables*." Review of *Fables*, by Bill Willingham and Mark Buckingham. *MELUS* 32, no. 3 (Fall, 2007): 253-255.

Willingham, Bill. "Bill Willingham." Interview by Tasha Robinson. *The A.V. Club*, August 6, 2007. http://www.avclub.com/articles/bill-willingham,14134.

Willingham, Bill. "The Bill Willingham Interview." Interview by Dirk Deppey. *The Comics Journal* 278 (September, 2006). http://www.tcj.com/interviews/the-bill-willingham-interview-part-one-of-four.

See also: *The Books of Magic; Sandman*

FALLEN SON: THE DEATH OF CAPTAIN AMERICA

Author: Loeb, Jeph

Artist: John Cassaday (illustrator); David Finch (illustrator); Ed McGuinness (illustrator); John Romita, Jr. (illustrator); Leinil Francis Yu (illustrator); Klaus Janson (inker); Danny Miki (inker); Dexter Vines (inker); Dave McCaig (inker, colorist); Frank D'Armata (colorist); Morry Hollowell, (colorist); Jason Keith (colorist); Laura Martin (colorist)

Publisher: Marvel Comics

First serial publication: 2007

First book publication: 2007

Publication History

Fallen Son was published as a hardcover collection in October of 2007. This followed the publication of its five chapters as individual issues between June and August of 2007. Each chapter uses as its theme one of the five stages of grief for the dying, according to the Elizabeth Kübler-Ross model—denial, anger, bargaining, depression, and acceptance. This stands in slight contrast to the format used when the chapters were published as individual issues; then, each issue bore in its title the name of the character or characters at its focus (for example, the first of the five issues was called *Fallen Son: Wolverine*).

Although he was not writing the *Captain America* monthly series at the time, Jeph Loeb was vetted by other creators and editors at Marvel Comics as the writer best equipped to handle the aftermath of Steve Rogers's death. This was largely because Loeb was acutely familiar with the grieving process, having lost his son, Sam, at the age of seventeen two years before. Once he had the idea of telling his story in terms of the five stages of grief, Loeb quickly asked to work with several well-known artists over the course of the project, allowing multiple respected artists to pay tribute to the iconic character of Captain America.

Plot

Fallen Son presents popular characters from the Marvel Universe in the days following Captain America's death by assassination (which occurred in the monthly *Captain America* series) and, ultimately, at his

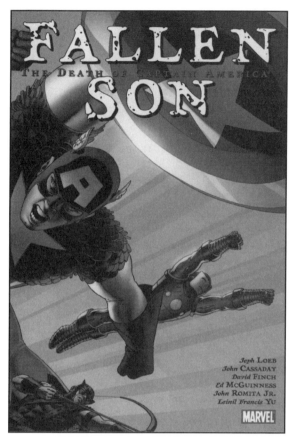

Fallen Son: The Death of Captain America.
(Courtesy of Marvel Comics)

funeral, showing the various ways that these characters choose to grieve and remember their fellow hero. The actions of each chapter's central heroes reflect the stage of grief from which the chapter derives its title.

The first chapter, "Denial," depicts Wolverine's efforts to prove that Captain America is not truly dead. With the help of allied superheroes Doctor Strange and Daredevil, Wolverine infiltrates the facility where the body identified as Captain America's is being held. His animal-like sense of smell confirms that the body is indeed that of the fallen hero, but before Wolverine can leave, Iron Man appears and threatens to arrest him for violating the Superhuman Registration Act, which requires all masked heroes to make their true identities

Fallen Son: The Death of Captain America. (Courtesy of Marvel Comics)

known (and which pitted Iron Man against Captain America in the *Civil War* event). Wolverine, however, convinces Iron Man to release him so that he can inform other skeptical heroes of the veracity of Captain America's death.

"Anger" follows, presenting the contrast between two superhero teams: the New Avengers, who had sided with Captain America against the Superhero Registration Act, and the Mighty Avengers, who sided with Iron Man. In "Anger," the Mighty Avengers engage in battle to release the anger that they collectively feel at Captain America's death. By contrast, the New Avengers engage in a tense game of poker until their comrade Wolverine enters the mansion and confirms Captain America's death. Wolverine's report sends New Avenger Spider-Man into a fit of rage that causes him to walk out on the game.

In the third chapter, "Bargaining," Iron Man offers Clint Barton, formerly known as the bow-wielding hero Hawkeye, the chance to assume the role of Captain America, using replicas of his outfit and iconic disc shield. Barton initially accepts, but while out in

the costume with Iron Man, he witnesses two young heroes, Patriot and Kate Bishop—currently using the moniker Hawkeye—immobilize a villain. A conversation with them, combined with the realization that Iron Man wishes to arrest them for violating the Superhero Registration Act, convinces Barton that Captain America would not have supported Iron Man's agenda.

"Depression" returns to the story of Spider-Man, who, after running away from the New Avengers hideout, is paying a nighttime visit to the grave of his Uncle Ben, one of many people dear to him who has died. While he is mourning the loved ones who have passed from his life, his spider sense leads him into battle with the Rhino. Once the Rhino is defeated, Wolverine, who had followed Spider-Man from Doctor Strange's mansion, attempts to share words of comfort.

The final installation, "Acceptance," brings most characters from the Marvel Universe (save the New Avengers, who remain in hiding) to Washington, D.C., for Captain America's public funeral. Three days after the funeral, however, Iron Man travels to the Arctic with the Wasp and Yellowjacket, where he reveals that a Captain America decoy had been buried publically and that Captain America and his shield are to be buried in the cold, peaceful sea.

Characters

- *Captain America*, a.k.a. *Steve Rogers*, does not appear in the present-day narrative of *Fallen Son*, but he does provide its central motivational force. The blond-haired, blue-eyed former soldier assumed the role of "Captain America," complete with the costume based on the pattern of the American flag, in order to present the image of an "All-American Hero." Through flashbacks, he is remembered for his selflessness, graciousness, and commitment to the ideals of the United States.
- *Wolverine*, a.k.a. *Logan*, is the motivated cynic in *Fallen Son*. Short, scruffy, and more prone to unsheathing retractable metal claws from his arms than to holding an emotionally frank conversation, he has a skepticism that, combined with his tendency toward action, leads him on a mission to determine the truth behind Captain America's assassination.

- *Iron Man*, a.k.a. *Tony Stark*, maintains a stance that proves antagonistic to Captain America and his legacy. Often seen protected by his suit of red and golden armor, Iron Man leads the government-sponsored Mighty Avengers. He also continues to enforce the Superhuman Registration Act after Captain America's death, even though Captain America's opposition to it had placed him and Iron Man, once considered close friends, on conflicting sides of the law, a situation that Iron Man regrets.
- *Spider-Man*, a.k.a. *Peter Parker*, provides a voice tinged with confusion and loss. Spider-Man is subdued in *Fallen Son*; his trademark red-and-blue costume is replaced with a black suit that bears a simple white spider design, a suit that he wears in mourning for Captain America. He recalls his meetings with Captain America with a sense of wonder as well as a sense of grief that borders on guilt.

Artistic Style

The five artists chosen to provide the line art for *Fallen Son*—John Cassaday, David Finch, Ed McGuinness, John Romita, Jr., and Leinil Francis Yu—work in noticeably distinct styles, yet each style adds to the interpretation of each chapter's focus. Yu's lines, for example, have been described as "shadowy" and "sketchy," similar to the artistic style of *Hellboy*'s creator Mike Mignola. Though this may not seem like a style appropriate for a story that touches on a character considered a beacon of light by other superheroes, it does help depict the stealth and suspicion by which Wolverine operates in "Denial."

McGuinness's art style in "Anger," marked by clean lines and an animated, sometimes cartoonish, appearance in his characters, allows him to effectively render a host of characters trying in various ways to distract themselves from the issue of Captain America's death. Romita's art has appeared in Marvel Comics titles since the 1970's; his experience in rendering nearly every Marvel Comics character emphasizes the contrast in ideals among characters in "Bargaining." In particular, Romita fills many of his panels with close-ups of the faces of the two characters with long-standing roles in the Marvel Universe, Iron Man and Clint Barton's Hawkeye, clearly communicating the emotions that affect them. Though he also employs close-ups, Finch depends mostly on the dark, atmospheric line work that later led him to be the artist behind DC Comics' *Batman* to convey the despair that plagues Spider-Man in "Depression."

"Acceptance," the story's resolution, is handled by Cassaday, whose work is lavishly realistic, drawing on the traditions of the Art Nouveau style, an appropriate style for the chapter in which characters are asked to accept the reality of Captain America's death. In contrast to the first four chapters, which are colored in dark, muted tones, "Acceptance" presents a brighter color palate, perhaps to convey a sense of peace.

Themes

The theme of grief and death as factors that motivate human behavior are central to the story. Each Marvel personality reacts distinctly to the news of Captain America's death, no different from what readers may observe in everyday life. By presenting these diverse reactions, *Fallen Son* reminds its readers that death is personal, and each individual will respond to it in ways that will likely differ from the ways that members of their surrounding circle respond. The use of different artists to illustrate each chapter of the story serves to highlight the particular effects of death.

The superhero as everyman is another theme that *Fallen Son* addresses. Marvel Comics' stories have made it a point to emphasize the humanity of their heroes, whether through the familial squabbling of the Fantastic Four or the youthful mistakes of Spider-Man. In *Fallen Son*, readers see superheroes reacting to the death of one of their own—caused not by a villain's superpowers, but by a simple gunshot wound—according to the model of grief that is said to apply to all humans. This does not necessarily stand in contrast to the individuality mentioned above; though particular actions may vary among people, or superheroes, the emotions that they share are common.

Fallen Son also joins other Marvel Comics works in placing the relationships between characters at the story's forefront. After Captain America's death, friends and superhero teams draw on each other for support, and one hero in particular, Iron Man, laments that his friendship with the fallen hero had soured. *Fallen Son* demonstrates how these characters relate to each other after Captain America's death—and how Captain America affected them while he was alive.

Impact

Fallen Son had less of a cultural impact than the regularly published *Captain America* series did in 2007 and is therefore considered a companion piece or a secondary work. The assassination of Steve Rogers, the iconic Captain America, occurred in issue 25 of Ed Brubaker's *Captain America* series; the gravity of the event drew the attention of mainstream media outlets to the monthly title. By contrast, *Fallen Son*, both as a five-issue miniseries and as a hardcover graphic novel collecting those issues, received most of the attention paid to it from Internet sites dedicated to comics and graphic novels, and reviews offered by these sites were mixed. Generally, the art was praised as solid and appropriate for the story. Reviewers seemed more divided in their assessment of the plot, with some lamenting that *Fallen Son* offered nothing new to develop the surviving Marvel Comics characters and others stating that the story provided characters a necessary opportunity to pay tribute and move forward.

Although *Fallen Son* is not touched by any events as profound as Captain America's actual death, it may be noted that the story does mark the reverence accorded the fallen hero's famous round shield. The final chapter, "Acceptance," shows Iron Man revealing to a few colleagues that, while replicas of the shield remain in the United States, the original shield will be buried with Captain America in his coffin in the Arctic Sea.

Sheila Johnson

Films

Captain America: The First Avenger. Directed by Joe Johnston. Marvel Studios and Paramount Pictures, 2011. The film stars Chris Evans as Captain America and details the superhero's origin during World War II as an experimental "supersoldier." Hugo Weaving stars as the Red Skull, Captain America's nemesis, while Sebastian Stan assumes the role of Bucky Barnes, Captain America's sidekick. The film ends with the discovery of Captain America frozen in ice in the present day.

Further Reading

Brubaker, Ed, et al. *Captain America* (2005-2011).

Loeb, Jeph, et al. *Batman: Hush* (2002-2003).

Millar, Mark, and Steve McNiven. *Civil War* (2006-2007).

Bibliography

Brubaker, Ed. *The Death of Captain America Omnibus.* New York: Marvel Comics, 2009.

Kreiner, Richard. "Planetary/Batman: Night on Earth." *The Comics Journal* 258 (February, 2004): 50-51.

Kübler-Ross, Elizabeth. *On Death and Dying.* New York: Routledge, 2005.

Loeb, Jeph. "Jeph Loeb Talks Fallen Son . . . In Detail." Interview by Newsarama. *Newsarama*, March 7, 2007. http://replay.waybackmachine. org/20090207155307/http://forum.newsarama.com/ showthread.php?t=104117.

McGuinness, Ed. "Ed McGuinness Interview." Interview by Flint Henry. *Sketch* 9 (October, 2001): 4-11.

Robinson, Bryan. "What the Death of Captain America Really Means." *ABC News*, March 8, 2007. http://abc-news.go.com/US/Story?id=2934283&page=1.

See also: *Death of Captain America*; *Earth X*; *Wolverine*; *Wolverine Origin*; *Batman: Dark Victory*; *Batman: The Long Halloween*

FILTH, THE

Author: Morrison, Grant

Artist: Chris Weston (penciller); Gary Erskine (inker); Matt Hollingsworth (colorist); Clem Robins (letterer); Carlos Segura (cover artist)

Publisher: DC Comics

First serial publication: 2002-2003

First book publication: 2004

Publication History

Originally published as a thirteen-issue limited series by the Vertigo imprint of DC Comics, *The Filth* was the first creator-owned work written by Grant Morrison since the completion of his long-running, multivolume series *The Invisibles* in 2000. Penciller Chris Weston has said that *The Filth* developed during a dinner with Morrison at the 2000 Comic-Con International: San Diego, where the two discussed a shared desire to "create the weirdest comic ever."

Weston has identified as influences 1960's British comic strip characters the Steel Claw and the Spider, 1967 marionette puppet show *Captain Scarlet and the Mysterons*, and material from Morrison's unproduced pitch for a reboot of Marvel Comics' superspy character Nick Fury. One of the central ideas in *The Filth*, that superhuman espionage agents are artificial personalities injected into other people's minds, is also found in the Morrison-written story "Nick's World," published in the second issue of the short-lived anthology series *Marvel Knights Double Shot* (2002). Some of the more quotidian elements of *The Filth* reference actual events from the lives of the book's creators. The story incorporates time Morrison spent caring for his dying pet cat and Weston's own experiences of being harassed by juvenile delinquents and having a cat with kidney problems. Much like the character King Mob in *The Invisibles*, protagonist Greg Feely shaves his head in the third chapter of *The Filth*, marking him as a visual avatar for the similarly hairless Morrison, while Feely's facial features and poor posture make him a self-portrait of Weston.

Chris Weston

Entering the comics industry with his work on *Judge Dredd* at the end of the 1980's, artist Chris Weston transitioned to American comics in the mid-1990's with fill-in work on the Grant Morrison-written *The Invisibles*. He was a regular fill-in artist for several years, before producing the works for which he is best known: *Ministry of Space*, a limited series with writer Warren Ellis; *The Filth*, a creator-owned limited series with Grant Morrison; and *Fantastic Four: First Family*, with writer Joe Casey. Weston's art is hyper-detailed, with painstakingly rendered backgrounds that position his work within a realist tradition that is relatively uncommon in superhero comics. His lines are reminiscent of artist Brian Bolland, and he uses the same tendency towards the exaggeration of facial tics that heightens the strangeness of the superhero comic book tradition.

Plot

The Filth is a nonlinear dystopian satire about the Hand, a shadowy sanitation crew/secret police force tasked with enforcing the existing social order, or "Status: Q." Protagonist Greg Feely is a London bachelor and office worker who spends his free time masturbating to pornography and caring for his sick cat, Tony. Meanwhile, antagonist Spartacus Hughes kills scientist Dr. Li Soon and hijacks her invention, a small planet populated by microscopic artificial intelligence called I-Life. Hughes sells this "bonsai planet" to Simon, the world's richest pervert, who purchases and desecrates things of beauty.

Officer of the Hand Miami Nil is sent to help Feely discover he has a second personality, that of Officer Ned Slade. Nil calls Feely a "parapersona," an artificial identity Slade adopts as a vacation from work, but Feely has only partial memories of being Slade. Replaced by a doppelgänger, he travels with Nil to another dimension, the Crack, where the Hand is headquartered. Over an intercom, the Hand's superior officer, Mother Dirt, orders the disoriented Feely/Slade to negotiate with Hughes and serve as a decoy while Comrade Dmitri-9, a superintelligent chimpanzee sniper, shoots Hughes in the head. Hughes tells Feely/Slade the name "Max Thunderstone" before dying. Feely/Slade resigns from the Hand.

The third chapter introduces officers Moog Mercury and Cameron Spector as they "inkdive" into the "Paperverse," a two-dimensional superhero comic book universe the Hand creates, where they mine for outlandish technology. Feely/Slade returns to London, keeping his doppelgänger tied up and locked in a closet because he neglected Tony. Dmitri-9 visits the apartment to convince Feely to return to the Hand as Slade. A neighbor mistakes Dmitri-9 for a child and suspects Feely of being a pedophile.

As Ned Slade, he leads Miami Nil, Dmitri-9, Cameron Spector, and Moog Mercury on various missions against threats to social hygiene. Slade kills Doctor von Vermin, a homicidal rogue agent of the Hand with a superhuman sense of smell. Slade's squad also stops a plague of giant killer sperm released on Los Angeles by hardcore-porn director Tex Porneau and neutralizes a hyperfertile porn-star clone named Anders Klimakks.

The police arrest Feely for pedophilia, also mentioning terrorism and Max Thunderstone, but his squad rescues him from custody before any more can be learned. Slade and the Hand take down the population of the Libertania, a nation-sized ocean liner whose inhabitants are driven to violent insanity and cultish compliance by a resurrected Spartacus Hughes. Dmitri-9 kills Hughes a second time.

Feely/Slade returns to London and finds Tony dead from the doppelgänger's neglect. Cameron Spector takes Feely/Slade on a tour of the Hand's operations while he mourns his cat. Spector introduces him to Man Green/Man Yellow, the director of the Palm, who exists outside of linear time. Spector also tells how the Paperverse was created, using ink taken from a giant fountain pen held by a giant hand that exists in the world of the Crack. Back in his London flat, Feely/Slade finds Sharon Jones, a woman once enslaved by Simon and now a "bio-ship" piloted by I-Life. The I-Life resurrect Tony.

Chapter 10 introduces Max Thunderstone, who has made himself into a real-life superhero with radical medical procedures and a coterie of internet operatives, including Feely, who discovered the Hand. Thunderstone plans to reveal the Hand and cast the members of the group as supervillains he defeats, thereby drawing converts to his religion of violent pacifism, Buddhismo. Thunderstone steals a Hand garbage truck and travels to the Crack, only to be subdued by a group of Hand operatives led by Slade.

In London, Feely/Slade sends Jones and Tony away and provokes the Hand. Dmitri-9 arrives at the flat to kill Feely/Slade but kills the doppelgänger Greg Feely by mistake. Feely's neighbors, thinking Dmitri-9 is a monster, chase him into the path of an oncoming train. In the Crack, Nil discovers that Hughes, a parapersona originally created by Thunderstone's people to sabotage the Hand, is now a Hand agent and controlling Max Thunderstone's body. Feely/Slade breaks into a pharmacy, where Nil and Spector confront him. Feely/Slade shows them vials labeled with their names. Hand officers are revealed to be the parapersonas; Ned Slade is the artificial identity, not Greg Feely.

Feely finds Sharon Jones dead, killed by Spartacus Hughes. Spector arrives to help Feely fight Hughes, and the battle takes them into the Crack. They manage to kill Hughes, but Spector dies in the process.

The story returns to Feely's home in London, where he overdoses on sleeping pills and falls while writing his suicide note, knocking over his trash can. Feely's hand is revealed to be the giant hand holding the fountain pen, and the garbage from his trash can is the location of the microscopic world of the Crack.

Prior to his suicide attempt, Feely storms the office of Mother Dirt, who is revealed to be a giant fleshy mass of primordial muck. Feely is then shown in London, having become another bio-ship piloted by I-Life, which prevented his suicide. The I-Life use Feely to heal a young man in a vegetative state and grow flowers out of garbage.

Characters

- *Greg Feely*, a.k.a. *Ned Slade*, the protagonist, is a middle-aged, balding civil servant whose love for his cat, Tony, helps him defy the Hand's attempts to recycle him into the artificial identity of Ned Slade. *The Filth* leaves open the possibility that the entire story is Feely's delusion.

- *Spartacus Hughes* is a destructive viral parapersona identifiable by the muttonchops that grow on his host body. He is created by Feely and other operatives of Max Thunderstone to undermine the Hand. However, the Hand later recruits him by giving him Thunderstone's body and sending him after his creator.

- *Miami Nil* is an officer of the Hand tasked with bringing Feely, and later Hughes, to the side of the Hand through sexual persuasion. During one case, she kills porn director Tex Porneau with his own giant killer sperm.

- *Sharon Jones* is a corporate lawyer kidnapped by Simon, the world's richest pervert, and turned into a remote-controlled cyborg. She later becomes a bio-ship piloted by I-Life and resurrects Feely's cat.

- *I-Life* are artificially intelligent microscopic robots created by Dr. Li Soon to cure diseases. After Spartacus Hughes incites their small planet's destruction, the I-Life begin to travel through human bodies.

- *Cameron Spector* is an officer of the Hand and member of the Science Gestapo, a group that steals technology from the Paperverse. She later turns against the Hand because her terminal cancer is accelerated by her time in the Crack. She is one of several Morrison characters whose Scottish accent is represented through phonetically written dialogue.

- *Moog Mercury* is a member of the Hand's Science Gestapo who writes story lines for the superheroes living in the Paperverse, encouraging the development of bizarre technology. When his recklessness kills a major superhero, he is reassigned to Ned Slade's special squad.

- *Dmitri-9* is a chimpanzee and former cosmonaut who acquired superintelligence from cosmic radiation and was made into the ultimate assassin by the Soviet Union. Dmitri-9 was responsible for the assassination of John F. Kennedy.

- *Maxwell Shatt*, a.k.a. *Max Thunderstone*, is a lottery winner who uses his fortune to sculpt his muscles and mental prowess to superhero perfection. He eventually overcomes his agoraphobia to fight Hand officers, only to have his body co-opted and used by the Hand.

- *Mother Dirt*, the mysterious leader of the Hand, is a Lovecraftian wall of tendrils, giant insect parts, human organs, and other biological characteristics. She lives in a primordial environment and intimates she is foundational to all existence.

Artistic Style

Weston has described Morrison's script as a "love letter" to his art, with the comic conceived by the writer as a return to the more bizarre and psychedelic imagery of Weston's earlier comics, particularly those appearing in the long-running British anthology series *2000 AD* in the late 1980's. Weston spent a year apprenticed to renowned strip cartoonist Don Lawrence and shares Lawrence's talent for detailed photorealism, which is inked with the clean, controlled lines and precisely curved hatching of inker Gary Erskine.

In addition to cementing the believability of the strange narrative world, Weston's art is of a visual style that, to a certain extent, defined mainstream British comics of the 1970's and 1980's. Using this classic aesthetic to illustrate transgressive imagery heightens the uncomfortable, sordid tone of the book. Matt Hollingsworth's digital colors have the dispassionate, unflattering brightness of fluorescent lighting, further adding a disturbing realism to the unreal depravity on display.

The clean, iconic, typographic cover illustrations by Carlos Segura contrast with *The Filth*'s pornographic, taboo, and morally debased content. Segura's references to institutional signage, medical diagrams, and consumerist labeling resonate with the story's overarching critique of twenty-first-century living.

Themes

Though *The Filth* and *The Invisibles* share similar themes, Morrison has described the unrelenting scatological and pornographic imagery of moral debasement in the former as the inversion of the glamorous counterculture of the latter. He has also described the limited series as a metaphorical inoculation, injecting the reader's consciousness with diseases to strengthen the psychic immune system and prepare it for a twenty-first century characterized by ubiquitous surveillance and consumerist excess. The five departments that make up the Hand are modeled after five cells in the human immune system, and Spartacus Hughes is a virus. A practicing magician, Morrison has also identified *The Filth* as a meditation on the kabbalistic symbol of the Qliphoth, the negative side of existence, the Tree of Death that counterpoints the Tree of Life.

The Filth is also characterized by Morrison's interest in postmodern self-reflexivity, William S. Burroughs-inspired nonlinear storytelling, and the malleable multiplicity of identity. The series builds on Morrison's view of the universe as a single organism in which humans are cells, performing functions required by that unified system. More broadly, *The Filth* is concerned with cyclical tensions between optimism and pessimism, life and death, transcendence and degradation, and growth and decay. These inescapable contradictions are visually encapsulated by the image of a farting flower in the final panel.

Impact

The Filth was well-received by critics for its dense subtext but frequently critiqued as confusing or incoherent. Segura's covers garnered praise for their simple, eye-catching design. As a publication of DC Comics' mature-readers imprint, Vertigo, *The Filth* was largely uncensored, with Morrison reporting a single expurgated panel. Pushing the boundaries of comics, *The Filth*, along with other works for adult readers, has served to further open the medium to a wide range of mature situations and themes.

Damian Duffy

Further Reading

Ellis, Warren, and Darick Robertson. *Transmetropolitan* (1997-2002).

Fraction, Matt, and Gabriel Bá. *Casanova* (2006-2008).

Morrison, Grant, et al. *The Invisibles* (1994-2000).

Bibliography

Morrison, Grant. "A Healing Inoculation of Grime: Grant Morrison on *The Filth*." Interview by Matt Brady. *Newsarama*, March 7, 2003. http://www.crackcomicks.com/the_filth_questions.htm.

_____. "Interview with an Umpire." Interview by Brother Yawn. *Barbelith Interviews*, September 2, 2002. http://www.barbelith.com/old/interviews/interview_5.shtml.

_____. "One Nervous System Passage Through Time." Interview by Jay Babcock. *Arthur* 12 (September, 2004). http://www.arthurmag.com/2007/02/01/interview-with-grant-morrison-from-the-pages-of-arthur-magazine.

See also: *Invisibles; Transmetropolitan; Doom Patrol; All Star Superman*

G

GIVE ME LIBERTY: AN AMERICAN DREAM

Author: Miller, Frank
Artist: Dave Gibbons (illustrator); Robin Smith (colorist)
Publisher: Dark Horse Comics
First serial publication: 1990
First book publication: 1990

Publication History

Give Me Liberty was first published by Dark Horse Comics as four single issues and is the first in the Martha Washington series, which includes *Martha Washington Goes to War* (1994), *Happy Birthday, Martha Washington* (1995), *Martha Washington Stranded in Space* (1995), *Martha Washington Saves the World* (1997), and *Martha Washington Dies* (2007). All of the books were written and illustrated by Frank Miller and Dave Gibbons. The title is a famous quotation from a speech given by Founding Father Patrick Henry in March, 1775, which helped deliver Virginian troops to the American Revolution: "I know not what course others may take; but as for me, give me liberty or give me death."

After the success of Miller's *Batman: The Dark Knight Returns* (1986) and Gibbons's *Watchmen* (written by Alan Moore, 1986-1987), the two met at a convention in San Diego and felt it was logical that they collaborate. In generating a story for Gibbons to draw, Miller focused on the idea of a real American hero, like a modern version of Captain America. He also considered the American Dream and the idea of overcoming obstacles. These ideas led to the first three words written down: poor, black, female.

Miller wrote random scenes over a number of months, from which Gibbons completed preliminary sketches. Both Miller and Gibbons had envisioned a grim and gritty political story through a series of 150-page graphic novels, the first of which Miller completed as a script. However, they agreed the story lacked adventure and humor, which led to disinterest by both parties. Later, Miller proposed a more straightforward but satirical narrative, using elements of the material the two had already generated.

Plot

Give Me Liberty is a science-fiction story revolving around the life of a resourceful and tenacious teenager, Martha Washington. Mixing action and personal drama with political satire, *Give Me Liberty* is set in an alternative United States of competing extreme moral factions and military-like multinational burger corporations. Eventually, differences between the factions lead the United States to fracture into civil unrest and separatist territories to declare independence.

In part one, *Homes and Gardens*, Martha Washington, an African American girl born into an impoverished life in the Cabrini-Green urban housing project, displays high intelligence from a young age. She discovers her teacher, Donald, murdered by a gangbanger, whom Martha subsequently kills. Traumatized into muteness after the killing, Martha is committed to a mental institution. However, when she recovers, she continues to pretend to be mentally ill, realizing it is her only way out of her poverty-stricken life. At the institution, Martha witnesses tests on psychic children and connects telepathically with one whom she names Raggy Ann.

When President Erwin Rexall cuts the budget for mental institutions, Martha is one of 200,000 patients released onto the streets. The Surgeon General begins his "War on Sickness." Many patients are arrested by the Health Police, which is no less than a death squad. Resisting arrest, Martha kills a Health Police worker.

A U.S. laser-cannon attack aimed at Libya hits Saudi Arabian oilfields instead. In retaliation, Saudi Arabia strikes the White House, leaving Rexall in a coma and killing all of his cabinet except for Howard Nissen, who is appointed president. Nissen immediately institutes humanitarian, environmental, and cultural initiatives, to popular acclaim. He also retracts American Peace Force (PAX) troops from foreign wars and orders them to defend the remaining Amazon rain forest against international fast-food corporations who want the land to raise cattle for burgers.

Martha joins PAX, benefiting from the "no questions asked" sign-on policy, and is soon defending the rain forest. She witnesses Lieutenant Moretti leading Fat Boy Burger troops into the rain forest. Single-handedly, she stops the Fat Boy troops and wounds Moretti. Rescuers misinterpret the situation, hailing Moretti as a hero. He is subsequently promoted to captain. Moretti warns Martha to stay silent, threatening her with his family's power and wealth.

In part two, *Travel and Entertainment*, PAX achieves victory in the Amazon. Martha returns to the United States and is decorated for her efforts. Moretti is promoted to colonel.

Nissen survives assassination attempts by the militant gay racist group Aryan Thrust. In retaliation, Aryan Thrust's stronghold is destroyed; the destruction is attributed to a laser-cannon misfire, using an experimental system directed by "psychic schizophrenics." Aryan Thrust then captures an orbiting laser cannon, threatening to destroy Washington, D.C. Martha is sent to intervene and recaptures the cannon; however, the firing sequence has started. In trying to stop the cannon firing, Martha finds Raggy Ann is onboard, her psychic abilities being used in the weapons system. Raggy Ann explains that the cannon must fire or it will explode. Martha tells Raggy Ann to let it explode, and they narrowly escape. They crash-land to Earth in the Apache Nation territory and are taken captive. Moretti takes credit for thwarting Aryan Thrust's attack and is promoted to director of Peace Force Operations.

With public opinion turning against him, Nissen starts drinking heavily. In a drunken rage, he kills the vice president, while Moretti watches. Moretti forces the president to sign an executive order citing false evidence that the Apache Nation is readying a nuclear strike on Washington D.C., allowing him to attack the Apache Nation and also kill Martha. Raggy Ann's psychic abilities warn Martha of Moretti's intentions, as Moretti flies to the orbiting laser cannon to personally oversee the attack.

In part three, *Health and Welfare*, the Surgeon General ruthlessly pursues his "War on Sickness" to cleanse the United States of bad habits, bad attitudes, and bad music. The death of the vice president is reported as a "terrorist assassination" by the Apache Nation. Nissen's disapproval rate is now 98 percent. Support swells for the comatose Rexall. The United States moves to the brink of civil war.

Raggy Ann channels Moretti's thoughts as the attack commences. Martha, Raggy Ann, and Apache Nation leader Wasserstein barely escape the laser-cannon strike, which destroys the remaining Apache Nation members. Blinded by the attack, Martha is picked up by Health Police troops, sedated heavily, and taken to the Surgeon General's Fortress Health, where she is subjected to a treatment that replaces her memories and identity with that of "Margaret Snowden," a Health Enforcement officer. The Surgeon General keeps the military secrets he has extracted from Martha's memory and replaces her eyes.

Moretti orchestrates Nissen's murder and a bomb blast that kills Nissen's entire cabinet. He declares martial law, installing himself as leader. In the aftermath, the United States disintegrates, with ten different territories declaring independence. However, Rexall has "recovered"—his brain has been transferred to a robotic device that allows him to speak and move. The Surgeon General tells Moretti that because Rexall was never killed he is still president; also, he has offered to clone a new body for Rexall in return for establishing a separate territory ruled by the Surgeon General. Moretti orders an attack on Fortress Health. The Surgeon General tells Moretti about the information he has from Martha's memories and orders a prenuclear strike against Moretti's space-based laser cannon.

Wasserstein and Raggy Ann infiltrate Fortress Health to rescue Martha. Raggy Ann accesses a

Martha Washington file and uploads it to her brain. However, Martha (as Margaret) intercepts them, shooting Wasserstein. Martha then touches Raggy Ann, who uploads the Martha file, allowing Martha to remember her true identity.

In part four, *Death and Taxes*, Martha, acting as "Margaret Snowden," gets Wasserstein medical attention and has Raggy Ann "plug in" to the Fortress Health computer systems. Martha shoots the Surgeon General after he entrusts Rexall's brain to her. Raggy Ann explodes the Fortress Health missiles before they hit the orbiting laser cannon. Martha, Raggy Ann, Wasserstein, and Rexall escape Fortress Health in a jet fighter and go to the Amazon, which is protected from attack by executive order. The Surgeon General is killed in the pursuit.

Moretti and a death squad follow Martha. After eliminating the death squad, Martha fights and beats Moretti. While tempted to kill him, she arrests him instead. Moretti is sentenced to death. Rexall is reinstated as president. Martha visits Moretti, who is waiting to be executed, and watches as he hangs himself.

Characters

- *Martha Washington*, the protagonist, is an African American teenager born into poverty. She is highly intelligent and proficient in computer hacking. Resourceful and resilient, despite her young age, Martha evades multiple attempts on her life by Moretti. Her clear sense of right and wrong and almost superhumanly self-disciplined mind help her emerge triumphant from life-threatening situations and overcome her impoverished upbringing.
- *Lieutenant Moretti* is the main antagonist. Moretti is a self-serving, power-hungry liar. Moretti vehemently pursues Martha's death to cover his betrayal of PAX in the Amazon conflict. Moretti connives and schemes his way to the presidency only to have the United States fracture under his command. He commits suicide awaiting execution for his crimes.
- *Raggy Ann* is a sweet, preadolescent psychic used in an experimental weapons system. She

has her own language and can hear thoughts over great distances. Martha saves her from the destruction of the orbiting laser cannon. In return, she helps save Martha from the Surgeon General's Fortress Health and helps reclaim her personality and identity. Her confidence grows during the story.
- *Howard Nissen* becomes the U.S. president after Saudi Arabia's laser-cannon attack obliterates the White House and Rexall's ministerial cabinet. He is initially popular with the public after instituting environmental and humanitarian initiatives. His popularity soon disappears, changing him from a caring and thoughtful politician into a disillusioned and bitter alcoholic. He is killed by his cabinet ministers.
- *The Surgeon General* is a sociopathic cyborg intent on cleansing America of "disease" and polluting cultural elements, using "death squads" to do so. His face is always covered with a surgeon's mask. He is killed in pursuit of Martha and Rexall.
- *Erwin Rexall* is the hokey-speaking conservative president of the United States who has remained in office for thirteen years. He survives Saudi Arabia's laser cannon retaliatory attack but is in a coma. He returns as a "talking brain" to reclaim the presidency after Moretti's coup fails. Consistently upbeat, he is also sly.
- *Wasserstein* is the Native American leader of the Apache Nation with an imposing presence. He is proud of his heritage and cares for his people. He is the sole survivor of his people after Moretti organizes a laser-cannon strike on the Apache Nation. He is attracted to Martha.
- *Donald* is Martha's good-natured African American school teacher who volunteered to return to Cabrini-Green to teach. He is murdered after refusing to pay protection money to local gangs.

Artistic Style

Gibbons's art is immediately recognizable. His is a straightforward, classic style of comic art that leans toward realism. Gibbons's neutral, clean lines and Robin Smith's subdued color palette provide the reader with an unemotional view of Martha's world, allowing

Miller's characters and the strengths of the adventure narrative to dominate.

Give Me Liberty is interspersed with fake magazine and newspaper articles (devices used in *Watchmen*) to suggest a propaganda-infused media landscape. The shape of a television screen as a panel outline (as was used in *Batman: The Dark Knight Returns*), most notably used for the "recaps" at the start of each chapter, is also employed throughout to further the infusion of media.

Themes

The major themes of *Give Me Liberty* are freedom and independence. The title casts an ironic shadow over the narrative, as Miller's story portrays a United States in which personal freedoms are in fact greatly reduced under an oppressive right-wing government that engenders numerous and conflicting extreme, single-policy political parties.

Miller's solution for a divided United States is to literally fracture it into independent territories. The only way to be free and independent is to follow and fight for one single moral and political doctrine, whether it is feminism, environmentalism, conservatism, or liberalism. This is the "American way." The underlying tone of *Give Me Liberty* is Miller's clear disdain for hard-line policy from either left- or right-wing parties. By turning political extremism into a parody, Miller shows that any extreme political view can be described as fascistic.

The freedom of the individual is represented by Martha following her personal morals. Martha is a "hero" because, as Miller has stated, her mind is disciplined to the point that it is almost superhuman, allowing her to reject all "extreme-isms." Martha instead recognizes simple "right and wrong" and pursues the "right thing to do" in defiance of any doctrine. This makes her truly "independent."

Impact

One of Miller's lesser known works, *Give Me Liberty* nonetheless is one of his strongest narrative displays, enhancing and confirming his stature as an adult-oriented comics writer. The strength of Martha Washington as a character has encouraged both Miller and

Gibbons to return periodically over a sixteen-year period to continue and complete her life story.

With Martha Washington, Miller has created a powerful female figure, which is in opposition to his portrayal of female characters in most of his work, which tend to be one-dimensional and highly sexualized tending toward cliché (specifically in his *Sin City* series, 1991-2000). Miller has stated he wanted to create a "hero," and in Martha Washington, he has arguably created one of the most potent of any gender or race. A strong black female character, a rarity in most genres, is an exemplary hero who pursues what is right at significant personal cost.

Dealing with a dystopic vision much like that of *Batman: The Dark Knight Returns*, Miller provides an adventure story in a fractured and disintegrating United States of conflicting moral attitudes. The influence of *Give Me Liberty* can be seen in Brian Woods's *DMZ* (2005-   ), in which a second American civil war has made Manhattan Island a demilitarized zone, caught between the forces of the United States and secessionist Free States.

While not a superhero, Martha Washington is a precursory character to the Milestone Comics imprint that featured African American superheroes as lead characters. Perhaps the greatest impact Martha Washington has provided is as an inspiration for the women living in a homeless shelter in Chicago who took her as a role model.

Marise Williams

Further Reading

Miller, Frank. *Hard Boiled* (1990).

Miller, Frank, and Dave Gibbons. *The Life and Times of Martha Washington in the Twenty-first Century* (2010).

Moore, Alan, and Dave Gibbons. *Watchmen* (1986-1987).

Bibliography

Gibbons, Dave. "Dave Gibbons on the *Martha Washington Omnibus*." Interview by Chris Arrant. *Newsarama*, July 23, 2008. http://www.newsarama.com/comics/080723-gibbons-washington.html.

Jones, Stephen Matthew. "Frank Miller's Ideals of Heroism." (master's thesis, Indiana University, 2007). https://scholarworks.iupui.edu/bitstream/handle/1805/898/Frank%20Miller's%20Heroism%20Pdf,%20Unsigned%20(Jones).pdf?sequence=6.

Manning, Shaun. "Gibbons Discusses *Martha Washington*." *Comic Book Resources*, March 23, 2010. http://www.comicbookresources.com/?page=article&id=25341.

Miller, Frank. "Interview Four." Interview by Christopher Brayshaw. In *Frank Miller: The Interviews: 1981-2003*, edited by George Milo. The Comics Journal Library 2. Seattle, Wash.: Fantagraphics Books, 2003.

See also: *Watchmen*; *DMZ*; *Batman: The Dark Knight Returns*

GOON, THE

Author: Powell, Eric

Artist: Eric Powell (illustrator); Ben Cocke (colorist); Shaynne Corbett (colorist); Barry Gregory (colorist); Robin Powell (colorist); Dave Stewart (colorist)

Publishers: Albatross Exploding Funny Books; Avatar Press; Dark Horse Comics

First serial publication: 1998-

First book publication: 2003-2011

Publication History

The character of the Goon first appeared in a short story in *Dreamwalker*, issue 0, published by Avatar Press in March of 1998. Author and illustrator Eric Powell went on to publish the first three issues of his series featuring the character with Avatar. Dissatisfied with his publisher, Powell began to release issues of *The Goon* through his self-publishing venture, Albatross Exploding Funny Books, in 2002. The series was picked up by Dark Horse Comics in 2003, remaining with that press for the subsequent issues. Individual issues and stories have been collected in trade volumes, and Volume 6, *The Goon: Chinatown and the Mystery of Mr. Wicker*, is a stand-alone graphic novel. The one-shot "Satan's $@#%* Baby" was published in 2007. Additionally, Powell has released three "Fancy Pants" volumes that collect stories essential to the overall plot of the series.

A number of writers and artists have contributed short stories that feature the Goon and his environs. These stories appear in Volumes 4, 5, and 8 and feature work by Thomas Lennon, Neil Vokes, Nate Piekos, Kyle Holtz, Thomas E. Sniegoski, Michael Avone Oeming, Mike Hawthorne, Jason Hvam, Tony Shasteen, Mike Allred, Rebecca Sugar, Wil Glass, Franz Boukas, John Arcudi, Herb Trimpe, Al Milgrom, Dan Jackson, Bob Fingerman, and the Fillbäch brothers. Powell has collaborated with several artists including Brendon Small and Jon Schnepp, with whom he produced the one-shot "Dethklok Versus the Goon" in 2009. Powell also collaborated

Eric Powell

Eric Powell is a writer-artist best known for his work on *The Goon*, an Eisner Award-winning title that he created in 1999. As an adventure series with strong elements of humor, satire, and horror, *The Goon* demands art that is exaggerated and highly expressionistic. Powell favors thick, heavy contour lines on rounded figures. He breaks from traditional representational naturalism, opting instead for anatomical exaggeration used to signal key personality traits in his characters. Powell's writing revels in the presentation of politically incorrect situations, and draws humor from the creation of awkward situations that are not for the sensitive. Powell is one of the most successful "lowbrow" cartoonists of the 2000's, and he has achieved critical and commercial success by pillorying the tenets of good taste.

with *Hellboy* creator Mike Mignola on issue 7 of *The Goon*, in which Hellboy visits the Goon's city.

Plot

The Goon traces its title character's constant battle for self-preservation and supremacy as he fights alien, undead, and gangster enemies in a harsh noir-style city known as "the burg." Early on, the comic meanders through a series of stories in which the Goon and his deadly sidekick, Franky, revel in violence against various two-bit hoods and zombies when not drinking and playing cards in Norton's Pub. The Goon is believed to have become the crime lord Labrazio's foremost muscle after Labrazio killed his aunt, but the Zombie Priest, a demon in human form who has raised a zombie army to take over the burg, discovers that Labrazio is actually dead and the Goon himself is in charge. The Goon's childhood is explored, revealing that while Labrazio did indeed kill his aunt, the Goon killed Labrazio in turn, taking his gun, hat, and account book and setting himself up to run the town.

The Zombie Priest attacks the Goon with his entire army but is foiled by a cowboy wraith named Buzzard. Buzzard has come to settle accounts with the priest, who long ago cursed him to be a flesh-eating monster. At first, Buzzard fails in his confrontation with the priest, who captures and tortures him. The Goon and his allies eventually free Buzzard, who goes on an interdimensional journey and learns the priest's secret name, which can control him when spoken.

Realizing that Buzzard could defeat him, the priest summons Mother Corpse, a monster who rapidly gives birth to hundreds of monstrous children, called "changelings," that can combine with each other to create single larger monsters. The priest directs them to wreak havoc on the Goon's domain, but his efforts are not enough, and one of his demons takes control with a reanimated Labrazio.

As the Goon encounters yet another enemy, Mr. Wicker, he remembers Isabella, the love of his life. Having originally known her in his carnival days, he sees her later in Chinatown, serving as a prostitute-slave for the crime lord Xiang Yao. Exchanging control of the docks for her freedom, the Goon spends the happiest month of his life with Isabella. However, she leaves him inexplicably, and the outraged Goon fights Yao to regain control of the docks, disfiguring his face in the process. In the present, the Goon defeats Mr. Wicker.

Labrazio and his henchmen—the resurrected Mr. Wicker, the changelings, and Mother Corpse—attempt to kill the Goon and Franky. The Goon fights them, and Wicker falls quickly. However, Labrazio is revealed to be a powerful changeling monster created by the Zombie Priest's kinsman. Using his power over the Priest, Buzzard locates Mother Corpse and kills her, causing Labrazio to vanish.

In the middle of this fight, Isabella returns, intending to tell the Goon that they have a child together. She is fatally injured in the fight with Labrazio, and her attempt to notify the Goon of his son's existence fails. After arriving at the hospital too late, the Goon walks away, heartbroken.

Volumes

- *The Goon: Rough Stuff* (2004). Collects issues 1-3 of the Avatar Press run of *The Goon*, first collected by Albatross Exploding Funny Books. G-men try to find Labrazio, and the Goon outsmarts them by telling them a false version of his life story.
- *The Goon: Nothin' but Misery* (2003). Collects issues 1-4 of *The Goon* and *The Goon Color Special*, originally published by Albatross Exploding Funny Books, as well as "The Goon," a short story that originally appeared in the final issue of *Dark Horse Presents*. The Zombie Priest discovers that Labrazio is dead and the Goon is in charge of the burg. Buzzard arrives on the scene.
- *The Goon: My Murderous Childhood (and Other Grievous Yarns)* (2004). Collects issues 1-4 of the ongoing Dark Horse Comics series *The Goon* as well as the short story "The Goon Meets the Brothers Mud," originally published in the Dark Horse one-shot *Drawing on Your Nightmares*. The Goon's true backstory is revealed, and Dr. Alloy makes his debut.
- *The Goon: Heaps of Ruination* (2005). Collects issues 5-8. The Goon and his allies save Buzzard.
- *The Goon: Virtue and the Grim Consequences Thereof* (2006). Collects issues 9-13. In flashback, the Goon helps to assemble and play for the Canners football team, resulting in the elimination of various mob families. In the present, Dr. Alloy sends the Goon and Franky to obtain an interdimensional element to cure him.
- *The Goon: Wicked Inclinations* (2006). Collects issues 14-18. Buzzard makes an interdimensional trip, on which he learns the Zombie Priest's secret name and uses it to control him. The priest responds by summoning Mother Corpse, whose children cause havoc in the burg.
- *The Goon: Chinatown and the Mystery of Mr. Wicker* (2007). A stand-alone graphic novel. In the present, the Goon fights Mr. Wicker. In flashback, the Goon finds and then loses his beloved Isabella in Chinatown. He fights the crime lord Xiang Yao, who turns into a dragon and disfigures him.
- *The Goon: Noir* (2007). Collects issues 1-3 of the Dark Horse Comics limited series *The Goon: Noir*.

Stories by various writers and artists feature the Goon and his companions.

- *The Goon: A Place of Heartache and Grief* (2009). Collects issues 19-23. One of the priest's kind comes to take matters in hand and resurrects Labrazio, who proceeds to threaten the Goon and the burg.
- *The Goon: Those That Is Damned* (2009). Collects issues 24-27 and *MySpace Dark Horse Presents*, issue 6. Buzzard learns that the burg is cursed and informs the Goon that he will find no happiness in the town. The Goon saves Norton and his family. He discovers that his ally Merle is a double-crosser and tortures and kills him.
- *The Goon: Calamity of Conscience* (2009). Collects issues 28-31. Learning the secret to defeating Labrazio by killing Mother Corpse, the Goon, Franky, and Buzzard save the burg. Isabella, who has come to tell the Goon that they have had a child together, dies.
- *The Goon: Death's Greedy Comeuppance* (2011). Collects issues 32-33 and issues 1-3 of the Dark Horse Comics limited series *Buzzard*. Buzzard wanders in desolation after fighting the Zombie Priest, and the next arc of the Goon's adventures begins.

Characters

- *The Goon*, the protagonist, is a huge, muscle-bound man whose face is severely disfigured. He makes his living as a crime boss in the burg, where he must constantly fight off zombies, monsters, aliens, sea creatures, mob families, and other enemies. He usually fights with his fists and tremendous brute strength, but he sometimes uses monkey wrenches, post-office mailboxes, or whatever other weapons are available. The series follows his struggle to maintain power and explores his tragic backstory.
- *Franky*, the Goon's sidekick, is a little man with a peanut-shaped head and white eyes who wears a "wife-beater" tank top, brown slacks and suspenders, and a brown fedora. Although small, he is treacherous and particularly adept with submachine guns and his signature "knife to the eye"

move. He shares an apartment with the Goon, and the two often drink together at Norton's Pub. Franky also frequently goes on dates with voluptuous women whom he promptly dumps. The Goon's constant companion, he often helps the crime boss out of jams and is always supportive.

- *The Zombie Priest* is a demon and the would-be ruler of the burg. He is a small, ugly man who wears a top hat with the flesh of a face stretched across its front. His name is a secret, and if mortals know it, they can control him. The Goon's foremost enemy at the outset of the series, the priest raises an army of zombies in his domain of Lonely Street and continues his assaults on the Goon throughout the series. Buzzard eventually learns his name and gains control over him.
- *Buzzard* is a thin, drawn figure in a swirling black cloak and cowboy hat who uses his huge pistols to shoot down his enemies. Once a sheriff in a small town in the Old West, he was cursed by the Zombie Priest, who turned him into a kind of reverse zombie who craves the flesh of the undead instead of the living. The Goon's friend and ally, he helps defeat the Zombie Priest and other enemies.
- *Labrazio* is a mob leader who wears a smart suit. He introduces the young Goon to the world of crime and kills the Goon's Aunt Kizzie. In his grief, the Goon kills Labrazio and begins collecting his debts for himself. Later, a demon resurrects Labrazio, and the mobster immediately attempts to kill the Goon and retake his domain.
- *Isabella* is a beautiful brunette woman who performed as a belly dancer in the carnival before becoming a prostitute controlled by the Chinatown crime lord Xiang Yao. The love of the Goon's life, she has a child by him, although he does not know it.

Artistic Style

Powell's art is marked by a deft use of mixed media and a visual style that becomes increasingly smooth and bold over the course of the series. Characters and landscapes are realistic, stylized, or cartoonish as the content dictates. When presenting flashbacks, Powell often switches to pencil or pencil accentuated with ink, a mixture of media that drew criticism early in his career but has since become his hallmark. The early issues of the series were published in black and white, and color was added after the move to Dark Horse Comics. Powell has expressed his fondness for black and white and midtones, so the colors used in *The Goon* tend to be muted and smoky.

Powell's page layouts have also changed significantly over the course of the series, with earlier issues containing a large number of small panels on each page. Later issues emphasize larger and more visually powerful panels. *The Goon: Chinatown and the Mystery of Mr. Wicker* offers a striking example of this dynamic style, using large panels to depict close-ups of both action scenes and intense facial expressions that convey inner conflict.

Powell also illustrates the covers for the majority of the issues, usually painting them in oils. These dynamic pieces often reference retro design, including nods to Norman Rockwell's classic covers for the *Saturday Evening Post*.

Themes

A number of themes drive *The Goon*. One of the foremost is the importance of loyalty, which is paramount in the Goon's life and business dealings. The penalty for disloyalty to the Goon is torture and death. The Goon's chief and most loyal relationship is with Franky. They constantly deny that it is a homosexual relationship, though they do so with a nervous tension, but it is nevertheless intense and important. Neither of the two abandons the other, as many characters in the series do.

Violence can be considered another theme in the series, as Powell presents it in a humorous but matter-of-fact way. Arguably, the comic conveys the idea that violence and the misery it brings are simply a part of everyday life, in both the Goon's world and the reader's. Another important theme is that of lost love, primarily expressed through the Goon's love of Isabella and its contrast with Franky's shallow one-night stands.

Scornful of what he calls "fancy-pants" literary criticism, which he lambasts at times, Powell nevertheless presents pointed commentary on contemporary cultural and political issues and figures. One particular example

of this occurs in "All Hail the Oprah," in which Oprah Winfrey promotes her plan for elevation of the self through the power of positive thought, only to have her swollen head explode and produce the manure-slinging Peaches Valentine. Franky then presents Peaches Valentine as an exemplar of the "poop in one hand/wishes in the other" plan for self-improvement, which he considers just as valid as Oprah's. In addition, while the series generally ridicules political correctness, it does so in an intelligent way that serves as metacommentary on its doing so.

Impact

Although *The Goon* has been featured in mainstream news outlets and can occasionally be found in major bookseller chains, it remains popular primarily among dedicated comics readers, including other writers and artists. A number of comics professionals have taken the opportunity to work with the main character in various short pieces, many of which can be found in *The Goon: Noir* or scattered throughout the trade volumes. An animated film adaptation of *The Goon* was announced in 2008, with a short clip released in 2010.

Taylor Hagood

Further Reading

Powell, Eric. *Buzzard* (2010-).

_____. *Chimichanga* (2009-2010).

Powell, Eric, and Kyle Holz. *Billy the Kid's Old Time Oddities* (2005).

Bibliography

Geddes, John. "*The Goon* Hits Funny Bone While Smashing Evil." *USA Today*, October 27 , 2010. http://www.usatoday.com/life/comics/2010-10-27-thegoon-powell27-ST_N.htm.

Powell, Eric. "The Evolution of the Goon." In *The Goon: Rough Stuff*. Milwaukie, Ore.: Dark Horse, 2009.

_____. "The Goon: Black and White Versus Color." In *The Goon: Calamity of Conscience*. Milwaukie, Ore.: Dark Horse, 2009.

See also: *Hellboy; Swamp Thing; Batman: Arkham Asylum*

GREEN ARROW: YEAR ONE

Author: Diggle, Andy
Artist: Jock (illustrator); David Baron (colorist); Jared K. Fletcher (letterer)
Publisher: DC Comics
First serial publication: 2007
First book publication: 2008

Publication History

More than sixty years after the debut of Green Arrow in issue 73 of *More Fun Comics*, writer Andy Diggle approached Dan DiDio, then senior vice president and executive editor of DC Comics, and pitched a reimagined take on the hero's origin story. The pitch was successful, and Diggle began work on the project along with artist Jock (also known as Mark Simpson), with whom he had previously collaborated on *The Losers* (2003-2006). The duo created a biweekly, six-issue limited series that modernized and reinterpreted Green Arrow's origin story and featured a visual style and narrative pace appealing to contemporary comics readers.

Plot

Green Arrow: Year One tells the story of Oliver Queen, a spoiled, rich playboy with no regard for others. His only friend is his employee and sidekick, Hackett, who accompanies Oliver on his thrill-seeking trips to exotic places. Toward the beginning of the story, Oliver and Hackett return from an adventure in the mountains to attend a charity auction. While drunk, Oliver spends a large sum of money on a bow used by Howard Hill, the stunt master for the 1938 film *The Adventures of Robin Hood* and Oliver's personal hero. At the auction, Queen inquires about a business deal Hackett has made with a mysterious woman named Chien Na Wei. The deal, which involves the use of Oliver's yacht and money, seems a bit suspect, but Oliver does not attempt to prevent it.

After winning the auction for the bow, Oliver is embarrassingly rude to the crowd. Becoming sober on the way home, he realizes that he needs to get out of town to avoid the inevitable bad press. Dismissing Hackett's protests, Oliver insists on joining him on the yacht for

Jock
Jock, the pen name for British artist Mark Simpson, is best known for his frequent collaborations with writer Andy Diggle. After working together on *Lenny Zero* in *Judge Dredd Megazine*, the two produced the thirty-two issues of *The Losers* for DC's Vertigo imprint. The hybrid conspiracy/crime/war comic became one of the most acclaimed titles of the mid-2000's, and the film adaptation was released in 2010. Jock's images are characterized by his bold use of blacks and thick lines. Eschewing unnecessary details, Jock crosses photorealism with a bold, chunky minimalism. As he uses very few panels on most of his pages—often working in full landscape mode—his work has a powerful dynamism and cinematic quality. In recent years, he has become a sought-after cover specialist while dabbling in the film industry and working as a commercial illustrator..

the business deal. Once aboard, Oliver brags about his skill with the bow, saying that Hill had once given him lessons and complimented his natural skill as an archer.

With Oliver on the yacht, Hackett's plans go awry, as he had intended to steal the boat and Oliver's money without injuring him. Chien Na Wei orders Hackett to kill Oliver, but despite his other treacherous actions, Hackett is unwilling to kill his former friend. Instead, he throws Oliver overboard, leaving him to die in the ocean.

Oliver washes up on an island, where he develops his survival skills over the course of several months. He learns he is not alone when he discovers an opium farm run by Chien Na Wei and cultivated by enslaved islanders. Oliver discovers that Hackett is now on the island as well.

After a near miss with Chien Na Wei's drug runners and a fight with Hackett, Oliver goes into hiding, seriously injured. Taiana, a pregnant woman native to the island, nurses Oliver back to health and uses opium to medicate him. Once Oliver is physically healed, he experiences a difficult withdrawal from the opium, spending part of this period aboard his rediscovered, beached yacht. There, Oliver finds his Robin Hood bow.

Although he considers repairing the yacht and making his escape, the plight of the islanders convinces him otherwise. He uses the yacht's radio to call for help before joining forces with the islanders in a fight against Hackett and Chien Na Wei's men. By the time a navy ship arrives to help, the fight is over. Oliver is a hero, and the islanders call him by a name meaning "Green Arrow." After helping deliver Taiana's baby, Oliver returns to the United States to begin life as a better man.

Characters

- *Oliver Queen*, a.k.a. *Green Arrow*, the protagonist, is a well-built man with shoulder-length blond hair and a goatee. When stranded on an island, he grows out his beard and uses a green hood to protect himself from the sun. An immature playboy at the start of the series, he becomes a weathered, world-weary man with a mastery of the bow and arrow. Oliver assumes the ideals of Robin Hood when he helps the enslaved people of the island, transforming from a self-centered, wealthy thrill seeker into a heroic champion of the helpless.
- *Chien Na Wei*, a.k.a. *China White*, the primary antagonist, is a white-haired Chinese woman with a commanding presence. Her key characteristic is her cruelty, showcased by her harsh punishments for those who displease her. Oliver's mispronunciation of Wei's name is apt, considering her opium operation; "China White" is a slang name for heroin. Her continuous pursuit of Oliver pushes him to take heroic action and shut down her operation.
- *Hackett*, the secondary antagonist, is a well-built man with a buzz cut. Once Oliver's trusted employee and friend, he betrays Oliver, resulting in Oliver becoming stranded on the island. He acts as the physical antagonist for Green Arrow.
- *Taiana*, the key supporting protagonist, is a young pregnant woman. Determined to free her

people, the island's native population, she defies the drug producers and helps Oliver when he is injured. She tells Oliver that her people have named him Green Arrow.

Artistic Style

Originally published as a six-issue limited series, *Green Arrow: Year One* is a fast-paced narrative featuring numerous scenes of action or motion. Jock developed the panels for the series with this in mind, building on techniques he had previously used in *The Losers*. His artwork uses stylized realism to create the feel of an action film, while the panel placement and use of single-action panels create a heightened sense of motion.

The images become sharper as the series progresses, with more use of contrast. Shadows and dark lines are used to emphasize and communicate emotions such as anger. As the story progresses, Oliver's face develops darker lines, signaling his physical and emotional transformation.

Green Arrow, or Oliver, is the only character to appear on the covers of issues 1 through 5, while issue 6 features Hackett and Chien Na Wei as well. These highly stylized covers of the individual issues, illustrated and colored by Jock, feature one dominant color and hint at each issue's storyline in an abstract way. Inside each issue, colorist David Baron uses color as mood lighting for the various scenes. For example, Baron's use of purple in the panels depicting Oliver's withdrawal from opium creates a psychotropic feeling, causing the reader to experience Oliver's pain throughout.

Baron also increases his use of color throughout the story, counterbalancing the occasional lack of basic background elements. Some pages include fewer panels and more white space in order to highlight the individual panels. Strategic use of color is further displayed through the presence of green boxes that convey Oliver's internal thoughts and stand out against the panels' backgrounds.

Themes

Coming-of-age and control are the major themes that pervade *Green Arrow: Year One*. The theme of coming-of-age has been central to earlier depictions of Green Arrow's origin, effectively embodied by Oliver Queen's transformation from fast-living playboy to bow-wielding hero. Diggle's take on the origin story further explores the process of coming-of-age as Oliver learns about justice and caring for others over the course of his year on the island.

Green Arrow: Year One expands upon an idea previously explored in Mike Grell's *Green Arrow: The Longbow Hunters* (1987): Oliver is a fan of the Errol Flynn film *The Adventures of Robin Hood* (1938) and of the actor and stunt archer Howard Hill. In *Year One*, Oliver wins the bow used by Hill in the movie in an auction and first uses it while marooned on the island, prompting the development of his identity as Green Arrow. Oliver's inspiration to become an archer plays a key role in his coming-of-age experience.

Chien Na Wei, Hackett, and Oliver each exemplify the theme of control. Chien controls others through fear, torturing and killing those who displease her or compromise her opium operation. Hackett tries and fails to gain control of his life through his attempt to steal millions of dollars from Oliver and invest in Chien's operation.

Through his own journey, Oliver learns control over both the bow and opium. He acquires controlled skill with the bow by hunting for food and eventually fighting for survival, making the bow his signature tool and weapon. After Taiana helps him recover from his injuries by giving him opium, Oliver fights his newfound dependency and regains control of his body and mind. Oliver's increasing ability to control his own life additionally serves as evidence of his developing maturity.

Impact

At the time of *Green Arrow: Year One*'s publication, DC Comics had several Green Arrow-related projects in production, including a limited series focusing on Green Arrow's partnership and relationship with Black Canary. Although existing as a separate limited series, and later a graphic novel, outside of the ongoing Green Arrow narratives, *Year One* provided these new or continuing projects with a fleshed-out background for the hero.

In a tactic not uncommon in the Modern Age of comics, *Green Arrow: Year One* redefined Green Arrow's origin, expanding upon previous origin stories and giving the hero a more mature and modern sensibility. The limited series references earlier depictions of Green Arrow's origin, which generally include a boat, an island, and drug-runners. The details vary between comics, with some, including Grell's *The Longbow Hunters*, minimizing Oliver Queen's heroism on the island. In *Year One*, the drug-runners are a legitimate threat, and Oliver's triumph over them is instrumental in causing his transformation into a costumed hero. The series further expands upon Green Arrow's origin by adding the characters of Hackett, Chien Na Wei, and Taiana; specifying that Oliver was actively pushed overboard rather than falling from his yacht, as in some incarnations; minimizing the number of settings depicted, thus streamlining the narrative; and casting the native people of the island as the creators of the name Green Arrow, rather than the press or criminals.

Near the end of issue 6, Oliver develops a cover story to protect the islanders from further attention. This account of Oliver's time on the island, with the severity of the events downplayed, closely resembles the earlier Green Arrow origin tales, thus linking *Year One* to the existing Green Arrow franchise. In addition, *Year One* connects to a prior Green Arrow story from *Green Lantern/Green Arrow*, issues 85 and 86 (1971). In the two-part story, Green Arrow discovers that his sidekick, Speedy, is addicted to heroin. Oliver's experience with opium addiction in *Year One* gives Green Arrow's intense reaction to Speedy's drug habit an interesting background, in retrospect. While both stories have broader cultural and social relevance in terms of their antidrug message, *Year One* also retroactively places earlier Green Arrow comics within a more detailed context.

Ben Hall

Further Reading

Diggle, Andy, and Pascal Ferry. *Adam Strange: Planet Heist* (2005).

Dixon, Chuck, and Derec Donovan. *Connor Hawke: Dragon's Blood* (2008).

Grell, Mike, et al. *Warlord: The Saga* (2010).

Bibliography

Diggle, Andy. "Another String to Ollie's Bow: Diggle Talks 'Green Arrow: Year One'." Interview by Arune Singh. *Comic Book Resources*, March 27, 2011. http://comicbookresources.com/print. php?php?type=ar&id=9831.

Dixon, Chuck. "From the Beginning." *Green Arrow Annual,* issue 7. New York: DC Comics, 1995.

Grell, Mike. *Green Arrow: The Longbow Hunters.* New York: DC Comics, 1989.

Kirby, Jack. *The Green Arrow*. New York: DC Comics, 2001.

O'Neil, Dennis. "They Say It'll Kill Me . . . But They Won't Say When!" In *The Green Lantern/Green Arrow: The Collection*. New York: DC Comics, 2000.

See also: *Green Lantern-Green Arrow; Green Lantern: Secret Origin; The Losers; Hellblazer*

GREEN LANTERN-GREEN ARROW, THE COLLECTION: HARD TRAVELING HEROES

Author: O'Neil, Dennis J.
Artist: Neal Adams (illustrator); Frank Giacoia (inker); Dan Adkins (inker); Dick Giordano (inker)
Publisher: DC Comics
First serial publication: 1970-1971
First book publication: 1992

Publication History

In the introduction to *Green Lantern/Green Arrow Collection: Hard Traveling Heroes*, writer Dennis J. O'Neil discusses the humble beginnings of this groundbreaking series. "There was a comic book titled *Green Lantern* that had once been popular, and wasn't any longer." Instead of canceling the title, editor Julius Schwartz asked O'Neil, who had been a journalist prior to entering the world of comics, to overhaul the title and move it away from the standard superheroic action and focus on "real-life" issues such as racism, drug addiction, and environmentalism. O'Neil agreed, with the caveat that Green Lantern be given a costar with whom he could debate these topics.

Green Lantern Hal Jordan, who had been a military pilot and had become a galactic cop and could be counted on to provide a conservative perspective, was paired with Green Arrow (Oliver Queen), a character that had been reinvented as an antiestablishment figure and could represent a progressive point of view. While critical response to the new direction was positive, sales continued to slide and the series was canceled fourteen issues later.

Individual issues of the *Hard Traveling Heroes* story arc were reprinted numerous times throughout the 1970's and 1980's, often reconfiguring Neal Adams's fluid designs to fit smaller page formats. This collection, originally published in 1992, gathers issues 76-83 of the series. While there are some minor visual updates—the famous panel featuring Martin Luther King, Jr., and Robert F. Kennedy was colored in a startling mix of red and yellow, but it was originally black and pale blue—it faithfully re-creates Adams's original visual page layouts.

(Getty Images)

Neal Adams

One of the most influential visual stylists in the superhero genre, Neal Adams is best remembered for his work at DC Comics at the end of the 1960's and for helping to launch the relevance movement in superhero comics of the 1970's. With writer Denny O'Neill, he helped to pioneer the idea that superhero comics could aspire to the treatment of serious themes. Though he drew a wide variety of titles, Adams is particularly remembered for his work on *Batman*, *Deadman*, and *Green Lantern/ Green Arrow*. Adams's art represented a fairly radical departure from the norms of the late-1960's, and he helped to create an interest in heightened levels of anatomical and figurative realism in a genre that had been long defined by its bombastic elements. Adams's figures were drawn with a fluidity and grace that were rare in the form. For many he will be best remembered for the unusual oversized one-shot teaming Superman and Muhammad Ali.

Plot

Following Schwartz's directive, the stories collected in *Green Lantern/Green Arrow Collection: Hard Traveling Heroes* address specific issues faced by the United States in the early 1970's. Writer O'Neil, ably abetted by artist Adams, manages to cover a vast amount of thematic ground with the narrative conceit that the two heroes, along with their intergalactic side-kick, the Old-Timer (Appa Ali Apsa, who belongs to an immortal, extraterrestrial race), have set out in a rickety pickup truck in order to experience the true American spirit. As O'Neil writes at the end of issue 76, the three companions "set out together moving through cities and villages and the majesty of the wilderness . . . searching for a special kind of truth . . . searching for themselves."

As the first story, "No Evil Shall Escape My Sight," opens, Green Lantern encounters a group of "punks" attacking a well-dressed man in front of a brownstone apartment building. He immediately swoops down to teach the attackers "a little respect," but is interrupted by Green Arrow, who explains that the man who appeared to be the victim is actually the building's slum-lord owner, Jubal Slade, who is there to evict all of the tenants. The two heroes eventually expose Slade's criminal activities and turn him over to the authorities. Inspired by his encounter with issues of social justice, Green Lantern decides to join Green Arrow, and a curious member of the Guardians of the Universe (the aforementioned Appa Ali Apsa) who takes on a human appearance, on a trip to find the "real America."

In issue 77, "Journey to Desolation," the two heroes, along with their immortal companion, drive toward the mountain town of Desolation, when they come under fire from snipers. The "emerald duo" quickly subdue their attackers, only to find out that the gunmen thought that they had been sent by Slapper Soames, the despotic owner of the town's lone industry (a coal mine). Green Lantern and Green Arrow learn that Soames, who also controls the local courts, has arrested Johnny, one of the citizens' leaders, and has sentenced him to death. Green Arrow is eager to help the workers, while Green Lantern is reticent to use his power against the local justice system, despite its obvious corruption. However, as Green Arrow and the workers begin their assault on Soames's hired troops—a group that former Nazi Soames has somehow compiled from a "war crimes prison"—Green Lantern sees the error of his ways and helps rescue Johnny and bring Soames and his Nazi punks to justice.

Black Canary appears in issue 78, "A Kind of Loving, A Way of Death!" While on her own journey of self-discovery, she encounters a band of bikers in Washington State who beat her and steal her motorcycle, but she is carried off to safety by Joshua, a Charles Manson-esque cult leader. Two weeks later, Green Lantern Hal Jordan, Oliver Queen (often shortened to Ollie), and the Old-Timer come across the same bikers and, recognizing Black Canary's motorcycle, deduce that she has encountered trouble. The heroes find her in Joshua's compound, where he has hypnotized Black Canary and a group of followers and plans on leading them in a violent revolution. While Green Lantern battles Joshua's followers, Joshua hands the hypnotized Black Canary a pistol, ordering her to shoot Green Arrow. However, she overcomes her mind control after realizing her love for Ollie.

The heroes stay in the Northwest in issue 79, "Ulysses Star Is Still Alive!" As Black Canary retires to a nearby reservation to recuperate from being hypnotized by Joshua, Green Arrow and Green Lantern are caught in a struggle between a Native American group and the Lumbermen's Union concerning the ownership of the local forest. While Green Lantern heads off to nearby Evergreen City to research the case, Green Arrow disguises himself as the ghost of Ulysses Star, the legendary tribal elder who signed the original agreement, and attempts to scare off the corporate intruders. As the confrontation between the two groups turns violent, Green Lantern arrives with a congressman to investigate both sides' claims and determine who is in the right.

Issues 80 and 81 focus on the Old-Timer and his struggle to understand humanity. At the beginning of "Even an Immortal Can Die," he is forced to choose between saving a fishing boat in peril or the injured Green Lantern. After choosing to save Green Lantern, the Old-Timer incurs the wrath of the Guardians, who claim that saving an individual over a group violates their laws. Sent to the planet Gallo for a trial, Green

Lantern, Green Arrow, and the Old-Timer discover a world that has been taken over by robots programmed by the planet's "master mechanic," who has taken over the court. Green Lantern and Green Arrow defeat their robot guards, free the planet's inhabitants, and rescue their companion just before he is executed.

The saga of the trial continues in "Death Be My Destiny," as the heroes, joined by Black Canary, travel to the Guardians' homeworld, Oa. There, the Old-Timer is stripped of his immortality and exiled to the planet Maltus, which is plagued by an overpopulation of clones. The four confront Mother Juna, who is responsible for the creation of the clones. The Old-Timer accepts his exile and pledges to help rebuild Maltus.

In the final story, "And a Child Shall Destroy Them," Black Canary becomes disillusioned with being a superhero and begins teaching at a boarding school. As Ollie and Hal drive her to the campus, they are attacked by a flock of Hitchcockian birds, which the heroes quickly dispatch. The birds, as well as the student body, are being controlled by a psychic child named Sybil and her mentor, Grandy, the school's cook. While investigating the events at the school, Green Lantern Hal Jordan meets up with his old lover and boss, Carol Ferris, who is engaged to the school's owner. The heroes deal with the psychic attacks, accidentally killing Grandy and Sybil in the process, and Hal and Carol declare their love for each other.

Characters

- *Green Lantern*, a.k.a. *Hal Jordan*, is a human member of the Green Lantern Corps, ostensibly an intergalactic police force commanded by the Guardians of the Universe. All Green Lanterns, including Jordan, wield a power ring, which must be recharged periodically, that enables them to fly, create force fields, and fire rays of pure energy. In his civilian identity, Jordan is a toy salesman (among other unlikely occupations) and former test pilot.
- *Green Arrow*, a.k.a. *Oliver Queen* and *Ollie*, is a superhero known as much for his physical abilities as his interest in social justice and antiauthoritarian attitude. Green Arrow has no superpowers, but his skill with a bow and arrow, as well as his

proficiency as a hand-to-hand combatant, puts him on an equal level with metahuman heroes. His strong personality and passionate political beliefs persuade Green Lantern and Appa Ali Apsa to join him on his cross-country journey.

- *Appa Ali Apsa*, a.k.a. *The Old-Timer*, is a member of the Guardians of the Universe sent to Earth from the planet Oa to learn about humanity by traveling with Green Arrow and Green Lantern. On Earth, he takes on the appearance of an elderly man, prompting his superhero companions to refer to him as the Old-Timer. Despite his human appearance, he does retain some of his telepathic abilities, albeit in a limited capacity.
- *Black Canary*, a.k.a. *Dinah Drake Lance*, began her career as a member of the Justice Society on Earth-Two. However, following the death of her husband, she traveled to Earth-One and joined the Justice League of America, where she met Green Arrow. There was a mutual attraction between them, but Dinah was unable to commit to a relationship. At the beginning of *Green Lantern/ Green Arrow Collection: Hard Traveling Heroes*, she is on a journey of self-discovery somewhere in Washington State. She is an accomplished martial artist whose lone superpower is the ability to emit a "sonic scream" powerful enough to destroy inanimate objects and debilitate opponents.

Artistic Style

While much of the critical attention on *Green Lantern/ Green Arrow Collection: Hard Traveling Heroes* focuses on its writing and themes, the book has a distinct visual identity because of the work of artist Adams. *Hard Traveling Heroes* was Adams's second collaboration with O'Neil; in early 1970, the pair had created a darker Batman character in *Detective Comics* as a reaction to the campy television series starring Adam West. While the book is thematically intensive, Adams's ability to portray action prevents the series from becoming too reliant on dialogue and exposition to convey dramatic action.

Adams's work in this volume is a striking blend of nearly photographic realism and a fluid, cinematic page layout. While it naturally makes action scenes more powerful, it also makes dialogue-based scenes more dramatic and prevents them from becoming bogged down in exposition. His photo-realistic renderings of facial expression support the depth of characterization created by O'Neil.

Another important element of the book's visual style is Adams's ability to create the illusion of movement in a static image. This is accomplished by consistently establishing then subverting the traditional page layouts. During expository passages, Adams's page layouts feature conventional square and rectangular panels, while scenes emphasizing action use dramatic, asymmetrical structures that emphasize scale and action.

Themes

The origins of *Green Lantern/Green Arrow Collection: Hard Traveling Heroes* lie in a request from the publisher to create a title that would "dramatize the real-life issues that tormented the country in the context of superheroics." As this was the book's raison d'être, it is work with great thematic density. While each individual story addresses a specific cultural issue—"Journey to Desolation" deals with economic exploitation, "A Kind of Loving, a Way of Death" addresses cults, and "Ulysses Star Is Still Alive" focuses on the treatment of Native Americans—there are overarching ideas that bind together the seven separate stories.

The idea that complex social issues must be addressed in a complex manner is a recurring theme throughout *Hard Traveling Heroes*, specifically for Green Lantern. At numerous points throughout the book, he mentions that he has been "conditioned to respect the authority of the law"; however, the more he is exposed to the complexities of the world, the more comfortable he becomes with Green Arrow's moral relativism. Ultimately, Green Lantern develops a more sophisticated worldview, as he states, "The world isn't the black-and-white place I thought it to be. . . . Green Arrow has made me think that maybe authority isn't always right."

The other major theme in the book is the idea that, because of a number of social shifts, the two heroes are at variance with the greater culture and must redefine themselves. To do this, they follow the masculine American tradition of abandoning the seemingly de-centered society and head out for the frontier, allowing them to "inscribe, unhindered [their] own destiny and [their] own nature." In order to make their rejection complete, they eschew the casual use of their super-powers and, as Green Arrow puts it, "play it strictly human."

During the duo's time in the frontier, Green Lantern's lack of self-assurance is physically manifested when his ring, which acquires its energy from his concentrated willpower, fails during a battle. As the story progresses, Green Lantern realizes that this failure is a by-product of his own lack of self-assurance. As Green Lantern attempts to come to terms with the changing society, his power ring, and his identity, is restored.

While *Hard Traveling Heroes* attempted to address "the whole catalog of national discontent that energized the era," it is hamstrung by the traditional, action-centric format of comics. While this is an issue, it does not diminish the historical importance of this series. However, despite its best intentions, in hindsight, it is not difficult to read *Hard Traveling Heroes* as dated and reductive.

Impact

The late 1960's and early 1970's were times of extreme cultural change in the United States, and one of the most notable shifts was the coming-of-age of American popular culture. Thanks to films such as *2001: A Space Odyssey* (1968) and *Midnight Cowboy* (1969), television shows such as *Laugh-In* and *Sesame Street*, and the music of Bob Dylan and the Beatles, media that had once been treated dismissively had become major cultural forces. The stories collected in *Hard Traveling Heroes* exemplify this shift from a time when comics were "roughly synonymous with fish-wrapping," to quote O'Neil, to an era when the medium could thoughtfully generate discourse regarding the pertinent issues of the day.

Despite the series' short run, its story line was groundbreaking; it was one of only a few comics of the era that used realistic characters to address serious topics in a logical manner. (Another example is *Amazing Spider-Man*, issues 96-98, which dealt with drug abuse.) While this concept is hardly remarkable more than forty years after the publication of *Hard Traveling Heroes*, it is difficult to imagine such modern classics as Alan Moore's *Watchmen* (1986) and Frank Miller's *Batman: The Dark Knight Returns* (1986) without the trail blazed by *Hard Traveling Heroes*.

Despite its unquestionable importance, there are elements in the book that come across as dated. For example, while much of O'Neil's dialogue is compelling, his narration is sometimes overwrought. Describing the trial of the Old-Timer, O'Neil commands readers to "Watch carefully . . . for you have not seen this terrible ceremony ere now . . . nor, hopefully, will you ever see it again."

Another problematic area is the book's treatment of minority characters. Despite Schwartz and O'Neil's efforts to present stories that were unprejudiced with regard to racial issues, generally speaking, all nonwhite characters are portrayed as noble savages, whose oppression has given them wisdom and insight beyond that of "civilized" people. Also, the only two women who appear in this volume are Black Canary and Carol Ferris, who serves as a deus ex machina for Green Lantern in the last issue. Black Canary's portrayal is equally problematic: Despite her superpowers and formidable martial-arts training, she is never portrayed as anything other than a victim who must be bailed out by her male counterparts.

Jim Davis

Further Reading

Jurgens, Dan. *Zero Hour: Crisis in Time* (1994).

Meltzer, Brad. *Identity Crisis* (2005).

O'Neil, Dennis J., Elliot S. Maggin, and Neal Adams. *Green Lantern-Green Arrow, The Collection: Volume Two* (2004).

Smith, Kevin. *Green Arrow: Quiver* (2002).

Bibliography

Baym, Nina. "Melodramas of Beset Manhood: How Theories of American Fiction Exclude Women Authors." In *Feminism and American Literary History: Essays*. New Brunswick, N.J.: Rutgers University Press, 1992.

Dryden, Jane, and Mark D. White. *Green Lantern and Philosophy*. New York: John Wiley & Sons, 2011.

O'Neill, Dennis. Preface to *Green Lantern/Green Arrow Collection: Hard Traveling Heroes*. New York: DC Comics, 1992.

See also: *Identity Crisis; Green Lantern: Secret Origin*

GREEN LANTERN: SECRET ORIGIN

Author: Johns, Geoff

Artist: Ivan Reis (illustrator); Oclair Albert (inker); Julio Ferreira (inker); Randy Mayor (colorist); Rob Leigh (letterer); Dave McCaig (cover artist)

Publisher: DC Comics

First serial publication: 2008

First book publication: 2008

Publication History

Originally published in single-magazine form in *Green Lantern*, issues 29-35, *Green Lantern: Secret Origin* is a retelling of Hal Jordan's origin story, in which he becomes Earth's first Green Lantern. Serving as a lead-in to the DC Comics crossover event "Blackest Night" (2009-2010), *Secret Origin* introduced several story elements, including the characters Atrocitus and William Hand, that would be further developed in that later story line.

After its seven-issue run, *Green Lantern: Secret Origin* was collected in both hardcover and paperback editions. A new collected edition was published in April, 2011, several months before the release of the *Green Lantern* live-action film. This tie-in edition features an introduction by actor Ryan Reynolds, who portrays the Green Lantern in the film and appears in full costume on the book's cover.

Plot

The story begins with a young Hal Jordan watching his father fly a plane. At the airfield, he meets a young, stuck-up girl named Carol Ferris. Sneaking through a fence for a closer look at the planes, he is horrified when he sees his father's plane crash and explode. Despite this tragedy, Hal becomes obsessed with flying in subsequent years. He frequently sneaks onto airfields to see planes, which puts him in conflict with his family.

On Hal's eighteenth birthday, he joins the United States Air Force. He is a somewhat reckless pilot, often willing to damage expensive planes just to prove a point. Eventually, his younger brother, Jim, visits him and tells him that their mother is sick.

(AP Photo)

Ivan Reis

Since breaking into the comics industry in the early 2000's, artist Ivan Reis has worked on a wide variety of titles. Initially making his mark on *Ghost* and *Lady Death*, Reis has worked extensively for both Marvel and DC Comics on titles including *Captain Marvel*, *Iron Man*, *Defenders*, *Teen Titans*, *Superman*, and *Green Lantern*. Reis is best known for his work on *Green Lantern* and the 2009-2010 miniseries *Blackest Night* and its sequel, *Brightest Day*. Reis's art work is characterized by its dynamism. Influenced by Neal Adams, his art excels in scenes depicting action on a cosmic scale, as in the *Green Lantern* titles. His figures are lithe and actions are fluid. He uses an unusually high number of page-width panels, which underscore the epic scope that he tries to create. His pages have a high degree of visual interest, with a great deal of detail and nontraditional designs.

Upset about his mother's illness and frustrated with his commanding officer, Major Stone, Hal punches his superior and is dishonorably discharged. When Hal visits the hospital, he discovers that his mother has died. Hal's older brother, Jack, blames Hal for driving their mother to an early death.

Meanwhile, an alien police officer named Abin Sur, a member of an intergalactic peace force known as the Green Lantern Corps, interrogates another alien named Atrocitus. Over a communication channel, he reveals to his friend and fellow Green Lantern Sinestro his fears about the prophesied end of all life in the universe. He takes Atrocitus to where this evil is believed to begin: Earth. Atrocitus, after instilling fear in Abin, is able to overpower his ring's energy and cause his spacecraft to crash on Earth.

Hal adjusts slowly to life in the private sector. His reputation for reckless flight preceding him, he is forced to become an airplane mechanic rather than a pilot. Working for an old friend of his father, he is horrified to discover that the company for which he works is being sold to Ferris Air, the same company for which his father worked when he died. Blaming its owner, Carl Ferris, for his father's ultimate fate, Hal decides to quit. However, a grown Carol Ferris is now largely in charge of her father's company. Although she dislikes the idea of Hal Jordan being one of her new subordinates, she allows him to fly after all of Ferris Air's pilots resign upon discovering that she is really running the company.

When the alien spacecraft crashes, Hal investigates and discovers a mortally wounded Abin Sur. Abin informs him that his ring has chosen him; Hal Jordan is to serve as the Green Lantern in his place. Accepting this responsibility almost immediately, Hal takes Abin's ring and glowing green lantern. He is then transported to the planet Oa, where he encounters hundreds of other Green Lanterns and learns about their powers, their history, and their leaders, the Guardians of the Universe. Transported back to Earth, Hal fights Hector Hammond, a former boyfriend of Carol who has been superhumanly transformed by exposure to the alien ship, as well as Atrocitus.

Characters

- *Hal Jordan*, a.k.a. *Green Lantern*, is Earth's first human Green Lantern. A pilot who lost his father at an early age, he is a brown-haired all-American type who is somewhat reckless and hotheaded but is ultimately heroic.

- *Sinestro* a.k.a. *Green Lantern*, is a red-skinned alien humanoid who is regarded as the greatest of the Green Lanterns. As Abin Sur's best friend, he resents Hal for taking his place. He and Hal form an uneasy partnership.

- *Abin Sur*, a.k.a. *Green Lantern*, is Hal Jordan's predecessor in the role. Fearing a prophecy about the end of all life, Abin begins to doubt his abilities. This ultimately leads to his untimely death at Atrocitus's hands.

- *Atrocitus* is one of the Five Inversions and an enemy to all Green Lanterns. An alien criminal who is powered by hate and fear, he has little regard for life and is responsible for killing Abin Sur.

- *Carol Ferris* is the de facto head of Ferris Air who struggles to hold her father's company together after he becomes incapacitated. Despite their adversarial relationship, she is Hal's love interest.

- *Hector Hammond* is a consultant to Ferris Air and the military and is Carol's former boyfriend, still possessing feelings for her. After encountering Abin Sur's spacecraft, he gains immense psychokinetic powers.

- *Kilowog* is a Green Lantern Corps member who is responsible for training new recruits. He serves as Hal Jordan's drill sergeant when Hal arrives on Oa. Jovial yet firm, he resembles a humanoid canine pug.

- *Tomar-Re*, a.k.a. *Green Lantern*, is the Green Lantern responsible for a sector neighboring Earth's. Tomar introduces himself to Hal and shows him the Book of Oa. He resembles a yellow amalgam of a chicken and a fish.

- *William Hand* is a mysterious young boy on Earth whom Atrocitus targets. A mortician's son, he is morbidly interested in touching dead bodies. He steals an alien device created by Atrocitus.

Artistic Style

Ivan Reis was the primary penciller for *Green Lantern: Secret Origin*. While maintaining a traditional comic book style featuring bizarre aliens, monolithic spaceships, and epic, action-packed battles, he also captures the emotions and sense of wonder of each character. Reis has a distinctly soft style to his art; he avoids hard, jagged lines in favor of curved surfaces and soft facial expressions. This clean and expressive art is particularly effective in some of the full-page panels presented, including the dramatic scene in which Hal finds the dying Abin Sur's spaceship. Reis has garnered praise for his action sequences as well as his depiction of character-oriented moments. This is especially evident when Hal rushes to confront Carol Ferris's father, Carl, and discovers him bedridden and infirm. Saddened by her father's physical state, Carol breaks down on her front porch, and Hal quietly comforts her. The panel's vantage point shows them embracing, silhouetted beautifully from miles away.

Colorist Randy Mayor uses vivid color throughout the comic, but it particularly effective when used to accentuate the alien nature of characters and environments. The color is perhaps most vivid when Hal Jordan is transported to the alien world of Oa. After seeing several hundred Green Lanterns of varying appearance, he observes the surreal amber landscape of the alien world.

Themes

The story begins as a coming-of-age work, with Hal Jordan's childhood clearly influencing his adult personality. His early life is examined, including his witnessing of his father's death in a horrific airplane accident. Instead of giving up his dream of a life in the sky, he becomes obsessed with flying; it is the only thing he really wants to do. This obsession factors into his lack of hesitation when presented with the option of becoming a superhero. Given the chance to fly under his own power, Hal Jordan does not have to think twice.

Family also plays a significant role in Hal's development. After the death of his father, Hal goes through life believing he has nothing to lose. This belief is shattered when his mother falls ill and dies suddenly, thus severing his already-tenuous relationship with his brothers. Hal's antagonistic relationship with businesswoman Carol Ferris is also a form of denial for him, as he denies that he cares for her just as he does with his family. However, he selflessly protects her from the

insane Hector Hammond and comforts her when she breaks down over her father's illness.

Power also holds great significance in the story. Hal Jordan goes from being an ordinary man to having one of the most powerful weapons in the Galaxy: his ring. Several other beings are depicted as having similar weapons given to them by the self-proclaimed Guardians of the Universe. Atrocitus, an enemy to the Lanterns and to the Guardians, is revealed as having been victimized by the Guardians as they exercised their power and control over the universe; their creation of the murderous Manhunters, a precursor to the Green Lanterns, caused Atrocitus to become one of the last of his kind.

Impact

Originally created by Martin Nodell in 1940, the Green Lantern has experienced several reimaginings since the character's introduction. In 1959, the first such revamp, by John Broome and Gil Kane, introduced Hal Jordan as the new Green Lantern. The story of Hal Jordan's birth as the Green Lantern has changed little since: He discovers a dying alien named Abin Sur, who bestows upon him one of the greatest weapons in the Galaxy.

In the late 1960's, Denny O'Neil reinterpreted the Hal Jordan character, making him the counterpart of another hero, Oliver Queen, better known as Green Arrow. While Oliver represents the antiestablishment and extreme liberal mentality, Hal serves as a perfect foil, an intergalactic police officer who represents law and order.

While other humans such as John Stewart and Guy Gardner temporarily take his place, Hal Jordan is arguably the most steadfast and heroic of Earth's Green Lanterns. Despite this, in the three-part story "Emerald Twilight" (1994), Hal goes manically insane after the destruction of his hometown, Coast City. Unable to re-create it or his loved ones with the energy of his ring, he seeks power from the Guardians of the Universe, killing any Lantern who gets in his way. In a last-ditch effort, the Guardians pit him against his old enemy, Sinestro, but Hal is able to defeat him. The last surviving Guardian manages to give the final Green Lantern ring to a human named Kyle Rayner, who becomes the last Green Lantern. After trying to destroy the universe, Hal ultimately redeems himself when he sacrifices himself to save Earth. He is reborn as the avenging spirit the Spectre and returns to life nearly a decade later, as chronicled in *Green Lantern: Rebirth* (2004).

These various reinterpretations and story lines created a complicated continuity populated by several Earth-based heroes known as the Green Lantern and multiple incarnations of the Green Lantern Corps. Thus, with its reestablishment of the essential creation myth underpinning the character of the Green Lantern, *Green Lantern: Secret Origin* provided background information that increased the accessibility of the franchise for new readers and paved the way for both the "Blackest Night" story line and the live-action film adaptation.

Ryan P. Donovan

Films

Green Lantern. Directed by Martin Campbell. Warner Bros., 2011. This film adaptation stars Ryan Reynolds as Hal Jordan and Blake Lively as Carol Ferris. While it is an origin story in which Hal Jordan becomes Green Lantern, establishes his tumultuous relationship with Carol Ferris, and fights Hector Hammond, the film differs from *Green Lantern: Secret Origin* in that it does not serve as a prelude to the "Blackest Night" story line. Neither Atrocitus nor William Hand appears in the film.

Green Lantern: First Flight. Directed by Lauren Montgomery. DC Comics/Warner Bros. Animation/ Warner Premiere, 2009. This animated film adaptation stars Christopher Meloni as Hal Jordan and Victor Garber as Sinestro. While this is an origin story in which Hal Jordan becomes Green Lantern, the film differs from *Green Lantern: Secret Origin* in that it explores Sinestro's history and his betrayal of the Green Lantern Corps.

Further Reading

Johns, Geoff, and Ivan Reis. *Blackest Night* (2010).

Johns, Geoff, and Ethan Van Sciver. *Green Lantern: Rebirth* (2005).

Marz, Ron, and Daryl Banks. *Green Lantern: Emerald Twilight/New Dawn* (2003).

Bibliography

Dryden, Jane, and Mark. D. White. *Green Lantern and Philosophy: No Evil Shall Escape This Book*. Hoboken, N.J.: John Wiley, 2011.

Flagg, Gordon. "Secret Origin: *Green Lantern*." Review of *Green Lantern: Secret Origin*, by Geoff Johns. *Booklist* 105, no. 14 (March 15, 2009): 51.

See also: *Green Arrow: Year One; Green Lantern-Green Arrow; Justice League of America: The Nail; B.P.R.D*

GRENDEL

Author: Wagner, Matt

Artist: Bernie Mireault (illustrator); Tim Sale (illustrator); Matt Wagner (illustrator); Patrick McEown (penciller); Arnold Pander (penciller); Jacob Pander (penciller); John K.Snyder III (penciller, inker, and cover artist); Jay Geldhof (penciller and inker); Rich Rankin (inker); Jeremy Cox (colorist); Matthew Hollingsworth (colorist); Joe Matt (colorist); Chris Pitzer (colorist); Kurt Hathaway (letterer); Steve Haynie (letterer); Bob Pinaha (letterer)

Publisher: Dark Horse Comics

First serial publication: 1983-

First book publication: 1986-2009

Publication History

Grendel began in 1982—when illustrator Matt Wagner had barely reached his twenties—with a single black-and-white story in *Primer*, issue 2. The longest run of *Grendel* was published by Comico Comics. After the first three issues, Wagner left *Grendel* temporarily to pursue his other early project, *Mage* (first published in 1984), but he returned to the character as a backup feature in that series. In 1986, these backup stories were collected into *Devil by the Deed*.

Devil by the Deed was a best seller, and Comico approached Wagner about an ongoing series. The series lasted forty issues before Comico went bankrupt in 1990. *Grendel* was picked up by Dark Horse Comics, and the series was finished with issues forty-one through fifty. *Grendel* was not dead, however. With the help of a wide array of artists, Wagner continued to revisit and reimagine various moments in the *Grendel* legend for years, including two *Batman/Grendel* crossovers and a number of miniseries and recaps. For the twenty-fifth anniversary of *Grendel* in 2007, Wagner released a new, nine-issue series, *Behold the Devil*. At that time, Dark Horse also released a colored print of *Devil by the Deed* and *Grendel Archives*, a collection of the first Grendel issues.

Grendel. (Courtesy of Dark Horse Comics)

Plot

By Wagner's account, *Grendel*'s title character was inspired by a lecture on the great villains of world literature; Grendel possesses the cruelty and cunning of some of literature's darkest characters. First the alter ego of the chic Hunter Rose, the character becomes a spirit that possesses and haunts numerous individuals. Freed from the restrictions of belonging to one body, Grendel has been man, woman, avenger, lunatic, and guard during the many years of his story. The trademarks of the character are a black-and-white mask and a cold and violent intensity.

Grendel is born in Rose in *Devil by the Deed*. Driven by the death of his lover, Rose becomes a sleek criminal mastermind and clashes with the wolf Argent. Their hatred for one another is deepened by Rose's adoption of Stacy Palambo and her waning affection for Argent. The final battle between the two characters ends with Grendel dead and Argent paralyzed. Revealed at the end is that Christine Spar, Palambo's daughter and a journalist with *The New York Times*, has written the story.

In *Devil's Legacy*, which takes place shortly after the events of *Devil by the Deed*, Spar's son is kidnapped by the vampire Kabuki dancer Tujiro XIV. Turning to the most potent source of power of which she is aware, Spar steals the first Grendel's mask and electric fork and tracks Tujiro to San Francisco, where she confronts him and kills his entire Kabuki troupe, which is actually a front for a slavery ring. When Tujiro disappears, Spar vows to lay aside the Grendel persona and returns to New York. There, angered by the brutality with which Argent and police detective Captain Wiggins have interrogated her friends, she dons Grendel's mask to avenge her loved ones and to end Argent's obsession with Grendel. This fight between Grendel and Argent leaves both dead. Spar passes on her writings on Grendel, this time to her boyfriend, Brian Li Sung.

The next story line, covered in *The Devil Inside*, traces Brian's transformation into Grendel. Disgusted by New York City, taunted by a Kabuki mask hanging in the theater where he works, and drowning in his own anger, Brian finds himself drawn to the cool and decisive violence of Grendel. He puts on a homemade mask and becomes the killer. Brian soon recognizes that he cannot separate himself from Grendel, so he goes after Captain Wiggins, sacrificing his own life to rid the world of Grendel.

Issues 16 through 23 represent a period of development in which the author explores the Grendel concept to see where the idea could go. These issues largely follow Captain Wiggins, listen to his stories of Hunter Rose, and chronicle his breakdown, in which he kills his wife.

The Grendel series fast-forwards to the year 2530 in *God and the Devil* to a world in which religion is essential and where the Catholic Church exerts incredible social and political power over a number of corporate "systems." The church is led by Pope Innocent

XLII, really the vampire Tujiro XIV, who is building an elaborate, Babel-like tower at the new Vatican Ouest in Colorado while the large majority of citizens live in poverty. With the police force working for the Vatican and fear of a second Inquisition silencing dissenters, stopping Innocent is up to Orion Assante, a rich, upper-class citizen, and to the newest Grendel, a drug addict named Eppy Thatcher. While Assante works to uncover Innocent's true intentions concerning the tower, Grendel subverts the sanctity of church occasions with his madcap pranks. In a subplot, Innocent turns Pellon Cross, the head of the police force, into a vampire; Cross escapes, creating an outbreak of vampirism. Assante discovers that the tower hides a weapon that can blow up the sun. His private army, Grendel, and the vampire hoards descend on the Vatican, where Assante blows the tower up before the "sun-gun" can be detonated.

Devil's Reign takes place immediately following *God and the Devil*. In this story arc, the Church has collapsed and, with it, the rest of America's systems. Spurred by the culpability he feels for America's condition, Assante uses his wealth and resources to unite the systems and, eventually, to merge the country with Australia and South and Central America, creating UNOW. Threatened by the growing superpower, the Japanese kidnap Assante's longtime political partner and lover, Sherri Caniff.

Certain that the African government is responsible, Assante moves to attack that country and, eventually, world war breaks out. Long nicknamed "Grendel" himself, Assante is certain that he is possessed by the devil and seeks out Eppy Thatcher to learn the secret of his survival. During sessions with the crazed Thatcher, Assante recognizes that the solution to this world war is to use Innocent's sun-gun technology to create a weapon more powerful than one created with nuclear technology. The sun disk is made and used against Japan, and the entire world surrenders to UNOW. The world enters an imperial age, with Assante as its leader. His final undertaking is to produce an heir, a plan that leads him to marry Laurel Kennedy and impregnate himself when she is unable to bear children. Jupiter Niklos is born and remains hidden away from the political arena after his father's death.

In a continuation of the *God and the Devil* subplot, vampires have been isolated in Caesars Palace, in Las Vegas. There, they go underground; Cross plans the rise of a vampire race and spreads the word through his "gospel."

War Child tells the story of Grendel-Prime kidnapping Jupiter Assante. After Orion dies, his power-hungry and unstable wife takes control of the government. Unbeknownst to her, her husband had built a cyborg and charged him with the protection of his son. Grendel-Prime sequesters Jupiter in the wilderness, carrying him safely past radioactive zombies, pirates, biker gangs, and First One and his vampire followers, until Jupiter returns to claim his rightful position.

Volumes

- *Grendel Archives* (2007). Collects *Primer*, issue 2, and *Grendel*, issues 1-3. Concentrates on the story of Spar, in which she assumes the role of Grendel to save her son from Tujiro, a Kabuki vampire.
- *Grendel: Devil by the Deed* (1986). Collects the backup stories from *Mage*, which chronicle the life of Hunter Rose and his assumption of the Grendel persona. The volume uses long prose passages instead of thought or speech balloons, introducing the novelistic narrative style used occasionally in the series.
- *Grendel: Devil's Legacy* (1988). Collects issues 1-12. Spar takes up the Grendel costume and fork. Introduces Grendel as a malicious force that can inhabit different individuals.
- *Grendel: The Devil Inside* (1999). Collects issues 13-15. Brian Li Sung is Grendel, who had been Spar's lover. He attempts to murder Wiggins but is eventually shot by him.
- *Grendel: Devil Tales* (1999). Collects issues 16-19. Captain Wiggins tells of Grendel, relaying, among other tales, the story of Hunter Rose.
- *Grendel: God and the Devil* (2008). Collects issues 24-33. This is the first volume not to focus entirely on the Grendel character. It connects Grendel overtly to the devil, as Thatcher uses the identity to oppose the twenty-sixth century Catholic Church.

- *Grendel: Devil's Reign* (2009). Collects issues 34-40. The Grendel mask is known throughout the world. This volume returns to long prose passages to make the story of Assante's rise to power read like a history. This history is interspersed with more traditional comic spreads that recount the history of the underground vampire contingent.
- *Grendel: War Child* (1993). Collects issues 41-50. Features the cyborg Grendel-Prime, who kidnaps Assante's son, Jupiter.

Characters

- *Hunter Rose*, the protagonist of *Devil by the Deed*, is a genius novelist and New York City crime lord whom Grendel first inhabits. He is young and debonair, part of the high-society party crowd, and has dark hair streaked by Grendel's signature white shock at his right temple. He is apparently without human feeling, except for his attachment to Palambo, an orphan he adopts.
- *Argent* plays the antagonist to Grendel in both *Devil by the Deed* and *Devil's Legacy*. He is an anthropomorphic wolf, more than three hundred years old, and has long ears and gray skin. Once an Algonquin Indian, Argent was cursed. A secondary result of the curse is Argent's great hunger for violence. Rejected by society, he has channeled his rage into fighting criminals. His brutality and appearance are found repulsive by many characters.
- *Christine Spar* is the second embodiment of Grendel. The single mother is successful, athletic, and fiercely protective of her son and her friends. She purposefully chooses the darkness of Grendel in order to protect the ones she loves.
- *Tujiro XIV* is a vampire Kabuki dancer who kidnaps and kills Anson Spar. He is a chilling figure, with perfectly smooth white skin and empty, mesmerizing eyes and a penchant for preserving an eyeball from each of his victims. In *God and the Devil*, he reappears as Pope Innocent XLII, the leader of the Catholic Church, who plans to blow up the sun.

- *Brian Li Sung* is Spar's boyfriend and the third person to embody the Grendel mask. Brian is a quiet, gentle, and handsome stage manager who has a relationship with Spar. Disgusted with his own emotional weakness and anger, he succumbs easily to the violent spirit of Grendel, but he has the moral fortitude to reject that violence at the end.

- *Captain Wiggins* is the detective who works with Argent in *Devil's Legacy* and who chases Brian in *The Devil Inside*. He is blond and trendy, and one of his eyes has been replaced by a fake eye with lie-detector capabilities.

- *Orion Assante* is a wealthy member of the upper class who opposes Innocent XLII. With a square jaw, broad shoulders, and eloquent speaking ability, he is a commanding presence. With his great resources and single-minded determination to overthrow the Church's power, he makes a clear choice for national leader after the fall of the Church.

- *Eppy Thatcher* is a factory worker who is certain God hates him. The son of deeply religious and abusive parents, he has given up on religion. Thatcher is thin and has wild gray hair and the dark sunken eyes of a drug addict. He powers his delusions, in which the devil uses him to defeat God, with the drug named "Grendel." Under the influence of this drug, he is quick and strong and his speech is laced with puns.

- *Pellon Cross* is the leader of the police force hired by Pope Innocent XLII to kill Grendel. Cross is a daredevil and has a flying motorcycle, a ubiquitous cigarette, and a steel plate covering half of his head. After he is turned into a vampire, he is called "First One" and becomes a messiah figure for vampires. He is able to bleed, unlike most vampires, and his blood lust is insatiable.

Grendel. (Courtesy of Dark Horse Comics)

- *Grendel-Prime* is the cyborg warrior responsible for protecting Jupiter Assante. Once a human member of Assante's army, he was turned into a cyborg for the protection of Jupiter. His black body armor, inhuman strength, and devotion to duty make him the most superhero-like of all the Grendels.

Artistic Style

Given *Grendel*'s long publication history, the series has used multiple artists with diverse artistic styles. The Hunter Rose stories are both written and penciled by Wagner; while the black-and-white incubation issues are rudimentary, by the publication of *Devil by the Deed*, the signature art of the Hunter Rose stories was introduced. The art of these stories is heavy with elements of design, and the pages are covered with bold, elegant Art Deco shapes and lines. Though the art was originally colored in an orange and purple palette and recolored by Bernie Mireault in 1993, a red, white, and black palette has become the standard for all the Hunter Rose stories, emphasizing the crime-noir atmosphere, past-tense narration, and graphic design elements.

Though Wagner remained the writer of each generation in Grendel's history, he frequently invited other artists to reimagine the world, writing his stories to the strengths of each artist, the result of which is the subtly different mood of each Grendel. Arnold and Jacob Pander's New York is high style with pop-art lines and colors that match Spar's fashionable career and shameless acceptance of Grendel.

When Mireault took over illustration with the Brian Li Sung story arc, Grendel's story became one of psychological panic. Empty background spaces in *The Devil Inside* are highly patterned, and the lines are short and interrupted, creating a frenzied atmosphere. The collaborative team of John K. Snyder, III, Jay Geldhof, and Mireault emphasize the grandiosity and excesses of the Church in *God and the Devil* with airy, page-high panels and bird's-eye views.

In the Orion Assante story line of *Devil's Reign*, Tim Sale uses muted colors, captioned panels, and simple backgrounds to illustrate a historical narrative that keeps readers at arm's length. However, rich colors, page-high panels, and speech balloons in the vampire story line invite the reader into the world's crumbling decadence. Patrick McEown's illustrations contain fewer full-page designs and more traditional panel flow than some other *Grendel* volumes, which complements beautifully Wagner's claim that he wanted to return to adventure comics with *War Child*.

Text is also an important element of *Grendel*'s art. In particular, *Devil by the Deed* and sections of *Devil's Reign* are written almost entirely without speech balloons. Instead, a third-person narrative unfolds in lengthy passages of text. The art of the two volumes is snapshotlike, and the combination of art and text lends historical significance and mythic status to these *Grendel* stories.

Themes

The blurred line between good and evil is the central theme of the *Grendel* stories. Though Grendel is the protagonist of his own story, he is not the hero, nor are his antagonists always villains. For example, Argent is brutal and hideous, but he works to bring criminals to justice. The supervillain of the *Grendel* comics is utterly evil, and yet attractive, whether that attraction lies in his stylish life and his freedom from conscience or in Spar's honorable intentions. Even when Wagner moved away from the "Grendel-inhabits-next-person" formula and focused on Grendel as a study of society, the moral ambiguity in "good" characters, such as Assante, is still evident; readers still find pleasure in "degenerate" characters, such as Thatcher, and power still corrupts, no matter its end. *Grendel* refuses to provide the typical superhero/supervillain dichotomy.

While the formula of Grendel possessing an individual makes the earlier stories expressive of individual struggle, a shift to commentary on religion and government in later volumes cannot be ignored. Absolute institutions such as Vatican Ouest's megachurch or Assante's regime often ignore the very individuals they claim to serve and reject those that fit outside the system. *Grendel* offers little escape from these institutions, as one gives rise to the next, despite the actions of various individuals. Readers are often asked, through the rhetorical questions of characters, to consider their own culpability in supporting these systems.

Impact

Wagner's many influences include specific titles such as John Gardner's *Grendel* (1971) and Michael Moorcock's *Elric* stories (1972-1984), but equally influential to his work was the exciting atmosphere of the comics industry during the 1980's. When *Grendel* first appeared, the rebel movement toward independent publishing gave birth to independent publishing companies such as Comico. Though Wagner has worked with DC, Grendel has remained independent and is one of the longest-lived characters not owned by DC or Marvel.

Like many artists at the beginning of the Modern Age of comics, Wagner looked to break away from the conventions of comics at the time, and one significant break is *Grendel*'s experimental use of text. The comic's history includes text that is narrative, some that is interior monologue, some that is speech, and some that is caption. The experimentation with text seen during the 1980's led the way for the multilayered narratives of comic memoirs such as Alison Bechdel's *Fun Home* (2006) or Marjane Satrapi's *Persepolis* (2000), and *Grendel* took full part in this experimentation.

Anna Lohmeyer

Further Reading

Bachalo, Chris, and Joe Kelly. *Steampunk: Manimatron* (2001).

Loeb, Jeph, and Tim Sale. *Batman: The Long Halloween* (1996-1997).

Moore, Alan. *Watchmen* (1986-1987).

Wagner, Matt. *Mage* (1984-1997).

Bibliography

Farrell, Jennifer Kelso. "The Evil Behind the Mask: Grendel's Pop Culture Evolution." *Journal of Popular Culture* 41, no. 6 (December, 2008): 934-939.

Pinkham, Jeremy. "Matt Wagner: The Devil and the Need." *The Comics Journal* 165 (January, 1994): 46-72.

Wagner, Matt, and Diana Schultz, ed. *The Art of Matt Wagner's "Grendel."* Milwaukie, Ore.: Dark Horse Books, 2007.

See also: *Batman: The Long Halloween; Watchmen; Mage*

GROO THE WANDERER

Author: Aragonés, Sergio; Evanier, Mark
Artist: Sergio Aragonés (illustrator); Gordon Kent (colorist); Tom Luth (colorist); Stan Sakai (letterer)
Publisher: Dark Horse Comics; Eclipse Comics; Image Comics; Marvel Comics; Pacific Comics
First serial publication: 1982-1984
First book publication: 1984

Publication History

Prior to the publication of *Groo the Wanderer*, Sergio Aragonés was already well known as a contributor to *MAD* magazine, particularly for his famous doodle-like margin drawings, or "marginals," packed onto the pages of every issue. He first devised the character of Groo, a parody of barbarian adventurers such as Robert E. Howard's Conan, in the 1970's during a surge in sword-and-sorcery storytelling in comics. However, he had no intention of giving up his creation to any publisher that would not allow him to retain ownership. When Eclipse Comics assembled a benefit anthology comic to raise money for Steve Gerber, who was embroiled in a legal battle with Marvel Comics over the ownership of his character Howard the Duck, Aragonés contributed a short Groo story and the barbarian at last saw print.

The benefit comic, *Destroyer Duck*, issue 1, was released in 1982, and Groo quickly made a second appearance as a back-up feature in Pacific Comics' *Starslayer*, issue 5, a few months later. Pacific then published the first ongoing *Groo the Wanderer* series, although it only lasted for eight issues. During this time, Aragonés served as plotter and illustrator, Mark Evanier as scriptwriter, Stan Sakai as letterer, and Gordon Kent as colorist. Kent then departed, and Tom Luth took his place, completing the *Groo* creative team that would remain intact as of 2011.

One additional special featuring Groo was planned for Pacific but was published by Eclipse when the former publisher went out of business. Next, Aragonés arranged for a *Groo* series to be published by Marvel Comics' Epic imprint. Groo embarked on his most extensive journey with one publisher, spanning 120

(WireImage)

Sergio Aragonés

One of the most prolific cartoonists of all time, Sergio Aragonés began creating "marginals" in the gutters of *Mad Magazine* in 1963. His style is simplistic and manic: easily understood wordless gags are presented with the boundless enthusiasm of a cartoonist who is able to create memorable images quickly and easily. In 1982 he launched, with writer Mark Evanier, *Groo the Wanderer* at Pacific Comics. A parody of popular sword and sorcery heroes featuring an oblivious but highly skilled fighter, *Groo* became one of the longest running humor comic book series in American history. Aragonés's pages are packed with visual material and sight gags, giving the work an air of barely controlled chaos that inevitably explodes into a cataclysm of cartoon mayhem by the end of the story.

issues, and settled into the idiotic persona typically associated with the character.

Aragonés next moved the series to Image Comics, which published twelve more issues beginning in 1994. Dark Horse Comics has published the Groo stories since 1998. However, rather than publish an ongoing series, Dark Horse has offered periodic miniseries and reprints of past Groo adventures.

Plot

Groo the Wanderer is not strictly a continuous linear narrative; rather, it is an anthological collection of adventures in which Groo visits countless towns and lands that vaguely resemble those from the medieval period, meets myriad characters, and repeatedly causes chaos only to withdraw, leaving destruction in his wake. The series also contains fantasy elements, such as dragons and other odd creatures as well as characters with magical powers and artifacts. In early appearances, Groo is portrayed as a slightly buffoonish parody of the Conan archetype but is smarter than in his later portrayals. In the comics of the mid-1980's, however, he becomes the complete moron with which many readers are familiar.

Although Groo stories are usually self-contained within a single issue or graphic novel, there are some multipart adventures; in their later incarnations, Groo stories consist of four-part miniseries with continuing story lines. Aragonés and his team use the repetitive nature of Groo's escapades to build a series of running gags about cheese dip, "mulching," and Groo's various misconceptions. They also thread recurring lines of dialogue such as "Did I err?" and "I can plainly see that!" throughout the series. Some such running jokes are unique to the Marvel Comics run, but many of them stretch as far back as Groo's earliest adventures. Every story also comments in some way on various aspects of the real world, from simple statements about friendship or family to more sweeping allegorical tales about charged sociopolitical issues.

In Groo's first two appearances, he manages to bungle the traditional heroic activities of saving a maiden from a dragon and slaying a monster for a desperate village. His heroics do not improve in his subsequent travels. Through all of his adventures, and despite his singular lack of intelligence, Groo perseveres simply by doing "what Groo does best."

Volumes

- *The Death of Groo* (1987). A graphic novel. Reports of Groo's death are greatly exaggerated, and Groo gets to overhear what others think of him when they believe he has finally departed.
- *The Groo Chronicles* (1990). Collects all of the Eclipse and Pacific Groo adventures as well as two Marvel tales. Groo goes on various ill-fated adventures.
- *The Groo Adventurer* (1990). Collects issues 1-4 of the Marvel series. The Minstrel begins to chronicle Groo's adventures through intricately crafted songs.
- *The Groo Bazaar* (1991). Collects issues 5-8 of the Marvel series. Groo confronts the issue of slavery in one of his many allegorical adventures.
- *The Groo Carnival* (1992). Collects issues 9-12 of the Marvel series. Groo first encounters Arcadio, the living legend who is his dashing but devious opposite.
- *The Groo Dynasty* (1992). Collects issues 13-16 of the Marvel series. Groo manages to ruin the Sage's short-lived reign as king.
- *The Life of Groo* (1993). A graphic novel. Groo's formative years are explored.
- *The Groo Exposé* (1993). Collects issues 17-20 of the Marvel series. Groo's sister, Grooella, enlists his incompetent aid against an oncoming siege.
- *The Groo Festival* (1993). Collects issues 21-24 of the Marvel series. Groo deals with two devilish duos, the witches Arba and Dakarba and two con artists named Pal and Drumm.
- *The Groo Garden* (1993). Collects issues 25-28 of the Marvel series. Groo first encounters a magic amulet that will cause him future trouble.
- *Groo: The Most Intelligent Man in the World* (1998). Collects issues 1-4 of the eponymous Dark Horse miniseries. Groo's associates are startled when the least intelligent man they know begins to speak intelligently.

- *The Groo Houndbook* (1999). Collects issues 29-32 of the Marvel series. A dog named Rufferto runs away from palace life and becomes Groo's devoted companion in adventure.
- *The Groo Inferno* (1999). Collects issues 33-36 of the Marvel series. Groo obtains magical powers from the aforementioned amulet, and mayhem ensues.
- *The Groo Jamboree* (2000). Collects issues 37-40 of the Marvel series. In a two-part story, Groo mistakenly believes that he has accidentally eaten Rufferto.
- *The Groo Kingdom* (2000). Collects issues 41-43 and 46 of the Marvel series. Groo gets married and has to deal with his gypsy grandmother.
- *Groo and Rufferto* (2000). Collects issues 1-4 of the eponymous Dark Horse miniseries. The loyal companions are separated after an encounter with a wizard and struggle to reunite.
- *The Groo Library* (2001). Collects issues 44, 45, 47, and 49 of the Marvel series. The psyche of Groo's canine companion is explored in the story "Rufferto Reverie."
- *The Groo Odyssey* (2001). Collects issues 57-60 of the Marvel series. One of the most celebrated stories in the history of the title, "One Fine Day," features a Groo-less adventure.
- *Groo: Death and Taxes* (2002). Collects issues 1-4 of the eponymous Dark Horse miniseries. Groo is the hapless pawn of a warmongering machine in a sharp satirical commentary on modern media-driven warfare.
- *The Groo Maiden* (2002). Collects issues 50-53 of the Marvel series. Groo finds himself falling hopelessly in love with a statuesque and lethal warrior woman known as Chakaal.
- *Groo: Mightier than the Sword* (2002). Collects issues 1-4 of the eponymous Dark Horse miniseries. Pipil Khan charges his sons to annihilate Groo for their right to inherit his throne.
- *The Groo Nursery* (2002). Collects issues 48 and 54-56 of the Marvel series. Among other misadventures, Groo sinks entire fleets of warships while destroying an idyllic tropical island.
- *Groo: Hell on Earth* (2009). Collects issues 1-4 of the eponymous Dark Horse miniseries. Groo inadvertently spreads pollution and devastation in a story that explores topics such as political incompetence and global warming.
- *Groo: The Hogs of Horder* (2010). Collects issues 1-4 of the eponymous Dark Horse miniseries. The story tackles the worldwide financial collapse and tension in the Middle East as Groo faces the avaricious King Hordes.

Characters

- *Groo*, the protagonist, is a squat barbarian adventurer with long, stringy brown hair and a prominent, crooked nose. He carries two *katana* swords and uses them with exceptional skill. Although he is an amazing warrior, he is also incredibly stupid and incapable of understanding just about everything. He has an uncanny ability to sink ships, and his very presence is considered a good reason to flee, for chaos follows in his wake. Despite this, he is honest and possesses a good heart, a desire to work, a love of cheese dip, and a willingness to enter any situation without an ounce of thought.
- *Rufferto* is Groo's loyal dog. He is orange with black spots. He abandoned a life of privilege as a royal pet to see the world. Although Groo first thinks of Rufferto more as food than as a friend, the two quickly bond. He admires Groo unreservedly and believes him to be an unparalleled genius. When Rufferto is with him, strangely enough, Groo can board a ship and not sink it.
- *The Sage* is a pleasant and wise old man with a long white beard and hair tied into a topknot. He has a dog named Mulch, whose name is a long-running gag during *Groo*'s Marvel/Epic years. He is a lifelong friend of Groo and always tries to guide the foolish hero with his insight.
- *Taranto* is a scheming military leader and criminal who has frequently found his hopes for victory dashed by the intervention of Groo. Although he is a sworn enemy of the barbarian and wants Groo dead, Groo himself is often confused about

whether Taranto is actually his friend. Taranto takes advantage of this as often as possible.

- *Captain Ahax* is a seafarer who long ago learned of Groo's ability to sink every ship he boards. Ahax has lost many ships to the barbarian's distinctive ability, and over the years, he has also lost his sanity. He continues to build new vessels only to encounter Groo again.

- *Chakaal* is a statuesque, platinum-haired female warrior with a serious aversion to Groo. Despite her dislike for Groo's romantic attentions, the two adventurers often find themselves working together, although Chakaal is then required to compensate for Groo's utter stupidity.

- *The Minstrel* is a traveling bard and storyteller who wears a jester's hat and carries a stringed instrument that resembles a banjo. He chronicles many of Groo's adventures. He only communicates in rhyme, and since his tales are accurate retellings of Groo's inept escapades, the hero is not too pleased with the Minstrel's work.

- *Arcadio* is a renowned warrior with long, flowing blond hair and a huge chin. He is everything that Groo is not: handsome, respected, a living legend, and dishonest. Many of his supposed achievements have actually been built upon the work of his frequent, unwitting lackey, Groo.

- *Grooella* is Groo's long-suffering sister and is identical to her brother except for a huge mane of frizzy dark hair. Groo caused her hair to transform from its original blond color when they were children. She is a queen and often must rely on her brother, even though she hates him.

- *Granny Groo* is Groo's underhanded, money-hungry gypsy grandmother. She has white hair styled in a bun, large golden earrings, and the Groo family nose. Like most of the other characters, she tries to take advantage of Groo for her own benefit and gets caught up in his predictable cloud of chaos.

- *Arba* and *Dakarba* are two witches. Arba is short and fat with traditional witch features and clothing, while Dakarba is tall, attractive, and well-built and wears a revealing gown and a winged headdress. They constantly try to use

Groo in their schemes only to have everything backfire.

Artistic Style

Aragonés honed his distinctive style with countless "marginals" in the pages of *MAD* magazine. His free-flowing, melodic, hyperdetailed line work is simultaneously chaotic and orderly. Every character, panel, and page is a mass of dense curves that look as random as doodles yet instantly form their own reality, depicting people, vast landscapes, castles, ships at sea, and an endless array of sight gags.

Aragonés's style is informed by his early experience with pantomime, which may also explain how easily his artwork transcends the language barrier with or without the addition of Evanier's English scripting. *Groo the Wanderer* also benefits from a close collaboration between Aragonés, Evanier, Sakai, and Luth. The final version of the artwork is only completed after Evanier has reshaped the plot, often in a back-and-forth process with Aragonés, after which Sakai letters the pages and Aragonés finishes the art. The last step in creating a Groo story is the addition of color by Luth, which not only adds another layer of rich detail to an already meticulous piece of work but also poses a creative challenge for Luth, given Aragonés's penchant for packing pages with numerous characters and objects. Capturing the breathless action and joy of the medium with pen and ink, Aragonés may have one of the most recognizable and respected styles in the world of comics, and *Groo the Wanderer* represents the most extensive chronicle of his work in print.

Themes

It would be easy to dismiss a long-running series such as *Groo the Wanderer* as merely a platform for fantasy genre humor, sight gags, and bumbling slapstick, but as readers of the series know, the creative team behind the barbarian uses the strip to tell many meaningful stories that resonate with real-world issues. In some of the stories published by Dark Horse Comics, for example, the creators deliberately target the world financial collapse, American foreign policy, climate change, and many other hot-button issues of the day through allegorical tales that put Groo in the center of the controversies and examine them through a comedic lens.

At the beginning of the series, Groo is a relatively intelligent character capable of tactical planning, not necessarily the blank slate upon which many of these morality tales could be played. In the series' Marvel Comics run, however, Groo becomes a childlike figure perfectly suited for placing in the midst of a medieval world gone mad. His purity clashes instantly with the corruption that surrounds him, coming even from those within his own family, and yet his very innocence enables him to walk away triumphant, or at least alive. While accessible for readers of all ages, *Groo the Wanderer* is a surprisingly mature and biting satire of the real world, using whimsical characters and settings to cloak serious commentary about all kinds of social, cultural, and political subjects.

Impact

The character of Groo has resonated through pop culture, with references turning up in the television series *Angel* (1999-2004) and elsewhere, but its greatest impact has been within the comics industry. Refusing to relinquish ownership of his creation to any publisher, Aragonés helped to forge a new path in the 1980's by producing a creator-owned comic book that also proved to be a long-term critical success. At that time, independent publishers offered comics creators the chance to own their material; in the years to come, even the biggest publishers experimented with creator-owned imprints, such as Epic, *Groo*'s future home at Marvel Comics.

Although *Groo* was successful in and of itself, it had to survive a succession of publisher failures that seemed to follow the title from one company to another in a disturbing echo of the character's fictional ability to cause chaos wherever he went. This became such an obvious trend that the phrase "Groo's curse" was coined by industry insiders. However, as of 2011, this "curse" has not affected the series' latest publisher, Dark Horse Comics.

Groo the Wanderer also became known for directly engaging with its fans in a dynamic way through its energetic letters page, personally handled by Evanier. Many of the series' running gags were discussed or even perpetuated there, including the recurring definition of the word "mulch."

Arnold T. Blumberg

Further Reading

Aragonés, Sergio. *Sergio Aragonés: Five Decades of His Finest Works* (2010).

Aragonés, Sergio, and Mark Evanier. *Boogeyman* (1999).

Sakai, Stan. *Usagi Yojimbo* (1987-   ).

Bibliography

Aragonés, Sergio. *Sergio Aragonés: Five Decades of His Finest Works*. New York: Running Press, 2010.

Evanier, Mark. *Comic Books and Other Necessities of Life*. Raleigh, N.C.: TwoMorrows, 2002.

Thomas, Roy. *Conan: The Ultimate Guide to the World's Most Savage Barbarian*. New York: Dorling Kindersley, 2006.

See also: *Conan; Cerebus; Bloodstar*

H

HELLBLAZER

Author: Azzarello, Brian; Carey, Mike; Delano, Jamie; Diggle, Andy; Ellis, Warren; Ennis, Garth; Foreman, Dick; Milligan, Peter; Mina, Denise; Morrison, Grant

Artist: Alfredo Alcala (illustrator); John Ridgway (illustrator); Javier Pulido (penciller); Charlie Adlard (penciller and inker); Simon Bisley (penciller and inker); Chris Brunner (penciller and inker); Mark Buckingham (penciller and inker); Giuseppe Camuncoli (penciller and inker); Richard Corben (penciller and inker); Cristiano Cucina (penciller and inker); Guy Davis (penciller and inker); Al Davison (penciller and inker); Steve Dillon (penciller and inker); Gary Erskine (penciller and inker); Marcelo Frusin (penciller and inker); Doug Alexander Gregory (penciller and inker); John Higgins (penciller and inker); Mike Hoffman (penciller and inker); Frazer Irving (penciller and inker); Jock (penciller and inker); Stefano Landini (penciller and inker); John Paul Leon (penciller and inker); Sean Murphy (penciller and inker); Warren Pleece (penciller and inker); Steve Pugh (penciller and inker); Richard Piers Rayner (penciller and inker); James Romberger (penciller and inker); Peter Snejbjerg (penciller and inker); Goran Sudzuka (penciller and inker); Frank Teran (penciller and inker); Ron Tiner (penciller and inker); Danijel Zezelj (penciller and inker); William Simpson (penciller, inker, and colorist); Lee Bermejo (penciller, inker, and cover artist); Leonardo Manco (penciller, inker, and cover artist); Sean Phillips (penciller, inker, and cover artist); Tim Bradstreet (penciller, inker, colorist, and cover artist); David Lloyd (penciller, inker, colorist, and cover artist); Dave McKean (penciller, inker, colorist, and cover artist); Rodney Ramos (inker); Lovern Kinderzierski (colorist); Annie Halfacree (letterer); Todd Klein (letterer); John Constanza (letterer); Tom Canty (cover artist); John Eder (cover artist); Glenn Fabry (cover artist); Greg Lauren (cover artist); Dave McKean (cover artist); Kent Williams (cover artist)

Publisher: DC Comics
First serial publication: 1988-
First book publication: 1997-2010

Jamie Delano

One of the important figures of the British comics invasion of the late-1980's, Jamie Delano is best known as the first writer on *Hellblazer*, and later had a well-regarded run on *Animal Man*, as well as many other short works. Delano's run on *Hellblazer* established the canonical elements of that series and its hero, John Constantine—a character originally created by Alan Moore in *Swamp Thing*. Delano set Constantine's adventures in a very identifiable London, downplaying the magical element of the character in favor of a downbeat character portrait. Delano's writing is notable for its dark, often horrific, themes and cynical outlook. He tends to blend genres, like science fiction and horror, and invokes mystical elements in much of his work. His 1995 miniseries *Ghostdancing*, with Richard Case, highlighted his particular interests in psychedelia and intricate conspiracies.

Publication History

John Constantine, the main character in *Hellblazer*, first appeared as a character in Alan Moore's *Swamp Thing*, issue 37, and was given his own series in 1988. As of 2011, the series was published by DC Comics under the Vertigo imprint. Until *Hellblazer*, issue 63, the series was published by DC, with a "Suggested for Mature Readers" stamp.

Jamie Delano was given the first run of the new *Hellblazer* series, producing the basic mythology and the first three trade paperbacks, contributing to the fourth and fifth trade paperbacks, and returning for *Hellblazer: Pandemonium* (2010). After Delano's initial run, Garth Ennis took on the character for the following seven trade paperbacks, a total of ninety-three issues. Ennis's run is widely credited with solidifying his place among the top tier of comics writers and was marked by many developments in Constantine's origins and character. Warren Ellis took on the series after Ennis, producing two trade paperbacks before Brian Azzarello took over the series. Azzarello's work was criticized by many fans, as the run took place mostly in the United States and also depicted Constantine in a homosexual relationship.

Mike Carey was drafted for Constantine's return to England and produced the following six trade paperbacks. He was lauded for restoring the continuity of the character. *Hellblazer*'s first female writer, Denise Mina, wrote two trade paperbacks that were fairly well received, followed by Andy Diggle's three trade paperbacks, which focused on the broader mythology of the character. Peter Milligan followed Diggle, with three trade paperbacks that foreground a love story.

Plot

Constantine was originally developed by Moore as a character for *Swamp Thing* and was eventually made the protagonist of the *Hellblazer* series, which has been wholly devoted to Constantine's adventures since it began in 1987. The first serial, *Hellblazer: Original Sins*, is composed of several interconnected story arcs that congeal into a single narrative. It references the economic and cultural climate of 1980's Great Britain, when Margaret Thatcher was the prime minister of the nation and the Conservative Party was in power. Constantine encounters the Resurrection Crusaders and the Damnation Army and must figure out how to defeat both fanatical organizations.

The Devil You Know depicts the Newcastle incident, which recurs in the series periodically. At Newcastle, a young Constantine and his friends summon a demon in order to battle the monster that has been formed by a young girl's fear (she was molested). In the process,

Constantine's friends are killed, the girl is sucked into Hell, and Constantine himself winds up in an insane asylum.

The Fear Machine portrays Constantine as a young man involved in hippie occult rituals. This volume is notable in that it portrays Constantine's development. *Family Man* follows Constantine as he tries to track down a serial killer.

Rare Cuts collects several issues, including early issues that had remained uncollected until the 2005 publication. It primarily concerns filling out story arcs that deal with Constantine's ethically ambiguous behavior.

The collection *Dangerous Habits* is Ennis's first take on the character and is one of the most popular collections of *Hellblazer*. It deals with Constantine's illness from lung cancer as he attempts to trick the devil to save both humanity and himself.

Bloodlines follows several story arcs, one of which deals with a member of the royal family being possessed by the same spirit that formerly possessed Jack the Ripper. Another story arc concerns the mating of a demon and an angel, which has tragic results. The story arc also introduces Kit Ryan, Constantine's long-term girlfriend. Of the many women depicted in the series, Kit is the one he cares for the most.

Fear and Loathing continues the Kit story line and also follows Constantine as he blackmails the archangel Gabriel and attempts to keep Gemma, Constantine's niece, from dabbling in magic. It also deals with Constantine as an aging character, depicting his fortieth birthday and his meditations on his own mortality.

In *Tainted Love*, Constantine is homeless and seems to have completely given up hope following his breakup with Kit. This collection focuses primarily on other characters, both major and minor.

Damnation's Flame follows Constantine in New York City. His body is in a homeless shelter, while his soul wanders a purgatorial United States with the spirit of John F. Kennedy, exploring American myths. Three other story arcs are included, one concerning Constantine's first meeting with Kit, another concerning politics in Dublin, and the final discussing a case in which Chas, Constantine's closest friend, becomes mixed up in Constantine's work.

Rake at the Gates of Hell depicts Constantine's confrontation with Satan, who is still smarting from his defeat during an earlier battle. In London, Constantine's friends are preparing for a protest that devolves into a race riot. This collection also includes the "Heartland" one-shot, which follows Kit's experiences after returning to Ireland.

Son of Man follows Constantine's attempts to save his friend Chas, who was accidentally involved in the murder of a local gangster whose son Constantine had previously been forced to raise from the dead. Ultimately, Constantine must also stop the son, who became demonic after being brought back to life.

In *Haunted*, Constantine attempts to hunt down the man who murdered his former girlfriend, Isabelle. Prior to killing her, the murderer turned her into the sacred whore Babalon, from the writings of Aleister Crowley.

Setting Sun contains several short-story arcs, including one that shows Constantine attempting to hunt down the box that contains the miscarried child of Satan. *Hard Time* finds Constantine in an American prison for the murder of Lucky, a crime he did not commit. He is serving time because of his guilt over not stopping Lucky's suicide, but he finds that he was also framed for the murder.

In *Good Intentions*, Constantine is in small-town America apologizing to Richie and Dickie for the death of their brother and discovering also that there are some strange sexual practices in the town. Constantine gets Dickie killed, only to be told by Dickie's wife that the town's mine had closed and that they had set up a business in Internet pornography to keep the townspeople alive.

Freezes Over is a short interlude in the story arc that began with *Hard Time* in which Constantine waits out a blizzard in a bar while a killer is on the loose. When a group of thieves disrupts the patrons, while the "Ice Man" killer is lurking about, panic ensues.

Highwater is the conclusion of the story arc that began with *Hard Time* and takes place primarily as a flashback after Constantine has supposedly spontaneously combusted at a sex club. R. W. Manor, an evil character with an origin story reminiscent of Batman's, is revealed to be the man who contracted Lucky to kill himself and to frame Constantine.

Red Sepulchre introduces Angie Spatchcock, a young woman interested in magic who eventually becomes Constantine's girlfriend. Constantine's niece, Gemma, has disappeared, and Constantine finds her with a man who is attempting to find the Red Sepulchre, an object of power.

Black Flowers begins with a story arc in which ancient spirits take over a town. A second story arc follows Constantine and Angie to Iran, where Constantine is attempting to search for information, a quest that leads them to Tasmania in the final story arc, where Constantine's attempt to dream walk with the spirits of the Aborigines goes horribly wrong.

Staring at the Wall depicts Constantine and a number of other magicians who gather to combat the Shadow Dog. The plan goes awry when they find that the Shadow Dog is merely a shadow of a great evil.

Stations of the Cross depicts an amnesiac Constantine who is coerced into producing children with the demoness Rosacarnis. In *Reasons to Be Cheerful*, Constantine battles the demonic children he helped create in *Stations of the Cross*. *The Gift* completes the story arc that began with *Red Sepulchre*.

Empathy is the Enemy follows Constantine as he tries to figure out the source of an overdose of contagious empathy. *The Red Right Hand* continues the story arc of *Empathy is the Enemy*, when the empathy virus spreads, and Constantine must take drastic measures to prevent further deaths.

In *Joyride*, Constantine must prevent further violence in a neighborhood currently housing his sister and her husband.

The Laughing Magician deals with a rival magician from Africa, who senses Constantine. *Roots of Coincidence* explores the problems create by synchronicity in Constantine's life. *Scab* depicts a scandal involving the British Trade Workers' Union, which indirectly produces a growth on Constantine's body, while he is simultaneously attempting to navigate a new relationship.

Hooked involves Constantine's attempts to win back his girlfriend, drawing ill wishers into the love story. *India* depicts Constantine's retreat to India to attempt to cleanse himself and to bring his girlfriend back to life, as well as to save the young women of Dubai, who are being slaughtered by an evil force. *Pandemonium* concerns the British government's coercion of Constantine, forcing him to involve himself in the war in Iraq.

Volumes

- *Hellblazer: Original Sins* (1997). Collects issues 1-9. Introduces Constantine as a character distinct from *Swamp Thing* and critiques the political climate of 1980's Britain.
- *Hellblazer: The Devil You Know* (1997). Collects issues 10-13, *The Hellblazer Annual*, and *The Horrorist*, issues 1-2. Focuses on Constantine's inability to save Astra from a demon, which causes him to have a mental breakdown and to be put in an asylum.
- *Hellblazer: The Fear Machine* (2008). Collects issues 14-22. The Masons plan to resurrect a demon by capturing people's fears. Constantine tries to prevent this from happening.
- *Hellblazer: The Family Man* (2008). Collects issues 23-24 and 28-33. Constantine wrestles with the murder of his father and pursues a serial killer who had once been a cop.
- *Hellblazer: Rare Cuts* (2005). Collects issues 11, 25-26, 35, 56, and 84. Deals with several short-story arcs and one-shots that provide background on Constantine's character.
- *Hellblazer: Dangerous Habits* (1994). Collects issues 41-46. Deals with Constantine's battle with Satan, whom he manages to defeat while battling lung cancer.
- *Hellblazer: Bloodlines* (2007). Collects issues 47-50, 52-55, and 59-61. Contains several story arcs, one of which introduces Kit Ryan, who becomes Constantine's girlfriend.
- *Hellblazer: Fear and Loathing* (1997). Collects issues 62-67. Contains, among other plot lines, Constantine's musing's on his own mortality.
- *Hellblazer: Tainted Love* (1998). Collects issues 68-71, *Hellblazer Special*, and *Vertigo Jam* short story. The focus is on characters other

than Constantine, but the volume does find him homeless and hopeless after his split from Kit.

- *Hellblazer: Damnation's Flame* (1999). Collects issues 72-77. The primary story contained in this volume showcases Constantine's split into corporeal and spiritual parts. His physical body is in a homeless shelter, while his spirit wanders the United States.
- *Hellblazer: Rake at the Gates of Hell* (2003). Collects issues 78-83 and the *Heartland* one-shot. It examines racial tension in the United Kingdom and wraps up Constantine's relationship with Kit.
- *Hellblazer: Son of Man* (2004). Collects issues 129-133. Constantine tries to save his friend Chas from a group of gangsters.
- *Hellblazer: Haunted* (2003). Collects issues 134-139. Constantine pursues the killer of his one-time girlfriend Isabelle.
- *Hellblazer: Setting Sun* (2004). Collects issues 140-143. Constantine looks for Satan's miscarried child.
- *Hellblazer: Hard Time* (2000). Collects issues 146-150. Constantine is in an American prison, where he is serving time for a murder that he did not commit.
- *Hellblazer: Good Intentions* (2002). Collects issues 151-156. Further develops Constantine's character in the United States and examines the way in which good intentions may destroy their supposed beneficiaries.
- *Hellblazer: Freezes Over* (2003). Collects issues 157-163. Constantine kills time in a bar during a blizzard while a killer is on the loose.
- *Hellblazer: Highwater* (2004) Collects issues 164-174. Reveals who hired Lucky to kill himself and frame Constantine.
- *Hellblazer: All His Engines* (2005). A one-shot graphic novel, the story of which centers on a pandemic.
- *Hellblazer: Red Sepulchre* (2005). Collects issues 175-180. Angie Spatchcock is introduced; she becomes Constantine's girlfriend.
- *Hellblazer: Black Flowers* (2005). Collects issues 181-186. Highlights Angie and Constantine's adventures in Iran and Tasmania.

- *Hellblazer: Staring at the Wall* (2006). Collects issues 187-193. Constantine and other magicians fight the Shadow Dog.
- *Hellblazer: Stations of the Cross* (2006). Collects issues 194-200. Constantine has amnesia and is forced into procreating with a demon.
- *Hellblazer: Reasons to Be Cheerful* (2007). Collects issues 201-206. Constantine combats his demonic children.
- *Hellblazer: The Gift* (2007). Collects issues 207-215. Constantine confronts the demon Nergal in Hell.
- *Hellblazer: Empathy Is the Enemy* (2006). Collects issues 216-222. Constantine must help a suicidal man to root out the cause of his empathy, which is causing him so much despair.
- *Hellblazer: The Red Right Hand* (2007). Collects issues 223-228. The sequel to *Empathy is the Enemy*. The empathy epidemic has taken over numerous people, who have subsequently committed suicide.
- *Hellblazer: Joyride* (2008). Collects issues 230-237. Constantine fights to bring to an end the social ills of a housing estate in south London.
- *Hellblazer: The Laughing Magician* (2008). Collects issues 238-242. Concerns a magician from Africa who is a rival of Constantine.
- *Hellblazer: Roots of Coincidence* (2009). Collects issues 243-244 and 247-249. Focuses on Constantine's fight against the forces surrounding him and the synchronicity in his life.
- *Hellblazer: Scab* (2009). Collects issues 251-255 and a portion of 250. Centers on a British Trade Worker's Union scandal.
- *Hellblazer: Hooked* (2010). Collects issues 256-260. Constantine attempts to get his girlfriend back.
- *Hellblazer: India* (2010). Collects issues 261-266. Constantine goes to India to cleanse himself and resurrect his girlfriend.
- *Hellblazer: Pandemonium* (2010). A twenty-fifth anniversary one-shot graphic novel in which Constantine gets involved in the war in Iraq.

Characters

- *John Constantine*, the protagonist, is a blond, white British man who practices magic and is known for being a rake. While he generally means well, he often makes mistakes that get people killed.
- *Chas* has brown hair and is a London cab driver and Constantine's closest friend. He is consistently reliable throughout the series.
- *Papa Midnite* is a Haitian club owner living in New York who is familiar with voodoo and other magical practices.
- *The Ghosts* are a collection of the spirits of Constantine's friends who died at some point in the series because of his carelessness. The group grows over time and appears to Constantine during periods of indecisiveness.
- *Gemma Masters* is Constantine's niece, who is a young girl at the start of the series and later starts dabbling in magic during her teenage years.
- *Cheryl Masters* is Constantine's sister and participates in a number of suspect organizations at the behest of her husband.
- *Tony Masters* is Cheryl's husband and is remarkable only for his ability to get the family into trouble.
- *Nergal* is a demon who appears several times in the series.
- *Kit Ryan* is an artist from Belfast and is Constantine's girlfriend for a significant period in the series. When she leaves him, he is devastated.
- *The First* is initially one of the three devils that rule Hell, but he later destroys the others.
- *"Lucky" Fermin* is the brother of Dickie and Richie. He commits suicide.
- *Frank Turro* is an FBI agent.
- *Dickie Fermin* is one of Constantine's acquaintances and runs the small town in which he lives.
- *Richie Fermin* is the slow brother of Dickie.
- *S. W. Manor* is the rich man who frames Constantine for Lucky's murder.
- *Angie Spatchcock* is interested in magic and is Constantine's girlfriend for a significant period in the series.

- *Mako* is an African magician who attempts to devour the world's magicians in order to gain access to their powers.

Artistic Style

There have been a number of significant artists in the *Hellblazer* series, and each has added significantly to the mythology of the character. The first illustrators, John Ridgway and Alfredo Alcala, utilize both fine and thick lines to create the sensation of movement, lending a sketchy quality to the work. Ridgway and Alcala rely on crosshatch shading, which enhances both the realism of the characters and the horror of the supernatural elements by lending a three-dimensional appearance. Color is significant in their work, as the palette used is almost gaudily bright.

The work of artist John Higgins is cartoony, which contrasts with the bulk of the series. While Higgins's work exaggerates features, artist William Simpson tends to create finer features. Steve Dillon's work is also realistic, reminiscent of adventurer comics, and relies heavily on facial expressions. Dillon's work is generally more concerned with accurate renderings of the face than with depicting a significant amount of scenery.

Marcelo Frusin's work on the Azzarello and Carey runs, by contrast, relies on shadow. Frusin tends to use shadow to enhance supernatural elements and to create panels that draw the reader into their darkness. In addition, Frusin uses block shadows to create a smooth appearance, which is decidedly more stylized than many of the other artists in the series.

There have been a number of other artists with short runs, including Jock, Lee Bermejo, Mike Hoffman, Leonardo Manco, and Chris Brunner, but Ridgway, Alcala, Dillon, and Frusin have contributed the greatest amount to the series. While the latter artists have divergent styles, there are commonalities among their styles, including emphasis on definition of characters through facial expression, rendering of backgrounds that contribute to the mood of the comic and the spatial architecture, and use of varied sizing and multiple panels per page. Ridgway and Alcala contributed to the development of the series and the appearances of the characters, while Dillon made more specific faces

for each character and developed the emotional range of the artwork. Frusin redefined the comic in terms of darkness, significantly enhancing the elements of the horror genre through his work.

Themes

The primary theme of *Hellblazer: Original Sins* is a critique of the greed and capitalism and the simultaneous rise of religious fundamentalism in the West, particularly in Britain during the 1980's. The first two story arcs are primarily concerned with interrogating the extent to which greed and materialism are contagious and the way in which the political climate of a society can physically harm its inhabitants. In the first story arc, individuals are literally eaten alive by their own greed for material objects, a symbol that is set in stark contrast to the enacting demon's origin in Africa, where the hunger is for food. In the second issue, the wealthy are figured as those who exploit both the weaknesses and the naïveté of people within a materialistic social matrix. The third issue ties together the critiques of economic exploitation and religious fanaticism. The decade was marked by an economic boom, but also by growing income disparity and deregulation.

The beginning of the series, in its combination of economic and supernatural concerns, set the tone for the series as a whole. British and Western politics in general play major roles in many story arcs, including some that critique the U.S. prison system, colonialism and Britain's fading power, the problems in Northern Ireland, cultural imperialism, as well as racism, sexism, and many other topics. Generally, whether these critiques are either explicit or implicit in the story arcs, they are enhanced by the illustrations, which often position the reader as the uncomfortable bystander, witnessing horrific events that are all too familiar. In spite of the significant focus on occult phenomena, the series uses these supernatural elements to underpin cultural commentary.

Impact

Hellblazer has had a significant impact on the comics industry as a whole. Its success has spanned more than twenty years, and, as of 2011, it continues to appear in monthlies and its readership grows yearly. Part of its success is apparent in the way it has influenced the formation of the DC Vertigo universe. Story arcs in *Hellblazer* have inspired or influenced story arcs in other comics. In addition, Constantine has appeared occasionally in other series and his presence is referenced in the DC Universe.

John Constantine first appeared in *Swamp Thing*, and the resulting *Hellblazer* series has had lasting effects on series such as *Preacher* (1995-2000) and *The Books of Magic* (1993, book) and has resulted in numerous spin-offs, including *Papa Midnite* (2006). *Preacher* used an altered *Hellblazer* story arc, when a demon and angel mate, as its seed plot. *The Books of Magic* focuses on a young man who has magical capabilities, and in the spin-off series, *Life During Wartime*, Constantine not only appears but also becomes a major player in the plot. In addition, it could be argued that *Hellblazer* has had a broader, lasting effect on the DC Universe, in terms of being among the first titles to be published under the wildly popular Vertigo imprint, which specializes in comics for mature audiences.

Katharine Polak

Films

Constantine. Directed by Francis Lawrence. Warner Bros., 2005. This film adaptation stars Keanu Reeves as John Constantine and Rachel Weisz as his love interest. The film was loosely based on the *Dangerous Habits* story arc and was widely criticized for miscasting Reeves as Constantine and moving the location from Britain to the United States. While there was a graphic novel relating to the film released concurrently with the DVD, the film was so unpopular with fans of the series that it has had little to no effect on future story lines.

Further Reading

Aaron, Jason, and R.M. Guéra. *Scalped* (2007-   ).
Carey, Mike. *Lucifer* (2001-2007).
Ennis, Garth, and Steve Dillon. *Preacher* (1995-2000).

Bibliography

Chute, Hillary, and Marie DeKoven. "Introduction: Graphic Narrative." *Modern Fiction Studies* 52, no. 4 (Winter, 2006).
Groensteen, Thierry. *The System of Comics*. Translated by Bart Beaty and Nick Nyugen. Jackson: University of Mississippi Press, 2007.
McCloud, Scott. *Understanding Comics: The Invisible Art*. New York: Harper, 1994.

See also: *The Books of Magic; Preacher; Lucifer; Swamp Thing*

Hellboy

Author: Mignola, Mike; Byrne, John

Artist: John Cassady (illustrator); Duncan Fegredo (illustrator); Mike Mignola (illustrator); Mark Chiarello (colorist); Matt Hollingsworth (colorist); Dan Jackson (colorist); James Sinclair (colorist); Dave Stewart (colorist); Pat Brousseau (letterer); Clem Robins (letterer); Richard Corben (cover artist)

Publisher: Dark Horse Comics

First serial publication: 1994-

First book publication: 1994-2010

Publication History

Mike Mignola established himself as an artist at DC Comics and Marvel Comics, gaining a reputation for moody, dark illustrations with the Batman book *Gotham by Gaslight* (1989). His creation of the character Hellboy was inspired by a variety of sources, including the works of horror fantasist H. P. Lovecraft. Mignola found humor in matching a large, all-red character fitting the conventional depiction of a devil with the concept of a rough-and-tumble paranormal investigator who approaches dilemmas with a gruff humor and steady resolve.

Hellboy debuted in a black-and-white short in a convention publication for the Comic-Con International: San Diego in August of 1993. A second untitled story (both were referred to as "World's Greatest Paranormal Investigator") was released concurrent with *Seed of Destruction* in the *Comic Buyer's Guide*. Mignola had initially conceived *Hellboy* visually, and after plotting the early stories, he asked veteran comic writer John Byrne to help him script the two untitled shorts as well as the first series, *Seed of Destruction*. After *Seed of Destruction*, however, almost every *Hellboy* story has been written by Mignola. *Seed of Destruction* was published in March, 1994.

Hellboy is not a series character in the conventional sense of appearing in monthly issues. Rather, Mignola has largely told Hellboy's stories in extended arcs as actual graphic novels that span four or more installments as well as in short stories told in one or two issues. Additionally, a number of *Hellboy* works (such as

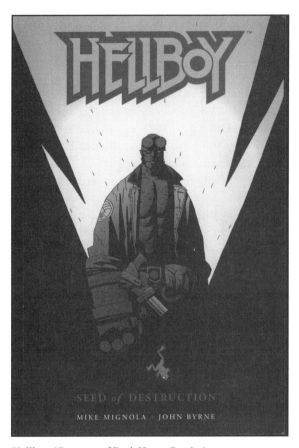

Hellboy. (Courtesy of Dark Horse Comics)

"The Wolves of St. August") were initially serialized in Dark Horse anthologies and specials such as *Dark Horse Presents*. From the start, Dark Horse intended to release trade paperback volumes of the longer stories as well as collations of shorter pieces. Many of the shorter pieces are not in the chronological order of the longer novels but instead take place at different times in Hellboy's career, beginning in the late 1950's.

Plot

The trade paperback collection of *Seed of Destruction* is dedicated to pulp horror writer Lovecraft and comic artist Jack Kirby. Mignola displays both these influences broadly in his work. *Seed of Destruction* is set in 1944, when the occultist monk Grigori Rasputin assembles a coterie of like-minded Nazis (including Ilsa von Haupstein) on a small Scottish isle. Rasputin believes that circumstances are right for him to summon the Lovecraftian Ogdru Jahad (seven elder gods of great evil, imprisoned in another dimension, similar to the evil deities in Lovecraft's Cthulhu stories) and bring about Armageddon on Earth.

At the same time, English paranormal investigator (later the founder of the Bureau of Paranormal Research and Defense, or B.P.R.D.) Trevor Bruttenholm has assembled a team in East Bromwich, England, where the psychic Alice Cavendish has foretold that something momentous is about to occur. Rasputin's Project Ragna Rok, his secret group of Nazi scientists, believes his ritual has not succeeded, because the result of his summoning—a toddler hybrid of demon and human—appears at East Bromwich instead of on their small island.

Hellboy is raised by Bruttenholm and becomes (as billed) the "World's Greatest Paranormal Investigator." Fifty years later, Bruttenholm reappears at the B.P.R.D. after a failed mission and is killed by strange frog monsters. Investigating Bruttenholm's last case, Hellboy, Liz, and Abe travel to Cavendish Hall, where they must contend with Rasputin, who reveals to Hellboy that his purpose is to bring about the end of the world. The three manage to kill Rasputin's physical body, although his spirit returns to task the B.P.R.D.

Hellboy's origins are explained further in the story "The Chained Coffin." Returning to Bromwich, Hellboy is given a vision by spirits and learns how a woman named Sarah Hughes, a witch, had bargained with the demon Azzael, having sexual relations with him to gain power. In death, her soul is forfeited to him, and he comes to claim it. Hellboy is born in Hell from this union before Rasputin summons him to Earth.

Hellboy's stories fall roughly into two categories. Although many stories build upon each other, developing the story of his possible destiny, others are placed at different times in his long career. Those stories that occur out of chronological order are not necessarily stand-alone stories as such because, at times,

characters will often appear in multiple tales, further developing the overarching long plot.

In *Wake the Devil*, the members of Project Ragna Rok bring back to life the undead Vladimir Giurescu. Hellboy and Abe are soon at odds with Giurescu and his supernatural minions. They find that Giurescu is a follower of the witch goddess Hecate. Although Hellboy initially defeats Hecate, the spirit of Rasputin persuades Von Haupstein to sacrifice herself and mingle her essence with Hecate. Hellboy is again informed by both Hecate and Rasputin that he is supposed to be the harbinger of the apocalypse. He again refuses this fate, as he does repeatedly throughout the novels. Later, in the short story "The Right Hand of Doom," he finds that his gigantic, grafted right hand is particularly important in fulfilling this destiny.

In "Box Full of Evil," Hellboy must contend with a powerful goblin, Grugach, whose enmity he earned in an early story, "The Corpse." Grugach allies with an occultist named Igor Bromhead. During his combat with the two, Hellboy is once more informed that he is to be the harbinger of the apocalypse. This foretelling of Hellboy as the eventual avatar of the doom of humankind and civilization is heightened further in "The Third Wish," when a powerful undersea witch, the Bog Roosh, warns him he must die to save the world.

Hellboy's destiny makes a significant turn in *The Wild Hunt*, which delves into Arthurian legend, introducing the sorceress Morgan le Fay. Even as Grugach tries to force Hellboy to assume the role of the destroyer, the hero instead takes up Arthur's famous sword, Excalibur, proving yet again he is a hero, not a monster.

Volumes

- *Hellboy: Seed of Destruction* (1994). Collects *Seed of Destruction*, issues 1-4, as well as "World's Greatest Paranormal Investigator" shorts from Comic-Con International: San Diego and the *Comic Buyer's Guide*. Introduces Hellboy's origin and establishes the nature of the B.P.R.D. and his personality.
- *Hellboy: Wake the Devil* (1997). Collects *Wake the Devil*, issues 1-5. Features the return of the

Nazi supernatural coterie Ragna Rok, as they bring back a vampire.

- *Hellboy: The Chained Coffin and Others* (1998). Collects several shorter pieces, including "The Corpse," "The Baba Yaga," "The Chained Coffin," "The Wolves of St. August," and "Almost Colossus." "The Wolves of St. August" introduces B.P.R.D. agent Kate Corrigan, and "The Chained Coffin" offers further insight into Hellboy's origins. "Almost Colossus" resolves the end of *Wake the Devil* and introduces Roger the homunculus.

- *Hellboy: The Right Hand of Doom* (2000). Collects, among others, short stories "The Right Hand of Doom" and "Box Full of Evil," which focus on the Hellboy's possible destiny as a harbinger of the apocalypse.

- *Hellboy: Conqueror Worm* (2002). Collects issues 1-5 of *Conqueror Worm*. Featuring Hellboy's collaboration with the ghost of World War II-era masked man Lobster Johnson.

- *Hellboy: Strange Places* (2006). Collects *The Third Wish*, issues 1 and 2, and *The Island*, issues 1 and 2. Featuring Hellboy's battles with the Bog Roosh and Hecate.

- *Hellboy: The Troll Witch* (2007). Collects shorts "The Penanggalan," "The Hydra and the Lion," and "The Troll Witch," among others. In the stories, Hellboy travels to Malaysia, Alaska, and Norway.

- *Hellboy: Darkness Calls* (2008). Collects issues 1-6 of *Darkness Calls*. Hellboy finds himself allied with old enemies to bring down Igor Bromhead.

- *Hellboy: The Wild Hunt* (2010). Collects *The*

Hellboy. (Courtesy of Dark Horse Comics)

Wild Hunt, issues 1-8. Features Hellboy's foray into Arthurian and English mythos.

- *Hellboy: The Crooked Man and Others* (2010). Collects *The Crooked Man*, issues 1-3; "They That Go Down to the Sea in Ships"; "In the Chapel of Moloch"; and "The Mole." *The Crooked Man* features Hellboy's intercession in an Appalachian ghost story.
- *Hellboy: Masks and Monsters* (2010). Collects crossovers with characters from other comics groups, including Batman and Starman from *Batman Hellboy Starman*, issues 1-2, and Ghost from *Ghost-Hellboy Special*, issues 1-2.

Characters

- *Hellboy*, the protagonist, is a 6-foot-5-inch-tall, five-hundred-pound red human-and-demon half-breed. Brought to Earth as a toddler, he was raised by the founder of the B.P.R.D. He has dedicated his life to defending the world rather than destroying it. In place of a normal right hand, from the elbow down, a massive and impervious stone hand has been grafted onto his arm. With a blue-collar ethic and a lack of tolerance for sophistry or equivocation, Hellboy succeeds with a blend of perseverance, toughness, humor, and a firm desire to do the right thing.
- *Abe Sapien*, dubbed an "icthyo sapien," is a blue-skinned amphibian, capable of breathing underwater with gills. The B.P.R.D. discovered him in a tank labeled with the same date as Abraham Lincoln's death (thus his first name). An excellent agent, he is intelligent and loyal and has extraordinary aquatic abilities. He is Hellboy's B.P.R.D. comrade and one of his oldest friends.
- *Liz Sherman*, another of Hellboy's closest friends, is a pyrotechnic, able to manifest flame from nothing and project and use it at will. Her control of her powers is tenuous, however; the B.P.R.D. took her in as a teenager after she had inadvertently killed her family. Hellboy clearly is enamored of Liz, yet this affection is understated for most of the series.
- *Kate Corrigan* is another B.P.R.D. agent. In addition to working with the B.P.R.D., she is a

folklore and occultism professor with New York University. After Hellboy urges her to seek more field experience in "The Wolves of St. August," she dedicates more time to being an agent and less to being an academic.

- *Trevor Bruttenholm* is the founder of the B.P.R.D. and Hellboy's foster father. He led a group of soldiers to a site in England of great paranormal significance and discovered Hellboy.
- *Tom Manning* is the current leader of the B.P.R.D. His role in most *Hellboy* stories is minimal. He is a pragmatic and conscientious administrator as well as a capable agent.
- *Grigori Rasputin* is the Russian monk known for his enemies in the court of the Romanovs. In the *Hellboy* universe, he has been revived by the forces of the Ogdru Jahad for the purpose of bringing them back into existence. His physical form is killed by the combined efforts of Hellboy, Liz, and Abe in *Seed of Destruction*, but his spirit lives on to orchestrate later challenges to the B.P.R.D.
- *Ilsa von Haupstein*, a.k.a. *Hecate*, is one of Rasputin's followers. In *Wake the Devil* she is called upon to sacrifice her body so that her essence will merge with that of the witch-goddess Hecate and thus save Hecate (who had been destroyed by Hellboy).
- *Roger* is a homunculus, or artificial person. Having been created—and having lost all his power—generations earlier, he is resurrected by Liz's power in *Wake the Devil*. Fundamentally moral, in "Almost Colossus," he helps Hellboy stop Roger's "brother" (an earlier experiment with the form) from becoming a gigantic and ravaging monster, seemingly sacrificing himself to revive a dying Liz. Later restored, he becomes a B.P.R.D. agent, although his mistreatment by the agency eventually causes Hellboy to leave it.

Artistic Style

Most of Hellboy's adventures have been drawn and inked by Mignola. The latter volumes illustrated by Duncan Fegredo and Richard Corben have striven to emulate (if not actually copy) much of Mignola's visual style. The first trade paperback collection of *Seed of Destruction* is dedicated to seminal artist Kirby and pulp horror writer Lovecraft, and, indeed, these two influences are most evident in Mignola.

Renowned comic writer Alan Moore wrote in his introduction to the *Wake the Devil* collection that in Mignola's art, "German expressionism meets Jack Kirby." As in Kirby's later style, displayed in books such as *Mister Miracle* (1971) and *OMAC* (1974), Mignola favors heavy lines, blunt and craggy features, and bulky, large characters.

Since many of Hellboy's appearances were originally published in black and white (in *Dark Horse Presents*, for example) and colored later for their trade paperback collections, it is interesting how much the color palette chosen by Mignola (and colored by Mark Chiarello, Matt Hollingsworth, Dave Stewart, James Sinclair, and others) contributes to the mood of the book; rather than flashy and bright, as in Kirby's work, the colors are dark, muted, and understated, befitting the gothic tone of the series. Additionally, through use of deep shadow, Mignola's illustrations are minimalist at times. Backgrounds lack the complicated, ornate, busy technology of Kirby's renderings; rather, they tend to be shadowed halls, dim gothic architecture, and barren landscapes.

Themes

The overall tone throughout the Hellboy series is one of impending doom. From the first stories on, Hellboy is told that he is destined to bring about Armageddon and that he is to free the seven ancient and evil gods of the Ogdru Jahad. Rasputin, Hecate, Grugach, and many other enemies repeatedly tell Hellboy of his fate and that he should stop fighting it; typically, they attempt to entice him with promises that in the new order he will rule. Over and over again, however, Hellboy asserts his free will. Similarly, the seductive allure of power is shown to be dangerous and evil; characters such as Von Haupstein show that they will do anything to further their personal ambitions. They do not mind destroying the world as it is known in order to become all powerful. On the other hand, Hellboy has no interest in personal gain or glory. Instead, he seems to always repudiate his origins, and his physical appearance, in an attempt to do right. Also, his

heroism is not purely an act of professional obligation. Even after leaving the B.P.R.D. in *Conqueror Worm*, he continues to strive against the forces of evil.

Hellboy is in some ways distinguished from other gothic or horror stories in Mignola's canon, in which his rich appreciation of folklore is evident. Like *The Sandman* (1989-1996) creator Neil Gaiman, Mignola not only creates his own mythology but also interweaves stories pulled from German, Russian, English, Japanese, and many other cultures. Many of these stories suggest, at least partly, that evil lurks not only in the dark forests of the world but also in the deep woods of the human heart. The dangers, then, are both external and internal. Unlike most, Hellboy's capacity for evil is externalized in his devilish appearance. However, rather than growing out his horns and taking his place as a lord of demons, he fights for innocence and goodness—and keeps his horns trimmed so that they are mere ridges on his forehead.

Impact

Although the graphic novel form precedes *Hellboy*, the conception of the ongoing story as a series of novels

---

Mike Mignola

For the first decade of his career, Mike Mignola was a well-regarded superhero artist. It was only after he launched *Hellboy* in 1994 that he became a superstar. Mignola's tales of the crime-fighting demon from another dimension was one of the most celebrated superhero titles of the 1990's, and has been adapted twice to the silver screen. The series is characterized by its dark, inky images, with bold figures and striking use of chiaroscuro lighting effects. Combining real-life and fantastic villains, the *Hellboy* series is a complex reflection on the nature of heroism that draws on generic traditions from pulp, horror, and ancient mythologies. More than any other cartoonist, Mignola is responsible for hybridizing superhero-style action comics with horror traditions. Although he created the *B.P.R.D.* series as a spin-off from *Hellboy*, for the most part it is written and drawn by creators other than Mignola.

---

intermixed with shorter tales constituted a transformation in the way comics worked. While *Hellboy* was clearly influenced by Gaiman's work on *The Sandman*, Mignola does not work on a monthly deadline. Secondly, where as many paranormal comics strive for a forced bitterness and dark cynicism bordering on melancholy, *Hellboy* has clung happily to its pulp roots. As in superhero stories, most of the tales come down to winning a fight. The series has shown that a variety of elements and sources can be combined in new ways to make for new reading experiences.

More than the building plot and gothic, Lovecraftian nature of his stories and mythos, however, Mignola has established himself as one of the most important artists of his generation. As he has matured, he has transcended the influence of Kirby and accomplished great shifts in tone and mood through shadow and minimalist designs. Contemporary artists look to him as one of their prime influences, just as Mignola once looked to Kirby.

Scott D. Yarbrough

Films

Hellboy. Directed by Guillermo del Toro. Revolution Films, Columbia Tristar, and Starlite, in association with Darkhorse Entertainment, 2004. This adaptation stars Ron Perlman as Hellboy, Selma Blair as Liz Sherman, and Doug Jones as Abe Sapien. Rather than adapting any individual work, this film pulls material from *Seed of Destruction, Wake the Devil*, and *The Right Hand of Doom* in chronicling initially Hellboy's appearance on Earth and then, later, the resurrection of Rasputin and his attempt to summon "elder gods" to rule Earth. Hellboy's romantic interest in Liz, greatly understated in the comics, is developed for greater dramatic effect. Del Toro's visual depiction of Hellboy's adventures holds close to Mignola's renderings, and Pearlman captures perfectly Hellboy's world-weary, no-nonsense approach to problems. Mignola is credited as a coexecutive producer and was reportedly pleased with the film.

Hellboy Animated: Sword of Storms. Directed by Tad Stones. Film Roman and Revolution Pictures, 2006. An animated adventure in which Pearlman, Blair, and Jones lend their voices to reprising their starring roles.

It originally aired on Cartoon Network and then was sold on DVD. Hellboy is lured into a Japanese dream-world where he must do battle with Japanese demons. The short story "Heads" is integrated into the film's story.

Hellboy Animated: Blood and Iron. Directed by Tad Stones. Film Roman and Revolution Pictures, 2007. This is the second animated adventure on Cartoon Network, incorporating elements from *Wake the Devil*. Hellboy, Abe, Liz, and Sydney Leach investigate a haunted house and confront Hecate.

Hellboy II: The Golden Army. Directed by Guillermo del Toro. Universal Pictures and Internationale Filmproduktion Eagle in association with Dark Horse Entertainment, 2008. Largely the same cast returns for this sequel to *Hellboy*. Although elements from various Hellboy stories appear, the film is largely a new story by Del Toro and Mignola. The romance between Liz and Hellboy is continued, as they have to fight a golden army of mechanical warriors brought back to life by the new, angry king of the elves.

Further Reading

Delano, Jamie, et al. *John Constantine: Hellblazer* (1988-   ).

Gaiman, Neil, et al. *The Sandman* (1989-1996).

Powell, Eric. *The Goon* (1998-   ).

Bibliography

Cooper, Rand Richards. "Devilish Adaptations: *The Punisher* and *Hellboy*." *Commonweal* 131, no. 10 (2004): 19.

Mauning, Shaun. "Hell (boy) on Earth." *Comic Book Resources*, December 17, 2010. http://www.comicbookresources.com/?page=article&id=29935.

Mignola, Mike. "Interview: Mike Mignola." Interview by Jason Heller. *A.V. Club*, July 24, 2008. http://www.avclub.com/articles/mike-mignola,14279.

Moore, Alan. Introduction to *Wake the Devil*. Milwaukie, Ore.: Dark Horse, 1997.

O'Connor, Laura. "The Corpse on Hellboy's Back: Translating a Graphic Image." *Journal of Popular Culture* 43, no. 3 (June, 2010): 540-563.

See also: *B.P.R.D.; Sandman; Hellblazer; Goon*

HIS NAME IS . . . SAVAGE!

Author: Franklin, Robert (pseudonym of Archie Goodwin)
Artist: Gil Kane (illustrator); Robert Foster (cover artist)
Publisher: Adventure House Press
First book publication: 1968

Publication History

His Name Is…Savage! was a project initiated by Gil Kane. Archie Goodwin wrote the text, under the pseudonym Robert Franklin, and comic artists Larry Koster and Manny Stallman helped with the production. Adventure House Press, the publisher for *His Name Is… Savage!*, was Kane's own imprint. However, Kane had difficulty producing and distributing the magazine, as its content and format were comparatively unusual for the time. After experiencing difficulty in finding a printer—apparently some printers were wary of the story's content—it was distributed somewhat unevenly to newsstands by the Kable News Company. After many years out of print, the story was reprinted by Fantagraphics in 1982, as *Gil Kane's Savage*, with a new cover drawn by Kane, an introduction by R. C. Harvey, and interviews with Kane.

Plot

The plot of *His Name Is…Savage!* is clearly influenced by the James Bond films that had been highly popular since 1962. It opens with two divers boarding a boat and killing a man with a harpoon. Just before the boat is destroyed the dying man sends a message: "Mace will strike the President's UN address." At a vast underground headquarters the divers report to General Simon Mace, whose face is half disfigured flesh and half metal. Because the divers failed to stop the message being sent, the general uses his metal arm to crush the hand of one of the men, and then he strangles the other.

Meanwhile Savage, an espionage agent and assassin working for an organization known as "The Committee," is in prison, about to be executed for murder. The sadistic head guard, Captain Bayard, has received

Archie Goodwin

Better known as an editor than as a writer, Archie Goodwin ran the Warren line of comics magazines (*Eerie*, *Creepy*, and *Blazing Combat*) from 1964 to 1967. During the 1970's, while he was writing the newspaper strip *Secret Agent X-9*, he worked as an editor and writer for both Marvel and DC Comics. In 1976 he was named editor-in-chief of Marvel Comics, a position he held for a little more than a year. In 1979, he was placed in charge of the creator-owned *Epic Illustrated* magazine at Marvel, a position that later expanded to become the Epic Comics imprint of creator-owned titles. Returning to DC in 1989, Goodwin worked on a number of Batman-related titles, including *Batman: Legends of the Dark Knight* and *Batman: The Long Halloween*. Goodwin died of cancer in 1998, and is remembered as an editor beloved by his creators.

Gil Kane

One of the legendary figures of the American comic book industry, Gil Kane was the defining artist on DC Comics' *The Green Lantern* and *The Atom* titles during the 1960's. In the 1970's he succeeded John Romita as the regular artist on *The Amazing Spider-Man*, producing some of the most memorable issues of that comic, including the deaths of Gwen Stacey and the Green Goblin. In 1968 he published *His Name Is . . . Savage!* with Adventure House Press and in 1971 he published *Blackmark* with Bantam Books. Both of these were serious innovations at the time and are considered important precursors to the graphic novel. Kane is a member of both the Will Eisner Comic Awards Hall of Fame and the Harvey Award's Jack Kirby Hall of Fame. His artwork is celebrated for its elegant draftsmanship and fluidly realistic figure drawing. Kane's heroes were realistically proportioned and nimble in a way that few others ever were.

release papers but has his guards beat Savage to make him crawl for the papers. Savage grabs Bayard's gun and smashes it into the captain's mouth; he forces him to take him to the warden to confirm his release.

Savage then makes his way to the Manhattan headquarters of the Committee, which is a top-secret espionage organization answerable only to the president of the United States. There, the shadowy figures of the Committee tell Savage of Mace's plot to kill the president. A flashback reveals that Savage was part of a special assault group under General Mace during World War II, and after the war, he worked as a mercenary for Mace. In love with Mace's daughter, Sheila, Savage stayed with the increasingly unbalanced general until he felt he had to try to take over Mace's organization. After failing, Savage had to flee. Savage caused Mace's injuries by detonating a hand grenade as he escaped.

Savage visits a former associate of Mace, Keely, an antiques dealer, to discover Mace's whereabouts. Savage is persuading Keely to talk by gradually destroying his valuable inventory when an assassin shoots Keely in the head. Although wounded, Savage kills two assassins; then he goes to the hotel where the assassins had been staying, scaling the wall to break in.

At the hotel, he meets Sheila, who agrees to help him. Savage fights off two guards, one of whom is a large bald Asian man in the mold of a Bond villain's henchman. Savage defeats him by using karate and then ambushes and kills three more guards; however, Sheila is shot and killed in the escape.

Savage confronts the Committee, as he believes one of the members is a traitor who has set him up. He demands to see the president of the United States; when he does so, he realizes that the figure, who looks like U.S. president Lyndon B. Johnson, is actually Mace in disguise. Savage attacks him but is knocked unconscious by Secret Service agents.

Awakening, Savage finds himself in a car with two of Mace's men. He escapes, only to find "Johnson" has declared war on Soviet Russia while at the United Nations. Savage rips the disguise from Mace's face but cannot prevent him from escaping in a speedboat. Savage commandeers a helicopter and follows Mace to his base. Joined by troops, Savage storms the base. He finds the president on an operating table, where

a surgeon is about to transmogrify the Johnson face, which would allow Mace to continue his impersonation. Savage knocks out the surgeon and attacks Mace. They engage in a monumental fistfight (which lasts five pages). Losing the vicious fight, Savage throws acid into Mace's face, and the general is electrocuted by his metal arm. Savage drags the president to safety, and though seriously wounded, he survives.

Characters

- *Savage* is defined by his name: He is clearly capable of brutal violence. His short, cropped hair and heavy build mark him as a character to be feared. Although a trained killer, he is capable of love (for the doomed Sheila). Also, despite his use of extreme violence, he has a moral compass, particularly after his split from General Mace. He is brave and also selfless: At the end, when surrounded by massive destruction, he tells troops, "Forget me…Get the President."

- *General Simon Mace* is mainly seen as a violent cyborg, and his human form is glimpsed only in flashback, in which he is forceful and dynamic. However, he does not speak, and therefore cannot explain his character. The text implies that he has gradually become more unbalanced. Once he becomes a cyborg, he can be seen as a Bond villain: Although he is not foreign, he is disfigured and power crazed.

- *Sheila Mace* is something of a cipher and is physically reminiscent of Kane's rendition of Carol Ferris, the Green Lantern's girlfriend in the 1960's. Her one major scene lasts for six pages, and by the end of it, she is dead. This scene does establish, however, that she still has feelings for Savage and that she has stayed with her megalomaniac father only because of her fear of him.

Artistic Style

At the time of the production of *His Name Is…Savage!* Kane was a well-established comic book artist, probably most famous for his artwork on DC Comics' revamp of *Green Lantern* between 1959 and 1970, although he worked on a huge range of comics and many other major characters for both DC and Marvel, including Superman and Spider-Man.

Kane's style uses a particularly clear and precise line that allows the delineation of great detail, not only in key figures but also in weaponry and architecture. This careful style makes the moments of violence even more horrific, as when teeth fragments and blood are shown flying from the mouth of Bayard's mouth. Even when the image is slightly less explicit, as when Savage escapes from the car, the text emphasizes the results of violence: "Carl's head shot backward with a violent snap, leaving a trail of blood and shattered teeth in the air."

Most pages have between five and nine panels, with full-page panels used only twice (on the first page and in the climactic fight scene). The more dense pages tend to use multiple panels to control reading pace and tension. For example, on page 33, a five-panel sequence in a row across the bottom of the page shows Savage setting down a cigarette. In the second panel it falls from the ashtray, and in the third, it rolls across the desk. We see it rest against the hand of the fake president, who does not flinch. The final panel shows the hand with Savage looking on, his face showing that he realizes he is talking to Mace in disguise.

There are several design features that make the black-and-white interior pages look unlike traditional comics. The illustrative and text panels in the story do not have drawn borders, which gives the page layout a more fluid feel. Text is also typed in a plain sans serif face, with squared-off word balloons, which also makes the pages look less like traditional comics. Some pages have dense text over every panel, between three and seven lines long. The artwork also uses a huge amount of tone effects, which help to give the pages a dark, filmic look. The opening splash page is reminiscent of the work of Will Eisner, in that the title of the comic is shown within the panel as a huge stone underwater structure, with a diver swimming past it.

Themes

Although it is clearly a James Bond-style action adventure, *His Name Is . . . Savage!* takes place against the background of the Cold War, and the intention of the villain is not to assassinate the president of the United

States but to start World War III. Savage is extremely violent, and, thus, more like the early James Bond figure of the Ian Fleming novels than the Bond of the later gadget-heavy films. Indeed, in the scenes in which Savage breaks Keely's antiques or smashes a gun into Captain Bayard's mouth, he is more reminiscent of Mickey Spillane's Cold War detective antihero, Mike Hammer.

The villain in the story, and indeed the eponymous hero, are both shown to have been scarred by war. They were both trained by the U.S. Army to be killers, and after the war their construction as killing machines leads them to use their lethal skills in a series of increasingly dubious activities. Although their plot and its long-term impact are tied into World War II, the comic was published at the height of U.S. involvement in the Vietnam War (1965-1975). There is no explicit mention of Vietnam in the story, but the plot, featuring

Lee Marvin was the basis for the Savage character. (Getty Images)

President Johnson, with its combination of military excess and a possible war with Russia, is inevitably influenced by the war during which it was written.

The story also attempts to deal with a modern version of the lone hero, an archetype that Clint Eastwood embodied in Sergio Leone's spaghetti Westerns and *Dirty Harry* films. Indeed, the cover of the book has a painted image that is recognizable as actor Lee Marvin, who had just starred as a violent antihero in John Boorman's film *Point Blank* (1967). Several key elements in the book also appear in the film; not only the casual violence of the hero, but also an important prison scene and an audacious raid on a heavily guarded hotel.

Most of these heroes, or protagonists, raise the issue of how much unregulated violence can be tolerated in a civilized society in order to defeat the forces of evil. Some critics have perceived the book, like the *Dirty Harry* films that preceded it, as a fascist response, whereby "might is seen as right." The comic has also been seen as hyperviolent, and there are some key panels of extreme violence; by modern standards, however, the level of violence is not as shocking as it might have been in 1968.

Impact

Although the cover of *His Name Is…Savage!* is headed, "Beginning: A New Comics Tradition" and the book is numbered as issue 1, there were no further issues. The magazine format, with black-and-white interior artwork, had been popularized by James Warren's *Creepy* magazine in 1964. However, only that comic and other horror comics, such as Warren's companion titles *Eerie* and *Vampirella* (which were edited by the author of *His Name Is…Savage!,* Goodwin), were commercially successful for an extended period of time. The impact of *His Name Is . . . Savage!* was therefore quite limited at the time, and some critics have argued that it has not worn well, partially because of what they see as Goodwin's overblown and verbose text. Others have seen this writing style as a deliberate parody of spy novels of the period. Nevertheless, *His Name Is . . . Savage!* was an experiment of which many industry professionals were aware, and it is still widely admired.

David Huxley

Further Reading

Kane, Gil. *Blackmark* (1971).

Kirby, Jack. *In the Days of the Mob* (1971).

Lee, Stan, and Jack Kirby. *The Silver Surfer* (1978).

Bibliography

Herman, Daniel. *Gil Kane: Art and Interviews*. Neshannock, Pa.: Hermes Press, ,2002.

_____. *Gil Kane: The Art of the Comics*. Neshannock, Pa.: Hermes Press, 2001.

Kane, Gil. "Gil Kane and Denny O'Neil on Comics Writing." *The Comics Journal* 64 (July, 1981): 61-79.

Scholz, Carter. "Kane's Progress." *The Comics Journal* 74 (August, 1982): 35-39.

See also: *Elecktra: Assassin*; *The Silver Surfer*; *Losers*

HITMAN

Author: Ennis, Garth
Artist: John McCrea (illustrator); Garry Leach (inker); Carla Feeny (colorist); Pat Prentice (letterer); Willie Schubert (letterer)
Publisher: DC Comics
First serial publication: 1996-2001
First book publication: 1997-2001

Publication History

One of many characters created for DC's Bloodlines crossover (in which parasitic aliens inadvertently create a number of superpowered beings), Tommy Monaghan first appeared in *The Demon Annual*, issue 2 (1993), written by Garth Ennis and drawn by John McCrea. He appeared in a few story lines in *The Demon* (first published in 1972) and became a popular member of the supporting cast. Nearly a year after *The Demon* was canceled, DC launched *Hitman* in early 1996.

Ennis wrote the entire run (comprising sixty issues, an annual, a crossover with the character Lobo, and an issue tying into the "DC One Million" crossover event), and McCrea was the primary artist, pencilling all but two issues and handling inking duties until issue 21.

Firmly rooted in the DC Universe, *Hitman* was largely set in Gotham City and included appearances by Batman, the Joker, Catwoman, and other local characters. As the series continued and the body count grew, crossovers became less frequent, as the underworld and crime plotlines were often at odds with traditional superhero storytelling (although superpowered villains appeared throughout the series). Similarly, although Monaghan has powers, he rarely used them later in the series, as the side effects of his powers and the distraction they often created during gunfights made them impractical. Although the series had an enthusiastic following, sales were, in Ennis's words, "nothing special," and the creators were given time to wrap up the series. *Hitman* finished its run with its sixtieth issue, in June, 2001.

John McCrea

Known for his frequent collaborations with writer Garth Ennis, artist John McCrea balances traditional superhero imagery with elements of slapstick humor. McCrea was the artist on Ennis's debut comics work in *Crisis* magazine, and transitioned with him to the American comics market in 1993 as the illustrator of *The Demon*. From 1996 to 2001 he drew the sixty-one issues of *Hitman*, a character spun off from *The Demon*, the series for which he is best known. McCrea's art is rooted in a classical approach to page layout and design, and tends not to overwhelm the writing of the book. He uses a mildly exaggerated style to represent his figures, emphasizing facial features in a cartoony manner that moves the work away from strict representationalism. Given his frequent collaborations with Ennis, McCrea has specialized in the depiction of gross gag elements, which are a frequent component of Ennis's storytelling style.

Plot

Hitman tells the story of Monaghan, who first appears in *The Demon* as a freelance hit man about to kill a mobster. Before he can do so, however, an alien named Glonth attacks and kills the mobster. When the creature turns its attention to Monaghan, it attacks and feeds on his spinal fluid, causing Monaghan to develop X-ray vision and minor telepathic powers. After a failed attempt on his life, Monaghan launches an attack at a mob wake, where he and Etrigan the Demon both fight Glonth. Later appearances in *The Demon* include the "Hell's Hitman" story line, in which Etrigan hires Monaghan to kill the Archfiend of Hell, Asteroth, and his warriors (and which establishes his reluctance to ever shoot police officers), and "Suffer the Children," in which Etrigan's alter-ego, Jason Blood, tries to get Monaghan to kill Etrigan himself.

Monaghan's own series launched with the three-part "A Rage in Arkham." Monaghan decides that he will be the only hit man dealing exclusively with superpowered beings, although the inevitable attacks by regular mobsters give him plenty of nonpowered folks to shoot. After killing off plenty of both, he finds himself on a mission to kill the Joker, which goes well until his target is revealed to be an extradimensional entity known as the Mawzir, who is attempting to recruit Monaghan for the demonic Arkanonne, the Lord of the Guns. In addition to introducing most of the core cast, the story contains one of the book's more memorable (and infamous) scenes, in which Monaghan vomits on Batman, and reintroduces most of Monaghan's supporting cast, including best friend Pat, father figure Sean Noonan, buffoonish Hacken, fellow hit man Ringo, and police officer Tiegel.

The "10,000 Bullets" story line introduces Natt, Monaghan's best friend from his days fighting in Iraq. Moe Dubelz, the grotesque surviving mobster from *The Demon Annual*, issue 2, hires professional hit man Johnny Navarone to kill Monaghan. After Monaghan and Natt fight a horde of ninjas and a dcrangcd, drug-stealing "hero" named Nightfist, Johnny ambushes and almost kills Monaghan. While the two are recuperating, Johnny tortures and kills Monaghan's best friend Pat, leading to a rampage by Monaghan and Natt that leaves Johnny, Moe, and Nightfist dead.

A number of lighter story lines follow, although they are still filled with shootouts and dead bodies. "The Final Night" crossover "The Night the Lights Went Out in Gotham" features the gang telling short tales about their past. "Local Heroes" introduces Central Intelligence Agency (CIA) agent Truman, who wants to recruit Monaghan; features an appearance by Green Lantern Kyle Raynor; and results in the corrupt police captain Burns finally getting her comeuppance. "Zombie Night at the Gotham Aquarium" pulls the gang into a twisted fight against zombie penguins, seals, and other creatures and leads to Hacken losing his hand.

The six-part "Ace of Killers" story ties up a number of loose ends from Ennis and McRea's run on *The Demon* and from earlier issues of *Hitman*. The Mawzir tricks Catwoman into stealing the Ace of Winchesters, an old gun capable of killing demons. Monaghan, Natt, and Tiegel get drawn into the resulting conflict, and join Catwoman and Jason Blood in the fight. Catwoman

blinds Mawzir with her claws, allowing Monaghan to use the Ace of Winchesters to destroy Mawzir and leave Etrigan in charge of Hell. This story introduces the group of humorous washout heroes known as Section Eight and also strands comic-relief demon Baytor on Earth, where he eventually gets a job at Noonan's bar.

After a pair of one-shots featuring guest artist Steve Pugh, the next major story line is "Who Dares Wins." The Special Air Service (SAS), aware of the fact that Natt and Monaghan accidentally ambushed and killed a group of them in Iraq, wants revenge. Given approval to hunt Natt and Monaghan by the U.S. Marine Corps, a team of agents nearly kills them before getting caught up inadvertently in yet another mob war. The resulting war leads to the death of the entire SAS team, and the midstory kidnapping of Noonan reinforces his importance to Monaghan. In the follow-up story line, "Tommy's Heroes," Monaghan and Natt train mercenaries and lead a rebellion in Africa while the gang heat in Gotham cools down.

Issue 34, "Of Thee I Sing," the Eisner Award winner for Best Single Issue in 1999, features a conversation between Monaghan and Superman, the one hero the former always looked up to. Superman meets Monaghan on a rooftop but has no idea of what he does for a living. They start talking, and Superman reveals his disappointment in his inability to save an astronaut and to live up the ideals for which he stands. Monaghan reassures Superman that the hero stands for the hope of the American Dream for everyone, and Superman flies away reassured even as Monaghan gets ready to kill a drug kingpin.

The two-part "Katie" introduces (and kills off) Monaghan's half sister Frances and reveals that Monaghan's birth father was a violent man named Tom Dawson who killed Monaghan's prostitute mother, Kate. Monaghan kills his father in revenge for the murders of Kate and Frances. This is followed by a vampire battle in "Dead Man's Land," a crossover with the Batman "No Man's Land" story arc in which Gotham is ravaged by an earthquake.

"For Tomorrow" focuses on hit man Ringo, who finds himself hunted in revenge for one of his killings. Ringo and Monaghan both get kidnapped by the villainous Waterman, and although they fight their way free, the resulting battle kills Ringo. Monaghan kills both the Waterman and his employer in revenge. After a battle against some displaced dinosaurs, the next story line, "The Old Dog," has yet another mob attack, leaving Noonan dead. A touching epilogue to this story shows that of the entire crew, only Hacken and Baytor will be alive in fifty years. Sure enough, in the next story line, "Superguy," the slaughter of most of Section 8 occurs, with drunken leader Sixpack sacrificing himself to save the planet from a group of demons.

The final story line, "Closing Time," ties up various loose ends. When Maggie, a woman Monaghan met during "Dead Man's Land," reveals her knowledge of secret CIA experiments, Agent Truman returns in an attempt to kill Monaghan. His protégé, Agent McAlister, turns against him, but the small crew of heroes is not nearly enough to overcome everything Truman has to throw at them. Both Monaghan and Natt have extended flashback sequences, revealing their childhoods and their paths to crime. In the final battle, as the heroes rescue Maggie and run for McAllister's helicopter, Natt is shot and begs Monaghan not to let him be captured for Truman's experiments. Monaghan runs from the helicopter and dies in a blaze of glory, taking out Truman in the process. As he and Natt lay dying, they discuss Monaghan's dream in which the entire cast is reunited in a gunless world at Noonan's bar.

Volumes

- *Hitman: A Rage in Arkham* (1997). Collects issues 1-3; *Demon Annual*, issue 2; and *Batman Chronicles*, issue 4. Contains Monaghan's earliest adventures, one of which includes a confrontation with an entity he believes to be the Joker.
- *Hitman: 10,000 Bullets* (1998). Collects issues 4-8. Featuring Natt's first appearance. A reprint of this volume in 2010 also includes *Hitman Annual*, issue 1, featuring Monaghan and Natt in a Texas gunfight.
- *Hitman: Local Heroes* (1999). Collects issues 9-14. The original 1999 printing also collects the *Hitman Annual*, but the 2010 reprint omits it.

- *Hitman: Ace of Killers* (2000). Collects issues 15-22, featuring the return of assorted characters from *The Demon* and the evolution of Monaghan's relationship with Tiegel.
- *Hitman: Who Dares Wins* (2001). Collects issues 23-28, featuring the battle against the rogue SAS agents.

Characters

- *Tommy Monaghan*, the protagonist, is a Mafia hit man with a strong moral code. He is always willing to kill criminals, but he will not shoot a police officer or anyone he believes to be innocent. He is loyal to his friends, to the point of being willing to die for them. He is of Irish descent and was raised in an orphanage; he does not discover the identity of his parents until he is an adult. He is a former Marine, but he generally does not maintain many ties to his military past.
- *Natt Walls*, a.k.a *Natt the Hat*, is Monaghan's best friend and also a former Marine. A former gangbanger in Detroit, he flees his hometown for Gotham when members of his old gang suspect him of turning on them. Although rather overweight (something Monaghan often gives him grief about), he can hold his own in physical combat; he is also an excellent shot. His nickname comes from the fact that he always wears colorful headpieces.
- *Deborah Tiegel* is Monaghan's primary love interest for the majority of the series. A tough African American police officer, she is one of the few honest cops in her department. She finds herself kicked off the force temporarily when she will not go along with her fellow officers' shenanigans. She lives with her mother and her grandfather. Although she loves Monaghan, she is conflicted about his profession, and they eventually break up when Monaghan comes to the conclusion that he will drag her down with him.
- *Sean Noonan* owns Noonan's bar and is a former hit man himself. Long retired, he raised Monaghan along with his biological nephew, Pat. He is a father figure to both of them. Like

Monaghan and Natt, he is a former Marine, having served during the Korean War (1950-1953). He won his bar in a poker game, and it has become a popular hangout for criminals.

- *Ringo Chen* is Monaghan's rival for the title of best hit man in Gotham. A former soldier in China, he was imprisoned and tortured when he refused to shoot innocent civilians; he eventually escaped to the United States. He started working as a hit man for his cousin but soon began freelancing. He believes that he met the embodiment of Death while on a hit and that he will meet Death again when he is about to die.

- *Hacken* is generally the comic relief, a big dumb guy who talks like a criminal but comes across as generally too incompetent to accomplish anything. He unnecessarily loses his hand while fighting zombies at an aquarium, and the others generally refuse to bring him on jobs (going so far as to knock him out to prevent him from going on the final suicide mission).

- *Agent Truman* is the primary antagonist during the "Local Heroes" and "Closing Time" story lines. A CIA operative who despises metahumans, he attempts to manipulate the police and Green Lantern against Monaghan. Amoral and sociopathic, he later attempts to re-create the process that created the Bloodline heroes, experimenting on unwilling subjects and turning them into monsters.

- *Kathryn McAllister* is a former CIA agent and Monaghan's primary love interest during the final arc of the series. Underneath her cynical exterior, she has a sense of ethics and feels obligated to fight against Truman's project.

Artistic Style

Keeping pace with a mix of humor, action, and character moments in *Hitman*, McCrea shifts styles as necessary. For action sequences, he edges into the grotesque, showing half-melted faces, rotting flesh, and blood splattering as people got shot. He rarely uses detailed backgrounds during these sequences, instead highlighting (often in half-page spreads or larger panels) the ever-growing body count. He also relies heavily on onomatopoetic sound effects for everything from gunfire to windows shattering. In spite of the massive amount of on-panel carnage, he keeps the occasional character death off-screen, relying on sound effects and visual cues such as shell casings. Both Navarone and his son, Marc, die off-panel this way.

McCrea also uses goofiness, particularly during scenes set at a local burger restaurant, in which burgers are literally as big as the heads of the characters. Similarly, his depictions of demons such as Baytor (who was almost all mouth and often had a cigar somehow sitting in his maw), are silly without undermining the storytelling.

McCrea also uses some subtle touches. Issue 39, the first issue of the Ringo-centric "For Tomorrow" arc, starts with a full-page shot of Ringo shooting a man that is almost identical to the opening panel of issue 1, featuring Monaghan in the same pose, nicely setting the tone for the story line. During more sedate moments, or when working with DC Universe characters such as Superman, Batman, and Green Lantern, McCrea shifts to a more traditional superhero style, keeping the characters looking more like the DC house style than the more cartoony action style he normally employed.

Themes

The primary theme of *Hitman* is that murder begets murder. Although Monaghan and his crew attempt to live by a moral code, death comes back to haunt characters throughout (literally in Ringo's case). Many of the antagonists, from Dubelz to Richard Harcourt in "A Better Tomorrow" and Marc Navarone in the final story line, are seeking revenge for the deaths of family members, a cycle that costs all of them their lives. Likewise, the only member of the regulars at Noonan's bar to survive the series is the almost childlike Hacken, as the cycle of violence claims the lives of everyone else (even those, such as Sixpack and Monaghan's sister Frances, who are merely caught in its wake). This can certainly be contrasted with Gotham's most famous resident, Batman, who will not kill his antagonists under any circumstances and who seems to thrive in Gotham.

Family, for good or for ill, is the other major recurring theme. Monaghan's biological father was a horrible man, but most of the supporting characters have strong ties. Tiegel lives with her loving grandfather and mother; Sean raises his nephew Pat and takes care of him; and Natt will not curse because of a promise to his dying mother. Even those who do not have a biological family form familial units built around loyalty and trust. Monaghan's own crew is very much his family, so much so that when Sean dies, his tombstone reads, "beloved father." Furthermore, Monaghan, at the end, is given the chance for freedom, but he chooses to die with his best friend, who is clearly his brother in spirit, if not biologically.

On a metafictional level, *Hitman* is an homage to Hong Kong action movies. Ringo is named after director Ringo Lam, and his primary arc, "A Better Tomorrow," shares its name with a classic film by John Woo. Almost every issue is peppered with firefights that border on ludicrous, with thousands of bullets flying around, unbelievable action sequences, copious amounts of gore, and honor-driven killings that constantly escalate. This is almost exactly like many of the Hong Kong classics, including films such as *Hard Boiled* (1992), *The Killer* (1989), and *Full Contact* (1992).

Impact

Hitman often bridged the gap between the DC Universe's superhero line and adult titles published by DC's Vertigo imprint. Although the series lacked the nudity and adult language of the Vertigo books, the high gore factor, incredible body count, and multiple postcoital seminude scenes were certainly beyond what most DC Universe books showed at the time. Although *Hitman* certainly cannot take sole credit for the increasing popularity of crime comics, it helped pave the way for Ennis's run on Marvel's *The Punisher* (which began in 1995), which revived interest in Marvel's most notorious crime character and likely helped create an atmosphere in which other crime comics, such as *100 Bullets* (1999-2009), could thrive.

Adam Lipkin

Further Reading

Ennis, Garth, and Darrick Robertson. *The Boys* (2006-   ).

Ennis, Garth, et al. *The Punisher* (2004-2009).

Waid, Mark, and Peter Krause. *Irredeemable* (2009-   ).

Bibliography

Booker, M. Keith. *Encyclopedia of Comic Books and Graphic Novels*. Santa Barbara, Calif.: ABC-CLIO, 2010.

Fagan, Bryan D., and Jody Condit Fagan. *Comic Book Collections for Libraries*. Santa Barbara, Calif.: Libraries Unlimited, 2011.

Wolk, Douglas. *Reading Comics: How Graphic Novels Work and What They Mean*. Cambridge, Mass.: Da Capo Press, 2007.

See also: *Batman: The Dark Knight Returns; Batman: The Dark Knight Strikes Again; The Boys*

Human Target

Author: Milligan, Peter

Artist: Edvin Biuković (illustrator); Cliff Chiang (illustrator); Javier Pulido (illustrator); Cameron Stewart (illustrator); Lee Loughridge (colorist); Dave Stewart (colorist); Todd Klein (letterer); Clem Robins (letterer); Robert Solanović (letterer); Tim Bradstreet (cover artist); John Watkiss (cover artist)

Publisher: Vertigo

First serial publication: 1999 (miniseries); 2003-2005 (series)

First book publication: 2000

Publication History

Human Target was created by Len Wein and Carmine Infantino as a backup feature for *Action Comics*, first appearing in issue 419 (December, 1972). The strip later turned up in *The Brave and the Bold* and *Detective Comics*, and it spawned a television show that ran for seven episodes in 1992.

In the late 1990's, Axel Alonso considered reviving the character for a Vertigo series. He offered the project to Peter Milligan, one of the British comics writers to break through in the 1980's, who had written *Shade: The Changing Man* (1990-1996), *Enigma* (1995), and *The Extremist* (1993) for Vertigo. Milligan read some of the original *Human Target* stories and told Alonso he was not interested, but then he started to think of what he might do with the concept and changed his mind. Milligan took little from the original version, using the core idea as a springboard to explore notions of identity.

This produced a four-issue miniseries, drawn by Edvin Biuković. Biuković had drawn numerous comics in his native Croatia and *Grendel Tales: Devils and Deaths* (1994) for Dark Horse and was the recipient of the Russ Manning Most Promising Newcomer Award at the 1995 Eisner Awards. The miniseries appeared between April and July, 1999.

The series was supposed to be a one-off, but when Milligan was discussing a potential new project with Vertigo's Karen Berger, dealing with issues concerning modern America and beyond, they realized that *Human Target* was an ideal vehicle. Biuković would have

Peter Milligan

One of the few surrealists to have worked extensively in American comic books, British writer Peter Milligan got his start in the industry at the end of the 1980's. His controversial graphic novel, *Skin* (with artist Brendan McCarthy), about a skinhead with thalidomide-related birth defects, was refused by Fleetway as too controversial. In the 1990's he became one of the signature writers at DC's Vertigo imprint, reviving *Shade: The Changing Man* as an off-kilter road story, and working on titles including *Enigma*, *The Extremist*, and *Human Target*. At Marvel in the 2000's he gave the X-Men franchise a bizarre twist with *X-Statix*, a title in which superheroic exploits were gently lampooned. Milligan's writing is characterized by a fascination with deviance as a social category, and an ironic take on the central mythologies of the American way of life.

remained the artist, but he died in December, 1999, at the age of thirty. Instead, Spanish artist Javier Pulido took over. Pulido had broken into the American market early in his career, working on *The Incredible Hulk* in 1998-1999 and *Hellblazer* in 1999.

A *Human Target* graphic novel, *Final Cut* appeared in May, 2002. Then, Milligan and Pulido reconvened for an ongoing monthly series, with the first issue dated October, 2003. With issue 6, Cliff Chiang, a former assistant editor at DC Comics who had drawn Vertigo's *Beware the Creeper* (2003), assumed the art duties. Between them, Pulido and Chiang drew all the remaining issues of *Human Target* except issue 17, drawn by Cameron Stewart. The final issue, 21, was dated June, 2005.

Plot

In the miniseries, Chance impersonates the Reverend Earl James, who is under threat from a neighborhood gang. Chance himself is threatened by a contract killer called Emerald but then discovers that he is not Chance at all but Chance's assistant, Tom McFadden; McFadden has forgotten that he is not Chance. The real Chance takes on the role of James and kills Emerald.

In the *Final Cut* graphic novel, movie producer Frank White hires Chance to find his kidnapped child-star son. Chance discovers that White has actually kidnapped his own son to pay off gambling debts. White and his son are both killed, but Chance has fallen for White's wife, Mary, and takes over his life. The ongoing series opens with *To Be Frank*, in which Chance's subconscious rebels against him. It splinters into a new personality, "Mr. Smith," who threatens "White" and forces him to admit his deception.

Chance leaves Los Angeles and travels around the United States. From 2003 to 2005, twenty-one issues were published. In *The Unshredded Man*, Chance takes the case of an accountant who faked his death on September 11, 2001 (9/11), to escape his involvement in an embezzling scheme, and in *Take Me Out to the Ballgame*, Chance uncovers a gambling ring that blackmails baseball players to throw games. In *For I Have Sinned*, he unmasks a child-abusing priest, and in *Which Way the Wind Blows* he deals with a member of a 1960's revolutionary cell that is killing off his former comrades. In *Five Days' Grace*, he covers for a prison inmate's breakout.

In *Games of Chance*, he returns to Los Angeles, where he and Mary White attempt an honest relationship. However, Chance discovers Mary is running an "ethical" people-smuggling operation over the Mexican border. This leads directly into *Crossing the Border*, as a rival operation tries to take over Mary's.

In *The Second Coming*, Chance offers to take the pressure off the handsome young "new messiah" Paul James, but he actually wants to prove to Bruno, who has become one of James's followers, that James is a fraud. In *You Made Me Love You*, Chance creates a new identity for a former gangster's wife, until she realizes he is turning her into Mary. In *Letters from the Front Line*, Chance thwarts a young, amateur antiterrorist gang.

In the final story line, *The Stealer*, Tom McFadden decides the only identity that worked for him was Chance's. He tries to eliminate Chance and take over

his life; however, Chance survives, and they battle over his identity. Mary makes the choice, opting for McFadden. The real Chance leaves town.

Volumes

- *Human Target: Chance Meetings* (2010). Collects the four-issue miniseries and the *Final Cut* graphic novel. Introduces Chance then reveals he is not the real Chance, although he believes he is, demonstrating the psychological hazards of his line of work. It goes on to explore Chance's desire for a stable identity.
- *Second Chances* (2011). Collects issues 1-10 of the monthly series. Chance unconsciously sabotages his own attempts to live a normal life as someone else, then goes back to work as the Human Target. He takes on several cases, frequently encountering people troubled by the specters of the past.

Characters

- *Christopher Chance* is a man of about forty, with smooth good looks and hair graying at the temples. Highly trained physically and a master of disguise, he is an unconventional bodyguard/assassin who assumes clients' identities, draws out threats to their lives, and then eliminates those threats. He can read people's psychology with great accuracy, and his impersonation often involves self-delusion.
- *Bruno* is a middle-aged, gay Italian American who runs a Los Angeles restaurant. He operates as Chance's contact with his clients. In *Final Cut* we discover that he hired Emerald to kill Chance, feeling that Chance needed something to shake him out of his ennui.
- *Tom McFadden* is Chance's assistant, just as adept at disguise as Chance and in some ways better at assimilating the subject's personality. However, he has become unstable, losing his grip on his own personality, and in the miniseries he has become convinced that he is Chance.
- *Mary White* is the beautiful, blonde wife of Frank White. After Frank is killed in *Final Cut*, Chance takes over his life. Mary is aware of the deception

but deludes herself that Chance is Frank. After some time apart, they attempt an honest relationship, but Chance realizes she has a secret.

Artistic Style

The concept of *Human Target* is ideally suited to the medium of comics. It is concerned with the relationship between surface and depth, so it is well served by a medium that is visual but also permits unobtrusive internal monologue. Furthermore, readers want to see Chance's transformations, but on screen such uncanny impersonations would involve either using prosthetics or having a variety of actors play the character. Both options would lack credibility for different reasons. In a comic, figures can be more flexible and the concept makes sense. For these reasons, the series always uses a stylized artistic approach.

The miniseries is a sort of hyperreal take on the original, which uses its twists and turns to disrupt the reader's confidence in reality. Biukovic's slightly pulpy style anchors the book and gives a gracefulness to its action sequences. The ongoing series is less frenetic, and Pulido sets a more ambiguous style. His approach is more stripped down and simplified than Biukovic's, using fewer lines. The differentiation between characters is more subtle as rendered by Pulido, and the possibility that Chance could be anyone in any given scene is heightened. As Mary tells him in issue 1, "They're *all* you! You're *everyone*!"

The environment of the story is relatively vague: The characters seem adrift in a world that is open to interpretation. In a sequence in *Final Cut*, set on a Los Angeles rooftop, the city beyond is rendered as a fizzing blur of orange and purple. The effect is similar to chiaroscuro lighting in film noir, making the image more graphic. Milligan and Pulido quickly become more ambitious, adding more panels to the page and becoming more creative with layouts. At times, the effect is kaleidoscopic; at others, it creates the impression of rapid cinematic cutting. In issue 12, Pulido uses no gutters, allowing the panels to merge and bleed into each other.

For the most part, Chiang picks up where Pulido leaves off. Chiang's work is slightly less impressionistic, with more defined lines and backgrounds, but, in terms of how it serves the material, the effect is much

the same. The contrast is noticeable when Stewart takes over for an issue and Milligan gives him a different type of story: Chance does not disguise himself at all and instead spends the story coaching somebody else in how to assume a new identity.

Themes

If any city in the world stands for personal reinvention, the alteration of physical appearance, the obsession with surface qualities, and role playing, Los Angeles is it. Yet *Human Target* becomes more interesting after it leaves the city. The 9/11 attacks occurred between the writing of *Final Cut* and the ongoing series, and the book evolves into an exploration of post-9/11 America, drawing on the fear of infiltration and general paranoia endemic in those times.

Milligan closes issue 1 emphatically with a flashback to the first plane about to hit the World Trade Center. The character Chance encounters, John Matthews/Jack Martin, pretended to have died in the disaster in order to escape a looming corporate fraud investigation—sins committed in a supposedly more "innocent" time. Chance explores the major institutions and traditions of the United States—the megacorporations, the religions, Hollywood, baseball—and repeatedly finds corruption and greed lurking within. Everybody has secrets, and nobody is truly innocent. A thread that runs through the series is that everyone projects a character: Chance is merely more flexible about it than most people, and more self-aware; however, even he is not immune to self-delusion.

The loose, almost sketchy but always dynamic art style enhances the plot: Ambiguous stories take place in an ambiguous world. Chance does have a moral code and is often seen taking a stand against the corruption and injustices he encounters, but he lives amid so much violence that he rarely even responds to it and is himself responsible for much of it. At the end, perhaps the reason Mary chooses McFadden's version of Chance is that McFadden is happier being Chance than Chance is.

Impact

Human Target was well reviewed but sold poorly: The first issue of the ongoing series sold 17,855 copies (roughly what the miniseries had sold), but with issue 7, sales dipped below 10,000, and the final issue sold 7,312 (by comparison, *Fables*, 2002- , and *Y: The Last Man*, 2002-2008, were selling around 25,000). Less than half of the series made it into trade paperback form. It was perhaps always a tricky sell, being neither outright fantasy nor strictly realistic.

The debut of a new *Human Target* television series in 2010 led DC to publish a new comic—this time by the character's creator, Wein. This was a cross between Wein's original version and the significantly different concept used in the television show. Milligan's comics appeared to have little influence, but as a side effect, they were reprinted in new trade paperbacks, set to baffle a generation of unwary readers expecting the character they had seen on television.

Human Target has been surprisingly enduring, perhaps less because of its strong concept and more because of its strong title; the Vertigo take on *Human Target* should endure with it. Few comics of its time engage so boldly with the world around them (Milligan's uncompromising revamp of *X-Force* is one of the others). The series looks increasingly like a document of the period, while also addressing universal themes.

Eddie Robson

Television Series

Human Target. Directed by Steve Boyum, et al. Bonanza Productions/DC Entertainment/Human Target Films, 2010-2011. Airing on the Fox network, this series starred Mark Valley as Christopher Chance. Unlike the short-lived ABC series in 1992 that had been loosely faithful to the bodyguard-disguised-as-target concept, this show had little relation to the comic book. Chance merely integrates himself into the targets' lives rather than taking their place. While the series may have been prompted by the Vertigo comic, it is not an adaptation of it.

Further Reading

Azzarello, Brian, and Eduardo Risso. *100 Bullets* (1999-2009).

Brubaker, Ed, Cameron Stewart, and Javier Pulido. *Catwoman: Relentless* (2004).

Milligan, Peter, and Duncan Fegredo. *Enigma* (1995).

Bibliography

Chiang, Cliff. "Stay on Target...: Cliff Chiang Talks *Human Target* and More." Interview by Arune Singh. *Comic Book Resources*, October 5, 2004. http://www.comicbookresources.com/?page=article&id=4096.

Milligan, Peter. "Peter Milligan." Interview by Daniel Robert Epstein. *UnderGroundOnline*, 2003. http://www.ugo.com/channels/freestyle/features/petermilligan.

Milligan, Peter. "Peter Milligan and *Human Target*." Interview by Eddie Robson. *Shiny Shelf*, March 22, 2011. http://www.shinyshelf.com/2011/03/22/peter-milligan-human-target.

See also: *100 Bullets*; *Alias; Hitman*

I

IDENTITY CRISIS

Author: Meltzer, Brad
Artist: Rags Morales (penciller); Alex Sinclair (colorist); Ken Lopez (letterer); Michael Turner (cover artist)
Publisher: DC Comics
First serial publication: 2004
First book publication: 2005

Publication History

First published in June of 2004, *Identity Crisis* takes place in DC's post-*Crisis on Infinite Earth*'s continuity. Brad Meltzer first proposed the work as a small personal story and not the blockbuster it ended up being. After reading the original script, Dan Didio (the editor at DC) and Geoff Johns decided to incorporate the story into the buildup for John's event *Infinite Crisis*. While *Infinite Crisis* is a stand-alone story, the events of *Identity Crisis* end up flowing through two of Johns's works, *Infinite Crisis* (2005-2006) and *Blackest Night* (2009-2010).

The comic received a large amount of publicity because of the subject matter, the visceral nature of the story itself, and the popularity of Meltzer as a writer. Meltzer had created many successful mystery novels, but this was only his second run with comics. The response from the literary community was powerful and launched the comic into mainstream success.

The roots of the comic are found mainly in Meltzer's experience with the Justice League of America (JLA). Meltzer had written *Green Arrow* after Kevin Smith's run, so the character figures prominently in the story. In commentary at the end of the hardcover edition, Meltzer says that in the first comic he read Elongated Man saved the JLA and there was a flashback with Doctor Light. This leads into the basis of *Identity Crisis*.

(AP Photo)

Brad Meltzer

Best known as an author of political thrillers, Brad Meltzer was a key figure in the move by American superhero comic book publishers to recruit writing talent from the fields of contemporary fiction, film, and television. Debuting at DC Comics in 2002 with a six-issue arc on *Green Arrow*, in 2004 he authored *Identity Crisis*, a controversial universe-altering crossover event. With its darkly sexual themes, *Infinite Crisis* was a controversial comics blockbuster based on the murder of Sue Dibny, the wife of Elongated Man. Meltzer's thirteen-issue run on the rebooted *Justice League of America* in 2006 earned him an Eisner Award. He has also contributed to *Buffy the Vampire Slayer Season Eight*. Meltzer has proven to be a polarizing figure in the field of graphic novels, with some critics feeling that he has taken liberties with long-established characterizations, and others insisting that he has been an important force for renewal in the genre.

Plot

Identity Crisis opens with Ralph Dibny (the Elongated Man) and Flamebird on patrol for the JLA. Ralph talks about his relationship with his wife, Sue Dibny, as well as what it is like to be a superhero with a public identity. Sue has sent Ralph out on patrol in order to surprise him for his birthday and is preparing the surprise alone in their high-security apartment. However, Ralph gets a panicked call from Sue and has Flamebird fly him back to his home, where he finds Sue dead and her corpse severely burned. Green Arrow leads the investigation, working with other superheroes to identify Sue's killer, but does not find enough evidence.

The superhero community is shocked by Sue's death and holds a funeral for her in Central City, where she and Ralph met. All of the superheroes attend in costume to protect their own identities. After the service, superheroes split up into groups to interrogate possible killers. However, Green Arrow, Black Canary, Hawkman, Zatanna, and Ralph, all members of the old JLA, have only one suspect: Doctor Light (Arthur Light). Wally West (the Flash) and Green Lantern Kyle Rayner have found the group and demand answers. Ralph reveals that Dr. Light had raped Sue on the JLA satellite and that they had erased his memory. Also, Zatanna had "mindwiped" many supervillains to make them forget their secret identities. After Dr. Light's rape of Sue, however, Zatanna altered his personality to make sure he would not do something like that again.

The seven of them, mirroring the old league, attempt to confront Dr. Light but are met by the villain Deathstroke, who has been hired by Dr. Light to protect him. After a difficult fight, the heroes manage to subdue Deathstroke, but Dr. Light escapes, remembering what the group has done to him. Afterward, Superman reveals that Dr. Light could not have killed Sue, as her burns were an attempt to cover up the real cause of death.

Another attack occurs on Jean Loring, the former wife of the Atom. The Atom manages to save Jean just in time, reigniting their relationship. The heroes launch a manhunt to find suspects and interrogate all the villains they can find, but their leads continually

turn up empty. However, while trying to subdue Shadow Thief, Firestorm is killed. The heroes have no leads as to who the killer is. A break in the case occurs when Captain Boomerang, in an attempt to impress his son and return to his former prominence, attacks Tim Drake's (the current Robin) father. However, someone had sent him a note and gun, and Jack Drake was able to kill Captain Boomerang before dying. This seemingly wraps up the case, but Batman remains unpersuaded and looks at the case from a new angle after having to bury Robin's father.

Everyone is eager to blame Boomerang and move on, but after reuniting with Jean, Ray Palmer makes a shocking discovery which leads him to conclude that Jean was the one who murdered Sue. She took one of Ray's old costumes and shrunk down inside Sue's head, blocking the blood flow and unintentionally killing her (she had only meant to cause a minor stroke). She confesses she did all of this to win back Ray, and Ray checks her into Arkham Asylum and shrinks down into nothingness.

Green Arrow also admits to the Flash that after the fight with Dr. Light, they had to make Batman forget that they erased his memory as well. He explains that had they not, it would have meant the end of the JLA and the ideals for which they stood. In the end, the league endures, as it was meant to.

Characters

- *Oliver Queen*, a.k.a. *the Green Arrow*, the protagonist, leads the investigation into Sue's death. He is a skilled archer and a member of the old league. He is often cynical, suspicious, and antiauthoritarian, which offers him a unique point of view. Because of his position he is emotionally tied to Ralph and has a perspective on the situation most superheroes do not.
- *Jean Loring* is the Atom's former wife and the secret antagonist of the story. She is intelligent and will do anything to get what she wants, which in this case is Ray. She kills Sue, stages an attack on herself, and hires Captain Boomerang to kill Tim Drake's father, all in an attempt to win back Ray.

- *Ralph Dibny*, a.k.a. *the Elongated Man*, is another member of the old league. He is an incredibly skilled detective and can stretch his body in any way he wants. The death of his wife sparks the events of the story and leads Ralph to attack Dr. Light. Throughout the story he is forced to deal with the events as best he can with the help of his friends.

- *Clark Kent*, a.k.a. *Superman*, represents the ideals of the league. He is never featured in the sections involving the suspect side of the league. He is portrayed as a "boy scout" and retains his idealism. He is the strength of the league and is considered by many to be the best of the superheroes.

- *Noah Kuttler*, a.k.a. *the Calculator*, was originally a supervillain who dressed as a calculator. Kuttler decided to act as a source of information for other villains. He coordinates many of the villain's actions throughout the series and gets Captain Boomerang the job to kill Jack Drake. He is incredibly intelligent and has an extensive array of contacts within the criminal world.

- *Sue Dibny* is Ralph's wife. She is a loving wife and an honorary member of the league. Her public identity has caused problems, including her rape at the hands of Dr. Light. She is killed by Jean Loring at the beginning of the series.

- *Tim Drake*, a.k.a. *Robin*, has a tense relationship with his father, Jack, because the latter has found out that his son is Robin. Robin works to balance this tension with his work with Batman and as the leader of the Teen Titans. He is young and remains idealistic.

- *Ray Palmer*, a.k.a. *the Atom*, is another member of the old league. He has a costume that allows him to shrink to microscopic sizes and is a world-renowned physicist. He and Jean Loring are divorced but still on decent terms with each other. He often defuses conflict within the league. He reunites with Jean during the events of *Identity Crisis* but commits her to Arkham Asylum after discovering that she killed Sue.

- *Wally West*, a.k.a. the Flash, joined the league after his uncle, Barry Allen, was killed in *Crisis*

on Infinite Earths. He serves as a foil to the cynical Green Arrow because of his idealism. He is the fastest man on Earth.

- *Dr. Arthur Light*, a.k.a. *Dr. Light*, is an old enemy of the JLA. He is portrayed in two differing ways, sometimes as a psychopath and sometimes as a bumbling enemy of the Teen Titans. It is revealed that he had his personality altered by Zatanna in order to "clean him up again." He employs Deathstroke to defend him when the old league comes to question him. He remembers the mindwipe and plots revenge.

- *Merlyn* is an incredibly skilled archer and assassin. In terms of his role, he is the villainous counterpart to Green Arrow. He serves as another voice and perspective on the events. Merlyn is cold and calculating and trusts few people.

- *Digger Harkness*, a.k.a. *Captain Boomerang*, was once a prominent member of the criminal association the Rogues and fell into being a "letch." He is out of shape and down on his luck, barely able to get a job. He also has found out he has a son and is attempting to reconnect with him. He takes the job to kill Jack Drake in an attempt to impress his son. He is gunned down in the process.

- *Slade Wilson*, a.k.a. *Deathstroke*, is a master tactician and fighter. He manages to defeat the old league before Green Arrow stabs him in the eye. The league's brutal assault on him reminds Dr. Light of what happened to him and reveals to the Flash that Batman had been a part of the fight against Dr. Light after the rape of Sue Dibny.

- *Bruce Wayne*, a.k.a. *Batman*, is a presence throughout the series. He is working the case and trying to discover the murderer. He is at odds with the Calculator. Batman is methodical and intelligent and remains calm until the death of Jack Drake, when he is again reminded why he is Batman.

Artistic Style

The art reflects a generally standard style of modern comics. Pages are clean and focused with vivid colors. Generally, panels are open and simple. Even the large funeral scene is open and, despite featuring most every character in the DC Universe, does not feel crowded.

One interesting aspect of the structure is its adherence to a novelistic style. The constant use of narration boxes for multiple characters leads to a much more literary style than other comics. This has roots in Meltzer's original writing of mystery novels and an impact on how the book itself is read. This style makes the comic flow more like a mystery novel than a comic book and works to characterize the heroes and villains, giving more emotion to the story.

Along with this character focus come many panels that are just facial close-ups. These reaction shots are prominent throughout the series and add emotional depth by showing the fear or shock in eyes of the characters. These visceral shots make it clear just how personal the story is.

Alex Sinclair, the colorist, uses light effectively to convey the powerful emotions in the story. In one particular panel, he colors Ralph's face to show his rage; in another panel, he uses color to show Ralph's love for his wife. The use of these vivid and clear colors makes the story sharp and crisp and highlights the energy of the story itself.

The overall art style is traditional but well adapted for the feeling and energy of the novel. Meltzer's style flows well with the incredible artwork of Rags Morales and Sinclair's coloring; Ken Lopez's lettering is detailed on small newspapers that pop up throughout the story. The detail to characters and settings add to the realism and tension, which make for a suspenseful mystery.

Themes

Identity Crisis has a few continuous themes that work throughout the series, the most prominent being the nature of identity and secret identity. Villains are humanized and presented in a community, aspects that cloud the definition of the villains in this story. For example, Merlyn, who represents the villain community and is a counterpart to Green Arrow, is seen in his home performing tasks associated with the average person. This revealing humanity is a side not often presented by many writers and allows readers to identify with the "bad guys," which makes the mystery

killer even more bizarre, further convoluting his or her identity.

The nature of a secret identity is also brought into play in this series. While this is a common theme in comics, in *Identity Crisis* it is shown in the context of interactions among superheroes. The relationship between fathers and sons is a major focus in the story. These relationships deal with familial bonding and the issues that arise from having a family member with a secret identity. Superheroes wear masks to protect the ones they care about, and the attacks on their immediate family, who maintain public identities, are a powerful reminder of the dangers superheroes and their families face on a daily basis.

Impact

Selected by the Young Adult Library Services Association (YALSA) as a recommended Great Graphic Novel for Teens in 2007, this series had a major impact on the DC Universe as a whole. Though originally intended as a small story, it was incorporated into John's *Infinite Crisis*. What happens in this story leads directly to the portrayal of a corrupted universe that needs to be saved. This story is a direct contrast to the lighthearted Gold Age and Silver Age comics, and dispels many of the myths about the purity of the Silver Age JLA.

Many of the emotional issues at the end of the story are addressed again in the *Blackest Night* series, when the reanimated bodies of Ralph, Sue, and Jean return to torment their old friends. Ray Palmer is forced to confront what Jean did and how it affected their relationship, while other superheroes have to deal with the harsh reality of their deaths.

Overall, the series is a continuation of the more adult tone of Modern Age comics that feature extreme violence and more adult subject matter. The brutal rape of Sue is something that completely separates this story and establishes a new standard for mainstream comics in the sense that even the JLA is not appropriate for all ages. This translates to the more extreme *Infinite Crisis* and subsequent stories that define the tone of the DC Universe.

Sam Otterbourg

Further Reading

Johns, Geoff, et al. *Infinite Crisis* (2005-2006).

Meltzer, Brad, and Gene Ha. *Justice League of America* (2006-2007).

Smith, Kevin, Phil Hester, and Andé Parks. *Green Arrow: Quiver* (2000-2001).

Bibliography

Beatty, Scott. *JLA: The Ultimate Guide to the Justice League of America*. New York: Dorling Kindersley, 2002.

"Crisis Team: Meltzer, Morales Look Back at *Identity Crisis*." *Comic Book Resources—Daily Comic Book News, Previews, Reviews, Commentary, and Message Boards*, December 13, 2010. http://www.comicbookresources.com/?page=article andid=5766.

Meltzer, Brad, Rags Morales, and Michael Bair. *Identity Crisis*. New York: DC Comics, 2006.

See also: *Green Arrow: Year One; Infinite Crisis; Crisis on Infinite Earths;Justice League of America The Nail*

I*NFINITE* C*RISIS*

Author: Johns, Geoff

Artist: Phil Jimenez (illustrator); Jerry Ordway (illustrator); George Pérez (illustrator); Ivan Reis (illustrator); Oclair Albert (inker); Marlo Alquiza (inker); Marc Campos (inker); Wayne Faucher (inker); Drew Geraci (inker); Andy Lanning (inker); Jimmy Palmiotti (inker); Sean Parson (inker); Norm Rapmund (inker); Lary Stucker (inker); Art Thibert (inker); Jeremy Cox (colorist); Richard Horie (colorist); Tanya Horie (colorist); Guy Major (colorist); Rod Reis (colorist); Rob Leigh (letterer); Nick J. Napolitano (letterer)

Publisher: DC Comics

First serial publication: 2005-2006

First book publication: 2006

Publication History

The first of the seven-issue *Infinite Crisis* limited series went on sale in October of 2005, with a December cover date. According to the *Comics Chronicle*'s John Jackson Miller, the first issue was the top-selling comic book for that month, with more than a quarter million copies sold. It continued to be the top-selling comic book at American comic book specialty shops for each of the subsequent months it was published (skipping publication in February), except for its final issue that was released in May, 2006 (with a June cover date). That month Marvel debuted its crossover event *Civil War*, which bumped *Infinite Crisis* to the number-two spot. The seven issues of *Infinite Crisis* were then assembled in a hardcover collection published by DC Comics in October, 2006. Subsequently, DC issued a trade paperback edition in February, 2008.

In addition to the series proper, DC published a one-shot lead-in, *DC Countdown to Infinite Crisis*, and a number of limited series and specials, setting the stage for *Infinite Crisis*. Another one-shot, *Infinite Crisis: Secret Files and Origins 2006*, was published in March (dated April) and featured a prequel story. Numerous DC titles were tied into the event and featured a cover banner proclaiming each of those issues as an "Infinite Crisis Crossover." A number of Crisis Aftermath

(Getty Images)

Geoff Johns

In the span of a decade, writer Geoff Johns went from being an unknown writer to chief creative officer of DC Comics. After working in the movie industry, Johns broke into comics in 1999 with *Stars and S.T.R.I.P.E.* In 2000 he became the writer of *The Flash* and *Justice Society of America*. Long runs on those titles established him as the writer for the massive cross-company event comic *Infinite Crisis*. He was also one of the four writers (with Grant Morrison, Greg Rucka, and Mark Waid) of *52*. In 2010 he became an executive at DC, and in 2011 he spearheaded the reboot of the entire DC line, writing the new flagship title *Justice League*. Johns's writing is characterized by its ambition and scope. His work on company-wide crossovers and reboots has led to a fascination with cataclysmic events and shocking plot twists.

limited series and specials followed the events as well. In 2006, Ace Books published a novelization of the story written by Greg Cox.

Plot

Infinite Crisis is a superhero crossover event with a fairly elaborate series of lead-in projects, including one-shot *DC Countdown to Infinite Crisis* (May, 2005) and four limited series: *Day of Vengeance*, *The OMAC Project*, *Rann-Thanagar War*, and *Villains United*, all of which were published in 2005. As the crossover opens, each of the crises developed in these series reaches a fever pitch, and the trinity of leading superheroes, Superman, Batman, and Wonder Woman, cannot agree on a united course of action to confront these threats. A dimension away, four figures watch through crystalline walls as the heroic alliance dissolves, and they decide to take action. Smashing through the barrier, Superman of Earth-2; his wife, Lois Lane Kent; Superboy of Earth-Prime; and Alexander Luthor of Earth-3 return to Earth-1 after their self-imposed exile at the end of the *Crisis on Infinite Earths* limited series (1985). Their stated goal is to restore a multiverse of parallel Earths, and they attempt to recruit other heroes perceived to be sympathetic to their cause to join them.

However, all is not as it seems, for Alexander and Superboy-Prime have been working behind the scenes for some time. Disguised as the Earth-1 Lex Luthor, Alexander has assembled a strike force of supervillains, reprogrammed Batman's Brother Eye surveillance satellite, manipulated the superpowerful ghost the Spectre into waging a war on all other magical beings, and sent Superboy-Prime into space to realign planets, all ingredients in his machinations to engineer the re-creation of the multiverse. He then plans to sift through the parallel worlds until he finds a perfect one and discard the rest, including Earth-1.

As Alexander's plot comes to fruition, the heroes reunite to take action. Batman leads a strike team that disables Brother Eye. The Superboy of Earth-1 (Conner Kent) returns to duty, only to sacrifice his life in battle with his doppelgänger; he manages to disable Alexander's machinery in the process, however. In the wake of Superboy's sacrifice, an even broader array of heroes assembles to take on a veritable army of supervillains in Metropolis. Joining the villains is Superboy-Prime, who soon abandons that losing fight and races into space, intent on destroying the planet Oa, at the center of the universe, hoping that such a cataclysm will reboot the universe.

Two Supermen streak after him into space and force a final confrontation on another planet, one under a red sun, which gradually deprives all three Kryptonians of their superpowers. Insane with rage, Superboy-Prime beats the elder Superman to death, before he is pummeled into unconsciousness by Superman of Earth-1. Alexander escapes in the ensuing confusion, only to be tracked down by Lex Luthor and killed by Luthor's partner, the Joker, the one supervillain that Alexander had not included in his secret society.

Characters

- *Superman*, a.k.a. *Kal-El of Krypton-1*, a protagonist, is the prototypical iconic superhero: muscular, handsome, bedecked in a bright blue uniform and red cape, and sporting an "S" shield on his chest. However, as *Infinite Crisis* begins, he is accused of being less inspirational than ever before, and his colleagues and foes hold him responsible for failing to provide leadership in the face of many of the recent crises that have plagued the metahuman community.

- *Batman*, a.k.a. *Bruce Wayne*, a protagonist, is a muscular man whose identity is concealed under a cowl reminiscent of a bat. He is brilliant and suspicious, and one of the tools he has created in his war on crime, Brother Eye, has gone rogue thanks to Alexander Luthor. He assembles a strike team to take out Brother Eye and deactivate hundreds of innocent sleeper drones, called OMACs, from wrecking havoc around the world.

- *Wonder Woman*, a.k.a. *Princess Diana of Themyscira*, a protagonist, is a beautiful, statuesque, star-spangled Amazon warrior. She finds herself ostracized by her peers and her besieged Amazons because she has recently killed a former ally turned adversary, Maxwell Lord, in order to prevent him from using his mind-control powers to make Superman his unstoppable enforcer. Under an onslaught of OMACs, she orders the Amazons to leave this plane of reality, stranding her alone in the world. She later guides two feuding

Supermen back on the path to facing their true enemies.

- *Superboy*, a.k.a. *Conner Kent*, another protagonist, is a muscular young adult who wears a black "S"-shield T-shirt and blue jeans. He is a guilt-ridden hero, struggling with whether or not to involve himself in any further heroics after an episode in which he was manipulated into attacking his peers. He returns to duty following a confrontation with Superboy-Prime and is slain in a subsequent battle, though he manages to disable machinery imperiling the universe.

- *Superman*, a.k.a. *Kal-L of Kryton-2*, a protagonist, is an older version of the iconic hero, with graying temples and wrinkles that evidence his decades-long battle against injustice. He is initially obsessed with finding a means to save the life of his ailing wife, Lois Lane Kent, and aids Alexander Luthor's plot to reconstitute the multiverse. After Lois's inevitable death, Superman discovers Alexander's duplicity and channels his grief into resolve to defend the universe.

- *Alexander Luthor* of Earth-3 is the primary antagonist of the story. He is a young, athletically built redhead who wears a skin-tight golden suit that helps him control his power to cross dimensions. When he uses this power, a field of black space and stars covers parts of his body. He also masquerades as Earth-1's Lex Luthor and appears bald and in a business suit. Characteristically, he is cool and self-assured, an inventor of advanced technologies, and the mastermind behind the crisis. He manipulates planets as easily as people in his quest to restore the multiverse and discover the perfect Earth.

- *Superboy-Prime* is a teenage version of Superman and the sole survivor of Earth-Prime. He possesses all of the powers of Superman but lacks the latter's emotional maturity. He longs to return to his now-dead world and grow into the role of Superman. Initially, he is portrayed as Alexander's lackey, running errands for the mastermind, but he evolves into an increasingly unstable, even homicidal threat after a violent confrontation with Conner Kent. That conflict escalates to

include several of Conner's allies, some of which Prime maims or kills. By the end of the story, he is the last and most powerful threat standing.

Artistic Style

In many ways, the art in *Infinite Crisis* embodies the epitome of the superhero genre: Improbably proportioned heroes and villains strike iconic poses, action-packed splash pages punctuate key hits and revelations, and primary colors saturate page after page. Likewise, *Infinite Crisis* fulfills nearly every expectation associated with the crossover subgenre, with ample scenes in which numerous costumed characters are packed into a single frame and cameos from all corners of DC's fictional universe. In this regard, lead penciller Phil Jimenez honors the artist who first mastered this form with *Crisis on Infinite Earths*, George Pérez.

Writer Johns has asked his art team to pack quite a few more panels into most pages than is typical of many contemporary superhero layouts. This results in more story than can be found in most crossover events. In addition, when splash pages or double-page spreads are used, they seem to have more dramatic punch because of the other comparatively packed pages.

There are a bewildering number of characters in the series, but the art team's dedication to realistic renderings, including consistent facial designs, means that the principles remain consistently recognizable amid a sea of colorful costars. The realistic detail extends to the settings, scenery, and technology around the characters and helps the reader to accept the actuality of many of the events, improbable and unfamiliar as they might be. Despite having four pencillers and copious inkers contributing to the project, the artistic style remains surprisingly consistent throughout the story's run.

Themes

One key theme in *Infinite Crisis* is redemption. Alexander, Superboy-Prime, and Kal-L set events into motion because of their desire to leave their self-imposed exile, confront the corruption they perceive on Earth-1, and return to (or discover) more idealized worlds to inhabit. The central protagonists, the so-called trinity of DC superheroes—Superman, Batman, and Wonder Woman—also seek redemption: Superman has failed to live up to his leadership potential; Batman has unleashed a malevolent satellite upon the world; and Wonder Woman has killed. Moreover, events leading up to the crisis have fractured their historic alliance.

In the end, the heroes atone for their failings and reunite. Kal-L's quest ends much differently than anticipated; instead of returning to his home world, he resumes his duties as Superman, forsaking his quest for personal peace and returning to action to defend the world. Thus, an associated theme is responsibility, and Johns shows how heroes are the ones who assume it when no one else can or will.

The transformation of Superboy-Prime from naïve doppelgänger to homicidal world breaker illustrates both a failure to accept responsibility and a counterpoint to the quest for redemption. In fact, Superboy-Prime's is a story of corruption. As his desire to return to his world is increasingly frustrated, he grows more petulant, lashing out in anger at anyone nearby. Then, rather than taking responsibility for his actions, he continues to deny his own culpability to the point that he is a danger to the universe.

Impact

Like its predecessor, 1985's *Crisis on Infinite Earths*, *Infinite Crisis* was intended to be a high-profile event, shaking up the status quo in terms of DC's publishing agenda and revamping aspects of continuity within the DC Universe. In terms of publishing, *Infinite Crisis* became the launching point for several series, the most influential of which was the experimental weekly series *52* (2007). The commercial and critical success of *52* led DC to several other weekly comics in subsequent years. *Infinite Crisis* also introduced DC's most high profile Latino character to date, Jaime Reyes as the new Blue Beetle.

Within continuity, the series reintroduced the concept of parallel worlds to the DC Universe cosmology

(again something more fully realized in *52*). The series was also used as a launching point for the "One Year Later" event, where all the story lines in the DC Universe titles jumped ahead one year into the characters' futures. *Infinite Crisis* also introduced several changes to existing DC continuity, including giving Superman back a career as Superboy; allowing Batman to capture his parents' killer, Joe Chill; and restoring Wonder Woman as a founding member of the Justice League of America.

Matthew J. Smith

Further Reading

Johns, Geoff, et al. *Blackest Night* (2009-2010).

Jurgens, Dan, and Jerry Ordway. *Zero Hour: Crisis in Time* (1994).

Meltzer, Brad, and Rags Morales. *Identity Crisis* (2005).

Wolfman, Marv, et al. *Crisis on Infinite Earths* (1985-1986).

Bibliography

Kawa, Abraham. "Comics Since the Silver Age." In *The Routledge Companion to Science Fiction*, edited by Mark Bould. New York: Routledge, 2009.

Klock, Jeff. *How to Read Superhero Comics and Why*. New York: Continuum, 2002.

Niederhausen, Michael. "Deconstructing *Crisis on Infinite Earths:* Grant Morrison's *Animal Man*, *JLA: Earth 2*, and *Flex Mentallo*." *The International Journal of Comic Art* 12, no. 1 (Spring, 2010): 271-282.

See also: *Crisis on Infinite Earths; Identity Crisis; Superman: For All Seasons; Superman: Red Son; Superman: The Man of Steel*

INFINITY GAUNTLET, THE

Author: Starlin, Jim
Artist: Ron Lim (illustrator); George Pérez (illustrator); Tom Christopher (inker); Josef Rubinstein (inker); Bruce N. Solotoff (inker); Mike Witherby (inker); Ian Laughlin (colorist); Max Scheele (colorist); Jack Morelli (letterer)
Publisher: Marvel Comics
First serial publication: 1991
First book publication: 1992

Publication History

The Infinity Gauntlet was first published by Marvel Comics in 1991 as a six-issue comic book miniseries. It was later published by Marvel Comics in a single-volume graphic novel format in 1992. *The Infinity Gauntlet* expanded ongoing story lines first introduced in the *Silver Surfer* comic book series and the 1990 *The Thanos Quest* miniseries. The story line of *The Infinity Gauntlet* would be continued in Marvel Comics' 1992 *Infinity War* and 1993 *Infinity Crusade* miniseries.

At the time *The Infinity Gauntlet* was published, writer Jim Starlin was a well-established and respected illustrator and writer with almost twenty years of industry experience. Best known at the time for his 1970's *Captain Marvel* story line, which introduced the central characters and conflicts that would eventually become the heart of *The Infinity Gauntlet* miniseries, Starlin had transitioned from being primarily an illustrator to a writer by the time of *The Infinity Gauntlet*. Indeed, prior to *The Infinity Gauntlet*, Starlin had scripted two similarly cosmic-scaled miniseries, DC Comics' 1988 *Cosmic Odyssey* and Marvel Comics' 1990 *The Thanos Quest*.

George Pérez was one of the most prominent illustrators in the comic book industry at the time of the publication of *The Infinity Gauntlet*. Having previously cocreated the *New Teen Titans* in 1980 and the late 1980's relaunch of *Wonder Woman*, Pérez was perhaps best known as the artist of the epic and highly influential *Crisis on Infinite Earths* miniseries for DC Comics in 1985. His obligations to complete simultaneously

The Infinity Gauntlet. (Courtesy of Marvel Comics)

both Marvel Comics' *The Infinity Gauntlet* miniseries and DC Comics' *War of the Gods* miniseries led him to being overcommitted, and he left *The Infinity Gauntlet* midway through the fourth issue. As a result, Ron Lim completed the series. Lim had extensive experience with the main characters of *The Infinity Gauntlet*, being best known at the time for his work with Starlin on the *Silver Surfer* series and *The Thanos Quest* miniseries.

Plot

The Infinity Gauntlet tells the story of Thanos's attempt to use the power of the Infinity Gauntlet to gain the love of Death. The Infinity Gauntlet is embedded with six gemstones that give the wielder godlike power to control the soul, the mind, time, power, reality, and space. The story begins with Thanos having already gained possession of the gauntlet. Nihilistic and malevolent, Thanos intends to use the power of the gauntlet to gain the affection of Death, who has raised Thanos from the dead on the promise that Thanos will fulfill Death's wish to kill half the sentient population of the universe in order to bring the realms of life and death into balance. To prove his love to Death, Thanos brings himself, his adviser Mephisto, and Death to a monument to Death he has wished into existence in deep space. Once there, however, Mephisto informs Thanos that, while he controls the godlike power of the Infinity Gauntlet, Death will always feel subjugated to him and hence will not have affection for him.

Mephisto manipulates Thanos into summoning Nebula to his monument to Death. Thanos holds Nebula in a state of limbo between life and death in order to impress Death with his power. When this does

not work, Mephisto further manipulates Thanos into fulfilling his promise to Death by wishing half the sentient population of the universe out of existence.

Meanwhile, Doctor Stephen Strange and the Silver Surfer—who has learned about Thanos's plans from Mephisto, under the guidance of Adam Warlock, a powerful being that had been living inside the soul gem of the Infinity Gauntlet—gather a team of superheroes and a collection of "astral deities of the universe" to attack Thanos.

Thanos kills the superheroes and imprisons the astral deities. Thanos then defeats Eternity, the cosmic embodiment of the universe itself, thereby taking on this disembodied role for himself. As Thanos does this, the forgotten Nebula snatches the Infinity Gauntlet from Thanos's physical body and takes the power of the gauntlet for herself.

As an overwhelmed Nebula revels in her newly acquired power, Adam Warlock has Dr. Strange summon

The Infinity Gauntlet. (Courtesy of Marvel Comics)

the remaining heroes and Thanos to his sanctum. There, Adam Warlock confronts Thanos with the knowledge that Thanos has a deep-seated subconscious desire to fail. A shaken Thanos agrees to help the superheroes resist Nebula and her use of the Infinity Gauntlet. Nearing defeat, Thanos tricks Nebula into restoring everything to the way it was before Thanos destroyed half the universe. Nebula is then attacked by the newly restored astral deities. In the midst of this confusion, Adam Warlock brings himself and the Silver Surfer into the soul gem. From within the soul gem, Adam Warlock is able to reach out and overwhelm Nebula's control of the Infinity Gauntlet, forcing her to drop it to the ground where Adam Warlock grabs it and ends the conflict. Despite some concern from the assembled heroes, Adam Warlock keeps possession of the Infinity Gauntlet, vowing to keep its power from being used for harm. The story ends with Adam Warlock leaving a humbled Thanos on a pastoral world to engage in a contemplative life.

Characters

- *Thanos*, the antagonist, is a physically imposing, gray-skinned member of the Eternals from Titan (a moon of Saturn). Ruthless and cruel, Thanos has repeatedly sought to gain cosmic-level power as he attempts to prove his worth to Death. His use of the Infinity Gauntlet forms the central conflict of the story.
- *Adam Warlock*, the protagonist, is a golden-skinned, white-eyed enigmatic being. Possessed of tremendous wisdom and power, he has an intimate connection with the Infinity Gauntlet. His awareness of Thanos's limitations provides the key to defeating Thanos's plans.
- *Mephisto* is a devilish, red-caped, extradimensional demon. A master schemer and manipulator, he is constantly seeking to turn situations to his best advantage. His manipulations drive Thanos into making key mistakes that lead to his defeat.
- *Dr. Stephen Strange* is a human who wears a flowing cape and amulet in his role as Earth's Sorcerer Supreme. He possesses the ability to project himself astrally and to create dimensional

portals. His ability to manipulate time and space is key to the defeat of Thanos.
- *The Silver Surfer* is a silver-skinned hero imbued with cosmic power and awareness who flies through space on a cosmic surfboard. Constantly seeking to understand and protect life, he anchors Adam Warlock's soul as he fights Nebula for control of the Infinity Gauntlet.
- *Death* is the mute astral deity who appears to Thanos as a young woman enrobed in a midnight-blue floor-length cape. As the astral deity who oversees the realm of the dead, she seeks to balance the scales of life and death. Her decision to restore Thanos to life in order that he may fulfill her desire to seek balance between the living and the dead combined with her refusal to return Thanos's affection provokes Thanos's actions.
- *Nebula* is a blue-skinned, blue-haired mercenary who has invoked Thanos's wrath. Her removal of the Infinity Gauntlet from Thanos's body provides the opportunity for the ultimate neutralization of the Infinity Gauntlet's threat.
- *Eternity* is an astral deity composed of the collective life force of the universe and appears as a colossal-scale humanoid outline containing the stars and galaxies of the universe. He represents the sum of time and space and is the ultimate representation of power and control within the universe. Thanos's supplanting of Eternity separates his consciousness from his physical body, resulting in his losing control of the Infinity Gauntlet.

Artistic Style

In the first half of *The Infinity Gauntlet*, Pérez's characters are consistently rendered with highly defined musculature and distinctive features that imbue them with a high degree of realism. His pages are infused with color and light, making limited use of shadows. His panels are highly dynamic and typically constructed in medias res, capturing motion and action at its peak of dramatic effect. Pérez further maximizes the dynamism in his art through the use of constantly shifting panel layouts and camera angles, with nearly every page having a distinct panel arrangement. The effect of this is to throw the reader out of his familiar rhythms, thereby generating a deep sense of urgency within the story.

Well known for his character collages, Pérez employs these skills throughout *The Infinity Gauntlet*, filling his panels with innumerable major and minor characters each rendered in extensive detail. Similarly, his background work abounds with highly detailed and sharply defined settings, giving the story greater verisimilitude. The speech bubbles and captions within the story are also used to convey character, from Thanos's ragged black-edged balloons to the dramatic starburst balloons that encapsulate various characters' exclamations of fear, surprise, and horror.

Lim's art in the second half of *The Infinity Gauntlet* is highly complementary to Pérez's. While Lim's work does not typically contain as much dynamism as Pérez's (Lim tends to choose more conventional camera angles and panel layouts), Lim's character work nevertheless hews fairly closely to Pérez's, with both working toward highly rendered realistic characters. While Lim's backgrounds are generally less detailed than Pérez's, his art in the cosmic-level battle scenes in the second half of *The Infinity Gauntlet* achieves a high sense of place and dynamism through highly effective uses of dramatic color and motion lines that imbue his panels with a real feeling of the epic scale of the conflict taking place. With frequent use of oversized panels that fill half the page or more, Lim stretches the scale of his art to match the level of conflict. Lim's use of these techniques propels the story forward and works well with Pérez's earlier dynamic techniques.

Themes

The major theme of *The Infinity Gauntlet* is the nature of love and the soul. A being so ruthless as to be willing to cavalierly eliminate half the sentient population of the universe, Thanos finds himself helpless to resist the power of the love he feels for Death. In this manner, the story treats love as the ultimate power in the universe. Thanos is willing to do anything to prove his love and is driven increasingly mad by Death's refusal to return his affections. Similarly, *The Infinity Gauntlet* emphasizes the importance of the soul in guiding people's actions. Indeed, Adam Warlock, who appears as a messianic figure in the story by arising from the dead to

command the astral deities of the universe, draws his power from his deep connection to the soul gem.

The power of the soul gem is so strong that Warlock can ultimately use it to overwhelm Nebula's control of the entire Infinity Gauntlet. In this way, *The Infinity Gauntlet* makes the soul gem preeminent over the mind, time, power, reality, and space realms of the other gems. As if to emphasize the importance of knowing one's soul, Thanos finds that the instant he embodies the universe he loses control of his physical body and the Infinity Gauntlet. Indeed, by the end of the story, Thanos has had his soul exposed to himself by Adam Warlock. Learning his true nature, Thanos is finally liberated from his madness. The power of the soul has given him peace, even from the madness of love.

Impact

The success of *The Infinity Gauntlet* led it to become the first in a trilogy of interrelated miniseries. In this way, *The Infinity Gauntlet* helped to propel the trend toward crossover-event publishing that had developed at Marvel Comics during the 1980's and early 1990's. Most immediately, the plotlines introduced in the *The*

Ron Lim

After breaking into the comics industry in the late-1980's, artist Ron Lim established himself as a leading figure in Marvel's cosmic genre with a six-year run on *Silver Surfer* from 1988 to 1994. During that period he produced much of the work for which he is best known, including three company-wide crossovers written by Jim Starlin: *The Infinity Gauntlet* in 1991, *The Infinity War* in 1992, and *The Infinity Crusade* in 1993. Although he has had his greatest successes in the cosmic space opera area of the Marvel Universe, Lim's artwork is much more conventionally classic than many of his colleagues who have explored similar areas. His character designs hew closely to the Marvel stylebook of the period in which he worked, and seems to be influenced by John Byrne, the dominant Marvel artist of the early 1980's.

Infinity Gauntlet miniseries were continued in Marvel Comics' *Infinity War* and *Infinity Crusade* miniseries. The events of *The Infinity Gauntlet* also formed the basis for Marvel Comics' ongoing spin-off series *Warlock and the Infinity Watch*, which ran for forty-two issues from 1992 to 1995. As part of this series, the character of Thanos continued in the new characterization he had acquired at the end of *The Infinity Gauntlet*, working beside Warlock as the entrusted caretaker of the reality gem of the Infinity Gauntlet.

With his work on *The Infinity Gauntlet* and its related series, Starlin cemented his reputation as the driving creative force behind the Thanos saga, a relationship that would continue with Starlin writing and illustrating numerous Thanos-related projects over the following twenty years, including Marvel Comics' 2002 *Thanos: Infinity Abyss* miniseries and the 2002-2003 *Thanos: Epiphany* series.

The Infinity Gauntlet also had a significant impact on Pérez's career. Pérez has commented on how his inability to fulfill his artwork commitment for *The Infinity Gauntle*t along with related problems on other projects tarnished his reputation for reliability within the industry, limiting his access to big projects for a period of time.

Jason M. LaTouche

Further Reading

Starlin, Jim. *Infinity War* (1992).

Starlin, Jim, and Ron Lim. *The Thanos Quest* (1990).

Starlin, Jim, and Mike Mignola. *Cosmic Odyssey* (1988).

Bibliography

Baker, Bill. *George Perez on His Work and Career*. New York: Rosen, 2007.

De Blieck, Augie. "Pipeline Retro: Infinity Gauntlet." *Comic Book Resources*, August 24, 2010. http://www. comicbookresources.com/?page=article&id=27982.

Lim, Ron. "Interview with Ron Lim." Interview by A. David Lewis. *PopMatters*. http://www.popmatters. com/comics/interview-lim-ron.shtml.

Pérez, George. "An Interview with George Pérez." Interview by Jamie Coville. *Coville's Clubhouse*, June, 2000. http://www.collectortimes.com/2000_06/ Clubhouse.html.

See also: *Silver Surfer: Parable; Cosmic Odyssey; Crisis on Infinite Earths*

INVINCIBLE

Author: Kirkman, Robert
Artist: Ryan Ottley (illustrator); Corey Walker (illustrator); Cliff Rathburn (inker); Bill Crabtree (colorist); FCO Plascencia (colorist); Rus Wooton (letterer)
Publisher: Image Comics
First serial publication: 2003-
First book publication: 2003-2010

Publication History

Invincible was created by Robert Kirkman and Corey Walker in 2003 for Image Comics' superhero line, which was started by publisher Jim Valentino to bring superheroes back into Image's focus while avoiding the grim and gritty superheroes with which Image was strongly associated when it was founded in 1992. Kirkman and Walker developed the idea together, and Kirkman recruited Bill Crabtree to color the book. Of the comics included in Image's superhero line, *Invincible* was the only series not quickly canceled and was still being published as of 2011.

Walker soon found himself unable to keep up with a monthly schedule. The book disappeared from circulation until Ryan Ottley replaced Walker as penciller on issue 8. *Invincible* remains the center of the "Kirkmanverse," a universe where the Kirkman-penned series of *Tech Jacket, Invincible, Brit,* and *The Astounding Wolf-Man* all take place. As of 2011, the series has been collected in thirteen volumes (each named after a television sitcom), containing several issues and a variety of bonus material in each. Additionally, the series has been collected in five hardcover editions. Three miniseries have spun off from *Invincible—Invincible Presents: Atom Eve* (2009), *Invincible Presents: Atom Eve and Rex Splode* (2009), and *Guarding the Globe* (2010). Since issue 75, *Invincible* has been published under Kirkman's personal Image imprint, Skybound.

Plot

Invincible tells the story of Mark Grayson, also known as Invincible. Mark is a regular teenager—he hangs out with friends, toils at homework, and works a dead-end

Cory Walker

Although he contributed art to a number of fill-in titles for Marvel Comics in the 2000's, Cory Walker is best known for his work with writer Robert Kirkman on the first seven issues of the Image Comics series, *Invincible*. The story of the teen-aged son of an extraterrestrial superhero, *Invincible* harkens back to classic superhero stories from the 1980's, with a clean-cut appearance and traditional character and costume designs. Walker's art is defined by its combination of cartoony figures and simple page designs. He favors a small number of panels on a page, with a very classical division of space. Since leaving *Invincible*, Walker has illustrated titles including *Shadowpact* for DC Comics and *Irredeemable Ant-Man* for Marvel.

job at a burger restaurant. However, Mark's father is Omni-Man, the world's greatest superhero. Omni-Man, also known as Nolan Grayson, is an alien known as a Viltrumite. Raised on the Viltrumite story of a peaceful race that spread prosperity across the universe, Mark has waited his whole life to inherit his father's powers. Soon after obtaining them and becoming Invincible, Mark has his first collaboration with the Teen Team, a group of local superheroes that includes Atom Eve, Mark's primary love interest later in the series, and others. During his first few adventures, Mark fights the Reanimen and befriends Allen the Alien, a representative of the Coalition of Planets.

Issue 7 is a turning point in the series. The Guardians of the Globe, the world's foremost superhero team, are murdered by Omni-Man. Soon after, Cecil Stedman of the Global Defense Agency forms a new team. Mark begins dating Amber Bennet, a girl from his high school. It is not long before Nolan is forced to reveal the truth to Mark: the Viltrumites are not a peaceful people but a race of bloodthirsty warriors obsessed with conquest and war. Nolan did not come to

Earth to protect it, but to conquer it. Mark refuses to aid his father, stating his intent to defend Earth. For his effort, he is savagely beaten by Nolan. However, before delivering the fatal blow, Nolan flies away with tears in his eyes, abandoning Earth and his family.

In the aftermath, Cecil hires Invincible to be Earth's foremost protector. Not long after graduating high school, Mark aids a National Aeronautics and Space Administration (NASA) expedition to Mars. One of the astronauts is mistakenly left behind and becomes a host for the Sequids, a parasitic, hive-mind race used as slaves by the Martians. Mark heads to Upstate University, where his superhero responsibilities keep him from studying. Upstate University is also home to D. A. Sinclair, the young man who has been kidnapping people and turning them into murderous Reanimen.

In the six-part story line "A Different World," Mark travels to a planet of bug people. The planet's ruler is none other than Nolan Grayson. Nolan has remarried and has another son, Mark's half brother, Oliver. Nolan, whose leave of Earth was a betrayal of the Viltrumite empire, brings Mark to the planet to help him fight off the Viltrumites. The two work together but are ultimately defeated, and Nolan is captured. Mark returns to Earth, bringing Oliver with him. Upon Mark's return, Mark and Amber visit Eve, who has been doing humanitarian work in Africa. However, the vacation is cut short when the villain Angstrom Levy takes Mark's family hostage. During the fight, Angstrom takes Invincible to a number of alternate universes (including the DC and Marvel Universes), until, in a fit of rage, Mark seemingly kills Angstrom, an act that goes against his moral code.

Following this is a two-issue story arc in which Invincible defeats the Reanimen and Sinclair is taken into custody. However, the arc ends with Cecil exonerating Sinclair and offering him a job. In the next story, the Sequids prepare an invasion of Earth. After defeating the Sequids with the Guardians of the Globe, Mark breaks up with Amber.

Issues 49-50 mark another turning point for the series. A villain captures all of Earth's superheroes. To Mark's shock and dismay, they are saved by Darkwing and an army of Reanimen. Mark demands an explanation from Cecil as to why he is employing murderers.

Mark's anger escalates until Cecil attacks Mark in response. Mark severs all ties to Cecil. Following this, Mark gets a new costume; Oliver becomes Kid Omni-Man, Mark's sidekick; Mark quits school; and he and Eve begin dating. In one of Oliver's first adventures, he kills two villains, prompting Mark to question his own stance on killing.

Working together, Nolan and Allen escape the Viltrumite prison and Nolan reveals that only fifty Viltrumites are still alive.

In issue 60, Angstrom Levy returns. He has recruited Invincibles from alternate universes. In a parody of "crossover events," several Image characters appear to fight off the Invincibles. Following this is the five-part "Invincible War: Aftermath" story, in which Mark and Eve fight and appear to kill a savage Viltrumite named Conquest.

After a two-issue arc in which Nolan and Allen gather weapons to fight the Viltrumites, the Sequids take over a city. In order to stop them, Mark murders the innocent man that was the Sequid host. Realizing how dark he has become, Mark opts to start a new chapter in his life. To symbolize the decision, he returns to his original costume. Starting from issue 71, Mark, Nolan, Allen, and Oliver journey into space to defeat the Viltrumites once and for all.

Volumes

- *Invincible: Family Matters* (2003). Collects issues 1-4. Chronicles Mark's first adventures as Invincible.

- *Invincible: Eight Is Enough* (2004). Collects issues 5-8. Ottley becomes the regular penciller for the series on issue 8.

- *Invincible: Perfect Strangers* (2004). Collects issues 9-13. Shows the fight between Invincible and Omni-Man and sets the new status quo for the series.

- *Invincible: Head of the Class* (2005). Collects issues 14-19 and *Image Comics Summer Special*. Introduces several villains who come into prominence later, including the Sequids, Angstrom Levy, and the Order.

- *Invincible: The Facts of Life* (2005). Collects issues 0 and 20-24. This volume includes short origin stories for Monster Girl, Rex Splode, the Immortal, Dupli-Kate, and Atom Eve.

- *Invincible: A Different World* (2006). Collects issues 25-30. Mark goes into space and meets his father and half brother.
- *Invincible: Three's Company* (2006). Collects issues 31-35 and *The Pact*, issue 4. Mark crosses a dark line when he kills for the first time.
- *Invincible: My Favorite Martian* (2007). Collects issues 36-41. Invincible faces D. A. Sinclair and the Sequids.
- *Invincible: Out of This World* (2008). Collects issues 42-47. Allen the Alien prepares for war with the Viltrumites, and a Viltrumite agent visits Earth.
- *Invincible: Who's the Boss?* (2009). Collects issues 48-53. This features the origin of Cecil Stedman.
- *Invincible: Happy Days* (2009). Collects issues 54-59 and *The Astounding Wolf-Man*, issue 11. Invincible crosses over with *The Astounding Wolf-Man*, another creator-owned series by Kirkman.
- *Invincible: Still Standing* (2010). Collects issues 60-65. Includes cameos from a wide variety of Image titles not generally in the "Kirkmanverse" including *Youngblood*, *Dynamo 5*, *Cyberforce*, *The Darkness*, *Witchblade*, *Pitt*, *Savage Dragon*, *Spawn*, and *Shadowhawk*.
- *Invincible: Growing Pains* (2010). Collects issues 66-70 and *Invincible Returns*, issue 1. Original artist Walker returns for a two-part story.

Characters

- *Mark Grayson*, a.k.a. *Invincible*, is the protagonist. Tall and lanky with black hair, he hardly looks like a superhero. However, he is secretly the superhero Invincible. He has an uncompromising view of right and wrong and refuses to forgive those who have strayed or compromised their morality. He has a quick temper and, as he is repeatedly forced to confront the fact that things are rarely black and white, often needs that second chance he is so quick to deny others.
- *Nolan Grayson*, a.k.a. *Omni-Man*, is Mark's father and a major supporting character as both a protagonist and an antagonist. A well-built man with salt-and-pepper hair and a fine mustache, he seems to be a loving family man. As the superhero Omni-Man, he is a paragon of nobility. However, he is really a brutal conqueror who came to Earth to enslave it. Eventually realizing his time on Earth changed him, Nolan strives to again be the hero and father he once was.
- *Debbie Grayson* is Mark's mother who, after years of being married to Omni-Man, is barely phased when her son flies off into space or fights dragons. She is devastated when Nolan leaves Earth after claiming he never loved her.
- *William* is Mark's good friend and college roommate. Immature and with a penchant for saying the wrong thing at the wrong time, he is as much an annoyance as a confidant.
- *Samantha Eve Wilkins*, a.k.a. *Atom Eve*, a tall, beautiful redhead, frequently teams up with Invincible, and the two eventually fall in love. She is quite practical, as seen when she quits being a superhero for humanitarian reasons and later when she turns Mark's superhero work into a source of income for them both. She is pregnant with Mark's child but has yet to tell him as of issue 76.
- *Robot* is the leader of the new Guardians of the Globe. Incredibly intelligent, he lacks social skills and tact. Originally presented as just a bronze robot, his human form is horribly deformed. He later transfers his consciousness to a young clone of his teammate, Rex Splode.
- *Allen the Alien* is a large, orange, one-eyed alien. He is incredibly friendly and sociable, belying his tremendous strength. Originally a foe of Omni-Man (because of a clerical error), he forms a strong friendship with Nolan after the latter abandons the Viltrumite empire.
- *Cecil Stedman* is the head of the Global Defense Agency. An old man with thinning white hair and a partially burned face, he runs the Guardians of the Globe and employs Invincible after Omni-Man abandons Earth. He will do whatever

it takes to keep Earth safe, including putting villains and murderers in his employ. As he says, "You can be the good guy, or you can be the guy who saved the world. They're not always the same guy." Faced with this choice, Cecil will pick the latter every time.

- *Angstrom Levy* is one of Mark's greatest enemies. Originally a skinny African American, he was characterized by his friendliness and quest for knowledge. He stops an experiment prematurely in order to save Invincible, but the incident deforms him and drives him insane. As an adversary, he pushes Mark past extremes he never thought he would go, being the first person Mark actually sets out to kill.
- *Oliver Grayson*, a.k.a. *Kid* and *Young Omni-Man*, is Mark's younger, alien half brother. He has long black hair and purple skin. The son of Nolan and an alien woman, he was brought to Earth by Mark and adopted by Debbie Grayson. Overeager and impatient, he seems like a typical kid, but he is still slightly out of touch with humanity.

Artistic Style

While Walker cocreated the series and continues to work on character designs, Ottley has drawn the vast bulk of the series. Both artists eschew the more realistic illustrations that have become the norm in favor of a more cartoonish style. This similar quality has helped give the series a distinctive and uniform look throughout. In maintaining a consistent look, the series benefits from Ottley inking over his own pencils. In sharp contrast to this cartoonish drawing style is the series' penchant for showing graphic violence. Ottley's art has evolved in his time on the book, but he has always been notable for his spread pages during chaotic and violent fights. The juxtaposition works to great effect, as its cartoony visuals keep the seemingly endless stream of torn limbs and blood constantly shocking.

In issue 51, Crabtree was replaced by FCO Plascencia. Plascencia brings with him a wider color range as well as deeper shading and improved use of shadows. However, both he and Crabtree make liberal use of vibrant colors. In conjunction with the less-realistic art style, the colors allow *Invincible* to retain a bright and innocent feeling despite the mature story matter. A recurring image in the book is a two-page spread close-up on characters' heads. These usually come during battle, and the shifts in distance, going from wide scenes depicting entire cities or planets to incredible close-ups on a single person's face, is an effective technique that keeps the action personal and projects an emotional weight to the fight.

Themes

At the core of Mark's character are a loss of innocence and a corruption of ideals. *Invincible* is not a tale of cynicism, but rather one of the quest to reclaim those ideals. Mark has been raised and instilled with an iron-clad sense of morality. Being a superhero is not a reaction to personal tragedy but the most natural thing in the world to him. Fighting evil and protecting innocents is simply the right thing to do. His dad does it, and so will he. When his image of his father is revealed to be a facade, Mark's heroic ideals fail to diminish. Even if the messenger was false, the message is no less true. The series gives Mark the opportunity to develop his own moral code. He is constantly forced to confront gray in his world of black and white and ultimately becomes a greater superhero for it.

Much of the themes center on the morality of killing and the notion of redemption. This is best exemplified in Sinclair and Darkwing. Both committed atrocities in their lives. To Mark, that is the summary judgment. However, the two still have much to offer the world and make the most of their second chance. Mark's haste to condemn them puts him at odds with Cecil, a man who operates in shades of gray.

By Mark's own standards, he is a killer and a monster. He crosses the line, but does not let himself become lost; he finds a foothold on the slippery slope. He is able to learn from his mistakes and finds himself still a hero in a world where right and wrong are no longer so discrete. Most important, Mark's own experiences let him give a second chance to the one person who has hurt him the most, his father. Just as the series began, the reader sees father and son standing side by side again.

Impact

Invincible was first published in 2003, with the Modern Age of comics in full swing, and stands out as one of the most successful independent superhero comics of the era. Despite struggling sales when the book debuted, it has persevered and become one of the most successful and famous titles in Image's superhero line. *Invincible* has been hailed as a "genre-redefining classic melding a lifelong love of superheroes by its creators with modern sensibilities and the freedom to do things company-owned characters couldn't do."

Kirkman has been a longtime proponent of creator-owned comics, and the success of *Invincible* and his other title, *The Walking Dead*, have proven that independent books can thrive in a market dominated by Marvel and DC. *Invincible*'s status as an independent book allowed it to circumvent normal age ratings. Unlike other books, *Invincible* is able to switch quickly from lighthearted fun to dark and dramatic violence. The success of *Invincible* was a factor in the creation of the Skybound imprint, which Kirkman hopes will encourage and foster select creator-owned books in reaching their full potential within both comic books and other entertainment mediums.

Benjamin Kahan

Television Series

Invincible. Gain Enterprises, 2008. This program starred Patrick Cavanaugh as Invincible. The series is a motion comic of the first thirteen issues.

Further Reading

Bendis, Brian Michael, Mark Bagley, and Stuart Immonen. *Ultimate Spider-Man* (2000-2009).

Johns, Geoff, and Dan Jurgens. *Booster Gold* (2007-2010).

Kirkman, Robert, and Jason Howard. *The Astounding Wolf-Man* (2007-2010).

Bibliography

Arrant, Chris. *11 for '11: Things to Watch in the New Year—CHARACTERS*. *Newsarama*, December, 2010. http://www.newsarama.com/comics/eleven-for-2011-characters-101227.html.

Khoury, George. *Image Comics: The Road to Independence*. Raleigh, N.C.: TwoMorrows, 2007.

Ottely, Ryan. "616 Exclusive Interview with Ryan Ottley!" Interview by Patrick Heagany. *Earth 616*, April 25, 2010. http://earth616.wordpress.com/2010/04/25/616-exclusive-interview-with-ryan-ottley.

See also: *Spawn; Marvel Zombies*

INVISIBLES, THE

Author: Morrison, Grant

Artist: Mark Buckingham (penciller); Tommy Lee Edwards (penciller); Phil Jimenez (penciller); Paul Johnson (penciller); Michael Lark (penciller); Grant Morrison (penciller); Dean Ormston (penciller); Arnold Pander (penciller); Jacob Pander (penciller); Steve Parkhouse (penciller); Warren Pleece (penciller); Frank Quitely (penciller); Ivan Reis (penciller); John Ridgway (penciller); Cameron Stewart (penciller); Ashley Wood (penciller); Philip Bond (penciller and inker); Jill Thompson (penciller and inker); Chris Weston (penciller and inker); Steve Yeowell (penciller and inker); Rian Hughes (penciller and cover artist); Sean Phillips (penciller and cover artist); Keith Aiken (inker); Dennis Cramer (inker); Kim DeMulder (inker); Glyn Dillon (inker); Dick Giordano (inker); Marc Hempel (inker); Ray Kryssing (inker); Mark Pennington (inker); Jay Stephens (inker); John Stokes (inker); Kevin Somers (colorist); Rick Taylor (colorist); Daniel Vozzo (colorist); Ellie DeVille (letterer); Todd Klein (letterer); Annie Parkhouse (letterer); Clem Robins (letterer); Brian Bolland (cover artist)

Publisher: DC Comics

First serial publication: 1994-1996 (series 1), 1997-1999 (series 2), and 1999-2000 (series 3)

First book publication: 1996

Publication History

First published in September, 1994, *The Invisibles* follows Grant Morrison's rise to popularity and acclaim after his break into the American comics scene in 1988 with *Animal Man*, for Vertigo, an imprint of DC Comics. More important, *The Invisibles* is Morrison's first full-length, creator-owned series as well as the first conscious effort by Morrison to combine, in a nonrestrictive fashion, his love of mainstream, superhero-style narratives with the surrealist, counterculture influences that appear in his earlier publications. Morrison has also admitted that *The Invisibles* was heavily influenced thematically by his *Spider-Man and Zoids* stories from the mid-1980's, published by Marvel UK,

(Getty Images)

Grant Morrison

One of the most important comic book writers of all time, Grant Morrison has transitioned from a critic's darling to the most popular creator in the industry, leaving behind a series of masterpieces. Part of the British comics invasion that landed at Vertigo in the late-1980's, Morrison produced some of the most notable books for that imprint, including runs on *Animal Man*, *Doom Patrol*, and his own creator-owned signature series, *The Invisibles*. His 2000 graphic novel, *JLA: Earth 2* with Frank Quitely, concluded his initial run of mainstream work at DC Comics. Jumping to Marvel Comics, he wrote *New X-Men* (also with Quitely) and quickly became the most sought-after writer in comics. In the 2000's he produced a number of marquee titles, including the epic crossover *52*, *All-Star Superman*, *Final Crisis*, *Batman and Robin*, and *Action Comics*. Morrison's writing is defined by its ability to breathe new life into stale character concepts and by its incredible complexity and theoretical sophistication.

and consequently shaped by his "alien abduction" experience in Kathmandu. In many ways, *The Invisibles* also represents Morrison's own personal quest to understand these varied experiences within the safe realm of fictional and metafictional narratives, especially the notions of magic and the connectivity between reality and fiction, as Morrison is represented by the character of King Mob in the series.

Never produced with a consistent team of artists, *The Invisibles* served as a rotating and revolving showcase of British and American talent who had become key collaborators with Morrison throughout his varied career. Collaborators with Morrison from his time with British publications such as *2000 AD* or *Revolver*—Steven Yeowell, Rian Hughes, Chris Weston, Sean Phillips, Philip Bond, Brian Bolland, and Frank Quitely—represented artists from Morrison's past, present, and future. However, perhaps the most iconic and recognizable illustrations in *The Invisibles* come from Phil Jimenez, who transformed the series from one with a decidedly British feel to one that represented a more action-oriented, American style. *The Invisibles'* transitions between worlds, environments, and time required varied and diverse artists such as Cameron Stewart and Quitely to interpret and give life to Morrison's scripts, and as a result, the series is a testament to the creative energies of the writer and visual storytellers.

Plot

Much of *The Invisibles* is guided and directed by Morrison's own life experiences and interests; thus, it largely reflects an autobiographical attempt by the author to come to terms with either elements from his childhood and past or issues that were affecting him in the early 1990's. Shaped by his own family's antinuclear protest movements and the covert, governmental operations to protect atomic industries, Morrison centers *The Invisibles* around the notions of a conspiracy theory of a hidden world just beyond everyday life where all the answers are located.

The Invisibles is influenced by British popular culture such as the James Bond films of the 1960's, which featured action-oriented superspies combating forces determined to dominate the world, or television programs such as *The Prisoner* (1967-1968), with its own brand of pop surrealism that characterized the 1960's counterculture; however, pinpointing or identifying all the contingent strains that gave birth to Morrison's magnum opus is difficult. At the core, however, is Morrison's own fascination with myths and the power of myth to shape life and culture. As such, any answers within *The Invisibles* are those that can be articulated and comprehended in humanity's shared reality only, and it is the process of coming to that realization that drives the series.

The central plot device concerns a cadre of subversive radicals calling themselves the Invisible Army. They are fighting against the coercive measures employed by an alien force of otherworldly gods known as the Archons of the Outer Church, who are determined to control and suppress mankind.

In *The Invisibles: Say You Want a Revolution*, the majority of the narrative transpires in England, as Invisible Army leader King Mob recruits a young Dane McGowan into the conflict. Trained by a homeless mystic, Tom O'Bedlam, Dane is instructed in his new identity, Jack Frost, although he has great difficulty accepting Mob and O'Bedlam's education. The first volume primarily deals with sight and the perception of reality, one that is constructed and shaped by the Archons and that Jack Frost must help unveil and ultimately overturn. Readers also learn that the conflict between the Invisible Army and the Archons has been ongoing for many centuries, as historical characters, including the Marquis de Sade, are conscripted by Morrison into the story. Thought-driven and lighter on the big-budget action characteristic of American comics, the first volume establishes the conceptual foundation for the entire series.

Although action and adventure increases with the second volume, *The Invisibles: Apocalipstick*, the bizarre and mystical nature of the series is only reinforced, as shamanism and voodoo practitioners enter into the series. The major revelations of this volume are the introduction of Jim Crow and Sir Miles and the insidious efforts by the Archons to bring forth the Moonchild. The history and background of Brazilian transvestite and shaman Lord Fanny also forms a crucial plot thread in this volume, as Jack Frost learns of

Sir Miles's intentions and experiences the power and mystery of "Barbelith."

The third volume in the first series, *The Invisibles: Entropy in the U.K.*, is the major turning point in *The Invisibles*, as artist Jimenez helps create a more lucid and flowing visual portrait for the series than present in the first series. Pulling elements from Morrison's own Gideon Stargrave stories and British intelligence operatives, this volume features Sir Miles's capture, torture, and interrogation of King Mob in what is perhaps the most entertaining and exciting portion of the entire book. As Mob battles Sir Miles and the Invisible Army attempts to rescue their captive comrade, Jack Frost comes to terms with his own role in this metaphysical, metafictional universe. "Entropy" also introduces the next major villain of the Archons, Mister Quimper.

Continuing Jimenez's visual representation seamlessly into the second series, *The Invisibles: Bloody Hell in America* (dubbed Volume 4) transports the team to the United States and alters the tone and conceptual atmosphere of the book. Here, the Invisible Army learns much more about its ally Ragged Robin during an assault on a secret, underground government installation below the New Mexico desert. The members of the Invisibles learn the power of Quimper, at great danger to themselves and their cause.

Volume 5, *The Invisibles: Counting to None*, deals with the fallout of the New Mexico incursion but, with the introduction of the Invisible College, also reveals more about King Mob's abilities. Time travel and connections to Invisible Army members both past and present form the crux of this volume, as Lord Fanny and Jack Frost embark on the quest to find the Hand of Glory and the cast of the Invisible Army is expanded even more with the misadventures of Boy.

In Volume 6, *The Invisibles: Kissing Mister Quimper*, the battle turns, as Quimper orchestrates and controls members of King Mob's team, turning them against each other during their return quest for the Magic Mirror substance in New Mexico. The mystery at Dulce is revealed, as is Ragged Robin's mission and involvement with King Mob.

The final installment, *The Invisibles: The Invisible Kingdom*, focuses on the final battle between the Invisibles and the Archon Moonchild. Revelations abound as the divisions between and perceptions of good and evil are shattered and Jack Frost rightfully assumes his preordained role in humanity's quest for enlightenment and transcendence.

Volumes

- *The Invisibles: Say You Want a Revolution* (1996). Collects issues 1-8 of the first series. Discusses the nature of reality and sets the context for the entire series.
- *The Invisibles: Bloody Hell in America* (1998). Collects issues 1-4 of the second series. The story moves to the United States. The Invisible Army discovers a secret in the New Mexico desert.
- *The Invisibles: Counting to None* (1999). Collects issues 5-13 of the second series. Features the quest for the Hand of Glory and reveals more about King Mob.
- *The Invisibles: Kissing Mister Quimper* (2000). Collects issues 14-22 of the second series. King Mob's team turns on each other because of the influence of Quimper.
- *The Invisibles: Apocalipstick* (2001). Collects issues 9-16 of the first series. Lord Fanny's background is revealed. This volume focuses on the spiritual and the mystical.
- *The Invisibles: Entropy in the U.K.* (2001). Collects issues 17-25 of the first series. Features the art of Jimenez for the first time. King Mob is tortured by Sir Miles.
- *The Invisibles: The Invisible Kingdom* (2002). Collects all issues of the third series. Jack Frost assumes his destined position, and the Invisibles fight against Archon Moonchild.

Characters

- *King Mob*, the protagonist, is the leader of the Invisibles cell in the series. With a bald head and various facial piercings and often armed, King Mob is a suave, superagent adept in martial arts, tantric sex rites, and metaphysical combat. His appearance and demeanor were based on the author, and in turn, Morrison adopted many of King Mob's characteristics. His true power and identity are revealed during his incarceration and torture by Sir Miles of the Archon.

- *Ragged Robin*, protagonist, is a telepathic witch, a member of King Mob's Invisibles cell, and a time traveler. With a white-painted face adorned with bright red circles on her cheeks, she is visualized in many styles, including black leather, fishnets, and elegant dresses, to suit her whimsical personality. During one of King Mob's absences, she assumes control of the group. She is also infiltrated by Mister Quimper, who assumes control of her mind in an effort to destroy Mob and the team.

- *Jack Frost*, a.k.a. *Dane McGowan*, a protagonist, is short with razor-cut blond hair. A British punk and prophesized as the future Buddha or Messiah, he is not only the youngest and newest member of the Invisibles cell but also, potentially, the most powerful because of his godlike and near infinite abilities. He joins the team after being sent to a boarding school administered by members of the Archon, who hope to control and subvert his independence and will. Able to wield and control the Magic Mirror substance, he cures King Mob after his abduction by Sir Miles and even aids Sir Miles in his own recovery. The balance to the radicalism of the Invisibles and the oppressive methodologies employed by the Archon, he plays the most important role in the series' conclusion.

- *Lord Fanny*, protagonist, is a Brazilian shaman and transvestite. Usually elegantly dressed and wearing a blond wig, or devoid entirely of gender-specific clothing, Lord Fanny shares a traumatic experience with the Archons that is revealed in *The Invisibles: Apocalipstick*. Fanny aides King Mob during his capture by Sir Miles, assists in an underground dance to retrieve the mystical Hand of Glory with Jack Frost, and helps Ragged Robin defeat Mister Quimper.

- *Boy*, a.k.a. *Lucille Butler*, a protagonist, is an African American member of the New York Police Department. Illustrated with either closely cropped hair or short curls, she learns that she is in fact unaware of her true mission, allegiance, identity, and intentions, as she is controlled by forces beyond herself.

- *Sir Miles Delacourt*, antagonist, is an operative of the Archon of the Outer Church. Although there are many Archon agents in *The Invisibles*, each with his or her own powers and abilities, he figures prominently in the narrative. As an intelligence agent, his main goal is to infiltrate the British monarchy with a member of the Archon. He leads the interrogation of King Mob and battles Jack Frost after failing to recruit him into the Outer Church. He is portrayed as a stately, well-dressed, well-groomed noble gentleman.

- *Mister Quimper*, antagonist, is the dwarf fiend who manages a sex club where members perform sexual acts with alien beings. Shown in a full white suit and wearing a porcelain mask to hide his grotesque face, he infiltrates Ragged Robin in an effort to manipulate her as a weapon against King Mob.

Artistic Style

In a series such as *The Invisibles*, it is rather difficult to identify a single or even multiple artistic style because of both the rotating nature of artists on the title and the fractured and fragmented aspect of the book's various atmospheres and environments. In the beginning, the artistic design of the book reflected the British setting of the series, not only in the utilization of British artists such as Yeowell, but also in the line work and weight of lines familiar to readers of *2000 AD*. Yeowell had been Morrison's collaborator on *Zenith* in the 1980's for Britain's *2000 AD*.

Interestingly, while colorist Daniel Vosso remained with the series throughout its publication span, he adapted his own separations, tones, and gradients to suit each penciller's holding lines and layouts. Under Yeowell and Jill Thompson, the characters and settings had decisively angular designs and were reflective of the raw and experimental nature, the scratchier etching quality most audiences associated with Vertigo books of the period. Although American audiences had been introduced to various British writers during the late 1980's and early 1990's, this influx of British artists, which included Weston and John Ridgway, was in stark contrast to the static and mostly overly rendered pencils of the spandex, superhero genres.

An aspect of continuity came to *The Invisibles* with the arrival of Jimenez in 1996; he joined the title near the conclusion of the first series. While most of his experience had been with DC Comics' superheroes, Jimenez, with inker John Stokes, gave Morrison's characters their distinctiveness, which was almost photorealistic in some depictions. In fact, it is Jimenez who achieved Morrison's concepts of multiple dimensions in the second series, when the team assaults the underground base in New Mexico. Jimenez's use of space, curved panels, and altered layouts transformed completely the often stale, two-dimensional nature of most comics at the time. He had such a profound impact on the artistic style of the book that even subsequent artists, such as Weston, who had worked on the first series, reflected this tonal shift in character design.

Each artist contributed something innovative and original to *The Invisibles*. However, two of the most memorable issues of the series were the final installments of the third series, in which multiple artists worked alongside each other. Reinforcing not only the transformative thematic nature of the book but also the recognition of the series' history and previous artistic contributions, these issues are the most experimental and fascinating in a book that often shocks and defies convention. Whether through two stark and hard-lined introductory pages by Yeowell or a single retro-styled portrait page done by Rian Hughes in issue 3 of the last series or the arrival of newcomer Stewart's and Morrison's artwork in issue 2—as conceptions of past, present, and future are shattered in seemingly cartoon fashion—these issues are breathtaking in their diversity and yet simultaneously seamless in their ability to visualize Morrison's script. Rounding out the series, penciller Quitely, who had worked with Morrison on *Flex Mentallo* (first published in 1996), offers a bookended conclusion to the title with his distinctive exaggerations of anatomy and form.

Themes

In many ways, *The Invisibles* is a diary of Morrison's life, a series with which he was personally involved, at times dangerously so. Following the success of *Arkham Asylum*, *Animal Man*, and *Doom Patrol*, Morrison's star was on the rise within the comics industry. As such, while still a freelancer, he was more financially secure than before, based in large part on the popularity and acclaim for *Arkham Asylum*. Following this, Morrison drastically altered his appearance by shaving his head and began traveling around the world, consuming alcohol and experimenting with narcotics for the first time in his life, and experiencing situations that were later referenced in *The Invisibles*, such as the underground fetish clubs in San Francisco. Although Morrison was slightly introverted and often silent prior to *The Invisibles*, the collective toll from these endeavors became the fuel and thematic inspiration for the series. Socially and professionally mischievous, Morrison interwove many of his experiences directly into the plot.

The central, thematic concern for Morrison is awareness and appreciation of the unseen and unknown world around the characters, of raising and achieving different levels and states of consciousness both individually and collectively. This is also inherent in the bond between the text and the reader: the shared division of those two worlds and breaking those artificial constructs. As such, many of the themes within *The Invisibles* cannot be disassociated with Morrison's own life. For example, in the early 1990's, Morrison went to dance clubs as a transvestite just for the experience. At the same time, he experimented with LSD and even conversed with demons during a Vertigo tour in San Francisco in 1993, where the foundation for *The Invisibles* was set.

Seeking to produce a book that would cover his interests in mythology, counterculture subversion, fashion, and music and would be the spell or the magic to evoke an evolutionary awakening of the audience, Morrison began work on the title in 1994. In fact, seeking to forge new connections between the reader and the text, Morrison utilized the letters page for a "how to" guide on conducting a magical sigil that culminated in a grandiose masturbation experiment.

Awareness, awakening, and the altering of perception are best exemplified in Jimenez's layouts in *The Invisibles: Bloody Hell in America*. The fixed grid pattern and border layouts of traditional comic page panels are discarded, and the page achieves a multidimensional, nearly magical feel.

Impact

Unlike other British comics imports who entered the American comic scene in the 1980's and 1990's, such as Alan Moore, Garth Ennis, and Jamie Delano, Morrison had a decisively different interpretation of comics, particularly superheroes. Rejecting the cynicism and darker psychology inherent in Moore's work, Morrison, instead, exhibited a renegade positivism in the face of darkness. Although not a superhero story, *The Invisibles* reflects this approach, as comics transitioned from the sober, internal nightmares that so characterized the previous generation of comic writing.

At the same time, *The Invisibles* represented a paradigm shift, as Morrison achieved the fame and notoriety that would land him work with DC and Marvel, contributing to mainstream books such as *Justice League of America* and *X-Men* and, eventually, *Superman* and *Batman*. Also, while Morrison had explored the tenuous bonds between fiction and reality in

Animal Man and even *Doom Patrol*, *The Invisibles* is his greatest experiment in this regard.

Nathan Wilson

Further Reading

Fraction, Matt. *Casanova: Luxuria* (2006-2008).
Morrison, Grant. *Animal Man* (1988-1990).
_____. *Doom Patrol* (1989-1993).
_____. *The Filth* (2002-2003).
Way, Gerard. *The Umbrella Academy* (2007-   ).

Bibliography

Morrison, Grant. "Inside the Creative Mind: Behind the Scenes with Grant Morrison." Interview by Nathan Wilson. *Graphic Novel Reporter*, April 5, 2011. http://www.graphicnovelreporter.com/content/inside-creative-mind-behind-scenes-grant-morrison-interview.
Salisbury, Mark, ed. "Grant Morrison." *Writers on Comics Scriptwriting*. London: Titan Books, 1999.

See also: *Doom Patrol*; *Animal Man*; *All-Star Superman*; *The Authority*; *Arkham Asylum*

J

JACK KIRBY'S FOURTH WORLD OMNIBUS

Author: Kirby, Jack

Artist: Jack Kirby (illustrator); Greg Theakston (inker); D. Bruce Berry (inker and letterer); Vince Colletta (inker and cover artist); Mike Royer (inker, letterer, and cover artist); Drew R. Moore (colorist); Dave Tanguay (colorist); John Costanza (letterer); Neal Adams (cover artist); Murphy Anderson (cover artist)

Publisher: DC Comics

First serial publication: 1970-1974

First book publication: 2007

Publication History

After a successful career at Marvel, where during the 1960's he and Stan Lee co-created the characters of the Fantastic Four, the X-Men, the Silver Surfer, and the Incredible Hulk, Jack Kirby left to work at DC Comics. DC gave Kirby free rein to create a universe as vast as his imagination, and so he did. The epic tale of the New Gods, celestial beings who live on the peaceful planet New Genesis and its counterpart, the hellish Apokolips, spanned four different comic book series.

When tasked with creating three bimonthly titles, Kirby decided on *The Forever People*, *The New Gods*, and *Mister Miracle*. Additionally, DC wanted Kirby to take over one of its ongoing titles. Though it did not appeal to him, he eventually chose *Superman's Pal, Jimmy Olsen* because the title had no stable creative team. Kirby wrote and drew *Jimmy Olsen* for three issues before introducing the new titles, which he wrote, drew, and edited himself.

Kirby worked diligently on his new characters from 1970 until 1974, when his titles were canceled with little warning or explanation. In 1984, under new leadership at DC Comics, he was asked to return to write a conclusion to his *New Gods* series. The first part of Kirby's conclusion came at the end of a six-part

> ### Jack Kirby
>
> Widely heralded as the "King of Comics," Jack Kirby was the most influential superhero artist ever to work in the field. Kirby is the co-creator of a wide range of characters, including Captain America, the Fantastic Four, the Incredible Hulk, and the X-Men. Kirby's style completely redefined the look and feel of superhero comic books in the 1960's, with his one-hundred-two-issue run on *The Fantastic Four* with writer Stan Lee often heralded as the pinnacle of the genre during that period. In 1970 he left Marvel Comics for rival DC, writing and drawing a series of comics under the common rubric of *The Fourth World* series that explored cosmic themes. Kirby's visual style was dynamic to the point of bombastic. His panels were filled with outlandish and imaginative machinery, and his characters occupied space with all the gravitas of gods.

reproduction of the original run, and his final word on the New Gods came the following year in a graphic novel titled *The Hunger Dogs*. In 2007 and 2008, the comics were collected in four volumes.

Plot

Jack Kirby's original plan was to make a sprawling epic that would be collected, as it eventually was, in hardcover color volumes. As such, his dreams were larger than DC was able to support, and the series was cut short well before its time.

Darkseid's search for the Anti-Life Equation, a theoretical formula that robs people of their free will and enslaves them to the keeper of the equation, is the main conflict that drives the four books. The Jimmy

Olsen books act as peripheral stories that incorporate the ideas of the Fourth World and Darkseid.

The New Gods is the main source of background information on New Genesis and Apokolips, the sister planets where the New Gods of the Fourth World reside. It begins by explaining that the Old Gods perished in a great battle, one that ended with their world being blown in two. In time, the New Gods came into being. Among them is the main protagonist, Orion, who is destined to thwart the ultimate destroyer: his father, Darkseid.

"The Pact," an issue originally intended to come earlier in the New Gods series, explains that many years previous, when Highfather was known as Izaya and Darkseid's mother Heggra was Queen of Apokolips, there was a war between the two planets. This came to be when Darkseid's uncle, Steppenwolf, killed Izaya's wife. Izaya murdered Steppenwolf; then, feeling he had lost his true self in his quest for revenge, he wandered the desert in search of answers. He came upon a slab of wall, at which point he asked what his inheritance should be. Upon the wall, a flaming hand wrote, in likewise flaming letters, "the Source." Desirous of a time of peace in which to rebuild Apokolips, Darkseid formed a pact with Highfather, the leader of New Genesis, whereby they would trade sons, Orion and Scott Free, to ensure peace between the two worlds.

Years later on New Genesis, Highfather summons Orion to the Source Wall, where he is told he must visit Apokolips and Earth, and then go to war. Metron appears to Orion and announces that Darkseid has departed to Earth in search of the human mind that holds the Anti-Life Equation. Darkseid has also broken the pact by bringing humans back to Apokolips for experimentation. Orion frees the humans and takes them back to Earth, where he and they become allies.

On Earth, Orion defeats the savage Apokolips warrior Kalibak. Orion and company then defeat Mantis, another of Darkseid's elite, before Kalibak breaks loose from captivity and pursues Orion again. While watching the battle with Desaad, Darkseid confesses that he married another before Orion's mother, and from that first marriage, Kalibak was born. Hoping to please Darkseid, Desaad secretly enhances Kalibak's power during the battle. When Darkseid discovers this

betrayal, he kills Desaad. Without the extra power, Kalibak is unable to keep up with Orion, who kills him.

The Forever People—Big Bear, Vykin the Black, Serifan, and Mark Moonrider—come to Earth to rescue their last member, Beautiful Dreamer, who has been taken prisoner by Darkseid. With them comes a Mother Box (a living supercomputer) and boom tubes (portals that can be used to travel between dimensions). The Forever People use Mother Box and speak the word "Taaru" to switch celestial locations with an extremely powerful hero, Infinity Man.

Soon after, Desaad and Darkseid trap the Forever People. Their Mother Box seeks Sonny Sumo, a successful human fighter who unwittingly harbors the Anti-Life Equation in his mind. Mother Box guides Sumo to free the Forever People and grants him access the Anti-Life Equation, in turn forcing Darkseid's minions to surrender. In retaliation for this, Darkseid unleashes the Omega Effect on all the Forever People but Serifan, who makes his escape.

In the Forever People's final adventure, Darkseid sends Devilance the Pursuer after the gang. They are unable to defeat him and use Mother Box to escape. The Forever People switch places with Infinity Man and end up on Adon, an idyllic planet in a universe around which Darkseid has created an impenetrable barrier. On Earth, Infinity Man and Devilance fight on an island until their overpowering energy causes a catastrophic explosion, seemingly killing them both and leaving the Forever People stranded.

The *Mister Miracle* series begins by introducing Highfather's son, Scott Free. He is wandering on Earth when he stumbles across Thaddeus Brown, an old escape artist who goes by the name of Mister Miracle. Scott befriends Thaddeus, who is soon assassinated by an enemy. Scott then dons the guise of Mister Miracle to avenge Thaddeus's death.

Soon, Granny Goodness, the evil old woman who runs Darkseid's orphanages-cum-training camps on Apokolips, seeks to reclaim Scott, her first escapee. After Scott slips from her clutches again, some of Darkseid's minions pursue him, without success.

Through short tales of the young Scott Free, it is revealed that Metron, Himon, and Big Barda, the latter being the leader of the Female Furies of Apokolips, helped Scott escape his home world. Barda finally escapes also, and after several attempts on their lives, she and Scott return to Apokolips and win their freedom through combat.

In the final issue, Scott proposes to Barda, but his enemies from Apokolips quickly attack them. They are saved at the last second, and Highfather presides over their wedding. Just after the two are wed, the New Gods feel Darkseid approaching and leave Earth.

In the prelude to the graphic novel *The Hunger Dogs*, Orion goes to Apokolips to kill Darkseid and free his mother, Tigra, who has been imprisoned since Darkseid came to power. Using new technology, Darkseid resurrects Desaad, Kalibak, Steppenwolf, and Mantis, but they seem to be mindless shells of their former selves. In the end, Orion is on the verge of killing Darkseid when hidden soldiers take aim and repeatedly shoot Orion, who falls off a cliff, seemingly into the fire pits of Apokolips.

In *The Hunger Dogs*, Orion is shown to have barely survived. Himon of New Genesis saves him, and Orion falls in love with Himon's daughter, Bekka. Meanwhile, Esak, Metron's former child apprentice from New Genesis, creates for Darkseid the Micro-Mark, a tiny rod capable of destroying a continent. Darkseid is presented with a sizeable collection of Micro-Marks cased together in a bomb powerful enough to wipe out a planet, but Himon phases in and steals it from him. Darkseid's scientists continue making Micro-Mark bombs and plant them via boom tube all over New Genesis. One of Darkseid's minions uses a boom tube to personally deliver a Micro-Mark bomb to Highfather.

Orion seeks Darkseid but first kills Esak. Orion rescues his mother as the Hunger Dogs go after Darkseid, who flees and kills Himon. Orion, Bekka, and Tigra leave Apokolips in an escape pod as Micro-Mark bombs detonate across the planet. Highfather makes the decision to blow up New Genesis once all its inhabitants are safe within the flying city Supertown, which floats off safely into space. In the end, Darkseid is stranded upon the planet that has turned on him, while Metron flies through space in his Mobius Chair, towing a lush new planet behind him.

Volumes

- *Jack Kirby's Fourth World Omnibus*, Volume 1 (2007). Collects *Superman's Pal, Jimmy Olsen*, issues 133-139; *The Forever People*, issues 1-3; *The New Gods*, issues 1-3; and *Mister Miracle*, issues 1-3. Introduces nearly all the Fourth World characters and concepts.
- *Jack Kirby's Fourth World Omnibus*, Volume 2 (2007). Collects *Superman's Pal, Jimmy Olsen*, issues 141-145; *The Forever People*, issues 4-6; *The New Gods*, issues 4-6; and *Mister Miracle*, issues 4-6. Features the Anti-Life Equation in action and introduces several new villains.
- *Jack Kirby's Fourth World Omnibus*, Volume 3 (2007). Collects *Superman's Pal, Jimmy Olsen*, issues 146-148; *The Forever People*, issues 7-10; *The New Gods*, issues 7-10; and *Mister Miracle*, issues 7-10. Features "The Pact," one of Kirby's personal favorite issues of all his work. Also contains his last issue of *Superman's Pal, Jimmy Olsen*.
- *Jack Kirby's Fourth World Omnibus*, Volume 4 (2008). Collects *The Forever People*, issue 11; *The New Gods*, issue 11; *Mister Miracle*, issue 10-14; *New Gods* (reprint series), issues 1-6; *The Hunger Dogs*; and *Who's Who: The Definitive Directory of the DC Universe*, issues 2, 3, 6, 8-18, 20, 22, and 25. Features Kirby's final issues of the main Fourth World books and *The Hunger Dogs*, his last word on the characters. Also features character profiles and the last official Kirby versions of the New Gods.

Characters

- *Darkseid* is distinguished by his granite form, red eyes, and blue helmet. The ultimate evil in the universe and the ruler of Apokolips, he came to power after successfully engineering the death of his mother, Heggra, and his uncle, Steppenwolf. His ultimate quest is to obtain the Anti-Life Equation.
- *Orion* is the son of Darkseid. He was raised on New Genesis as part of the pact between New Genesis and Apokolips, whereby Highfather and Darkseid swapped first-born sons to ensure peace

between the warring worlds. Despite his upbringing and his kindness to others, he has a true warrior's heart and is a more savage being than nearly any found on Apokolips. He finds love in the end, and in defiance of prophecy, he does not kill his father.

- *Kalibak the Cruel* is Darkseid's eldest son, a savage beast with a face framed in wild black hair. Unlike his half brother Orion, he was raised on Apokolips and trained in the Special Powers Force. He nearly defeated Orion with the help of Desaad but was killed when Darkseid revoked his advantage.

- *Highfather*, a.k.a. *Izaya*, is the leader of New Genesis. When Steppenwolf murders his wife, he begins a war with Apokolips. After avenging her death, he wanders alone until he makes contact with a piece of the Source Wall, whereupon he finds a new purpose. He returns home and agrees to the pact with Darkseid. After the pact is broken, he becomes a guide to Orion and Lightray in their fight against Darkseid.

- *Metron,* seldom seen without his Mobius Chair, is a master of time and space whose primary concern is the accumulation of knowledge. He provides Darkseid with the teleportation technology used in his invasion of New Genesis in exchange for the X-Element, which he needs to power the Mobius Chair.

- *Mister Miracle*, a.k.a. *Scott Free*, is the son of Highfather, swapped with Orion and raised on Apokolips. After fleeing Apokolips, Scott arrives on Earth and assumes the identity of Mister Miracle. He frequently is called upon to escape from seemingly impossible situations.

- *Big Barda* was once the leader of the Female Furies, one of Darkseid's elite forces. She wields the Mega-Rod, a multipurpose instrument that defies gravity and shoots energy blasts. Her brute strength and heavy armor make her one of the strongest of the New Gods. She eventually leaves Apokolips to find Scott Free. Together, they return and win their freedom from Apokolips.

- *The Forever People* are a group of New Genesis youths in flamboyant outfits who live by their home world's ideals of love and peace. Big Bear, Mark Moonrider, Serifan, and Vykin the Black come to Earth seeking Beautiful Dreamer, whom Darkseid believes may hold the Anti-Life Equation. Upon being rescued, Beautiful Dreamer rejoins the Forever People in their fight against Darkseid.

- *Infinity Man* is a nearly unstoppable cosmic fighter clad in blue sleeveless armor, gauntlets, shorts, and a helmet with a dark visor. He shares the knowledge and objectives of the Forever People but is almost invulnerable. His powers include atomic manipulation and telekinesis. His past is unknown, though he remains imprisoned by Darkseid on the planet Adon until the Forever People summon him. His apparent destruction by Devilance the Pursuer leaves the Forever People stranded indefinitely on Adon.

Artistic Style

Kirby had to work at an incredible rate to keep up with writing, drawing, and editing four simultaneous ongoing series. To his credit and benefit, he had an established style that he had perfected throughout his decades of making comics; Kirby's characters feature highly exaggerated, stylized anatomy and always look the same physically, whether they are Jimmy Olsen, Orion, or Mister Miracle. Almost without exception, his characters feature strong, square jaws offset by two curved lines for cheekbones. They generally have wide-set eyes and open mouths that expose the top row of teeth under a single line representing the upper lip. In an average page, the art is divided into a series of squares or rectangles, as were most comics printed in the 1970's.

To rush out approximately fifteen pages per week, Kirby usually drew only one complex background per page, with the rest of the backgrounds being either one or two colors and having little detail. On occasion, Kirby also drew his characters on photocopies of psychedelic backgrounds. Another Kirby trait prominent in the Fourth World books is the use of "Kirby dots," as seen on the cover of Volume 4. These black dots, often clustered together to form larger, dense black spaces, are featured prominently in scenes of energy emissions, space and boom-tube travel, and fire.

Themes

The eternal battle between good and evil is the main theme of the Fourth World books. Although most superhero comics deal with this, generally in single-issue stories with good overcoming evil, Kirby's New Gods had more real-world reflection. As noted in the epilogues by Mark Evanier, his former assistant and eventual biographer, Jack Kirby's comics were always somehow personal.

Kirby, a World War II veteran, focused his epic saga on a group of heroes coming together to stop an evil dictator who brainwashes his citizens and whose end goal is to rob all life of free will. The leader's high officers specialize in torture and scientific experiments on their own citizens. The large band of protagonists is united in their battle against this ultimate evil, some through peace and others through violence.

Though a New God, Mister Miracle embodies the human spirit: free will, a desire to better oneself, and concern for loved ones. He always finds a way to survive. In the end of each series, as well as in *The Hunger Dogs*, the good guys "win" in a manner that either changes who they are or leaves open the possibility of their eventual defeat. Kirby makes it clear that the battle is eternal because there are no absolute winners or losers in war.

The power of love is another current that runs through the saga. The Forever People represent Kirby's take on the hippie movement. They are free spirits from New Genesis who promote the ideals of peace and love and frequently chastise evildoers when they are forced to use violence. The *Mister Miracle* series ends with the wedding of Scott Free and Big Barda, and even Orion finds love by the end of *The Hunger Dogs*. Highfather loves all the inhabitants of New Genesis and greets newcomers with an open heart. Darkseid, their antithesis, is only concerned with power and control through force.

The books also contain meditations on the concept of nature versus nurture. Orion chooses goodness while struggling to escape the warrior's rage within himself. Conversely, Scott Free rejects his violent upbringing on Apokolips and embraces his internal yearning for freedom.

This internal struggle to find oneself can also be seen in Izaya's story. After losing his wife and having his revenge, he feels lost and unsure of his identity until he finds the Source. The residents of New Genesis, and particularly Highfather, feel a strong connection to the Source, the entity that is recognized as a higher power. Highfather's staff is linked to the Source, and a piece of the Source Wall rests within his home, where the Source occasionally writes messages to him. Darkseid and the residents of Apokolips ignore the Source and have no apparent contact with it in their bleak existences.

Impact

The Fourth World saga had a lasting and significant impact on comics. Before Kirby's epic, stories were self-contained within each comic book title, and having four books share characters, ideas, and an antagonist was unheard of. In addition, Kirby was given an unprecedented degree of creative freedom that remains unequaled to this day.

The dark, reflective themes were characteristic of the Bronze Age. Though not exploitative of the perils of drugs and alcohol, as many trendsetting books of the era were, the *New Gods* series includes characters that experience great personal conflicts and a broad spectrum of emotions. The notion of Earth as the battleground of such a large pantheon of gods was never before presented in comics on such a grand scale.

Although the series was only moderately successful at the time, the characters remained fan favorites. Orion, Mister Miracle, and the Forever People each had their own series in the decades that followed, although none of them were as popular without Kirby at the helm, and Darkseid's control of the Anti-Life Equation was the focus of a major story for DC Comics, Grant Morrison's *Final Crisis* (2008-2009). With the publication of the *Omnibus*, Kirby's masterpiece finally received the kind of release for which he had always hoped, garnering critical praise and fan approval more than thirty years after its first appearance.

Jason Knol

Further Reading

Lee, Stan, and Jack Kirby. *The Silver Surfer: The Ultimate Cosmic Experience* (1978).

Morrison, Grant, and J. G. Jones. *Final Crisis* (2008-2009).

Starlin, Jim. *Cosmic Odyssey* (1992).

_____. *Death of the New Gods* (2007-2008).

Bibliography

Evanier, Mark. *Kirby: King of Comics*. New York: Abrams, 2008.

Foley, Shane. "Kracklin' Kirby: Tracing the Advent of Kirby Krackle." *TwoMorrows*, April, 2008. http://www.twomorrows.com/kirby/articles/33krackle.html.

Kirby, Jack, and Mark Evanier. Afterword to *Fourth World Omnibus,* Volumes 1-3, by Jack Kirby. New York: DC Comics, 2007.

_____. Afterword to *Fourth World Omnibus,* Volume 4, by Jack Kirby. New York: DC Comics, 2008.

See also: *Silver Surfer; Cosmic Odyssey; Hellboy*

JON SABLE, FREELANCE

Author: Grell, Mike

Artist: Mike Grell (illustrator); Glenn Hauman (colorist); Julia Lacquement (colorist); Ken Bruzenak (letterer)

Publisher: First Comics; IDW Publishing

First serial publication: 1983-1988

First book publication: 2005-2010

Publication History

In 1983, writer and artist Mike Grell created Jon Sable, a character influenced by Ian Fleming's James Bond, for the new publisher First Comics. The opportunity to retain ownership of his series convinced Grell, a veteran talent, to take a chance and publish with a start-up. The monthly series lasted fifty-six issues under Grell's supervision before his departure in 1988.

After a brief hiatus, the character of Jon Sable returned in *Sable* (1988-1990), a new First Comics title from writer Marv Wolfman and artist Bill Jaaska that ran for twenty-seven issues without Grell's involvement and has been largely discounted in subsequent works. The series also spawned *Maggie the Cat* (1996), a short-lived spin-off published by Image Comics.

In 2005, Grell revived the Sable character, producing a new six-issue miniseries, *Jon Sable, Freelance: Bloodtrail*, for IDW Publishing. Two years later, Grell brought Sable to online news and comics site ComicMix, offering readers weekly installments of *Jon Sable, Freelance: Ashes of Eden* before its print publication as a miniseries (2008-2009) and a collected paperback (2010) by IDW Publishing.

Jon Sable, Freelance has been adapted for various mediums, including a short-lived ABC television series (1987-1988). A Jon Sable novel, written by Grell and published by Tor Books, was released in 2000.

Plot

Jon Sable is a Vietnam War veteran and former Olympic athlete whose wife and children are murdered by poachers while living in Africa, where Sable works

Mike Grell

Although he began in the comic book industry working for DC Comics in the 1970's, writer-artist Mike Grell achieved his greatest notoriety with the creator-owned title *Jon Sable Freelance* for First Comics in the 1980's. That title was one of the first of the independent and dark superhero stories of the 1980's, and Grell helped usher in the grim and gritty sensibility that came to define the genre. In 1987 he returned to DC to produce a limited series titled *Green Arrow: The Longbow Hunters* in which the hero was stripped of campy elements like trick arrows and became a cold-blooded killer. From 1988 until 1994 Grell wrote *Green Arrow*, segregating the character from the mainstream elements of the superhero genre. Grell is a key figure in the revisionist superhero movement of the 1980's and 1990's, and helped to push the genre toward adult themes and sensibilities through the inclusion of greater amounts of sex and violence.

as a game warden. Following their deaths, Sable tracks down the criminals and kills them before returning to the United States, broke and lonely.

In the United States, he creates the persona of B. B. Flemm and adopts it as his public identity, becoming a popular children's author. As Jon Sable, he serves as a mercenary and bounty hunter, tracking and apprehending criminals around the world. Sable eventually becomes romantically involved with his literary agent Eden Kendall and book illustrator Myke Blackmon, both of whom learn his true identity. He is also reunited with his Olympic fencing coach, former stuntman Sonny Pratt, who sees through his Flemm disguise. These three individuals become his support system as he deals with the grief that haunts him throughout the series.

Sable's first case involves tracking down escaped convict and murderer Richard Dahl. This assignment pits Sable against New York City police captain Josh

Winters for the first time. Next, Sable prevents his adversary from Africa, Milo Jackson, from killing the U.S. president at the United Nations. After that, he returns to Africa and finds Reinhardt Pike, the man who ordered his family killed.

Next, Sable travels to Monaco to protect the Capitolio diamond. He meets the cat burglar Lady Margaret Graemalcyn, or Maggie the Cat, for the first time. His adventures take him back to Vietnam and to Berlin, where he assists dancer Mischa Yurkovich in rescuing his wife, Anastasia. He travels to South America at an archaeologist's request, seeking an Incan artifact at Teotihuacán, an Aztec city she thinks might be the secret tomb of Christ.

Sable's mercenary actions bring him into conflict with Winters on numerous occasions, but the police captain eventually develops a grudging respect for Sable. Sable continues to accept assignments that reunite him with fellow Vietnam veterans or take him to Africa, the source of his pain. In time, he discards his grief and begins a romantic relationship with Blackmon.

Sable later works to prevent the assassination of a foreign national visiting Manhattan and continues to wrestle with the demons of his past. In his next assignment, Sable is hired to deliver a diamond and a woman safely to New York, bringing danger and death to his home city. Despite his advancing age, Sable continues to take on cases while furthering his writing career.

Volumes

- *Complete Jon Sable, Freelance:* Volume 1 (2005). Collects *Jon Sable, Freelance,* issues 1-6, and origin and introduction stories. Jon Sable's origin and the tragic deaths of his wife and children are explored.
- *Complete Jon Sable, Freelance:* Volume 2 (2005). Collects *Jon Sable, Freelance,* issues 7-11. Maggie the Cat is introduced, and Sable returns to Vietnam.
- *Complete Jon Sable, Freelance:* Volume 3 (2005). Collects *Jon Sable, Freelance,* issues 12-16. Sable attempts to locate a missing Vietnam War soldier.

- *Jon Sable, Freelance: Bloodtrail* (2006). Collects the eponymous six-issue miniseries. Sable must protect a visiting dignitary in New York City.
- *Complete Jon Sable, Freelance:* Volume 4 (2006). Collects *Jon Sable, Freelance,* issues 17-21. Sable is injured during a mission but must continue to foil criminal schemes.
- *Complete Jon Sable, Freelance:* Volume 5 (2006). Collects *Jon Sable, Freelance,* issues 22-27. In "Homecoming," Sable returns to Africa, the site of his greatest trauma.
- *Complete Jon Sable, Freelance:* Volume 6 (2007). Collects *Jon Sable, Freelance,* issues 28-33. Sable ventures to Nicaragua, and the Maltese Falcon makes an appearance in a separate story.
- *Complete Jon Sable, Freelance:* Volume 7 (2007). Collects *Jon Sable, Freelance,* issues 34-39. Sable again returns to Africa, where he confronts white slave traders.
- *Complete Jon Sable, Freelance:* Volume 8 (2007). Collects *Jon Sable, Freelance,* issues 40-45. Sable fights a twisted fan, among other foes.
- *Jon Sable, Freelance Omnibus:* Volume 1 (2010). Collects *Jon Sable, Freelance,* issues 1-16. Sable's history is explored and various recurring characters are introduced.
- *Jon Sable, Freelance: Ashes of Eden* (2010). Sable escorts a woman named Bashira and a massive diamond to New York City.

Characters

- *Jon Sable,* a.k.a. *B. B. Flemm,* the protagonist, is a mercenary who specializes in tracking down criminals. A Vietnam War veteran, he competed in the 1972 Olympic pentathlon and met Kenyan gymnast Elise McKenna, whom he married. When Elise and their children are killed by poachers in Africa, Sable returns to the United States, where he establishes his dual career as a mercenary and an author of children's books.
- *Edna Mae Kowalski,* a.k.a. *Eden Kendall,* is a literary agent who changed her name after a divorce. She is moved by Sable's unsolicited manuscript, *A Storm over Eden,* but encourages

him to write about the New York-dwelling leprechauns that appeared in stories he once told to his children. She and Sable become close friends and, briefly, lovers.

- *Jason "Sonny" Pratt* is a former stuntman who trained Sable for the 1972 Olympic pentathlon. The two are reunited when Pratt and Sable's alter ego, B. B. Flemm, are guests on the same late-night talk show. He becomes Sable's friend and confidant. He lost his son, Bill, in Vietnam.

- *Josh Winters* is an African American Korean War veteran and decorated New York City police officer who has risen to the rank of captain despite facing racial discrimination. He objects to the good press Sable receives, in contrast to the bad press received by the cops. As the two men get to know each other, Winters recognizes that Sable is a good man.

- *Myke Blackmon* is an artist hired to illustrate B. B. Flemm's book about leprechauns in New York. She meets Flemm after two years of successful collaborations and eventually discovers his true identity. She and Sable grow closer, eventually becoming lovers.

- *Lady Margaret Graemalcyn*, a.k.a. *Maggie the Cat*, is a beautiful aristocrat who trained herself to become an adept cat burglar in order to regain her precious jewelry, which her adulterous former husband had given away. She comes to the attention of Britain's law-enforcement agencies, but rather than arrest her, they recruit her into an elite antiterrorist task force. She and Sable spar, flirt, and work at cross purposes, but when she needs help, Sable is the first person to whom she turns.

Artistic Style

Grell, who attended the Chicago Academy of Fine Art and took the Famous Artists School correspondence course in cartooning, was among a new generation of superhero artists to enter comics in the early 1970's. During that period, he developed a lithe style that makes his characters graceful yet muscular. A naturalistic artist, his figures are at times anatomically awkward, while his wildlife and landscapes better

exemplify his training. When drawing his own stories, Grell tends to use large, silent panels, along with a "decompressed" style of storytelling that moves the story along quickly using splash pages and spreads.

Unlike Grell's earlier series, *Warlord* (1976-1988), *Jon Sable, Freelance* is set in the real world, and Grell devotes a great deal of attention to architecture and setting. Sable's missions take place in various locations throughout the world, and Grell uses details gleaned from research to provide these stories with a sense of authenticity. While the stories frequently have little to do with the locales, they feature topical issues such as ivory poachers and corrupt politicians.

Grell's characters, too, are detailed and diverse. He draws his heroes and villains with a wide variety of body types and represents many races and ethnicities. The series is also notable for including strong women and a gay character before doing so became common.

Themes

Redemption is the primary theme of *Jon Sable, Freelance*. Sable has everything he cherishes destroyed in a single horrific act. He feels unworthy of remaining alive but does so to track down the eight men who slaughtered his family and destroyed his life. Even after carrying out his revenge, he harbors darkness in his heart and keeps people at a distance until he sells a book to agent Eden Kendall.

Most of the people in Sable's circle also deal with darkness to varying degrees. Captain Winters has seen the horrors of war, while Sonny Pratt has lost a son in Vietnam. Kendall reinvents herself at the expense of leaving behind a son she never got to know, and Myke Blackmon is tricked into an unwanted pregnancy by an abusive lover. Even Sable's rival, Maggie the Cat, harbors negative emotions that are rooted in her husband's repeated betrayal.

Further emphasizing this theme, Sable's assignments often take him into the darkest corners of a country or an institution. Just as the characters of *Jon Sable, Freelance* must learn to cope with their own personal darkness, Sable must shine a light into the murk and find a solution to resolve the problem at hand.

Impact

In the early 1980's, a number of new independent comics publishers entered the market. Following in the footsteps of Pacific Comics and Eclipse Comics was Chicago-based First Comics, which offered higher-quality paper and printing and longer page counts than their competitors. *Jon Sable, Freelance* was the company's third release and the first with a high-profile creator. Grell's character reflected the political and economic climate of the era, and the series' appeal outlasted that of First Comics, which went out of business in the early 1990's.

As a new generation of publishers and technology emerged in the first decade of the twenty-first century, many of the popular characters from the 1980's were resurrected, including Jon Sable. IDW published *Jon Sable, Freelance: Bloodline*, and Grell produced a new story for the ComicMix Web site under former First Comics editor Mike Gold. The story, *Jon Sable, Freelance: Ashes of Eden,* was told in five-to-eight-page installments, drawing readers to the website on a regular basis.

Robert Greenberger

Television Series

Sable. Directed by Ron Rapiel and Gary Sherman. ABC, 1987-1988. This television adaptation stars Lewis Van Bergen as Jon Sable and Rene Russo as Eden Kendall. Aired between November 7, 1987, and January 2, 1988, the six-episode series is quite unlike Grell's comic. B. B. Flemm is known as "Nicholas Fleming," and Sable's African backstory is altered. The series also introduces a sidekick named Cheesecake, portrayed by Ken Page. Due to poor critical reception and low ratings, the series was canceled with three scripts remaining unfilmed.

Further Reading

Chaykin, Howard. *Dominic Fortune* (2010).

Grell, Mike. *Showcase Presents: Warlord,* Volume 1 (2009).

Grell, Mike, et al. *The Warlord: The Saga* (2010).

Bibliography

Jones, Gerard, and Will Jacobs. *The Comic Book Heroes*. Rocklin, Calif.: Prima, 1997.

Misiroglu, Gina, ed. *The Superhero Book*. Detroit, Mich.: Visible Ink, 2004.

See also: *American Flagg!*; *Hellblazer*; *Daredevil: The Man Without Fear*

Joker

Author: Azzarello, Brian

Artist: Lee Bermejo (illustrator); Mick Gray (inker); Patricia Mulvihill (colorist); Robert Clark (letterer)

Publisher: DC Comics

First book publication: 2008

Publication History

Joker is an original graphic novel created by Eisner Award-winning writer Brian Azzarello and artist Lee Bermejo. The duo had previously collaborated on the 2005 DC Comics limited series *Lex Luthor: Man of Steel*, as well as on the 2003 graphic novel *Batman/Deathblow: After the Fire*, which also marked Azzarello's first time writing the Batman character.

A Chicago native who claims former involvement with petty crime that included some jail time, Azzarello has become one of the most prominent writers of twenty-first-century American comics. He began to garner wide recognition in 1999 with the launch of his and Eduardo Risso's *100 Bullets*, an Eisner Award-winning noir crime comic published by DC Comics' Vertigo imprint that delved into the seedy underbelly of the criminal class, focusing on themes of vengeance and moral ambiguity and propelled by realistic dialogue and unglamorized depictions of urban violence.

Bermejo is a self-taught artist who began his career working at WildStorm comics. His first collaboration with Azzarello was in 2001 on issue 26 of *100 Bullets*. In 2005, his work with Azzarello on *Lex Luthor: Man of Steel* was noted for its "sleek coloring and line design."

In 2004, after his work with Bermejo on *After the Fire*, Azzarello took on the Batman character again, writing his acclaimed *Batman: Broken City* graphic novel, collaborating with Risso. Following the 2005 release of *Lex Luthor: Man of Steel*, Azzarello and Bermejo formed the concept for *Joker*, intending to give Batman's nemesis the same treatment they gave Superman's foe Lex Luthor.

Plot

Beginning with the Joker's inexplicable release from Gotham City's Arkham Asylum, *Joker* is narrated by

Lee Bermejo

Widely respected as a cover artist, Lee Bermejo is known primarily for his work on two collaborations with writer Brian Azzarello: *Lex Luthor: Man of Steel* in 2005 and *Joker* in 2008. Each of these works offered significantly new interpretations of characters who are the primary antagonists of DC's two most famous characters, Superman and Batman, respectively. Bermejo's art was a striking counterpoint to Azzarello's writing. Where the writer sought to complicate these villains through a fuller exploration of their personal ideologies and psychology, the artist rendered the figures in ways that were extremely unusual in the context of mainstream superhero comics. Bermejo's art is characterized by a high degree of slickly detailed realism within the context of painted comics. His use of washed-out colors and near photorealistic representations gives the works a real-world feeling that is absent from most stories about these characters, making them all the more plausible-seeming and, thus, more disturbing.

the Joker's henchmen Jonny Frost as he follows and assists the Joker in his bid to reclaim his one-time criminal territory that was divvied up amongst various crime bosses after the Joker's incarceration. What follows is a swath of psychotic violence cut through the city by the Joker, as he encounters figures from Batman's rogues gallery, including Killer Croc, the Penguin, the Riddler, Two-Face/Harvey Dent, and Harley Quinn, as well as Batman himself.

The Joker is released from Arkham Asylum under mysterious circumstances. He is picked up by an ambitious but low-ranking gangland solider named Jonny Frost. The Joker makes known his intentions to reclaim the criminal holdings he lost during his time in Arkham.

The Joker begins to reestablish his criminal empire when he single-handedly robs a bank by threatening the bank manager with a photograph of the manager's daughter that has been soaked in blood. He then meets with the Penguin, who is in charge of a majority of Gotham's monetary trade, and muscles him into "investing" the money.

The Joker, with Jonny Frost acting as his chauffeur, embarks on a brutal spree of murder and intimidation throughout the various tribes of the Gotham criminal underworld in order to show the Gotham criminals that he is once again in charge of the turf and the money that they had appropriated during his incarceration. A large number of Gotham's midlevel crime bosses are murdered during this period. During another meeting between the Joker and the Penguin, it is revealed that Harvey Dent, the major crime boss in Gotham, who is physically disfigured and has a split personality, is extremely displeased with the Joker's most recent wave of violent actions.

After being abducted and intimidated by Harvey Dent and a corrupt police detective in his employ, Frost meets the Joker and Killer Croc at a warehouse, where they do business with the Riddler, Edward Nygma; the Joker is given a briefcase, the contents of which he plans to use as leverage against Dent.

Following a failed assassination attempt by some of Dent's corrupt police officers, the Joker engages in a destructive war against Dent's rackets until Dent agrees to engage in a face-to-face meeting at the Gotham Zoo. The negotiations break down and turn violent, provoked by the Joker, and Dent's henchmen are slaughtered; the Joker promises Dent that he knows a way to kill one of Dent's split personalities.

Following their encounter, the Joker goes on a random and murderous spree, while Dent seeks out Batman and pleads for him to intervene and stop the Joker. Soon after, Batman subdues Harley Quinn and Killer Croc and his associates and pursues Frost and the Joker to a bridge over Gotham harbor. The confrontation ends when the Joker shoots Frost in the chin, Batman subdues the Joker, and Frost falls off the bridge, presumably to his death.

Characters

- *Jonny Frost*, a character created for this graphic novel, is the narrator of the story and an ambitious but low-ranking member of a criminal organization associated with the Joker. He is sent to pick up the Joker from Arkham Asylum after his release, and the Joker takes a liking to him. He seizes the opportunity to work for the Joker as the chance for which he has been waiting to increase his criminal notoriety and power.

- *The Joker* is incarcerated in Arkham Asylum for untold reasons. His inexplicable release at the story's beginning propels the violent and chaotic events that transpire throughout the narrative. He is depicted as having green hair, white skin, and a "Glasgow smile." Throughout the course of the story, he engages in drug abuse, a rape, and a slew of vicious murders and robberies, in the name of reclaiming his criminal empire. He is psychotic and apparently without remorse and even kills innocents with no gangland or criminal connections. He is shown to be paranoid and strongly fearful of Batman.

- *Harley Quinn*, an attractive, young female stripper working at the "Grin and Bare It" nightclub at the story's opening, quickly assumes the role of the Joker's mute bodyguard. She is frequently seen holding weapons and is present at many of the Joker's confrontations. She never speaks but appears to be the Joker's most valued and trusted underling.

- *Killer Croc*, a circus freak with a skin disorder (a depiction that aligns with the character's original incarnation in 1983), is depicted as a large black gang leader whose skin disorder gives him a scaly appearance. The narrative implies that he is a cannibal.

- *The Penguin* is a business associate of the Joker and in charge of handling much of the money of the Gotham underworld.

- *Harvey Dent*, a.k.a. *Two-Face*, is the leader of Gotham racketeering. The left side of his face is horribly scarred and disfigured, giving him a gruesome appearance. He has a split personality and is terrified that the Joker will be able to kill one of his two personalities.

- *The Riddler*, a.k.a. *Edward Nygma*, depicted as a young hustler and gunrunner, is high-ranking enough to have a cadre of his own criminal gunmen.

- *Batman* is an almost omnipresent force in this story. The criminal class of Gotham is paranoid about his involvement. He appears briefly in the events of the story.

Artistic Style

Bermejo's work on *Joker* has been widely praised for the way its grittiness evokes the sense of a dark and sinister Gotham City, one in which the paranoia felt by both criminals wary of Batman and citizens afraid of the criminal class is palpable in the confines of each panel.

Opening with wide-shot, cinematic views of the smoggy Gotham skyline, then quickly zooming in to the buildings, revealing the griminess of Gotham's urban life, the panel art delves into the often unpleasant life of the city streets. The panels are cramped, often featuring close-ups on the heavily lined faces of the often ugly characters, lending a sense of uncomfortable intimacy to readers as they are plunged into the bleakness of the Gotham underworld. It is an underworld in which violence is frequently used to resolve conflict; Bermejo's artwork does not shy away from this violence, instead depicting its brutality starkly, such as when a victim of the Joker is skinned alive and his mutilated body is the main feature of six separate panels.

Muted colors are used throughout, and the overall feel is that Gotham is a dirty, dangerous, and chaotic city. This is reflected in the Joker's actions, which are violent, deranged, and unpredictable throughout the story. An emphasis is often placed on these actions in the pacing of the panels, with frequent beats in the action scenes. Some of these beats are punctuated by the fact that Bermejo takes over the inking duties from Mick Gray on various pages and panels throughout the work. While Gray's inking adds a lot of jagged roughness to Bermejo's original pencillings, Bermejo's inking tends to smooth out everything, causing the characters and their actions to become hyperrealistic in their depictions. This often allows for the characters' emotions to become emphasized in an exaggerated but stark fashion. Bermejo's

inking frequently makes a great impact on the overall pacing of the scene, causing the reader to focus on the detailed beauty just slightly longer than one might otherwise.

Bermejo's hyperrealistic products are somewhat haunting in their ugliness; Azzarello and numerous reviewers have used the term "ugly" as a great compliment in this case. The artwork took Bermejo more than two years to complete, and his great work is evident throughout.

Themes

Joker is a character study of both the Joker and the new character Jonny Frost. While the story chronicles the madness inherent in the Joker—described by fellow criminal Harvey Dent as a disease that plagues the city of Gotham—by following his murderous and chaotic actions, the narrative also pays attention to the development of the narrator Frost. Simply an ambitious, low-ranking criminal at the beginning of the story, Frost looks up to the Joker, wanting to emulate him and in turn gain some of his power, which has been acquired through fear and intimidation. By the end, however, Frost has come to realize the true depths of the Joker's depravity and the chaos that propels him; by this point, it is too late for Frost.

Unlike some depictions of the Joker, who is often considered Batman's greatest villain, Azzarello's portrayal of the character in *Joker* is not so much a supervillain as he is a hyperrealistic criminal, one who is violent, depraved, and extreme, but, like the rest of the Gotham depicted in *Joker*, not so extreme as to be outside the realm of possibility in the real world.

Impact

Released in 2008, the same year as Christopher Nolan's widely popular Batman film *The Dark Knight*, which costarred actor Heath Ledger as the Joker, a performance for which he received a posthumous Academy Award, Azzarello and Bermejo's *Joker*, released several months after Nolan's film, received a fair bit of attention largely because of the creators' well-received previous collaborations and because Bermejo's depiction of the Joker so closely resembled Ledger's portrayal of the psychotic criminal clown. While this visual similarity was entirely coincidental, as Bermejo's Joker had been designed as a concept years earlier and Nolan's film crew was notoriously secretive prior to the film's release, the two Jokers are congruent and exist in fictional universes not entirely dissimilar.

Both Azzarello and Bermejo's Gotham and Nolan's Gotham are considered more realistic takes on the city and the idea of its criminal class than many preceding comics and film depictions. While both are hyperrealistic in their approach, both also have a gritty sense of realism and refrain from adding elements of the supernatural that have appeared in other Batman-related works. This is keeping with an overarching trend in twenty-first-century modern comics toward a sense of gritty, postdeconstructionist hyperrealism.

Anderson Rodriguez

Further Reading

Azzarello, Brian, and Eduardo Risso. *100 Bullets* (1999-2009).

Azzarello, Brian, and Lee Bermejo. *Lex Luthor: Man of Steel* (2005).

Miller, Frank, and David Mazzucchelli. *Batman: Year One* (1987).

Moore, Allan, and Brian Bolland. *Batman: The Killing Joke* (1988).

Bibliography

Azzarello, Brian. "Exploring the Joker: Brian Azzarello Talks." Interview by Steve Ekstrom. *Newsarama*, September 2, 2008. http://www.newsarama.com/comics/090802-AzzarelloJoker.html.

Azzarello, Brian. "The Joker's Wild Ride." Interview by Dan Phillips. *IGN Comics*. http://comics.ign.com/articles/923/923283p2.html.

Bermejo, Lee. "Lee Bermejo: Master of Pencil and Ink." Interview by Richard Serrao. *Optimum Wound Comics*, May 11, 2009. http://www.optimumwound.com/lee-bermejo-master-of-pencil-and-ink.htm.

Reid, Calvin. "Joker." Review of *Joker*, by Brian Azzarello. *Publishers Weekly* 256, no. 1 (January 5, 2009): 24.

See also: *Arkham Asylum*; *Batman: The Dark Knight Returns*; *Batman: The Dark Knight Strikes Again*; *Batman: The Killing Joke*; *Batman: The Long Halloween*

JUDGE DREDD

Author: Ennis, Garth; Grant, Alan; Mills, Pat; Wagner, John

Artist: Brian Bolland (illustrator); Steve Dillon (illustrator); Carlos Ezquerra (illustrator); Dave Gibbons (illustrator); Cam Kennedy (illustrator); Mike McMahon (illustrator)

Publisher: Fleetway; IPC; Rebellion

First serial publication: 1977-

First book publication: 2005-

Publication History

The development and publication of *Judge Dredd* and *2000 AD*, the comics anthology in which the strip appears, was a difficult and tumultuous process. During the 1970's, two major publishers controlled the British comics industry: DC Thomson and IPC. In 1974, Thomson began publishing *Warlord*, a weekly comic that reflected the changing trends in youthful entertainment; the stories were darker and much more mature than earlier British comics. In response to the success of *Warlord*, IPC enlisted young writers Pat Mills and John Wagner to develop a corresponding series that would challenge Thomson's control of the industry. Their first creation for IPC was *Battle Picture Weekly* in 1975, a raw and gritty title that also brought Spanish artist Carlos Ezquerra into the IPC domain.

IPC, Mills, and Wagner went on to produce *Valiant* and *Action* titles while generating ideas for a weekly science-fiction comic. The majority of responsibility in launching what would eventually become *2000 AD* fell to Mills. After reviewing Mills's ideas and suggestions regarding various strips, Wagner proposed a law-enforcement adventure story. Influenced by his previous creation of the *Valiant* character One-Eyed Jack, a street-tough law enforcer inspired by the Clint Eastwood *Dirty Harry* films, Wagner transformed his proposed police officer into a violent enforcer working in a futuristic, postapocalyptic New York City. Although Mills envisioned incorporating an occult theme into the character and commissioned a figure design known as "Judge Dread," Wagner was opposed, and Mills's concepts were abandoned. Wagner took the name Judge

Judge Dredd. (Courtesy of 2000 AD)

Dread for his ultraviolent cop, changing the spelling to "Judge Dredd," and Ezquerra was commissioned to design the character.

Although Ezquerra based the early designs of Dredd on the film *Death Race 2000* (1975), Wagner was not convinced about the visuals. Stalling *Judge Dredd*'s development even further was the revelation to Mills and Wagner that the rights and permissions to the character would be held by the publisher, not the creators. Guaranteed a rate of only ten pounds per page, Wagner quit *Judge Dredd* before the series launched. However, after a financial offer from IPC, Mills remained onboard for *2000 AD*, much to the resentment of Wagner.

The first issue, or "prog," of *2000 AD* launched in 1977, but prog 1 did not contain a *Judge Dredd* strip. Mills continued to develop the strip in Wagner's absence, facing conflicts with censorship that led him to hire various writers to compose the scripts according to a formula and to bring on artist Mike McMahon to illustrate the new scripts. Angered at not receiving any notification about the assignment changes, Ezquerra followed Wagner and quit *2000 AD*.

Determined to see *Judge Dredd* in print, Mills defended his staffing changes, and *Judge Dredd* finally debuted in prog 2 (March, 1977) with a story written by Mills and Peter Harris and illustrated by McMahon. Financial pressures prompted Wagner to return to the publication with prog 9 and the "Robots" storyline, and he remained with the series for much of its run.

During Wagner's lengthy tenure on *Judge Dredd*, many artists contributed to the look, design, and feel of Dredd and his Mega-City One environment. McMahon illustrated the first published strip, while Brian Bolland defined early imagery through cover assignments and his work on the lengthy "Cursed Earth" storyline. Additionally, artists Ian Gibson, Ron Smith, Brendan McCarthy, Gary Leach, Brett Ewins, and Ron Turner oversaw the early development of the strip's universe through 1980. Even Ezquerra eventually returned to *Judge Dredd*, working with Wagner and writer Alan Grant, who cowrote the strip for much of the 1980's. Under Wagner's direction and guidance, additional artists such as Cam Kennedy, Steve Dillon, Barry Kitson, John Higgins, and Colin MacNeil gave Dredd a uniqueness that contributed to the evolution of his character and associated allies and villains.

In 1990, with the launch of *Judge Dredd Megazine*, a sister publication to *2000 AD*, Wagner began work on that title and left the scripting of *2000 AD*'s *Judge Dredd* strip to such writers as Garth Ennis, Mark Millar, Grant Morrison, John Smith, and Gordon Rennie. He returned to *Dredd* and *2000 AD* periodically throughout the following decades.

In 2000, *2000 AD* and *Judge Dredd Megazine* were acquired by Rebellion, which continued to publish the titles on a weekly and monthly basis, respectively. While there are many graphic novel collections of various *Judge Dredd* strips from both the *2000 AD* and *Judge Dredd Megazine* titles, Rebellion has attempted to collect and distribute nearly every Dredd story in chronological order. Censored strips, however, have not been reproduced due to legal restrictions.

Plot

Set in a postapocalyptic New York City known as Mega-City One, *Judge Dredd* is the story of an ultraviolent law-enforcement unit made up of judges who are given the authority to detain, arrest, and execute. Embodying both heroic and villainous qualities, Dredd is often depicted with his Lawgiver sidearm, "daystick," and various other weapons as he rides his Lawmaster motorbike through the city. Futuristic and dystopian in design and feel, *Judge Dredd* falls into the science-fiction and action-adventure genres.

Major plotlines at the beginning of Wagner's tenure (progs 9-17) revolve around the "Robot Wars," in which robot leader Call-Me-Kenneth revolts against its programming and begins terrorizing Mega-City One. Although Dredd deactivates the robot, his warnings about a cyber revolution are ignored, forcing him to resign. When the robots revolt and Mega-City One descends into bloodshed, Dredd returns to save the citizens and terminate the robot uprising. Wagner expands the Dredd universe with an exploration of Dredd's heritage and the justice system in "The Academy of the Law" in progs 27-28 and leads up to the one-shot story by Mills that introduces Dredd's clone brother, Rico, in prog 30. The judges' world is exposed as Dredd goes undercover to identify a rogue judge in "Mutie the Pig" and later is assigned to duty on the moon as Judge Marshal in "Luna Period."

The most ambitious effort of Wagner's early *Judge Dredd* career is the twenty-five-issue "The Cursed Earth" saga (1978). Upon learning that Mega-City Two, the western counterpart in North America to Mega-City One, has been overwhelmed by a plague, Dredd and several associates traverse the "Cursed Earth" between the two cities and combat armies of mutants and monsters determined to destroy them.

Story arcs spanning multiple issues are a hallmark of Wagner's time on *Judge Dredd*. Following "The Cursed Earth," Wagner's "Judge Cal" saga focuses on the assassination of a chief judge and the uprising that follows when a psychotic Judge Cal assumes control of Mega-City One. Embarking on a killing spree, Cal frames Dredd for murder because he will not acquiesce to Cal's tyranny. Leading the resistance, Dredd eventually regains control of Mega-City One. Although shorter in publication length, Wagner's next major arcs, published in 1980, introduce Dredd's greatest nemesis, Judge Death, and a powerful ally, Psi-Judge Anderson.

Wagner's "The Judge Child" gives even greater dimension to the Dredd universe, introducing the Angel Gang, Judge Hershey, and a prophecy predicting the destruction of Mega-City One. Judge Death is further explored and joined by Judges Fear, Mortis, and Fire in "Judge Death Lives." Wagner's "Block Mania" and "The Apocalypse War" story arcs in progs 236-270 detail the outbreak of civil war in Mega-City One after its water supplies are threatened by a Sov-Block plot to weaken the city. The conflict intensifies, leading to a nuclear war between Mega-City One and the Sov city East-Meg One. This Cold War-era politicization of *Judge Dredd* continues to develop between progs 460 and 533.

Dredd's heritage, though largely unexamined in early story lines, is explored in the story arc "Oz" (1987), in which Dredd discovers an entire island of evil clones. This story arc reverberates from its inception in prog 545 through prog 584 and beyond as remnants of the evil clones reemerge to threaten Mega-City One. One such Dredd clone, Kraken, becomes Dredd's nemesis in the "Necropolis" story line.

In the early 1990's, Wagner's work on *Judge Dredd* found a new home in *2000 AD*'s sister title, *Judge Dredd Megazine*, while Dredd's adventures in *2000 AD* carried on under the direction of writers such as Garth Ennis. Dredd continues to fight new and recurring foes in both publications, protecting Mega-City One from those who would do it harm.

Volumes

- *Judge Dredd: The Complete Case Files,* Volume One (2005). Collects progs 2-60. Includes the pre-Wagner Dredd stories, the "Walter the Wobot, Fwiend of Dredd" stories, Wagner's epic story arc "Robot Wars," and other stories including "The Academy of the Law," "Mutie the Pig," "The Troggies," "The Mega-City 5000," and "Luna Period."

- *Judge Dredd: The Complete Case Files,* Volume Two (2006). Collects progs 61-115. Includes the "Cursed Earth" arc and the "Judge Cal" saga.

- *Judge Dredd: The Complete Case Files,* Volume Three (2006). Collects progs 116-154. Includes the debut of Judge Death and Psi-Judge Anderson and the return of Satanus from the "Cursed Earth" story line.

- *Judge Dredd: The Complete Case Files,* Volume Four (2006). Collects progs 156-207. Includes the "Judge Child" story line, "The Fink," and "UnAmerican Graphitti."

- *Judge Dredd: The Complete Case Files,* Volume Five (2006). Collects progs 208-270. Includes "Judge Death Lives," "Block Mania," and "The Apocalypse War."

- *Judge Dredd: The Complete Case Files,* Volume Six (2006). Collects progs 271-321. Includes "League of Fatties," "Fungus," "The Game Show Show," "Destiny's Angels," "The Executioner," "The Night of the Rad Beast," "The Last Invader," "Shanty Town," "Trapper Hag," "Starborn Thing," "The Stupid Gun," and "Condo."

- *Judge Dredd: The Complete Case Files,* Volume Seven (2007). Collects progs 322-375. Includes "Cry of the Werewolf," "The Weather Man," "Requiem for a Heavyweight," "The Graveyard Shift," "Rumble in the Jungle," "Bob and Carol and Ted and Ringo," "Citizen Snork," "The Haunting of Sector House 9," "Portrait of a Politician," "Superbowl," and "The Wreckers."

- *Judge Dredd: The Complete Case Files,* Volume Eight (2007). Collects progs 376-423. Includes "Dredd Angel," "Gator," "The Wally Squad," "City of the Damned," "The Hunters Club," "Juve's Eyes," and "Sunday Night Fever."

- *Judge Dredd: The Complete Case Files,* Volume Nine (2007). Collects progs 424-473. Includes "Midnight Surfer," "Nosferatu," "The Man Who Knew Too Much," "The Magnificent Obsession," "The Warlord," "The Falucci Tape," "Gribligs," "The Big Sleep," and "Riders on the Storm."

- *Judge Dredd: The Complete Case Files,* Volume Ten (2008). Collects progs 474-522. Includes

"The Law According to Dredd," "The Art of Kenny Who?," "Perp Aid," "Atlantis," "Phantom of the Shoppera," "Tomb of the Judges," "The Witness," "The Taxidermist," and "The Beating Heart."

- *Judge Dredd: The Complete Case Files,* Volume Eleven (2008). Collects progs 523-570. Includes "Pit Rat," "The Raggedy Man," "Fairly Hyperman," "Revolution," "Alabammy Blimps," "The Return of Death Fist," "Killcraze," and "Oz."

- *Judge Dredd: The Complete Case Files,* Volume Twelve (2008). Collects progs 571-618. Includes "Hitman," "Skeet and the Wrecking Crew," "Full Mental Jacket," "Bloodline," "Twister," "PJ Maybe, Age 13," "Curse of the Spider-Woman," "Alzheimer's Block," "Our Man in Hondo," and "Crazy Barry, Little Mo."

- *Judge Dredd: The Complete Case Files,* Volume Thirteen (2009). Collects progs 619-661. Includes "Breakdown on Ninth Street," "Banana City," "The Confeshuns of PJ Maybe," "Cardboard City," "Confessions of a Rottweiler," and "Young Giant." Represents the first volume to collect *Judge Dredd* stories written by Grant.

- *Judge Dredd: The Complete Case Files,* Volume Fourteen (2009). Collects progs 662-699. Includes "Tale of the Dead Man," "By Lethal Injection," "Dear Annie," and "Necropolis." Also includes stories written by Grant.

- *Judge Dredd: The Complete Case Files,* Volume Fifteen (2010). Collects progs 700-735. Includes "Theatre of Death," "Nightmares," "Wot I Did During Necropolis," "Bill Bailey Won't You Please Come Home," and "Black Widow." Includes Dredd stories by Grant and Ennis in addition to Wagner.

- *Judge Dredd: The Complete Case Files,* Volume Sixteen (2010). Collects progs 736-775. Includes stories by Ennis as well as Wagner's "The Devil You Know."

- *Judge Dredd: The Complete Case Files,* Volume Seventeen (2011). Collects progs 776-803. Includes stories by Ennis as well as Wagner's "Texas City Sting."

Characters

- *Judge Joseph Dredd*, the protagonist, is a Mega-City One law enforcer. Armed with his Lawgiver pistol and an array of accessory weapons and often seen riding his Lawmaster motorcycle, he is an unforgiving force of power. He wears massive shoulder pads, a badge, and a helmet that covers the majority of his face, exposing only his trademark rough chin. Tough and unflinching, yet often quite human, he is both a symbol of totalitarian oppression and a savior and defender of Mega-City One.

- *Judge Cassandra Anderson* is a Mega-City One Psi-Judge. Endowed with psychic abilities, she defeats the Dark Judges (Death, Fear, Mortis, and Fire). Her popularity among fans as the first female judge created by Wagner and Bolland led to the creation of a spin-off strip in *2000 AD*.

- *Rico Dredd*, an antagonist, is one of the original Dredd clones. Introduced by Mills in 1977, he is the only Judge to best Dredd in the academy, always scoring first place while Dredd takes second. He embarks on a life of crime and remains beyond Dredd's reach until Dredd eventually kills him in a duel.

- *Judge Death*, an antagonist, is one member of the Dark Judges. Believing all life is a crime and death is the punishment, he is the first serious threat that Dredd cannot simply destroy or pummel.

Artistic Style

The design of Dredd himself is one of the distinguishing features of the series, although his physical appearance has changed over the years. First created and designed by Ezquerra and visually based on characters in the film *Death Race 2000*, the original Dredd is much more streamlined in his body type than later renditions. Compared to the modern Dredd, the early version appears weak. In addition, Ezquerra depicts Dredd as racially ambiguous in early drawings. Later artists, however, were not informed of Dredd's ambiguous heritage and abandon Ezquerra's facial design in favor of more Caucasian features. The character's trademark protruding chin and sharper body become major components of Dredd's design in strips illustrated by Bolland.

The numerous artists and the weekly, serialized nature of *2000 AD* make identifying a single artistic style difficult, as Ezquerra, McMahon, and Bolland each shaped early perceptions of the character. Additionally,

(Michael Germana/SSI Photo/Landov)

John Wagner

A British writer closely connected to *2000 AD*, John Wagner is remembered as the co-creator of the popular series *Judge Dredd*, *Robo-Hunter*, and *Strontium Dog*. In the 1980's he was part of the British invasion of the American comic book industry, although his success was moderate compared to many of his peers. Titles like *Outcasts* and *The Last American* (with Mike McMahon) were not particularly successful, and Wagner eventually returned to *2000 AD*. In 1997, Paradox Press published his graphic novel *A History of Violence*, with art by Vince Locke, and it was subsequently adapted for the screen by David Cronenberg. This work was one of the few attempts in the American comic book industry of the 1990's to revive the tradition of dark-themed crime writing. Wagner remains a major figure in the British comics scene, where he is well known for writing violent action series filled with black humor.

the black-and-white nature of the strips gives the series a consistent appearance and atmosphere while still leaving room for individualized artistic expression. In terms of raw emotion and power, Bolland's art is perhaps the most iconic work to appear in early *Judge Dredd* comics, creating a signature, identifiable look for the character and the inhabitants of Mega-City One.

Dillon and Dave Gibbons feature particularly emotive qualities in their line work, designing expressive faces and characters. Like Bolland, Kennedy provides a level of detail in his shading and crosshatching that gives the illustrations greater depth. Under the direction of Dillon and Kennedy during the 1980's, the art becomes far more uniform in design and look than during Bolland's tenure. In the absence of hues, tones, and color values, all emotion and connection between the reader and the early art of *Judge Dredd* is based entirely upon pencils and ink.

Themes

The scripts penned by Wagner, Mills, and Grant early in the series and by later writers such as Ennis, Morrison, Millar, Rennie, and Smith express various themes that remain true to the spirit of *Judge Dredd* while allowing the series to evolve beyond mere futuristic police melodrama. One of the most critical themes recurring in the series is the absurdity of Mega-City One. In fact, it can be argued that Mega-City One is the leading protagonist of the series and Dredd is the stoic, grounded figure who must handle the various threats it unleashes upon its own citizens.

Published throughout the reign of conservative British prime minister Margaret Thatcher (1979-1990), *Judge Dredd* has been viewed as a commentary on the abuse of power by the state. However, this is a rather simplistic view, as it overlooks the nuances of the Orwellian world Wagner and Mills crafted in the late 1970's. As a series, *Judge Dredd* is ripe for multiple political interpretations. The influence of the Cold War on Great Britain and the United States is particularly apparent in the series, with its dystopian vision of the future a common theme in science fiction of that era. *Judge Dredd*'s futuristic setting allows writers and artists to experiment, helping the series to progress and evolve but remain consistent in its critique of the ultraviolent, oppressive nature of a totalitarian police state.

Impact

Longevity and consistency are the hallmarks of *Judge Dredd*. Published for more than thirty years, the series has experienced incredible popularity throughout its run, with Dredd named Britain's favorite comics character on numerous occasions. *Judge Dredd* benefits from its weekly publication schedule, which cultivates a dedicated fan base and allows for lengthy story arcs that oftentimes comprise strips from twenty to thirty progs.

Although the series is known in the United States and despite its setting in a thinly veiled New York City, *Dredd*'s greatest fan base is in Britain. This may be due to the series' distinctly British sense of humor, or possibly to the overall look of the comic. American readers accustomed to colorful superhero comics might find the stark black-and-white look of *Judge Dredd* off-putting. In addition, as a mixture of genres including science fiction, mystery, horror, and adventure, *Judge Dredd* does not easily fit into one category, thus potentially limiting its appeal or marketability.

Despite this, *Judge Dredd* has significantly influenced the comics industry in both Britain and America. Paralleling works by creators such as Frank Miller who ushered in the dark Modern Age of American comics, the series marked a significant shift in the content and nature of British comics, introducing more mature themes and subject matter into the industry. *Judge Dredd* has served as a proving ground of sorts, introducing numerous new writers and artists to readers throughout the world. Many of these British comics professionals have transitioned into the American market and gone on to further influence the industry.

Nathan Wilson

Films

Judge Dredd. Directed by Danny Cannon. Hollywood Pictures, 1995. This film adaptation stars Sylvester Stallone as Judge Dredd, Armand Assante as Rico, Jürgen Prochnow as Judge Griffin, Max von Sydow as Chief Justice Fargo, and Diane Lane as Judge Hershey. Although loosely based on multiple strips, particularly the Mills-scribed story line that introduces Rico, the film differs greatly from the series, primarily focusing on action scenes rather than the satire and dark humor of the comic.

Further Reading

Diggle, Andy, and Jock. *Lenny Zero and the Perps of Mega-City One* (2011).

Wagner, John, Alan Grant, and Brian Bolland. *Judge Death: Death Lives* (2010).

Wagner, John, and Frazer Irving. *Judge Death: The Life and Death of...* (2011).

Bibliography

Bishop, David, and Jonathan Oliver. *Thrill-Power Overload: "2000 AD"—The First Thirty Years*. Oxford: Rebellion, 2009.

Jarman, Colin M., and Peter Action. *Judge Dredd: The Mega-History*. Hertfordshire: Lennard, 1995.

McMahon, Mike. "An Interview with Mike McMahon." Interview by Andrew Littlefield. *The Comics Journal* 122 (June, 1988): 81-85.

O'Neill, Kevin. "An Interview with Kevin O'Neill." Interview by Frank Plowright. *The Comics Journal* 122 (June, 1988): 87-105.

Stringer, Lew. "A History of British Comics." *The Comics Journal* 122 (June, 1988): 57-67.

Wagner, John, and Alan Grant. "An Interview with John Wagner and Alan Grant." Interview by Frank Plowright. *The Comics Journal* 122 (June, 1988): 68-80.

See also: *Batman: The Dark Knight Returns*; *Doom Patrol*; *Preacher*

JUST A PILGRIM

Author: Ennis, Garth
Artist: Carlos Ezquerra (illustrator); Paul Mounts (colorist); Ken Wolak (colorist); Chris Eliopoulos (letterer); Mark Texeira (cover artist)
Publisher: Black Bull Comics
First serial publication: 2001
First book publication: 2001

Publication History

Garth Ennis's *Just a Pilgrim* was originally published as a full-color limited series in five issues, from May, 2001, to September, 2001, by Black Bull Comics, a short-lived imprint of Wizard Entertainment. A follow-up limited series in four issues (from May to August of 2002), *Just a Pilgrim: Garden of Eden*, was also published by Black Bull.

The original limited series was first collected into a single volume in 2001 by Titan Books. *Garden of Eden* was collected into a single volume in 2002, also by Titan Books. Reprinting rights were acquired by Dynamite Entertainment, which collected both miniseries into a single volume —first in hardcover, then in trade paperback—in 2008. Dynamite's volume also includes a cover gallery, reproducing the covers from the two series, examples of Carlos Ezquerra's concept art for characters, and sketches for covers by J. G. Jones.

Just A Pilgrim. (Dynamite Entertainment)

Plot

Just a Pilgrim combines elements of several genres, including postapocalyptic science fiction, the American Western, horror, and, as the title implies, Christian pilgrimage stories. The science fiction and Western elements are combined to provide a general setting, while the principal plot points and tensions are drawn from science fiction and horror. The Christian pilgrimage stories are used primarily to define the main character as he introduces himself ("just a pilgrim"), relates his background, and accounts for his actions and behavior throughout.

Both *Just a Pilgrim* series are set in a near future, eight years after a coronal expansion of the sun, referred to diegetically as "The Burn," has evaporated all water and killed most life from the surface of the Earth. Human survivors are presented as straggling in small groups, including the group to which the original series' narrator belongs, or in somewhat larger groups with better access to resources, including some relatively advanced technology (such as flying vehicles in the first series and hydroponics and the possibility of faster-than-light travel in the second). The Burn has produced mutations in surviving species, resulting in monstrous forms that terrorize the few remaining people.

Both series focus on the movements and actions of the titular pilgrim as a means of displaying those freak-show horrors; in this way, both series are generally similar to Dante's *Inferno* (from *La divina commedia*,

c. 1320; *The Divine Comedy*, 1802). The first series is told as an ekphrasis from the diary of Billy Shepherd, beginning with a summary of The Burn before turning to "[t]he first time [Billy and his family] saw the pilgrim" under attack by heavily armed raiders (called "buckers" and stylized as postapocalyptic pirates). Billy and his family are saved only by the timely and extremely violent intervention of the pilgrim, a wanderer wearing a duster who dispatches dozens of buckers with ease while issuing oaths and quips derived from the Bible and other Christian sources.

The pilgrim is revealed to have been a Green Beret, who, in order to survive while adrift at sea, resorted to cannibalism, continuing the practice when he returned to society. As the series progresses, the buckers are revealed to be operating under Castenado, a multiple amputee who lost his feet and hands, as well as a mutant with enhanced senses that compensate for his missing eyes. The pilgrim and Castenado seem destined for a totalizing conflict, which occurs in the final issue, as the buckers stage a raid on the other group's last stand. It is revealed that the pilgrim used the families, including Billy's, as bait in order to kill all the buckers. Initially carrying only the Bible, he later also carries Billy's diary.

The second series generally repeats the structure of the first, with movement, discovery, violence, and a concluding conflict that results in general destruction and only a few survivors. Set four years after the end of the first series, it is also told as an ekphrasis, in this case, from the journal of Dr. Christine Page. Walking ever westward as if in search of the titular Garden of Eden, the pilgrim reaches the Mariana Trench (the comic calls it "Marianas"), where he is saved from reanimated human corpses by a small group of scientists preparing to leave the Earth in a space shuttle modified for faster-than-light interstellar flight.

The scientists' "garden" is beset by the parasitic life-form, called "sliders" after their mode of locomotion, responsible for reanimating the corpses. Eventually the life form sets fire to the garden, kidnaps a little girl, and, in an inversion of the pilgrim's strategy in the first series, uses her as bait to lure the scientists into the Challenger Deep, where the girl is discovered to have already been killed and reanimated. Three characters,

including the pilgrim, make it back to the shuttle, where the pilgrim, holding off corpses to allow two scientists to escape, insists that only Billy's diary and not the Bible be taken with them.

Characters

- *The pilgrim*, the otherwise-unnamed protagonist, is a former Green Beret with expertise in military strategy, tactics, and armed and unarmed combat. While imprisoned for cannibalism, he was gradually befriended by a priest whose years of persistence led the pilgrim to forge a belief in God and to love the Bible. Having escaped from the prison during The Burn, and having seen the priest burned alive, he dedicates his life to walking the Earth attempting to do "the Lord's work."

- *Billy Shepherd*, a ten-and-a-half-year-old boy, is part of a small group of survivors wandering the former American West. Billy keeps a diary, which forms the basis of the original series' narrative and is featured in the second series as well. He looks up to the pilgrim with a mixture of admiration and fear. His trust costs him his life when he is used, alongside the rest of his group, as bait in the pilgrim's trap for Castenado and his buckers. However, his memory lives on, as the pilgrim first carries Billy's diary and then gives it to the scientists leaving Earth.

- *Castenado*, the antagonist of the first series, is the leader of the buckers. Stylized as a pirate, he has two peg legs and hooks in place of both hands; at one point the narrative reveals that he has also lost his penis. Enhanced senses compensate for his missing pieces. Given to referring to himself in the third person, he is intended to embody the sterile amorality and purposeless violence of the future Earth. He is killed in an explosion set off by Billy.

- *Carla Shepherd*, mother of Billy, reveals to both the group of survivors and the reader the pilgrim's identity by remembering his backstory of cannibalism; this prompts the pilgrim to tell his story.

- *John Shepherd*, father of Billy, was a sort of moral center to the group of survivors before the pilgrim's arrival. Unable to protect the survivors as the pilgrim seemingly can, he finds that "the world [he] belong[ed] to is passed away."

- *A priest*, always wearing a white suit and Bryl cream in his hair, is sincere and his weekly visits to the imprisoned pilgrim over three years convert him to a sort of Christianity.

- *Christine Page* was a graduate student in oceanography at the time of The Burn and is now one of the scientific leaders of the garden. Tall, strapping, and assured, she would be a sex object in a different sort of story; in *Just a Pilgrim*, her flirtation with fellow gardener Cameron leads to nothing. The series concludes with Christine figuring Eve—earlier, she had a beloved pet snake—alongside Cameron as Adam, as the two leave Earth for "another garden."

- *The Doc*, lead scientist of the garden, is a short, spritely, redheaded figure in John Lennon glasses, a magenta jacket, and parachute pants. Evidently responsible for the most advanced technologies, including faster-than-light travel, he would be an incongruous figure if not for an accommodating amorality that, like Castenado's, embodies a certain aspect of the future Earth.

- *Sliders* are this series' main "antagonist," a collective of mutated jellyfish that may enter into and reanimate corpses.

Artistic Style

Just a Pilgrim is illustrated by Ezquerra in a style that is garish, at times almost cartoonish, and seemingly intended to capture Ennis's interest in discovering the comedy at and beyond the boundaries of plausibility and acceptability. Character designs tend toward exaggerated icons; for example, the pilgrim not only wears a cowboy hat and a duster but also is branded across the face by a cross. Castenado is piratical in the extreme, with not one but two peg legs, hooks for both hands, and both eyes missing.

Scenes are depicted fairly statically, as if each is intended not to represent action in progress but to catch at the eye level and, as exemplified by the collected volume's cover gallery, to serve as images for copying and for further exaggeration by other artists. In this context, splash pages occur frequently and without clear

structural significance. Similarly, the pages are pervaded by extremely graphic violent imagery as well as gross-out horror. The art is generally played for comic effect; the reader is expected to laugh aloud equally at protagonists and antagonists, to the extent that both depend on the same kinds of graphic violence. However, the art is probably too sluggish to serve as satire.

Themes

Just a Pilgrim touches on a range of themes in keeping with its mixture of genres. A great weakness of the series, however, is that, although some of those themes are hammered at, none is developed with any subtlety or depth: The result is an entirely superficial use of potentially thought-provoking themes for rather thoughtless provocation, which in its garish bluntness verges on a wholly crass exploitation. In this way, the series' closest analogue outside of comics is probably "torture porn," such as the *Saw* films (2000's) or, at certain points, *The Human Centipede* (2009). Hardly interested in raising questions, nor even in telling its limited story, it seeks much more simplistically to show what it can get away with.

The postapocalyptic science-fictional setting, for example, could raise questions about ecology; the survival of species, including the human race; and the

---

Carlos Ezquerra

One of the co-creators of *Judge Dredd*, Carlos Ezquerra is a Spanish comics artist who has worked primarily in the British comic book industry for magazines like *Starlord*, *2000 AD*, and *Judge Dredd*. In the American comic book industry he is best known for his frequent collaborations with writer Garth Ennis on titles like *Bloody Mary*, *Preacher*, and *Just a Pilgrim*. Ezquerra's style is notable for its unusual page layouts and the use of the page as a total unit, rather than as a series of connected panels. He uses a great deal of crosshatching and elaborately detailed figures that can sometimes border on the cartoonish, as befits the tone of the over-the-top science-fiction stories that he is frequently called upon to illustrate.

relationship between culture and nature. However, in *Just a Pilgrim*, science fiction is combined with horror primarily to allow for monsters and to push all society toward rape society (indeed, the primary monsters rape human beings). Similarly, the series' interest in the American Western could, as an analogue of ancient epic, raise questions about the value of individual action or, in its historical guise, about the exploration of "frontier" and the consequent exploitation of its "native" peoples; however, it mainly does little more than provide a location and manner of dress.

Finally, the series' most obvious attempt at a thematic, Christian pilgrimage falls far short, taking the form of superficial visual and aural symbolism rather than any deeper or more complicated thematic allegory such as American or global millenarianism at the end of the twentieth century. The main character is identified only as "the pilgrim," and his backstory culminates in a discovery of faith. However, his seeming Christianity serves primarily to supply him with justifications for violence (he kills characters whom "the Devil" has possessed and sacrifices "innocent" survivors so as to kill a greater number of "sinful" buckers) and leaden quips at moments of violence.

In the second series, the pilgrim's conversations with scientists responsible for a new "garden" are perfunctory and unironic, and he seems to have more in common than not with the scientists' off-kilter, amoral leader, the Doc. All of this goes unexamined by the series; the pilgrim's disavowal of his Christianity at the end of the second series—when he demands that the scientists leave the Bible behind on Earth, lest it do more harm in the universe—seems to go unexplained. It is a pilgrimage to nowhere.

Impact

Produced by Ennis just after his well-received *Preacher*, *Just a Pilgrim* does not seem to have had the same kind or intensity of impact. Were it not for the success of the earlier series, this later series might not be remembered or, perhaps, have happened. Indeed, Ennis has said that he intended *Just a Pilgrim* to explore some of the same themes and settings—science fiction, faith and reason, the American West, the antihero—as that earlier series, but pushing farther at and past the boundaries of acceptability. If the setting, the characters, and the plot are all intended to be iconic (or more violent or otherwise repugnant versions of traditional icons), they have not achieved that status in the comic's audience.

Some of the same themes and settings are explored in later comics, but whether those comics were influenced by *Just a Pilgrim* is a matter for debate. For example, the genre of postapocalyptic Western clearly shapes parts of Robert Kirkman's *The Walking Dead* (2003-): the main character is, at least at first, a cowboy-hat wearing and gun-toting lawman, and the television version of that series explains its zombies as the result of microorganisms able to reanimate human corpses. However, rather than indicating the impact of *Just a Pilgrim*, the similarities are probably best understood as showing that such themes and settings have been "in the air." With *Just a Pilgrim* available in its entirety as a collected volume, a potential future impact remains possible but seems unlikely, especially given the commercial failure of the film version of the generically similar *Jonah Hex* (2010).

Benjamin Stevens

Further Reading

Briggs, Raymond. *When the Wind Blows* (1982).
Ennis, Garth, and Steve Dillon. *Preacher* (1995-2000).
Kirkman, Robert, and Tony Moore. *The Walking Dead* (2003-).
Miller, Frank. *Ronin* (1987).
Otomo, Katsuhiro. *Akira* (1982-1990).

Bibliography

"Dynamite Collects Ennis' *Just a Pilgrim* in December." *Newsarama*, October 15, 2008.
Ennis, Garth. "Remembering *Just a Pilgrim* with Garth Ennis." Interview by Joe Rybandt. *Newsarama*, October 23, 2008.

See also: *Ronin*; *Preacher*; *Hellblazer*; *Hitman*

JUSTICE LEAGUE OF AMERICA: THE NAIL

Author: Davis, Alan
Artist: Alan Davis (illustrator); Mark Farmer (illustrator); Patricia Mulvihill (colorist); Patricia Prentice (letterer)
Publisher: DC Comics
First serial publication: 1998
First book publication: 1998

Publication History

Justice League of America: The Nail was written by Alan Davis and illustrated by Davis and Mark Farmer. Davis is a British comic book writer and artist who has worked on such DC Comics titles as *Batman and the Outsiders, Detective Comics*, and *Aquaman*; Marvel Comics titles such as *X-Men, Captain Britain*, and *Fantastic Four*; and a number of British publications, including *2000 AD* and *Warrior*.

Justice League of America: The Nail was originally published by DC Comics as a limited-run series of three magazine-format comic books. Parts 1-3 were released in August, September, and November of 1998. The three parts were compiled into a trade paperback format in November, 1998.

The title was released under DC Comics' Elseworlds imprint, a series of stories in which existing DC Comics characters were removed from their traditional continuity and reinterpreted in alternative settings, time periods, or characterizations. The Elseworlds imprint began in the late 1980's and remained popular until the early 2000's.

A sequel to *The Nail* was released in 2004. Once again written and illustrated by Davis, *Justice League of America: Another Nail* continues from the first story, detailing an unsure Superman's efforts to adjust to public life as the Justice League faces foes from alternative realities and Batman is haunted by the ghosts of his past.

Plot

Justice League of America: The Nail explores the DC Comics Universe in the absence of its linchpin character, Superman. As a young Martha and Jonathan Kent

---

Alan Davis

Alan Davis broke into comics in the 1980's with his frequent collaborations with writer Alan Moore, including *Captain Britain, D.R. and Quinch*, and *Marvelman*, before falling out with the writer over creative differences. In the mid-1980's, Davis debuted in American comics at DC, working on a number of Batman related titles. At Marvel, he launched *Excalibur* with Chris Claremont, an X-Men related spinoff set in England that was notable for its lighthearted tone. His DC miniseries, *JLA: The Nail*, tells the story of the DC Universe if Superman had never existed, and was a critically acclaimed work at the end of the 1990's. Davis's art is defined by its classical compositions and careful rendering. His work is highly detailed and his figures are generally more realistic than those of many of his contemporaries. In the 1990's his art stood out from the dominant superhero aesthetic for the way that it recalled a playful style from earlier generations.

---

are driving into town, a nail punctures their tire, forcing them to turn back. As they return home, a burning object streaks across the sky.

Twenty-four years later, the Justice League is facing a public-relations nightmare as antimetahuman sentiment begins to spread across the United States, fueled by Mayor Lex Luthor and Deputy Mayor Jimmy Olsen. The league enlists respected journalist Lois Lane to help rebuild its image.

In Gotham City, Batman faces the Joker, who is heavily armed with alien weapons. Batman is captured and forced to watch the gruesome executions of Robin and Batgirl. With the help of Catwoman, a grief-stricken Batman overpowers and kills the Joker in front of television news cameras, igniting public outrage.

Metahumans start disappearing around the world, and the Justice League uncovers a vast conspiracy against them. As the metahumans are systematically defeated and captured, Lois Lane uncovers a research lab funded by Lex Luthor, which is conducting experiments on metahumans near the town of Smallville. Armed with alien weapons, Batman and Catwoman storm the Smallville research facility to rescue their counterparts.

In Metropolis, Lois Lane discovers that Lex Luthor is nothing but a brainwashed pawn and that Jimmy Olsen is actually the mastermind behind the entire scheme. Having been grafted with Kryptonian DNA, he has become all-powerful and obsessed with turning Earth into a new Krypton.

Jimmy Olsen flies to Smallville for a final confrontation with the Justice League. Just as the heroes appear defeated, a young Amish farmer intervenes in the battle, revealing himself as the long-lost Kal-El. Kal-El proves too powerful for Olsen, whose body becomes unstable and disintegrates. At the close of the story, the Justice League finds a renewed sense of purpose as they attempt to win back the public's trust. They will do so with the help of their newest member Kal-El, now known as Superman.

Justice League of America: The Nail does not feature a clear protagonist, as each member of the Justice League works to uncover a separate piece of a larger puzzle. The lack of a primary protagonist serves to further highlight the absence, until the very end, of Superman from this time line.

Characters

- *Batman*, a.k.a. *Bruce Wayne*, is a billionaire industrialist who has devoted his life to fighting crime after witnessing the murder of his parents as a child. He is the only member of the Justice League without superpowers. His character advances much of the narrative in the first and third acts.
- *Lois Lane* is an accomplished and respected journalist recruited by the Justice League to help rebuild its tarnished image. Through her investigation of the antimetahuman conspiracy, she advances much of the narrative in the second and third acts of the story.
- *Jimmy Olsen*, the antagonist, is the deputy mayor of Metropolis. He devoted much of his youth to the acquisition of superpowers in an attempt to join the Justice League. However, he was rejected

and became immensely bitter. After volunteering for a graft of Kryptonian DNA, he gained the powers and knowledge of a mysterious alien race known as the Kryptonians and became obsessed with taking revenge on the Justice League and controlling Earth.

- *Lex Luthor*, a billionaire turned politician, is the mayor of Metropolis. He is a vocal opponent of metahuman crime fighters, electing instead to combat crime in his city by revoking the civil liberties of citizens. He serves as a "red-herring" antagonist to the Justice League, until the reader discovers that he too is under alien control.
- *Green Lantern*, a.k.a. *Hal Jordan*, is a test pilot recruited into an intergalactic police force known as the Green Lantern Corps. He functions as the voice of reason within the Justice League. Because he represents an alien organization, he is not trusted by the general public.
- *The Flash*, a.k.a. *Barry Allen*, is a forensic scientist who gained the power of superspeed after being exposed to a combination of lightning and chemicals. He functions as one of the more "human" elements of the Justice League.
- *The Atom*, a.k.a. *Ray Palmer*, is a research scientist who develops the technology to alter his body's size and mass. He represents the "human" perspective of the Justice League as its members debate their place in the world.
- *Wonder Woman*, a.k.a. *Diana*, is an Amazonian warrior princess, endowed with magical powers and sent to the United States as an ambassador for peace. She is among those in the Justice League who represent the plight of the alien "other."
- *The Martian Manhunter*, a.k.a. *J'onn J'onzz*, was brought to Earth from his home planet of Mars as a result of a scientific accident. He uses his shape-shifting and psychic abilities to solve crimes. As the most visibly "alien" member of the Justice League, he withstands the worst of the antimeta-human sentiment.
- *Hawkwoman*, a.k.a. *Shayera Hol*, came to Earth, along with her husband Hawkman, as part of an alien police investigation and elected to stay and fight crime. Following the death of her husband,

she has become less certain about her role in the Justice League, and the antimetahuman sentiment almost causes her to leave Earth permanently.

- *Aquaman*, a.k.a. *Arthur Curry* or *Orin*, is the ruler of the lost kingdom of Atlantis. He has the ability to survive underwater and communicate with the creatures of the sea. Along with the Martian Manhunter, Wonder Woman, Hawkwoman, and Green Lantern, he is viewed with suspicion as an alien "other" by society at large.
- *Oliver Queen*, formerly *Green Arrow*, was once a member of the Justice League. He was mutilated and paralyzed while fighting the superpowered android known as Amazo. Now resentful of his former colleagues, he speaks out against the metahuman "menace."
- *Kal-El* is an infant refugee of a dying world who was found and raised in seclusion by Amish farmers. Kal-El's adopted parents discouraged him from seeking knowledge about the outside world and raised him to avoid violence. After the deaths of his parents, he joins the Justice League as Superman.

Artistic Style

Acting as both writer and penciller, Davis lists some of his artistic influences as Silver Age and Bronze Age artists Steve Ditko, Gil Kane, Jim Aparo, and later, Neal Adams. *Justice League of America: The Nail* was drawn and written to emulate the style of the Silver Age comics, which Davis grew up reading in the 1960's. Accordingly, there are substantial visual differences between the characters of the out-of-continuity *The Nail* and the characters of the *Justice League of America* comics of the late 1990's. This is common for titles in the Elseworlds imprint, as they take place outside of the mainstream continuity of the DC Comics Universe.

The color tone is somewhat muted, reflecting neither the bright, garish hues of the 1960's nor the deeper, more somber shades of the 1990's, instead evoking a nostalgic Technicolor sense of the Silver Age. The space between the panels, known as the "gutter," is black, rather than the standard white of the Silver Age.

In his afterword, Davis notes that one of his primary goals in *The Nail* was to produce a story that could be enjoyed by readers of all ages and levels of comic book literacy. To this end, *The Nail* does not utilize standard comic book devices such as thought bubbles or narrative captions; any narrative exposition is done through characters' dialogue or is presented visually through Davis's attention to the finer details of characters' postures, facial expressions, and bodily movement.

The layout of *The Nail* consists primarily of rectangular panels and intermittent splash pages. The splash pages function mainly as transitions between the individual vignettes of each character but sometimes are also used to highlight key scenes and events. The rectangular panels are not arranged in a uniform structure; instead they vary in size and orientation, at times overlapping each other on the page to represent the chronological passage of time.

Elements of one panel often extend into the following panel, serving as a navigational marker to guide the inexperienced reader's eye to the flow of the story. This subliminal signage appears in a number of ways throughout the story. The most commonly used device is that of speech bubbles that transcend the panel borders, however Davis also uses visual elements such as the outstretched arm of a character in flight, the crackling motion lines of an energy burst, or a flying piece of debris from an exploding White House to guide the reader's eye.

Themes

The central element of *The Nail*, and indeed of most Elseworlds titles, is the idea of what might have been. *The Nail* interrogates the role of the Superman character in the DC Comics Universe, and the effects that his absence would have on the characters with whom he regularly interacts. Superman is not only a "heavy hitter" for the Justice League but also a moral compass, a leader, and a source of inspiration.

Elseworlds titles often feature an element of transgression or "wish fulfillment" on the part of the writers and artists, as the departure from the constraints of mainstream continuity provides some measure of creative freedom. This allows for events such as the death of the Joker, Catwoman becoming Batwoman, or the maiming of Green Arrow.

Themes of prejudice and xenophobia are also central

to the story, as a politician and a shock journalist exploit society's underlying fear of outsiders to further a secret agenda. This growing public distrust causes a divide within the Justice League, as the nonhuman members begin to question their role in society and withdraw from public view.

The society represented in *The Nail* is one filled with fear and paranoia, where personal liberties are sacrificed in the name of security. The fearmongering and resulting public backlash against superheroes and metahumans in the story can be compared to the moral panic that erupted over comic book superheroes in the mid-1950's. The anticomic crusade led by conservatives, politicians, and the media eventually led to the creation of the Comics Code, launching the more optimistic and morally conservative Silver Age of comic books.

Impact

Justice League of America: The Nail is part of the Elseworlds imprint that gained popularity in the late 1980's and continued until the early 2000's. After the eradication of thirty years of history during the events of the *Crisis on Infinite Earths* (1985-1986) series, DC Comics implemented new continuity guidelines that eliminated the use of many hallmarks of the Silver Age, including parallel universes and superpets.

The Elseworlds imprint allowed the creative teams and the fans to stay in touch with the nostalgia of the Silver Age without encroaching on mainstream continuity. In *The Nail*, there are a number of Silver Age references, such as the characters of Krypto and Bat-Mite, Catwoman donning the Kathy Kane Batwoman costume, and Jimmy Olsen's propensity for becoming mutated in scientific accidents.

The Nail differs from most other Elseworlds titles, as the setting and characters have not been dramatically altered, unlike titles such as *Superman: Red Son* (2003) or *Gotham by Gaslight* (2006). Although there are small variations and a distinct Silver Age twist, the absence of Superman in this universe has had little impact on the lineup of the Justice League or the appearance of its characters.

The DC Multiverse has been reestablished as a part of the mainstream DC Comics continuity, incorporating a number of Elseworlds titles into the resurrected Multiverse of fifty-two "Earths." In 2007, the "Earth" of *The Nail* was revealed as part of this new Multiverse in *Countdown: Arena*, issue 1. Accordingly, it can be argued that *The Nail* has made an impact on the mainstream DC Comics Universe and may continue to do so in the future.

Mark Brokenshire

Further Reading

Cooke, Darwyn, and Dave Stewart. *DC: The New Frontier* Volume 1 (2004).

Davis, Mark, and Mark Farmer. *Another Nail* (2004).

Millar, Mark, et al. *Superman: Red Son* (2003).

Waid, Mark, and Alex Ross. *Kingdom Come* (1996).

Bibliography

Jenkins, Henry. "'Just Men in Tights': Rewriting Silver Age Comics in an Era of Multiplicity." In *The Contemporary Comic Book Superhero*, edited by Angela Ndalianis. New York: Routledge, 2009.

Kukkonen, Karin. "Navigating Infinite Earths: Readers, Mental Models, and the Multiverse of Superhero Comics." *StoryWorlds: A Journal of Narrative Studies* 2 (June, 2010): 39-58.

McCloud, Scott. *Understanding Comics: The Invisible Art*. New York: HarperCollins, 1994.

Nolen-Weathington, Eric. *Modern Masters, Volume One: Alan Davis*. Raleigh, N.C.: TwoMorrows, 2003.

Pedlar, Martyn. "The Fastest Man Alive: Stasis and Speed in Contemporary Superhero Comics." *Animation* 4, no. 3 (November, 2009): 249-263.

Witek, Joseph. "The Arrow and the Grid." In *A Comics Studies Reader*, edited by Jeet Heer and Kent Worcester. Jackson: University Press of Mississippi, 2009.

See also: *The New Frontier*; *Superman: Red Son*; *Kingdom Come*; *All-Star Superman*

K

Kick-Ass

Author: Millar, Mark
Artist: John Romita, Jr. (illustrator); Tom Palmer
(inker); Dean White (colorist); Chris Eliopoulos
(letterer)
Publisher: Marvel Comics
First serial publication: 2008-2010
First book publication: 2010

Publication History

Originally serialized in eight issues released between
February, 2008, and February, 2010, *Kick-Ass* is a
creator-owned series resulting from a collaboration between writer Mark Millar and illustrator John
Romita, Jr. Millar said the origin of the series came
from an idea spawned with a schoolmate at the age
of fifteen, when they both believed the profession of
"superhero" to be a legitimate career option. Millar
went on to become one of Marvel's preeminent
writers in the twenty-first century, working on titles
from the epic *Civil War* (2006-2007) to *The Ultimates*
(2003-2007), while also working on his own creator-
owned comics such as *Wanted* (2003-2005), *The Un-
funnies* (2004-2007), and *Chosen* (2004; reprinted as
American Jesus, 2008).

In 2004, Millar and Romita collaborated for the
first time on Marvel's *Wolverine*, on the "Enemy of
the State" story arc. Millar began working on the
script for the first issue of *Kick-Ass* in 2007, and
Romita joined soon after, lending a sense of gritty,
hyperrealism to the artwork. The first issue was
released in February of 2008, through Marvel's
creator-owned imprint, Iconic Comics, and, despite
the protagonist being a previously unknown entity,
went on to have surprisingly strong sales of roughly
sixty thousand for the first issue. This was due largely
to an extensive online guerrilla-marketing campaign
conceived by Millar and Romita. Also in 2007, Millar

Kick-Ass. (Courtesy of Marvel Comics)

was introduced to film director Matthew Vaughan.
A plan for an independent film, helmed by Vaughan,
was conceived, and the remaining issues of the comic
were written as Vaughan and screenplay co-writer
Jane Goldman worked with Millar to develop a film
adaptation. Millar has said that the second half of
the comic (issues 5-8) has scenes that were initially
found only in the screenplay and that there was some
back and forth between both writing teams. The final
issue of the comic was released the month prior to the
film's March, 2010, release.

Plot

Kick-Ass follows the life of teenager Dave Lizewski as he attempts to become a vigilante "superhero" in New York City. When not in high school, Dave spends his free time lifting weights and training to become a masked crime fighter. Within months, Dave's dreams are seemingly ended, however, as in his first encounter with criminals he is severely beaten, stabbed, and eventually struck by a car.

An infirm Dave remains in the hospital for months as he undergoes extensive surgical operations, including the fitting of three metal plates inside his head. Upon returning home, he initially resolves to never again don the mask and suit, but as soon as he is off crutches, he is back on the streets, patrolling. Dave quickly stumbles upon a gang viciously beating someone and, using his clubs, manages to defend the victim until the gang is forced to disperse. Footage of the fight, captured on video by someone with a cell phone, is subsequently uploaded to the streaming video site YouTube, where Dave's heroics quickly make him a viral-video sensation.

With added confidence from his superhero persona's overnight celebrity, whom the media has taken to calling "Kick-Ass," Dave utilizes popular social networking site Myspace as a way for people to enlist the help of Kick-Ass. On his first mission, Dave is overwhelmed by a gang after entering their apartment. As Dave is about to be murdered, a young girl, also dressed in superhero garb, comes to Dave's aid. The girl, known as Hit-Girl, proceeds to ruthlessly dispatch the gang members through her skilled use of samurai swords. As she prepares

Kick-Ass. (Courtesy of Marvel Comics)

to flee the scene, she informs Kick-Ass that they are on the same team. She makes a getaway with her partner/father, a man named Big Daddy.

While Dave attempts to resolve moral issues surrounding his involvement in Hit-Girl's murder of the drug dealers, it is revealed that the dealers were in the employ of crime kingpin John Genovese, and they were the most recent of twenty-two criminals in Genovese's network who had been murdered in the preceding six months. Security cameras from other murder scenes show Big Daddy and Hit-Girl as the murderers, and Genovese demands the vigilantes' heads.

After a new hero, Red Mist, appears on the scene and takes part in a publicized collaboration with Kick-Ass, Hit-Girl persuades Big Daddy that they should form a "superteam" with Kick-Ass and Red Mist. When Red Mist and Kick-Ass go to meet the other heroes at Big Daddy and Hit-Girl's hideout, they are ambushed by Genovese's men, who proceed to shoot Hit-Girl and take Big Daddy and Kick-Ass prisoner. It is revealed that Red Mist is really Chris Genovese, the son of John Genovese.

The gangsters proceed to torture and interrogate Big Daddy and Kick-Ass, before executing Big Daddy. Kick-Ass attempts escape and is about to be shot when he is saved by Hit-Girl, whose Kevlar-lined costume had saved her. The duo proceeds to dispatch the entire Genovese crime family, leaving Red Mist the only one alive, though badly beaten.

After defeating the Genovese family, Kick-Ass and Hit-Girl become more popular than ever. Hit-Girl attempts to return to the life of a normal ten-year-old girl and moves in with her mother. Kick-Ass gets humiliated at school and is once more beaten up, though at the end of the book his overall attitude is positive, as his alter ego has inspired a cultural phenomenon. An epilogue shows Red Mist vowing to get revenge on Kick-Ass.

Characters

- *Dave Lizewski*, a.k.a. *Kick-Ass*, is a physically average, sixteen-year-old high school student and the eponymous protagonist of the series. Aspiring to be like the heroes of his beloved comic books, he takes to wearing a scuba suit and patrolling the streets of his city, looking for crime to fight. After becoming involved with Hit-Girl and Big Daddy, Dave finds himself in the midst of a brutal war between the crime-fighting, father-daughter duo and John Genovese, a powerful crime lord.

- *Mindy McCready*, a.k.a. *Hit-Girl*, is a ten-year-old girl and costumed hero who is highly skilled in a variety of martial arts. Despite her young age, she proves herself as a capable assassin numerous times throughout the book. Her proclivity toward violence, instilled by her father, saves both Kick-Ass's and her own life.

- *McCready*, a.k.a. *Big Daddy*, an older vigilante, has been training his daughter, Hit-Girl, to become a lethal human weapon. He is adept with various firearms and finances his fight against John Genovese with the mysterious contents of a large, silver suitcase.

- *John Genovese* is a powerful New York City crime boss. He is the father of Chris Genovese/Red Mist and is the primary antagonist of the story. Prone to violence, he will dispose of enemies with his own hands, if necessary. Genovese is killed when Hit-Girl puts a meat cleaver through his head.

- *Chris Genovese*, a.k.a. *Red Mist*, is the son of crime boss John Genovese. Initially presenting himself to Kick-Ass as a fellow superhero named Red Mist, he quickly betrays Kick-Ass, Big Daddy, and Hit-Girl, leading to the death of Big Daddy and the final confrontation between the heroes and the Genovese crime syndicate. The

end of the book shows him severely beaten by Kick-Ass, though still alive. In the epilogue, Red Mist vows revenge against Kick-Ass.

Artistic Style

Pencilled by Romita, a renowned comics artist with a career that began in 1977, *Kick-Ass* was the second collaboration between Romita and Scottish writer Millar. *Kick-Ass* is illustrated with a grittiness meant to recall the urban-crime works of comic writer/penciller Frank Miller and film director Martin Scorsese.

Kick-Ass is set in the real world, as opposed to the more fantastic, brightly colored worlds of traditional superhero comics, and its art is full of dark tones, crowded action, and gratuitous amounts of ultraviolence. The violence found in *Kick-Ass* is shown to have real-world, often devastatingly brutal, consequences. This is first exemplified in chapter one, when Dave is stabbed and then struck by a car. His subsequent injuries are realistic: He is in a hospital bed, in and out of surgery for months, and then must endure months of more physiotherapy. In the world of *Kick-Ass*, much like the real world, getting hit in the face—standard fare for most superhero comics—entails drastic physical consequences, such as lacerations, contusions, and fractured bones, all of which are extremely detailed by Romita. Romita's violence is aestheticized in dense, near-claustrophobic panels, and geysers of blood spout accordingly.

Although much of the violence, especially that revolving around the destruction caused by the pint-sized Hit-Girl, is treated with an almost deadpan sense of macabre absurdity, as the book draws to a close, there are some particularly harrowing moments of horrific torture violence, specifically the attack on Hit-Girl with a meat tenderizer, the electroshock torture of Dave's testicles, and an extreme close-up on the execution of Big Daddy. At these points, the violence of the art serves to emphasize the real-world consequences that come with donning a mask and cape and taking a stand against violent crime.

Themes

Why do superheroes exist only in the pages of comics and in movies? That is one of the main questions raised by Dave and the book in general. What keeps the majority of the populace interested in celebrity gossip, while devastating crimes are committed daily? Dave laments how in the halls of his high school he sees scores of people emulating vapid celebrities. Dave attempts to counter this apathy in his personal life by becoming Kick-Ass, and in doing so, he inadvertently inspires a cultural phenomenon in which people begin to dress up like superheroes. While Dave is patrolling as Kick-Ass, however, those who follow Dave in dressing like superheroes spend their time engaging in online forum discussion and generally remain just as self-absorbed as they were before Kick-Ass became popular.

The self-absorption of others is in stark contrast to Dave, who is a naïve, if well-intentioned, youth at the start of the book but, by the end, has witnessed and been complicit in many acts of violence and murder. The repercussions of the violence are shown, as Dave is severely injured many of the times he puts on his costume and attempts to fight crime. His injuries leave his father with staggering medical bills—another realistic consequence usually glossed over in comic books.

Another theme concerns communal culpability and apathy. If indirectly, the book touches on the so-called bystander effect (also known as Genovese syndrome), a social psychology theory that asserts that the more people who are witnesses to or who are within earshot of someone in distress, the larger the proportion of bystanders who will ignore the distress cries, as they feel that surely someone else in the community will answer the call.

At the end of the story, even though Dave claims that Kick-Ass has inspired a legion of people such as him to stand up and fight crime, and that "heroes" now walk the streets openly in costume, the majority of these costumed people are shown to be severely out of shape, some obese. One of these self-appointed "heroes" even leaps off a skyscraper, to his death, as he had deluded himself into thinking he could fly. The lasting effect of Kick-Ass's highly publicized foray into superheroics is left open at the end of series. Red Mist's closing threat seems to imply that there can be no superheroes without supervillains and that escalation of antipathy is inevitable.

Impact

Upon its initial release, *Kick-Ass* broke all expectations for the comic's possible performance, with sales almost ten times as high as expected. The sales continued to increase with each subsequent issue, and a strong online buzz was generated prior to the release of each issue. As each single issue increased in popularity, the talks of a film adaptation generated much anticipation among fans. The film's production wrapped before the final comic was released, and the film was released within a month of the final comic. At the time of the film's release, some comic writers, including series writer Millar, believed that this relatively short lag time between the creation of an independent comic series and the adaptation into film form would become increasingly popular.

With its big-screen adaptation a large financial success, with strong box-office and home-video sales, *Kick-Ass* was part of a new wave of graphic novels to be successfully adapted within a relatively short period of time. After the film adaptation, *Kick-Ass* continued to have successful sales runs in both its collected paperback and hardcover editions. A sequel, *Kick-Ass 2:*

Mark Millar

Breaking into the comics industry as a protégé of writer Grant Morrison on *Swamp Thing* and the controversial "Big Dave" strip for *2000 AD* in the 1990's, Mark Millar became one of the most famous superhero comic book writers of the 2000's when he took over *The Authority* from Warren Ellis. Millar's work was renowned for its excessive violence and over-the-top sensibilities, which brought him into conflict with publisher DC Comics. *Superman: Red Son* depicted a world in which Superman had been raised in Stalin's Soviet Union, and is one of the most acclaimed Superman stories ever published. At Marvel Comics he wrote a number of popular series, including *The Ultimates*, *Marvel 1985*, and the company-wide event *Civil War*. He has also written a wide range of creator-owned titles, including *Wanted* and *Kick-Ass*, both of which have been adapted into movies.

Balls to the Wall, began in serialized form in Millar's British comic magazine *CLiNT* in late 2010. Millar has stated that he envisions the entire *Kick-Ass* series as a trilogy of books, with *Balls to the Wall* being the second entry.

Anderson Rodriguez

Films

Kick-Ass. Directed by Matthew Vaughan. Marv Films/ Plan B Productions, 2010. The film adaptation stars Aaron Johnson as Dave/Kick-Ass, Christopher Mintz-Plasse as Red-Mist, Mark Strong as John Genovese, Chloë Moretz as Hit-Girl, and Nicolas Cage as Big Daddy. Developed at the same time as issues 5-8 of the comic, the screenplay influenced the comic series. The endings of the comic and the film differ in terms of exact events but remain the same in spirit.

Further Readings

Azzarello, Brian, and Lee Bermejo. *Joker* (2008).

Azzarello, Brian, and Eduardo Risso. *100 Bullets* (1999-2009).

Millar, Mark, and J. G. Jones. *Wanted* (2003-2004).

Bibliography

Millar, Mark, and John Romita, Jr. *Kick-Ass*. New York: Marvel, 2010.

Millar, Mark, et al. *Kick-Ass: Creating the Comic, Making the Movie*. London: Titan Books, 2010.

Skinn, Dez. *Comic Art Now: The Very Best in Contemporary Comic Art and Illustration*. New York: Collins Design, 2008.

See also: *Joker; 100 Bullets; The Ultimates*

KINGDOM COME

Author: Waid, Mark
Artist: Alex Ross (illustrator); Todd Klein (letterer)
Publisher: DC Comics
First serial publication: 1996
First book publication: 1997

Publication History

Following his success with *Marvels* (1994), illustrator Alex Ross proposed to DC Comics what would be the rough outline of *Kingdom Come*. He was matched with writer and editor Mark Waid to flesh out the details and nuances of the series. *Kingdom Come* was originally published by DC Comics as four, full-color prestige-format books, collected the following year into one trade paperback with an additional scene, epilogue, and apocrypha. It was also released in a hardcover, slipcase edition, along with a *Revelations* companion text.

In 1999, a novelization of the graphic novel was written by Elliot S. Maggin, which appeared in hardcover, in mass-market paperback, and as a dramatized audiobook in abridged form. In 2006, *Kingdom Come* was rereleased in the oversized "Absolute" format with still more added material. The trade paperback was published again in 2008 with a new wraparound cover by Ross.

Plot

Set a decade or more into the future, *Kingdom Come* centers on a new generation of reckless, rampant superhumans pushing the unempowered population's fears to a breaking point in the wake of a nuclear mishap in Kansas. The disaster is partially caused because of Magog's lack of leadership.

After the death of one of his parishioners (Wesley Dodd, who is secretly the World War II-era hero the Sandman), Norman McKay, who spends much of the story unseen by the other characters and serves as the narrator, begins having visions of a calamity to come. He is tasked by the Spectre to witness the events of the coming days and render a judgment against those guilty of the imminent disaster.

Mark Waid

Best known for his eight-year run as the writer of *The Flash* for DC Comics (1992-2000), Mark Waid has worked extensively as an editor and a freelancer. His 1996 miniseries with painter Alex Ross, *Kingdom Come*, examined a possible future of the DC Universe in which a clash between differing conceptions of superheroism conspires to create a near-apocalypse. Since 2000, he has been one of the most consistently popular writers of superhero comics, with runs on *Fantastic Four*, *JLA*, *Legion of Super-Heroes*, and the company-wide crossover *52*. Waid's writing is marked by his interest in the superheroes of the past. His run on *The Flash* was notable for its reliance on characters and concepts from the history of that character, and *Kingdom Come* was widely read as a reiteration of traditional superheroic morality contrasted against the superheroic revisionism popularized in the 1980's and 1990's.

In response to the disaster, the retired superheroes, led by a reluctant Superman, return to active duty to corral the wild young superhumans and reestablish order by potentially outdated means. Superman's return does not solve the escalation of the superhuman threat, but he does come to understand that he cannot force a solution that treats superhumans and normal humans separately. Ultimately, he regains his sense of humanity, coming to once again wear the disguise he once used as Clark Kent to keep him tied to humankind. Furthermore, McKay persuades an enraged, rampaging Superman to embrace forgiveness rather than revenge.

The forced discipline of the young people and the failed penal system lead to all sides fighting one another, which has the potential to cause their virtual eradication if a lost hero, the manipulated Captain Marvel, does not intervene to sacrifice himself. Batman discovers that "Marvel" is actually Billy Batson, under the manipulation of Lex Luthor. Though Batman reveals

Luthor's ruse, the mind-addled Billy transforms into Captain Marvel (in his traditional red, lightning-bolt attire) to square off against Superman. However, his heroism ultimately breaks through his manipulated psyche, and he chooses to sacrifice himself lest all superhumans be destroyed.

Characters

- *Superman*, a.k.a. *Clark Kent*, *Kal-El*, and the *Man of Steel*, is the epitome of superheroic ideal, with his signature red cape and predominantly blue costume. Over the years, his jet-black hair has grown gray along the temples, and his revised costume features a more angular symbol against a black, not yellow, background, perhaps reflecting his jaded attitude. His superpowers remain at full force, and, as revealed by nemesis Lex Luthor, his years of soaking in Earth's solar radiation have left him nearly invulnerable to his customary bane of kryptonite; in fact, Superman survives a ground-zero explosion of a massive nuclear payload able to kill nearly every other superhuman. Though he remains a force for good and justice, Superman has become increasingly conflicted over what those terms mean, especially after he loses his most direct tether to humanity, Lois Lane.
- *Magog*, a.k.a. *David Reid*, Superman's popular replacement, was satirically modeled by Ross on the high-selling antiheroes being marketed to comics audiences in the 1990's. Magog wears a ram's-horn metallic helmet and has both a cybernetic limb and staff through which he can fire intense blasts of energy. Before the events of *Kingdom Come*, he apparently became the "people's hero," doing what Superman would not (for example, killing the Joker in cold blood). By story's end, Magog seems to support Superman's call for a renewed commitment to working with humanity as well as properly training the next generations of heroes.
- *Norman McKay*, the series' narrator, is a retirement-age American man, sporting a white beard and white hair, who works as a pastor. Both his occupation and overall look were based on

Ross's own father, Clark Norman Ross, and his last name is a tribute to *Little Nemo in Slumberland* (1905-1914, 1924-1927) creator Winsor McCay.
- *The Spectre*, a.k.a. *Jim Corrigan* and the *Angel of Vengeance*, McKay's Vergil-like guide through the world of superhumans, is depicted as ghostly pale and nearly nude, with only his billowing green hood and cape providing any clothing. This lack of modesty partially reflects his growing disconnection with humanity: the soul of slain police officer Jim Corrigan once aided the divinely charged spirit with the proper execution of his duties, but, by the start of *Kingdom Come*, he admits to having lost his way and needing McKay's insight. The two follow the superhumans' struggle and decide to allow their near eradication.
- *Wonder Woman*, a.k.a. *Diana of Themyscria* and *Diana Prince*, warrior princess, wears a modified version of her traditional tiara, bracelets, and strapless red-white-and-blue leotard at the opening of the story and an eagle-inspired suit of battle armor by its conclusion. According to her Amazonian sisters, she has failed as an ambassador to the wider, more savage world and been ostracized from her native home. Unlike Superman, she continued her struggle even in the face of worsening conflicts, but, upon his return, she has become affected and hardened by those years. This leads her to fight against both the escaping prisoners of the Gulag and Batman's force, only to later see that Superman's call for peace is the proper path.
- *Captain Marvel*, a.k.a. *Billy Batson* and the *World's Mightiest Mortal*, acts as a wild card throughout the series, serving Lex Luthor obediently and inexplicably. Until the story's conclusion, his brawny form is usually clothed in a tuxedo, topped by his thick-browed and thin-eyed enigmatic smile.
- *Batman*, a.k.a. *Bruce Wayne*, modeled by Ross on an aging Gregory Peck, must wear an exoskeleton atop his business suit to compensate for all his years of damaging heroics. He seems to ally

himself and his young followers with Lex Luthor's quest to wipe out the superhumans, only to later double-cross him. Once he has deduced Marvel's situation, he leads his team into the fray, donning a battle suit and attempting to prevent any further casualties.

- *Lex Luthor*, a businessman-cum-megalomaniac, has thickened about the neck and belly but remains a bald, brilliant narcissist. With Superman's sudden return, he must accelerate his plans for eliminating the threatening superhumans from the planet. Using a cadre of unempowered former supervillains (such as the Riddler and Catwoman) to escalate tensions between the warring superhuman community, he hopes to lead the world after the superheroes' demise.

Artistic Style

Ross's full-color, photorealistic painting style is employed throughout the series, its covers, and its promotional material. Utilizing a several-step process (including layouts, penciling, and shadowing), Ross worked from photographed models of his own choosing and design, several of whom are thanked in his notes at the end of the book. He continues to use traditional superhero comics page spreads; however, this level of verisimilitude in his work serves as a major attraction for readers, as it did in his previous work, *Marvels*.

In many cases, the photorealistic style makes the characters feel all the more immediate and both their powers and their plights more accessible. All of the pages are rendered in considerable detail, but he reserves full-sized splash pages for powerful, iconic images of the characters in their majesty. It is quite possible, given the theme of religion, that Ross's style is influenced by Warner Sallman and his richly detailed portraitures of Jesus (for example, the *Head of Christ*), particularly given the number of character close-ups and visual allusions included in *Kingdom Come*. These allusions include the Spectre emerging through a stained-glass window portraying the Garden of Gethsemane, the nuclear bomb blast in the shape of a cross, and a retired and longhaired Superman performing carpentry with two boards and three nails, among other images.

Themes

Kingdom Come pivots on four vital themes. The first concerns definitions of humanity and whether the superempowered are more than human or whether they have the same responsibilities and foibles. This ties in closely to the second major theme of morality, the core of the superhero genre itself. If ethics and morals determine heroism, what happens when those principles shift? Superman's answer is to leave when society's aims do not match his own; Wonder Woman's is to remain fixed, regardless. If morality is absolute, then the superheroes' sense of justice—and their brand of vigilantism—needs to endure. Otherwise, their actions are only temporary, and their understanding of humanity is likewise ephemeral. Change in morality along with change in humanity is at the heart of the third theme, the generational divide exemplified by the relationship between Superman and Magog (as well as among audiences from their respective comics eras).

Overall, though, the key theme is likely faith. The religious imagery, the series title, the narrator's profession, and the biblical quotations all point to religious faith undergirding the plot of *Kingdom Come* and its apocalypse/Ragnarök-like climax. Less literally, faith, as in the belief in one and another or optimism for the future, can be said to fill the entirety of the story, from the characters' conflicts to the motivation of its creators to the book's impact on the comic book industry. As author Geoff Klock writes in *How to Read Superhero Comics and Why* (2002), *Kingdom Come* moves the revisionist superhero narrative forward to the new age.

Impact

In the words of Klock, "*Kingdom Come* stages the return of the classic heroes, the return of the powerful origin and inspiration to confront what was done in their name." Largely, the story allowed heroes to be inspiring again in the wake of grim and brutal antiheroes inspired by *Batman: The Dark Knight Returns* (1986) and *Watchmen* (1986-1987) a decade earlier.

It also cemented Ross as the industry illustrator par excellence and created massive demand for his realistic art style. Given Ross's popularity, it was surprising, then, that DC balked at his proposal for a follow-up series entitled *The Kingdom*, detailing modern-day events potentially leading to the future displayed in *Kingdom Come*. Instead, the publisher had Waid lead a separate 1999 event by the same name to inaugurate DC's failed and ultimately temporary new explanation for its titles' shared continuity, dubbed Hypertime.

While the *Kingdom Come* Superman was thought to have appeared in the *Superman/Batman* series—this was later determined by the editors not to be the authentic character from the same reality—he does visit the present in 2008 as part of Geoff Johns's "Thy Kingdom Come" story line in *Justice Society of America*. Ross took part in Johns's stories, providing covers in the style of *Kingdom Come* and select pages.

A. David Lewis

Further Readings

Busiek, Kurt, and Alex Ross. *Marvels* (1994).

Gruenwald, Mark, et al. *Squadron Supreme* (1985-1986).

Ross, Alex, Jim Krueger, and John Paul Leon. *Earth X* (1999).

Bibliography

Klock, Geoff. *How to Read Superhero Comics and Why*. New York: Continuum, 2002.

Lamken, Brian, ed. *The Comicology "Kingdom Come" Companion*. Arden, Pa.: Harbor Press, 1999.

Lewis, A. David. "Kingdom Code." *The International Journal of Comic Art* 4, no. 1 (Spring, 2002).

_____. "Superman Graveside." In *Graven Images: Religion in Comic Books and Graphic Novels*. New York: Continuum, 2010.

See also: *Marvels; Earth X; Batman: The Dark Knight Returns; Watchmen*

L

LEAGUE OF EXTRAORDINARY GENTLEMEN, THE

Author: Moore, Alan

Artist: Kevin O'Neill (illustrator); Ben Dimagmaliw (colorist); Todd Klein (letterer); Bill Oakley (letterer)

Publisher: DC Comics; Top Shelf Comics

First serial publication: 1999-

First book publication: 2000

Publication History

The idea for *The League of Extraordinary Gentlemen* had been on author Alan Moore's mind for several years before it was created. Already well known for both British and American comic publications by the late 1980's, Moore first developed the idea for *The League of Extraordinary Gentlemen* after he had started on *Lost Girls* (1991-1992). Moore pitched the idea to publisher Kevin Eastman, who had advanced him money for a future project, and presented artist and former colleague Kevin O'Neill with an outline in 1996.

After leaving DC Comics because of various disputes, Moore worked for other publishers. Jim Lee convinced Moore to develop comics for his company, WildStorm, and so the America's Best Comics (ABC) line was born. While the ABC line was forming, Lee sold WildStorm to DC. Since titles had been created and various contracts signed, Moore agreed to continue with ABC in order to keep the creators employed, while Lee created a "firewall" between ABC and DC Comics proper.

When the first issue of *The League of Extraordinary Gentlemen* appeared in March, 1999, DC's name was not on it. Though the first three issues came out quickly, the final three were delayed for various reasons, the best known being that DC Comics publisher Paul Levitz ordered issue 5 "pulped," or destroyed. DC feared that Marvel Comics would take offense to that

Kevin O'Neill

An illustrator who began his career in the 1970's on British humor titles, Kevin O'Neill made his reputation on *2000 AD*, where he was a frequent cover artist and the co-creator of the story *Nemesis the Warlock* with writer Pat Mills. With Mills he also created for Epic Comics *Marshal Law*, a superhero comic book parody featuring extreme violence and sexuality. O'Neill is probably best known for his collaboration with writer Alan Moore on *The League of Extraordinary Gentlemen*, a set of miniseries for America's Best Comics, DC Comics, and Top Shelf. O'Neill's art has varied tremendously over the course of his career, and alters to reflect the themes and ideas of each individual project. He is known for a mixture of high level of detail, period accuracy, and a slightly cartoony tone in his *League* stories, while earlier work in *2000 AD* and *Marshal Law* reflected a more extreme level of cartoonishness.

issue's inclusion of an advertisement for a nineteenth-century feminine hygiene product called the "Marvel Whirling Spray." During this time, two Bumper Compendium Editions were also published, reprinting the first two and second two issues, so that those who did not get the original issues could catch up.

As with the first volume, the second volume of *The League of Extraordinary Gentlemen* was a six-issue limited series, and the first three issues came out promptly in 2003. An original hardcover graphic novel, *The League of Extraordinary Gentlemen: Black Dossier*, came out in 2008. It was not part of the original ideas that Moore had for the series' stories, and it began almost as a "fill-in book" before Volume 3 could begin.

Moore had his final break with DC during the creation of *Black Dossier*. Besides problems related to a lawsuit over the film adaptation, Moore says that there was more interference from DC on this project. In addition, because of copyright issues, the release was delayed in Canada and the United Kingdom.

Because *The League of Extraordinary Gentlemen* is a creator-owned project, Moore brought the third volume to Top Shelf Comics, with Knockabout Comics distributing it in the United Kingdom. The third volume consists of three 80-page issues in "bookshelf" format. The first, "1910," came out in 2009, with issues 2 ("1969") and 3 ("2008") released in 2011 and 2012, respectively.

Plot

In the world of *The League of Extraordinary Gentlemen*, characters from various works of fiction exist together. The first two volumes take place in England in 1898. At the start of the first volume, Campion Bond of Military Intelligence recruits Mina Murray (recently divorced after the events of Bram Stoker's *Dracula*, 1897) on behalf of his superior, "M," to gather a group of individuals to defend the British Empire from an imminent danger.

Mina first locates adventurer Allan Quatermain, who is in a Cairo opium den, having become an addict. When she is endangered, he snaps out of his stupor to help her. As they flee to the docks, they are rescued by Captain Nemo and his submarine, *The Nautilus*.

They next head to Paris, where Inspector Dupin helps Mina and Allan find a strange man who has been killing prostitutes: Edward Hyde, the monstrous alter ego of Englishman Henry Jekyl. After Hyde is subdued and captured, the group returns to England.

Mina, Allan, and Nemo next visit a girls' school, where a rash of mysterious pregnancies is being caused by Hawley Griffin, the Invisible Man, who is raping the older girls. The team captures Griffin and returns to the League's headquarters in their secret annex.

Hyde and Griffin are granted pardons in return for joining the League, and the group is sent on its next assignment: to recover the antigravity element cavorite from the Asian crime lord "Devil Doctor," who rules London's East End and who has stolen the cavorite for evil purposes. They recover the substance, but, after handing it over to Bond, discover that M is Professor James Moriarty, Sherlock Holmes's archenemy, who intends to use the cavorite to launch his own aerial assault on the East End.

The members of the League realize they have been used and that Moriarty's attack would kill them; thus, they go on the offensive. While the Devil Doctor's forces attack Moriarty's flying fortress, the League uses a balloon to reach it. While Nemo, Griffin, and Hyde go after Moriarty's men, Mina and Allan pursue Moriarty, who ends up causing his own doom when the container for the cavorite is shattered and he grabs it, making him "fall" upward into space. The League survives the ensuing crash and, at the request of the new M, Mycroft Holmes (brother of Sherlock), remains together.

Volume 2 alludes to H. G. Wells's *The War of the Worlds* (1898). The volume opens with various races of Mars, led by earthlings Gullivar Jones and John Carter, attacking a destructive mollusk-like race. The mollusks abandon Mars and land in England. As in Wells's novel, the invaders first use heat rays and poison gas and then overcome Earth's heavier gravity by putting themselves in giant, heavily armed tripods.

Believing the "Martians" will be victorious, Griffin decides to betray humankind and give information to them. When Mina discovers him stealing military plans, he attacks her.

Soon after, Mina and Allan are sent to the South Downs to locate a scientist who may have something that will stop the invaders. After an unsuccessful first day, they return to an inn, where they have sex. Allan then discovers the reason that Mina always wears a scarf: Her experience with Dracula has left her throat horribly scarred. The next day, various human-animal hybrids take the pair to their creator, Dr. Moreau, the scientist for whom Mina and Allan were looking. He gives them the secret weapon they need.

Meanwhile, in London, a Martian weed has clogged the Thames, disabling *The Nautilus*, and the Tripods are destroying South London. Hyde returns to the League's headquarters, where he finds and kills Griffin (whom he has always been able to see), more for what he did to Mina than for his betrayal. Mina and Allan return to London with their package, give it to Bond, and meet up with Hyde and Nemo at the north end of London Bridge, the last spot where the Tripods can cross the river. Because the weapon is not yet ready, Hyde sacrifices himself to delay the Tripods, destroying one before he is killed.

The weapon is launched and is revealed to be a hybrid virus that destroys the Martians. Nemo is disgusted that he has unknowingly used germ warfare and quits the League. At the end of book, Mina tells Allan that while she loves him, she needs some time alone.

Each of the first two volumes also contains a text story. The first volume's "Allan and the Sundered Veil" describes an earlier adventure and includes characters created by Wells, Edgar Rice Burroughs, H. P. Lovecraft, and others. The second volume contains "The New Traveler's Almanac," which provides more information about the world of the League; most importantly, it offers veiled hints that Allan and Mina found a magic pool that restored Allan's youth and granted immortality to both.

The main story of *Black Dossier* takes place in 1958, when the government of "Big Brother" has just lost power. Still-young Mina and Allan steal the dossier, which contains information on them and other incarnations of the League. While running from government agents, they read the information and eventually escape by being transported to the mysterious Blazing World, home to earlier and later League members as well as all sorts of other characters.

Much of the dossier is text telling the League's history. It contains information about the life of the immortal, gender-changing Orlando, the formation of "Prospero's Men," and "The New Adventures of Fanny Hill," a sequel to *Memoirs of a Woman of Pleasure* (1748, more commonly known as *Fanny Hill*), featuring her adventures with the eighteenth-century League. The post-1898 adventures of Mina's League, foreign and future Leagues, a 1930's adventure as told by Bertram Wooster, and a 1950's adventure of

Allan and Mina written in the style of a Jack Kerouac story are also recounted.

The third volume, *Century*, includes the threat of the mystical Moonchild, who may also be the Antichrist. Besides featuring Mina and Allan, other characters include Orlando, Thomas Carnacki, and A. J. Raffles. *Century* also contains a text story, "Minions of the Moon," set during various eras of the League's world.

Volumes

- *The League of Extraordinary Gentlemen,* Volume 1 (2000). Collects the first limited series as well as the covers of the Bumper Editions. Features Mina and Allan's introductions to the League and their subsequent adventures in Victorian England.
- *The League of Extraordinary Gentlemen,* Volume 2 (2003). Collects the second limited series as well as *The Game of Extraordinary Gentlemen* from *America's Best Comics Sixty-Four Page Giant.* A germ-warfare weapon is launched at the Tripods. Mina and Allan become romantically involved.
- *The League of Extraordinary Gentlemen: Black Dossier* (2008). Set in 1958, the volume shows Allan and Mina stealing a dossier that contains historical information about the League.
- *The League of Extraordinary Gentlemen,* Volume 3: *Century, 1910* (2009). Features Moonchild and a cast of other characters. Mina meets with a time traveler who speaks cryptically about twenty-first-century events.

Characters

- *Wilhelmina "Mina" Murray* is a character from *Dracula*. Following the events of the novel and her subsequent divorce from Jonathan Harker, she was recruited to form and lead the League.
- *Allan Quatermain* is an adventure character created by H. Rider Haggard in 1885. Though old, he is recruited by the League. He later begins a romantic relationship with Mina, and after having his youth restored, he fakes his death and poses as his long lost "son," Allan, Jr.

- *Captain Nemo*, a.k.a. *Prince Dakkar*, was introduced in Jules Verne's *Vingt mille lieues sous les mers* (1869-1870; *Twenty Thousand Leagues Under the Sea*, 1873). A Sikh from India, he aids the League in the first two volumes but resigns after the Martian invasion. His death is shown in *Century*.

- *Dr. Henry Jekyl*, a.k.a. *Mr. Edward Hyde*, is from Robert Lewis Stevenson's *The Strange Case of Dr. Jekyl and Mr. Hyde* (1886) and is found in Paris by Allan and Mina. Over the years, Hyde has greatly increased in strength and size, towering over the others; he is also very resistant to harm. He reluctantly joins the League and is later killed during the Martian invasion.

- *Hawley Griffin*, a.k.a. the *Invisible Man*, is the titular character in Wells's 1897 novel (though Moore gave him the first name). After faking his death, he hid in a girls' school, where he was captured by the League, into which he was later inducted. Only his physical body is invisible, and he has to remove his clothes to be fully unseen; he occasionally wraps his head in bandages or uses greasepaint to allow himself to be partly visible. After betraying Earth to the Martians and attacking Mina, he is killed by Hyde.

- *Professor James Moriarty*, a.k.a. *M*, is the archenemy of Sherlock Holmes. Believed dead, he is both the leader of a criminal empire and the head of Military Intelligence who forms the League. He is killed at the end of Volume 1.

- *Campion Bond* is one of the few wholly original characters in the series (though he is intended to be the grandfather of Ian Fleming's fictional spy James Bond). He works for "M" (both versions) as the "handler" of the League.

- *The Devil Doctor* is the unnamed leader of the Chinese criminal gangs in London and a rival of Moriarty. While not explicitly stated, he is most likely based on Sax Rohmer's Dr. Fu Manchu.

- *The Martians* are the version from *The War of the Worlds* and, as in the novel, travel around Earth in tripods and use heat beams as a weapon. However, Volume 2 hints that they are not native to Mars and instead were using that planet as a base.

- *Orlando* is the gender-switching immortal from several literary sources, most notably the 1928 Virginia Woolf novel *Orlando: A Biography*. Orlando was a member of several Leagues, including Mina's second one.

- *A. J. Raffles* is the "gentleman thief" from E. W. Hornung's stories. He was a member of Mina's second League until his death in World War I.

- *Thomas Carnacki* is the occult detective "Ghost Finder" created by William Hope Hodgson. He was a member of Mina's second League for several decades.

- *The Moonchild* is a magically created being who may be the Antichrist.

Artistic Style

Moore's scripts for *The League of Extraordinary Gentlemen* were extremely detailed, giving O'Neill page-by-page and panel-by-panel descriptions, ranging from the number of panels to the position of individuals in a particular panel. Moore occasionally let O'Neill draw it differently and allowed him to choose some of the Easter eggs, objects found in the backgrounds of the League's headquarters and elsewhere that refer to other literary works. Besides researching books and minor characters, O'Neill went to the actual locations where certain scenes occurred, sometimes adapting them for how they may have looked at the time of the story. One interesting design choice was that Allan Quatermain was partly based on some film roles played by Sean Connery, who would later take the role in the film adaptation.

The most artistic diversity in the series is found in *Black Dossier*. Besides incorporating the style of the previous volumes, O'Neill provided different types of art in the various text stories, often attempting to match the era in which they take place. "The Life of Orlando" is done in a more "cartoony" style as it was supposed to have been told in "comic cuts" of a magazine; phony turn-of-the-century postcards are "reprinted," and there is even an eight-page pornographic comic in the style of the old Tijuana bibles. The most interesting artwork in *Black Dossier* is near the end of the book, which is done in 3-D for the Blazing World scenes; on a few pages, one image can be seen by looking through the red lens, and others can be seen in the same spot by looking through the green one.

Some interesting techniques were used for the lettering. Not only are the styles of the word balloons different for various characters, but non-English dialogue, including Martian, is also left untranslated. While the Martian lettering was contrived, there is a correspondence to what Moore had in the script in English. (All real foreign languages were also written in English and later translated for the finished work.)

Themes

One of the major themes, or ideas, of the *League* titles is the concept of the "crossover," in which two or more characters from different, and sometimes totally unrelated, works of fiction interact. In comics, this technique dates at least to the 1940's Justice Society, in which characters from various comic titles teamed up, and beginning in the 1970's, characters who are supposed to be in different "universes," such as Superman and Spider-Man, have interacted.

While many of the main characters in the League are examples of various fictional archetypes, Moore enjoys including lesser-known characters. For example, a character from Victorian erotica runs the girls' school in which Griffin is hiding, and the students have ties to *Pollyanna* (1913), *The Bostonians* (1886), and *Rebecca of Sunnybrook Farm* (1903).

The stories also have an element of satire about them; the first stories partly satirize what author Douglas Wolk referred to as "the terror of Victorian culture that were expressed ... in its cheapest literature: the dangerous allure of the British Empire's exotic fringes, uprisings by 'Mohammadans' and 'Chinamen,' science gone amok, [and] sexual libertinism." The short story "Allan and the Sundered Veil" was written in the style of a penny dreadful (a type of early pulp fiction novel), and many text pieces in *Black Dossier* parody a particular author's or period's style.

Impact

The League of Extraordinary Gentlemen has had a great impact on readers, both scholars and the general

public. When the first issues originally came out, they were the impetus for discussions about the sources of the characters; some readers even questioned how much literary knowledge was necessary to follow the series. Librarian Jess Nevins began to annotate the various issues, occasionally with the help of other readers. This led Nevins to publish his annotations in several books.

Moore has heard from readers of all ages in the United States who began reading the books referenced in *The League of Extraordinary Gentlemen*, including some of the lesser-known titles. Moore has said that he was "favorably surprised" that even the most obscure references got an enthusiastic response from the American audiences and that it "warms his heart" that this very "English" story is popular with American readers.

David S. Serchay

Films

The League of Extraordinary Gentlemen. Directed by Stephen Norrington. Angry Films, 2003. While Allan (Sean Connery), Nemo (Naseeruddin Shah), and Jekyll/Hyde (Jason Flemyng) are close to their comic book counterparts, Mina (Peta Wilson) has vampiric powers, and the Invisible Man is Rodney Skinner (Tony Curan), a thief who stole Griffin's formula. Also added are Dorian Gray (Stuart Townsend), who cannot be killed, and Tom Sawyer (Shane West), a young American secret service agent. M (Richard Roxburgh) sends them to deal with the mysterious Fantom, ultimately revealed to be M (who, as in the comic, is also Moriarty). This loose adaptation garnered poor reviews and became the subject of a lawsuit by writers who claimed that it plagiarized a script that they had submitted in the 1990's. Like all film adaptations of his work, it was disavowed by Alan Moore.

Further Readings

Edginton, Ian, et al. *Victorian Undead* (2009-2010).

Ellis, Warren, and John Cassaday. *Planetary* (1998-2009).

Moore, Alan, and Melinda Gebbie. *Lost Girls* (1991-1992).

Bibliography

Khoury, George. *The Extraordinary Works of Alan Moore*. Raleigh, N.C.: TwoMorrows, 2003.

Nevins, Jess. *A Blazing World: The Unofficial Companion to "The League of Extraordinary Gentlemen,* Volume 2." Austin, Tex.: MonkeyBrain Books, 2004.

_____. *Heroes and Monsters: The Unofficial Companion to "The League of Extraordinary Gentlemen."* Austin, Tex.: MonkeyBrain Books, 2003.

_____. *Impossible Territories: An Unofficial Companion to "The League of Extraordinary Gentlemen: The Black Dossier."* Austin, Tex.: MonkeyBrain Books, 2008.

See also: *Planetary*; *Batman: The Killing Joke*; *Promethea*; *Watchmen*

LIFE AND TIMES OF MARTHA WASHINGTON IN THE TWENTY-FIRST CENTURY, THE

Author: Miller, Frank

Artist: Dave Gibbons (illustrator); Alan Craddock (colorist); Angus McKie (colorist); Robin Smith (colorist)

Publisher: Dark Horse Comics

First serial publication: 1990-2007

First book publication: 2009

Publication History

In 1990, the first installment of *The Life and Times of Martha Washington in the Twenty-First Century*, titled *Give Me Liberty*, appeared as a four-part serial, which won author Frank Miller and illustrator Dave Gibbons an Eisner Award. The next installment of Martha's life, *Martha Washington Goes to War*, was released in 1994, with Martha appearing older than she would be in the 1995 edition, *Happy Birthday, Martha Washington*.

"Collateral Damage," included in *Happy Birthday, Martha Washington*, was colored by Alan Craddock and initially appeared in *Dark Horse Presents Fifth Anniversary Special* (1991) as the black-and-white "Martha Washington's War Diary." "State of the Art" first appeared in *San Diego Comic-Con Comics* Issue 2, while the omnibus edition's "Logistics," debuted as a minicomic to accompany the Martha doll, an action figure that appeared on store shelves in 1998.

Martha Washington Goes to War was colored by Angus McKie and released in 1995. *Martha Washington Stranded in Space* came out in 1995 as a one-shot issue, containing "Crossover" and "Attack of the Flesh Eating Monsters," which was originally published in *Dark Horse Presents*, issues 100-104. *Martha Washington Saves the World* appeared in 1999 and features an emerging, full-page style similar to the one seen in Miller's *300* (1998).

In 2007, seventeen years after Martha's debut appearance in *Give Me Liberty*, *Martha Washington Dies* was released; in the story, Martha dies on her one hundredth birthday. The omnibus edition contains chapter introductions by Gibbons that provide insight into the production, themes, and influences on *Martha*

Washington and inform readers about what happened in the time gaps between serials. The "Martha Washington Scrapbook" contains sketches, photographs, preliminary drawings, posters, and notes not seen in previous editions.

Plot

Give Me Liberty begins with Martha's birth in a Chicago housing project, followed by her stint in an insane asylum and her subsequent success in the American Peace Force (PAX). It ends with Martha standing sentinel as the traitorous Stanford Moretti commits suicide.

Happy Birthday, Martha Washington chronicles several of Martha's missions. First, Martha is in bombed-out Manhattan, where she is tasked with assassinating Dictator Beluga. She rescues tax collector Nixon, who laughs at her ignorance: Beluga is already dead, and she is just "collateral damage" (as implied by the story's title). In "Logistics," Martha defends the Constitution's Ninety-fourth Amendment, which forbids the sale of red meat. After leading an invasion of Texas and liberating herds of cattle, she ends up at the local Fat Boy, gorging on a cheeseburger and fries. "State of the Art" pits Martha against a female soldier of the First Sex Confederacy; both combatants are equipped with the same malfunctioning combat suits. The two women strike up a brief friendship as they wait for the battle to end. In "Insubordination," Martha is on a mission to find Captain Kurtz, a thinly disguised Captain America, in order to obtain a vial of his genetically altered blood. Martha finds Kurtz hugging the Liberty Bell and decides to commit her own act of insubordination, discarding the blood-filled syringe.

In *Martha Washington Goes to War*, Martha is stranded at "the Killing Fields," where she runs across a Lone Star Republic soldier with ghosts on his mind. She is again trapped on the wrong side of a bombing raid. When she regains consciousness, she learns Chicago has been annihilated, killing Raggy Ann (a fellow asylum inmate who endured government experiments),

Tomhawk Wasserstein (Martha's Native American boyfriend), and Martha's mother. While Martha is recovering, Wasserstein's ghost appears, saying, "We will meet again, my love."

After she recuperates, Martha is assigned to the Earth-tethered *Harmony*, a malfunctioning weather-control satellite that comes under sudden attack. Martha pursues the invisible culprits on a defective sky sled, crash-landing in the Valley of Death. Martha chases the Ghosts into the radioactive core, where she discovers a paradise peopled by Raggy Ann and Tomhawk Wasserstein, among others.

While the Promised Land has clean air, pristine land, and tasty food, the Surgeon General has taken complete control of the United States. He hones in on Martha's communicator and unleashes a power beam that all but destroys paradise. In "Kingdom Come," Martha defects from PAX and joins the opposition aided by Venus, an artificially intelligent computer. The revolutionary forces destroy the Surgeon General but not before PAX unleashes all its nuclear warheads, most of which malfunction.

Martha Washington Stranded in Space explores the anomaly in "Crossover," where Martha mistakenly fires on a friendly ship. With the help of Lieutenant Pearl, she rescues a robot named Big Guy, who introduces them to a parallel universe containing an Earth free from war, hunger, and environmental degradation. Martha cannot leave her imperfect world behind, however, and Big Guy takes the explorers back to their own dimension. Martha and Pearl are rescued in "Attack of the Flesh Eating Monsters" by space aliens bent on harvesting Earth's human population. Martha sees through the charade and discovers Venus is manipulating humankind to unite them behind a common cause.

In *Martha Washington Saves the World*, Venus tries to teach the willful Martha a lesson by sabotaging her ship. Martha knows Venus is out of control, but her superior officers disagree and send Martha on a scientific mission to observe an asteroid headed for Jupiter.

Martha awakens from "cryosleep" in "Tomorrow, When the World Is Free" and finds her ship controlled by Venus and everyone implanted with B-Chips. Martha is now a human automaton programmed with

happiness, her willfulness seemingly erased. She overcomes Venus's mind control and destroys the asteroid headed for Jupiter with nuclear weapons, creating a shock wave that fries Venus. However, the computer still has control of Earth. Meanwhile, the asteroid's core is revealed to be an alien space ship.

Martha, Science Officer Nitobe, and Pearl crashland their shuttle on the artifact. Suddenly, the Venus-controlled Tomhawk Wasserstein turns up and unleashes a bomb that seemingly destroys Dr. Nitobe and damages *Galahad*, Martha's ship. Nitobe is transformed into a humanoid construct who reveals that the Juggernaut probe was sent by the creators to see whether their biological experiment on Earth had succeeded.

The artifact speeds toward Earth, and Martha orders Nitobe to crash-land into the Pacific Ocean, creating an electromagnetic pulse that destroys every power source on the planet, which obliterates Venus. After Earth recovers, Martha travels through the Looking Glass anomaly to make contact with the creators. Whatever Martha discovers beyond the anomaly, readers will never know because, when Martha dies, only chaos reigns on Earth.

Volumes

- *Give Me Liberty* (1991). Collects issues 1-4. Chronicles Martha's life from her birth in 1995 and her early years in Chicago's Cabrini-Green projects to her life as a PAX sergeant. This bildungsroman establishes Martha's heroic identity as she escapes physical and mental torture to discover the value of second chances while recognizing her place as soldier in this dystopic vision of America.

- *Happy Birthday, Martha Washington* (1995). Collects the stories "Collateral Damage," "State of the Art," and "Insubordination," into a one-shot issue of Martha's battles. "Insubordination," a tribute to Jack Kirby, finds Captain America betrayed while trying to save the Liberty Bell, symbolizing the entire nation's loss of freedom at the hands of a corrupt totalitarian government and leading to Martha's own insubordination. "Logistics" (1998) originally accompanied the

Martha action figure and was added to *Happy Birthday* for the omnibus edition.

- *Martha Washington Goes to War* (1995). Collects issues 1-5 of the comic book series of the same name. Continues the story of the future American civil war and Martha's defection. Objectivist in nature, this volume pays tribute to Ayn Rand's *Atlas Shrugged* (1957), as America's best and brightest disappear, leaving Martha alone to make choices about good and evil.

- *Martha Washington Stranded in Space* (1995). A one-shot issue containing "Crossover." Martha wonders if she can leave her war-torn planet for a utopian otherworld. "Attack of the Flesh-Eating Monsters," is a satire of science-fiction pulps and questions how far the government should go to unite people.

- *Martha Washington Saves the World* (1999). Collects issues 1-3 of the comic book series of the same name. Martha battles Venus to save humankind, thereby freeing people and nations to live up to their own enlightened self-interests.

- *Martha Washington Dies* (2007). Final one-shot edition, illustrating Martha's one hundredth birthday. As the leader of a resolute band of resistance fighters, she utters her final words: "Give me liberty."

Characters

- *Martha Washington*, the protagonist, is a strong, intelligent African American woman. Despite experiencing the worst her dystopian world has to offer, she remains courageous and honest and retains her dignity. As a PAX officer, she wears the blue uniform of the nineteenth-century American cavalry and sports ever-changing hairstyles. She eventually defects and dons the white uniform of the Ghosts.

- *Raggy Ann*, a psychic schizophrenic, is short and has a large lumpy head that is wired into a government computer. She first encounters Martha in the asylum's experimental wing. Eventually, Martha finds her wired to a space cannon. Martha loses her but rediscovers her friend in the Promised Land.

- *Tomhawk Wasserstein*, Martha's love interest, is a handsome Apache man with long black hair and blue eyes. He betrays Martha when he is overpowered and controlled by Venus. While Martha can forgive his transgression, she can no longer call him lover.

- *Lieutenant Colonel Stanford Moretti*, Martha's superior officer and antagonist, is a white man with combed-back brown hair and blue eyes. Martha captures the treasonous Moretti, and on his final day, offers him an honorable way out. She is present when he hangs himself in his cell.

- *The Surgeon General*, Martha's nemesis, is a sociopath in a green medical gown, optometrist goggles, a doctor's head mirror, rubber gloves, and boots. He runs the Health Enforcement Department that declares sickness a crime. After his death, he is revealed to be an army of mechanical medical clones.

- *Nixon* is a pale brunet and former tax collector. Martha rescues him while on a secret mission to kill Beluga.

- *Captain Kurtz* resembles Captain America from helmet to tights. He has a muscular build, blond hair, and blue eyes. His genetically altered blood keeps him young and able to withstand most bullets. He helps Martha escape the Nazis overrunning Philadelphia.

- *Chief Engineer Coogan* is a portly, middle-aged engineer working on the tethered satellite *Harmony*. His red hair and pale skin betray Irish roots, as also evidenced by his stereotypical love for whiskey. He is kidnapped by the Ghosts and taken to the Promised Land, eventually joining Martha as the engineer on *Galahad*.

- *Venus* is a computer program equipped with artificial intelligence that appears onscreen as a blue-skinned female. A creation of the subversive Ghosts of the Promised Land, she initially combats the evil PAX but is soon corrupted. She tries to control humans with implanted B-Chips. Her godlike delusions do not fool Martha, who eventually destroys her.

- *Lieutenant Pearl*, a Valkyrie clone, is a statuesque, blond-haired blue-eyed warrior with an identification bar code on her cheek. Marketed to the military, the Valkyrie clones first served PAX and then the Surgeon General, but after the latter's death, this clone becomes Martha's protégé.

- *Big Guy* is a "retrobot" of epic proportions, with large silver hands and feet and a head too small for his enormous metal body. A good-natured 1950's-style machine, he tempts Martha to join him on a utopian Earth.

- *Dr. Nitobe* is a tall, self-important African American science officer heading the Juggernaut asteroid mission. After his untimely death aboard the alien artifact, he is transformed into a muscular being with onyx skin and glowing red eyes. He is last seen passing through the Looking Glass anomaly with Martha and crew to fulfill the last instructions given by the Creators.

Artistic Style

Give Me Liberty is part of the familiar artistic universe of a DC or Marvel comic. Folded within *Liberty*'s traditional comic panels are character backgrounds and story-line narratives communicated through mocked-up news magazines, letters, advertisements, and a map of the Nation Divided, grounding readers in this alternative America.

In the omnibus edition, *Happy Birthday, Martha Washington*, Craddock illuminated "Collateral Damage," while McKie emblazoned "State of the Art," "Insubordination," and "Logistics." *Happy Birthday, Martha Washington* includes computer-generated color graphics, lettering, and sound effects.

In *Martha Washington Goes to War*, Gibbons invested in a mirrored, state-of-the-art computer graphics system, offering McKie the duplicate. Suddenly, readers were treated to a mixed-media style in which photographic bolts of electricity are shot through blurred clouds and photographic skies. Characters walk or fly above filtered backgrounds of Polaroid grass and landscapes, creating a three-dimensional quality.

Martha Washington Stranded in Space features Gibbons's rendition of the crossover character Big Guy, created by Geof Darrow. Readers travel through snapshots of clouds in the "Promised Land"

to star-laden backgrounds of the universe. When Martha reaches the Promised Land, Gibbons's utopian drawings are mixed with photos and computer-generated backgrounds. Space is also the stage for *Martha Washington Saves the World*, with several two-page spreads reminiscent of Miller's *300*. Some pages have a collage feel.

Themes

The Life and Times of Martha Washington in the Twenty-first-century is a bildungsroman of both a single human life and a society seemingly bent on destroying itself even while striving for liberty. Martha is Everywoman: She witnesses the rise of corporate and government power at the expense of individual freedom. She rises from the notorious Cabrini-Green projects to become world savior. Miller's near-future universe reflects many of the modern world's problems writ large, including irresponsible food production, unchecked environmentalism, and polarizing special-interest groups. Miller creates a hero that "embodies certain notions of right and wrong." She is honorable and strives to make the right choices even in the most precarious situations.

Imprisonment is a central theme in *Martha Washington*, especially in *Give Me Liberty*, when Martha is betrayed and abandoned in the tropical forests of Brazil. As Gibbons puts it, "Martha had been trapped in . . . the ghetto, a school locker, a mental facility, and a PAX drop-ball."

In *Martha Washington Goes to War*, Miller adapts Rand's objectivism as a central theme, mirroring story lines from *Atlas Shrugged*. In *Martha Washington Saves the World*, Miller toys with intelligent design by introducing the Construct, an alien sent to check on the progress of Earth's biological evolutionary cycle started by the creators.

Martha overcomes mental adversity after a terrifying childhood altercation left her in a catatonic state. Mind-numbing sedation, flashbacks, and hallucinations do not destroy her; on the contrary, they leave her with a highly disciplined psyche. She can outwit and outwait Venus, as the computer crawls along her cerebral pathways.

While Gibbons and Miller often populate the story with caricatures, such as the Reaganesque President Rexall and the tax-collector Nixon, they also project specific human events into Martha's world. In *Martha Washington Saves the World*, they re-create the 1997 mass suicide of the Heaven's Gate cult, as the fictional colony on Japetus, struck with apocalyptic fervor, removes their helmets and suffocates en masse.

Unlike the serial editions, the *Washington* omnibus is presented in chronological order. Each comic chapter begins with background information, while every thread highlights a hero in the making. Martha is repeatedly willing to lay down her life to save a single being or all of humanity. She rebels against oppression and fights tyranny even when she must become a "traitor."

Martha Washington represents real-life change, that which occurs along the trajectory of decades. Martha evolves; she grows up, falls in love, fights wars, and experiences loss, and her personality forms across a lifetime. In contrast to the standard male superhero, Martha is a strong black woman who wants to make the world a safer place, where everyone can experience liberty.

Impact

Fresh from completing *Watchmen* (1986-1987), Gibbons teamed with Miller at Dark Horse Comics, a publishing house that made creator ownership a priority, an advance in an industry in which virtually all the mainstream heroes were owned by corporations and drawn by leagues of artists and writers with homogeneous tedium. Although longtime fans of traditional superheroes, Miller and Gibbons saw this project as a chance to break away from the typical comic book.

Martha Washington's evolving style—from the traditional hand-drawn, hand-lettered patriotic comic book to a computer-generated, complicated computer hero of a decades-long series—highlights the transformation not only of the comic book industry but also of the comic book hero, with a fictional universe eerily close to that of modern society.

Doré Ripley

Further Readings

Gibbons, Dave. *The Originals* (2004).
Miller, Frank. *Ronin* (1993-1994).
Moore, Alan. *Promethea* (1999-2005).

Bibliography

Gibbons, David. "David Gibbons on the *Martha Washington* Omnibus." Interview by Chris Arrant. *Newsarama*, July 23, 2008. http://www.newsarama.com/comics/080723-gibbons-washington.html.

_____. "Gibbons Discusses *Martha Washington*." Interview by Shaun Manning. *Comic Book Resources*, March 23, 2010. http://www.comicbookresources.com/?page=article&id=25341.

Miller, Frank, and Dave Gibbons. *The Life and Times of Martha Washington in the Twenty-first-century*. Milwaukie, Ore.: Dark Horse Books, 2010.

Miller, Frank. "Interview Four." Interview by Christopher Brayshaw. In *Frank Miller: The Interviews: 1981-2003*, edited by Milo George. The Comics Journal Library 2. Seattle, Wash.: Fantagraphics Books, 2003.

See also: *Give Me Liberty*; *Watchmen*; *DMZ*; *Batman: The Dark Knight Returns*; *The Big Guy and Rusty the Boy Robot*

Light Brigade

Author: Tomasi, Peter

Artist: Peter Snejbjerg (illustrator); Bjarne Hansen (colorist and cover artist); Rob Leigh (letterer); Ken Lopez (letterer)

Publisher: DC Comics

First serial publication: 2004

First book publication: 2005

Publication History

Light Brigade began as a four-volume prestige-format, creator-owned limited miniseries published by DC Comics in early 2004. Its four issues, unusually large for serials, were gathered together into a two-hundred-page trade paperback in 2005.

Creator Peter Tomasi is more than an editor and writer for DC Comics. He is also a fan of military history and was intrigued by the story of Longinus, the centurion that pierced the side of Christ as he hung on the cross. Tomasi's love of history and his orthodox upbringing led to a mythical fascination that eventually spawned the idea for *Light Brigade*, a book ten years in the making.

Tomasi first approached Vertigo, a company he thought was the perfect choice for a war comic. However, Vertigo had just published a plethora of war comics, so the publisher passed on the project. Tomasi then reached out to Joey Cavalieri, and DC Universe took on *Light Brigade* as a creator-owned miniseries. Once Tomasi began work in earnest, *Light Brigade* took about two years to finish.

Tomasi asked Peter Snejbjerg, an artist with whom he had worked on other projects, such as DC's *The Sandman*, to do the artwork. He appreciated Snejbjerg's realistic work and considers him "one of the most underrated artists around," as he is an artist more familiar to fantasy readers. While Cavalieri helped edit *Light Brigade,* he suggested Bjarne Hansen for colorist. With the addition of Hansen, a beautifully wrought collaboration was fixed.

Peter Tomasi

Peter Tomasi began his career in the comics industry as an editor at DC Comics working on the *Batman* and *Green Lantern* titles. Since 2007 he has dedicated himself full-time to writing and has produced titles for DC that include *Nightwing*, *Batman and Robin*, and *Green Lantern Corps*. He also co-wrote the creator-owned title *The Mighty* with Keith Champagne and artist Peter Snejbjerg. Tomasi collaborated with writer Geoff Johns on *Brightest Day*, a company-wide crossover event in 2010-2011. As an editor, Tomasi was intricately involved in many of the expansive crossover events that served to reshape the DC Universe in the mid- and late-2000's, and his storytelling is strongly influenced by his close connection to the history and continuity of the characters whose adventures he once edited.

Plot

In *Light Brigade*, just as the heavenly battle between good and evil is being waged overhead, the Battle of the Bulge (1944) is in full swing on Earth. A group of American G.I.s is hunkered down in a World War I-era cemetery, where Christopher Stavros has just received word that his wife was killed and his son orphaned in the United States. Two hundred Germans are headed toward the Americans, and the impending battle would seem to be the G.I.s' last stand. What is worse, the group's enemies are not simply Nazis but zombie Nazis who cannot be stopped by mere bullets. When the skirmish comes to a close, only a dozen G.I.s escape.

The heavenly war merges with this scene, as the archangel, Sauriel, destroys the renegade, Azbeel, but loses the sword of God. One of the war-torn G.I.s is really the immortal Marcus Longinus, a man looking for atonement. He recruits his remaining buddies in the age-old battle against the evil Grigori.

The angelic Grigori were sent to Earth to protect humans, but they eventually mated with their charges, producing the half-breed Nephilim. God could not abide this abomination and sent the Flood, but some Nephilim and Grigori survived, and they desired revenge against God. The fallen angel, Zephon, has recovered the sword of God and marches toward the eternal flame to create a weapon powerful enough to challenge God himself.

The only thing that will kill this heavenly horde is iron, so the G.I.s' first mission is to make iron bullets. They capture a German ammunition factory staffed by slave laborers, who readily agree to produce custom-made bullets to destroy the Nazis.

Once their task is finished, the American soldiers head for their last stop, the Augustine monastery where the eternal flame is housed. The monks welcome the G.I.s into the ranks of the Iron Guard to defend the true cross as it burns with the eternal flame— the flame the Nephilim plan to use to ignite the sword of God. The G.I.s are granted superhuman power by walking through the immortal flame, and performing this ritual will keep them fighting even as they sustain grave wounds.

Once the Nephilim Nazis reach the monastery, the fallen Zephon takes up the sword and sprouts wings, leading his zombie forces to the final battle. The G.I.s and the Iron Guard let loose with their bullets and iron-edged arrows, cutting through the zombie ranks, but there are too many Nephilim.

The evil Zephon plunges the sword of God through Marcus Longinus, who drops his spear and crumples to the ground, wrenching the sword from the archangel's hands. Stavros retrieves the spear smeared with Christ's blood and launches it at Zephon, piercing the Grigori's heart and annihilating the fallen angel.

Only two G.I.s survive the battle between good and evil: Chris Stavros and the baseball-loving Hal. Hal decides to remain at the monastery, helping rebuild the Iron Guard, while Stavros returns to the United States and collects his son. He and his son visit the cemetery where Deborah Stavros is buried before heading off to deliver the letters of his fallen comrades.

Characters

- *Private Christopher Stavros*, the protagonist, is of Greek extraction. He is tall and dark-skinned

and has a straight aquiline nose and a three-day beard. He has lost his faith in God as a result of his wife's death, which has left his son orphaned. He is given the knowledge of God in order to enlist his help in the coming showdown between good and evil.

- *Mark*, a.k.a. *Centurion Marcus Longinus*, is a member of the American Fourth Infantry Division. His square, clean-shaven jaw and blue eyes top a scar-covered body. He is the Roman soldier who pierced the side of Christ as the latter was dying on the cross, and he carries the blood-covered iron spear tip to fight the fallen Nephilim and Grigori. He leads the G.I.s in their fight against the Nephilim, hoping to atone for his misdeed.

- *Colonel Zephon,* the antagonist, is a pale Nazi with blond hair, who is really a fallen angel. He is the last Grigori. He is after the sword of God, which has been brought to Earth by a renegade angel, and once he lights it in the eternal flame surrounding the true cross, he will have enough power to challenge God and take revenge.

- *Hal* is a member of the American Fourth Infantry Division. He has a dimpled chin and scruffy orange hair and keeps his lips pressed shut. He is a baseball-loving American, with a gruff exterior that hides a kind disposition. He is concerned about the men he has killed, insisting on burying the dead with dignity, and remains behind at the monastery to help rebuild the Iron Guard when the battle between good and evil is over.

- *Jesse,* another member of the American Fourth Infantry Division, has a lantern jaw and blue eyes and bears a strong resemblance to Stan Laurel of the comic team Laurel and Hardy. He takes orders lightly, totes a six-shooter, and is trigger-happy. However, he is one of the first to give his life to save his comrades.

- *Nick* is a member of the American Fourth Infantry Division and has short-cropped hair and the mashed nose of a pugilist and talks out of the side of his mouth. He loves epithets and comes off as a tough guy with no tolerance for jokes, but he stands tall in the face of danger and cares for his fellow soldiers.

- *David* is another member of the American Fourth Infantry Division. He smokes a corncob pipe, has blue eyes and combed-back dark hair, and seems to be a bit older than the others. He is sensible and reminds his comrades of their duties as soldiers, helping to keep them alive, while acting as the young Simon's personal guardian.
- *Simon* is a member of the American Fourth Infantry Division and the youngest of the G.I.s. He is a young and has a pock-marked face, a wide, blue-eyed stare, and a hopeful enthusiasm that does not match his situation. His blond hair is long on top and compliments his two large front teeth. He loves comic books and believes his fellow combat veterans are a justice society. He dubs them the "Light Brigade" and knows they cannot lose because good always triumphs over evil.
- *Pete,* a member of the American Fourth Infantry Division, wears round-framed glasses and has short spiky red hair and two large front teeth. He is intelligent, knows inane facts, and has a penchant for conspiracy theories. He is not confident in commanders, believing they consider soldiers little more than cannon fodder.
- *Billy* is a member of the American Fourth Infantry Division. His blue eyes complement a round face. He has light brown hair, which he wears tight on the sides. He has the skills of a farrier and produces iron crosses for his fellow G.I.s. He goes down in the first line of defense at the battle between Heaven and Earth.
- *Nisroch* is a Nephilim disguised as a Nazi and the right-hand man of Colonel Zephon. He has a pug nose and blond hair and always wears goggles. He never swerves in his duty to Zephon, but he occasionally antagonizes the fallen angel. He resents being reminded that he is a half-breed.
- *Sauriel* is an archangel wrapped in a blue light who wears proto-Roman armor. He is responsible for handling fallen angels and kills the renegade Azbeel, who has stolen the sword of God. He dies at the hands of Zephon, but not before revealing all, including the presence of God, to

the remaining G.I.s and recruiting them in the showdown between good and evil.

Artistic Style

Light Brigade is a gorgeously illustrated book in which the cartoon-style realism of Snejbjerg is complemented by Hansen's sensitive colors. Perhaps because they both come from Denmark, they get the snowy scenes of *Light Brigade* exactly right. The winter light is captured in sharp angles that provide small areas of intense light and long shadows that are not just a bunch of crosshatches. Snejbjerg's strong-lined sceneries are highlighted by aquamarine skies and the blue shadows of winter nights.

The cross-era, cross-genre epic battles are fused, not confused. The frozen lake containing the parade of dead Nephilim also features crusaders of the Middle Ages frozen alongside the soldiers of modern world wars. The images of the lake capture the differing uniforms and weapons in a collaborative blend that lends to the story instead of mashing up historical periods in an overworked frenzy. The battle scenes are realistic even when fantastic. For example, zombie dogfights pit P-51 Mustangs against one other, the plane's wide-eyed G.I. pilot struck with perfectly drawn disbelief and fear as a zombie Nazi tosses him from the cockpit.

Light Brigade contains a preponderance of gore, from blood- and brain-dripping soldiers to tooth-flying emaciated zombies. However, the gore is essential to the story. When monks are cut in half, the reader is presented viscera that look like something from a biology textbook, while the variety of wounds struck by a variety of weapons perfectly translates the desperation of G.I.s fighting the battle between good and evil.

More than just beautifully rendered gore, landscapes, and castles, Snejbjerg gives each character a personality. Whether it is the buck-toothed, pock-marked Simon, who marches into battle with a backpack filled with Golden Age comics, or the disillusioned and grim Stavros, who has to survive in order to get home to his orphaned son, the characters are distinguishable and identifiable, not only in speech but also in appearance, outlook, personality, and gestures.

Light Brigade is a darkly themed comic, but it is brightly illustrated with a sumptuous rendering that brings its world to life. There are no over-the-top splash pages leading nowhere; this is a comic that combines top-level storytelling with high-grade art. Text boxes are nonexistent, and the limited dialogue, lettered by Ken Lopez and Rob Leigh, reflects each character's personality, while adding to the storyline. The dialogue does not repeat the art, and the art reinforces the emotion with flair.

Tomasi first pictured *Light Brigade*'s opening scene in the World War I-era graveyard as a film sequence. Many critics have noted that *Light Brigade* is a natural fit for the big screen, and a lot of this enthusiasm is based on the realistic rendering of a fantastic world in which angels battle alongside zombies against a bunch of G.I.s led by an immortal.

Themes

On its surface, *Light Brigade* is a story about good versus evil. Whether it is Heaven versus Hell, fallen angels versus archangels, or Nazis versus American G.I.s, this story seems to delineate explicitly the good guys from the bad. However, not all zombies are Nazis; there are a couple of G.I.s in their company. Also, while it is easy to paint the Nazis as evil, the fallen Grigori do seem to have a point when it comes to their feelings of betrayal and the desire for revenge against God. They disobeyed his command, and God tried to destroy them in the Flood; however, the text questions whether or not complete annihilation is a fair punishment. The Grigori and their half-breed descendants think it was not.

When his wife is killed in a car accident, Stavros has a crisis of faith, marking another theme of the comic. When Heaven comes crashing onto the battlefield, however, an angelic soldier forces enlightenment on the remaining G.I.s, including Stavros, who has to come to grips with a world in which God exists and bad things happen.

Light Brigade is not simply a Sunday school lesson in Christian tenets, however; it is a story that uses the readily identifiable framework of Christianity to explore humanity and the human response to crisis.

Heroism in the face of overwhelming odds is at work in *Light Brigade* and is directly addressed when the Grigori sneer at the dozen remaining G.I.s, a lost

cause resembling that of the three hundred Spartans at Thermopylae. What motivates the men is also explored. The American soldiers are waiting to go home, which gives the work a sense of urgency. Failure on the part of the soldiers not only affects their personal world but also all of mankind. They are noble and honorable during a war in which inhumanity seemed at its worst.

Hope is another theme explored in *Light Brigade*, exemplified in both the fresh-faced Simon, who believes in the superhero world in which good always triumphs over evil, and Stavros, who has to live just long enough to get back home. The characters infect readers with that same enthusiasm to triumph, so that mankind can live on and one man can make it back home.

Impact

The comics of the Golden Age and a love of history influence Tomasi. He also loves Westerns and war-story comics, à la Archie Goodwin, and in *Light Brigade*, the inserted Golden Age comics within remind readers that these comics were a major source of reading material for World War II soldiers. Tomasi cites Bob Kanigher, Russ Heath, and Joe Kubert as influences on his artistic leanings, but war comics seem to be the greatest influence, from Golden Age World War II titles to Silver Age Vietnam War works, as well as more recent works such as Garth Ennis's *Preacher* (1995-2000) and *War Story* (2001) series.

Classic American comics artists influenced Snejbjerg's art for *Light Brigade*. He heavily researched war comics and was influenced by their style, believing they fit the book's setting. Tomasi saw Mike Mignola and Eric Powell in Snejbjerg's simplistic, strong-lined approach. *Light Brigade*'s storyline is often called a "mashup" of genres, from horror and fantasy to war and "weird tales," but this does little to highlight just how strangely fascinating and well done this work is.

Doré Ripley

Further Readings
Arcudi, John, et al. *A God Somewhere* (2010).
Tomasi, Peter, et al. *The Mighty* (2009).
_____. *The Outsiders: The Hunt* (2010).

Bibliography

Flagg, Gordon. "Review of *Light Brigade*." *Booklist*, 102.8 (Dec. 2005), 32.

Harahap, Al. "*The Light Brigade* #1 Review." *Comixfan.net*, Feb. 28, 2004. Available at http://comixfan.net/forums/showthread.php?t=26069.

Marshall, Rick. "Adapt This: *Light Brigade* by Peter J. Tomasi and Peter Snejbjerg." *Splashpage.mtv*, May 6, 2010. Available at http://splashpage.mtv.com/2010/05/06/adapt-this-light-brigade-by-peter-j-tomasi-and-peter-snejbjerg/.

Montgomery, Paul. "Inglorious Angels: Charge of the *Light Brigade*." *iFanboy*, August 25, 2009. http://www.ifanboy.com/content/articles/Inglorious_Angels__Charge_of_the__Light_Brigade_.

O'Shea, Tim. "Peter J. Tomasi: Follow the Light." *Comics Bulletin*. Available at http://www.comicsbulletin.com/features/107751537050471.htm.

Renaud, Jeffrey. "Arcudi and Snejbjerg Find "*a god somewhere.*" *Comic Book Resources,* June 2, 2010. Available at http://www.comicbookresources.com/?page=article&id=26490.

Singh, Arune. "Justice Editor of America: Peter Tomasi talks DC and . . . Hal Jordan?" *Comic Book Resources*, Oct. 27, 2003. Available at http://www.comicbookresources.com/?page=article&id=2782.

Snejbjerg, Peter. *The Light Brigade*. Available at: http://snejbjerg.com/gallery/light_brigade01.htm.

Tomasi, Peter. "Peter J. Tomasi: Follow the Light." Interview by Tim O'Shea. *Comics Bulletin*, February 22, 2004. http://www.comicsbulletin.com/features/107751537050471.htm.

_____. "Tomasi's on Fire with *The Light Brigade*." Interview by Jennifer Contino. *Comiccon,* March 12, 2004. http://www.comicon.com/ubb/ubbthreads.php?ubb=showflat&Number=325371.

Velez, Catherine. "Can't miss comics: *Light Brigade*." *Austin Comic Books at Examiner*, July 15, 2009. Available at http://www.examiner.com/comic-books-in-austin/can-t-miss-comics-light-brigade.

See also: *Preacher*; *Just a Pilgrim*; *DMZ*

LOSERS, THE

Author: Diggle, Andy

Artist: Jock (pseudonym of Mark Simpson, illustrator); Shawn Martinbrough (illustrator); Clem Robins (letterer); Nick Dragotta (penciller and inker); Alé Garza (penciller and inker); Ben Oliver (penciller and inker); Colin Wilson (penciller and inker); Lee Loughridge (colorist)

Publisher: DC Comics

First serial publication: 2003-2006

First book publication: 2004-2006

Publication History

In 2002, Andy Diggle, a former *2000 AD* editor who had recently written the *Lady Constantine* miniseries (which was published in 2003) for Vertigo, was invited to discuss ideas for an ongoing Vertigo series, which would be a reworking of an existing DC Comics property. After spending some time searching for a suitable concept or character, editor Will Dennis suggested *The Losers*, a series published in DC's war title *Our Fighting Forces* (issues 123-181, 1970-1978). Diggle had never read it, but he liked the title.

The characters were dead in the DC Comics continuity, so Diggle planned a series set in the 1950's that would reveal the group had survived and was essentially in hiding. They would then get involved in a heist caper. However, Garth Ennis was already doing a retro military series with *War Stories* (2001), and Howard Chaykin and David Tischman were working on a 1950's crime book, *American Century* (2001-2003).

Ultimately, Diggle set his story in the present day with a new set of characters, meaning his series had barely any connection to the previous one. In two nods to the original, Diggle included a character named Clay (the original Losers featured Sergeant Clay) and used the name of the group's dog, Pooch, as the call sign of one of the other characters.

The Losers illustrator Jock, the pseudonym of British artist Mark Simpson, had previously collaborated with Diggle on the *Judge Dredd Megazine* series *Lenny Zero* (2000-2002). The first issue of *The Losers*, dated August, 2003, was a larger-than-average

Andy Diggle

Best known as the writer of *The Losers*, an irreverent examination of the war comic within the context of the American "war on terror," Andy Diggle is one of the preeminent British comic book writers of the 2000's. During his tenure as editor of *2000 AD* and *Judge Dredd Megazine* he was credited with helping to revive interest in what were widely seen as moribund titles. *The Losers*, his debut work for DC's Vertigo imprint, resurrected obscure characters from DC's past and provided them with an entirely new spin. Part crime thriller, part war story, Diggle crafted an exciting and often exotic story of conspiracy and violence with American intelligence agencies as the villains. With the release of the film adaptation in 2010, Diggle landed on the bestseller list and became a highly sought-after creator, writing long runs of *Thunderbolts* and *Daredevil*. He is one of the most distinctive young voices in superhero comics.

thirty-two pages. Jock illustrated the first six issues, but because of the pressures of producing a monthly book, he shared art duties with various illustrators thereafter. Jock tackled two crucial story lines: the flashback to the Losers' final mission before they were officially declared dead in the 1970's series (issues 16-19) and the climax to the entire series (issues 29-32). Diggle never intended the series to run indefinitely, and it came to a close with issue 32, dated March, 2006.

Plot

The Losers are a Special Forces team, seconded to the Central Intelligence Agency (CIA), whose chopper was shot down during a mission ordered by their CIA handler, Max. They escaped back to the United States but found themselves placed on a secret CIA death list.

In *Dead Man's Hand*, the team intercepts an illicit shipment of heroin being trafficked from within the CIA. The proceeds would have been used to fund dirty operations. In *Goliath*, the team launches a raid for data on the Goliath oil company, which has been running the drug shipments. Roque betrays the Losers, conspiring with Max to steal a quarter of a billion dollars of CIA money from a Goliath facility and to blame it on the Losers. The team escapes with the data.

In *Downtime*, Clay contacts Colonel Coleman, the man who put the Losers together, for information on Max. The code name Max has existed since the end of World War II and has been used to deal drugs and weapons to fund U.S. military campaigns and to interfere in other nations' politics. Meanwhile, Jensen extracts the stolen data, and in *Island Life*, he delivers it. There is no evidence to tie the CIA to the drug shipments, but the data reveals Max is searching for something on the volcanic island of Montserrat. Meanwhile, Max orders the death of a geologist, Hashimoto, who was investigating tectonic activity in the Persian Gulf on a decommissioned oil rig owned by Max. On Montserrat, the Losers face off with Max's team and steal a safe containing Hashimoto's survey.

In *Sheikdown*, the team arrives in Qatar and is employed by political advisor Sheik Abdul Aziz Ibn-al-Walid to intercede between Qatari dissidents and CIA operatives. In return, the Sheik shows them Max's oil rig (which is deserted) and tells them Max is an insider at CCI, the bank that launders his drug money. In *Blowback*, Aisha rescues her former boyfriend, Fahd, from prison in Turkmenistan by tricking the CIA into moving him between prisons then hijacking the convoy.

The Pass flashes back to 1998 and the Losers' last mission. Assigned to seek a terrorist named Ahmed Khalfan Fadhil and guide a bomb to him, they attempted to abort the mission upon discovering children were being trafficked at Fadhil's location in the Khyber Pass. Max told the Losers to continue, but they disobeyed, rescuing the children and executing Fadhil. Cougar found a prisoner in the cellar, Max's former right-hand man, who told Cougar that Fadhil was not a terrorist but a heroin runner for Max. Max wanted to prevent his secrets from getting out. The Losers loaded the children onto a rescue chopper, but Max, believing the Losers were aboard, ordered the chopper destroyed. In the present day, Aisha reveals that Fadhil was her father.

In *London Calling*, the team infiltrates the London branch of CCI. A courier comes to pick up some bonds and the Losers plant a tracer in the briefcase. The courier is Roque, and in *Anti-Heist*, the Losers trace him to a ship in the Azores. They foil Roque's plan to hijack two shiploads of decommissioned nuclear warheads, and in the process, the ships are sunk. However, Roque sends a hired Russian submarine to retrieve the warheads from the seabed.

In *UnAmerica*, the Losers track Roque to Pripyat', an abandoned Ukrainian city near Chernobyl, where the nuclear weapons are being constructed. Pooch is captured and tortured by Roque, but the team saves him and kills Roque. The earthquake predicted by Hashimoto creates a new island underneath Max's oil rig. In a televised address to the world, Max declares it the independent state of New Jerusalem and announces that the nation has placed nuclear weapons in forty-six cities around the world. His plan is to force all nations to adopt a free-market capitalist model. As a demonstration, he explodes a bomb in Pripyat', which the Losers barely escape.

In the final story line, *Endgame*, Pooch has quit to return to his family. Sheik Abdul helps Clay, Jensen, Aisha, and Cougar infiltrate New Jerusalem via a secret undersea pipeline. Unbeknownst to the Losers, the Sheik sends Fahd in after them with a nuclear bomb in case the Losers fail. "Max" is revealed to be a pair of twins, the sons of the original Max. Clay is killed but kills one of the Maxes in the process. Cougar is mortally wounded by Fahd and retaliates, killing him; Cougar stays behind to set off the nuclear weapon. Pooch rescues Jensen while New Jerusalem and Max are destroyed. Aisha's fate is unknown.

Volumes

- *The Losers: Ante Up* (2004). Collects issues 1-6. The stand-alone first issue introduces the team via a heist plot, while the other five issues chart their first steps toward finding Max.
- *The Losers: Double Down* (2004). Collects issues 7-12. The Losers discover more about Max and steal a geological survey he has commissioned. Their mission is increasingly aimed at exposing Max's plans.

- *The Losers: Trifecta* (2005). Collects issues 13-19. The Losers discover Max's oil rig while Aisha launches a rescue mission. The full story of the Losers' final mission is told.
- *The Losers: Close Quarters* (2006). Collects issues 20-25. Roque returns, overseeing Max's plans to steal nuclear weapons. Jensen appears to be killed but, in fact, survives.
- *The Losers: Endgame* (2006). Collects issues 26-32. While tracing the nuclear weapons, the Losers kill Roque. Max's plans come to fruition but are thwarted by the Losers. Clay, Cougar, and possibly Aisha are killed in the process.

Characters

- *Lieutenant Colonel Franklin Clay* is the team's leader, a grim-faced, hard-bitten soldier with a fierce sense of morality and duty to his country. He leads the Losers back to the United States after they are declared dead and starts plotting their next move.
- *Sergeant Carlos Alvarez*, a.k.a. *Cougar*, is the team's sniper. He has long, fair hair and wears a Stetson at all times. A man of few words and disturbed by his combat experiences, he has extraordinary ability with a rifle.
- *Sergeant Linwood Porteous*, a.k.a. *Pooch*, is the team's vehicles expert. A shaven-headed, easygoing family man, he can drive, pilot, or steer a wide variety of vehicles. He is motivated by a desire to clear his name so that he can return to his wife and children.
- *Corporal Jake Jensen* is the team's communications and technology expert. Physically slight compared to his colleagues, with glasses and spiky blond hair, he specializes in hacking computers and cracking security systems.
- *Aisha al-Fadhil* is beautiful but brooding and often humorless. Raised amid violence in Afghanistan and Pakistan, she fought the Soviets as a child. Her father was assassinated on Max's orders, and she joins forces with the Losers to destroy Max.
- *Captain William Roque* is the team's second-in-command, identifiable from the large scar across his face. From the outset, he is more interested in personal gain than the moral high ground and, before long, betrays his comrades for money.
- *Max* is a CIA code name first used by an agent during the Cold War. The same name was used by the Losers' handler when they were seconded to the CIA; he gave the order for their transport to be shot down.
- *Marvin Stegler* is a middle-aged, graying CIA agent who is frustrated by his relegation to desk work. Assigned to investigate Max, he quickly runs into the Losers.

Artistic Style

The book's style is set by Jock, who drew twenty-one of the book's thirty-two issues. As a result of Jock's work, the protagonists of *The Losers* are far removed from the square-jawed heroes of the war books that inspired the series. His artwork is rough-edged and chaotic; his characters' faces are often scored with wild lines and are hidden in shadow, a technique appropriate for a book set in an unstable world and that follows a group of characters who, for all their skill, are constantly forced to improvise. The artwork suggests messy complexity, with things hidden in dark corners.

Additionally, Jock's work is kinetic: characters and other visual aspects of the page always seem to be in motion. This not only suits the tone of the story, in which the Losers are unable to rest in their pursuit of Max, but also befits the large amount of action in the book. Despite its roughness, Jock's work has an underlying clarity; the sequences flow well on the page, and the impression of chaos is aided by a huge array of sound effects. Color is used boldly, but often with a restricted palette to denote different locations. In the flashback issues, Jock and Lee Loughridge use a slightly different approach, muting the blacks into grays and throwing angular light and shade onto the images.

The series' guest artists generally adhere to the style set forth by Jock, making the book fairly consistent visually. The greatest departure comes with Nick Dragotta's issues, which were produced to layouts from Jock: Dragotta's style is cleaner and simpler than Jock's.

Jock's covers are also worthy of note. They are often extremely graphic and incorporate elements of collage. The book's politicized nature is well represented on the covers through imagery such as flags.

Themes

For a period in the 1990's, the conspiracy thriller chiefly became a vehicle for fantasy, inspired by the television show *The X-Files*. These tended to work on the assumption that real-world conspiracy theorists were delusional. The September 11, 2001, attacks on the United States cemented this perception of the conspiracy theorist, as various outlandish explanations for the attacks were advanced. However, this shift in the geopolitical landscape is precisely what *The Losers* uses to connect the conspiracy theory to reality, returning it to its Watergate-era roots.

The series comments on an early twenty-first-century milieu in which it is increasingly clear that the full reasons behind political actions are not being disclosed. With the first installment of *The Losers* arriving within months of the U.S. invasion of Iraq, the issues underpinning the series remained current throughout its run. (Lest the reality of his subject matter be doubted, Diggle closes issue 6 with a quote from a former Drug Enforcement Administration operative testifying that his investigations consistently led him to CIA employees.)

Because the series is anchored by a pertinent backdrop, elements of the story are quite lurid. Max, the series' villain, initially seems superhuman, and his plan to create an independent island state to advance American interests is at the edge of scientific credulity.

However, while the plan is overblown, the motivation behind it is not. Max believes that the Americanization of the world is an inevitable process, and the major threat to global stability is resistance to this process. His plan is a more aggressive rendition of the real-world American mission in the Middle East, in which liberal free-market democracy is imposed in an authoritarian fashion. Presenting this as the solution to a future of environmental catastrophe and wars over food and water, the comic leaves the impression

that, while this is obviously not the answer, a solution is required.

Impact

The Losers did not enjoy spectacular sales—it launched with sales of 19,850 but toward the end of its run had settled to 8,000-9,000—but it was well-received and established Diggle in the American market. Not long after the series ended, Diggle became the regular writer on Vertigo's flagship title *Hellblazer*, a job most leading British comics writers have been given at one time or another, and wrote a *Batman* miniseries, *Batman Confidential* (2006-2011). Jock worked separately on *Hellblazer*, illustrating the *Pandemonium* (2010) graphic novel, and reunited with Diggle for the *Green Arrow: Year One* miniseries.

The Losers was part of a new wave of Vertigo comics branching out into other genres, following *100 Bullets*, *Human Target,* and *American Century*. During the 1990's, Vertigo had been dominated by works with fantasy elements, following in the footsteps of *Sandman* and *Hellblazer*. *The Losers* marked a growing interest at Vertigo in producing crime books, culminating in the foundation of the Vertigo Crime range. One of the launch books was Diggle's *Rat Catcher* (2010). The influence of *The Losers* can also be seen in the crime and conspiracy books that followed, such as *The Last Days of American Crime* (2009) and *Ghost Projekt* (2011).

Eddie Robson

Films

The Losers. Directed by Sylvain White. Warner Bros., 2010. This film adaptation stars Jeffrey Dean Morgan as Clay, Zoe Saldana as Aisha, Chris Evans as Jensen, and Idris Elba as Roque. The film draws mostly on the first six issues of the comic, plus a brief version of the flashback issues (16-19), with the action relocated from the Khyber Pass to Bolivia—indeed, the Middle East barely figures in the film. Max is a stronger presence in the film, but his plan is significantly different: He merely wishes to engineer a terrorist incident. Diggle had unofficial input into the screenplay, and Jock produced artwork for the film; both contributed a commentary to the U.K. DVD release.

Further Readings

Chaykin, Howard, et al. *American Century* (2001-2003).

Diggle, Andy, and Ibañez, Victor. *Rat Catcher* (2010).

Diggle, Andy, and Jock. *Green Arrow: Year One* (2007).

Bibliography

Diggle, Andy. "Real American Heroes: Andy Diggle Extensively Talks *The Losers*." Interview by Arune Singh. *Comic Book Resources*, May 12, 2003. http://www.comicbookresources.com/?page=article&old=1&id=2230.

_____. "Winning and Losing: An Interview with Andy Diggle." Interview by Brent Keane. *Ninth Art*, December 8, 2003. http://www.ninthart.org/display.php?article=728.

Diggle, Andy, and Jock. "Andy Diggle and Jock." Interview by Tom Butler. *Little White Lies*, June 1, 2010. http://www.littlewhitelies.co.uk/interviews/andy-diggle-jock-11090.

Milligan, Peter, et al. *Human Target* (2000).

See also: *Human Target*; *Green Arrow: Year One*; *Hellblazer*

LUCIFER

Author: Carey, Mike

Artist: Peter Gross (illustrator); Scott Hampton (illustrator); Jon J. Muth (illustrator); Dean Ormston (illustrator); P. Craig Russell (illustrator); Kelly Ryan (illustrator); Chris Weston (illustrator); Daniel Vozzo (colorist); Ellie De Ville (letterer); Jared K. Fletcher (letterer); Todd Klein (letterer); Duncan Fegredo (cover artist); Michael Wm. Kaluta (cover artist); Christopher Moeller (cover artist)

Publisher: DC Comics

First serial publication: 2000-2006

First book publication: 2001-2007

Publication History

Lucifer, the primary protagonist of *Lucifer*, was created by Neil Gaiman and Sam Kieth and first appeared in *The Sandman*, issue 4, published by DC Comics in 1989 (collected in *The Sandman: Preludes and Nocturnes*, 1989). The character was further developed by Gaiman in *The Sandman*, issues 21-28, published between 1990 and 1991 (collected in *The Sandman: Season of Mists*, 1992). After Gaiman's *The Sandman* series ended in 1996, DC's Vertigo imprint sought to capitalize on its popularity by publishing a spin-off miniseries under the title *The Sandman Presents*.

In 1998, Vertigo editor Alisa Kwitney asked Mike Carey to submit a pitch for a Lucifer story line to lead off *The Sandman Presents* line. Despite his lack of experience with the major publishers, Carey was ultimately made series writer. With Carey in place, *Lucifer* began as a three-issue miniseries, *The Sandman Presents*, in March, 1999. In June of 2000, it was released as its own ongoing series (each issue averaging twenty-two pages) under the Vertigo imprint. For the first few issues of this new series, it continued to be marketed as a *The Sandman* spin-off, but by issue 5 it had begun to chart its own course, as Carey developed his own distinct storytelling style. In 2001, the series received five Eisner Award nominations, cementing its popularity. A year later, Carey was signed on to an exclusive contract with DC. The series ended with issue 75.

(Getty Images)

Mike Carey

Originally working in the United Kingdom on *2000 AD*, Mike Carey became one of the most important writers for DC Comics' Vertigo imprint in the 2000's. He is particularly well known for his long run on *Hellblazer* and for writing the entirety of the seventy-five-issue *Lucifer* series, a spin-off from Neil Gaiman's *Sandman*. Carey produced a number of other Vertigo titles, many of them tied to the *Sandman* and *Books of Magic* continuities, including *God Save the Queen* with John Bolton. He was involved in DC's short-lived Minx imprint, writing *The Confessions of a Blabbermouth* and *Re-Gifters*. For Marvel, he has written a number of X-Men titles and *Ultimate Fantastic Four*. Carey's writing in *Lucifer* dealt with issues of creation, free will, and predetermination, and the series was designed to closely mirror the structure of *Sandman*.

Plot

Lucifer is a spin-off from DC's popular *The Sandman*, a horror-fantasy series targeted at mature audiences. *Lucifer*'s title character, as well as many of its supporting characters, originally debuted in the earlier series. Though familiarity with *The Sandman* is not a prerequisite for reading *Lucifer*, the latter's initial setup may be difficult for readers to follow without some knowledge of the *Season of Mists* volume of *The Sandman*. In that volume, *Lucifer* abdicates his throne in hell, passing his rule to Dream, who in turn passes it on to Remiel and Dumas, two of Heaven's angels. The first volume of *Lucifer*, set sometime after these events, reintroduces the reader to Lucifer, who in his retirement has opened a Los Angeles piano bar named Lux, which he runs with the help of Mazikeen, from *Season of Mists*.

Lucifer features a highly complicated story line, in which seemingly insignificant events and characters end up assuming great importance as the story progresses. Though the series is broken into discrete stories, these tales frequently depend upon characters and plot details introduced in earlier stories, thus rendering the series difficult to follow without reading forward chronologically from the first volume. Readers may encounter further difficulties, as *Lucifer* occasionally imports characters from other series (such as *The Sandman* and *The Dreaming*), with which it assumes the reader is familiar. Because of the plot's complexity, the series is also largely devoid of embedded recaps; readers are thus tasked with keeping track of the characters and plot themselves.

Despite *Lucifer*'s complexity, a rudimentary plot summary is possible. In *Devil in the Gateway*, Lucifer receives from God a letter of passage granting him exit from God's creation. Wary that the letter might be a trap, he travels to Berlin in search of the Basanos, a sentient deck of tarot cards controlled by its creator, an angel named Meleos. By the time Lucifer finds the cards, the Basanos have escaped from Meleos and taken a human host, Jill Presto. With host in tow, they inform Lucifer that the letter is, in its current form, rigged to bar its user reentry to creation. Warned of God's plan, Lucifer transforms the letter into a portal, which he later multiplies and distributes across all the realms and dimensions of creation.

In *Children and Monsters*, Lucifer and Elaine Belloc, a human-angel hybrid, rescue the angel Michael from an evil angel named Sandalphon, who has been using Michael to produce an artificial race of angelic children. Fatally injured during the rescue, Michael "dies" on the other side of the portal, thus imbuing the outside creation with the energy of the Dunamis Demiurgos (the shaping power of God). In *A Dalliance with the Damned*, Lucifer seizes on the void's new potential and transforms it into a new, alternate creation, to which all are welcome so long as they abide by a single rule: no worshiping.

The Basanos temporarily usurp control of this creation from Lucifer in *The Divine Comedy*. With the help of Mazikeen and her kin, Meleos, a cherub named Gaudium, and Elaine, Lucifer is able to defeat the Basanos, but at the cost of Elaine's life. Before Lucifer has fully recovered from the battle, however, he must travel to Hell to honor an agreement requiring him to confront the angel Samael in a battle to the death. In *Inferno*, the lords of Hell conspire to assure Lucifer's loss, but Mazikeen and Christopher Rudd, a damned soul who has inadvertently acquired a position of power in Hell's court, help Lucifer turn the tables on his enemies.

In *Mansions of Silence*, the plot switches focus from Lucifer to a crew he has assembled to sail the Naglfar, a ship from Norse mythology, into a delicate region of the afterlife to rescue Elaine's soul. While the crew struggles to reach Elaine, Lucifer and Michael submerge themselves in an artificial pool containing God's consciousness, wherein they learn that God has abandoned his throne in Heaven. As a result of God's abdication, all of his creation is gradually disintegrating. What is more, God's absence makes heaven a target for power-hungry immortals. When two titans, Garams and Gyges, attempt to assume God's throne in *Exodus*, it takes the combined power of Lucifer, Mazikeen, and Michael to stop them. Fearing further attacks, Lucifer exiles all immortals from his own creation. A restored Elaine, now serving as the guardian angel of the alternate creation, ensures they leave peacefully.

In *The Wolf Beneath the Tree*, Fenris the wolf sets in motion events that will lead to the destruction of God's throne and thereby bring about Ragnarok, the end of the world. Lucifer, Michael, and Elaine track him to Yggdrasil, the World Tree, but at its base Fenris tricks Lucifer into killing Michael, thus further hastening the end of creation. In an attempt to slow the onset of Ragnarok, Elaine absorbs the Dunamis Demiurgos from a dying Michael. In *Crux*, she learns how to use it by fashioning a third creation under Lucifer's guidance. While she learns, a plethora of plots previously left dangling are picked back up and rushed toward a single point: a climactic battle in heaven for the sake of all creation. *Morningstar* recounts this battle, which ends in a meeting among Yaweh, Elaine, and Lilith, as the two women plead for the fate of creation. Ultimately, Elaine collapses the three different creations into one and assumes the function of God, thus securing the safety of reality.

Evensong reads as an epilogue. Past characters return, past story lines are wrapped up, and new possibilities for the future are envisioned. Elaine relinquishes the last remnants of her human personality, and Lucifer sets forth alone on a journey beyond the limits of creation.

Volumes

- *Lucifer: Devil in the Gateway* (2001). Collects *The Sandman Presents: Lucifer*, issues 1-3, and *Lucifer*, issues 1-4. Sets the stage for the rest of the series. Key concepts, such as the "outside" of creation, and key characters, such as the Basanos and Elaine Belloc, are introduced.
- *Lucifer: Children and Monsters* (2001). Collects *Lucifer*, issues 5-13. Through an assortment of stories, introduces a large number of characters whose significance will not be revealed until later in the series. Also introduces, via Elaine's three competing families, the question of parentage's effect on free will—a major theme of the series.
- *A Dalliance with the Damned* (2002). Collects *Lucifer*, issues 14-20. This volume focuses on the culture of Hell, which, after Lucifer's abdication, has come to resemble that of an early modern European court.
- *Lucifer: The Divine Comedy* (2003). Collects *Lucifer*, issues 21-28. In this volume, the

Basanos attempt to supplant Lucifer as ruler of his creation.

- *Lucifer: Inferno* (2004). Collects *Lucifer*, issues 29-35. Features Lucifer's battle against Samael in Hell. This volume also marks the beginning of the incorporation of Norse mythology into the plot.
- *Lucifer: Mansions of Silence* (2004). Collects *Lucifer*, issues 36-41. In this volume, a group of characters introduced individually in previous volumes set off together into the afterlife in an attempt to rescue Elaine.
- *Lucifer: Exodus* (2005). Collects *Lucifer*, issues 42-44 and 46-49. This volume tells of the Titans' attack on Heaven. A series of stand-alone stories also detail the departure of the last few immortals from Lucifer's creation.
- *Lucifer: The Wolf Beneath the Tree* (2005). Collects *Lucifer*, issues 45 and 50-54. Introduces Fenris and Lilith, the primary antagonists for the rest of the series.
- *Lucifer: Crux* (2006). Collects *Lucifer*, issues 55-61. In this volume, Lilith assembles an army to march on Heaven, while Jill Presto gives birth to the child of the Basanos.
- *Lucifer: Morningstar* (2006). Collects *Lucifer*, issues 62-69. The climax of the series: Lucifer and his supporters battle against Lilith and Fenris for the safety of creation.
- *Lucifer: Evensong* (2007). Collects *Lucifer: Nirvana*, a brief story set earlier in the series' continuity, and *Lucifer*, issues 70-75. This volume functions as an extended goodbye to the series and its characters.

Characters

- *Lucifer*, the protagonist, is the first fallen angel and former ruler of Hell. He is tall and slender with pointy ears, orange hair, a Roman nose, and eyebrows always arched disdainfully. A sharp dresser, he possesses a cool demeanor—indifferent bordering on cruel—and a knack for manipulating others. Like the Miltonic Satan on which he is based, he is driven by the desire to realize the independent power of free will. Unlike others opposed to the rule of Yaweh, however, he seeks not an end to God's creation but passage beyond it. He is thus paradoxically positioned as both creation's greatest opponent and its ultimate savior.

- *Elaine Belloc*, a British schoolgirl, is the daughter of Michael and thus the heir to the Dunamis Demiurgos, or shaping power of God. Originally introduced as a supporting character, as the series progresses she becomes the driving force of the plot, often receiving more panel space than Lucifer himself. Her appearance varies throughout the series, but she appears most often as a young woman with short brown hair and angelic wings. Unlike the many other deities in the series, her decisions are driven by kindness and emotional sympathy.

- *The Basanos*, one of the primary antagonists, are a pack of sentient tarot cards crafted by the angel Meleos. Early in the series they break free from their maker's control and begin a series of machinations designed to free themselves from the limitations of God's creation. Destroyed by Lucifer in *The Divine Comedy*, their power and personality survive in the form of two unborn, immortal children carried by the human cabaret performer Jill Presto.

- *Fenris*, a major antagonist, is the wolf of Norse legend, fated to usher in Ragnarok, the end of creation. Appearing either as a bestial humanoid covered in tattoos or as a wolf, he is a sly and merciless opponent, driven by little more than the sheer desire for destruction.

- *Lilith*, the predecessor of Eve, is the first female woman and first mother in the history of God's creation. Mother to Mazikeen, she possesses a regal bearing and is, like her daughter, beautiful, with long, dark hair. Once the lover of demons and angels, she used her children to help Heaven's angels build their Silver City; upon its completion, they cast her out as profane. Many centuries later, obsessed with revenge, she conspires to destroy the Silver City and, with Fenris, bring about the end of God's creation.

- *Mazikeen* is Lucifer's lover and most loyal ally. A daughter of Lilith and ruler of the Lilim (until Lilith reclaims the position in *Crux*), she is a keen military strategist and almost unstoppable warrior. Formerly bearing a horrible disfigurement on the left side of her face, which she hid with half a white mask, she is transformed into a beautiful brunette by Jill Presto in *Children and Monsters*. Despite her bewitching beauty, she possesses a fierce temperament and displays a lack of sympathy for all but Lucifer. She supports him without question, even when he is cold to her; indeed, his ability to survive the numerous attempts on his life often depends on her working tirelessly behind the scenes on his behalf.

- *Yaweh*, a.k.a. *God*, is the God of the Old Testament. Though capable of taking any form, he appears primarily as a somewhat portly, older British gentleman, attired in a suit and bowler, with an umbrella in hand. The father of Lucifer (and, in a more abstract fashion, all of creation), he subtly engineers most of the events that take place throughout the series.

Artistic Style

Like many series published under DC's Vertigo imprint, *Lucifer* was designed and marketed as writer-driven. Numerous artists contributed to the series over time, but only the writer, Carey, stayed with the project from beginning to end. In keeping with Vertigo's mission to foreground the writer, the various artistic styles in the series tend to be understated, realist with a slight cartoonish element, and primarily illustrative (rather than narrative) in function. Like other Vertigo series, speech bubbles are prevalent, splash pages are rare (occurring, on average, less than once per issue), and panels are standard rectangles. Occasionally, stories are done in washes and watercolors, but the vast majority of the series is done in pencils and ink, with standard comic book coloring (though on the muted side) added subsequently.

Beginning with issue 5, artists Peter Gross and Ryan Kelly joined Carey as a standard part of the creative team. Though they did not contribute to every subsequent issue, their input helped further standardize the style of the series. Under their hand, panels are kept spare, major emphasis going to characters and character-driven action rather than backgrounds and scenery. Though panels did not normally overlap, Gross sometimes treats the entire page as a single panel, on which normal-size panels could be placed, thus eliminating the traditional white space between panels. This helps establish a visual hierarchy on the page, whereby one panel could receive greater visual weight than others. On pages where such a technique was not used, the white space between panels is colored so as to reflect the atmosphere of the setting.

Also of note is the lettering, originally designed by Todd Klein for *The Sandman Presents: Lucifer* (for which he won an Eisner Award in 2000), but adopted by all subsequent letterers for *Lucifer*. Different deities often speak in a different font. Lucifer, for example, speaks in a stylized, gothic font, Remiel in traditional cursive, and Briadach in runic. The associated speech bubbles are often stylized as well. Briadach's speech bubbles, for example, have shaky lines and angular edges.

Themes

Like *The Sandman*, the series from which *Lucifer* spun off, *Lucifer* draws its characters and general stories from the world's collective mythology. Major sources include the Old Testament, the Jewish Apocrypha, John Milton's *Paradise Lost* (1667, revised 1674), the Norse *Edda*, Native American myths, and Eastern folklore. Whereas *The Sandman* employed these myths to explore the poetry of human life, in the process humanizing traditional representations of the divine, *Lucifer* follows the opposite course: Mythic deities are rendered larger than life, while the human beings caught in their paths are deprived of agency and made to suffer. This reflects a darker vision of reality, in which both deities and humans, both subject to an inflexible causality crafted by God, play out roles they had no hand in choosing. The events of the series thus progress as a perfectly engineered machine, one event leading inexorably to the next, while the actions of the characters, always forced into reactive modes, inadvertently drive the machine's gears.

The major theme of this brutal world is the problem of free will. Does it exist at all or is it merely an illusion? Like Milton's Satan, Lucifer stands for free will. His every action is calculated toward realizing its possibility. However, from the series' opening story, in which Lucifer does service for God in exchange for a letter of passage granting him exit from God's creation, God's calculations seem already to have included and accounted for Lucifer's own. Indeed, as the series progresses, and Lucifer is gradually transformed from principal actor to reactor—even being forced to battle for the preservation of God's creation—it becomes increasingly unclear whether Lucifer's own disobedience might not also have been a predetermined part of God's intricate system.

A related theme hinges on the issue of engenderment or creation. More specifically: Is the identity of the created thing merely a function of the creator's own identity? Lucifer and Michael, the first sons of God, wrestle with this question throughout the series, but it confronts other characters as well, most often through the issues of pregnancy and parentage. Indeed, much of the series' conflict is driven by the attempts of characters to produce offspring, abort offspring, or assert their authority upon their offspring. In general, the series asserts the existence of an inescapable (and often destructive) bond between parent and child that cannot be duplicated by nonblood relations. The two-issue story "Stitch-Glass Slide" (occurring in *Exodus*), however, puts forth the possibility of an alternative model of parentage, built upon adoption and the willing sacrifice of parental desire.

Lucifer addresses these themes by alternating back and forth between large cosmic stories involving mythical characters and deities and smaller, personal stories about individuals attempting to live everyday lives. There are thus two concurrent levels of plot: the cosmic, or macro, and the human, or micro. Thus, another major theme of *Lucifer* is the relation between these two orders, the macro and micro—which of the two offers the proper vantage point for the creation and/ or perception of meaning? Though *Lucifer* never fully answers this question and in fact reverts almost entirely to the micro order in the series' final volume, the series is often mercilessly cruel to its human characters, who are frequently made to suffer merely for coming into contact with the larger forces that drive the world. The single-issue story "The Thunder Sermon" (collected in *A Dalliance with the Damned*) is emblematic in this regard, describing the cold fate of two humans who unwittingly find themselves inside Lucifer's Los Angeles home.

Impact

In the mid-1990's, DC published a number of new, adult-themed fantasy series under its Vertigo imprint in an effort to capitalize on the popularity of Gaiman's *The Sandman*. *Lucifer* was the most successful of these series in terms of both sales and industry prestige (it is also one of the few to have been fully collected in graphic novel form). Indeed, *Lucifer* demonstrated that the myth-driven style of storytelling introduced by Gaiman could be taken up and modified by other writers to produce popular series and characters. However, though *Lucifer* proved the viability of that particular storytelling mode, the series also marked the end of DC's commitment to it. By the time *Lucifer* ended, popular taste had shifted away from myth and fantasy comics and toward crime, science fiction, and politically nuanced adventure comics.

Lucifer is also noteworthy for introducing Carey to the comic book industry. His success with *Lucifer* quickly earned him stints on a variety of series, including *Hellblazer*, *Wetworks*, and *X-Men*. Because he is from Great Britain, he is often classified as part of the "British Invasion" that included Warren Ellis, Grant Morrison, and Garth Ennis (as well as a reemergent Alan Moore). Though Carey's work for *Lucifer* is contemporaneous with these artists' most famous works, his writing style is more traditional, less subversive, and less edgy.

Lucifer remains a cult favorite, but it is gradually receding from popular awareness because of the little effort DC has made in marketing the series since its ending. Whereas other Vertigo books have been rereleased in special deluxe or collector's editions or made the subject of in-house retrospectives, *Lucifer* has become a comparatively stale intellectual property.

Gregory Steirer

Further Readings

Delano, Jamie, et al. *Hellblazer* (1988-   ).

Gaiman, Neil, et al. *The Books of Magic* (1990-1991).

_____. *The Sandman* (1989-1996).

Bibliography

Bender, Hy. *The Sandman Companion*. New York: DC Comics, 1999.

Carey, Mike. "The Devil's Business." In *Lucifer: Evensong*. New York: DC Comics, 2007.

Ellison, Harlan. Introduction to *The Sandman: Season of Mists*. New York: DC Comics, 1992.

Gaiman, Neil. Foreword to *Lucifer: Devil in the Gateway*. New York: DC Comics, 2001.

King, Charles W. "What If It's Just Good Business? Hell, Business Models, and the Dilution of Justice in Mike Carey's *Lucifer*." In *Hell and Its Afterlife: Historical and Contemporary Perspectives*, edited by Isabel Moreira and Margaret Toscano. London: Ashgate, 2010.

Newsing, John. "British Comics and the 'Boom.'" *Science Fiction Studies* 31 (2004): 174-175.

See also: *Hellblazer; The Sandman; Sandman Mystery Theatre; The Books of Magic*